SEMIOTEXT(E) NATIVE AGENTS SERIES

Published by Semiotext(e)
PO BOX 629. South Pasadena, CA 91031
www.semiotexte.com

Special thanks to Marwa Abdul-Rahman, David Buuck, Luka Fisher, Peter Gizzi, Will Hall, Michael Malone, and Kit Schluter.

Cover Design by Hedi El Kholti and Lauren Mackler
Cover Photograph by Robert Fischer
Layout by Hedi El Kholti

ISBN: 978-1-63590-218-1

10 9 8 7 6 5 4 3 2

Distributed by The MIT Press, Cambridge, Mass. and London, England
Printed in the United States of America

Kevin Killian

Selected Amazon Reviews

Edited by Hedi El Kholti and Robert Dewhurst

Introduction by Wayne Koestenbaum
Afterword by Dodie Bellamy

Semiotext(e)

CONTENTS

Introduction by Wayne Koestenbaum

ON THE TAKE

Kevin Killian's *Selected Amazon Reviews*—a star turn that transforms, in one boa-clad swoop, the premises of cultural criticism—takes a stand against prizes and pecking orders. Killian is not interested in "the best." Having no wish to winnow, he pursues reviewing as an act of love, not carnage: critique as caress. His assemblage puts forth a philosophy of responsiveness—how to pay attention, how to expand those capacities by using them again and again, replenishing the ability to regard (and to caress, and to critique) by promiscuously multiplying the occasions.

* * *

Above all, Killian charms—stylish flights, commonsensical spasms, outré details, a fabulist's dazzle, and a gossipy confidingness. Charming itself is this book's carnival of juxtapositions—a consequence of the editorial decision to arrange the reviews chronologically rather than by genre or subject. The leaps between different echelons of evaluated object (book, gadget, high/low, abject/lofty) teach a reader how *not* to differentiate, how to savor, repeatedly, the moment of scission, and how to recognize that a flotilla of desires—a plurality—composes a valorous life.

* * *

Killian's reviews originally appeared on Amazon's web hub. Whether or not he foresaw the posthumous aggregation of his *Nachlass* in a book, or whether he savored, instead, the online, piecemeal buildup, review by review, he was steadily engaged in making a site-specific artwork—responding to the conditions and colossi of his time, as if wrapping, festooning, or "tagging" a building (think of Warhol's *Thirteen Most Wanted Men* or anything by the Christo team), but politely, not angrily. With a delicacy of guerilla consciousness, Killian engaged in a nonviolent act of squatting, or the appropriative act that Michel de Certeau, in *The Practice of Everyday Life*, called "la perruque"—doing creative work, surreptitiously, while on the company's payroll. Occupy Amazon is the action that Killian performs, squatting on Amazon with a radical-faerie insouciance. Generous and genial his reviews may be, but their insistent profusion suggests a revolutionary will to destroy barricades. He enacts a cosmophagic critical practice, doing a Sontag but without the severity. Not siding with the sublime, Killian opts for the grandeur that comes with a *horizontal* viewing practice, eschewing the verticality of hegemonic evaluations (top, bottom, first class, steerage).

* * *

Killian's opus takes part in the tradition of vernacular criticism bibles, endurance acts of obstinate taste-making, like Boyd McDonald's *Cruising the Movies.* Killian's cultural cruising consists of unfettered speech shaking its tush at the capital-controlled bazaar of Amazon, its riverine greed and imperial plunder diverted or stopped (a finger in the dike?) by his assiduous impertinence, his nonstop bestowal of opinion, dish, chatter, digression, and wisdom. By reviewing "difficult" experimental poetry alongside domestic appliances and Hollywood flotsam, he jams the PR structure of mainstream reviewing outlets, organs that push the offbeat arts into shadow. He prognosticates an era, perhaps ours, when normcore organs have withered away, and online "takes" are the salvation or death knell of all cultural products.

* * *

Killian's reviews, stowaways on Amazon's boat, could be considered self-published. Self-publishing remains among the most radical acts within the literary marketplace. Instead of awaiting the luxury of an imprimatur, Killian commits to a zine mentality, an internet replay of the Mimeo Revolution, and thereby shoves gatekeepers off their thrones. Usurper, careening from attachment to attachment, he hugs every object in his garrulous path. Without fanfare or institutional backing, he ends up constructing a critical edifice as sizeable and encyclopedic as the oeuvres of Pauline Kael, Serge Daney, Harold

Bloom, Edmund Wilson, Robert Burton (*The Anatomy of Melancholy*), J. Laplanche and J.-B. Pontalis (*The Language of Psycho-Analysis*), and Robert Duncan (*The H.D. Book*). Killian parks his omnibus, however, not at the *New Yorker* or *Cahiers du cinéma* but at Amazon's love motel.

* * *

Critique attains individuality when it takes place in zones relatively free from surveillance—when it retreats to those stolen culverts where a body can enjoy a paradoxical privacy. In the permission Killian's performance gives for unleashed speech to flourish, his tome bears an oblique resemblance to Dennis Cooper's epistolary novel *The Sluts*. Killian, like Cooper, memorializes and darkly celebrates the libidinal-oracular-demotic language that flourishes in chat rooms, threads, DMs, WhatsApp, Telegram—sites housing a verbal surplus that asserts language's deathlessness. We love idiosyncratic language because, like a weed or a cockroach, it can thrive everywhere. Killian demonstrates literature's wiliness, its hydra-headed body reappearing wherever there arises a terrain on which to squat.

* * *

Unorthodox speed-dating-style juxtapositions animate these assembled reviews, electrified by an abundance of what Killian calls (in reference to the work of Susan Howe) "the sizzle of disjunction." Sizzle produces a jump-cut paradise: Tallulah Bankhead next to *Airport Planning & Management*, *The Night of the Iguana* next to *How to Make Your Pet a Star*, *Valley of the Dolls* next to Gerber baby food, Paul Bowles next to *Kate's Cake Decorating*, straightening boar-hair brush next to Maggie Nelson, Bruce Boone next to towel warmer, Aveda conditioner next to Barbara Guest, Yeats next to three-story escape ladder, Clint Eastwood next to crochet stitches, Chris Kraus next to *Batman Returns*, potato salad next to Eileen Myles, copper fire bowl next to Rae Armantrout, Robert Altman next to Aalto vase, *I Married a Witch* next to white mint box with window, Louis Zukofsky next to genie headpiece with veil, *Autumn Leaves* next to Abraham Lincoln costume, charm bracelet link next to Aaron

Shurin, Holiday Celebration Barbie doll next to *Bonjour Tristesse*, Advil next to Ammiel Alcalay, John Wayne next to *The Girl on a Motorcycle*, multipurpose duct tape next to Patti Smith, *A Star Is Born* next to sterling-silver stud earrings, *A Man and a Woman* next to Robert Duncan, Liv Ullmann next to *Wild West Hero: A Gay Erotic Novella*, Cid Corman next to Pilot ballpoint pens, Fortuny next to Akilah Oliver, Stevie Nicks next to Hergé. Though the book's chronological structure determines these juxtapositions, the craving for dissonance is echt Killian, who writes, in a review of a NARS Multiple Orgasm makeup kit, "The famous Orgasm blush, the color of pale, demure, Staffordshire pottery, is sitting next to the florid bronze tanner, like two squares in the old game show of *Hollywood Squares*. Never have two contestants seemed so disparate, so unlikely to get along." Killian understood his procedure's TV talk show randomness, and the profundity that comes from artfully pursuing the unplanned.

* * *

Like the Black Sparrow Press edition of James Schuyler's art reviews (edited by Simon Pettet), *Killian's Selected Amazon Reviews* is a covert autobiography—a diary of a sensibility, a defense of errant taste. Nothing more perverse, nothing more hardwired to the individual, than the delicate, unjudicable matter of desire—the etiology of why one cherishes, and the embarrassing overabundance of things cherished. Killian's pleasure thermometer indicates a high fever; we see the signature of heat not just in his Amazon reviews but in his *Tagged* project. This ongoing series—photographs of writers and artists posing nude while holding a Raymond Pettibon drawing of male genitalia—demonstrated a steamy, enumerative thoroughness, a wish to consume multitudes, to stuff a smorgasbord into a genre's capacious gullet.

* * *

Did Killian really grow up in France? In several reviews, he brags that he spent his childhood there; he uses a droll Norma Shearer tone when he sketches these early (and I presume fictional) idylls. Reviewing a "Dynasty" necklace, Killian reminisces about a farcically improbable *temps perdu*: "As an American boy growing up in France, I became mesmerized by an enchanting painting of an ancestor that hung never very far from the hearth. The painting, smudged by smoke and damaged by Vichy occupation of the château, showed a very thin and angular woman, her face like something reflected in the bowl of a spoon. ... 'Who is this woman?' I used to wonder out loud ... as my grandmother passed through the room looking for our vanished cat, Gateau." The unsung, never-mourned Gateau! Here Killian returns to his New Narrative roots—messing up the distinction between autobiography and fiction, between critical essay and roman à clef romp.

* * *

In these reviews, Killian tries on a variety of personae and interlocutors. He seems especially fond of saying "my wife." On a couple of occasions, he mentions his (fictional?) kids. Sometimes he addresses other Amazon reviewers, or the online reader, or the writer of the book under review. To his appraisal of Chris Kraus's *Torpor*, he appends the title "Twenty Questions for Chris Kraus," as if with a daffy, Joe Brainard–esque proceduralism: "If only I could ask Chris Kraus my twenty questions! Among them would be, 'How would you describe the form you work in? It's very distinctive, very Chris Kraus, but what is it?'" Kevin could have called up Chris and asked. But he enjoyed the umbrageous space of the go-between, Amazon as duenna, a love letter slipped over the transom.

* * *

Sometimes Killian mentions fictional products, such as a "Hepburninator," a device that can remove all the Katharine Hepburn scenes from one of her movies. In a review of George Cukor's *Holiday*, Killian notes: "I never really liked this movie much until my wife and I invested in one of those newfangled 'Hepburninators' on TiVo, which allow you to watch a full-length Katharine Hepburn movie in half the time by eliminating all scenes in which she appears." Killian doesn't defend his distaste for Hepburn; such idiosyncrasies of palate and preference sneak into the reviews like short-sheeting roommates when the patsy's back is turned.

* * *

A couple of times, my own name pops up in Kevin's pages. We're always reading each other, you and I, writer and writer, behind each other's back. Literature is a conversation among distant and sometimes dead bodies; the conversation happens when we read the works of others and when in writing we reproduce or pay homage to them. In a review of Andrew Epstein's critical study *Beautiful Enemies: Friendship and Postwar American Poetry*, Killian writes: "friendship is always a bag mixed to brimming with competition, adoration, a Wayne Koestenbaum sort of erotics, and a perfect period panache." I hadn't known that I typified a specific flavor of eroticism. I wish I'd read this review in February 2007, when Kevin wrote it. I could have asked him what sort of erotics he thought I adumbrated. Maybe the erotics of the "sort of"?

* * *

Killian achieves distance from self without pushing away the pleasures that the puritanical and the dull condemn as narcissism: as a consequence of a gregarious, Whitmanian self-scrutiny that also accommodates the wish to commingle with others, Kevin permits narratives (fictional or otherwise) of "self" to manifest in reviews where his eye is ostensibly trained elsewhere. The stream of Kevin can flow without Kevin actually speaking about himself, and part of that torrent is the arresting phrase, the unlikely comparison. "Alert as a caterpillar," a simile that might have delighted Marianne Moore, is Killian's description of a Lorca scholar, Jonathan Mayhew. Alert as a caterpillar is Kevin, too, crawling selflessly over other people's sentences.

* * *

I keep wondering whether Killian's reviewing-engine project, its size-conscious ambition, its *Passagen-Werk* oddity, qualifies as academic, shadow academic, anti-academic, mimic academic, parodic academic. His critical morsels bristle with bibliophilic erudition: even if the artifacts under consideration are not always textual (more than a few are household products), he expresses his enumerative desire in language haunted by literature. (My definition of literature? Language haunted by prior language. Language that knows itself to be the consequence of other people's language. Language that might wish to differentiate itself from other people's language but that yearns to return to an intimate relation with it. Language that persists in the fantasy that the language I'm uttering now is a solitary edifice.) Literature is the hospitality agent hosting Killian's adulations. But could such a book, or such a critical mode, find a place inside the university, even if we could differentiate *inside* and *outside* the university, an institution impossibly protean, compromised, obstinate, to be loved and also to be avoided, amended, upended? "Peer review" is the timid antithesis of Killian's machine, his Trojan horse, flouting the pedigreed tribunals. No advancement on any career ladder can be achieved by writing Amazon reviews—except posthumously. Only now can Killian's pieces be culled, with editorial love, into a burnished fascicle, exhibiting a sage completeness, Dickinsonian in its serene open-endedness and its sphinxlike assertion of closure on its own terms.

* * *

Killian acknowledges Amazon's homophobia. He quips, in a review of a Michael Curtiz film, *This Is the Army*: "when I heard about the Amazon dustup or glitch in which hundreds of gay and lesbian titles were deranked earlier this month, this was the first item I checked up on because it is definitely the gayest thing on sale in all of Amazon. I was glad to see it remained available right through the whole fracas, vibrating with the lavender vibrations of a genuinely revolutionary object." To vibrate with a fey, insurgent intensity: that is Killian's aesthetic credo. And his political credo is to stage that vibration on a site—Amazon—whose structure and underpinnings (monopolistic, cannibalistic) quash innovation, smallness, and community. As important as are Killian's critical pronouncements and asides, most crucial is their occupation of Amazon-owned turf. The reviews may have been written for catharsis, out of friendship and compulsion and the pleasure of exercising his own artfulness, but their effect, en masse, in situ, is to untie the suffocating sash enmeshing capital and culture.

* * *

Killian's text often addresses itself to his fellow Amazon reviewers by acknowledging their co-presence with him, choristers all, on the Attic stage: "Other reviewers recommend Advil for its ease of use, but I'm here to tell you the main reason to buy it is that it is tasty and sweet." Here and elsewhere he alludes to a subculture of Amazon reviewers, unpaid workers lauding what they love and panning what they detest, building up feedback loops—enfranchising, kibbitzing, clustering—to forge an underground society. Witnessing Killian's performance, a reader understands its waste, its satisfied (cheerful, not resigned) knowledge of itself as waste, as a byproduct of the Amazon machine but also a belligerent interruption. A text that knows itself as waste is a text that might have the gumption to earn lastingness. Language itself, indestructible fertilizer, is the hero and heroine of Killian's comedy.

* * *

Ever in pursuit of happy endings, his selected reviews (and the collected reviews of which this book offers a foretaste) achieve a human bulk, as if symbolizing his forfeited body. These spunky bonbons could have been lost, as all our bodies will eventually be lost, but this fleshy book now remains, asserting its monumentality. Online text is intrinsically vulnerable, buried by the profusion of other online material, and by the murderous whims of websites that arise and vanish: into the good night of the internet we gently go with our textual outpourings, without rage we go, willing to let our language disappear. Killian's reviews, claimed and resuscitated here, thus become an elegiac stand-in for all lost speech, syllables eaten alive on the internet and then evacuated.

* * *

In a review of Pierre Bourdieu's *Masculine Domination*, Killian recounts attending an Anthony Bourdain reading: "I made a fool of myself when, after waiting in line a good fifteen minutes, I asked the famous TV chef to autograph *Masculine Domination*! He looked at it in disgust, curling his lip and letting loose with some salty language, and his handlers whispered 'This is not by Bourdain, it is by Pierre Bourdieu.'" This mix-up encapsulates the shifts and torsions of

Killian's enterprise: the critique of masculinity is the strain—the nourishing tributary—underlying many of these reviews. The mythic Amazons were women warriors, but the Amazon Prime on whose shores Killian lies is a dominatingly masculinist fundament. Killian aims to confuse: the Bourdain/Bourdieu mix-up typifies Killian's anti-academic yet library-loving streak, but this flub offers an allegory of *the slip-up* as central to the practice of criticism. Revering the slip-up, Killian lets whimsy win the tournament. Opinionatedness can make a person cranky, but it can also make a person a counter-cultural seer—especially when this streak of giddy opinionatedness (the willingness to be partial, to hold certain objects dear and to discard others) is pursued with pedestrian indefatigability, in dim-lit and noncentral locales, debased spaces, the malls and mail-order catalogs of the slip-prone mind.

* * *

Killian's tone sometimes resembles Frank O'Hara's in "Ave Maria" ("Mothers of America / let your kids go to the movies!")—a mock-populist, pervy, *Summer Stock*–style enthusiasm about public scenes of consumption and exhibition. Killian teaches us to open up our voice to make its posited addressees seem a larger population than the kaffeeklatsch of faithfuls actually listening to the poem. Widen the voice, he suggests, as a way to widen the audience; throw the voice into amphitheater proportions. Call Killian's critical voice Amazonian in its ambition, size, and flow—its rippling inevitability. Could such a book *not* have come into existence? And yet it only barely made it here alive.

* * *

Nor did he buy on Amazon all the stuff he reviews. In a consideration of *A Magick Life: A Biography of Aleister Crowley*, Killian admits that he bought it for one dollar at a sale run by children in an abandoned building in San Francisco. "It seemed that a charitable agency was having a book sale for the wee ones of our city. A few adults stood prowling the street corners but otherwise the sale was entirely organized and manned by these children—none more than twelve years of age, and most barely out of kindergarten." Whether or not his account of the book's provenance is fictional, by announcing as fact that he bought *A Magick Life* offline, Killian charmingly rebuffs Amazon's intrusive ubiquity, meanwhile putting in a good word for the visionary capacities of the puerile. Amazon, not necessarily Killian's supplier, is merely the deposit dump for his opinions. He camps his critical pup-tent on Amazon's elephantine back, while simultaneously refuting the company's umbrella ambitions, its wish to be the nipple for every need. On rare occasions, Killian acknowledges Amazon's collaborating role as his Mephistophelian dance-partner: "I bought this book basically because of pressure from Amazon, or maybe 'pressure' isn't the mot juste, but you know when it tells you that 'People Who Bought This Book Also Bought,' and it shows you four photos of other book jackets?" Amazon represents a seducer as well as a grand inquisitor—a juridical beast, a toothsome lover.

* * *

His longest review, I reckon, is of Hitchcock's *Vertigo*, perhaps because doubling (the two Kim Novaks) is a conundrum as vast and iconic as the mirroring maze of Killian's relation to his doppelgänger, the Amazon in the looking glass, the Amazon who must be obeyed, the sister/mother *Chinatown* slapped face of star indistinguishability: Which Kim Novak am I when I look in the mirror? Which Kevin am I when I look in Amazon's mirror? Am I a poet, a prophet, or a sybarite when I pour my linguistic fervor into Amazon's filthy craw? Am I Amazonian, amazed by my own transformation into the corporate body that upholds me?

* * *

Killian's critical divertimenti are rich with digressions and reroutings. In a review of a TC Tolbert poetry book, Killian changes the subject to reminisce about another beloved poet: "John Wieners told me he had to stay 'on the take' to find all the poems he wound up writing, and through the sometimes difficult patches of his life, there was this one tendency that allowed him to live—the habit of acquisition." According to the online *Cambridge Dictionary, on the take* means "trying to profit in a personal and usually financial way from a situation."

In Killian's case, and in the case of some of his devoted readers, including me, the situation is life, and the profit is poetry. The situation is Amazon, and the profit is the review. Killian is *on the take* via a practice of issuing hot takes (though most of these reviews probably precede the popularity of the tart phrase "hot take"). Killian literally squeezes profit (in the nugget form of Amazon reviews) from a dire situation, a status quo in which Amazon has co-opted, with a strangler's grip, the satisfaction of desires. Amazon monopolizes bookselling: Killian squeezes that monopolization and lets drip from the squeezed Amazonian bladder the fine droplets of his takes. Criticism is not a parasitic art; it is a way of saving one's own life, justifying one's own taste, by scraping nourishment from capitalism's talons. Killian, who was much involved in San Francisco's Small Press Traffic, knew the inside story of the war between small presses and Amazon. The entire corpus of Killian's reviews offers a death's-door critique of what it means to publish today—the Gordian knot of being-published or not-being-published. Killian's stentorian way of saying no to the double bind of being-published / being-unpublished was to barnacle his *Anatomy* upon Amazon's brackish, horned hide—Killian's criticism taking vampiric root on the bloated body of a corporation's corpse structure. (To this extent, criticism *is* parasitic: it blood-sucks the empire.) We come away from witnessing Killian's performance with a sense of having received a sustenance that will keep on replenishing us as long as we write in cesspools, in ignored corners, in dumpsites, in the dirty fosses of Amazon's dire offices. I keep getting Christological when I think of this book's almost martyred extravagance—its willingness to lay everything on the line for no known reward. Isn't Kevin's hospitality a species of communion, a method of sacrificing symbolic bodies, repeatedly, for the sake of saving the world he loves, a world on the edge of extinction, a world still bursting with products and personages to love? Here's the parsley, here's the egg, here's the wafer, here's the sentence: Kevin has served us his Last Supper. As Elaine Stritch once put it, in a moment of musical extremity: everybody rise.

Kevin Killian

Selected Amazon Reviews

Ghost Girl
by Amy Gerstler

★★★★★
The Words Flower from Her Mouth

October 1, 2004

The cover shows us a young girl blindfolded with her fingers poised over a planchette, some kind of Ouija-board game with a pencil attached so that it writes too. I suppose the idea is to suggest that the poet brings us messages from another world as does the medium. Amy Gerstler has written a number of fine books but this is perhaps the best she's ever given us, partly for the reason that she seems so invested in exploration of this concept. Not only does the concept allow free rein to her trademark humor and irony, but she allows something genuinely chilling to creep into her work and thus I disagree with the *Publishers Weekly* review printed above, I don't think that Gerstler has a Billy Collins problem at all, although I can see why the reviewer battened on this aspect of her cultural production. Not every poem, after all, is as successful as the best of them, but here she keeps her readers happily engorged in a very high average, and the poems are not just simple one-trick ponies, she has earned our esteem with some quite long and complicated sorties toward what might be called her version of the "serial poem."

"Listen, Listen, Listen" is an extended meditation on the nature of sound, its manufacture and reception. Gerstler has always been a poet of exquisite verbal interplay, and now she parts some of the obfuscation to examine close up the way her effects are born. In the same vein, "On Wanting to See Ghosts" reflects not only a cynicism and resistance to the mystic, but a tender vulnerability and a deep appreciation of human nature and our need to reach out and find more on the other side of death. Ectoplasm is comical, let's face it. "What's that stuff erupting from her mouth now? Wadded up wedding veil? Celestial drool? One of heaven's tiny geysers?" Many of Gerstler's poems have a dramatic edge to them, as though Browning were leaning in on that planchette too, whispering in her ear. She is half a novelist and the book is filled with stories told as vignettes, end rhymes, enjambments. *Ghost Girl* reflects the way metaphors of poetry and of femininity are deeply embedded into popular discourses of spiritualism.

And the implications are staggering. I love the way Gerstler hints that the practice of poetry is now being delimited by "professionalism" among poets what with the rise of MFA programs and the increasing competition among poets for a handful of positions "teaching poetry" in the AWP: "Only mediums who have been investigated and found conscientious and reliable," she writes wisely, "may advertise in these pages."

There will be few books in this decade with the éclat or the brilliance of *Ghost Girl*. She's so good she doesn't even have to try and yet she does, again and again.

The Good, the Bad, and the Ugly (Extended Cut) (1969)
dir. Sergio Leone

★★★★★
Makes You Long for More

October 1, 2004

It's great that so much of the director's print has been discovered and fit in so seamlessly with the rest. And the documentary outlining the reconstruction of *GBU* is super, what a treat to see old Eastwood and even older Wallach mouthing their young dialogue into their young mouths in the cushy recording studio, a far cry from the plains of New Mexico. It makes you long for more, for there is probably another ten minutes of the complete version to be found, restored, and interpolated with the new extended version so splendidly presented here.

The movie itself is one of the masterpieces of both Italian and US cinema, and how many films get to boast of that? When I was a boy, the Morricone whistling theme became a top pop single, a feat that very few Westerns of recent vintage can aspire to. It's a haunting melody and watched with Leone's trademark close-ups and then sudden cutaways to long grand vistas, it gives you the chills of sudden fear from your spine to all your extremities.

Afeni Shakur: Evolution of a Revolutionary
by Jasmine Guy

★★★★★
A Great Conjunction

October 4, 2004

A great conjunction of author and subject, *Afeni Shakur: Evolution of a Revolutionary* will surprise those who think they know it all about Tupac Shakur, or even those who have taken his hint and done a bit of research on his mom, the legendary Black Panther of Oakland. For the actress Jasmine Guy has written a remarkable book, giving us the illusion of actually knowing Afeni Shakur and participating in her struggles for equality and Black hegemony in the last third of the twentieth century. I didn't know Jasmine Guy could write so well, but here she is, page after page of careful, extensive research plus such a winning way of drawing out her mysterious, courageous subject. This is a book with heart and soul.

Psycho (Collector's Edition) (1960)
dir. Alfred Hitchcock

★★★★★
RIP Janet Leigh, a Great Beauty, a Great Actress

October 4, 2004

We loved you in *Psycho* and cried when Marion Crane stole the money, thinking all along this was a bad move for her and would lead to trouble down the pike, we just didn't know how soon. And your beauty in *Words and Music* was so great you seemed to fill the MGM Technicolor screen with a ravishing light, like the rose of the world. We applauded your attempts to expand your screen image with risky roles such as your kooky, driven part in *The Manchurian Candidate*. And we admired the way you jumped into working with an amazing array of directors, everyone from Sternberg to George Sidney to John Carpenter. *Touch of Evil* was another favorite of your fans.

In addition, you brought forth into the world two other excellent screen actresses, Kelly and Jamie Lee Curtis. Today your fans from all over the world feel a sadness in our hearts because you have left this earth for a better place than this, having done your best to improve us, entertain us, make us smile, cry, and even scream. Go into light, Janet Leigh.

Back to School (1986)
dir. Alan Metter

★★★★★
Farewell, Rodney, You've Graduated at Last

October 6, 2004

As the word reaches us that Rodney Dangerfield has died without waking up from his coma, we take this occasion to salute him by viewing one more time his comedy classic *Back to School*. Adrienne Barbeau is in it, playing a trophy wife of yesteryear, grasping and unfaithful, she's only in it for the money anymore. Thornton Melon runs a men's store called "Tall and Fat," and I would have liked to see a whole sequel to *Back to School* that focused on the day-to-day life of running this haberdashery. Anyway he's rich enough to be able to afford to hire Kurt Vonnegut Jr. to write a term paper for him. Sam Kinison is in the movie too as the history professor—crazy and out of this world! And Sally Kellerman is more subdued than usual playing Diane Turner, the English professor who, in a memorable scene, makes Rodney analyze the meaning of Dylan Thomas's famous poem "Do Not Go Gentle into That Good Night."

Robert Downey Jr. is in the movie too, he's always good for a laugh or two. And Keith Gordon plays the son, maybe his best part after the young son of Angie Dickinson in *Dressed to Kill*. But most of all the picture belongs to the one and only Rodney Dangerfield. Rodney, we will miss your attitude and your "I get no respect" whining. You always saw things the way the common man did. We salute you for your tremendous achievements. As Dylan Thomas said,

And you, my father, there on the sad height,
Curse, bless, me now with your fierce tears, I pray.
Do not go gentle into that good night.
Rage, rage against the dying of the light.

Amy Lowell: Selected Poems
by Amy Lowell, ed. Honor Moore

★★★★★
"The Foxgloves Were like Tall Altar Candles"

October 10, 2004

This new edition of Amy Lowell's poems is a dazzling success in every way imaginable, and I hope people take it up in earnest thanks to the prestige of the Library of America and perhaps of Lowell's new editor, the distinguished memoirist and poet Honor Moore. Moore's introduction to the volume hits just the right notes and she is perhaps the ideal candidate to tell us why we should bother ourselves in the work of one of America's natural-born plutocracy who literally never had to work a day in her life. Despite all her advantages, Lowell was from the first interested in the ongoing "revolution of the word" that Pound, Flint, Hulme, and others were promulgating, first overseas and then, bringing it all back home, here in the USA. And Lowell was ready every step of the way, not only with her money but with her amazing talent. Lowell's best writing is scintillating, sharp as anything Pound did in the way of imagism, and yet she had something Pound lacked, perhaps a heart and certainly an openness to writing about sex experience that old Ez shied away from. Ezra Pound could never, for example, have written the poem Honor Moore includes here by Amy Lowell from 1919, called "Balls." At times Lowell and Pound seem to be occupying the same cultural space, as when Lowell proffers her own version of the ballad of the fisherman's wife, and when set head to head, Lowell seems to be, well, not quite as smart as Pound, but in her own way she is just as splendid and her life was terribly cut short when she was still (as these things go) sort of young, and it's interesting to speculate on what would have happened to an American poetry in the 1930s that had Amy Lowell working in it!

The book is very handsomely done and I can't think of anyone who won't walk away from it with a new respect for Amy Lowell, and a renewed puzzlement over the byways of publicity and mania that make Robert Lowell (say) so well known and his cousin Amy (say) kind of a relic from out of the closet.

Superman (1978)
dir. Richard Donner

★★★★★
RIP Christopher Reeve, Fine Actor, Exemplum of Courage

October 11, 2004

We will miss you, Christopher Reeve, and we will mourn your passing as we would any other noble soul's. We loved you as Superman, you were perhaps the only actor we would have "bought" in the role, both as dweeby Clark Kent and the chisel-chinned Man of Steel, and your floating over Metropolis taught us all that if we found the right love we too could fly. You won America's heart playing the part with all the conviction and vulnerability in the world, and so when your riding accident happened we were there for you too and we cheered on your fight against immobility and pain.

You fought against government inertia and inaction, and you made ordinary people aware of the great divide between the able bodied and the disabled, a divide that doesn't have to exist. In some ways you were even more splendid a hero in your later years than when you were mightier than a speeding bullet. Losing you is an event we were none of us prepared for, because I think we were all expecting one day to see you walk again, so titanic were your reserves of heroism and courage. Alas, that day was not to be, but now you are in the hall of the Valkyries, flying high overhead with the other heroes we have loved and lost. Sail on, sail on, Superman!

Arts and Letters
by Edmund White

★★★★★
A Treasure Trove

October 18, 2004

In *Arts and Letters* veteran novelist Edmund White shows again why he is one of the most inventive English-language writers. It's a salmagundi of commissioned pieces and articles that originally appeared in a variety of slick and gay magazines. Take them all together, and you get a lot of insight into White's own irresistible personality, even more so than in some of his celebrated autobiographical novels and memoirs. Plus, it's like being at the same party with some of the most intriguing personalities in the world today, as well as some dead immortals. White's style when he profiles these luminaries is never fawning— well, maybe once or twice, but he does it so well you forgive him anything. He's fearless, and asks the people in question exactly the kind of questions you think you'd ask yourself, if you were there on the scene and you had balls of brass. Cleis Press is to be commended for bringing out this jumbo volume. I only wish there were more.

There's just enough of a selection of White's writing about art to make you wish he'd jump in and write a whole book about the art and artists he admires. It's hard to find anything new to say about (for example) Jasper Johns or Robert Mapplethorpe, but after reading White's articles on both you will be viewing their work with new eyes. And he provides wonderful introductions to artists whose profiles may not be quite as high as these guys—Rebecca Horn, perhaps, or Steve Wolfe.

One after another of these articles are stunners—there's a fine piece on the half-forgotten French New Novelist Alain Robbe-Grillet, which takes you back to the day in which he was regarded as a wunderkind of depthless talent, and then shows today why he is still a writer worth studying.

White is not always Mr. Goody Two Shoes either. In one case, the Ned Rorem profile, you watch in helpless delight as Rorem gets skewered on the high kebab spears of White's erudition and wit. I also thought that printing a brief review of James Baldwin's *Just above*

My Head and labeling it "James Baldwin" leads the reader to think JB will be getting the full-blown profile treatment and instead it rebounds and just makes the review seem skimpy. And in some cases the reader will disagree, perhaps violently, with White's assessment of this or that subject, and you will still feel he has won the right to deliver it. I don't believe for an instant that James is the equivalent of Cavalcanti crossed with Noël Coward, but it's amusing to hear someone say so.

By and large these essays are compelling, entertaining, and wise. It's a book that deserves all the praise it will doubtless receive.

The Tinkerbell Hilton Diaries: My Life Tailing Paris Hilton
by Tinkerbell Hilton (as told to D. Resin)

★★★☆☆
Tinkerbell Released

October 25, 2004

This book is pretty cute, all things put together, and D. Resin, whoever he may be, has a cunning way of seeing events from a chihuahua's point of view. I enjoyed the different chapters about filming *The Simple Life* and the discovery that Paris had made a sex tape, and how her handlers were going to spin that for maximum publicity density. Resin understands as few others do that people like Paris not because she's socially aware, but because she treats life like a game and she always seems like a good sport.

Tinkerbell complains about the Pomeranians who live with her in the LA house. She explains how you have to be extra patient with Pomeranians because they're so dumb. And she deplores the way people associate chihuahuas with Pomeranians. "Unfortunately, because they're small, yappy, and ubiquitous, they're the ones most people picture when they hear the term 'toy dog.' Real fond of barking at nothing and getting freaked out by their own tails. Not exactly Lassie. In fact, if they had done that show with a Pomeranian dog, it would have been much simpler: Timmy would fall down the well, Lassie would furiously lick itself for forty minutes, and then Lassie would turn around and psychotically challenge a small rock to a fight, which it would ultimately become intimidated by." Needless to say, Paris isn't likely to use the word "ubiquitous" in a sentence any time soon, nor has she probably heard of Lassie. She's great, and as Tinkerbell points out, she has a "slack, blank, almost Zen sort of ease that's like wallpaper to read" but is sublimely easy to get along with. I hope that instead of being ashamed to be seen reading this book, as most people doubtless would be, more people pick it up and give it a good read. Virginia Woolf wrote *Flush* on much the same grounds, she wanted to paint a picture of a famous person (in her case Elizabeth Barrett Browning) from the point of view of her kidnapped dog. If it worked for Woolf, why can't it work for Resin? I say it does!

Hallelujah! The Welcome Table: A Lifetime of Memories with Recipes by Maya Angelou

★★★★☆
A Poet in the Kitchen

November 2, 2004

Here in San Francisco folk with educated palates still talk and reminisce about Maya Angelou's stint cooking at the Creole Café, back during the height of the Creole movement westward bound. A wandering people had reached the blue Pacific but hungry Louisianans still yearned for a little bit of home. Of course Angelou was not from Louisiana herself, as we all know she is from Arkansas which is why Bill Clinton asked her to read "On the Pulse of Morning" for his first inauguration, but her family's recipes saw her through some difficult times. And when times got tough for her, San Francisco diners reaped the benefits. Now, sixty years later, she finally reveals the secrets that made her own brand of Creole food so good. (Our local columnist the late Herb Caen wrote about Angelou first as a cook, later as an exotic dancer and singer, finally of course as a famous poet.) The truth is, she did a little bit of everything and you can taste it in her cooking.

I tried the homemade potato salad and found that, for me, speaking personally, there was maybe too much parsley and not enough pickles, relish, or celery, but it had a delicious flavor never-theless and I'm not surprised she has called it her favorite picnic food. Brian Lanker's photographs of the food she made herself decorate nearly every chapter, and he is of course the famous *Life* magazine photographer who made the award-winning documentary about artists who work for the US government (and independently) in combat. Here his photographs are more relaxed, though still gritty and reliable. He is a firm photographer, with definite slants to his insight, and so he is a good matchup for Maya Angelou, who now must be nearly eighty and with a lifetime of achievement to look back on. Even the famous food writer M. F. K. Fisher gave Maya Angelou a great compliment, saying she is one of the ten best cooks she ever met. (Both women were Bay Area residents during the '50s and '60s, and were quite fond of each other, odd as it seems.) There is one recipe here for every year of Maya Angelou's life, and I hope that the success of this volume calls forth for a sequel, one in which the recipes are arranged seasonally, and perhaps a few fewer tales of compliments that guests gave her, because it does sound a little vain, as though she were patting herself on the back in the pages of her own book.

Ariel: The Restored Edition
by Sylvia Plath

★★★★★
"Love Set You Going," She Wrote, "like a Fat Gold Watch"

November 9, 2004

Now at long last, we get the *Ariel* we deserve. Plath's admirers have been waiting a long time, since at least the early 1980s when Ted Hughes first revealed that he had changed the order of the poems in his wife's final manuscript. He had added some poems—the final, freezingly depressing ones—and then rearranged the bulk of the book to leave an impression of a woman gone over the brink into a chilling fugue state. Now Frieda Hughes, Plath's daughter, when her mother killed herself, has performed a ritual act of atonement to her mother's memory and given us the original, "happy" (relatively speaking) *Ariel* which we have never been able to see.

At $24.95, the book's a little expensive, but it feels as though money had been spent on its planning and execution, so you don't feel rooked. In one section, the gray paper on which the facsimile materials are printed is easy on the eyes, aiding the eye as it struggles with Plath's numerous emendations. We get the notes Plath wrote for her own use when she had to do that reading at the BBC toward the end, the more-British-than-thou reading we have grown to love and hate at the same time. Frieda Hughes contributes an interesting and contextualizing introduction in which she seeks to reconcile the differing viewpoints of her mother and father—a challenging task, but she's up to it. The book ends up with four of the beekeeping poems—and another in the appendix, "The Swarm," which Sylvia kept changing her mind about including. Should she leave it in? Take it out? The title is in brackets. Thus the book ends with a hopeful note, with the freshness of Devon instead of the bleak London winter. It ends, pleasantly enough, with the words "They taste the spring."

The Holy Grail: Charles Bukowski and the "Second Coming" Revolution
by A. D. Winans

★★★★☆
Good Book on Two Important US Poets
November 29, 2004

Have you been curious to find out how SF Beat poet A. D. Winans came to know the Los Angeles rabble-rouser Charles Bukowski? In this book you can find out the whole in and out of their relationship, in which they were sort of like the Hemingway and Fitzgerald of a nascent poetic movement which Winans has called "the *Second Coming* revolution," after his own magazine, the long-gone, and sadly missed, *Second Coming*, which might be said to have started a revolution in letting the common people speak in the language of the human tongue. But maybe "revolution" is the wrong word. Plenty of fine photos stud this book, some of the talented San Francisco poet Harold Norse and other figures around the legendary fifty-year-old bookstore City Lights on Columbus Avenue, where "Hank," as his intimates called Bukowski, made some of his most colorful public appearances. But A. D. Winans got to know Hank in private too, and some of the most telling stories in the book concern the way Winans counts it up and realizes that, actually, he only met with Bukowski a handful of times, and that he got to "know" him mostly through his letters and through his many volumes of verse.

There is also an explanation of why Winans is bitter today, for rightfully so he feels ignored, and plus he had a spiked drink some time ago and was jailed by malicious SF cops who put him in a cell with deadbeats and dangerous felons, and subjected him to a nude body search which was humiliating. But he survived his ordeal and has since then written over two dozen books. Though Bukowski is dead now, Winans lives on to dare to dream the visions of glory dreamt by the knights of the round table who wanted to find ... "the Holy Grail."

Cartouche (1962)
dir. Philippe de Broca

★★★★★
RIP Philippe de Broca, Farewell, À Bientôt
                                                    November 29, 2004

In *Cartouche* you made the rest of the '60s filmmakers seem out of date, and in Belmondo and Cardinale you found the perfect actors who could add the bubbles to your brand of filmic champagne. Now that you are gone, we think back to all the pleasures you have given us over the years, from your little parts in *Breathless* and *400 Blows*, to your most recent work discovering the Welsh coal miner's daughter Catherine Zeta-Jones, and we are grateful to you for your inspired interventions and pizzazz. Not since Ernst Lubitsch has flair been filmed so perfectly and gallantly, and not since Clouzot has action been so well blended with nail-biting suspense. Our hearts are sad today and we wish your extended family well in these difficult days. Belmondo and Cardinale are still with us and thanks to you, we will always have them in excelsis, as the perfect man and woman *au cinéma*. Merci, de Broca!

Alexander (2004)
dir. Oliver Stone

★★★★★
"Dreamers Exhaust Us ..."

November 29, 2004

"Dreamers exhaust us," says Ptolemy (Anthony Hopkins, looking like an elderly Yoda at the library in Alexandria), "we must kill them before their dreams kill us all." Call me crazy, but I loved *Alexander*. I went in with incredibly low expectations based on dismal reviews, and instead I wound up sitting there with my hand frozen halfway to my mouth, fist stuffed with popcorn, not moving a muscle until the picture was over. The movie may be "bad," but it's bad in a personal way, with lots of colorful sequences and some camp howlers that just move the action along as vigorously as anything DeMille could have turned out in his heyday. If you thought the acting was bad in *The Ten Commandments*, and yet you can't stop watching that picture every Easter, you will be crying with joy when you see *Alexander*, nearly as long and twice as pagan. Colin Farrell looks so young at first—he's good playing nineteen or twenty, and it's only when he ages that his acting starts falling apart. I thought Angelina Jolie was fantastic, unashamed of her part, putting herself into it with her whole heart and soul.

She looks wonderful, even when dozens of white, pasty, slug-colored snakes writhe and wrap around her marvelous body—were these all CGI or did she actually work with them? She certainly gives the impression of a mother whose priorities were (1) having fun with snakes and (2) the welfare of Alexander. Val Kilmer was great, whether he was trying to rape Olympias or taking little Alex through a mural tour of the great heroes of Greek history—Oedipus, Prometheus, Medea, no one was spared. The actor who plays Bagoas or whatever his name was—the boy who looks like a girl—has the strangest body, and both he and Rosario Dawson, who plays Roxane, Alexander's barbarian bride, seem to be in a competition for who can cast smoldering looks the farthest.

All the actors really threw themselves over the cliff in this one, and I as a moviegoer appreciated it, there's too much irony in the movies nowadays and hardly anyone gives that kind of balls-to-the-wall performance like they used to. Well, here there are at least a dozen of them, and Colin Farrell's thighs are serious competition to all the other Best Supporting Actor nominees of 2004. I also liked the way Oliver Stone told the story so that none of the central questions of the film are ever answered and we are thrust back onto the prongs of our own curiosity about this marvelous "Mager Alexandrum."

The Unsubscriber
by Bill Knott

★★★★☆
Good Work from Knott

December 6, 2004

I enjoyed a lot of *The Unsubsciber*, though some of the poems are weak. FS&G are promoting this book (well, sort of, actually they are sneaking it in under the radar) as though it were the work of an underground genius like Bill Hicks whom they are magically bringing into light, but the truth is that many poetry readers have been familiar with Knott's work for a long, long time.

Unlike the reviewer from *Publishers Weekly*, I thought the best part of the book was its last section, entitled "Poems After," each one inspired by a poet who has gone before—most of them now deceased. Knott has a thick, rich, whiskey-soaked voice and his various tributes and homages or "profiles" as he calls them are generally pitched in a lower key than the original. I liked especially his poem called "On the Road" in which he takes the characters and zeitgeist of Kerouac's poetic novel and castigates them for doing too much driving and using too many fossil fuels: "faster faster never slow / on the road to ecocide." It's not something I had ever thought of before.

Knott has wonderfully thorny poems about the difficulties of growing up and growing older, and one of the best in the book is his memory poem about grade school called "Mrs. Frye and the Pencil-sharpener," which I wish I could quote in full to you. He is endlessly quotable, and he embodies some of the lessons of transparency that the Russian poets like Mandelstam and the South American fictionists like Borges were so good at. When he is clumsy and awkward you often feel that he meant to be so, for some unspoken yet unchallengeable reason, like John Wayne's acting.

The Polar Express (2004)
dir. Robert Zemeckis

★★★★☆
"When Christmas Comes to Town"

December 6, 2004

The Polar Express is the picture of the year in IMAX 3D. I can't imagine how it might look any other way. The compositions would be the same, but the dimensionality of the movie really floors you, knocks you out, and I think perhaps the 3D effects help you enjoy Alan Silvestri's music more, even down to the magical sleigh bells that our little hero cannot hear.

The songs are to be cherished. I couldn't make out the lyrics of the choral number "Spirit of the Season," but it is something I would like to have the choir in my church sing during their rehearsals for *The Nutcracker Suite*. One of my favorite music numbers is the bizarre, minimal "Hot Chocolate" barked out by Tom Hanks and a chorus of singing waiters in a takeoff of an old Cotton Club / Cab Calloway style. Hanks really doesn't have a good singing voice, does he, and he's straining himself trying to get through a number even where all he has to say is "Hot, hot" a dozen times. In general, when Hanks was off the screen I liked the movie better. I couldn't help but think that he was hogging up all the action by trying to put his brand on every male character in the show, right down to the evil Scrooge puppet, and trying to play one character and the father to that character is stupid, if you ask me, but they say Warner Bros. paid him $25 million dollars to play in the show, so maybe they figured they would milk him for all he's worth. Peter Sellers used to play many characters—and Alec Guinness—I didn't like it when they did it either, to tell you the truth.

Steven Tyler from Aerosmith has a few cute moments as an elf singing "Rockin' on Top of the World."

The movie has you in tears from approximately 40:15 on. When the little Black girl and the poor boy who's afraid of Christmas disappointment get together at the back of the club car and sing "When Christmas Comes to Town," it is the signal to unleash all the tears you've ever wanted to shed about the world's injustice and also the beauty of the world that the young girl seems to be arguing in favor of. If the Christmas season can produce such wonderful feelings of love, then it is a shame it cannot last all year.

The Legend of Leigh Bowery (2002)
dir. Charles Atlas

★★★★★
Riveting

December 15, 2004

I knew only a little about Leigh Bowery going in, having seen some of Lucian Freud's large-scale paintings of him, and also seeing *Wigstock*, the drag queen documentary in which Leigh Bowery makes an astonishing appearance, giving "birth" to Nicola, his assistant, through an amazing theatrical stunt. I couldn't believe my eyes in either case.

The film is terrifically exciting both as information and as entertainment. Atlas has an artist's eye and, or so it seems, a tremendously sympathetic, yet dispassionate, insight into the personality of the mysterious and enigmatic Leigh Bowery. Bowery emerged rapidly from what must have seemed in comparison the very outback of Australia to the trendy, gender-bending nightclubs of '80s London, one of which he started himself—the infamous Taboo. He wore a variety of wigs and costumes, but that's understating it because the costumes took on a life of their own and indeed no other human could have worn them. Interviewees claim that even though some of the costumes were painful in the extreme to wear for more than a few minutes, Bowery carried on for hours in them, having the time of his life.

One nice thing is that Atlas has footage from every period of Bowery's artistic life, from his challenging one-man show at Anthony d'Offay Gallery, in which viewers could watch him through a one-way mirror preen and primp himself all day on a chaise lounge to die for, all the way to his last performances with the rock group Minty. His death from AIDS is treated very sparsely and, I thought, most movingly. One minute he was here, the next he was gone, poof! Like a dandelion. The speakers are all extremely cogent and it seems as though they wanted to put their best foot forward for their late chum, for all of them look fantastic, from Damien Hirst to Boy George. The painter Cerith Wyn Evans steals the show however—he is totally photogenic and, though no longer young, is the sexiest man in the movies right now. Sorry to add a lascivious note to this somber review, but I just have to. He's as riveting as the documentary he appears in.

Jay DeFeo and "The Rose"
ed. Jane Green and Leah Levy

★★★★★
Jay DeFeo Lives

December 22, 2004

Jay DeFeo spent many years of her life painting one picture, first called *Deathrose*, then just plain *The Rose*, and it grew so heavy with paint that it had to be hauled out of her studio on Fillmore Street in San Francisco on a crane. The proceedings were filmed by the artist Bruce Conner, a longtime friend of DeFeo's, and assembled by him into a film called *The White Rose: Jay DeFeo's Painting Removed by Angelic Hosts* (actually Bekins movers).

After a few showings, the painting was stored at the San Francisco Art Institute and eventually plastered over to stabilize its shifting masses of paint and also to protect it from student graffiti. For many years it hid behind this plaster and its absence became a giant statement. DeFeo herself began to think of Conner's film as a kind of displaced substitute for her work, and Jane Green and Leah Levy, the editors of the present volume, are astute enough to let this fact speak for itself. In a great act of showmanship, Lisa Phillips, a Whitney curator, not only restored the painting but bought it for the Whitney where it can be viewed today (sometimes).

This book contains many essays by people who were close to DeFeo, as well as some by those who never met her. Bill Berkson's essay imagines the 1959–60 *Sixteen Americans* show by Dorothy C. Miller (which featured DeFeo, as well as her husband Wally Hedrick, in addition to giving national exposure to the likes of Frank Stella, Jasper Johns, Robert Rauschenberg, but was missing *The Rose*, which DeFeo did not send saying it was not yet finished). Lucy Lippard's essay considers similarities between DeFeo's production and that of her contemporaries Eva Hesse and the Lees—Lee Bontecou and Lee Lozano— relating her depressing years of inactivity (1966–70) to the nascent women's art movement. It is provocative to say the least. The University of California Press has printed many fine photos to go with the book, including some color images which I had never seen.

Windblown World: The Journals of Jack Kerouac 1947–1954
by Jack Kerouac, ed. Douglas Brinkley

★★★★☆
Comedown, Sorrow, and Truest Love
December 23, 2004

Two of Kerouac's journals, published together and finally available for the lay reader to pick up and delve into. Editor Douglas Brinkley does a fine job putting this material into context, even if he makes overstated claims for it, and even if he seems so needlessly to kiss John Sampas's ass, even dedicating this book to him among others of his cohort. We learn a lot about Kerouac from these journals, a lot that's valuable and a lot that shows us just why so many fell in love with his mind and his thoughtful, sometimes halting way of proceeding, always trying to do the right thing despite innumerable obstacles. I think also he had a natural inclination to be sort of the bad boy, and then he had the specter of his dead brother acting on him as a kind of good angel always steering him right. With utmost seriousness he tried to plot out his life and his course of spiritual action; of course, as we see, women, booze, guys, and wanderlust got in his way, caused him to stray from the path.

His very earnestness however is endearing: "This is why life is holy," he states on p. 211 (think of the irony on top of which such a statement would be laden today by Kerouac's so-called successors), "because it is not a lonely accident. Therefore, again, we must love and be reverent of one another, till the day when we are all angels looking back." He sounds an apocalyptic note: "Those who are not reverent now may be the most reverent then (in their other, electrical, spiritual form). Will there be a Judgement Day? No need to judge the living or the dead; only the happy and the unhappy with tears of pity." Kerouac seems to have seen clearly what escapes all of us but the most enlightened, that we are all creatures of sorrow and of what he calls "electricity," the charge that makes us human.

But not all of *Windblown World* is so solemn, there are some hilarious tidbits and routines, such as the curriculum JK develops in October 1949 (pp. 226–28) for a kind of "new School for Comedians," with imaginary courses that might be given by Burroughs ("How to Play the Horses") and Huncke ("Modern Drugs"). His own courses were more poetic: "Riddles and Roses" and "The Myth of the Rainy Night." The requirements to get into the school? "Sixty points in elementary realization, largesse, comedown, sorrow, and truest love."

The Long Goodbye (1973)
dir. Robert Altman

★★★★☆
Reinvention of Marlowe

January 1, 2005

I really enjoyed the featurettes that came with the DVD, one with Altman and Elliott Gould, the other with cinematographer Vilmos Zsigmond who discusses technical points that added to my appreciation of the movie. It's one of the few movies from the hippie era that hasn't aged badly, because the naked girls doing yoga on the balcony are as perplexing to Marlowe as they are to the viewer of today. The female star, Nina van Pallandt, who plays Eileen Wade is genius casting. In fact the actor who plays Roger Wade, Eileen's husband, is also beautifully cast—Sterling Hayden. One wonders what the film would have been like if Dan "Hoss from Bonanza" Blocker had played the part of Roger Wade. In the featurette Altman reveals he nearly abandoned making the picture after Blocker's death, and he is listed in the credits in a weird sort of way. But back to Hayden and Van Pallandt. He is a man-mountain with a big *Lord of the Rings*-style beard, he could have played the tree thing in *Fellowship of the Ring*. He has a long monologue on the beach with a bottle of frozen aquavit that's fantastic as anything he did for Coppola or Kubrick. And Nina van Pallandt—who had been a kind of Danish folk singer and then one of the principals in the Howard Hughes / Clifford Irving forgery scandal of Ibiza—looks utterly gorgeous in the film, always wearing some ethnic hippie gown with sixty yards of material, always looking Scandinavian, with bogs of great sorrow in her dark eyes. She should have won the Oscar—that's plain to see nowadays. She's also great in Altman's *A Wedding* as the drug-addled mom.

And how many cigarettes does Elliott Gould smoke in this movie? It's as if he has discovered a new brand of acting which involves expressing oneself solely through cigarettes. No wonder Sterling Hayden calls him "Marlboro Man."

And the theme song is terrific, the lyrics by Johnny Mercer among Mercer's best. Between Johnny Mercer's contribution and those of Sterling Hayden and Leigh Brackett, Altman garnered the best of the 1940s and brought it into the 1970s for a last hurrah.

Going Once: A Memoir of Art, Society, and Charity
by Robert Woolley

★★★☆☆
A Bygone Era in Auctioneering

January 5, 2005

I feel sorry for the people who came to him during one of Sotheby's *Antiques Roadshow*-style days, for he was withering when confronted with the junk people offered him off of Aunt Tillie's mantelpiece. He is fairly fearless when it comes to painting a portrait of himself as the ultimate New York society queen. Poor guy died of AIDS not long after this book was published, and I still find it enjoyable. It seems as though a lot of Sotheby's secrets went to the grave with him, for he certainly knew where most of the bodies were buried. His account of the Andy Warhol–estate auction is mind boggling, so you will forgive him his gaucheries and his nonstop bitchiness. Another good story is how he auctioned off (for charity) the services of David Hockney, who volunteered to paint your swimming pool, and how the film producer Lester Persky had to be shamed into bidding for what was on the face of it an incredible bargain. We all love auction stories, for they remind us that maybe someday we will find a bargain worth bragging about, whether in the world of the decorative and visual arts, or in romance, as I did when I married my present wife.

Wood Diner Birdhouse
by Meadow Creek Trading

★★★★★
And All You Have to Do Is Provide the Seed!

January 6, 2005

The Diner Birdhouse is one of those products you wish you would have thought of, for how cute is it to have a diner setup for birds that dispenses birdseed round the clock?

As the sign says outside, "Open 24 Hours"! Many fine birdhouses were available to us, but this is the one we chose. My grandmother owned an actual diner, in Jamaica, Queens, and we put this up on our pole to honor her memory and to remember all the delicious ways she served up humble people food. Comes with hand-painted medallions and accoutrements, including picnic tables lining the diner frontage, with gay red-and-white-checked picnic tablecloths for that festive summer effect. But this is one birdhouse that looks grand with snow capping its roof too. Just make sure to keep the door open for birds looking for a quick bite, or maybe just to get in out of the cold for a spell.

The things you do for these birds, after all, you do for Saint Francis, who loved his feathered friends as he loved the moon and the sun.

Check out the merry silhouettes of the customers manning the booths inside the diner, you can spot them eating right through the painted windows.

"Shakes … Hamburgers … Welcome"!

Bottoms Up: Writing about Sex
ed. Diana Cage

★★★★★
Knock Yourself Out

January 10, 2005

"'My dreams are small,' said Olly. 'They can only scratch.'

'Well, cheers to that,' said Mr. Devine. 'To scratchy dreams! A house specialty. Bottoms up.'"

This pair of paragraphs from Jess Arndt's lovely story "The Unheard Arms of Olly Malone" suggests some of the extraliterary quality of this collection of twenty-first-century erotica, ably assisted by San Francisco editor Diana Cage, herself a very fine writer who shouldn't have been so demure, she should have included some of her own work. But that's just my peeve. Outside of that, I think you will find *Bottoms Up* a provocative and intriguing collection, one that includes some of today's best and most well-respected authors, as well as a bevy of young talent with lots and lots of skill. "Robin" by Eileen Myles is a story that has been around for some time, but still over-powers one with the specificity and the brilliance of Myles's powers of description and connotation (i.e., she pulls you into the story with image)—"I call her Robin because she is red and black and angular and resembles a bird in her speed and her cruelty. I fell in love with her briefly last year. I'm just not in love with her anymore but there's this residue." Similarly Robert Glück's account of the Folsom Street Fair has some of the haunting quality of folk fairy tale material and was originally written for an anthology of fairy tales rewritten and made up to date by gay male authors. It is called "The Glass Moun-tain" and its sparkle and its sheer impassibility calls to mind the mountain of its title. Haven't we all been in love a little bit like that. You can't go up, you can only go around. "I can reach myself only through the medium of a brittle young man whose shadow touches what it falls on, the grass rising again after it passes."

Among the writers who are newer to me, I will evince "Cruising" by Myriam Gurba as a tiny masterpiece of danger, psychic pain, and physical fulfillment. The young woman who tells us this tale brings to mind poor Elizabeth Short, "the Black Dahlia," who, we hear, once cruised these same tawdry beaches and amusement galleries in a slickly drawn Long Beach. Shoshana von Blanckensee brings "Billy," a story of multiple sexualities and multiple paragraphs, each one outlining an erotic possibility that should, but cannot, cancel the other out. She is like a Julio Cortázar excerpt with, well, much more sex LOL. Tennessee Jones's story is very tangibly an excerpt and thus leaves you longing for more, for its grittiness and sheer perversity brings to mind the near-gothic, southern writing of William Goyen or Flannery O'Connor. It is a story of boxcar sex and prison longing, redolent of scents and stench. I look forward to hearing more from Mr. Jones. I could tell you a little bit about each story, but I don't have the time or space, so I should close by citing the unusually structured, and enchanting, "Knockout" by San Francisco's Sarah Fran Wisby. "Knockout" perceptively tells the story of a young sex worker whose knowledge of being seen, of the male gaze, increases her power over men and her own inner desire to bring into clearer focus the nexus of her family. It has a final line that will make the hair stand up at the back of your neck à la Emily Dickinson.

Here's to all the dynamite writers who have come together for this splendid occasion, in *Bottoms Up*. I hope it's a great success. "To scratchy dreams!"

Nazarín (1959)
dir. Luís Buñuel

★★★★★
Goodnight, Señora Ofelia Guilmáin

January 14, 2005

The sad news spreads that you have left this planet, Ofelia Guilmáin, at age eighty-one. Born in Spain, you became a naturalized Mexican in the 1940s and embarked on a stellar career on the stages of Mexico City and provinces and in a series of Mexican films, among them several by the Spanish émigré Luis Buñuel. We recall you best of all in *Nazarín*, as the sometimes cynical, sometimes credulous landlady of the inn where Nazarin stays. As Chanfa, Ofelia Guilmáin's acting in what might have been a rote part shows you once and for all that there are no small parts, just small actors. The wronged girl who finds herself pregnant tries to hang herself from a beam in the ceiling. In a typical Buñuel setup, the beam snaps and the girl lives. Sobbing, on the floor, she looks up startled as she is discovered by Ofelia Guilmáin who smirks and comments "If you wanted to kill yourself, you should have found a better beam," a wry comment on the virility of the girl's cowardly suitor. Chanfa provides the note of the "real world" in contradistinction to the saintly impulses of the tortured priest, Father Nazario. Buñuel revered Ofelia Guilmáin and used her again to good effect in his 1962 epic *The Exterminating Angel*, and she appeared in several classic Mexican horror films including most memorably *The Brainiac*, where as the wife of a foundry owner she becomes the victim of the Terror Baron's revenge (warning, this is a pretty gruesome film). In person she was lovable, courageous, modest about her amazing career. She kept on working right until the end. Lovers of Buñuel will miss her, but we know that in *Nazarín* you light up the skies of *realismo* with your passion, Señora Guilmáin. Viva Ofelia Guilmáin!

I Believe in You
by Kylie Minogue

★★★★★
"I Don't Believe in Magic, It's Only in the Mind"

January 17, 2005

> *The joker's always smiling*
> *In every hand that's dealt*
> *I don't believe that when you die*
> *Your presence isn't felt*

The reiterated negatives ("don't," "isn't," etc.) in Kylie's lyrics convinces us that she's thought hard about what she believes in and, maybe more crucially, what she doesn't. She's been around for a long time (for a pop star) and she succeeds in making you believe she has an old soul—maybe reincarnation has brought her to this earth many times before. The accompanying video isn't as good as the song itself, but it isn't awful. We see Kylie in a kind of huge fifteen-foot cage, the shape of a pumpkin, made out of sinuous Lalique-style wires that reveal her swirling form. She doesn't dance, but the cage revolves at a measured, steady pace. Well, it's a kind of dance, I suppose—her feet don't move, but she performs a series of imaginative arm movements that will remind elderly viewers either of the hula or the kind of "modern dance" movements Paul Taylor used to teach his dancers. They're very skilled, but it's hard to say what Kylie has in mind while delivering them. Emotions cross her face, but in general she wants you to think "She's radiant," full stop.

It's a good comeback for her, after the messy, hurried effort of *Body Language* (which could have been so good!) and the tunes that will follow this number (like "Giving You Up" and "(Everything) I Know," if that is ever released) show promise. Kylie's had a great knack for seeking out the right collaborator, and here Jake and Babydaddy work wonders for her, replete with yodeling Heidi-style and a relentless pop beat. Despite her sometimes bland manner during interviews, she's an amazingly bright person and it shows in this gorgeous track.

Darwin the Wizard Marionette (Created by Artist Daniel Oates)
by Bozart Toys

★★★★★
I Love This Puppet

February 9, 2005

Puppets and marionettes make even the oldest of grown-ups into children. No one knows this fact of life better than master creator Daniel Oates, the renowned artist. I bought Darwin on a whim, wanting to produce some magic spells to get myself a raise at work. I figured with all the kids bragging about how Oates's four-string system made his marionettes impossible to tangle that even I could manage to take him out of the box. I liked what I saw and went ahead and ordered the whole lot of Oates's magical "dolls"—all of them boasting names that begin, like his, with the letter *D*.

There's a wonderful full-size puppet theater you can buy with shifting backdrops of medieval scenes. It's a little like *Shrek* come to life. The lovely Princess Destiny, her fuchsia hair almost silvery in the moonlight of San Francisco, is guarded by her knight, Sir Dorric. The strange and weird oversized raven, Dave, caws out a greeting to any who come to my apartment in the Mission. Dexter the Jester will tell a few jokes and mouth some warped wisdom, like the fool in *King Lear*. The extravagant unicorn, Delilah, loves Princess Destiny and will often approach her to try to tease some barley sugar out of her long, elegant, fingertipped hand. As you ring the doorbell of the moat, watch out for Dunstan, the playful dragon. He'll breathe fire all over you if you don't watch out. In this way my medieval fantasies go unchecked, thanks to the mastery of the one and one Daniel Oates.

Kinsey (2004)
dir. Bill Condon

★★★☆☆
Biopics Are Always a Little Disappointing …

February 10, 2005

No matter how well scripted, they're hidebound by having to stick to the outward facts of their subject's life. I haven't seen a good one since *Lady Sings the Blues* and even that wasn't awfully good, though it was fascinating. So is *Kinsey*, I expect, though people don't seem to want to go to it. My friend Wayne and I went last night and three women sitting behind us and to the left were laughing at themselves and their own naïveté because, as it turned out, they had come to the theater thinking they were seeing Kinsey Millhone, the Sue Grafton heroine, brought to life by Laura Linney. They didn't know whether to laugh or cry when they discovered they were in for a picture showing how America gradually opened up to the idea of sex when supported by science.

Another rule of thumb is most movies starring John Lithgow and Veronica Cartwright as the parents are probably going to be pretty overplayed. This was the case here. Seeing this movie was like going into a time tunnel of the cinema—so many of the actors haven't been in an A movie in ages. Timothy Hutton, Lynn Redgrave, John Lithgow, Katherine Houghton (the young girl from *Guess Who's Coming to Dinner*, now looking unimaginably aged), and even Chris O'Donnell from the

Batman movies. How did he get another job? He's looking good. But Peter Sarsgaard provokes most of the attention by slipping out of his clothes in a cheap hotel room and heading for the shower. Kinsey doesn't know which way to look but you can see where his eyes are straying to. Peter Sarsgaard isn't the luckiest guy in the size department, but he's got nothing to complain about, and once his pants come down, you can predict what's going to happen through the rest of the movie. I wonder if the real Clyde Martin is still alive? If so you'd think he'd ask for someone with a bigger endowment to play him. Oh well, he (Sarsgaard) is extremely good in the movie and many fans will beat a path to his door.

Linney and Neeson are good, too, but they are often harshly lit and made up to look awful. Laura Linney in particular has been given some nice hairdos and '30s and '40s dresses, but then they blotch her skin with a disgraceful aging makeup that makes it hard to believe she's not supposed to be playing a homeless person without access to moisturizer or even soap. As for Neeson, how old is he anyhow? Playing a young man he looks older than Walter Huston, and he doesn't get any better as he ages.

All in all the movie is too ambitious and tries to cover too much territory. *Gods and Monsters*, Bill Condon's previous biopic, took the subtler approach of limiting the story to the events of the last days of James Whale's life. This story might have worked better with a little restraint, though I can see Condon pushing for that epic feel which he just misses—what a pity.

Romeoland
by Lil' Romeo

★★★★☆
Sticks in Your Head, like Butter

February 17, 2005

Soon there will be a movie based on "My Cinderella" and it will be called *Lil' Romeo and Lil' Juliet*, starring the one and only Lil' Romeo, I wonder whom Hollywood will get to play Lil' Juliet, unless by then there is an actual rap personality with this name. In the meantime, fans of Lil' Romeo will be playing *Romeoland* again and again until the thing just falls apart. Hopefully Nick Cannon (who adds his own style on the track) will be featured in the new *Romeo + Juliet* movie too as he could add some respectability to the product. It's a beautiful song in which he says that before he's twenty-four he can rule the world, but only if he can find the perfect little shorty to reign at his side as his queen. "I'm willing to grow, to the mountaintop, if you're willing to go." His dad the famous Master P produces some of the other tracks. Who dares criticize Master P for having a son more famous than he is? That's like saying George W. Bush is more famous than his dad who was also president. Lil' Bow Wow's got nothing on that. He is his own rival and worst enemy.

Hidden Florida Keys & Everglades: Including Key Largo & Key West
by Candace Leslie and Ann Boese

★★★★★
"Buried Treasure"

February 18, 2005

Not every guidebook on the keys would feature such an unassuming place as Jim & Val's Tugboat Restaurant in Key Largo. Jim & Val's Tugboat is one of the true "buried treasures" of Florida, and this guidebook has enough sense to put it in bold. Wonder if we'll see the place overrun by "foodies" who will go anywhere to try something new.

Long ago, pirates prowled the waters around the Keys, and nowadays, it's chic to blame the congestion of the Keys on tourists, but sometimes it's just people drawn to the good food (like the steak au poivre which is simply out of this world) or people trying to find out what drew poet Wallace Stevens back, year after year, to the Key West hotel about which he wrote such a haunting poem. This guidebook will be a nice souvenir for you, even if you haven't been in Key Largo for some time. It will bring it all back to you—the salty creosote smell, the cerise skies that turn inky at night, the stars that twinkle right above your head, you can almost catch one by the toe.

If a Man Answers (1962)
dir. Henry Levin

★★★★★
Farewell to a Great Beauty and a Lovely Lady

February 20, 2005

CNN and other news networks have announced the sad news that our beloved Sandra Dee has died this morning at 6:00 a.m. of complications of kidney disease and pneumonia. She was with her son, Dodd Darin, who made the announcement to the press some hours later.

For those of us who admired her work in films, this is a sad day indeed. She was "before my time" but I never saw a Sandra Dee picture I didn't love. She was a child model, and a teen star, and she married the pop singer Bobby Darin while still carving out her own screen career, so perhaps she wasn't lucky in her own life, since she seemed to have grown up too fast and to have missed the normal life of the child, but we her fans were extremely lucky. We got to thrill with her as the first girl surfer in *Gidget*, and to root for her against her selfish mother in the second version of *Imitation of Life*, and to cry a little as she romanced Troy Donahue and "went all the way" in the majestically corny *A Summer Place*. And so many other films, good and bad.

A few years back she and Troy Donahue made a personal appearance at the Castro Theatre here in San Francisco, where she seemed frail but happy to greet the hordes of fans who poured in from all over the country to thank her for the decades of pleasure her cinematic legacy has given us. She even sang a little bit of that ironic song from *Grease* that mocked her virginal image, "Look at Me, I'm Sandra Dee." She was in fine form that night, and signed autographs and posed for photos until she begged off due to fatigue.

If a Man Answers may not be one of her best movies, but it shows her considerable comic abilities, and if she was ever happy at all, it might have been during this period when she was often teamed alongside her then-husband, and both seemed to be sitting on top of the world. Alas, today a little light went out of the world but I know that tonight I'll look up into the night sky and I'll see a pale new star, directly overhead, with the luminous intensity that was Sandra Dee's alone.

Singin' in the Rain
by Cliff Edwards

★★★★★
The Saddest Story

March 3, 2005

Wait till you hear the passion and the wit with which Cliff sings the famous Billy Rose number "The Night Is Young and You're So Beautiful." I love the optimism and the subtlety of the lyrics: "When the lady is kissable, and the evening is cool, any dream is permissible—in the heart of a fool." Elsewhere the track uses the word "over-amorous"—when was the last time you heard that in a song lyric?

Cliff was born in Hannibal, Missouri, and had the class to brag that he hailed from the same burg as none other than Tom Sawyer. Like Tom Sawyer, he was a boy at heart. Even his trademark uke had a boyish charm to it, and he could wield it like nobody's business. It is said that at the top of his popularity, music stores were selling ukuleles at a rate of 250 a week, a feat unmatched ever since.

This LP, made in the '40s while Cliff's voice had attained a golden luster, shows him at his best. It's simple, and unadorned, but you will surely get a tear in your eye when you hear him whisper:

> *Like a bolt out of the blue, fate steps in to see you through*
> *When you wish upon a star, your dreams come true.*

It didn't happen for Cliff Edwards, but it can still happen to you.

Dig! (2004)
dir. Ondi Timoner

★★★★☆
A Gallery of Genius and Gallantry

March 3, 2005

Dig! showcases two bands and makes you believe that the Dandy Warhols were a sellout group, whereas the insane Anton Newcombe, leader of the BJM, is a misunderstood and cruelly ignored genius on the order of Artaud or Blake. But when you get through the hype of the narrative, how much of this thesis holds up? The documentary seems designed to argue a thesis, but viewers can't help wishing for a little bit of the other side of the story. I think Courtney shows good manners throughout, even consenting to narrate a film that tries to make him look like a jackass at every juncture.

That said, the picture grows on you and lets you into a number of secret places along the way. Jeff Davies (of BJM) was born to play leading roles in front of the camera; his damaged, wounded face and his large kissable lips are like movie magic, he simply burns up the screen, and you don't even care what he's on half the time. Miranda Lee Richards, who has a great LP of her own music, makes a fascinating impression as well. She is as enigmatic and naturalistic as Jeanne Moreau in an early Louis Malle movie. She doesn't say a lot, but her gaze and her stance say plenty. As for Anton Newcombe, the filmmakers do their best to paint him as the Beethoven of modern rock, but they give him enough rope to hang himself and indeed he does.

Duel in the Sun (1946)
dirs. King Vidor & William Dieterle

★★★★★
Bigger than Any Other Movie

March 4, 2005

—and a little bit hollow, too, for the filmmakers try to blow up an ordinary love triangle into a social and economic canvas the size of *Gone with the Wind*, but it's just too small to fill that much space. However on all other fronts the film is magnificent and it is definitely one of the strangest pictures of the entire postwar period. The colors are rich, troubled, seething with pixels, and the musical score shouts and clamors what we all knew at heart, the West is another word for s-e-x. Selznick cleverly cast a number of silent film veterans, to trace the long history of melodrama in the movies, most notably Lillian Gish but also Lionel Barrymore, Harry Carey Sr., and the incomparable Herbert Marshall, who plays Pearl's gambler father, Scott, during the first reel or two.

The younger generation, as represented by Cotten, Jones, and Peck, all visibly strain trying to be colorful, and in the case of Jones and Peck, they are rewarded with twin triumphs of overacting and sheer ham. Selznick must have sat Jennifer Jones down and force-fed her the complete filmic works of her predecessor, Maria Montez, to get her to be so over the top. As for Peck, the whole audience explodes with gasps and laughter when we hear him whistling, mournfully, "I've Been Working on the Railroad" after we see him blowing up an entire train just for the hell of it. In contrast, Cotten's a little flimsy and distracted in his part—he doesn't hold up his end of the triangle very well. Maybe Robert Walker would have been better, or Montgomery Clift, one of many to whom Selznick offered the part.

When I first saw *Duel in the Sun* I was about fifteen and it blew me away. Contemporary films rarely feature the kind of soak-through Technicolor that Rosson and Garmes (and I guess Sternberg, who worked on the film for many months) were able to produce here. The dancing (by Ottilie "Tilly" Losch, the European answer to Martha Graham) is out of this world, and the oracular voice of Orson Welles blows the whole narrative into another dimension the minute his narration begins.

Shadow of a Doubt (1943)
dir. Alfred Hitchcock

★★★★★
RIP Teresa Wright, 1918–2005

March 9, 2005

With great sadness we find out today that Teresa Wright has died, in Connecticut, at the age of eighty-six. She wasn't necessarily a legend like some of her peers, but her acting embodied a warmth and a skill much like her somewhat later counterpart Patricia Neal, who oddly enough also (like Wright) made her name on the Broadway stage in Lillian Hellman parts. When Teresa Wright first came to Hollywood, the studio system was alive and kicking and it gave her initially the best roles of her career. She arrived in Hollywood with the rest of the *Little Foxes* company, and stayed around to make little pictures like *The Pride of the Yankees* and *Mrs. Miniver*.

One of her husbands was Niven (*Duel in the Sun*) Busch, who wrote wonderful parts for you in *Pursued* and *Track of the Cat*, two films which parlayed your ingénue perfection against Robert Mitchum's sexual bravado. It is said that he wrote *Duel in the Sun* for Teresa Wright to play, though I can't imagine her writhing across the desert with the élan of Jennifer Jones. Another husband, Robert Anderson, made memorable use of her screen image in *I Never Sang for My Father*. For some reason she was a writer's actress, and many of Hollywood's top screenwriters vied for her services. No one did better for Teresa Wright than Thornton Wilder, the Pulitzer Prize–winning playwright who wrote *Shadow of a Doubt* with the teen specialist Sally Benson. Wilder's memorable portrait of a small town, filled with ordinary people, which becomes the churning pool of a serial killer, was instantly acclaimed upon its release in 1943, and in the years since has come to be seen as one of Alfred Hitchcock's finest and most revealing pictures. And Teresa Wright gleams at the center of the whirlpool as Charlie, on the surface an innocent enough teenager in a small Northern California town, but with secret depths that link her filmically to Uncle Charlie, the part Joseph Cotten played so beautifully. It's not only that their names are the same, but they seem like two halves of the same person; and the audience senses this without being hit over the head with it due to careful writing and brilliant staging by Hitchcock. In its own way *Shadow of a Doubt* is as disturbing and transgressive as any of the contemporary film noir pictures, and will haunt you forever once you see it.

Goodbye, Teresa Wright, your powers of shadow and light will live forever. You are an actress for the ages.

Picnic-Themed Gift Basket

★★★★★
Best Bargain on Amazon?

March 15, 2005

Possibly the best bargain on all of Amazon. Just the basket alone must be worth a good $150, and then on top of it, it's stuffed with goodies for your next picnic—indoor or outdoor. There are some delicious apples, don't forget the relish and mustard, you will love the tangy winter pears and you will appreciate the newfangled "pear chips" that are the healthy person's substitute for potato chips (no grease). The cheese just melts in your mouth, you hardly need to spread it. But if you do, there are plenty of surfaces to spread it on, from sesame sticks to Irish soda crackers. Well, you can see the photo but I'm here to tell you, this photo tells only half the story. Maybe you have a fire at your picnic, maybe not, but you'll cherish the cunningly wrapped sausages and the boxes of cashews and other nuts.

Then I hope you still have an appetite, for there's still a chocolate decadence cake to be divvied up among you. Each bite is like a trip to Willy Wonka's Chocolate Factory. They say eating this cake increases your supply of endorphins, so that there's practically no calorie intake (just kidding).

Anyhow the cake is large enough for a large party, and small enough so that you won't be tuckered out having carried your deluxe basket to the nicest picnic since Kim Novak and William Holden did the "Moonglow" dance in *Picnic* way back when, melting into each other's arms while Rosalind Russell as Rosemary fumed and got drunk.

As I say, what a bargain—and you can use the basket again and again, or save it as a souvenir of a happy, carefree time.

The Devil and Miss Jones: The Twisted Mind of Myra Hindley
by Janie Jones

★★☆☆☆
Witches Brew

March 16, 2005

Janie Jones was one of the original Windmill Theatre girls and she made a number of pop records in the 1950s and 1960s, including a minor hit called *Witches Brew*, from which it is said Miles Davis derived that repetitive chord that begins *Bitches Brew*. You can get a good collection of Jones's greatest hits on the import LP *We're in Love with the World of Janie Jones.* She later turned to the more lucrative world of prostitution and went to prison, where this book really takes off because she befriended a notorious child murderer called Myra Hindley. First she stumbled across Myra's body—Myra had been assaulted and beaten by other prisoners, for everyone in England hated her for the crimes she had committed about ten years before Jones met her.

Then Myra began confiding in her and opening up. Well, Jones listened and listened, and sympathized with her, and agreed to help her appeal for parole, joining the venerable Lord Longford in fighting to get Myra freed. But later, when she had time to think about it, Janie Jones changed her mind and wrote this nasty little book. She (Janie) also made a great record with the Clash (UK rock group), who admired her trashy demeanor and limited vocal ability. Look for that, skip this awful book.

The Movie Queen Quiz Book: A Trivia Test Dedicated to Fabulous Female Film Stars
by Ed Karvoski Jr.

★★★★☆
Where's Ed?

March 24, 2005

We used to depend on Ed Karvoski Jr. to pull through for us whenever we wanted trivia about gay and lesbian entertainment. This is the most recent of his five fabulous books and as far as I can tell, he hasn't published anything since this one, *The Movie Queen Quiz Book*. I wonder what happened to him, I would try getting in touch with him via his website, but it too seems to have evaporated. Don't you hate getting those messages that say "The page you have requested is no longer available"? I just hope he's OK.

As far as trivia-quiz books go, Ed Karvoski Jr. always has the best, and *The Movie Queen Quiz Book* is no exception. The questions are provocative and funny, and even those of you who know all about Liz Taylor, Katharine Hepburn, Barbra, and so on are bound to be stumped by some of the zingers he throws at you. And yet he plays fair, one hundred percent. Hope you have your medical insurance paid up, for your thumb will be sore from having to turn to the answers so often but hey, that's life, and as we all know, deep knowledge of movie trivia is not a sport for sissies. And your stomach will be sore from the laughter and the fun he brings to the oldest game of all, the trivia quiz. Fabulous indeed.

Maltese: A Comprehensive Guide to Owning and Caring for Your Dog
by Juliette Cunliffe

★★★★☆
Wherefore Art Thou, Juliette?

March 24, 2005

Though she steadfastly guards her own privacy, Juliette Cunliffe has established a reputation as one of the world's great experts on toy and rare breeds. *Maltese*, which she wrote for the Kennel Club Dog Breed Series, is a fine example of her work. Perhaps not as carefully researched as *Pug* or *Shar Pei*, two of her other classic works, the love is obvious as you turn over the pages of her book. She cares for the humble Maltese, with its so-called bridal veil of white fur that tumbles over its brow and forms a fringe over its cute little black eyes, eyes which sparkle with affection and aristocratic breeding. On the other hand, you never get the feeling that Cunliffe has actually owned a Maltese herself, whereas her feeling for the bichon frise emanates throughout her handbook *Bichon Frise* and the *Cavalier King Charles Spaniel* book has a similar warmth to it which is oddly lacking in *Maltese*.

She is also very good at the racing dogs and her books *Whippet* and *Greyhound* have some good tips in them. Of course the little Maltese will never be a race dog. His heart is closer to the ground! And once you own one, as she admits from watching friends with Maltese breeding, you don't give your heart easily to any other breed no matter how handsome or lordly.

Haunted San Francisco: Ghost Stories from the City's Past
ed. Rand Richards

★★★★★
Fascinating Compilation

March 26, 2005

While some may complain that *Haunted San Francisco* is a misbegotten salmagundi, blending fact and fiction in a manner deleterious to them both, to me it is a splendid concordance of the ghosts which every sensible person will admit still haunt our city. Mark Twain, Ambrose Bierce, Gelett Burgess, and Jack London are but a few of the more famous names of those who have written up these spooks over the past 150 years, and Rand Richards includes tales by all here. The front cover gives the clue, it is a ghostly photo by Larry Moon which was recreated in Hitchcock's famous thriller *Vertigo*, likewise set in a San Francisco that is even now becoming a dream, the SF of the immediate postwar era when gaslight was still within the memory of living man and woman.

There are also interesting reminiscences of the bell tower of the San Francisco Art Institute, written by Antoinette May. Ms. May interviewed several artists who happen to be quite well known, among them Bill Morehouse, Hayward King, and Wally Hedrick. Alas, since they testified about the 1947–48 apparitions of the bell tower ghosts, both King and Hedrick, two of the six artists and poets who began the famous Six Gallery in San Francisco, the place where Allen Ginsberg first read "Howl," have passed on. Richards rings the multicultural bell by including Hayward King in his book, for so often when compiling ghost stories the experience of African American participants is neglected, and King was one of the notable Black artists of the 1950s through the 1980s.

I also like the story of the haunted penthouse of Pat Montandon. In May another book will appear called *Oh the Glory of It All* in which young Sean Wilsey, the son of Pat Montandon, will expose her as a kind of second-rate Auntie Mame, but this book glorifies her haunted penthouse as a sort of atelier of ghostly ambition. In San Francisco there are always stories within stories, and once in a while a drop of truth squeezes out like a tear.

Northwest Passage
by Stan Rogers

★★★★★
Stan Rogers Lives

March 28, 2005

His tunes will live forever, and the warmth in his voice. He was not a matinée idol in terms of his looks, but because of his tragic death, so young, aged only thirty-three, we will continue to think of him as cut down by fate (and smoke) in the prime of his youth and just when his talent was about to ignite the whole world. I sometimes feel that listening to the later music of the US singer Jeff Buckley that Rogers had everything Buckley had, except for US citizenship. Otherwise he (Rogers) would be as big a name as Buckley is today.

The songs are outstanding, from the sad, bitter "Lies" (like an Alice Munro short story put to music) to the anthemic a cappella threnody of the title song, "Northwest Passage." It has many admirers, of course, but it is still little known in the USA, even though we too are always going for the Northwest Passage, which some characterize as the easy way out, while others see it as a quixotic "impossible dream." Rogers's song preserves this ambiguity while adding a beauty unique to his own time and place.

Before the Poison
by Marianne Faithfull

★★★★★
Crazy Love

March 28, 2005

We saw Marianne Faithfull last night at the Fillmore Auditorium here in San Francisco, where she greeted her fans in support of the new LP *Before the Poison*. "Here I am, back in my darling San Francisco." How do the new songs sound live? For the most part, they were winners: she incorporated about half of the new LP into her set, including "The Mystery of Love," "No Child of Mine,"

"Last Song," and "Crazy Love." She kept telling us "This is a very lovely song written for me by Polly Jean Harvey." She'd tip her glasses back onto her nose to study the lyrics out of a black notebook. "She'd be very cross if I were to f—k it up."

The show closed with an ecstatic rendition of "Crazy Love," at the end of which she sank to her knees, apparently overcome by the devotion of her fans, and extended her hands to those in the mosh pit underneath, thanking them for their spirit.

Faithfull has apparently quit smoking and her voice has regained something of an upper register, and the difference is noticeable even since her appearance just this past summer in the Tom Waits / William Burroughs / Robert Wilson extravaganza *The Black Rider*. She has so much more power and energy now, she is like Axl Rose used to be! Except, of course, she's, you know, Marianne Faithfull!

PS: The set list, for those curious, was "Trouble in Mind," "Falling from Grace," "The Mystery of Love," "The Ballad of Lucy Jordan," a rare "She," "No Child of Mine," "The Last Song," an exquisite "Times Square," a blistering "Working Class Hero," an awkward "Incarceration of a Flower Child," "Strange Weather," "Guilt," "As Tears Go By," a showstopping "Sister Morphine," and "Crazy Love." As expected the encores were fan favorites "Broken English" and "Why D'Ya Do It?"

Crossfire Laser
by Black & Decker

★★★★★
The Answer to a Nightmare

March 28, 2005

Did you ever get yourself in a jam when hanging a picture, and no matter where you put up the nail in the wall, the picture still wound up looking crooked, even from far across the room? We had this nightmare happen to us on Wednesday, and after a few temper tantrums I remembered that we had the Crossfire Laser still sitting in its box from Christmas under the stairs.

It didn't take a minute to figure out how to use the thing, and as you are aware twin lasers appear and trace any ninety-degree angle you like. You'll be surprised that you won't need any chalk (or ballpoint pen) to put the mark on the wall, and it measures perfectly the distance from the floor and ceiling with ease, without having to squint to see the bubble line in the tube as we used to do for a level—in that tube that always looked like an oral thermometer. This one is far less messy. (As a sidelight, we found indeed that the reason the picture always hung crooked is because the frame itself wasn't perfectly rectangular but instead was made in a slightly rhomboid shape! Who would have guessed it, and without the Black & Decker Crossfire we still would be kicking ourselves.)

I can see using this for so many things that need doing around the house, inside and out. It's easy to understand, it's lightweight, and it's accurate, almost scarily so. It's the answer to a common household nightmare.

Au Masculin Eau de Toilette Spray
by Lolita Lempicka

★★★★★
Smells So Fine

April 6, 2005

It's not the scent that attracts you first about Lolita Lempicka, it's the way it holds in your hand, firm and sensual at the same time, as though the designer had taken a mold of your fist and poured liquid glass into your folded-up palm.

The lavender color may turn off some guys, but to me it looks like a scientific specimen preserved in some natural history museum, a primitive relic carved out from the ice, a fossil of some ancient igneous fuel source. It looks remarkably resistant to time, heat, or age. Hold it in your hand, I dare you to keep yourself from trying to undo its stopper.

The scent itself is sort of woodsy, warmer than you'd think. I don't think it will sweep the nation, but it'll look great in your medicine chest or on the hood of your car.

Lolita Lempicka Au Masculin also has a deodorant which I have tried often, it is just as effective as the spray. I played a round of golf, then got on my horse (if you know what I mean, and I think you do) and never had to use it twice.

I wonder if Lolita Lempicka is related to the futurist painter Tamara de Lempicka whose pictures are going for zillions of dollars now. I can kind of relate the heft of the bottle to Tamara's style.

Peyton Place (1957)
dir. Mark Robson

★★★★★
Without Compare

April 7, 2005

Mark Robson is definitely one of Hollywood's least respected directors but I could watch his films over and over again. It's a scandal that he is not better known or loved. He could take trash, like *Peyton Place* or *Valley of the Dolls*, and whip it up into something with emotional resonance, and he could direct actors easily as well as Sidney Lumet (for example). All of his pictures are worthy, but it is *Peyton Place* which has lasted longest in our imaginations. For many it has replaced the earlier *Rings Row* (also a good film) as *the* sexposé of small-town American life, its seamy side and its hidden scandals behind the lace curtains.

The casting is pretty great, even where it's fairly ludicrous, like asking Lana Turner to play a woman afraid of sex. Lana should have won the Oscar for this part, that is clear, and her handling of the deeply neurotic Constance MacKenzie is always spot on. I think she might actually have won if she had been playing opposite someone other than Fox discovery Lee Philips, fine here but without the spark of a true star. Lana's especially good in the one scene where she comes home unexpectedly and Allison is having a hot spin-the-bottle party with lovers pairing off together in the shadows of the living room, while the LPs spin and the couples are slow dancing and drinking booze.

The young people are terrific, especially Hope Lange playing against type as Selena, and Russ Tamblyn also playing against type as the neurotic (gay?) mama's boy. Terry Moore may be a bit old to be playing teenage Betty Anderson, but she throws her sexuality all over the place and has a ball doing so. She's also interesting on the commentary, with a lot of stories and still very much an exotic, like someone from the day of Lili St. Cyr or Tempest Storm. Diane Varsi is appropriately twisted playing Allison MacKenzie. Among the adult characters, no one in the movies of the 1950s was as scary as Arthur Kennedy playing the man who rapes his own stepdaughter, ugh, how repulsive is that.

The movie is beautiful on every level; the photography is dreamy and resonant, like Franz Waxman's haunting music. And with all its flaws, *Peyton Place* has some of the virtues of the old-fashioned Victorian three-decker novel: it tells a cross-stitched quilt of sin, memory, and ultimately, the forgiveness without which none of us can learn to live.

Poets of the Civil War
ed. J. D. McClatchy

★★★★☆
McClatchy the Master Editor Does It Again

April 8, 2005

J. D. McClatchy, who has edited many volumes of poetry, and written some poems of his own, is one of our very best editors. His book of Longfellow is the best selection since the 1950s. Now comes a more comprehensive, and at the same time more intimate book. The sheer breadth of poets who might be said to be "poets of the Civil War" is astonishing, and this is not even counting the many British, French, Caribbean poets who wrote on the war as well, this is just the Americans (both North and South). You can see the years pass by as the book begins with a not very memorable poem by William Cullen Bryant, who was born securely in the eighteenth century, while several of the poets made it through all the way into the twentieth century, not within living memory but sort of. Anyway McClatchy hit on the idea of arranging the poems by the birth year of the poets who wrote them, and this really points up in an elegant way the mechanisms by which attitudes toward the war seem to shift by generations.

The older poets, people like Bryant who might be described as being old even when the war began, have a very different take on it than those who were teens or even children when the war broke out. We can see this paradigm shift recapitulated in the case of a single poet, say Walt Whitman, who, as McClatchy cleverly points out, was all gung ho about the war at first, but later on in life saw the sadness and the tragedy of the war. "Drum-Taps" indeed.

This writing teeters on the edge of modernism, and in fact, a fascinating sequel might be compiled, perhaps by McClatchy once again, in which the early US modernists (Amy Lowell, T. S. Eliot, Pound, Moore, etc.) might be seen to be echoing the Civil War as a subject in their poetry. Like Robert Lowell's poem about his Civil War ancestor. In the twentieth century, McClatchy claims, poetry narrowed to the "increasingly oblique and intimate lyric." Yes, but this is only a partial truth. Plenty of poems were written on a national and epic scale, but they were increasingly devalued by partisans of New Criticism. Check out Cary Nelson's work in this area.

Though the work on view here in this book is indeed second rate, as McClatchy is eager to admit, it is not negligible, and in fact it's often thrilling, particularly the well-chosen poems by Emily Dickinson, Herman Melville, Ambrose Bierce, Francis Miles Finch, Julia Ward Howe (the famous "Battle Hymn of the Republic"), Emerson's "Boston Hymn," and four great poems by the incomparable H. W. Longfellow.

Becoming Something: The Story of Canada Lee
by Mona Smith

★★★★★
Becoming a Terrific Book

April 11, 2005

Though he died, sadly and miserably, before I was even born, the greatness of Canada Lee cast a long shadow over my early life on Long Island (a suburb of New York). Lee was but one of the victims of the tragic blacklist, and the HUAC hearings which tore apart the country, especially the entertainment world in which many well-meaning folks had taken part in various charitable organizations before and during

World War II only to find themselves suspected of Communism or merely "premature anti-Fascism." It was a time in which, to paraphrase playwright Lillian Hellman, you had to cut your conscience to suit this year's fashions, and such a time may be coming around again. If so, the Canada Lees of today are going to come to a terrible end.

What a world! And yet, as Mona Smith shows us, there is redemption for even the most miserable of us, and Lee was able again and again to triumph over the ingrown and casual racism of the film world by finding parts that made him more than just a grinning servant à la the underrated Stepin Fetchit. He refused to play a servant and thus suffered many privations and was denied many roles, along with his better-known compatriot Paul Robeson, also a famous athlete before turning to acting.

Lee's greatest films included Hitchcock's *Lifeboat*, in which he plays the only sane man in a lifeboat filled with hysterical excuses for human beings. This film, written partially by John Steinbeck, is one of those movies that seem more and more central to Hitch's career as time goes by—to Steinbeck's too.

Mona Smith's account of how she came to write the life of Canada Lee, as set forth in her preface, is heartbreaking. Unbelievably, Canada Lee's widow was still alive and was able to share with Ms. Smith a mountain of personal papers. It is truly one of the miracles of the archival process, and it makes her book not only a showbiz biography, but a study in civil rights and in American history and human endurance.

I recommend this book to everyone, of all ages, who wants to learn about redemption and sacrifice.

Joe: A Memoir of Joe Brainard
by Ron Padgett

★★★★★
Excellent Memoir

April 11, 2005

Poet Ron Padgett is also an interesting biographer and knows how to tell a good story. In *Joe* he does a fine job in recounting the basic facts of Joe Brainard's life, and his arrangements and paragraphs are written with a poet's eye to detail and piquancy.

Everyone loves Brainard's art and his writing, and the difficulty insofar as I can see it is that the book loses a little something after Joe meets Kenward Elmslie and his career moves into high gear. As Padgett admits, his closeness to Joe began to unravel slightly at this juncture. (The two had been high school pals in Oklahoma and had moved to New York together, with the poets Dick Gallup and Ted Berrigan, from Tulsa very early in the 1960s.) Once Joe stops worrying about money, a little of the tension disappears from the story. Until then it has the high drama of a Dickens tale, even down to the story of Joe reduced to begging in the Boston streets and being too embarrassed actually to ask people for money. After his success, he goes to Vermont every summer, he can afford tables at the finest restaurants, he meets Jackie Onassis and Willem de Kooning, the whole nine yards of NY social success, and eventually he stops painting.

His death from AIDS is briefly discussed. I have the feeling that Padgett did not want to make this into an AIDS story, and wanted instead to celebrate his gay friend's life and work, but as he admits many aspects of Joe's sexuality were occluded from himself and from Pat (Padgett's wife). Whenever Joe gets close to a woman he has fantasies about taking the next step into having sex with her, but this seems to have occurred seldom if at all. In the meantime he continues writing his book *I Remember* and its many sequels and extensions, and launches into a long-running affair with the actor Keith McDermott. Many other figures grace the book, including Andy Warhol and Frank O'Hara. Through every detail Padgett retains his equanimity, never letting the bathwater drown the baby. I wish he would write a memoir of all his friends (and relations, having enjoyed his book about his own father, a bootlegger and a real Oklahoma "character" like Curly or Jud).

Many anecdotes, many insights, in *Joe*. I love the tale of Padgett asking Joe, a notoriously hard person to shop for, what he would like for Christmas. Joe says, "Stairs. I don't like sitting in chairs, but I always like sitting on stairs, and I'd buy some, only I never see them for sale in shops." That would be charming enough, but then amazingly Padgett gets out his carpenter's tools and builds Joe a set of four stairs each about thirty inches wide and hauls them over to

Joe's loft a few days before Christmas. It is this kind of affection and amazement that pervades this book and, indeed, pervades our reading of Ron Padgett, no matter what he writes, poetry, memoir, translation.

It seems that on every page Joe is expressing his love for Pat and Ron by giving them painting after painting, drawing, collage, sculpture, you name it, they must have the world's biggest art collection. Good for them!

Little Caesar: A Biography of Edward G. Robinson
by Alan L. Gansberg

★★★★★
Fine Biography

April 11, 2005

Edward G. Robinson seemed tough, but he had a sensitive side too that was most obviously expressed in his love of modern art; his collection of Renoirs alone was for many years the most impressive west of the Mississippi. He was said to have bought a masterpiece every time he made another film for Warner Bros., to reward himself with some beauty for dipping himself in dreck. And yet Robinson's films still startle with their magnificent energy and passion. They too are works of art every bit as much as his Soutines and his Picassos.

He was not a ladies' man in the traditional sense of the term, but as Gansberg's fine biography shows, he was interested in all forms of beauty. And part of the reason he could so well play obsessed characters (such as his films with Joan Bennett in the noir cycle) is that he too was prone to obsession.

The blacklist (or more strictly speaking, the graylist) affected his career badly. For some time offers of employment dried up, even though he was never a Communist or anywhere near it. The mere idea is laughable. Cecil B. DeMille of all people, the director and producer often thought of as a right-wing nutcase, was the one who gave Robinson a solid job playing in his own remake of *The Ten Commandments*. No other mogul in Hollywood would have had the balls to cast Robinson so prominently, not at that time when men walked scared of HUAC and its minions. It took a compassionate conservative to restore Robinson to the high echelon of film stardom to which he rightfully belonged.

Robinson's own book, *All My Yesterdays*, was famous for revealing so little about its subject. Author Gansburg gets right down to ground zero with Robinson's psyche, exploring his ups as well as his well-chronicled downs. I wish I had been a fly on the wall when Gansburg interviewed some of his many witnesses. Among his many films, *Two Weeks in Another Town*, *The Violent Men*, *Scarlet Street*, *Soylent Green*, and *Nightmare* have all undergone recent critical revision, while *Double Indemnity*, *Key Largo*, and *The Woman in the Window* remain American masterpieces of the highest order.

Splendor in the Grass (1961)
dir. Elia Kazan

★★★★★
And Glory in the Flower

April 13, 2005

Deanie is another inspired creation by Natalie Wood, and the one in which she shows off her acting skills with a newfound confidence. Anyone who's read anything about Wood knows she had a profoundly controlling mother, and some of this tangled relationship seems to have seeped into Wood's portrait of a young girl with real issues around her mom. Few of us who have seen the film will ever entirely forget the scene in which she stands up, dripping wet, in the bathtub to defy her mother, and to send the mother the message that she is no longer a little girl but a woman with a grown woman's needs. In its day this was shocking and some thought Natalie had lost her mind along with the rest of her wardrobe, for nudity was still a very rare thing in the straitlaced Hollywood cinema of the 1950s. Director Elia Kazan was perhaps the only man who could have elicited such a strong performance out of her. Kazan himself saw this film as the culmination of a long line of movies he himself had shepherded through to success, a group of films which did much to put the "adult" back into movies, everything from *Baby Doll* to *Wild River*.

Indeed, *Splendor* was his last real success, either on the screen or stage, for the 1960s left him behind in more ways than one, even though he lived another forty years his best days were long behind him (though surprisingly in recent years there has been a burst of acclaim for the garish *Arrangement*, the film he thought his most personal but which was his biggest flop). As for Warren Beatty, with whom Wood was in real life "involved" as they say, this film showed him off at his best and might have been written especially for him, by a smitten William Inge, the Broadway playwright who had had four great hits on the stage, but who had never before attempted a screen original. This too was Inge's last success, but for Beatty it was only the beginning to a fine career. And for Wordsworth? *Splendor* did for the nineteenth-century Romantic poet what *Four Weddings and a Funeral* did for W. H. Auden—put him, however briefly, on the bestseller list, after a scene in which poor Deanie is forced to recite in class a section from Wordsworth's "Intimations of Immortality," and halfway through she realizes that its implications have hit home in a devastating way, and she breaks down, crying, in front of her teacher and fellow students. It is one of the great moments in screen acting and should have won Natalie Wood the Oscar that year.

Phyllis Diller is also pretty good in the movie, but her part is so strange you wonder why it was even included.

Now, Voyager
by Olive Higgins Prouty

★★★★☆
A Forecast of Things to Come

April 15, 2005

Olive Higgins Prouty would not have appreciated her books being regarded as pulp! But she would have been happy, I think, knowing that people were reading them again and enjoying them.

She is one of those cases where a novelist could be extremely popular in her own lifetime and then almost forgotten. Meanwhile the movies made from her books (including *Stella Dallas* and *Now, Voyager*) show how original and striking her plots were, how unique she was. Sylvia Plath, who wrote her many flattering, almost gushing letters so long as Prouty was giving her money, was vicious about her in private (and in the pages of *The Bell Jar*, in which Prouty appears as a menacing elderly lesbian, almost like Shelob the spider). It's funny how the encounter between Plath and Prouty has taken on mythic proportions, and how indeed Prouty's best work approaches that of Plath in terms of its insight into the human condition, especially of suffering, illness, pain, and madness. Anyone who reads *Now, Voyager*, or its "prequel," *Lisa Vale*, will see that Prouty was intimately familiar with neurosis. Plath might have been taken aback had she realized that Prouty herself had been hospitalized for mental illness when she was a teenager, way back at the turn of the century. In many ways, Prouty's whole life foreshadowed Plath's. We note in *Now, Voyager* the way that Charlotte's stifled New England ways explode when she encounters the debonair, sexy European man who turns her on to Lawrentian sexuality and rebellion—Sylvia and Ted much?

Now if only someone would reprint (among others) *White Fawn*, *Home Port*, *Good Sports*, and *Pencil Shavings*! Olive Higgins Prouty could write and it's time the world realized it.

The Beautifully Worthless
by Ali Liebegott

Hosanna

April 15, 2005

I remember going to see David Wojnarowicz reading from *Close to the Knives* and thinking that never again would I experience a reading of such power and such vast seismic changes of mood and register. And until two weeks ago, I still thought so. Then I went to see Ali Liebegott and had the same kind of earthquake experience all over again. She's insanely talented, it's mad.

If any of you enjoyed Anne Carson's "novel in verse," *Autobiography of Red*, I imagine you will like this book too. It is coming out of the same impulse, to find the lyric heart lurking inside narrative and to display it, to glory in it, to foreground that which is ordinarily hidden. *The Beautifully Worthless* crisscrosses the USA, like *Close to the Knives*, like Kerouac, desperately seeking out everything occluded and driven, a frenzy of seeking frozen into poetry. The sequences late in this book are written in language as stately and magnificent as the Psalms (King James Version).

Before this reading I wasn't very aware of Ali Liebegott and now I'm like Saul of Tarsus, I've seen the light and I'm here to spread the word. Whatever we were looking for, all the basic reasons we are drawn to reading, for escape, for commitment, for pleasure, for passion, she's got them good, like fever.

Long Day's Journey into Night
by Eugene O'Neill

★★★★★
A Mother Done In by Addiction

April 25, 2005

Long Day's Journey into Night is a great play, but sitting through the acting of all the acts can be a very tough experience. It is a heart-wrenching tale of a pair of brothers who are as different as night and day. When I was in high school a lack of girls required that I play the challenging part of Mary Tyrone, once a youthful beauty reveling in her ability to love and be loved, her body a wonderland as they say nowadays, but now only a shriveled-up hag, left on the shelf, who finds solace in her needle full of morphine. Her husband, she thinks, doesn't understand her. The surprise in the play is that she finds out oh yes, he does understand her—only too well.

She wears bedraggled clothes of the turn-of-the-century period, which she has pathetically tried to keep clean, ironed, and pressed, but which her morphine habit have caused to look wrinkled and generally disheveled. She knows how she has fallen apart and it is part of her agony that she no longer looks very trig. Poor thing, she is always fussing with her hair—in my case, a long gray wig which my mother attempted to tie up in the middle like an old-fashioned chignon. It kept falling out of its ribbon as I attempted to totter across the stage, imitating someone in the last throes of drug addiction, about which I knew very little. I imagined that I would always be seeing invisible people and monsters, like Ray Milland in Billy Wilder's *Lost Weekend*. And I would misplace things like my yarn and my spectacles, dropping them on what I thought was a bookshelf but was actually thin air. I feel sorry for my fellow actors, three lovely guys totally upstaged by my antics, but I didn't know any better. The play lasted a considerably long time. We only had three performances, though, and for the third we brought on two understudies for my two sons had quit the play and joined the basketball team instead, less stress.

The Grudge (2004)
dir. Takashi Shimizu

★★★★☆

Good Horror Movie, and Grace Zabriskie Is Awesome

April 25, 2005

If you haven't seen the original and just want to watch an American remake, this is the one for you, plus it has the bonus of featuring one of America's finest actresses, one often underused or ill utilized by directors who don't know what to make of her sterling talent. I'm not talking about Sarah (*Buffy*) Michelle Gellar, not this time, but instead I speak today of Grace Zabriskie, the actress who plays the elderly woman who sleeps on the floor and seems so haunted by the violent deaths of everyone she knows.

Grace Zabriskie has one of those faces you've seen over and over again, often playing disturbed or satanic mothers along the lines of Angela Lansbury's character in *The Manchurian Candidate*. Her other forte is playing supportive, rather helpless and pathetic mothers who are nevertheless sweet and loving. I first became aware of Ms. Zabriskie's sweeping talent while watching the US soap opera of the 1980s, *Santa Barbara*. She took a nothing part and filled it with every kind of theatrical, filmic gesture, elevating an ordinary show into the kind of thing you would tape every day just on the off chance that she would make an appearance on it. (That's actually not fair to *SB*, which in many ways was one of the most innovative shows on TV.) Then my friends whom knew I liked Grace Zabriskie would call me and tell me they had spotted her in other shows and films. She played one of the hardened factory hands in *Norma Rae* and she excelled in *Drugstore Cowboy*. She was the mother of Laura Palmer in the series *Twin Peaks*, and she was Debra Winger's mother in *An Officer and a Gentleman*. Need I say more? For twenty-five years she has been giving us her all, and in *The Grudge* she gives no quarter to the general shoddiness of the production. She attacks the part as though she were playing Gertrude in *Hamlet* (which she is in a way). Watch her as she turns white, and her struggles for breath, and her anguished pleas to Sarah Michelle Gellar, the costar with whom she seems to have the most empathy. If they had an entry for *greatness* in the dictionary, there would be a little picture of Grace Zabriskie to illustrate the noun.

By the way, she is a talented writer too, much more talented than the screenwriters of most of the movies, and she's made almost a hundred!

The Essential Leontyne Price: Spirituals, Hymns & Sacred Songs
by Leontyne Price

★★★★★
The Price Club

April 27, 2005

"I am here," said Leontyne Price when interviewed as she opened the new Metropolitan Opera with Samuel Barber's underrated *Antony and Cleopatra*, "and you will know that I am the best and will hear me. The color of my skin or the kink of my hair or the spread of my mouth has nothing to do with what you are listening to." Back in the 1960s Price was one of the greatest divas in all of opera, and it wasn't just her voice but her magnificent stage presence, combined with her social activism. All of the above come into play in this collection of secular songs and ditties, some of them traditional plantation chanties and others art songs and a scattering of pop music. And some of them, like Gershwin's "Summertime," cross the ever-permeable boundaries between Broadway and classical. These recordings were made at different times in Price's career, and her voice, while always angelic, has different shadings and reaches a different range of timbre on each separate recording date, but there is no question that as time goes by, she is able to impart a richness of life experience noticeably absent from some of her earlier work.

"Ave Maria" sounds heavenly no matter which way you slice it, and as for "I Wonder As I Wander," it brings tears to your eyes. If you have a heart that's beating, you will be moved by this rendition. "Ein feste Burg" is pretty strong, but Price seems more comfortable with the traditional spirituals, though perhaps it is the slightly off-kilter sounds of the Ambrosian Singers (what a name) who back her up on many of these tracks that detract slightly from the experience. Compare "Lead, Kindly Light" for a clear sense of what constitutes authority vs. what is a wee bit overproduced. If you had this compilation, and perhaps one of Leontyne Price's Christmas albums, you could attain nirvana any time you wanted to, just flip a switch and close your eyes, let her lift you up on wings of song.

Lust for Life
by Iggy Pop

★★★★☆
Legendary Creatures

April 29, 2005

Lust for Life has some terrific tracks, and real staying power, but I remember when it came out it seemed to lack the punch and "raw power" of *The Idiot*, which boasted some super Bowie-type tracks like "Sister Midnight" and "Funtime." Heard in the wake of *The Idiot*, *Lust for Life* seemed a little lackluster. However, today the positions reverse themselves. Maybe we were not yet ready for the stripped gears of Bowie's production approach when it came to *Lust for Life*. The goofy angelic grin Iggy wore on the cover seemed mindless back then, vapid in the face of *The Idiot*'s Dostoevskian take on fate, the state, the drive toward Thanatos. But now I'll go for that grin and remind myself, "It's only a movie, Ingrid." Advertising spots and *Trainspotting* put that inane title tune in our minds all the time, and I bet when the sad day comes and Iggy dies that will be the song they play on CNN to accompany that cover photo with his dates on a banner under his chin. For this is how we remember the legendary creatures of our youth.

Gaslight (1944)
dir. George Cukor

★★★★★
Cukor Doing a Hitchcock

April 29, 2005

Cukor's *Gaslight* has been thought of as an anomaly in his career, the one film of his which might honestly have been mistaken for a Hitchcock thriller.

Perhaps some of this confusion is set off by the presence of Bergman, one of Hitchcock's favorite actresses ("It's only a movie, Ingrid") together with Joseph Cotten, with whom Hitchcock teamed Bergman in the later *Under Capricorn*. The one-word title of *Gaslight* is also reminiscent of how many one-word titles Hitchcock employed over the years. Cotten and Bergman (as well as Hitchcock) were contracted to the former MGM head of production David O. Selznick, who was making *Since You Went Away* (also with Joseph Cotten) at the same time that Cukor was shooting *Gaslight*, so that Cotten was available to him only in the evenings.

For an MGM release in 1944, *Gaslight* is oddly bereft of MGM stars! Angela Lansbury made her debut here, but where are the other MGM notables? We know that during the war many of MGM's leading men were tied up in the service, but were there many MGM releases in 1944 in which none of the three leading players were under studio contract? I don't think so! This is definitely an odd duck among MGM's wartime films.

We have also long known that this was a remake of an older British film made by the esteemed director Thorold Dickinson, and some have cattily assumed that Cukor stole all of Dickinson's directorial flourishes in a paint-by-numbers, Gus Van Sant–does-*Psycho* kind of carbon copy of the original. This DVD shows us both films side by side, and at last we can all judge for ourselves. I like Diana Wynyard, who's very good in the Dickinson *Gaslight*—she has a very different style than Bergman, but both are quite effective. Isn't the time ripe for a full-scale Wynyard revival? Let's see her make a comeback via DVD!

"Paula," the name of Ingrid Bergman's character, is a favorite name of Cukor's. Viewers will recall that the young society girl caught up in a destructive affair with drunken rouse John Barrymore in *Dinner at Eight* was also called Paula. And later on in life, perhaps, this fondness would explain why Cukor allowed Paula Strasberg onto the set of the film *Something's Got to Give*, to coach the insecure Marilyn Monroe, with Cukor's compliance.

The Yearling (1946)
dir. Clarence Brown

★★★★★
Learning to Live Again

May 6, 2005

The Yearling, so beautifully shot and scored, is one of the very best postwar US films. It will have you welling up in tears, and the acting is awfully good. Some say that Claude Jarman Jr. didn't deserve that honorary kids' Oscar he got for playing little Jody, but I think his performance was outstanding. When he's romping around with Flag, the young deer, you wonder how director Clarence Brown got him to be so natural in this, his first movie. I also liked him with Lassie and Jeanette MacDonald in *The Sun Comes Up* and he was very believable as the young trouper torn between admiration for his dad (John Wayne) and devotion to his flamboyant mother (Maureen O'Hara). Jarman was one of the few child actors with the talent to make it into acting in adult parts, and yet for some reason he did not go on, and we will continue to remember him as Jody Baxter. In *The Yearling* his parents are in a similar situation to his parents in *Rio Grande*. Here they are not divorced or estranged, but the mother (Jane Wyman) seems locked in the past, unable to deal with the grief of multiple miscarriages and infant births, while Penny (Greg Peck) has to go on being both mom and dad to young Jody. That he does so without resentment is part of the reason that, for many of us, watching *The Yearling* is a lesson in growing up, from making the passage between boyhood and manhood. Peck is endearing, and I don't think that even Spencer Tracy, who originated the part in an earlier, scrapped MGM version of the novel, could have bettered the performance Peck offers up here. (Nor do I think Anne Revere could have come up to the level of emotion that Jane Wyman displays, for better or for worse, as the preoccupied mother who comes to understand, a little too late, that we should hold on to what we have instead of dreaming of lost yesterdays.)

That's Margaret Wycherly in the small part of Ma Forrester. Poor Margaret Wycherly was always playing "Ma" in the movies, and here she was about a year before her ultimate role as Ma Jarrett, the all-time strangest movie mom, in *White Heat* with James Cagney. In *The Yearling* she's a little bit softer, with that backwoods accent she also used playing Gary Cooper's mom, Ma York, in *Sergeant York*.

The Sunshine on My Face: A Read-Aloud Book for Memory-Challenged Adults
by Lydia Burdick

★★★★★
Not Only for One's Parents

May 9, 2005

Let me second the enthusiasm for Burdick's delightful book, which indeed will bring back some haunting images from even the most caved-in mind. It is not, however, solely geared for family members and I would encourage all to buy a copy of this book, you do not need to have a mother or father with Alzheimer's, it is perfect for reading along with any friends of yours, even younger people, who are troubled by memory challenges in the Alzheimer's range. For example, I took this book with me on my visit to the local elder hostel near my home, offering to share it with anyone who would like to read a good book, and once we were snuggled up on a park bench overlooking a pool swimming with koi, the "two lap" approach found me reading aloud to a white male stranger who might have been in his early eighties, a dignified man whose clothes were impeccable, if somewhat out of style, and obviously he had memory problems as he could not tell me his name. We sat down and began to pore through the book, with its lovely illustrations—not child-like, just very clear and nostalgic. After a few pages he told me that he had been in the Normandy Invasion! There are other suggestions in the book, tips on how to say things in ways which don't threaten the memory-challenged adult, and to my astonishment the man was telling me about a friend of his who had drowned in the surf on Omaha Beach, and he (my new friend) had climbed to safety on the back of his dead buddy. When we got to the part about his favorite song, he began to sing "My Buddy," a song which I did not know but he sang it so loudly that others in the park turned their heads and a few chimed in.

Some residents said that this man had not spoken aloud in years, and one said this was the first time anyone even knew that my new friend was an American. He spoke so little that, based on his name, many had thought he was a Frenchman marooned in this country by dementia. That day we truly felt "the sunshine on our faces." Even though it was not (strictly speaking) a good memory, it was still a precious one.

Lost: Lost and Found Pet Posters from around the World
by Ian Phillips

★★★★★
He's a Genius

May 16, 2005

I love his work and collecting these pet posters is a stroke of genius. Any-one who's ever had a pet and who has had to write one of these posters will be blinking back tears of sympathy, even if you acknowledge the ugliness of other people's pets, for some here are real lollapaloozas. Mostly you take your hat off to the eternal virtue of hope, for some of these people have faith deeper than rivers if they believe that you'd be able to recognize their cat or dog from the miserably scanned old photo of the animal, sometimes off in a corner of a photo looking completely anonymous or so dark you can't tell what you're supposed to be looking at. The texts Phillips collects are as heartbreaking as the photos, and again for every clear-cut description of an animal, there's quite a few in which it's like the old parable of the blind men and the elephant.

As you pore through this book, you can only hope all of these owners found their pets in this world and if not in this world, maybe in the next. *Lost* is a postmodern assemblage with old-fashioned heart and soul, it looks good and it feels good too.

Radio Controlled Helicopters: The Guide to Building and Flying R/C Helicopters
by Nick Papillon

★★★★★
New and Improved and a Must-Have

May 19, 2005

Papillon's book has been revised substantially, but even the old one was a keeper. The new one has more information and less of the risible Anglicisms that peppered the text of the previous edition.

Nick Papillon, an Englishman with a French name (meaning "butterfly," hilarious for someone so involved in model helicopters), has a finely developed sense of what we hobbyists want from a book like this one, and he knows what to leave out, too. Here in San Francisco we have a club, the Flying Goobers, that meets monthly—and in the summer, weekly—at Baker Beach, and I would say about 40 percent of our members already own one or both of Nick's handbooks. Sometimes the air is awash with the sound of seagulls and the hovering buzz of our RCs. Indeed sometimes we adjourn somewhere else when the air is too filled with static, etc., too many speedboats patrolling the Bay seem to suck the energy right out of the controls. Feels like earthquake weather.

If you want to know about aerobatics, beyond your simple push-pull, up-down "flight patterns," he's got it all down in language that is fairly easy to understand even for the tyro. His chapter "After the Crash," while sobering enough, is one of those classic stop-feeling-sorry-for-yourself-and-get-out-there-and-do-it-again sort of pep talks. When I started I didn't know the difference between a transmitter and a receiver, they'd call me "the late great Johnny Ace" with a sneer. Now the shoe is on the other foot as I explain to the newbies why lithium is cheaper in the long run, et cetera, all knowledge I got either from fellow Goobers or from pal Nick's RC handbook.

Men's Khaki Shorts
by Michael Kors

★★★★☆
If you don't mind yellow

May 20, 2005

Feeling flush last month I bought two pairs of these before I realized what an idiot I looked like wearing these big long shorts in khaki, with bright-yellow stitches all over them like a flock of yellow butterflies had settled on my crotch. They're what we used to call beachcomber pants and they're a pale-orange khaki rather like the color of St. Joseph baby aspirin, in a nice blend of linen and very fine cotton.

After a while I grew to like the look and now I wear them everywhere. In San Francisco you can wear just about anything, but too often the crisp cool weather precludes wearing something that bares your knees. Michael Kors does a lot of different style clothes, and he must have thought it would be amusing to see a lot of grown men running around with yellow embroidery all over their ass. What's good about them is the drawstring waist and the mesh pockets, you could put literally the whole contents of your knapsack into your pockets, say if you were out hiking or climbing rock.

The Pink Panther (1963)
dir. Blake Edwards

★★★★★
The Women of *The Pink Panther*

May 20, 2005

Peter Sellers, David Niven, both great, but for my money the women stars really steal the show. Claudia Cardinale is effervescent as the princess, she looks like a million lire. If only real princesses could borrow some of Cardinale's joie de vivre, I'm sure monarchy would not be so endangered. Her dresses and casual clothes, by Yves Saint Laurent, are among the finest examples of his classic mid-'60s period and could be studied for profit by today's ambitious young designers.

(Who, for example, is designing Kristin Chenoweth's or Beyoncé's costumes for the 2006 Steve Martin *Pink Panther*? I wonder! Oh, now I see it's Joe Aulisi, a competent designer who did *Charlie's Angels* and who also does fine character work, for example, he's the one who put Meryl Streep in rags for her homeless turn in *Ironweed*.)

Capucine, playing Madame Clouseau, is also outstanding in this, the very first of the *Pink Panther* films. Capucine is not ordinarily thought of as a great actress, but you can't take your eyes off of her, no matter what she's playing, or trying to play. Here she's got her best part ever, the adulterous wife who's married to Sellers but would rather be spending all her time with the Phantom. Her gaze as she lies in bed at the hotel, with Sellers bumbling beside her, says it all. Something of the real Capucine's bisexual glamor lingers over the whole movie, rendering it far different from all the other films in the series (save that in which she reprises her original role, looking a bit beat up, as though the '70s were hard times for her, poor thing). But here she is very striking, the epitome of European glamor. What was she, anyhow? She couldn't have been French. Was she from Vienna or somewhere? I felt sorry for her while she lived, having had a rough time being thrown over for younger faces; and then when she died, it was like a little part of me died too. When I watch her in *The Pink Panther*, it is like having an old, faded dream come to life once again, her sumptuous beauty forever ours to watch and possess.

Ancient Echoes: Music from the Time of Jesus and Jerusalem's Second Temple
by SAVAE (San Antonio Vocal Arts Ensemble)

★★★★★
God Tubwayhun You

May 23, 2005

Listening to this CD is like being transported out of your comfortable suburban lifestyle and plunged through time and space back into the Holy Land. You can almost sniff the figs and dates and the offerings made to the temple, the goat tethered down to the barbecue heap, and the wailing of the holy priests as they make offerings to God, as

Abraham was prepared to do to Isaac before he was stopped by a merciful Father. From the very first track you will feel viscerally that this was a very different world than ours, and yet the hunger for worship is strong in all cultures. The unusual instrumentation and play of voices may remind you of some of the modern Eurovision entries which depend on minor-key melodies and Middle Eastern harmony, and then again listeners of an older generation who like pop music will realize that Cole Porter and other Broadway composers borrowed these Middle Eastern modalities for their more mournful or sensual numbers.

San Antonio has reason to be proud. It is one of the great multicultural capitals of our continent, and as such must have some psychic connection to the sprawling, multifaith and multicultural world of old Jerusalem. You can hear the spirit in the impassioned play of voices, a mosaic of creeds and colors. Bewildering as some of the music may be at first, the longer you listen to a track like "Tubwayhun l'ahbvday sh'lama," you will soon be humming right along with the wonderful technicians of the Vocal Arts Ensemble. So many of the tunes have the word *tubwayhun* in them (it means "sacred," or "blessed by God") you may find yourself using this ancient word in your secular vocabulary. Say when somebody sneezes, where you might say "Gesundheit," now you will be saying "God tubwayhun you."

The Harvey Girls (**1946**)
dir. George Sidney

★★★★★
John Hodiak Appreciation Thread

May 23, 2005

Not much written nowadays about John Hodiak, who plays Ned Trent in this 1946 George Sidney musical, but he was a wonderful presence in the Hollywood cinema of the 1940s, and all of his pictures are worth a look. He seems strangely modern, natural in his appeal, with some of the cocky good looks and charm of our own John Travolta. *The Harvey Girls* is one of his rare ventures into musical comedy, and moviegoers often recall him in tougher parts: playing opposite Tallulah Bankhead in Hitchcock's *Lifeboat*, you know you'd have to have balls of steel to carry off that assignment, or zipping through Mexico with Lucille Ball in Jules Dassin's noir road-trip adventure *Two Smart People*. With Judy Garland he is noticeably gentler than he usually gets on-screen; you can almost feel the effort involved. He seems more like an Angela Lansbury sort of guy, hard, attracted to the glitter, out for a good time. Then something clicks and he and Garland really start to click and the picture picks right up.

The DVD features the abysmal "March of the Doagies," a piece which has so many things wrong with it you can see why Freed cut it out, but it's fascinating in its own right and it's great that they saved it. The song is bad, the singing isn't very good, the choreography pretty basic, and it seems they tried to save it by adding more and more elements to the number, you almost expect to see if not the kitchen sink, then the village pump, added to the mix. I suppose they were also trying to accommodate Hodiak's limitations as a dancer. He's no Ray Bolger (and no John Travolta). But his magnetism carries all before it, like a buffalo stampede.

Hodiak had the misfortune to be prominently featured in some of the era's most notorious failures, like *Song of Russia* and *Marriage Is a Private Affair*, but in a way this has proved his salvation for he is not cursed with the overfamiliarity with which we disregard someone we've seen a zillion times, no matter how worthy, like Clark Gable or Gary Cooper. He's always fresh and exhibits new facets to his screen personality. He died in 1955, still a stranger, after a well-publicized marriage to a fellow thespian (Anne Baxter, with whom he starred in the low-key charmer *Sunday Dinner for a Soldier*).

The Court-Martial of Billy Mitchell (1955)
dir. Otto Preminger

★★★★★
Elizabeth Montgomery on DVD

May 31, 2005

She is one of the most beautiful of all Hollywood actresses as well as among the most beloved, thanks largely to her years playing Samantha on *Bewitched*. She was Hollywood royalty, the daughter of the dashing patriot Robert Montgomery, a man with huge influence in the movie world, an actor of light comedy who matured during the war years into a serious actor, then a director and producer with enormous resources. And yet Elizabeth Montgomery's large-screen appearances can be counted on the fingers of one hand. What happened?

She is simply sublime in this, her very first movie role (though some say she appears in *They Were Expendable* in the short bit where Robert Montgomery remembers his family back at home). She made a big impression on moviegoers, and Otto Preminger took every care to make her look luscious, designing her period clothes with care and giving her many close-ups, some of them quite extraneous to his story of a man on trial for vilifying the armed services with his rash Cassandra-like predictions of doom for the air force. People must have wondered what Elizabeth Montgomery's character was even doing in the picture? It is certainly dragged in from left field. And yet she was a welcome attraction in this movie. That one pink-and-orange Schiaparelli concoction Preminger dressed her in made her look like a tall, cool parfait. And yet what happened after this movie? Nothing—not another movie for ten years—not until *How to Stuff a Wild Bikini* (1965) where she's only in the movie for like twenty seconds! It's totally unfair.

It is said by those in the know that Elizabeth was in line to play the parts Preminger was planning for her to take in his upcoming films, *Bonjour Tristesse* and Shaw's *Saint Joan*. She would have been perfect in both, of course. Was it that she wouldn't go along with his notorious casting-couch system and that's why she lost both parts to the unbalanced and yet quite talented Iowan Jean Seberg? And was relegated to appearing on TV dramas including her own father's vanity showcase? Poor Miss Montgomery married the much older Gig Young and tried to get away from her golden trap, and yet she never could until she unleashed Gig Young (who had been a bosom buddy of her dad's) and stopped playing daddy's little girl, much like Jane Fonda had to do later on in the 1960s. Anyway let this wonderful film stand in as a testament of a career that took a much different direction. But it could have been Elizabeth Montgomery who played all the parts that, say, Shirley Jones or Natalie Wood later did. She was just squelched.

A Summer of Faulkner: Three Novels by William Faulkner;
"As I Lay Dying," "The Sound and the Fury," "Light in August"
by William Faulkner

★★★★★
Black and White in Color

June 3, 2005

Three of Faulkner's greatest novels repackaged to take advantage of Oprah Winfrey's massive promotion. As we know, Oprah has so much street cred she could propel a shopping list to the top of the bestseller list, so let's see what she can do for Faulkner, a writer who has sometimes been criticized for relying on stereotyped depictions of Black characters. And at least two of these three novels face that explosive issue head-on. In *The Sound and the Fury*, the multiple neuroses of the (white) Compson family are always being counterposed to the nurturing and loving family of (Black) Dilsey and the rest of the servants. No matter what awful thing happens to one of the Compsons, Dilsey will always be hugging them to her bosom and singing plantation spirituals to cheer them up, ignoring her own systemic arthritis the better to give them the love and affection their own parents don't know how to dish up.

In *Light in August*, the racial identity of its protagonist, Joe Christmas, is a contested site, for no one knows if he's Black, white, or what. Commentators have often associated Joe with Jesus Christ (right down to the same initials) and his posture of martyrdom can still bring your heart into your throat, it's a very harsh look at Southern life at the beginning of the last century and Faulkner doesn't shy away from cruelty. He does show that patience and love do overcome almost any obstacles, or at any rate they wear down the obstacles to the degree that they transmogrify into something else. But was he counseling patience for Black people, telling them to go slow in their struggle for civil rights? Like any modernist text, *Light in August* is ambiguous and does not give up its answers very clearly.

As I Lay Dying, which takes the narrative form of *The Sound and the Fury* and explodes it further, is not as direct as the other two books in terms of its navigation of Black and white relations in the US. *As I Lay Dying* is more private, less social, more of a lyric meditation on family and the great cavern of death. No one yet has bettered Faulkner in his ability to enter into the heads of so many disparate characters and this book might be the tour de force of all time. Even the mother (dead when the book begins) speaks from beyond the grave, almost as a ghost might, but a ghost still attached to her own body, as her boys trundle her coffin from one far place to another. (Like Lena Grove's journey in *Light in August*.)

I'm happy Oprah is doing this! Maybe she can get Jonathan Franzen on her show and he could explain how *The Corrections* is really a postmodern remake of the Compsons. The truth is that most US novelists, and many writers from overseas, owe a huge debt to William Faulkner. Even those who don't know it yet. He is a fact of our landscape, like the weather.

At Hell's Gate: A Soldier's Journey from War to Peace
by Claude AnShin Thomas

★★★★☆
From There to Here

June 7, 2005

Once a highly decorated war hero, Claude Thomas had been sexually abused as a child and carried the scars of this abuse to Vietnam, where he commanded an elite helicopter unit for fourteen months at the height of the American incursion there. He wound up with a chestful of medals (twenty-seven) and a burnt-out shell of a man, returning to the US, a girl spat on him. One thing led to another and Thomas began questioning his own claims to his life. It wasn't until he met the famous Vietnamese sage Thích Nhat Hanh that he began to get a clue as to his spiritual path. Through mindfulness he became aware that he was a victim of Vietnam just as we all were, and just as generations unborn during the war continue to suffer from its political and cultural fallout. Today he is a Zen priest and has written an interesting memoir.

Like Claude AnShin Thomas, when we saw Thich Nhat Hanh, we burst into tears on the spot. And not because of any identification with his pain. I think I was just feeling emotional that day. Thomas has an amazing story to tell, but it is not all that well written and has many Buddhist clichés that spoil the thrust of the tale for me.

And could they have picked a scarier-looking portrait of Claude AnShin Thomas for the cover? I've seen him in person, he isn't that bad looking, he has sort of the look of Nelson Rockefeller, you know, not a matinée idol, but not a face from *Creature Features* either. I think Shambhala was definitely trying to go for the macho market here, making Thomas look like he was a serial killer coming out of the shadows to slit your throat then creep away. We know that Buddhism can sometimes be a dangerous practice, for you're standing in the middle of the fire trying to confront the real, but enough is enough, and this is a kind of visual crime if you ask me.

The Graduate (Special Edition) (1967)
dir. Mike Nichols

★★★★★
Farewell to a Great Actress

June 7, 2005

Today the news came we were dreading to hear but which we knew was coming, that our wonderful Anne Bancroft has died, at age seventy-three. It is said that she came to resent the way she was remembered by the mass public only for her role in *The Graduate*, bemoaning the fact that even her best screen work (playing Annie Sullivan in Arthur Penn's film of *The Miracle Worker*, for which she won the Oscar) was in its shadow. Any real fan of Anne Bancroft can remember dozens of great performances she gave us over the fifty years she spent in show business, all the way from screaming her lungs out in *Gorilla at Large* to her suicidal existentialist in *The Slender Thread* with Sidney Poitier as the psychiatrist who tries to help her.

Everyone knows that she was not the first choice to play Mrs. Robinson and that Mike Nichols lobbied hard to persuade Doris Day to take the part. Similarly, she only wound up playing the lead in John Ford's "Eastern" *Seven Women* (his last narrative film) when Patricia Neal had her terrible stroke. Bancroft was gallant, reliable, game for anything, and she was also extremely magnetic. The other day we were watching *The Turning Point*, Herbert Ross's ballet movie slash continual catfight, which cast her opposite the redoubtable Shirley MacLaine. No disrespect to Miss MacLaine, but when Bancroft is on the screen, as the aging prima donna Emma Jacklin, there's no way you can take your eyes off of her.

She was memorable also in *Agnes of God*, with Margaux Hemingway in *Lipstick*, and book lovers everywhere identified with her Helene Hanff, the American woman with a thing for London bookstores and the men who staff them, in *84 Charing Cross Road* opposite Anthony Hopkins.

No matter what the part, big or small, Bancroft was always amazing, and always classy, and that's what made her such a good screen partner (and life partner) to the unapologetically vulgar Mel Brooks. Together they formed a Hollywood relationship unlike all the others. We mourn her death and extend our condolences to him and to their family. Tonight we will look up toward the heavens and we'll see a new star burning in the sky with a fierce intensity. Goodnight, Anne Bancroft, shine on, shine on.

Doctor Zhivago
by Boris Pasternak

★★★★★
In Praise of Marina

June 10, 2005

Out of Zhivago's loves, I always liked Marina the best, and when the movie came out, I was puzzled to see that David Lean and Robert Bolt had left her out, excised her completely. It made me wonder why, why leave out the enchanting figure of Marina, the only one in Zhivago's world who was as faithful to him as a dog is to his master, one who was there at the beginning.

Maybe they thought that audiences were already being asked to swallow too much. Yuri Andreievich had married Tonya already, and had Sasha with her, and then the good doctor had found himself madly in love with Lara. That tragic romance ended badly and then Yuri finds himself completely without friends or family and he stumbles, like a bum, back into the life of Marina. I guess the filmmakers thought that they were painting Lara and Yuri to have the greatest love of all time, so where did Marina fit in? Anyone who's read the book knows that Marina's love for Yuri was stronger by far than the crazy, tender, adulterous love of Lara. Zhivago is such a good poet that Tonya, Lara, and Marina are all aquiver when he draws near them.

Marina is more mature (when she reencounters Yuri) and it's hard to imagine what actress of the mid-'60s would have best been able to essay her character—had Lean and Bolt been more faithful to the novel and included the Marina-Yuri story in it. She is a woman whom time has touched, but lightly, and she has seen the ravages of the revolution firsthand, while still remaining touched and open to the possibilities of new love. If they could have gotten her, Audrey Hepburn would have been a good choice, sort of the Audrey Hepburn of *Robin and Marian* and *Two for the Road*. Another performance that comes to mind is Claudia Cardinale in *Once upon a Time in the West*—women who have lived and suffered and whose spirits still flame and seek the higher ground. But perhaps Hepburn and Cardinale were too beautiful (or glamorous) and Pasternak wanted us to find the beauty in a plainer woman.

The book is a very different experience than the movie; structured as a poem, the novel moves laterally from time period to time period, while individual associations link disparate stories. We remember that Pasternak was writing about characters of another generation than his own, and that he had already seen the death of Stalin and the public demolition of the dictator's relationship when he published his novel at last. As a boy he had dreamed of becoming a musician, and it is said that he aped Scriabin in his earliest works. Certainly some of Scriabin's theories of synesthesia carry over into the marvelously sensual passages of *Zhivago*, where everything—smells, tastes, the pressures of flesh—all blends into image.

Guys Gone Wild

★★★★☆
To Sum It Up for Next Time

June 10, 2005

While we wait for the sequel, *Spring Break Explosion*, here's my impressions of the first *Guys Gone Wild* disc. And maybe a lesson or two for the makers of the first one, because it let us down quite a bit and maybe with *Spring Break* they will make some reparations. First, the plusses. For the most part the *GGW* guys are great looking, with a few duds sprinkled in here or there to keep us grounded. It's true, after a while they all begin to look alike. They have the same body type, the same haircut, the same goofy expressions frozen on their faces as their jaws try to speak in words after twelve tequilas, they shrug, they give up speaking, they concentrate hard on opening the drawstring to their pants. The sound equipment the interviewers use is horrible, and this is one DVD that might be better viewed with the mute button completely off. The interviewers can be heard screeching extremely loud, but the boys' answers are pretty mumbled, and it's not only the liquor that makes them sound underwater, it's the lack of attention placed on getting the audio right. To a lesser degree the same is true of the video. These girls can get a guy to strip off his boxers and get down to nothing at all in ten seconds flat, but they can't photograph him worth a darn.

Hire someone who can work both ends of a camera is what I say. The camera's bobbing up and down like it's on a buoy out in a storm, it's like the *Blair Witch Project*, and when you can see anything, it's just for a flash. The other problem is the running time is under an hour. I guess a fool and his money are soon parted but in this day of six-hour porn DVDs, who is going to be fooled twice with a fifty-minute short? Get some extra footage in there pronto.

I can't wait until these guys, who have all presumably signed releases, try to get work as adults. Hopefully they won't be running as congressmen or anything that would require full disclosure. Granted we all go a little crazy when we're juiced up, but doing it for video, that's a lapse in judgment—however it's one I'm glad they made. It will give a picture of what American youth thought appropriate in the year of our Lord 2005. Now let's just have more of it and I will rest happy. Oh, and to really add a star, girls, get them to have sex with each other on camera. How hard could that be?

Spellbound
by Paula Abdul

★★★★★
You Give Love, You Get Love

June 16, 2005

When I was young and in a vulnerable place in my life, Paula Abdul's music meant a great deal to me and helped me to see the bright spots in a dark cloud that was then passing over my life. Paula didn't have the greatest voice in the world, but engineering technology helped her over the hump. Her dancing style seemed so original, but she taught it to Janet Jackson first, and Janet did it better than she did, so that oddly enough Paula seemed like a clumsy imitator of Janet's moves, and her voice seemed even weaker than Janet's. The truth is that both of them are great, but for different reasons. And nothing will replace the masterpiece that is *Spellbound*. I love the graphics on the cover that show Paula under attack by the kind of typeface that Prince used to use to show emotional distress. This is the period when she was experimenting not just with different techno beats, but with different photo looks too—partly caused by fluctuating weight gain and loss—remember the video which anamorphically stretched her out so she looked like she was eight feet tall?

"Rush Rush," the great hit single, had a romantic video of its own with Paula pursued by heartthrob Keanu Reeves; some cynics disputed whether Keanu, who looked so stoned in the video, even knew he was being photographed at the time. It is one of the key ballads of the twentieth century, right up there with "If Ever I Would Leave You" by Lerner and Loewe, "But Not for Me" by Gershwin, and Cole Porter's "Night and Day." "Rush Rush" brings it all home, and it's not just about sensual longing, it's about philosophy and the pull of narrative and the way storytelling is the key to a long life:

"Here's my story, and the story goes: You give love, you get love, and more than Heaven knows." The music perfectly complements the words and imitates the adrenaline rush of that moment when you fall in love for the very first time. For me it represented the moment when someone I loved died, a miserable death of a tragic disease. I would sit in his room and play "Rush Rush" over and over again until he felt momentarily at peace. The lamp was set low so the shadows played over his face and his twitching hands. We had a joke that someday Paula Abdul would burst into the room eight feet tall and extremely thin. Or perhaps Keanu might just fall in.

Gothic Forbidden Dragon Athame Dagger Pendant Necklace
by Silver Insanity

★★★★★
Necklace of a Thousand Dreams

June 17, 2005

I bought this necklace for a close friend who loves dragons, and she wears it every day (except when she's working). She says it gives her a thousand dreams! As she moves through the day strange visions come to her of living in another time, close to the elements. At night, as she shuts her eyes and touches the dragon's head, slumber overtakes her and she feels that she's back in some medieval fantasy along the lines of Robert Jordan's Wheel of Time series.

It's an attractive piece, made of sterling silver, and cunningly carved out of silver by expert workmen. Wagner lovers and opera fans in general will want to wear one of those pendants while attending the *Ring* cycle live; you'll feel the breath of Fáfnir on the back of your neck as you touch the intricate folds and lines of the dragon's glaring face.

In his heart a garnet beats and you'll feel the counterpulse of a dagger, gleaming at your side. Looking for a little crystal energy in your life, to counterbalance the ugly planet energies? This is the one dagger-pendant necklace that you'll want to have. It's hard to describe the workmanship, but frankly, the photo here isn't very good and makes the necklace look like a gimcrack prize from a Cracker Jack machine. But in actuality it is precious looking and your guy or girl will think you've spent a whole lot of money on them if you give them this Forbidden Dragon as a birthday present or whatnot. Or if you're a parent with goth children, trust Kevin, they will be loving you after you give them one of these.

The Ivan Moffat File: Life among the Beautiful and Damned in London, Paris, New York, and Hollywood
by Gavin Lambert

★★★★★
Admiration and Mystery

June 21, 2005

Moffat called his autobiography *Absolute Heaven*, from a phrase his parents often used when he, as a child, asked them what they had done the night before, in the glittering London social scene they inhabited. "Went to a party, darling. It was absolute heaven." Moffat wrote his memoirs out by hand in a series of notebooks, and one of them has disappeared, so the book takes an awfully big jump right at an exciting part, and we land down again ten years later. Gavin Lambert, the novelist and biographer, fills in the gaps in his own way. Lambert knew Moffat himself, and also interviewed many of the survivors: people who had known him, from all walks of life.

If you have recently read *The Other Chekhov*, the biography of acting coach Michael Chekhov, and you've been curious about Dartington Hall, the experimental British art and drama school at which Chekhov worked, you will find a lot more of it in *Absolute Heaven*, for Ivan Moffat was a student there, and very close to Beatrice Straight and her family (the patrons of the hall). I found Moffat's late-in-life passion for Caroline Blackwood very touching, and the realization at the end of his life that he was actually the father of Caroline's daughter Ivana is wonderfully told and imagined. Another fine section details his work with the Hollywood director George Stevens on the US Army filmmaking unit that traveled and filmed everything they could from D-Day to Auschwitz to Stalingrad. Talk about high adventure!

The mystery that remains is the unevenness of Moffat's artistic production. After the war, his work with Stevens on the scripts of *Giant*, *Shane*, and *A Place in the Sun* is exemplary, and Lambert mounts a welcome defense of *They Came to Cordura* and the ill-fated *Bhowani Junction* that makes you want to see these pictures once again. And yet, at the end of the day, Moffat remains fairly opaque, as though his life had been led at such a clip there was no time for him really to make any sense out of it, especially in the painted bungalows of Hollywood and the traffic lights of the Sunset Strip. This isn't Gavin Lambert's masterpiece (that would probably be *The Goodbye People*) but in some ways it feels closer to autobiography than Lambert's own memoir pieces do. He is always a writer worth reading and one of the only living writers whose hand I would like to shake.

Imitation of Life (Two-Movie Collection) (1934/1959)
dir. John M. Stahl / Douglas Sirk

★★★★★
A Difference of Intention

June 24, 2005

Claudette Colbert, as an actress, dazzles with Gallic polish and style, but Lana Turner has a quality that is more expressive than Colbert's charm. Like the actress who plays her daughter (Sandra Dee), what people often criticize as Turner's "nonacting" is really the best kind of screen acting, a simple way of presenting oneself that the camera loves and a dignity that will withstand even the most ludicrous dialogue and situations. Sirk knows how to play this up—I imagine changing the character from a businesswoman into an actress is his way of accentuating how phony and self-absorbed Lora Meredith can be, and yet Turner makes us realize that this is the way that Lora has been forced to live her life to evade the Depression and to come out on top. We're cheering for her every step of the way, just as we would any dumb animal who's been beaten down and is looking for a ray of sunshine. When the *neorealismo* director approaches Lora Meredith to tell her that, of all the actresses in the world, he has selected her because of her innate gifts, it's so ludicrous it makes us look around at others in the movie theater to see if they are registering the same kind of shock: the world has jumped a little on its axis. It's the product of a moviegoer's imagination: someone must have remembered the seismic repercussions when Rossellini asked Ingrid Bergman to star in *Stromboli* eight years earlier. Certainly the Bergman-Rossellini collaboration hangs heavy over the *Imitation of Life* remake, as every scene seems to have its parallel in some earlier Bergman films, be it

Voyage to Italy, *Fear*, *Europe '51*, or *Joan of Arc at the Stake*. The love-less marriages and the striving for a divine connection forecast individual scenes in Sirk's *Imitation*, and yet Sirk has something that Rossellini doesn't—he injects race issues into the script, and in doing so brings out some shadows of American life that Bergman and Rossellini, it can now be seen, evaded by fleeing the United States in 1950. Sirk is a little bolder, though some have questioned whether, in casting Susan Kohner rather than a Black actress such as Fredi Washington in the 1934 version, he too was seeking to escape box office punishment and Southern rejection. Kohner is superb, her sulky lip furious in its threat, heartbreaking when she cracks. Hers is one of the great performances of the postwar era, it's blistering like red paint. In the Stahl film Fredi Washington seems more restrained, toned down after the outrageous spectacle she presented in *The Emperor Jones*, but on the other hand Kohner got lucky and the scriptwriters decided to include a white boyfriend for her to react against (Troy Donahue), and his rage matches hers, galvanizes it—there's no corresponding scene in the Stahl film.

Comparing the performances it is easy to see that Warren William (1934) is miles better at acting than John Gavin (1959), and yet Sirk uses Gavin's hangdog pretty-boy looks better than Stahl was able to maneuver his way around Warren William's impetuous danger signs.

The Bells of St. Mary's (1945)
dir. Leo McCarey

★★★★★
Sequel Time

June 28, 2005

Ingrid Bergman looks lustrous, her skin aglow, as though they fed them nothing but cream in that convent. No wonder she turned a million little American boys on to Catholicism and boxing at the same time. Bing Crosby can't take his eyes off of her, and this gives the movie an interesting tension; to doubters I say that Leo McCarey could have hired any actress to play Sister Benedict—a Helen Hayes, an Ethel Barrymore. Or younger, it could have been Rosalind Russell.

But instead McCarey just happened to hire the sexiest, most beautiful actress in the movies! You know he wanted those sparks. The two
stars are said to have conducted a romance whenever they heard the
word "cut." Who could blame them? McCarey's sets were generally
easygoing affairs, with great catering and plenty of cocktails served
twice a day. This was the last of Crosby's four 1945 pictures. They
kept them busy in those days! (Besides which, of course, he was starring the whole time in his own Philco-sponsored radio program every
week.) *The Bells of St. Mary's* was a step up in quality from his other
1945 efforts (except for *The Road to Utopia*, which has its own
surrealist charm and serious fanbase). Bergman was similarly overworked, having just released *Spellbound* as well as *Saratoga Truck*
(filmed earlier and delayed due to glut of studio releases during the
war years). She was at the height of her beauty and fame, and it
seemed she could do no wrong. The confidence of her portrayal of
Sister Benedict underlines this.

The movie, a sequel to *Going My Way*, lit up the box office and
became the biggest hit of the year. However, Crosby felt he had gone
to the well enough and declined to star in a third installment which
would have matched Father O'Malley with an orphaned set of twins
(his niece and nephew). Even in the 1950s when he could have used a
hit, he told his manager he would never make a third O'Malley film.

Late in her life I asked Ingrid Bergman which was her favorite
movie of all those she had made. She laughed. In Sweden? She named
a film. I did not recognize its title. With Rossellini? She said *Europe '51*.
In America? There were two, *Notorious* and *The Bells of St. Mary's*.

Loteria
by The Hangmen

★★★★★
Hangmen Also Die

June 29, 2005

The way people feel about Iggy I feel about Bryan Small, a rock icon
I have loved forever. He is notorious for the number of major labels
who have dropped his contract after the records failed to chart due to

lousy promotion. But a small cadre of worshippers adore his every move and hail his songwriting as the best to come down the pike since the heyday of Lou Reed back in the late 1960s. *Loteria* isn't his best LP but it ushers in a new configuration of Hangmen, and this one sounds like it could do Small's material justice in the long run (or live shows, the Hangmen's forte.) None of the tracks have the sway of "Bent," their tremendous anthemic single which ushered in the new millennium, and yet "Wild Beast" is pretty memorable and will have you hollering in the car as you skim along the 405 at 4:05 a.m. Angelique Congleton is a mighty fine bassist and her voice is like honey on fire.

The sentiments of living too long and for too little ring true to me, and anyone who's heard his songs knows that Small's been to see the hooting owl and lived to kiss the snake. The band here is a different mix-up of players than those that appeared on *We've Got Blood on the Toes of Our Boots*, but they seem capable and you know they have to be good with people if they can make it through a whole LP with King Spooky, Bryan Small. The way he sings it's like all of your heart got mushed up into a little ball then strained through a handkerchief.

At a recent show someone in the crowd told me that Robert Johnson made a pact with the devil that he would sell his soul to him in exchange for coming back as Bryan Small.

The Life of Helen Stephens: The Fulton Flash
by Sharon Kinney Hanson

★★★★★
Impressive Account of One of America's Finest Athletes

July 2, 2005

Wow, before opening this book I had never heard of Helen Stephens, and now that I've finished Sharon Kinney Hanson's fine book about her life, I feel as though I have known her forever! They called her "the Fulton Flash" because of her great speed, and her ability to sprint took her out of Missouri and catapulted her to the great stages of the world. Like a comet streaking across the sky she represented the United States in the now-legendary Berlin Olympics of 1936, where she appeared in front of Adolf Hitler and, no doubt, gave him a few ruminations about the power and speed of America. The Olympics were actually far from a rout for Germany, as Hanson reminds us. Nowadays we think that because of Jesse Owens and other great American performances, Germany had its ass handed to it at the games, but far from it, they actually did very well and Hitler must have been quite proud! In women's track events, Germany won seven medals, the US only two—both courtesy of Helen Stephens. Conceivably she could have won more medals, but some events later open to women competitors in later Olympics were closed to them in 1936 (like shot put, at which Stephens was a great champ).

Photos show she was an astonishing beauty, with great bones, perhaps a little Amazonian and androgynous. Some people thought she was a man, and this irked her no end. She sued *Look* magazine and the funny comeuppance for *Look* was she went out on a date with one of *Look*'s lawyers. After several drinks things got hot and heavy. As the author reports, "Helen told her friend Gertrude Webb, 'I had a sense he was trying to find something. So this ole country girl let him roam around awhile 'til he found what he was lookin' for. I just wanted to settle it then and there!'"

Nevertheless, Stephens was a lesbian in a homophobic society and stood her ground with dignity and courage. It was hard for such a woman to "come out" but inevitably she did, or almost did. The whole tragedy of women's sports in the twentieth century is a story that Sharon Kinney Hanson tells with distinction and clarity. She brings all her skills to her on-point account of the apparently intersex sprinter Stella Walsh, killed by a robber's gunfire in 1980, and because of the violent death subjected to an autopsy in Cleveland of all places, which revealed her ambiguous genitalia. Stella Walsh, one of the greatest Olympic heroines, was one of the closest friends of the Fulton Flash, and her death apparently had great impact on Helen. I won't reveal any more of the story, except to say it is an amazing one, the kind that makes you put down the book and just say "Holy moly."

i never knew what time it was
by David Antin

★★★★☆
Talking Head

July 5, 2005

I keep going back to this collection, again and again, mining it for its virtues. Antin is a master at talking, and these essays were apparently written first as improvisations, then polished over and over till they attain the shine of fine old silver. He has a way of describing things that make them seem brand new. His mind skips from one thing to another, exploring their connections, and yet he's light on his feet, like a stone skimming across the surface of a beautiful pond. His "manifesto" on postmodern practice turns out to be an account, rather like Mark Twain in comic richness, of himself and his wife trying to buy a bed and not knowing how to select the best one, and the awkwardness of trying out a bed in a furniture store, even with salespeople encouraging you to lie down and get comfortable on their samples. Never explicitly does he explain how this Jean Kerr–type story might be an allegory for postmodernism, but Antin is wise enough to let the tale speak for itself.

His memories of figures varied as John Baldessari and Herbert Marcuse are quite amusing. Best of all is Antin's line, without the benefit of capital letters, and sentences floating in scraps of phrases like comic book dialogue freed of balloon mooring. He approximates the free-floating effect of talking to someone who has absolute authority over thinking, and how liberating it is to submit to such a man. Reading the essays in this book, we long for more of such talk transcription. Apparently there are many, many more talks waiting for publication, and of course Antin happily is still very much with us planning more. He calls these talks "poems" and of course that is his right.

My caveat is that he spends too many pages repeating himself on the zaniness and spiritual emptiness of California, and he seems to be patting himself (and his wife, performance artist Eleanor Antin) on the back for bringing culture to San Diego way back when—in the 1970s. This thrust seems shortsighted and an insult to San Diego. However, this is a book for the ages and I expect will bring pleasure to anyone who can get into it.

Alien Green Ring
by Body Candy

★★★★★
Body Candy Does It Again

July 5, 2005

I had had enough of the popular Body Candy Cross Dangle ring, which was always getting caught in whatever I was wearing across the midriff. Or even if you were walking around bare midriff, the tips of the cross (where the hands of the crucified god might be if there was a body nailed to the cross) kept getting caught in the car door, on brambles, going past a picket fence, it would fly toward the left or right and slow me down. I wanted to get something that would set me off from the crowd and yet not be so Madonna-oriented as the cross-dangle piece I had worn so long. (I had the Old-World Solar Blue ring.) I toyed with the notion of buying one of the beer-mug danglers, but it just might call attention to my incipient beer belly, why tell people all about it when they can see it with their eyes open!

The Alien Green ring is just what the doctor ordered. On the beach or at the gym, the first thing people ask me is, "What is that on your navel?" It has a lurid, luminous green like kryptonite, two eyes perfectly symmetrical and round, and it stares at you like aliens are watching you. I shaved my "treasure trail" so it looks as though the aliens landed on a perfectly smooth runway. Just apply a little talcum powder and you're "it" for the duration. Best thing, with the round construction of the balls, they don't catch on any-thing. Hey, maybe Mother Nature had the same idea when she dreamed up the whole testicle idea (make 'em round).

Sure, some people stare and some people preach at you, but my philosophy is if you have to do it, might as well do it with Body Candy. I'd do TV commercials for this firm if I had to, that's how good they are. As for the haters, well, they can move on, there's no room for hate on my navel.

Alice in Jeopardy: A Novel
by Ed McBain

★★★★★
Farewell to the King

July 8, 2005

There will be another novel, *Fiddlers: A Novel of the 87th Precinct*, to follow in September, and who knows how many collections of short stories and republications of older material. But as we try to comprehend the news that Ed McBain died today, it is a staggering blow to anyone who loves the detective story in general and police procedurals in particular.

Alice in Jeopardy has received mixed reviews, and maybe some were disappointed by the book's disjointed structure. Others read it as an ambitious experiment in combining several genres of crime writing. Its heroine, Alice Glendinning, whose husband disappeared in a boating accident eight months ago, and whose children have just been kidnapped, is not your typical heroine and seems to ward off the reader's sympathies throughout. The mysterious villain is unmasked in a late chapter but probably most of us knew who it was going to be, we just didn't know how that obliquity would be undone. Thus *Alice* turns into a novel of inverted suspense. It would have been easy for McBain to make this a conventional novel of abduction and despair, but he was always after something different. People point to Picasso and say that he could be so experimental because he could draw like an angel. Same was true of Ed McBain. He knew so much about people that he realized he could write in clipped sentences, chapters that revolved like pieces of a kaleidoscope, and his readers would follow him anywhere, because we trusted his instincts.

It is a sad day for mystery lovers. This was a giant who has left us, and we shall not see his like again. Farewell to the king.

Spa Experience Gift Basket
by Wine Country Baskets

★★★★★
Top of the Line, Reports Client

July 11, 2005

I gave this gift basket to a client and got a new account! The timing was perfect, for my client, for whom I had already done a number of small favors, was about to take a week off from his job just to give himself some much needed "me time." I sent this basket off to his apartment and Amazon timed it so it would get there on his first day off. The products are everything they should be and the packaging, well, you can see for yourself that they do a good old job on their baskets. These are the original Wine Country people who've been doing this for eons and now they have perfected the art of spa bathing also. My client reported that everything was unopened and looked pristine, very important in our days of heightened security fears. Especially if you're giving something intimate that the other person plans to use on his skin while naked.

You don't want any impurities, and Wine Country Baskets just smells clean all over! The body scrub that they give in this arrangement includes a special kind of exfoliating soap that gives your skin the softness of a baby's bottom. Salt from the Dead Sea couldn't have been more useful. I almost did not recognize this fellow when he called me into his office to award the new portfolio based on my thoughtfulness. He was all aglow, like a man half his age. He expressed gratitude for the plush terrycloth bathrobe, the Provençal lavender hand lotion, and just the general luxury of the whole package.

He said he would keep the basket by his fireplace and keep logs in it, that's how sturdy it is. Anyway thanks to Wine Country Baskets and Amazon, we parlayed one man's "me time" into an account worth many times its value.

Bullet Park
by John Cheever

★★★★★
"Paint me a small railroad station, then"

July 12, 2005

I remember reading this book when it came out and feeling disappointed that it wasn't a more powerful, apocalyptic novel. Those were the '60s, after all, a time when we still looked to our novels for the answers to the day's problems. Cheever wasn't interested in solving problems. As we now know, he was torn in a psychic split between different parts of his identity—the average family man, colorless and yet possessed by a love divine, vs. the bisexual swinger who lives for sensation and the authenticity of the gutter.

Bullet Park represents this conflict in allegorical terms, and now I can see that the two neighbors and antagonists, Nailles and Hammer, form two halves of the same person. Well, that's a crude way of putting it, but at any rate reading back into the biography they perhaps represent two of Cheever's warring personalities, and in their conflict over the future of Tony Nailles, the appealing teenage son, they are going to war themselves. At stake is nothing less than the future of American literature.

I always thought this would have been a good movie—back in the day I wrote Cheever a note asking him to make sure that Burt Lancaster and Kirk Douglas would play Hammer and Nailles in the film version. He was polite but noncommittal. And I don't know who would be good among today's actors. I picked Lancaster and Douglas because those two, who of course made many pictures together, gave off the almost intangible sensation of somehow having been made for each other, like the way Plato wrote that we are all looking for the other half of the soul we were once part of. Thus even when they were playing antagonists, Lancaster and Douglas still seemed to be seeking each other out, not in an erotic way especially, but in a search for meaning that would never end.

Viva Poncho: Twenty Ponchos and Capelets to Knit
by Christina Stork and Leslie Barbazette

★★★★☆
Knitting for Foggy Weather

July 20, 2005

Viva Poncho, that's a clever title guaranteed to sucker male knitters in, with its bilingual pun on a popular old-fashioned Spanish phrase still current in many parts of California at least (don't know how this book will do in Middle America, where Spanish is less spoken). Anyhow I sat down with the book and breezed through the attractive pages looking for a cool-weather poncho for the cold San Francisco summer nights. There are plenty of outdoor events which take place late into the night, say, the recent fireworks at Crissy Field, and why not dress warmly with a newly knitted poncho? Lucinda Williams came and gave a free concert in Golden Gate Park, and I wasn't the only guy there wearing a decorated poncho in honor of Stork and Barbazette's new guide.

It was a great idea to hire David Verba to do the photos. He's famous for his Western photos of desert stretches and big throbbing moon shots, no one since John Ford has made Monument Valley look so good. But here in the knit department he does a good job, makes you look twice, expecting to see salamanders gliding across the model's boot.

The real reason ponchos are so popular among knitters is there's practically nothing you can do that will go wrong. No amount of dropped stitches are going to make the poncho look deformed or like anything else but what it is, a sort of rhomboid shape with a hole for your head to poke through. *Viva Poncho* has many of these, though some are clearly designed for women and few men, even in our liberated San Francisco, are going to wear some of the capelets in the book. In fact one or two of them no one but a runway model could wear without looking like an idiot. They're "too" stylish if such a thing might be and you know it might for sure!

No matter if you prefer mohair or alpaca, or just yarn from Marks & Spencer, you'll find something to make. Now, boys, get out those needles and set off some sparks!

Bright Boulevards, Bold Dreams: The Story of Black Hollywood
by Donald Bogle

★★★★★
It Will Change the Way You View Hollywood Film

July 24, 2005

I feel like I had never really seen a Hollywood picture before, now that I have read Donald Bogle's marvelous study of Black life in Hollywood on- and off-screen. The other day for example I saw an inconsequential Fox comedy of the 1950s written by Nunnally Johnson, *Oh, Men! Oh, Women!*, and in it a spoiled white heiress played by Barbara Rush refuses to exit a New York cab until the driver finds her the correct change. For the moment, the focus of the film is on the hassled driver, who has to contend with Miss Rush's airs, and also with the honks and screams of a dozen other cabs jammed up behind him. Finally he lets her out for free and he absorbs the cost of his mistake. I didn't recognize the actor who played (briefly) the cabbie, so I waited for the credits. It was Joel Fluellen. A name which would have meant nothing to me, if I hadn't just finished reading Bogle. Joel Fluellen! The forgotten man of the movies dead, alas, too soon, and way before he could reveal his true sexuality.

This performance, brief as it was, is totally calibrated and brings an energy into a movie which sadly needs some! In a way this scene might be an allegory for Bogle's thesis, which is that, even if they were given insulting little to do, African American actors did it stunningly well and the shame of it is how very few of them managed to catch a break all the way to stardom. A few of them did: Lena Horne, Dorothy Dandridge, Sidney Poitier. Because the book basically breaks off circa 1960, we don't get to hear later success stories such as Will Smith or Denzel Washington. This book is all about forebears.

A few nights later I watched a picture of an earlier vintage, *Crash Dive* with Tyrone Power. Oddly for its time, the movie gives a fair amount of screen time to a Black actor called Ben Carter. If you read *BBBD*, you will find out Carter's whole story, the way he parlayed his limited experience as a theatrical agent into representing some of Hollywood's biggest Black names—and often enough stealing their parts from them, because he'd nab the script and secure the part first if he thought it worth his time!

If you've got one film book to read this year, make it Donald Bogle. You'll find it an amazing intervention into a quickly disappearing history.

Overlord: Poems
by Jorie Graham

★★★★★
Her Best Book Ever

July 24, 2005

Often attacked for her headstrong ways and because, to be frank about it, she is a woman, Jorie Graham is triumphing over her current, well-publicized difficulties with a collection that adds new shadows and depths to what is already a distinctive voice and allusive, almost invisible storytelling. She has hit on the idea, the trope, of *Overlord* and managed to succeed at an unlikely target, a combination of historical detail like Stephen Ambrose, with her trademark exploration of consciousness, and a new attention to her long, long line which often reads as though thought itself was being examined and twisted along a wire, like a centipede on a tightrope, high above a crowd all of whose mouths hang gaping open. Let's look at an example, shall we?

In "Europe *(Omaha Beach 2003),*" Graham evokes the famous Normandy landings by picking out the appropriate, sometimes surreal, nouns: "Boats, surf, cries, miles, pools, bars, war." It is vivid, like the first reels of Steven Spielberg's *Saving Private Ryan.* "No / container, friend," she adds. "No basic building blocks 'of / matter.' No constituent particles from which everything / is made." Then, quick as a wince, she corrects herself: "No made." (Note the hidden word *nomad* in the middle of this, crouching like a Bedouin.)

Perhaps recent events in world history have left US poets feeling nomadic, as though there were no real place for us anymore on American soil.

Where would she be without Peter Sacks? He took a lovely photograph of her in Normandy in the very fields through which the

Allies poured on June 6, 1944, and then again he made some kind of spectral collage for the book's cover, random (perhaps?) newsprint torn and remounted, then superimposed with bold, Asian strokes of maroon, white, and black paint. The field is yellow, stained with age and water damage, like the shipborne invasion itself.

With the double consciousness of a wound, Graham has made an interesting investment in reclaiming a crucial battle of World War II from the Tom Brokaws and the Gerald Fords who have claimed it as their own, and returned it to poetry where it belongs.

Snow White and the Three Stooges **(1961)**
dir. Walter Lang

★★★★★
Unexpected Delight

July 25, 2005

I'm no movie snob, but I never thought I'd enjoy a movie called *Snow White and the Three Stooges*! I remember even when I was a little boy, I refused to go to see this one, even when the other kids on the school bus said it was awesome. Well, I finally gave in and I was confounded to see that it was practically an "A film," with lots of stylish touches and a genuinely well-acted script by the ever-reliable Noel Langley (from the Brothers Grimm classic). Langley also wrote (and directed!) one of my grandma's favorites, the proreincarnation docudrama *The Search for Bridey Murphy*.

No dwarfs in sight, but Carol Heiss is a haunting Snow White, limited in range but with a strange beauty, like Gene Tierney's in *Laura*. No wonder little boys and girls alike were drawn to her. I wonder if she could still be alive, what a shame she made no films after this one, but she must have been hard to cast, having so little acting talent. Edson Stroll is super, and he really can act! He was also in the Three Stooges' venture *In Orbit* the following year—wonder if he was sleeping with someone at the top? Whoever put him in those russet tights knew what he was doing!

The song that his little puppet, Quinto, sang to Snow White is so touching! And Stroll does a great job of making it seem as though the

Prince (disguised as the peasant, Quatro) really is performing ventriloquism, moving the muscles in his tightly closed mouth while staring passionately at Carol Heiss while Quinto bleats out the love song. Musical fans will notice the strong resemblance (strong enough for plagiarism?) between this main love theme and the Cole Porter tune "True Love" that Bing Crosby and Grace Kelly performed in *High Society* a few years earlier. Whatever, it is a gorgeous number and well sung by all concerned—little Quinto, handsome Stroll, and lovely Carol Heiss.

Yes, she is an atrocious actress, but there's something appealing about her, you want to save her from her own bad acting. Her voice isn't very modulated, but she's great on ice and the fantasy sequence where she dances on the multicolored ice rink is an unbelievable Technicolor spectacle.

I don't know, I liked the kinder and gentler Stooges. The scene where they have to tell Snow White about Prince Charming's supposed death is truly a heartbreaker. Moe Howard acquits himself as an ace actor, he really should have gotten an Oscar nomination for Best Supporting Actor. As for Patricia Medina, she is way over the top, and not that great at it. Her outfits are so loud she nearly gets lost in them. I realize I'm in the minority here but I didn't care for her here. She's much better when she works for Orson Welles, and her book, *Laid Back in Hollywood*, is first rate. But as the wicked Queen, she's merely OK.

Wuthering Heights (1939)
dir. William Wyler

★★★★★
Geraldine Fitzgerald–1913–2005

July 26, 2005

In the wake of Geraldine Fitzgerald's death earlier this month, we turn to our DVDs of *Wuthering Heights* and the "extra" feature on this disc looks more and more valuable—the interview with the aged Fitzgerald in which she looks back, after sixty years, to her memories of making this William Wyler classic. Wits of the day said that she was the only cast member who seemed to have read the Emily Brontë novel it was based on. In the on-screen interview she remembers a tumultuous set filled with the off-screen romantic shenanigans of Oberon and Olivier, who were each caught up in "important romances," Olivier's with Vivien Leigh, the woman he thought should be playing Cathy. Poor Merle Oberon usually gets the short end of the stick and is sometimes harshly criticized for being inadequate in the part, but Fitzgerald is kinder and gentler, and perhaps gives a truer yardstick toward that pivotal performance.

We admired Fitzgerald for generations; she was nominated for the Oscar playing Isabella; she continued to thrill us all through her years slaving away at Warner Bros., including playing Bette Davis's affectionate pal in *Dark Victory* and the wealthy noir doll in *Nobody Lives Forever* with John Garfield. Was she blacklisted? There was a strong leftist streak in her, and her movie credits die out during the period of HUAC activity; when she returned to the screen, she was playing older parts, some of them not quite dignified, but meanwhile she was returning to her stage roots and playing on the Broadway stage. After I saw her in *Long Day's Journey into Night*, I had the thrill of my life when she auditioned me for her Everyman Theater project—it was sort of a hippie venture to play Shakespeare in the streets, not just regular Shakespeare but a juiced-up acid-rock extravaganza heavily influenced by her understanding of Brecht. She was a brilliant director and conceptualist and one of the most vital people I ever met. Now that she's gone, a whole high-toned spirit has disappeared with her, out of the stage, out of the darkened cinema palace. Tonight I'll watch *Wuthering Heights* one more time, enjoying the larger-than-life melodrama, the beauty of Oberon and Olivier, but tonight out of respect to a magnificent actress and rebellious flame now quenched.

La bête humaine
by Émile Zola

Trainspotting

July 27, 2005

Jacques seems like a normal man from the outside, and judged by the standards of his contemporaries he is. It's the Second Empire and as Zola has foreseen, the rise of the steam railway has created enormous changes in the fabric of the social order. To analyze this phenomenon more deeply, Zola hit on a lovely idea, to investigate the lives of those who work on the railroad and its linked industries. What he didn't expect was what he came up with, a clear link between sex, murder, and high-speed railways. This link was to give rise within a few years of *La bête humaine*'s publication to the so-called Trunk Murders. As Jacques realizes, trains make it possible to remove one of the awkward social reasons why men do not kill—because in general it was impossible to remove oneself from one's victim's body fast enough to avert suspicion. You could bury the body, but it could still be traced back to you. Now in the 1880s, really all you had to do was put it on a train and science would steam it away from you at great rates of speed, putting infinite distances between you and your crime.

Agatha Christie took some elements of *La bête humaine* and modernized them a bit in her 1950s thriller *4:50 from Paddington*. Both novels share the same surrealistic image—the murder scene framed in the window of a passing train that you see, so vividly, for one moment only, then it's gone as though it never happened. (Freudians interpret this discomfiture as another version of the so-called primal scene.) Christie's murderer is a sort of updated Jacques, a man on whom the veneer of civilization is only as thick as his bank account and his convenience.

But, in *La bête humaine*, if you think Jacques is bad wait till you meet up with Séverine, the "heroine" of the book, a woman so bad she makes other noir protagonists look like Pollyanna. She is beautiful, selfish, conniving, self-absorbed, and yet what makes her tick is her acute understanding of her social position and the way things get done, and undone, by forces we cannot control. The negotiation of such tricky, slippery moral slopes is something that a sociopath can handle with ease. No wonder this novel made such good "noir" movies later on, one by Renoir, one by Fritz Lang.

Her Greatest Hits
by Belinda Carlisle

★★★★☆
Almost Perfect Except

August 2, 2005

Why can't I find an album which has the best of Belinda Carlisle's solo material together with her greatest hits while still with the Go-Go's? People like me love her in both incarnations and we don't want to have to seek out two different greatest-hits compilations with completely different material on each one. Surely some budget label could combine all of the above. Maybe they do that in England, where (or so my friend told me recently) Belinda C. is still considered a major force in pop, selling thousands of records a year. Talk about an alternate universe!

In the meantime, until my next trip to a British record store, that is, I will be playing this collection—a lot. Whenever I'm down or depressed, all I have to do is listen to "Heaven" and I get high right away. Besides being a feel-good song, it unveils any number of intriguing theological speculations: "They say in heaven that love comes first, we'll make heaven a place on earth." Belinda begs the question of how to conjoin the two different worlds, but I think the upfront romanticism of the track is what has made it a favorite of gay men all over the world. We all are looking for a world without borders where "love comes first." And that ain't happening here on this planet, not anytime soon. Indeed the walls keep climbing higher and higher. "The world's alive with the sound of kids on the street outside." I'm not a kid any more, and neither is Belinda I'm sure, but we still cherish our dreams of youth when anything seemed possible.

The whole LP is filled with brilliant touches and the ecstatic lyricism of the 1960s combined with the persuasive synthy percussions of the '80s. Today these sound a bit out of place, but the LP has the power to move you back in time. Her best tracks evoke the poetry of California beach life, its transience and ecstasy, like "Circle in the Sand" or the Spector-influenced "Summer Rain," with its claustrophobic, hypnotic mantra: "Every time I see the lightning / Every time I hear the thunder / Every time I close the window / When this happens in the summer, the night is so inviting / I can feel that you are so close I can feel you when the wind blows right through my heart." We've all had that epiphany, and whenever summer comes along, it's always time for a good dose of Belinda Carlisle.

The Heiress (1949)
dir. William Wyler

★★★★★
Needed, a DVD Transfer

August 2, 2005

Miriam Hopkins, no longer young and with lines of age gathered around her mouth and her expressive, huge eyes, dominates the first part of *The Heiress* with her firefly impression of Catherine's loving aunt. She darts around the dance scene, trying to make sure her wallflower niece has enough men's names signed up to the tiny dance card that hangs on a gold string from her wrist. Inevitably she gets caught up in the music herself, and through Hopkins's sensitive movements you can watch her character disappear for a moment to the waltzes of her own youth, before remembering and "coming to" again to see to her beloved niece. William Wyler, the director, is said to have driven most actors mad with his insistent need to film scenes dozens of times, over and over, until he got some particular nuance that he wanted out of their performance. And yet actors loved him once they saw the results. And he was loyal too, sometimes providing the only work an actor might hope to get after his star had fallen for whatever reason (and it happens to nearly every actor). Most of Miriam Hopkins's later parts—the best of them at any rate—were undertaken for Wyler, for whom at the peak of her stardom she had made *These Three* back in 1936. There was her wonderful Lavinia here, in *The Heiress*, a luminous portrayal indeed; then there was a darker part as Olivier's wife in *Carrie* (1952); finally she was the unbelievably selfish and egocentric Aunt Lily in *The Children's Hour*—a range that shows her getting worse and worse as she got older, so perhaps Wyler wasn't entirely good for her after all.

But here, at least, Hopkins fans have little to complain of. Though only 14 years older than De Havilland, in movie terms she was a whole other generation. De Havilland was maybe 31 or 32 when she played Catherine Sloper and, although she's no girl, she was still able to call up some girlish naivete and whole-heartedness while playing the scenes in which she falls headlong for young Morris Townsend. When he plays her mother's piano for her you can watch her heart leap up into her throat: an astonishing display of the physical, nearly Actors Studio response De Havilland puts into play when working with Clift.

And oh, that wonderful Copland score, I can't say enough about it. There are some scores which sweep you away and let their magnificence do all the "directing," and then there are the simple, lovely ones like *The Heiress* which never detract, which only illuminate, the performances they undershadow. There's a grand CD of Copland's movie music by the St. Louis Symphony Orchestra, in which *The Heiress*'s score is miniaturized down to something under ten minutes. Listen to it, and everything precious about this great film will come to you via osmosis and through Copland's tonal color.

Rebecca **(The Criterion Collection) (1940)**
dir. Alfred Hitchcock

★★★★★
Rebecca Fantasy

August 3, 2005

As I watch the film for the umpteenth time, I sometimes slip into a fantasy wondering what would have happened had one of the other Rebecca "hopefuls" whom Selznick tested been given the plum role of the second Mrs. de Winter. Happily the screen tests are among the extras to this Criterion edition (at least, there are some excerpts here, it would be great to see the unedited screen tests) so we have a chance to see what some of the screen's great ladies might have done had they been given a chance. (Again, Selznick tested many others besides the "stars" excerpted here, including some "nonactresses" of the period, including debs Brenda Frazier and Cobina Wright Jr., but their footage is not included here in this now-deleted Criterion edition.

Perhaps when it returns to print we will see the expanded gallery of screen tests.)

Anyhow, it is a strange set of luck that gave us Joan Fontaine as Rebecca because, as others have mentioned, she is not the best Rebecca on the evidence of the "screen tests" alone. Of course she rose splendidly to the occasion at the end of the day, but she's not too prepossessing here. Vivien Leigh seems to be giving it everything she's got—we learn elsewhere that she was determined to get the role, so she could be closer to her new love interest Laurence Olivier, who had already nailed down the role of Max de Winter. You wonder, "How'd *that* happen, was he such a great star even then?" Leigh might have been good, but equally she might have run roughshod over the fabric of the movie as she did elsewhere during her short movie career. She was truly larger than life, with an enormous physicality, and she seems to be shooting off sparks in her test and simultaneously trying to disguise her charisma under a cloak of artificial shyness. You can practically hear the buzzer going off when the test is over.

Anne Baxter is all right, but hopelessly American, her square jaw never more prominent. Baxter wasn't hopelessly beautiful, and she might have made an OK mouse, but at this stage in the game her acting chops weren't too sharp. I prefer Margaret Sullavan, though she seems a bit old in the role—and she wasn't all that old in real life—not even thirty I imagine; maybe she was just having a bad day. Here she looks as though she might have made a good Mrs. Danvers, or is that too catty?

My prize goes to Loretta Young, an actress often underrated, but one who could slip in and out of personae with the ease of a Ruth Draper. Yes, she is probably too gorgeous to play the second wife; yes, this might have been an enormous challenge for her, and Hitchcock probably paused long and hard before even deigning to test her—for after three thousand glossy Fox romances she was definitely "typed" by 1939. But anyone who has seen Young in either her great pre-Code parts or her interesting "noir" career after the war knows she was infinitely adaptable and could be more "real" than any number of her peers. I think I'll settle on my one fantasy, a Loretta Young who croons "Last night I dreamed I went to Manderley again." That'll tide me over, in my gallery of films that never were.

The Lost Weekend (1945)
dir. Billy Wilder

★★★★★
On The Straight And Narrow

August 4, 2005

Like *Crossfire*, which was based on Richard Brooks's antihomophobic novel *The Brick Foxhole*, but which took every scrap of homosexuality out of it by switching its story from gay-bashing among US veterans to anti-Semitism, Billy Wilder's *The Lost Weekend* remains one of those crypto-gay films that tries but ultimately cannot quite manage to erase the gay subtext of the novel it was based on.

Charles Jackson's book is compelling, no more frank or harrowing than the movie, but anyone who reads it can quickly see what becomes occluded in the film—a little bit cloudy and mysterious, as though you went out for popcorn and missed a key scene. Anyone reading the book would know that alcoholism is not the only reason Don seems to want to ditch Helen and her quiet support, and instead escape to a series of seedy downtown cocktail lounges. It's because he's gay but can't admit it, not even to his understanding bro, Wick. He can't tell it to Helen either, even though she halfway knows in her heart of hearts. Instead Don just dives deeper into the bottle, seeking forgiveness and oblivion both. And while he's plowed, he manages to have a whole bunch of sex with a whole bunch of GI Bill, postwar, Cold War guys who just want to have fun.

It was an alcoholic culture and in it, a certain amount of homo-sexuality could flourish. In Wilder's film, the bartender played by Howard da Silva is absolutely heterosexual, and yet he stands in for the Virgil-like figure Charles Jackson envisioned, the older man who would take Don deeper and deeper into, well, "Birnam Wood" (just like Shakespeare's *Macbeth*). The male nurse played by Frank Faylen keeps some of his queer camaraderie too, as he slaps down Don into a sort of bondage—all very friendly and palsy. As the hero, Ray Milland shows that he was one of the best period actors. Often mistaken for a lightweight, he has the loathsome imagination and fear of the very greatest actors. He can imagine the horrors, and what the Hays Code wouldn't allow us to know for sure, the expressions of dumb lust and swank that play over Milland's face give us a different kind of evidence. Wilder, in fact, was the master of a queer kind of cinema; has any other straight director made so many classics with lasting gay appeal?

The Rose Tattoo (1955)
dir. Daniel Mann

★★★★☆
The Movie—Not So Good—the Stars—Excellent
August 9, 2005

I wonder how Magnani won the Oscar when so much of her dialogue has been redubbed? Half the time it's her real voice, the rest of the time I guess she spoke so harshly that test audiences couldn't understand her, probably Marni Nixon took over. Tennessee Williams wanted to tell the story of how love, once betrayed, can bloom again like a phoenix shot down in flames, if the right man comes along with his hair smelling like roses. I agree with this so watching this movie was like preaching to the converted. Magnani is out of this world, though she looks appalled throughout, as though this was her first glimpse of America and she didn't like what she was seeing, and Burt Lancaster, well, he certainly showed none of the finesse of *The Leopard* in this role. And yet they say Visconti picked him to be the Leopard based on a hasty screening of this film. He must have seen something in Alvaro's goofiness and sunniness that he thought might be interesting if completely turned around, like the negative to a photograph.

However, film fans, feast your eyes on the young sailor with whom Marisa Pavan is in love. "Jack Hunter" indeed—notice how Williams inserted the sly sexual pun right in the very heart of his name. Anyhow, Jack is played by the angelic one and only Ben Cooper—be still, my heart! Cooper played lots of roles in the 1950s, mostly cowboys and renegades, soldiers, this and that, riffraff parts, sort of a sub–Sterling Hayden kind of guy, but young. Indeed he played Turkey alongside Sterling Hayden in the unbelievably Freudian Western *Johnny Guitar* for Nicholas Ray. Imagine being nicknamed "Turkey," it could only happen in a Nick Ray film. As Jack Hunter, he wears his heart on his sleeve and is the only actor in the film capable of sharing the screen with Magnani without getting his ass kicked. He is totally in possession of the role, that of a red-blooded American man who promises not to try to have sex with Marisa Pavan on Magnani's say-so. And yet we still respect him, because he is Ben Cooper. Cooper makes the most of this plum part, probably his best role until his masterwork as the country bumpkin in *Chartroose Caboose*, the country musical with Molly Bee, Edgar Buchanan, and Slim Pickens. In that film Ben Cooper and Molly Bee make country music as exciting as tango. He is red hot and *The Rose Tattoo* is as good a place as any to make his acquaintance. Ben Cooper, are you still among the living? We have lost so many of the live wires that once made going to the movies fun.

Separate Tables (1958)
dir. Delbert Mann

★★★★☆
Not the Best Rattigan but It Will Do

August 10, 2005

Wendy Hiller perhaps preserves best what we love about Rattigan's stage works, her dignity, her bitterness, the "insideness" of her despair, and her unfailing good manners and diplomacy. She's excellent. Most of the others, even Gladys Cooper and David Niven, seem to have been injected with essence of ham and turned loose on the set. They are way over the top! It's as though the actors were each trying to outact the others in a giant free-for-all. Rita Hayworth is probably the most obvious case of bad acting, but she is actually quite moving in her part. Ann *knows* she's from a different world, *knows* that the others will resent her beauty, glamour, and flame, so she's defiant. And Hayworth can break your heart even in her beauty, particularly as it began to fade after the Aly Khan years. Here she's trying to whip Burt Lancaster (John, her former husband) into a sexual frenzy, and all of a sudden Rita—not Ann—doesn't really feel up to it. Some say she should not be receiving top billing in this movie, but I disagree. Watching her is the best reason to see this show.

The other reason is to see how American filmmakers tiptoed around homosexuality in the late 1950s. Niven's character is a retired soldier who hangs around the hotel acting terribly British and stiff upper lip, while Deborah Kerr's Sybil hangs on to his every word though he doesn't seem to encourage her affections. Then a small newspaper article appears claiming that he is in remand for a sex crime. In the movie you never really find out what Niven has done. All we know is that he was bothering girls in a cinema. In a sense it doesn't matter what he's done, dramatically the point is that this crime separates him from respectable society, and the boarders of the hotel make up a petition to get Wendy Hiller to ask him to leave, and the plot hangs on whether or not Deborah Kerr will join the haters, or whether she'll forgive Niven for his attentions to the young girls and cast her lot with his, or whether her hateful selfish mother (Gladys Cooper) will prevail.

In the play, the crime Niven committed was picking up boys—underage boys of fifteen or sixteen, I guess. Well, not picking them up but "groping" them. I wonder how this would go down today. Obviously it was too strong for moviegoers of 1958. Would Niven have won the Oscar if he played some kind of homosexual deviant? Would Deborah Kerr have pledged her love to him nevertheless? What about Megan's Law—wouldn't all the other boarders have been able to track his comings and goings on the internet? Rattigan's plea for tolerance is a loaded gun standing in the corner just waiting to explode.

Gigi
by Colette

First Love

August 12, 2005

Gigi was the first novel I read in French, and at the time that I read it, probably it was the raciest book I ever read, I was a mere lad of I don't know, eleven or so. I couldn't figure out exactly who was who. I tried reading *Gone with the Wind* in French but that was too long. *Gigi* was perfect. She was, after all, a young girl, though from a different world than mine. She had several aunts who wanted to train her into the high-level world of the courtesan. A good parallel would be the recent novel *Memoirs of a Geisha* by Arthur Golden.

What distinguishes Colette from Golden is that the French writer built a legend around herself in terms of the beauty and poetry of her language. Not only did she possess a stern and acute mind from which no nuance of regret or longing escaped her gaze, but she wielded a pen like an angel. She was incapable of writing a phony sentence, and like the American modernist poet William Carlos Williams she found beauty in the ordinary and the common-place. A swatch of wildflowers growing in the graveyard where Gigi's mother lies becomes the palette of an artist, with the dap-pled colors suggesting possibility. Gigi's hopes, dreams, and fantasies lie mingled, like sooty water, with the harsh realities of her existence. Basically she must find a rich man to cling to, or lose all her status.

For a young boy reading her story, and trying to puzzle through the evocative French, I found myself stumbling at times, but at the end I became convinced that I knew this girl, and I took pleasure in her small triumphs and her enemies became mine.

Today many of Colette's works have been translated but she is still very much caviare to the general. Another couple of books I can recommend to you are *Chéri* and its sequel, *The Last of Chéri*. (Chéri's a guy despite his name which to me seemed feminine before I got the drift of things.)

Ship of Fools
by Katherine Anne Porter

★★★★★
"Ship of Fools on a Cruel Sea"

August 16, 2005

I got into *Ship of Fools* back in the day when I was a Deadhead and followed the band around from stadium to stadium. "Ship of Fools" as many know is one of their loveliest ballads and would never fail but put me in a trance. At one bookstore in the Bay Area I spotted lyricist Robert Hunter and I gathered together all my courage to approach him and to tell him how much his lyrics had meant to me and my kind. Somewhat to my surprise he asked me to name one of his songs that I loved. "Ship of Fools," I said. In the years since I have sometimes wondered why I didn't ask about "Row Jimmy," since that is even more puzzling. But anyway Hunter couldn't have been more receptive and even charming. I asked him where he found the inspiration to write "Ship of Fools" and he mentioned the Renaissance or medieval tradition of the ship of fools journeying out into the main without a solid plan and how it's a metaphor for the religious voyage of life. He mentioned other works based on this legend including Lewis Carroll's "The Hunting of the Snark" and, finally, Katherine Anne Porter's novel *Ship of Fools*, which he said he had read in the 1960s, close to when it came out originally.

Ship of Fools tells the story of a group of German nationals on a boat from Bremen to the USA, and it is apparently based on a real-life voyage. Jews by the boatload were attempting to escape from an atrocious and repressive regime, and what they did not realize is that the shipboard lifestyle was a microcosm for the pains of the rest of the world. We meet dozens of characters, some more skillfully developed than others, including a young American couple through whose eyes we get to see the whole tragedy unfolding.

There is a tragic romance between a middle-aged countess and the ship's doctor, and a sense of foreboding about the whole voyage. The champagne and the crêpe paper and the sparklers are out over the dark Atlantic, but we sense the lights going out all over the world.

Porter worked over thirty years writing this, her only novel, and when it came out it was a commercial success and a Book-of-the-Month Club selection, though in general the critics were disappointed that it did not hit the heights of the short stories that had made her name starting in the 1920s. Some have criticized this book as too slow and too portentous. To me it hits the right note over and over again. There is a movie version of this novel, directed by earnest, plodding Stanley Kramer, but I think if I saw it, it could not begin to compare to my experience of either the novel nor the song. "Now I cannot share thy laughter, ship of fools."

Tallulah! The Life and Times of a Leading Lady
by Joel Lobenthal

★★★★★
A Book for the Ages

August 16, 2005

Joel Lobenthal's book is a remarkable feat. He has rescued Tallulah Bankhead from her fans.

I can't understand the horrid reviews this book has gotten from others on the site. I found his work utterly compelling and a vast improvement on every other book I've seen (all of which I've enjoyed, by the way). It's just that Lobenthal has done something no other biographer has attempted—he has gone back and attempted to recreate the actual performances that she gave, by various means, including locating fellow castmates, some of them of extreme age but all of them with amazing, never-before-heard memories and anecdotes. They build up a picture of Bankhead as being the exact opposite of the coke-addled, personality-driven dilettante we have been used to for a long, long time.

And Lobenthal's research has deep roots! He worked on this project for close to thirty years, and it shows. He seems to know everything not only about Bankhead but about American and British theater throughout the twentieth century. Plus, he has persuaded his witnesses to spill all the beans and you'll find things out in this book which you never imagined about all of your favorite actors, writers, and directors.

What a roller-coaster ride Bankhead had for a career. Things looked pretty bleak for her by the mid-1930s and then in rapid succession she landed a series of parts which put her once again in the thick of the theatrical action and even returned her to movies. As Regina Giddens in Lillian Hellman's *The Little Foxes*, she brought her Southern gentility into play and got out the claws. As Lily Sabina in Thornton Wilder's *The Skin of Our Teeth*, she brought European expressionism onto the Broadway stage during World War II. Philip Barry's *Foolish Notion*, though not a commercial success, was an amazing dream play in which Bankhead's character imagined herself acting out alternative scenarios à la Pirandello. She made a personal success out of Noël Coward's *Private Lives*, eclipsing the memories of Gertrude Lawrence and replacing them with a raw wit that attracted many gay fans.

These fans, who stuck with her thick and thin, responded to something about her—both her emotional fragility and her perdurability. When she came to play Blanche in *Streetcar* for Jean Dalrymple, in the 1950s, this claque dismayed her by hooting and carrying on as though they were watching Dame Edna. Bankhead's attempts at shading Blanche with vulnerability found purchase in the wall of knowing laughter that greeted her every speech.

Soon we will have the first DVD of *Lifeboat*, a propitious moment for those of us who, intrigued by Lobenthal's account of her acting, want to see it firsthand. (We also have the late products *Fanatic*, aka *Die! Die! My Darling!*, and the animated *The Daydreamer*, for which Bankhead provided a character's voice.) Let's get those early Paramount films available, and *A Royal Scandal*, and number one on my want list *Main Street to Broadway*, in which she apparently plays herself, advising a young playwright on breaking into the writing biz.

He is a master biographer, the theatrical equivalent of a Robert Caro or a Leon Edel. If he decided to write the life of his cat, I'd line up for a copy.

Airport Planning & Management
by Seth B. Young and Alexander T. Wells

★★★★★
The Book of Choice for Students and Dreamers

August 22, 2005

Like many young men, and I daresay women, I was drawn to airport management after exposure to Burt Lancaster's sterling portrayal of a harried airport manager in the Ross Hunter classic *Airport*. Lancaster showed us that a man could handle a million problems all at once, if he had the right combination of grit and gray cells. It wasn't only the glamor, it was the idea of helping people get through their day—even when the people in question were six or seven miles up in the air—that made me consider airport management as a major at school.

Other factors prevented me from achieving my goal, but I continue to pick up textbooks and manuals to keep abreast of the way airports have changed over the last thirty-five years. From a technical point of view, one of the best resources for the lay manager is the Seth Young book *Airport Planning & Management* (*AP & Management*) coauthored with Alexander Wells, both of them prominent in the field—and the airfield—today. This book brings you thoroughly up to date on the way the skies (and the terminals) have changed since the day of infamy, 9/11. Their information is laid out with dispatch, not a wasted word between them. In addition, they know their stuff, that's for sure. Over five hundred pages and I could detect only a few minor inaccuracies.

If you were assigned to develop your own airport in some understaffed part of the world, this would be the volume you would bring with you. If you were limited to bringing one textbook with you. Of course, the old joke among airport-planning students is, What CD would you bring? Why, Brian Eno's *Music for Airports*, of course.

I Know Where I'm Going! (1945)
dir. Michael Powell and Emeric Pressburger

★★★★★
A Devotional Experience

August 22, 2005

Wendy Hiller plays Joan Webster, a rather chilly, upwardly mobile Englishwoman whose dad is a bank manager. Even he seems a bit alarmed by his daughter's mercenary soul; there doesn't seem to be much there, and he accuses her early on, in a marvelously modernistic nightclub setting, of acting more sophisticated than she really is. He's spot on, for as the movie progresses, we learn that (though not *why*, which is interesting in and of itself) she has gradually over time built up a facade in which she actually believes that money is more important than love. The thrust of the plot, and of Powell's dizzyingly vertiginous direction, is to disorient her into smashing the mirror and seeing the pieces of her real self, even if some of them are unpleasant.

I don't know which scenes Hiller is better at—being cold, or warming up! Both kinds do her ample justice and I imagine the part of Joan was actually written with her in mind, just as Powell and Pressburger must have created Catriona for Pamela Brown alone. Brown, with her cascading weirs of wild red hair and her stranded fey gaze, strides through the movie as though she owns it, shotgun over one shoulder, savage dogs at heel; but she knows when to stop. Brown's later scenes are all banked fire. She knows that Torquil has fallen for Joan and with that simple act he's effectively taken the hope out of her life, and yet she carries on. It's heartbreaking, or would be except that the moviemakers aren't interested in breaking your heart. What they're after is something more difficult and abstract.

And yet they use preposterously romantic ways of making you think about it! The legend of the whirlpool, with three kinds of ropes that break in three different ways; the old fashioned device of keeping the Ralph Bellamy character off of the stage; the disguise of the Laird (Roger Livesey) so that Joan doesn't know he's secretly a nobleman until after she's known him for a bit; the Highland setting, the three pipers, the postponed wedding, the white gown flung into the sea almost like a sacrifice, the twenty-pound difference between a life for the two young ingénues and their being separated for years; even Petula Clark, miles from "Downtown," in the absurd oversized spectacles of Alfalfa. The movie throws everything at us, we either start ducking or we start accepting it all, like Saint Sebastian his arrows. For Michael Powell, cinema is a devotional experience; you get what you come for, only you don't know what it's going to be when you pay the price of the ticket.

Midnight Cowboy (1969)
dir. John Schlesinger

★★★★★
Genre Item in Disguise

August 26, 2005

The film is structured along familiar genre lines, basically it's a rape-revenge picture, only disguised at either end. So the backstory is kept from us for a while, and thus we have no idea of the horrors Joe Buck left back home, nor what has driven him into this shortsighted, pathetic lifestyle of hoping to service women sexually on Times Square. Once the revelation happens, and we discover the shocking secret of Joe's past, and that of his girlfriend, played so beautifully by the one and only Jennifer Salt, we sympathize. (Apparently Salt was the daughter of *Midnight Cowboy*'s screenwriter, Waldo Salt, and all you can think of is, "He wrote this part for his daughter?" Something weird there.)

As Annie, Jennifer Salt does wonders with a small role. Most famous for her long-running Eunice Tate on the popular TV sitcom *Soap*, she also starred in four Brian De Palma films, most notably *Sisters* in which she plays the intrepid reporter Grace Collier who tries to penetrate the Margot Kidder mystery. As Annie, she has a more naturalistic role, clearly inspired by the then-notorious Caryl Chessman, who was executed for crimes committed at lovers' lanes in California.

Later, when Joe gets more and more perturbed about being a hustler, he has a dramatic encounter with a gay man and a heavy telephone. You can see clearly that Joe is seeking revenge for his own rape (if that's what it was; Schlesinger's photography all but covers up the ghastly deed, as though it belonged in the shadows) and we all know that the cycle of abuse never ends.

When you consider how affected Hoffman and Voight both became in their acting, the freshness and lightness of their performances here is a wonder. They're still great, but their tricks are no longer new. However, in *Midnight Cowboy* they achieve the kind of screen greatness we think of as emanating from the actors in Renoir films.

Midnight in The Garden of Good and Evil (1997)
dir. Clint Eastwood

★★★★★
My Favorite Christmas Movie

August 26, 2005

I wonder if there are cases where directors take novels and make the characters gay who were heterosexual in the book. That never seems to happen, just the other way around, like in this case where John Cusack plays a society reporter who in the book was certainly more drawn to covering the waterfront. He's been summoned to Savannah to write a puff piece for a lifestyle magazine on Jim Williams, the society dandy who has built up some run-down parts of Savannah and restored one of the most beautiful antebellum mansions, the Mercer House (built for the great-grandfather of songwriter Johnny Mercer).

Director Eastwood punctuates the Christmassy Savannah back-drop with some of Mercer's loveliest compositions, delivered in some jazzy renditions. Mercer is often thought of as the "poet of Tin Pan Alley," and his lyrics have the soft thickness of the best American poetry of the first half of the twentieth century. (The poet Conrad Aiken was a friend and mentor.) He wrote the lyrics for "Moon River," for example, as well as many lyrics whose internal rhymes and puns spin them to the brim of sense—a controlled madness, which Eastwood apes in his compositions, balancing the mad eccentrics of Savannah with the Apollonian neatness and classicism of the court-room and the legal system.

When Jim Williams kills a no-good boyfriend at Christmastime, the whole town picks up talking just as they've been talking for a hundred years about outsiders and insiders.

Kevin Spacey, as Jim, takes on a daring role. Was he worried that people would think he himself was gay? Or was this a complex dou-ble bluff to take the edge off people's suspicions and preconceptions about him? He seems to be playing all the angles as he figures as defendant in one of the biggest trials ever to hit the state of Georgia. John Cusack finds Eros with a young jazz singer played by Alison Eastwood, the director's daughter, who functions in this film roughly as Asia functions in the films of *her* father—as a surrogate leading lady, when no such animal existed in the book. Still she's wedged in there, and her natural style of acting goes down smooth, like the blond in her hair. She's irresistible, and I'm only sorry the picture did so badly at the box office, for I would have liked to have seen her and John Cusack reteamed again and again, as the old MGM bosses would reteam William Powell and Myrna Loy, for we go to the movies for many reasons, but chief among them is to witness sparks.

Lady Chablis, she's not a patch on the drag queens I've known here in SF and in New York. Don't get me wrong, she's OK, but only a man who's never met any other drag queens would have cast her as herself.

Midnight Express (1978)
dir. Alan Parker

★★★★☆
Dream Couple

August 29, 2005

Billy Hayes went to my high school, a few years ahead of me. This was an all-boys school on Long Island and when he was in jail at that Turkish prison, we used to joke that it was better than being stuck in our high school, and also that on the whole the freshman class did more hashish every day than Billy Hayes was able to smuggle across the entire width of his body. We were encouraged to pray for the soul of our fellow schoolmate William Hayes who was languishing in prison, unjustly convicted. Good-looking guy, though not so sublime as Brad Davis, who plays him in the movie.

Billy's girlfriend Susan, who joins him in a half-baked scheme to smuggle moderate quantities of hashish out of Istanbul, is played by the incredible Irene Miracle. A year or so later she was to come into her element fully as Rose Elliot in Argento's masterful *Inferno* but here she is more subdued, though still ravishingly beautiful. She and Brad Davis have got to be the hottest couple ever put on film. Of course their love gets torn apart once the jail portion of the movie begins, around reel 3. Giorgio Moroder, whose soundtrack is one of the epochal moments of 1970s cinema, wrote a beautiful love theme for Billy and Susan, it is tender and filled with longing and frustration. Sometimes I hear that theme played even on elevator Muzak and even now it brings back all the sorrow of lovers violently parted from each other, like Nino Rota's theme from the Zeffirelli *Romeo and Juliet.*

Is the movie racist for depicting Turks as menacing, ugly, brutish thugs? Maybe so. Maybe that's the lure of the movie, to suck you in telling you this is a true story and thus letting your moral judgments get go off the hook. The book on which this book is based shows a different angle on the story (in addition, Billy admits to enjoying sex in prison with men, an element that Oliver Stone excised out completely, later making up for it I suppose by including Jared Leto in his movie *Alexander*), but while watching *Midnight Express* all you experience is fear. I'm sure that the success of this movie led to the depressing statistic that only 19 percent of Americans own or use passports. The rest of us are too terrified of going overseas and being hung upside down naked in chains and flogged by Turks.

Permanent Midnight (1998)
dir. David Veloz

★★★★☆
Permanent Love Team

August 29, 2005

In *Permanent Midnight*, director David Veloz smooths out the hard edges from Jerry Stahl's riveting autobiography of the same name. Obviously he was going to try for some casting surprises, so a gang of comedians are brought in and asked to play serious parts, and if they're not funny comics, they're supermodels trying to act. All these people trying to "act seriously" pushes the movie over the edge into spectacle; but that's better than your average movie which doesn't offer any spectacle at all.

Maria Bello tries to prove there's more to her than drop-dead gorgeousness on the Cybill Shepherd line. Verdict? Not in just yet. In subsequent movies Ms. Bello has shown that she's competent, and in one or two something more, but here she doesn't especially impress. Elizabeth Hurley looks beautiful, and actually manages to achieve a state of peevishness that looks convincing; maybe the director told her that her L'Oréal ration was being suspended. And even Cheryl Ladd, top model of another era, is somehow squeezed into the movie, I guess to remind us that in Hollywood, even tiny parts are filled by the good looking. The trouble is, this is something we found out years ago from Burt Bacharach songs: "And all the stars / that never were / are parking cars or pumping gas." Such as Janeane Garofalo who made quite a few movies and then disappeared from the screen after Dennis Kucinich's candidacy sank like a stone.

The other point of *Permanent Midnight* is that heroin is bad for you and hurts the family structure. However, the hegemony of the US cinema by twin Pleiades Ben Stiller and Owen Wilson will never be destroyed, and their friendship here is a thing of intense contemplation. Long ago they decided that each one was the psychic twin of the other, and ten movies later, they have outlasted Hepburn and Tracy as the screen's great love team. It's a permanent thing with the tensile strength of steel.

A Midnight Clear (1992)
dir. Keith Gordon

★★★★☆
Second Favorite Christmas Movie

September 8, 2005

A Midnight Clear is nearly my favorite Christmas movie. I was born on Christmas Eve and have had a sentimental attachment to movies laid during Christmas time. Some reviewers have suggested that this movie is not sentimental, but I think automatically once you have two opposing armies laying down arms in the spirit of Christmas, it gets a little gooey. Ethan Hawke, so good in the recent remake of *Assault on Precinct 13*, again battles the snow in *A Midnight Clear*, as he and five other US grunts try to make sense out of the quandaries of a slow-moving war right before the Battle of the Bulge in the Ardennes Forest. His commentary reveals that the movie was actually filmed in the rocky ridges of Utah.

The war's almost over, the invasion a success, admittedly a great, unexpected resistance from German armies means that there's a long winter ahead of them, but as in Wharton's novel when they occupy (and more importantly, to secure) an ancient chateau and start to feel comfortable, an eerie sound floats through the crystalline night air at night—the sound of German laughter. They are not alone. Hawke plays a sergeant really not far removed from boyhood, while the Germans, who soon become their prisoners in name, are a mixture of older man and really young boy, for the prime specimens of "Aryan manhood" were long ago drained off into the draft and likely as not killed in Stalingrad, and now (at any rate in this battalion of the German army) you see the dregs and the far fetched. A children's crusade.

Children all, and their "mother," Wilkins (Gary Sinise, doing some interesting work), strips down to nothing in the snow hoping to get a Section 8 (discharge for madness). As we find out, he has had some terrible news from the States and just wants to get home as quickly as possible. Arye Gross, a capable actor who used to be in every other movie back then, plays the Yiddish-speaking Stan, the only man among them able to communicate with the Germans. As his fellow soldiers start calling Will Knott "Won't," naturally the viewer starts thinking of him as Melville's Bartleby, the man who politely refused to cooperate and thereby threw a monkey wrench into capitalism. But this analogy is far fetched as the concept of a "separate peace" at Christmas. Nevertheless, when the title song breaks through on the soundtrack, my eyes start to mist over because I know that something awful will come to break the peace. After you see this movie you will never look at a snowman with the same happy gaze.

Midnight Ride
by Paul Revere & the Raiders

★★★★★
Charm of Nostalgia

September 9, 2005

This LP used to be my favorite, until one day it didn't seem cool and I pushed it to the back of my record cabinet with some other records I was ashamed of. They were trying too hard to be like the Stones is what I figured, and they weren't cutting it. Oh boy, how wrong I was. But as it turned out, most of the records I was ashamed of loving then have come back from the valley of shame and are now my favorites! Isn't it funny?

Before the remastered reissue with the extra tracks, the final song on side B *used to be* the instrumental "Melody for an Unknown Girl," heavy with saxes, a tune I thought the ultimate in romance, sort of like "Caroline, No" was for the Beach Boys' *Pet Sounds*. I'd play it on my little mono player again and again. The needle would click, click, click after the last groove while I was lost in a silence that grew more tenuous and romantic with every minute that passed, while I thought of the way that eventually I would become a teenager and be out there falling in love every day and a half and breaking hearts and getting my heart broken too I suppose. It was the idea of the "unknown girl," tantalizingly mysterious in the mist of anticipation, parallel to the Tomb of the Unknown Soldier which my dad took me to see, which also broke my heart.

I liked "Kicks" then too, from a child's perspective the song was filled with an older boy's looking back to a time long past when "Kicks" weren't quite as hard to find as nowadays; I had regret that I was too young to live in that time—the hedonist's utopia, some archetypal time before the expulsion from Eden. If that sounds far fetched, the lyrics to verse 2 are all about the way the girl in the song is looking (through drugs, I used to think) "for another piece of paradise." We're all looking for that time before our own births in which sin and death had not yet corrupted our innocence. Maybe that's why those old albums and the pop tracks they contained now have the place of pride on my iPod.

Midnight Desert Young Style Car Seat
by Recaro

★★★★★
For Children Who Like to Rock and Roll

September 13, 2005

It's one thing to buy a high-style car seat for an infant under twenty inches, and another to make sure your baby is getting the proper amount of protection, inside and out, from a car seat that's no longer big enough for the little lad (or lady). Once the baby is bigger than twenty pounds—and with modern feeding practices that comes faster than ever nowadays, for as my grandma says as our cars get bigger, and everyone is driving an SUV, our babies grow correspondingly bigger as well—with the Midnight Desert Young Style Car Seat, you can ditch the puny little car seats that you had before when baby was one year young, here comes the heavy duty model.

I hesitated at first, not sure if the flaps (or "wings") would be sturdy enough for the little chap to see over, say if he developed his neck muscles, as some toddlers have a tendency to be impatient with the wings and want to see all the action happening out of the side windows (an encouraging sign, by the way, for moms and dads worried about possible later signs of dullness). Such activity is a sign for rejoicing, but it doesn't make your toddler easier to strap in for road trips, does it? But with Midnight Desert you don't have to worry. That protection shell you get with MD is just about the largest on the market and unless your baby is baby Superboy, he's not going to get out of the hard, resistant plastic and foam shell. Nor will his toys be able to dent it or rip it open as may happen with some other, flimsier car seats.

In defense of the other, more expensive and unnecessary toddler car seats, some of them are indeed prettier. One or two are true works of art. But I always say, baby doesn't need to be framed like the *Mona Lisa*! Baby just needs to be safe during your drive through the woods to grandmother's house. Now's the time to protect your toddler, he will learn about art and beauty later in life, or my name isn't Kevin Killian. Plus, if you're the tidy sort, you'll enjoy the washability of the cover that slips on and off easily for you to get it clean, 'cause it's made of microfiber just as though it had been tailored by Coco Chanel.

Midnight Cookies (Key Lime Coolers in Special Edition *Midnight in the Garden of Good and Evil* Tin)
by Byrd Cookie Company

★★★★★
Featuring the Famous *Bird Girl* Statue That Looks like an Angel

September 14, 2005

In Savannah you have to hand it to the locals, they have discovered the way to live. Recently on a trip to Florida we stopped off at the famous Bonaventure Cemetery in Savannah to see the statue that inspired the famous book *Midnight in the Garden of Good and Evil*. We weren't the first and you could barely see the statue because of a bus filled with daytrippers who were posing on the statue. One woman urged her twin toddlers to climb up into the angel's arms; these were hefty tots who probably would have broken off the arms of the poor angel if allowed to roam unchecked. Everywhere there were video cameras or cell phones turned on each other, trying to capture some action. A guard told us this was the most photographed statue in the world. He said it was not strictly speaking an angel, but a bird girl, but that indeed it had performed some miracles and that the types of people who used to go to Lourdes could now go to see the *Bird Girl* and pray to her, perhaps rub their bad limbs against the statue, and it was well known that cures resulted, people throwing away crutches, etc. This same guard offered us some delicious key lime cookies from a strangely familiar tin box.

It turned out he had ordered this box from Byrd Cookie Company. It's a handsome tin, capaciously filled with luscious Key Lime Coolers, and the selling point beyond the tasty treats is the exact replica of the famous statue! Thus, it looks just like the popular book which made bestseller history and turned Savannah from a backwater town to one of the most sought-after tourist cities in the USA. Can't say enough good things about Byrd.

They make a nice line of Artichoke Parmesan Biscuits that melt in your mouth like gravy, but on a hot day like we've had all summer long, nothing goes down as well as a few Key Lime Coolers and perhaps a pitcher of lemonade sweating nearby a hammock. Buy this box and leave it on your divan or coffee table and your guests will be agog with wonder, or maybe a better word would be *curiosity*.

Sunshine after the Rain (1996)
dir. Mike Esser

★★★★☆
Everybody Loves Johan

September 23, 2005

Everybody loves Johan, but this video doesn't represent his finest moment on film. In fact you might save your money and buy instead the saucy compilation *Moments with Johan*, which features probably the best clips from *Sunshine after the Rain* and also five or six other movies as well. What's wrong with a bargain? However, if you're into this film for more reasons than just the one (watching Johan), you might find plenty of reasons to kick back, make yourself a stiff drink, and spend just over an hour watching the action of this puzzling film.

Perhaps in days to come there will be a restored version of the movie that explains what the plot is supposed to be. As it is, you have the jacket copy on the back cover that says this is supposed to be happening all on one day to a bunch of schoolmates who have worked together and played together, and this is their last fling. That explains why some of the gorgeous European youth are crying tears of regret. The missing reels might add in actual scenes in which you could tell whom each bright god is supposed to be portraying. Otherwise they're running around like seven or eight Tadzios (from *Death in Venice*), with nary a strawberry mark to distinguish them. No, I can't say that. One or two of the boys look positively swarthy, not quite as blond, and another one looks as though he'd sorted out what he wants from life now that he's reached the ripe old age of nineteen. He smirks through the soft core as though he'd rather be making the big bucks in something like *The Apprentice* with Donald Trump.

You'll know the one I mean when you watch the video. Anyhow I can heartily recommend this to anyone interested in the '90s star Johan Paulik, who was sort of like the Josh Hartnett of Prague, only without Josh's ever so slightly daring note of rebellion or possible danger. In Bel Ami terms, Johan was their superstar and I don't think they have ever really recovered from his turning into a man. *Sunshine after the Rain* doesn't really show anything, but that's OK, after all, erotica's all in the head, isn't it? A few of the young pups on display, frolicking on the beach or on divans, went on to careers elsewhere, and some I guarantee you will never see again on-screen or off.

Now back to my eternal search for the missing reels of *Sunshine after the Rain*. Let others search for the footage cut from Orson Welles's *Magnificent Ambersons*, I will follow Johan's traces.

Too Far
by Mike Lupica

Anal Rule in High School

September 26, 2005

In *Too Far* veteran sports writer Mike Lupica has written a thriller from a moral high ground, a plea for tolerance and against sadistic hazing. In the wake of the notorious Mepham High School football scandal, this book comes as a wake-up call. It would be fair to say that actually this novel is nothing more than the Mepham case with the names changed and the athletic action switched from the gridiron to the hoops; it's pretty transparent that way. Well, Upton Sinclair wasn't subtle either. Nor is any man on a crusade against sodomy.

Old-school print journalist Ben Mitchell gets interested in the death of a high school basketball player on Long Island, whose body has floated ashore. With the help of student reporter Sam Perry, Ben quickly maps out the lay of the land in a perverted, though very starry, b-ball organization. Its pecking order is maintained by a strict system of threats and balances, and a pivotal part of team control lies in systemic anal rape of fellow teammates. In one genuinely creepy scene, the boy reporter is lured to a desolate park in the woods where he is assaulted and sat on, his pants and shorts removed. From behind, a broomstick, its handle coated in mineral ice to improve lubrication, enters his rectum as he squirms and cries, just an inch, that's all, enough to show him who's in control. When he agrees to lay off his investigation, his attackers laugh sadistically and promise him that if he doesn't obey their threats to the letter, that broomstick gets shoved in all the way.

It's no idle threat. They've already made their will known by using a basketball summer camp as a rape staging area, pressing a pinecone up the ass of one outnumbered boy, whispering to him "You like to be close to nature, don't you?" The trouble is that this campaign of intimidation can continue indefinitely, since each raped boy would (literally) rather die than have his assault reported, for fear that other boys would say he enjoyed it. Sam is taunted with the nickname "Broomstick Boy." Others try suicide.

Lupica links this isolated case to a nationwide system of sexual abuse among teammates, citing dozens of real-life cases. He suggests provocatively that such abuse is built-in to teams with multiple "stars," since such teams have a radical instability that implodes on itself. Shaq and Kobe, he says, dislike each other, because on any team there can be only "one f—ing man." These codes of masculinity may seem outdated, but to the guard with blood dripping out his butt, staining the radiant white of his uniform shorts, it's no laughing matter.

Reunion in France (1942)
dir. Jules Dassin

★★★★★
From Spoiled Mistress to Heroine of the Resistance

September 26, 2005

The conventional wisdom about this movie and its follow-up (*Above Suspicion*, which pairs Crawford with Fred MacMurray in Europe) is that they were deliberately bad features planned by the moguls to force Crawford out of pictures. But neither film deserves its bad reputation. Indeed in hindsight I find them fully as interesting as any other of Crawford's MGM vehicles, and by no means do they seem cheap or ill thought out.

Well, it's kind of silly having Crawford playing the richest girl in France, in a movie when everyone else is playing up the French accent so much so that at times you can't understand what they're saying, and meanwhile she, Joan, doesn't even try. Why should she? She's Joan Crawford. The only time she tries to go French is when she carefully pronounces the name of her fiancé: "Row-bear." Outside of that, she uses her regular, broad American accent with its weird dips and slurs, the voice we know from a hundred movies. When the picture begins, she's sitting, bored silly, on the dais during some kind of fundraiser honoring those who made the Maginot Line possible in May 1940— the night it broke. She rushes home to dismiss the modistes who have been waiting for her for two and a half hours, for she is off to Biarritz for a holiday. Well, by the time she crawls back, having been bombed and brutalized, Paris has fallen to the Nazis and it's a new day of deprivation for the glamorous Michele de la Becque, and "Row-bear" her boyfriend (Philip Dorn) is looking strangely like a collaborator.

Michele's million-franc mansion has been commandeered by Vichy forces, and she is told to sleep in this crummy little concierge studio, a room with a door on the street that doesn't lock. It's filthy, grim, and dangerous, for any Nazi could come in at any time. She takes a job at the couturiere she used to patronize—sort of a left-wing Coco Chanel, very chic but no threat to Joan in the looks department. German women are buying up all the gowns in the shop, big heavy Walküre-style creatures who look like pigs suckling at a trough. Then John Wayne (as Pat) escapes from a POW camp and stumbles, sick, nearly hallucinating, into Joan's arms and she has to shield him from the gestapo. John Wayne looks hot in this movie! He could put his boots under my divan any old time. She moves him right into her apartment with only a cursory thought to propriety, it's sort of refreshing. People in World War II, even Hollywood people, must have thought that they had entered into a new world which would be totally given over to the fight against Fascism, and that all other considerations were secondary to this mission. Jules Dassin, the director, embodies this pulpy material with real conviction and some wiseass camera setups—real wit, real grit, and two fantastic, out of this world stars.

Kramer vs. Kramer (1979)
dir. Robert Benton

★★★☆☆
Listless

September 27, 2005

They used to give out Juvenile Awards at the annual Oscars—that is, if a performer stood out ahead of the pack and gave an outstanding performance. Shirley Temple won the first one, and in subsequent years Judy Garland won another, so did Mickey Rooney, Deanna Durbin, right down to Hayley Mills. Instead of the full-size Oscar we know, the juvie Oscars were tiny little things, cute and pint size. Too bad they stopped this custom, and instead decided to throw the kids right in with a pack of sharks they call adult actors. Justin Henry, who played the little boy in *Kramer vs. Kramer*, was nominated for an Oscar in 1979. He ran opposite ancient Melvyn Douglas, and even oddly enough against Mickey Rooney, the preeminent boy star in Hollywood, then all grown up and a sad prophecy of what would happen to a child star who had seen better days.

Poor little Justin shouldn't have been put in this position. If the Academy had just given him his special Oscar, we might not have had the unpleasant experience of watching his career stall like a Duesenberg in Katonah River mud. Years later, when he played the little brother in

Sixteen Candles, American gasped in horror remembering how sweet he had been as the abandoned Kramer Jr., with his sheepdog hair and his forever-trembling lower lip, like a strawberry. As the brat in *Sixteen Candles* he rolled onto the screen like a tumbleweed, overweight, sulky, a dead zombie look in his eyes, throwing sexual innuendo in every direction, the parents' worst nightmare, as if to say "This is what would happen if your mother let your father bring you up in the dog-eat-dog world of Manhattan advertising."

Meryl Streep (selfish) and Dustin Hoffman (selfless) played the parents, and both of them are fine, though you really, really, *really* have to love Hoffman to sit through this picture without gagging. Not since the glory days of the 1940s "weepies" has a saint been presented in cinematic form with such humorless and melodramatic close-ups as Hoffman gets here, his beady eyes welling with tears that shine luminously as the human spirit itself.

Meryl Streep explains that she had to go find herself. It was a brave part especially at the beginning of a long career. No one who saw *Kramer vs. Kramer* when it first came out ever was able to look at her again without thinking in the back of their heads "There she is, the selfish one. Thinks only of herself."

Sixteen Candles, by the way, was a much better picture than this critical darling. As the years go by and more and more couples get divorced or never even bother marrying in the first place, the movie has lost some of its punch. It was always a fairy tale, now it's just listless, a Beast without Beauty.

The Midnight
by Susan Howe

★★★★★
Hanging in the Balance

September 29, 2005

Just about the best of Howe's recent books, *The Midnight* is jam-packed with allusion, drama, and poetry, sometimes withdrawn seductively from the reader, hidden in a clutch of quotations, and at other times lowered, as if from a great height, tantalizingly in your face. She has always been one to look underneath the surface of things; as an actress her training was in the Poets Theatre of Cambridge, and her mother was the famous Mary Manning of Dublin's Abbey Theatre. Thus there's a tendency to examine, sometimes at length, the underside of process, the thickness of what we do and especially what we say, when writing takes place, as the wind that reveals the silver underside of the leaves we'd otherwise never notice.

The Midnight is fairly shaking with sadness, regret, and the stern obligations of memory, as Howe again scans the marginalia of another. This time it's her late uncle and the books he left behind in a seemingly otherwise blank (or pathetic) existence, specifically his copies of R. L. Stevenson—the novelist admired above all others by Howe's hero Henry James. As she turns the pages of the novel, parts of her uncle's life (and family photographs) seem to pop out like something from a Nick Bantock novel, but it's all part of Howe's finely tuned poetry machine, the unexpected choice of word and quotation, the sizzle of disjunction and more than anything else, the shiver of anticipation that one is getting something from this poetry unavailable elsewhere, a direct pipeline into a strain of American experience that the past has otherwise denied us. It's suspenseful, and fun too, like an *Indiana Jones* movie. Don't let people tell you differently.

Schwarzenegger Syndrome: Politics and Celebrity in the Age of Contempt by Gary Indiana

★★★★★
The Last of the Tall Timber

September 30, 2005

Gary Indiana's incisive anatomy of California politics and the celebrity culture in which our state operates should be required reading for everyone in the USA. But that won't happen, because of "democracy," in which people "like" Arnold Schwarzenegger the same way they are said to "like" Bush, for once we like someone, there's no point in trying to change our mind, we're vapid. The book explores the rise of Arnold from movie star to governor, and the disingenuousness with which the populace has perceived this change. You get everything in this volume, from Wendy Leigh, to the famous *Premiere* article, to the concerted attempts by the *Los Angeles Times* to ruin Arnold's candidacy in the final days of his campaign. The Florida anthrax story is worthy of a book all by itself, and it is still puzzling, one of the few authentic mysteries of modern times.

The book is comprehensive and written beautifully. I don't think Indiana gives enough allowance to the way that Arnold's gubernatorial victory was a comeback for him over the crumbling of the box office beneath his feet. Once the greatest star in Hollywood, his career had become a disaster area you couldn't look away from—*Batman & Robin*, anyone? Indiana gives sensible, and prescient, analyses of several of Arnold's movies, both hits and flops, but I don't think his exegesis of *End of Days* and *The Running Man* goes very far past the most obvious places, the way people used to watch Don Siegel's *The Killers* to watch Reagan whomp Angie Dickinson across the kisser. In this regard Indiana, one of America's greatest critics and thinkers, pinpoints Arnold's appearance in August 2003 to announce his candidacy as emblematic, for it occurred during a taping of *The Jay Leno Show*.

He further cites Richard Hawkins, the LA artist who has a vast appreciation of Arnold as a, well, as a force to be reckoned with; as part of Hawkins's conceptual-art project he got Arnold to sign autographs on copies of Plato's *Symposium* and Arthur Symons's *Love's Cruelty*. That Arnold obliged Hawkins is a sign (as in *End of Days*) of a sort of identification slipperiness that has facilitated his rise in politics. Liberals were slow to pick up on his true nature because, well, not only are we vapid but he did pose nude for *Playgirl* or whatever.

If you enjoyed reading the social satire, combined with a novelistic appreciation for textures and shadings, of something like Joan Didion's *White Album*, I expect you'll enjoy this short book very much indeed. While Indiana is pretty much a dyed-in-the-wool New Yorker, he has set several of his lively, penetrating novels in California, and obviously the state fascinates him, the way that Medusa is said to have exerted a hypnotic, horrified pull over all those who gazed naked on her face. With such an enthralled gaze, he has seen things invisible to those of us who live among its rarefied airs, who walk blindly and blithely in its fogs.

Occasionally the breadth of his thought pushes too far across the page, disappearing at the edges into a kind of Möbius strip of contempt. On one page he is chastising media commentators for making scandals disappear by claiming that "it is nothing that hasn't happened before," claiming a grasp of history they don't have; a hundred pages later he's mocking the propensity of the media to find "bellwethers" everywhere, particularly in California. To me these two tendencies are in opposition to each other, and if Gary Indiana doesn't think so, he could at least explain why. But what a tiny fault, which won't distract from the pleasure you'll get from this amazing book. It opened my eyes, that's for sure.

E. E. Cummings: A Biography
by Christopher Sawyer-Lauçanno

★★★★★
A Man of Means

October 3, 2005

Cummings is a wonderful poet and three cheers for C. Sawyer-Lauçanno for attempting to give us a full-scale new reading of the complete works, while trying to clear a space so we can understand his complicated life a bit better.

I wound up seeing the life clearly, and noticing for the first time the extreme high reaches of class privilege that made Cummings's poetry possible. I suppose I had been reading this through the screen of Cummings's novel, *The Enormous Room*, with its bleak descriptions of prison poverty and deprivation, so without really thinking about it I just assumed that E. E. Cummings was sort of our American Genet, born of poverty, a hero of the underclass, an outsider artist who just scraped by, like Darger. Far from it, Sawyer-Lauçanno reveals. Everything he did seems to have been paid for by generous friends or family, and even in the French jail he was able to buy cartons of cigarettes, razors, books, and fruit from the concierge, because he had a huge trust fund.

Later, during the 1920s when he was writing all his masterpieces, the discerning Scofield Thayer became his patron. Thayer was a complicated case; as editor of the *Dial* his taste helped usher in a new American modernism. He married a beautiful and refined heiress, Elaine, and when Cummings fathered her daughter through an adulterous union, he assumed paternity of little "Mopsy" in an act of upper-class generosity. A few years later, he granted Elaine a divorce and she married Cummings, although only for two months. Thayer began a descent into madness that lasted until his death in 1982. He had apparently been gay the entire time and nurtured a secret passion for underage boys which got him in hot water from time to time, and perhaps he was in love with Cummings himself. Why not, everyone else was. Cummings must have had something, erotically speaking, for many women were drawn to him and not a few men. In any case we can see, bleakly, how spoiled and privileged Cummings was. No matter what harm he did to others, or to himself, someone would come along with a large checkbook and clean up after him. It's appalling the selfishness, and yet if great poems come in the wake of such self-love, what real harm and what real benefit? It's a stumper.

Sawyer-Lauçanno argues that Cummings's play *Him* is a major ignored work of the American theater. Such is his conviction that it fairly sweeps the reader into feeling the same way, or at any rate wanting to see a first-rate production. My idea is that *Him* might make a really good movie—by Lars von Trier perhaps. I can see it on the screen of my imagination, thanks to Sawyer-Lauçanno's persuasive, always elegant argumentation.

As for the reviewer in the *Washington Post*'s Book World, I honestly don't know what to make of someone whose idea of the three great American poets is Whitman, Frost, and Cummings. What kind of mind comes up with that combo? It's like the boys who formed the "Troika" in the later episodes of *Buffy*.

Board Game Three-Pack: Alibi, Elixir, La Strada
by Mayfair Games

★★★★★
Best Italian Trading Game in Yonks!

October 5, 2005

Did you ever wish that you lived and worked in old Italy? Here's a role-playing board game that will have you crying out "MAMMA MIA, that's a spicy meatball!"

Mayfair Games are always reliable, and many of us who used to swear by Clue now have thrown the old Parker Brothers standby right out the window and now we pledge allegiance to Mayfair's Alibi game, which is roughly the same idea but fiendishly clever and much more thrilling. It's like Clue with *CSI* thrown in. Another worthy game is called Elixir, which helps you bide your time waiting for the next *Harry Potter* movie to come out; it's fun, frivolous, involves fairies, and makes players do stunts, like Madonna's *Truth or Dare*, while under the spell of magical herbs, sort of the way the lovers in Shakespeare's *A Midsummer Night's Dream* all have to change partners due to Titania and Oberon's wishes. Anyhow my lips were already therefore moist when I heard about La Strada, the Italian-village-industry game from Mayfair, in which you decide how to proceed with building your own business in the land of pasta and vino. It's before the days of motorcars, so you do your peddling out of a horse-drawn buggy, reminding us of Ali Hakim, the Persian peddler who loves the ladies in Rodgers and Hammerstein's classic *Oklahoma!* You are the master of fleets of wagons, and the fate of a vast Italian commercial empire rests on your shoulders. Have you got the *cogliones* (Italian for, well, you can just imagine) to carry it off?

I have seen grown men cry after bringing their wagon to the fair and coming up empty. And yes, children cheer when they manage to do well on La Strada. Don't confuse this game with the popular "road movie" starring Giulietta Masina, the wife of Fellini. Just enjoy it, the way you once enjoyed playing Clue or UNO.

Cardinals Baseball Pennant

★★★★★
A Magic Carpet of Pride

October 11, 2005

A kind friend brought over the flag pennant knowing my love of the Cardinals and of bright, cheerful things in general. This baby is no pushover, either. It's nearly a square yard of flapping, screaming Card fever. I have three poles outside my window, and this pennant fits nicely via the top sleeve so that neighbors can't help but notice that a

Cards fan lives in their hood. One or two of them have teased me, saying that my Cards banner seems to be slightly larger and hung higher than the traditional US flag (the "Stars and Stripes Forever"), but as I tell them, that is just an optical illusion due to the color red being so prominent on the banner, both on bird and background, what you might call the "field."

Even those who don't follow the ball games will recognize the familiar red bird, its good nature and its competitiveness with other birds. The cardinal, as we all know, has staying power. It's the team that boasted over the years such Hall of Famers as Stan "the Man" Musial and Grover Cleveland Alexander, not to mention Cy Young himself, Dizzy Dean, Rabbit Maranville, Leo Durocher, the "Fordham Flash" Frankie Frisch, and Enos Slaughter, just to name a few. The banner is as big as a magic flying carpet; let it take you away on a never-ending tour of imagination and baseball firepower.

First thing in the morning, I will order another one through Amazon.com and take my chances. Which of my neighbors and/or fellow Cards fans shall I gift with this red surprise? Not everyone has the big personality it takes to display a red flag outside your front door, especially here in dim, foggy old San Francisco, where our own ball team has plenty of vociferous boosters. Well, we'll see. In the meantime, let the red bird soar and to all who know better, better luck next year.

The Bad Seed (1956)
dir. Mervyn LeRoy

★★★★☆
A Medal for Rhoda

October 14, 2005

If you watch *The Bad Seed* with a sympathetic eye, you can see why, out of all actresses (and indeed actors) in the world, Greta Garbo picked Nancy Kelly to represent her when she was awarded the life-time-achievement Oscar and, too reclusive to appear in person, she was asked to name a modern substitute who would accept it for her at the Shrine Auditorium. And in a way, if Nancy Kelly's acting seems stagey and dated today, I've been in theaters where Garbo's mannerisms have also elicited shrieks of laughter and howls of amusement from modern audiences.

The Bad Seed seems directed not as a movie at all, but as a play, by Mervyn LeRoy, the most up-and-down of classic Hollywood directors. With LeRoy you never knew what you were getting into. Sometimes he buckles down for business, at other times he seems to have been asleep at the wheel during the shoot. In *The Bad Seed* he lets his stars go to town, and they truly raise eyebrows today with their unadulterated ham. Nancy Kelly is not the worst offender. Patty McCormack is so evil she telegraphs it a mile away. No shadings here. And what about Eileen Heckart as the drunk mother of little Rhoda's unfortunate playmate? As Hortense Daigle, she turns in a performance as grotesque as her name. It's like every drunk scene in every other movie, combined. However, none of these "flaws" detracts one bit from the power of the film nor its fascination as a document of horror. Watching *The Bad Seed* reminds us of how little, when you get down to it, nurturing counts; apparently it's all in genetics. This movie must have frightened millions of people away from adoption, that's for sure. (As well as shrinking the number of people who wanted to name their little girls "Rhoda" after this one.) I don't want to give away any spoilers, but as Christine Penmark comes to realize, there was a broken link in the chain of DNA and that broken link was herself! She stands up and tries to bear the burden of that tragic knowledge, and soon, we realize, the turmoil inside is unbearable for her.

We saw *The Bad Seed* a few years back, with Patty McCormack in attendance. She commented on the film and how it took its toll on her, not only on her career (for she found it hard to get other parts after being typecast as Rhoda Penmark), but on her mental health as a little girl, having done this play every day for years, then having to make the film version. Did you know that Orson Welles was impressed by her and cast her in his never-released film of *Don Quixote*? McCormack is now a grown, beautiful woman. Sharp-eyed viewers have spotted her as poor Adriana's mother in reruns of *The Sopranos*.

Shampoo (1975)
dir. Hal Ashby

★★★★★
Shining, Gleaming, Streaming, Flaxen, Waxen
October 20, 2005

Shampoo harks back to the glory days of Hollywood to the famous incident at Ciro's (the night club) when Paulette Goddard added spice to her career by slipping under a table to give an evening's worth of excitement to director Anatole Litvak, thereby sealing her reputation as a party girl who really didn't care what anyone thought. (In another version of the story, Goddard and Litvak both vanished under the table simultaneously and had sex on the nightclub floor on the feet of their friends.) In any case, *Shampoo* recalls this incident by having Julie Christie slide out of her banquette to take care of the hairdresser, George Roundy (played by Warren Beatty), even though her "boyfriend" (Jack Warden) is hovering dangerously close by.

Shampoo also takes its cues from British Restoration comedy like Wycherley and Congreve, a world of cuckolded gentlemen, odious bourgeoisie, discontented wives, and boys on the make, relocating the center of the gilded universe from London to Los Angeles in the late 1960s. As in Congreve, the husbands believe it's safe to leave their wives and daughters alone with George because he's a dandy/aesthete/hairdresser. That suits him down to the ground, for on the bodies of these ignorant women he can have his revenge on the men who treat him as a tradesman, a social inferior. The picture has a slightly dated air, as if to say "We're different now than when the action of this film is laid," which might be difficult to apprehend today.

Beatty is fine, though his haircut doesn't recall the 1960s as much as the mid-'70s when the film was produced. As the typically '60s sex objects George dallies with, Julie Christie and Goldie Hawn are perfectly cast, almost too perfectly, they hardly seem to be acting at all; their haircuts and their clothes set the scene and call "cut" at the end of each take. Kathryn Blondell, the insanely talented Hollywood hairdresser, did the real hair work here, at the beginning of a long career which has included just about every movie Goldie Hawn has done since (Kate Hudson too!), as well as such period pieces as

Apollo 13 and *Bird*. She is the master at making women look great on-screen, and not just leading ladies, but supporting players and extras too. But this might be her best work—other than the futuristic styles she gave to Paul Verhoeven's *Starship Troopers*.

The Night of the Iguana (1964)
dir. John Huston

★★★★☆
In the Frightened Heart of Me

October 20, 2005

The Night of the Iguana opens in far-off Mexico and was filmed in the enchanted province of Puerto Vallarta, which enjoyed a brief vogue as a tourist spot after the publicity of filming the movie there catapulted the sleepy resort into the pages of news and gossip magazines all over the world.

In this mysterious, pleasure-loving, bigoted town, Ava Gardner, as Maxine, runs a boarding house or hotel replete with lots of chickens and some cute Mexican guys who turn dangerous after dark. Maxine's a drunk, the last of the good old broads.

Deborah Kerr isn't especially good playing Hannah Jelkes, but she's sufficiently different from Ava Gardner so that you can tell them apart. She is a painter who trundles from town to town asking non-Mexican people if she can paint their portrait in the bazaars of the primitive towns. She does this as a way to support her elderly grandfather, Nonno, who is waiting to die, but refuses to go until he can finish his poem. There must have been some subterranean connection hotwired into Tennessee Williams's brain between "Mexico" and "poetry." Look at *Suddenly Last Summer* where Sebastian has to go to Mexico once every year to write his one annual poem. As Nonno, the world's oldest man, Cyril Delevanti is, not to put too fine a point on it, wretchedly bad. Delevanti was everywhere in the 1960s, playing one of the Three Wise Men in *The Greatest Story Ever Told*, camping it up in *Mary Poppins*, acting grim in *Bye Bye Birdie*, and disapproving of Bette Davis in *Dead Ringer*. He just never let go! And here in the Huston film he is so annoying you just wish he would die, with or without reciting the last lines to his interminable, if somewhat charming, poem.

If you are a poet, you owe it to yourself to watch this film and see how a poem is really made. I watched it once with a group of friends and we agreed that it was an allegory, or perhaps a film à clef, of the life of Louis Zukofsky. Check it out! Don't forget it took Nonno twenty years to think of these final lines for his poem: "And still the ripe fruit and the branch / Observe the sky begin to blanch / Without a cry, without a prayer, / With no betrayal of despair. // O courage, could you not as well / Select a second place to dwell, / Not only in that golden tree / But in the frightened heart of me?"

You know, as a poem it's not so great, but it's touching coming from the lips of the world's oldest man.

Watching the movie now, it's hard to see where Richard Burton won a reputation as a romantic leading man. He's handsome in a battered, acned way, but he's a little guy, must weigh 125 pounds soaking wet. Next to Ava Gardner he's definitely a piece of nothing much. She could toss him over her shoulder like a dishrag.

StarPet: How to Make Your Pet a Star
by Bash Dibra

★★★★★
Shining Stars with Shining Fur

October 26, 2005

We picked up this book during our research about how to get our two cats, Ted and Sylvia, jobs in the entertainment industry, for we had agreed among ourselves that they are supercute, and if we liked them, and we are very picky, why shouldn't the world?

You get a lot for your money with *StarPet*. At first I thought author Bash Dibra was from India; his name sounds like a Bollywood star. But, as he reveals, he grew up in a refugee camp in his native Albania, where he became obsessed with dogs and how to train them properly for entertainment. Growing up, he went to Hollywood where he met the legends of StarPet training, including Rudd Weatherwax, the man behind Lassie, and Frank Inn, the man who trained Benji. The Old Masters, Bash calls them. They told him their secrets and now he passes them on, like a baton made of beef jerky.

Bash works training the pets of a dozen or more Hollywood and music stars, including the pets of Jennifer Lopez and Mariah Carey. Catfight? He doesn't reveal, but I would hate to see those two cats pitted against each other, for it is said their owners aren't too fond of each other. Bash holds private StarPet workshops where he will work with you individually, but we are so far from Hollywood it's good he has condensed his training into nearly four hundred pages, illustrated with dandy photos and some cleverly conceived line drawings. Bash reveals the three keys to motivation—the three *P*s, he calls them—persistence, praise, and patience, but never punishment. He doesn't believe in cruelty to animals, even in the service of making them stars. That would be crossing the moral line.

He envisions a world in which you and your pet can enjoy the sort of truly creative, collaborative work done by "Strasberg and Monroe or Scorsese and De Niro." That's aiming a little high, but you get the idea. A heartwarming book by a man with old-fashioned show business charm and moxie.

PS: We decided not to train Ted and Sylvia for stardom after all, but they are still probably the most appealing cats in North America.

It's One O'Clock and Here Is Mary Margaret McBride:
A Radio Biography
by Susan Ware

★★★★★
Doing the Products

November 7, 2005

I couldn't put the book down and took it with me on a flight to Seattle, then finished it on another flight to San Diego. What a ride! Susan Ware, one of the editors of *Notable American Women*, has gone back way in the past for this one. McBride was the premiere radio interviewer in the US in the 1940s and 1950s; as Ware astutely observes, she was yesteryear's equivalent of Oprah Winfrey, but plus ... plus what? Through the privileged relation then of radio to home,

McBride created an intimacy with her listeners—70 percent of them women—which even Oprah can't approximate, though she's certainly tops at what she does. Even Oprah's struggles with her weight, which have endeared her to millions of us, had their original rehearsal in McBride's huge girth, and in one famous incident in 1948 she got caught in a zipper and had to delay coming onto her own show—with complete honesty and charm she told the studio audience what had happened, and people loved her even more.

She came from a rocky girlhood in Missouri, and Ware is at her best showing us how she survived all kinds of grim childhood tragedies with a poignant determination to escape poverty. She never looked back (well, except to pen a series of bestselling memoirs of her youth à la Maya Angelou); and she brought her family with her, making sure all were well taken care of. Her mother was a frequent guest on her program, and when the mother died all America cried with her.

Mary Margaret never accepted advertising from any sponsors whose products she had not personally tried and approved. Every episode of her show had her interrupting herself constantly to talk about up to fourteen different ad campaigns. She called this "doing the products," and she believed in sponsorship religiously.

Ware is very good at showing how McBride helped to bolster, indeed create, middlebrow culture, but her distinctions are problematic. McBride, like Oprah, specialized in book promotion, and Ware says that she shunned highbrow culture and never had Hemingway, Faulkner, Thomas Wolfe, or Eugene O'Neill on the program. And yet as Ware allows, McBride welcomed William Carlos Williams, James Thurber, Tennessee Williams, Zora Neale Hurston, Marjorie Kinnan Rawlings, and Erskine Caldwell. Not to mention the cultural figures like Orson Welles, Martha Graham, etc. Like it or not, these authors are just as much a part of "modernist culture" as Faulkner and Company. There's a strange diffusion to some of Ware's arguments in this direction; if she wants to argue one thing, she reads Evidence Item X to prove it, but she then turns around and uses the same item to argue something completely different. In this case, it's arguing for McBride's disdain of modernism and yet her sympathy for writers of color; of course the paths intersect more than Ware wants to admit.

The same diffusion is present also during her discussion of whether or not Mary Margaret McBride might have been a lesbian, or were she and Stella Karn (her producer) just "girlfriends" of a different sort. Ware's conclusions on this topic vary from chapter to chapter.

I love her story about Langston Hughes, present during a taping during which McBride was advertising Dromedary Gingerbread Mix, and she urged him to help her out, and he responded with a perfect ad-lib poem (that does not appear in his *Collected Poems* you may be sure):

"Dromedary, help me carry news of chocolate cake / Also, news of gingerbread / For all the folks who bake." Ware's research (she listened to hundreds of hours of the program to transcribe wonderful tidbits like this) is fantastic. It is a book well done and so provocative in today's radio climate.

Fashionista Yarn
by Moda-Dea

★★★★★
You Can't Beat the Quality

November 9, 2005

And you can't beat the price either. I was at a loss, for none of the yarns I had on hand were anywhere near the natural quality in my mind. I was on the prowl for a particular look. I knew it had to be nylon, and I knew it had to have that hand-dyed look. It was going to be put through all kinds of weather hell, so the colors had to be fast, and yet not the unnatural dye you see so often on your cheaper pulls. I didn't want a yarn that screamed out that it was lab colored. I liked the soft Shetland colors of a highland kilt. A friend suggested I go for the ticker-tape look of a crocheted hand knit, and gifted me with a plentiful wicker basket piled high with Moda-Dea Fashionista yarns. All kinds, all colors, for me to plunge in, hook tucked behind my ear like a spatula.

Did you ever see a kid on Christmas morning when Santa's piled the gift-wrapped presents, still warm from the sleigh, high under the tree? That's how I felt, like a kid in a candy store. My fingers felt the difference immediately. Stroking one of these Moda-Dea yarns is like your first touch of silk, or even like your first kiss, it sure does go down smooth. Impatiently I discarded the yarn I had already been using for half a crocheted suit and decided on "Charade," a complex blend of straw yellow, moss green, blue, and sort of a morning-sun-pink color. It reminds you of a day at the farm, the perfect, Platonic farm that does not probably exist on earth but which you can now create with your crochet hook and about twenty dollars' worth of Charade.

That's the illusion, that's what all of us are looking for, subconsciously or not, when first the crochet hook begins to dance under our fingertips. We're all looking for some kind of escape from the busyness of our lives, looking for a time when things didn't move so fast and didn't cost so much time and money, a time when we lived off the land and had a more natural relation to the things of wool, and in this case, fine nylon spun waterproof, spun as finely as a silkworm in Japan. I told my mother, "You know my theory, Ma, about how they got the name Moda-Dea for their product?" "No son," said she, "tell me." I told her it sounded like the first fumbling words of a baby struggling to form his little lips around the simple words "Mother Dear." It's all for her.

Annie (Special Anniversary Edition) (1982)
dir. John Huston

★★★★★
Santa Claus? What's That? Who's He?
November 16, 2005

Annie is better today than when it came out. Little Aileen Quinn seems like a real child, and whenever the camera is on her, there's always some real emotion in her face and in her voice. Her singing voice isn't perfect, but it's real.

Too bad the movie doesn't keep its focus on the children more.

Carol Burnett is insane in the part of Miss Hannigan, sheer genius, and she staggers, coughs, sucks down booze like Lee Remick in *Days of Wine and Roses*. Every time she sees a man, she gets high, her endorphins flying around the room. She's got to be the easiest girl in town, and she makes it all seem natural. It's a brave performance, and I notice that when she reforms at the very end, John Huston has her do so in miniature, at the bottom of the screen while quarreling with Rooster, almost as if to say he doesn't believe it either.

Most of the numbers are very well done, except perhaps for the bizarre "I Think I'm Gonna Like It Here" sequence. Sorry, I just don't believe for a minute all those servants cavorting and dancing with the sheer joy of serving Oliver Warbucks. It's a spectacle without any foothold in reality. What are we supposed to think about the plutocratic rich? My sympathies are with the bearded anarchist who throws the bomb over the balustrade, the assassination attempt thwarted by that darn Sandy. The whole moral of the story is, as Ann Reinking suggests to Albert Finney, that his priorities aren't correct. "Why do you love only money and power and capitalism? They'll never love you back." The truth is, they do love back. The movie could have shown that capitalism is, not to put too fine a point on it, evil; in fact, viewed in one way, *Annie* is a spectacular, near-Brechtian demonstration of the evil of money.

Everyone's very good, excepting perhaps Ann Reinking, who plays the sweet, refined Grace Farrell, Warbucks's secretary. Reinking is a fine dancer but not a movie star, no way. Even on stage she seems ill at ease. She was the '70s version of Ann Miller, and both of them hailed from the same Land of Wood. She's got one number, "We Got Annie," in which she shows off the dancing Fosse taught her. Everything else is just splinters.

I remember how awful this movie was said to be back in the day, but give it a shot, there are some wonderful elements to it, and dream of the day when we can see it wide screen to appreciate the inventive choreography in the "Hard Knock Life" number, which looks so difficult and anarchic. If this isn't John Huston's very best film, it's in my top three or four by him. Is that impossible to imagine?

Our Town: A Play in Three Acts
by Thornton Wilder

★★★★★
My Little Town

November 18, 2005

Our Town gives us American experimental theater in its most easily graspable form. Once you get the general drift of the thing, you remain interested, for Wilder has planned it so. He gives us a little at a time, like a fisherman letting out his reel, slowly now, then for yards at a time once we are hooked. The Stage Manager orders the actors about, and we seem to be let into two different worlds at once: the backstage look at the theater and also, at the same time, God pulling his puppets from one end of the stage (birth) to the other (the tragic death that ends the play). Thornton Wilder, born in Madison, Wisconsin, grew up in China (Shanghai and Hong Kong) and made a study of Eastern religion at Yale, later at Princeton. All his life he remained fascinated by the patterns of things: birth, marriage, death.

Our Town shows us a different view of small-town life. Did you ever take an embroidered sampler off the wall and perhaps turned it around so you could see the back side, the knots and tangles, the rough switches, the mistakes hidden from plain sight? It's not a pretty picture, but without the fortification of error, we wouldn't have the homespun homily on the front side, under the glass. "God Bless This Home." In the play *Our Town* we see, simultaneously, both sides of the picture. It's scary to turn up the rock and see the underside. Live things wriggle there. And death comes quickly too. As George and Emily maneuver through life from childhood to dating to a wedding, the Stage Manager rushes us through, always pulling at another curtain. What comes after love? More love or no love? *Our Town* is all about sequence, but it illuminates sequence by asking us to imagine all life and death jumbled up on top of one another as though everything were happening at the same time. And yet still, none of us know, for a single second, the whole ecstasy of even one moment of our own lives.

Ninotchka (1939)
dir. Ernst Lubitsch

★★★★★
"With Ina Claire"

November 21, 2005

For Ina Claire, *Ninotchka* was a last chance to show posterity what she could do, for there wouldn't be many film opportunities offered her. She'd been a leading lady of the stage for nigh on thirty years, and her elegant beauty, very much a high-bred, Dina Merrill–type look, was still aglow. She was one of Carl Van Vechten's favorite subjects and he took photo after photo of her, staring imperiously against a wall of baize, or reclining on a lace pillow as fleecy as her beautiful blond hair.

She suffered the ultimate indignity the following year at MGM, when her part in *I Take This Woman* was taken away from her and given to the cheaper Verree Teasdale. Her director, Josef von Sternberg, was also let go, and in fact the whole picture was redone so many times studio wags called it *I Re-Take This Woman*! The "woman" in question was Hedy Lamarr; after Ina Claire's hilarious showdowns with Garbo in *Ninotchka*, the studio might have thought her perfect for the part of Lamarr's central European rival. A year or so later, and Edmund Goulding put her to work as Dorothy McGuire's mother in the charming, underrated *Claudia*, but that is definitely a mother part and, as such, put an end to Ina Claire's film career.

As the countess Swana she gets lots of Billy Wilder's best lines and laughs. She's not afraid of anyone, much less Garbo. Much has been written about the chemistry between Garbo and Melvyn Douglas, indeed a delightful mix, but the picture would have lacked a lot of its edge without Swana's steely, icy hauteur and her adroit manipulations.

In real life Ina Claire lived on to a great old age. She was ninety-two when the last curtain fell for her, and here in San Francisco, where she spent most of her life, all the lights in her building went off for an hour, precisely at 8:30 p.m., while her fans stood on the street, devoted and vigilant in our own way as the fans surrounding the Dakota Hotel when John Lennon died.

---

*My Fifteen Minutes: An Autobiography of a Child Star
of the Golden Era of Hollywood*
by Sybil Jason

★★★★★
Many New and Startling Stories from Hollywood's Golden Age

November 23, 2005

How often now are you going to get to read the real skinny about the Golden Age of Hollywood from one who starred opposite AL JOLSON and has plenty to say about him! Sadly most of his real-life costars have passed away long ago, but the children who knew him still remember him. Little Sybil Jason was a British charmer who made sixteen movies for Warner Bros. and Fox way back when (in the 1930s), and her memoirs are outstanding!

You owe it to yourself to read her account of making her very first American movie *Little Big Shot* (1935) with Glenda Farrell and Ward Bond! As she tells the story, Michael Curtiz set one of the scenes at a real-life Hollywood orphanage and, in the interests of realism, recruited real orphans to mingle with the child actors. Thus did you know that little Marilyn Monroe can be glimpsed in *Little Big Shot* a dozen years before her first "officially recognized role"? It's just one of hundreds of startling facts you'll find in this book.

Little Sybil had her favorites, and she's not afraid to name names if someone hurt her back then. She has some beautiful tributes to Jack Warner, Roddy McDowall, Peggy Ann Garner, Judy Garland, etc. She was there when, after starving herself all day, Judy was denied food at a Hollywood party by a MGM flunky who was assigned to take food out of her hands if she should try to eat something! No wonder Judy G. was troubled. Barbara Stanwyck comes off as self-absorbed, Errol Flynn as charming, even to children.

William Dieterle was the type of director a child feared, and Bogart thought of a way to punish him for his many cruelties! In this book Sybil Jason reveals that during a scene together Bogart unbut-toned his fly and hauled out his "equipment" while the cameras were rolling just to prevent William Dieterle from filming him when he was not ready. Poor Sybil, I think, saw an eyeful that day and she wasn't even ten years old.

That film footage would be interesting viewing today.

Shirley Temple's mother ruined poor Sybil's career, merely by telling Fox bosses that it was either Sybil or Shirley. After Sybil ran away with the notices for *The Little Princess* and *The Blue Bird*, Ma Temple made sure that Sybil never worked again!

Sybil was also very good playing Kay Francis's artistically inclined daughter in the superb James Wong Howe–lensed *Comet over Broadway*. She makes you laugh and makes you cry, often within a single frame.

A Day at the Races (1937)
dir. Sam Wood

★★★★★
For the Love of Ivy

November 23, 2005

Groucho, Harpo, and Chico try their best to cheat on the horses but with limited success. Maureen O'Sullivan, one of the most beautiful and underrated of the MGM stars, gives a lively performance here as Judy Standish. She's appealing, strong willed, yet with a vulnerable streak that found its ultimate expression in the waifishness of her daughter Mia Farrow. O'Sullivan's blond beauty seems designed to play off both Allan Jones's clean-cut, all-American appeal, but also the garish, sexually charged performance of Groucho as Dr. Hackenbush. Was there ever a more suggestive actor in the movies? In the '30s, there was Clark Gable, and there was Groucho for when you wanted to get serious about the body. When a guy taunts him "Are you a man or a mouse?" Groucho doesn't turn a hair, just snaps out "Throw a piece of cheese on the floor and you'll find out," exactly the kind of repartee you'd get on a good day on Craigslist.

His grimaces, astonished glances, the quick swivel and point of his chin when challenged (or aroused), his bristling hair and beetle-like spectacles here combine with the stethoscope of his "medical fantasy" to produce a vision of the id gone wild.

They don't call it a day at "the races" for nothing, for few MGM films had as many Black actors working alongside the white ones. True racial harmony. The magical moment here is the only appearance (as far as I know) in a full-length film of the incandescent Ellington singer Ivie Anderson, singing "All God's Chillun Got Rhythm." I know, what a title! But it is one of the most dazzling musical numbers ever captured on film. Ivie Anderson (here billed as "Ivy," but it seems she was one who honestly didn't care that much who spelled her name wrong or right) had one of the world's great voices, and she's given her due in this Sam Wood–directed number. Alone it would be worth buying just for this track. (There's also an Ellington short with Anderson singing Arlen's "Stormy Weather," but this is miles better.)

The Letters of Robert Lowell
by Robert Lowell, ed. Saskia Hamilton

What Next?

December 1, 2005

Saskia Hamilton, a New York–based poet, proves her mettle as an editor with this fat collection of Robert Lowell's letters.

He wrote great letters, and this surprised me a bit, but every one of them shows an insane desire to please, to flatter, to make the recipient feel good about himself or herself; he's marvelously attentive to nuance and knows exactly how to push the right buttons of his correspondents, telling them just what they want to hear. And he's sincere, which is a plus. Over and over again I was impressed by the facility with which he was blessed, or maybe he worked it up over time, because the earliest letters aren't that great, it's not until he gets into the 1940s that the familiar Lowell manner takes over.

This volume explains so much! Mostly how it was that, with all the truly awful things Lowell did, people still loved him. If it wasn't red-baiting the director of Yaddo and forcing the board to impeach her in 1947, it was publishing all those poems about Elizabeth and Harriet against their wishes, or it was wanting to marry Jackie Kennedy or whatever. Apparently all these were episodes of a manic nature in his bipolar disorder, including the car wreck that permanently disfigured wife #1 Jean Stafford. Well, of course none of them were really his fault, but still. And now this book of letters unveils his real private voice, gently coaxing, reassuring, making sense of the world, interpolating and penetrating the consciousness of whomever he was writing to at the time. The older and the famous got one style of letter; his peers got another.

Hamilton's notes are sparse, but seem sensible. However, printing over seven hundred of these letters is out of control. Like the Bidart- and Gewanter-edited *Collected Poems*, the book physically becomes too big to handle, it takes two strong men just to lift it off the shelf. Why so many? Plus, one gets the feeling that this is just the tip of the iceberg as far as the letters go, and that in a year's time we may have the first of many annual sequels, *More Letters by Robert Lowell*. Never underestimate how many times a manic genius (with, as he boasts, unearned income and lots of free time) will reach out to others to make himself heard and understood. The word is the life.

Miss Lulu Bett, and Selected Stories
by Zona Gale, ed. Barbara H. Solomon and Eileen Panetta

★★★★★
A Grand Revival

December 19, 2005

It's great to have *Miss Lulu Bett* back again. It is one of the classics of the original suffragette era, and has a wonderful title role in it. Cheerier than Edith Wharton, Zona Gale nevertheless shared some of Wharton's incisive social satire as well as a great heart for human dignity and courage. For even a trod-upon "old maid" like Lulu Bett can suddenly rear up and take command of her own life as she does in this book. The things she has to put up with are so awful, and what's heartbreaking is to think that the life she leads is just typical of unmarried women of the day. She is really nothing but a slave in the household of some people who are no better than she is, only they're married so that makes them better than she is automatically, under the legal and social codes of the day. While reading through Lulu's struggles I was also reminded of Dorothy Parker's wit and expansive humor, though Parker was apparently incapable of extending herself to the length of a whole novel: a new reader might think of *Miss Lulu Bett* as the novel Parker might have written with a wee bit more self-discipline and less gin.

Barbara Solomon and Eileen Panetta provide a sensible introduction that gives us something of the flavor of Gale's unique personality, sketching in the background of the literary scene in which Gale took such a prominent place. And they do their best to explain why she was so quickly forgotten, even her bestselling, Pulitzer Prize–winning works hardly a memory any longer.

On the other hand, "selected stories" is a little bit of a misnomer, or if not a misnomer, a rip-off, since only four stories are included! This from a writer whose short stories are among the best of the twentieth century! One story alone, "The Need," is so beautifully and starkly written it might have fit into one of Willa Cather's collections. It tells the story of a suburban couple newly installed in a tight little town where they don't know anyone, and the husband orders the wife to throw a party, only she can't think of anyone to invite, and there's the rub. Sounds simple doesn't it, but Gale takes this unpromising material and makes of it the most poignant demonstration of heartbreak since Katharine Hepburn made a fool out of herself putting on a showy dinner to impress Fred MacMurray in George Stevens's *Alice Adams*. And yet would it have hurt the editors (or the publishers) to give us a "selected stories" worth its name?

To Sir, with Love (1967)
dir. James Clavell

★★★★★
Out of this World

January 3, 2006

If asked for my favorite movies I never think of this one, and yet should *To Sir, with Love* show up on TV while I'm flicking channels, that's it, I never flick again, I stay put until the whole show is over and I'm still there a helpless ball of tears on the couch. I could have plans and I just cancel them, how can I go out when *To Sir, with Love* is on and even though I've seen it probably forty times it's so brilliantly constructed that I can never remember how it ends. Mack Thackeray (Sir) takes a job with civil engineering? Or will he stay in the horrid slum school he's been assigned to? Either way it would be a brilliant movie, mostly because of the writing I guess, but also it's superbly directed by someone who really loves kids, for each of the young actors in the film has a different personality, and each of them gets to shine. Of course Lulu has a big part, and she's pretty bad at acting, yet she's so over the top I always think, "Well, maybe there were actually slags that loud and vulgar." The young actor who plays Denham, Thackeray's nemesis, is sort of like Britain's answer to our own Michael Parks, both of them eye candy of a specialized sort, and above all the other youngsters is Judy Geeson, forever immortal for her playing of Pamela Dare, the one student who really gives her heart to Sir, for he's the only one who has given her a reason to think of herself as a human being. Every year that goes by she looks more beautiful and her outfits more trendy and fetching. Just tonight I was watching the big schoolyard scene where Denham throws the tin can at Sir, cutting his palm, and the kids are saying "Look, Chimney Sweep is bleeding red blood," and Pamela has a fit screaming at them for how racist they are. Anyhow she's wearing, well, is it supposed to be a slum outfit? It's a perfect, charcoal-colored, short-sleeved sweater that sets her figure off to perfection, and a charcoal skirt, almost a miniskirt but not quite, and I'm here to tell you, Yves Saint Laurent couldn't have done it better.

She is exquisite in every way, and almost her match is Suzy Kendall, so great in Argento's film *The Bird with the Crystal Plumage* and so great here as Poitier's colleague. Check out the dress she wears to the kids' museum trip: puff sleeves, tiny silk-covered bone buttons, white, white, white like some unbelievably tempting pastry. She has gumption in the movie and she's not afraid of what people say and she's not afraid of Judy Geeson's mad love for a forbidden temptation!

The music is great and I would like to know, Who is singing that song in the students' recess hall where Lulu and that dorky boy start dancing in a parody of courtly dancing of the eighteenth century, him kissing her hand, and then they break into current pop dancing of the 1960s? Is it the Mindbenders too, because that track is out of this world—just like the whole film which I could watch every minute of all over again, and will.

Tab Hunter Confidential: The Making of a Movie Star
by Tab Hunter (with Eddie Muller)

★★★★★
Fate Is Tab Hunter

January 6, 2006

What made Tab Hunter's career so unusual was his dual role as one of the final contractees to Hollywood's studio system (at Universal) and his generally adventurous own nature, so he ventured rather farther afield than, say, his contemporary Robert Wagner. Thus he appeared in the very last films of a number of ancient Hollywood greats, and yet on the other hand he forecasted, as did his sometime boyfriend Anthony Perkins, the beginnings of the New American Cinema of the 1970s. Hunter points this out himself in a typically insightful passage: "I was on the set for the last roars of so many old lions—[Raoul] Walsh, [William A.] Wellman, [Stuart] Heisler, [Jacques] Tourneur—as well as for the first forays of young Turks who'd inspire a whole new style of filmmaking: Frankenheimer, Lumet, Penn. My career fell smack in the middle of the changing of the guard."

His book is worth reading just for the insight into the methods of Luchino Visconti, for whom he seems to have had a serious penchant. Tab denies that he ever lay down on Henry Willson's casting couch, but how about Visconti's casting gondola? He draws the veil discreetly over these disappointments, but it's pretty clear that the up-and-coming (and complaisant) Helmut Berger stole some of Tab's thunder in a pinch. It brings us to the startling alternative universe in which Tab Hunter, not Berger, starred in such Visconti titles as *The Damned*, *Ludwig*, and *Conversation Piece*. Could have been!

Hunter seems like a nice guy, and his performances in vehicles as disparate as *Damn Yankees*, *Track of the Cat*, and *Polyester* show he had not only range but a quiet intensity that occasionally blazed into incandescence. Writer Eddie Muller brings Hunter's life into occasional coherence, but one comes away thinking that they might have brought their subject, Hunter's contested star status in a time of state-mandated homophobia, into a clearer light. Basically Tab is saying "I was always out. It was Tony who was in the closet." The great thing about their book is the new look at some of the great legends with whom Tab worked, including a gallant salute to the amazing, unforgettable screen beauty Linda Darnell, who costarred with him early in his career and gave him the confidence to fill up the screen.

Hitler's Piano Player: The Rise and Fall of Ernst Hanfstaengl, Confidant of Hitler, Ally of FDR
by Peter Conradi

★★★★★
Ouch

January, 8 2006

Readers of Djuna Barnes should pick up this important biography right away, for those of us who admire the brilliant, bisexual US modernist will discover, in Putzi Hanfstaengl, one of the central figures in Barnes's life and an original of *Nightwood*. When the two of them met, shortly before World War I in a very different New York City, aristocratic, thrill-seeking Harvard grad Ernst Hanfstaengl was like no one else Barnes had ever met, and even though she was already identifying herself pretty much as a lover of women, she managed still to bring him under her erotic spell. Author Conradi relays Andrew Field's story (from his authoritative Barnes biography) that he was so attracted to her that, while slow dancing with her, he suffered an embarrassing and infinitely painful little "sex accident." To put it in layman's terms, his erection exploded. Now, that's erotic enslavement!

Conradi's best guess is that Putzi and Djuna dissolved their engagement because she would not become German enough for him, but he outlines the various possibilities.

She is said to have contemplated killing herself by leaping from her window when he left her to return to Germany at the outbreak of World War I.

There he married the unsatisfactory, hapless Helene, whom he led a merry chase till she finally divorced him to find happiness with another.

The main story of the book, Hitler's friendship with Putzi and his eventual downfall at the hands of the Allies, is competently told. How much of it shall we believe? Whatever, it is a story more thrilling than any fiction, except perhaps *Eye of the Needle* and *Shining Through*. The Thomas Mann of *Buddenbrooks* might have written the early part of Putzi's life, but the last half of it could only have been dreamed up by a combination of Ian Fleming and John Cheever.

The Last Titan: A Life of Theodore Dreiser
by Jerome Loving

Titanic

January 21, 2006

I have to disagree with the *Publishers Weekly* reviewer who states that Loving doesn't seem interested in finding out what made Theodore Dreiser tick. I walked away from this hurricane of a book feeling I knew TD inside out (and incidentally more than a bit about Loving as well)! A difficult figure to classify, Dreiser has been cursed for decades by having a friend like H. L. Mencken, a man who praised him to the skies on the one hand, but on the other let the whole world know his real opinion, that Dreiser was an oversexed drunk who couldn't write his way out of a paper bag. Mencken's tributes to Dreiser's "power" were like Norman Mailer's tributes to Muhammad Ali, to be honored more in the breach than in the observance. And thus generations of students and readers have only picked at Dreiser warily, feeling that some of his low-class trashy ways might rub off on them.

Loving at least has no fear, and walks in like an angel to a landscape littered with the corpses of previous biographers. He focuses Dreiser's development right at the mirror stage, as it were, with his intense relationship with Sarah, his mother, and a brooding, quarrelsome batch of siblings. Among them was the Indiana songbird Paul Dresser (who changed his name from "Dreiser" for showbiz reasons), who wrote many hit tunes for Tin Pan Alley before an untimely death. For some reason Loving feels it necessary to state, more than once, that Paul Dresser is forgotten today, but how true is that? Not very! And a film like *My Gal Sal*—with Victor Mature and Rita Hayworth, Phil Silvers and Carole Landis, a Fox biopic of the songwriter—is every bit as good a film as the more portentous pictures drawn from Dreiser's own writings. I love Wyler's *Carrie* and Stevens's *Place in the Sun*, but even Dreiser's greatest fans would admit they're heavy sledding.

Loving takes particular pains with the first half of TD's life, the formative years, and lets the last half of his life slip by in a mere hundred pages, so he's actually skimming a bit, but one feels that the balance is essentially correct. I can't imagine a better biography of our weirdest novelist. Loving makes you want to read even the later books, like *The Stoic* and *The Bulwark*, books that haven't been cracked open since 1947. He explains the reasons why Mencken turned on Dreiser—basically Dreiser came to Baltimore to visit at a time when Mencken's mother was very sick, on her deathbed, upstairs, and he didn't even have the politesse to ask after the old woman. He was self-centered, true. Loving is also very good about explaining how old two-fisted Dreiser wound up editing women's magazines at the turn of the century and how he changed their course, and how the demands of the profession changed his own writing, perhaps required him to spend more time thinking about women. Loving states that Dreiser was the first important US writer to have descended from a country other than England. Interesting, but it sort of negates the achievements of some Black American novelists I think.

Futureworld (1976)
dir. Richard T. Heffron

★★★★★
One of Fonda's Finest

January 23, 2006

The more I see of Peter Fonda's '70s films, the more I'm beginning to feel that he had a more interesting career than either his father or his sister during that decade. In *Futureworld* he's a seasoned print journalist who's constantly comparing his prowess with the superficial nose for news displayed by his adorable ex-girlfriend Socks, played with élan by a game Blythe Danner. The two of them clash often and frequently during the first half of the movie, but then like *His Girl Friday* they decide to lie down with the lambs and from then on their chemistry grows by leaps and bounds. One needs the other's talents, and Fonda and Danner fully inhabit the characters of Tracy (Socks) and Chuck. They go to Futureworld on an all-expenses-paid business trip to drum up publicity for the $1.5 billion dream-vacation resort, which had died a death in the wake of the Westworld debacle. It seems that world leaders are arriving in droves to escape earthly problems, and Peter Fonda begins to suspect that, just like Roach Motel, you can Czech into Futureworld but you can't Czech out.

Some have said that the production values of *Futureworld* betray a poverty of MGM resources. I think on the contrary it looks more expen$ive than *Westworld*. It can't have been cheap to hire Yul Brynner to do that strange dream tango. Someone told me that they probably only had Brynner's services for one weekend, or else he died in the middle of filming, because otherwise why not give him a bigger part? It would have been awesome if he had come out at the end, as the gunslinger, to kill all the robots who wanted (SPOILERS AHEAD) to replace all the world leaders with Delos-friendly hybrids.

The acting was great all the way through, and the love story between the Stuart Margolin character and his friend, robot Clark (named after Clark Kent, "the Man of Steel") was heartbreaking, worthy of Heath Ledger and Jake Gyllenhaal in *Brokeback Mountain*. It's rare to find a good gay love story in the middle of a 1970s sci-fi actioner, but here you go, if it had teeth it would bite you.

Runner Mack
by Barry Beckham

★★★★★
Soul Force for the Ages

January 27, 2006

Runner Mack is one of those books that convinces you of the true power of literature, for while reading the book you are really walking a mile in the other man's shoes. In this case, the other man is called Henry Adams—no, not the quintessential American dilettante and thinker who wrote about Mont-Saint-Michel and Chartres and who knew Henry James.

Nor is it the famous brewer Henry Adams!

This Adams is a contemporary Black man faced with difficult and revealing decisions about his place in a largely white world which spurns his very existence. And it's also a baseball novel, centered on Adams's need to join the "Stars," a brilliant coinage on the part of the author Barry Beckham, who wrote this novel way back when, but it hasn't dated a bit, except perhaps today it's easier for Black athletes to get into pro baseball than it was back then. Picture the book as a sort of cross between Malamud's *The Natural* and a fiery, deeply felt (and Henry Adams–like) confession like *The Autobiography of Malcolm X*. In fact the central bond between Henry Adams and the title man, Runner Mack, reminded me a bit of the sometimes strained relationship between pioneer Jackie Robinson and martyred militant Malcolm X.

What makes *Runner Mack* stand out, however, is not its fidelity to the locker room ethics of pro baseball, nor to its heroes' vague similarity to figures from some Black History Month poster, but for its postmodern writing style. Beckham is fully the equal of writers like Thomas Pynchon or Ralph Ellison, and stepping into his world you go breathless with speed, dexterity, and a mind-blowing use of adjectives and verbs. Henry's relationship with Beatrice is a true classic, and brings out the very best in Beckham's heartfelt gravity. "Wasn't this a spirit that he was considering: an emotional makeup, a soul force whose bearing was as automatic as it was inexplainable, phantomlike in the vigor with which it sticks to one's bones, becomes a sixth sense; wasn't it—hell, wasn't it endowed or ancestral, this spirit, marching through the ages with the stride of an ineradicable heritage?" This writing brings you to your feet cheering; it doesn't make any excuses for itself, nor does it talk down to you, it treats you like you were actually smart as Barry Beckham, which is doubtful, and to think that this book, published long ago, nearly a quarter of a century ago, is still relevant, alive, and musical today. Oprah should pick up on Barry Beckham, forget your James Freys, go with the gusto!

Foxes (1980)
dir. Adrian Lyne

★★★★★
"A Hole in Your Old Brown Overcoat"

January 29, 2006

Jodie Foster is directed carefully by Adrian Lyne to break out of her typical cerebral mode and thus give a performance of real physical depth. You'll notice in almost every scene she's in, she's always touching, feeling, caressing the bodies of the other performers, the boys and girls alike, she can't take her hands off them, even when she's speaking of something else. And yet her need to feel flesh doesn't suggest sexual hunger, it seems instead related to a maternal instinct, for she's the one who's always taking care of everyone else, even her own mother (Sally Kellerman). The scene where Jodie Foster climbs into bed with sleepy, nerve-racked Kellerman and reads to her out of Plato—of all philosophers!—touches something real in all of us who have ever wondered, "Who is the other half of myself?" Yes, now and then Lyne crosses over the border into a realm of David Bailey bad taste, especially in the opening-credit sequence that so lovingly explores the bodies of the four sleeping "foxes" who are having a sleepover. It might almost be an erotic thriller from Showtime. However, that's what happens when you experiment, you risk bad taste, and I'd rather have a picture that was all bad taste as long as it was doing something unique. And most of the time the photography serves the characters well, showing the weakness as well as the strength, the maturity as well as the traces of childishness, on the faces of all his young stars.

Scott Baio never changes expression in the movie, but we feel we know his thoughts anyhow and can feel what he's thinking in every scene. Part of this is to the credit of an exceptionally literate screenplay. People always brag on about, oh, I don't know, Peter Greenaway, but he's done nothing as good as *Foxes*. Maybe it's the title, but *Foxes* doesn't get much credit, does it? Jodie Foster should have gotten the Oscar for this movie, she does better work here than in either of the films for which she actually won Academy Awards. Cherie Currie is fantastic too, she actually manages to seem like she's in some documentary about her own life, fragile, endangered, willful, ultimately inexplicable like all human beings.

And the whole milieu of an as yet ungentrified LA feels lived in, like an Altman landscape. You really believe these four girls live in this ugly, parched, and commercialized space, so that when they visit Randy Quaid's canyon place, it really must feel to them like another world.

Safestud: The Safesex Chronicles of Max Exander
by Max Exander

★★★☆☆
Look into the Past

January 30, 2006

Walking down Eleventh Street I literally stumbled across a copy of this book, here in a neighborhood where its author, now long gone to us, had so many friends. Out of curiosity I picked up the book and plunged right in. The experience took me right back to a very different time, to a strange new world in which many of us had to relearn and rethink everything we had been brought up to let go unchallenged. Max Exander was a "porn name" for the novelist Paul Reed, and Reed as well as many other intellectuals had at that moment to make a choice between a radical, modernist disengagement with society or with direct political action in the name of fighting AIDS. When it came to diverting sexual impulses, they were all walking into murky waters. John Preston, the famous pornographer, came up with an anthology called *Hot Living*, in which he got all his contributors to write sexy stories extolling the medically approved "safe sex," while others argued that because porn is only a fantasy anyway, why not let unsafe sex live on in writing at any rate, if not in life.

This question was so debated during the first half of the 1980s that rereading *Safestud*, yet another product of the era of reeducation, gives one a vertiginous feeling. I see angry faces all around me, the faces of those of us who had to curtail our sex lives or die, the faces of those dying, raging in an indifferent sea of government inertia or opposition. They, the state apparatus, tried to play it as though human rights were now in opposition to sexual rights. I had forgotten how much of *Safestud* does not speak the language of porn, how much of it borrows from Reed's "straight" writing, as it were, to tell the story of a gay community not only coping with the plague while trying to find the silver lining to new, restrictive sex practices, but just being ordinary guys living life in 1980s San Francisco. The characters go to see *Ghostbusters*, *Indiana Jones*, *Gremlins*, etc. They're reading Jackie Collins's *Hollywood Wives* as well as Milan Kundera. Phone sex must have just been invented, for they spend hours talking to each other (and to strangers) on these newfangled phone lines, one hand dipped in lube, the other rapid dialing.

It might almost be an age when Ansel Adams was still alive, for Max and his boyfriends and cohorts spend safe-sex weekends at all the fabled Ansel Adams sites in Northern California and Nevada. If I remember right, Paul was a protégé of the lesbian novelist May Sarton and had dozens and dozens of letters back and forth from and to her, her advising him on how to write a novel, etc. None of her advice really worked, did it, for he never wrote anything especially distinctive, but he was always a sturdy craftsman and he had something more than that, perhaps an earnestness and a sense of humor that his friends found delightful. You wanted him in your corner.

The new ways of having sex that Max discovers in this novel didn't last that long, I don't think. Deprived of bodily fluid exchange, he finds pleasure in being ordered to pleasure himself. In one vivid scene he is led to the middle of a warehouse and strange commanding voices order him to spank himself while they watch. This turns him on. I just found it, I don't know, it seemed distant. In the end Max finds a boyfriend, Eddie, who believes in safe sex as much as he does. They share a sexual faith that, they hope, will lead them out of the valley of the shadow of death. Alas, we know what happened.

The Secret Life of Oscar Wilde: An Intimate Biography
by Neil McKenna

★★★★★
Blood, Sweat, and Tears

February 13, 2006

I guess I'll read any life of Oscar Wilde, as I will of Kipling, Robert Frost, Frida Kahlo, or Frank Lloyd Wright, just because their lives were so twisted and strange that everyone has their own take on why, what happened. Just hand me one and don't come back for days, I'll be lost to you. Neil McKenna's new biography, which dwells clinically, unflinchingly on the sexual side of Wilde's passion for young men, wore its reviews on its sleeve when I came across it, and I was thinking, "Oh, it sounds awful." But I was mildly surprised right at the beginning when

McKenna skips all that stuff you've heard a million times, the subject's ancestry, parents, and childhood, three topics on which most biographers spend pages and pages. McKenna leaves all that out and goes right to the meat, to Oxford, where he first finds Oscar having sex with men.

It's a bare-bones approach which leads to amazing results, as I suppose any intense focus will. Wilde's feelings are of no particular interest in this life, yet instead McKenna finds plenty of gay knowledge when he looks at the particular sex acts Wilde engaged in, which now become pretty explicit with the recent discovery of the witness statements in the first and second trials. These accounts of semen, Vaseline, and excrement can make for pretty grim reading on the one hand, and yet they bring to life as never before exactly what it might have been like to have sex with Wilde (and with Lord Alfred Douglas as well, for it seems that if you went for one, you were going to have to give in to the other as well).

Some have complained that *The Secret Life of Oscar Wilde* lacks the wide-ranging inquiry into Wilde's works and genius that was the principal feature of, say, Richard Ellmann's biography. Well, that's OK, we've had all that. We haven't had Wilde's body until now though. Now it's here. And in addition we finally divine what McKenna calls Wilde's "sexual faith," his conviction, shared by other contemporary "Uranians," that sex itself is (or might be) a "magical act." Thus the drawing room fripperies of Lady Windermere might coexist with the unearthly portrait of Dorian Gray, the happy prince with the infanta.

Greene on Capri: A Memoir
by Shirley Hazzard

★★★☆☆
Cats on an Island

February 14, 2006

Really no more than a very, very long *New Yorker* sort of profile blown up to book size, *Greene on Capri: A Memoir* is an irresistible sort of book and pure opium for those of us who like to read about people with so much money they can afford to live on several continents at once. Shirley Hazzard writes so creamily that it was only after several chapters that I started asking myself, "Where is all this money coming from?" For none of the characters, save the distantly observed fishermen, have anything to do with their time but sit around all day at one of Capri's many colorful cafés, sip aperitifs, and cap each other's quotations from the Brownings.

It's a form of literary sleight of hand that at its best is positively alluring, but when the illusion falters for even a minute a certain distaste sets in. All travel writing is sort of alike, and there are two sorts of readers, one who loves nothing better than a book about Capri and the other who would rather undergo a Brazilian body wax without anesthesia than have to read a book like this one. Beyond this certainty, there are a few other problems with Hazzard's book. One is the problem noticed by most reviewers: that she really doesn't care much for Greene, so you ask yourself, "Then why write a book about someone whom you just can't stand?" The feeling creeps in that she was fascinated by his bad manners and his egotism, but that she was too drawn to his fame (the way her husband, Francis Steegmuller, became known as a permanent barnacle of the fame of Cocteau) to resist.

Another debit is the photo selections which render Shirley Hazzard, not a bad-looking woman, as the victim of a truly evil costume designer. No matter what decade it is, you see her wearing blouses with long Peter Pan–style collars in which the tabs droop down practically to her breasts, a bizarre style which makes her look like a bejeweled and preening horse. It must have been Graham Greene's revenge. Probably long ago, in 1962, in Capri, he might have sent her a little *care* package from some demented designer in Antibes, and advised her it would make her look less like Lillian Hellman. His unpleasantness was legendary, the "irrational and cruel paroxysm of the playground," as Hazzard hazards. The odd thing is that Greene went to Capri at all! He was of the generation of Englishmen, she avers, who were actually blind to the beauty of physical surroundings. Perhaps they thought it unmanly. He was just there because it was "away." Her explanation isn't very convincing, but she does provide some interesting sidelights, such as the fact that Greene thought Olivier a terrible actor, much preferring the mundanities of Ralph Richardson or Paul Scofield. Hazzard also provokes a chuckle when she talks about how bad Graham Greene's own performance is, in Truffaut's *Day for Night*. "In a companion scene of the same film, a cat does far better."

Alcatraz: The True End of the Line
by Darwin E. Coon

★★★★★
Prisoner: Cell Block H

February 16, 2006

I too met Darwin E. Coon during a recent trip to Alcatraz, which was brilliant. Coon sat in a shack on the pier with a young man who claimed to be his "nephew." This nephew did all the talking and would occasionally nudge old Darwin, who sat beside looking stolid and bored, with his elbow, prompting him to answer some questions from a countless stream of fans who, right off the boat from the island prison, wanted to ask him a zillion questions. Apparently he found his way to the souvenir shack every Saturday so you could often meet him, shake his hand, and get him to autograph a copy of *Alcatraz: The True End of the Line.* Otherwise he's sort of like Iron Eyes Cody, a man of few words. The nephew said to me, "My uncle wants to know if you want him to sign your copy of the book with his prison number." "Sure," I replied, after a glance at my companion, the video artist Karla Milosevich. "That number thing would be awesome." Darwin Coon took pen from nephew and scrawled his number on the front free endpaper of my book: "#1422." We looked at it in awe. "I had no idea the numbers were so short."

Darwin Coon looked at me impassively, as though to say "*Life* is short, you little pipsqueak."

His book is great and tells you all about the different animals kept by the Alcatraz inmates. No other book I know goes into such detail about the different pets smuggled in by prisoners. There's a great story about Sam, the fellow who found a lizard and trained it to be his pet, and every day he would walk the lizard around the prison on a gold chain, rather like the French symbolist poet Gérard de Nerval who walked around the Luxembourg Gardens with a pet lobster on a leash. In Sam's case the ending was tragic, for a seagull swooped down and carried off the little lizard!

Another prisoner made a tiny tuxedo for his pet mouse, complete with top hat! They were like a bunch of male Beatrix Potters over there; their love of animals will warm any human heart.

Harvard's Secret Court: The Savage 1920 Purge of Campus Homosexuals
by William Wright

★★★★★
Persecuted, Expelled, Abandoned, Friendless, and Made to Feel like Scum

February 19, 2006

Even though the facts are new, there's nothing really shocking about the three-week secret court of 1920 at Harvard. Homophobia, if that's what we can agree to call it, has been a part of human history for eons, and I wasn't surprised to find that deans of the college had interviewed thirty students, teachers, and Cambridge outsiders about their sex habits, only to expel fourteen of them later down the pike. It was horrifying but not really a shock.

As Wright notes, it's bizarrely confusing at first because some of the main characters have names that rhyme—"Say," "Lay," "Day," and "Gay." It must be a Harvard thing.

Wright, the author of the best biography of Lillian Hellman, surely knows human cruelty as have few observers since Montaigne. His picture of Lawrence Lowell is magnificent. Lowell was the best and the brightest, and the most obdurate of antigay hatemongers, and yet oddly enough his sister, the great US modernist Amy Lowell, was certainly a lesbian, and very much an in-your-face "out" case. And his relations with her were just fine, but maybe, as Wright suggests, he was taking out on the poor students his fury at feeling unable to keep Amy's gay passions under check.

The whole affair began when one student, Cyril Wilcox, killed himself mysteriously at home, and his family was shocked to find some compromising letters sent to him from fellow students. One of them boasted about trying to seduce his fiancée's younger brother, saying that once he and Bradlee were in bed together, he wouldn't be "taking it out for two days and two nights"! OK, sort of rough stuff for your mother to find on top of your dead body in 1920, but it led to untold privations for a group of tagged and persecuted men, whose only crime was really that they managed to find a moment or two of sexual bliss in a dark and hateful era.

The only downside to this book was a few chapters worth of invented dialogue—needless, and spoiled the sober effect; and also a certain amount of p-a-d-d-i-n-g and repetition. You feel like saying "All right already." But all in all, a story of fascination, and you feel with the three suicides that those boys are still on the march, seeking vengeance right now on a homophobic nation. This time I'm with the ghosts.

Babes on Broadway (1941)
dir. Busby Berkeley

★☆☆☆☆
Burning Down the Robert E. Lee

February 27, 2006

I saw this one last night after a long ride home from the airport, in teeming rain, and one of my shoes had split its sole so I was squelching puddles in every step on the pavement. What I wanted was to get warm and forget about my worries, and usually a good Busby Berkeley movie will do that for me. I noticed that this picture isn't among the Berkeley films featured on the upcoming boxed DVD set, but since that release concentrates on the Warner Bros. years, I assumed that was why. But no. I forgot there was a blackface number ("Waiting for the Robert E. Lee") that not only sneaks into *Babes on Broadway* but in fact forms the finale, so you can hardly skip it or avoid it. Maybe that's why it's not being rushed into DVD, especially during Black History Month!

People say that Busby Berkeley had every right to use blackface at the time he did, citing the example of Al Jolson and other white stars who rose to fame in blackface parts. But watching *Babes on Broadway* you get the feeling that the kids playing the parts were all born after the heyday of blackface and that this discarded genre was deliberately revived especially for this film, and that's a puzzler. Nineteen forty-one was not the heyday of blackface. Indeed Jolson had already become a has-been—his own revival would come after the war, with the blackface played down, down, considerably down. Perhaps the germ of the idea stimulated Berkeley's pictorial imagination: row after row of plinking banjos, strutting harlequin costumes, haystacks, and the churning wheels of the big riverboats. It's pretty hard to sit through, though I don't know (strictly speaking) if it's the absolute worst of all the Busby Berkeley numbers I've seen, for there are others that flirt with the absolute calamity of tastelessness. People say if it wasn't for that very lack of taste—I guess really it's whatever the opposite of taste *is*—there wouldn't be a Busby Berkeley, that having no inhibitions allowed him to come up with the surrealist inspirations for which we love him so.

I don't know about that. People say that Shirley Temple might have played the Barbara Jo part that here is played by MGM stalwart Virginia Weidler, whom you either love or hate in *The Philadelphia Story*, and don't ask me which camp I'm in. I think Shirley found out she'd have to smear black makeup over her face in the finale and something, perhaps the whispered advice of her mentor Bill "Bojangles" Robinson, still resonated in her ear and she just stuck out her chin and said, "Mr. Studio Driver, take me back to the Fox lot please."

Virginia Weidler does a fine job, by the way. I'm just kidding about her unlikability in *The Philadelphia Story*.

Body Double (1984)
dir. Brian De Palma

★★★★☆
The King's Two Bodies

March 3, 2006

De Palma should have hired Tom Hanks to play the part of Jake Scully. He would have been perfect with his neo–Jimmy Stewart persona and bumbling charm that might have so easily turned to obsession. He wasn't averse to Hanks, hiring him later for the fiasco that became *The Bonfire of the Vanities*. Maybe he just liked Craig Wasson's look (if you can call it a look). The only time Wasson looks halfway appealing is in his "Pee Wee" outfit, in a tight striped sweater and bowtie, at the beginning of the video for "Relax," by Frankie Goes to Hollywood, one of the seriously demented sequences in *Body Double*.

We watched this DVD not long ago and I was surprised to see that Melanie Griffith, whose name and image are all over the box, does not appear in the movie until after an hour of footage and exposition. Indeed she makes her first appearance at 1 hr. 12 mins. I'm still debating whether or not she appears in disguise earlier in the movie, but I don't want to reveal any spoilers here so I'll just post my wonder in a series of expostulating, highly verbal question marks. Griffith isn't good and she isn't bad, playing what (after *Blow Out* and *Dressed to Kill*) must have been considered the "Nancy Allen" part, the blowsy, down-to-earth comic role, who free of deadly romanticism herself brings a breath of fresh air to a neurotic male lead. It's a refreshing conception, but I think Nancy Allen does it better. And that's saying something, considering how awful Nancy Allen is in everything, including the aforementioned films, and yet we keep watching her because she's so fearless and alive. Melanie Griffith is said to have beat out some actual porn stars to land the role of Holly Body; she must have studied some porn footage, though she isn't called on to perform anything hard core.

And speaking of hard core, isn't that Lane Davies (later Mason Capwell on *Santa Barbara*) as one of the aspiring actors looking for a job? He's pictured glowering on a set of steps in a pair of blue jeans and sporting the most outrageous basket I've seen in the movies since the old Steve Reeves peplum movies! Whatever happened to Lane Davies? He was for a brief period the best American actor going. Then all of a sudden he just seemed to disappear.

The Toys Sing "A Lover's Concerto" and "Attack!"
by The Toys

★★★★★
Body and Soul

March 5, 2006

We were watching *It's a Bikini World* (1967) on TV, truly one of the 1960s' most inspired and subversive youth films. Stephanie Rothman directed a cheapo cast including Bobby Pickett, Tommy Kirk (in two roles, hip and square), and the one and only Deborah Walley, and in true *Beach Party* fashion the film manages to incorporate many great pop acts of the day. This one has Eric Burdon singing "We Gotta Get Out of This Place," the Castaways with their catchy "Liar, Liar" number, and many more, a few of which have certainly not stood the test of time, yet such is the energy of *It's a Bikini World* that viewers forgive all sins. Anyhow the Toys appeared and my heart went right out the window. I had almost forgotten about them, but when they sang their second hit "Attack" in the film, a whole era came back. The lead singer Barbara Harris is, to make a long story short, among the half dozen most distinctive voices of the century.

I can see why, or so it is said, the Supremes felt threatened when "A Lover's Concerto" hit the airwaves in the autumn of 1965, and had their songwriters attempt to imitate the successful Toys formula, which to my ears melds together the falsetto-and-horns sound of the Four Seasons with a gospel "realness." White America, I suppose, felt reassured at hearing that "A Lover's Concerto" took its melody from a Bach piece, as though to reiterate that in a time of seething social change and anger, Black people were appreciating the dead white males and their "timeless" music. Anyhow the Supremes hit right back with "I Hear a Symphony," but if you ask me, it's not half as good as the song it sought to ape. And when the Toys released "Attack" a few months later, they launched one of the strangest and most incandescent pop records of all time.

"All's fair in love and war," sing the Toys, and the real message seems to be "All's fair in pop." Barbara Harris tries to wrap herself around the lilting, twisty, difficult melody, but she's no perfectionist, for I imagine that to properly sing the octave-climbing melody of "Attack" you would have to record it one note at a time, the way Dusty Springfield was said to record. Harris attacks the tune as though her life depended on it, and if her hold on some of the notes seems slippery, it's all the more beautiful because you feel something is at risk. Yes, she's straining, and in *It's a Bikini World* even her miming looks uncomfortable, but if you think Tina Turner sang "River Deep – Mountain High" with conviction, you're talking pallid imitation of Barbara Harris in "Attack." "River Deep" and "Attack" also share a similar lyrical mise en scène, the singer talking about a love that has lasted through childhood, a love that time has made stronger than time itself, a sinewy vine that simply cannot be severed or cleaved. The other Toys provide suitable support, they're lovely, but really the song belongs body and soul to the lead singer, and eternal star, Barbara Harris (not the white actress whom I also like).

The First Lady of Hollywood: A Biography of Louella Parsons
by Samantha Barbas

★★★★★
Ministry of Fear

March 9, 2006

For Christmas a good friend gave me this exciting biography (hi there, Mac!) and ever since New Year's I've been on a race to finish it. But some books are so good you don't like them to end, and for the past few weeks I've been envying my former self who still had the whole book in front of him instead of a rapidly dwindling few pages.

Louella Parsons was a woman of iron determination who summoned up the inner strength to leave her shame behind in the small town where she'd grown up and go to New York where nobody would know her. With her she had a second husband and a small daughter, Harriet, who, quietly like a pet, watched her mother with a mixture of fondness and venom. I wonder if *Harriet the Spy* was named after her! It sounds improbable on the face of it but both *HTS* author Louise Fitzhugh and Harriet Parsons formed part of the same glamorous lesbian New York underground in the late 1950s, early 1960s, the years of Harriet's inception. Anyhow Louella soon rose to the top of the Hearst newspaper empire by an unbeatable combination of loyalty, native smarts, and an earnest brownnosing that is almost endearing to view today, although how it must have irked her professional rivals way back then.

Samantha Barbas is no Joan Didion but she lays out the facts with a great deal of skill. She has done her homework and even conducted a handful of new interviews, such as one with Mamie Van Doren, a Hollywood starlet who claims to have been one of Louella's victims. For Louella (I suppose I should call her "Parsons") was very much a bogeyman, a prop employed by the studio system to keep errant stars in line. She crucified Orson Welles, who had the temerity not only to make a jackass out of Hearst in *Citizen Kane* but also to lie about it to Parsons's face. "It deals with a dead man," he told her when she pressed him about the rumors that *Kane* was going to be a demolition of Hearst. She never forgave left-wing-leaning stars like Chaplin. And yet she had a soft side and people could cozy up to her, particularly the unpleasant songwriter Jimmy McHugh. Samantha Barbas shows us how McHugh "dated" Parsons for years, always stringing her along, never actually taking her emotional needs seriously but palming her off with a ditty called "Louella" which made her feel like a schoolgirl. It's a shame a once distinguished press like UC Berkeley can't afford a proofreader nowadays. Or else Dr. Barbas isn't very familiar with the stars of Hollywood—Parsons's beat—otherwise she wouldn't have written "Frederic March," would she?

But what she's terrific at is discovering the roots and the extent of Parsons's feminism, which went far and wide and early. Even before women's suffrage (1920) Parsons was in there fighting for women's rights, and she did help a lot of women journalists find their way. Good for her, too bad she turned into a tragic old harridan figure, half–Miss Havisham, half-Cassandra, nearly forgotten by the time of her death. I feel sure that *The First Lady of Hollywood* will remain the standard biography for at least the next few years, for what could supplant it? Anyone writing in the future on Parsons will be like a pygmy standing on the shoulders of a giant.

I hope Dr. Barbas continues to give us more, perhaps next she should turn to the life of Harriet Parsons and clear up the speculations about *Harriet the Spy*?

***

Vintage Ondaatje
by Michael Ondaatje

★★★★★
And the best is yet to come.

March 9, 2006

I wish there were a way I could give a copy of this book to everyone who wants to write in America. I don't know how many years I've been reading Ondaatje's books, but it must have been in college I picked up a copy of his *Billy the Kid* book and plunged in, getting high on the strangeness and weirdness and, what I didn't immediately perceive, its Canadianness. The poetry of the book made its story come alive in dazzling ways, like great gardens of tumbleweeds springing up from the sand and beginning to roll at a word. *Vintage Ondaatje* brings together a lot of work from the beginning of his career to excerpts from his latest novel, *Anil's Ghost*, which I'm sure will rank as one of his finest achievements, even though it didn't have perhaps the cultural oomph of its predecessor, the Booker Prize winner *The English Patient*.

Even from the limited sections printed here in *VO*, *Anil's Ghost* reveals itself slowly, deliberately, as though emerging from a film of water, or through the smoke of burning sandalwood. If throughout his body of work Ondaatje has celebrated and critiqued the modern world's nomadism, *Anil's Ghost* reworks some familiar concepts and makes them new again. Cunningly the poems sometimes serve as a sort of garnish for the longer prose works, and at other times the poems themselves seem like the polished, refined quintessences of glorious mystery. I think of him as I think of D. H. Lawrence, a marvelous poet whose artillery, or arsenal, of poetic effects and knowledge is even better put to serve in the making of a series of brilliant modern novels. That's not to say I'd throw out *Birds, Beasts and Flowers* to make room for, say, *Women in Love*, I'm just saying you couldn't have the latter without the former.

I can't believe I'm the first to speak up about this book. As I say, I hope that in the future everyone will receive a copy of this book at birth. It should be an essential human right like access to clean water and no more circumcision.

Valley of the Dolls (1967)
dir. Mark Robson

★★★★★
"Well, Broadway Doesn't GO for Booze and Dope!"

March 17, 2006

After *King Kong* I suppose there was really nothing great from Hollywood's Golden Era to bring out on DVD except for this, the Mount Everest of '60s film musicals. And soon, June 13, right in time for summer, we will be able to feast our eyes at last on the most addictive cinematic treat ever made. I know there are some who say it's the worst movie ever made, and I used to be in that party as well. But every time

I watch it now, and it's always on AMC, I have new respect for the makers of the film, especially director Mark Robson, who really is trying to bring life and reality into a somewhat bizarre script. Robson has plenty of prestige credits to his name; he started working with Val Lewton and then climbed out of B movies with the noir explosion of the late '40s, when right in a row he knocked out *Champion*, *Roughshod*, *Home of the Brave*. Something of the raw power of these films clings to *Valley's* frilly edges; not just in the over-the-top voyage of Neely O'Hara down to the alleys of San Francisco's North Beach, where she staggers from bar to bar looking for a jukebox to play one of her bygone hits. "I used to be Neely O'Hara!" Now, if Brando had said that, everyone would have believed it, but Patty Duke, perhaps she was a little too young to be playing the part. Anyhow the San Francisco of *Valley of the Dolls* is long gone now, and the alleys and fleabag hotels where Neely shacks up with any stranger have been replaced by expensive, sterile boutique tourist hotels, and yet we can still identify with her panicked sense that the world has gone by a little too fast for comfort. We all wake up and wonder, "What hit us, what happened, where did it all start going wrong?"

Mark Robson was Canadian and could view American problems with a gimlet eye, an inherently cinematic one at that. Audiences shriek with pleasure at the montage sequences of *Valley*, like the one where Neely exercises frantically in a series of improbable gym outfits, while learning musical numbers and berating Martin Milner in between. The truth is we are exhilarated by Robson's mastery of one of the cinema's oldest tricks, fast motion to make life seem more precious and magical. Méliès perfected it; Robson just brings it to life once again with that incredibly earnest André Previn soundtrack.

So, about Patty Duke I'm of two minds, but basically, when I see the show now, I am always impressed by how totally she gives herself to the role, even if she can't always stretch her talent all the way across its other side. Her wisecracks and her "sexiness" are tasteless, but her singing voice is ebullient, filled with life, fun, you can imagine, yes, she might have been a Broadway star. She's so short though that occasionally you catch the set designers rearranging chairs (giving them longer legs, etc.) to make her look less like a little girl and more like a mini Bardot.

She still brings me to tears every time she's in the sanitarium and Tony's there and she has the inspired idea to sing "Come Live with

Me" directly to him and somehow he remembers who he is for a minute and manages to croak out a few bars. It doesn't seem like something the thoughtless Neely would do, but we forget she's basically good at heart, she's just been hurt too early in life.

Anne Welles (Barbara Parkins) has another fantastic montage, when she becomes the Gillian girl on TV and they dress her in dozens of colorful caftans and minidresses while the backgrounds shift from one psychedelic-light-show-based blob to the next. She maintains her Canadian cool throughout. I only really love Anne when she gets herself concerned about poor Jennifer.

Jennifer North (Sharon Tate) is exquisite in every scene. There is no question in my mind that she should have won the Oscar for playing in *Valley*. People shrugged and said, "She can't act." That's true, but only in a very limited way. Mark Robson had the patience of a saint and really helped Sharon overcome her natural shyness and false self-consciousness. The scenes where she has to act in a trailer for a French "nudie" movie while at the same time she's watching the trailer in disgust are awesome, and how about when she and Tony are leaving Lincoln Center and he falters, then collapses. I've heard from several sources that Robson filmed the scene without telling Sharon Tate that Tony was going to fall down, thus capturing what looks like honest surprise and consternation and worry. Perhaps the DVD will show the screen tests that Jean Seberg did for Jennifer. *That* would be a coup!

All this and "I'll Plant My Own Tree," "Give a Little More," and that world-beating swinging love song, "It's Impossible."

And George Jessel. "Goodbye, pussycat—meow!"

Tender Harvest Sweet Potato Baby Food
by Gerber

★★★★★
Mmm-Mmm Good

March 20, 2006

Tender Harvest is one of Gerber's bestselling lines, and I believe the sweet potatoes form their all-time bestselling specialty item. Why? Because of its tantalizing blend of organic goodness and a soft, piquant flavor to the root vegetables puréed within that makes you think of a big sweet potato pie with all the fixings. You'll be asking yourself, "Is there sugar in this?" It's as resolutely sweet as a twenties Irving Berlin standard, but if you search the ingredients from the label you'll find zero added sugar, it's all in the starch and the starch itself has this robust bite, as though if you dipped your collar into the open jar, it would emerge forever crisp and dapper, suitable for office wear.

I first was introduced to Gerber as a wee laddie, when Mom never dreamed I'd ever graduate to anything but baby food, for I would sit in my high chair and refuse to eat anything but mashed-up Gerber vegetables. If Mom, Dad, or our extended family attempted to sneak something else onto my tray, wham! It would hit the opposite kitchen wall. Back then, sweet potatoes were not on every baby's bill of fare, they were thought to be too tough for baby's delicate stomach, but since then stronger minds have prevailed. Let's face it, a baby will eat a license plate if it wants to, and many in our Native populations believe in feeding an infant a tiny amount of dirt every day, believing in the old saw that we all have to eat a peck of dirt before we die.

Disappointingly gift wrapping is not available with this item, so if you order it, be prepared for just getting the plain jar with no fancy party flavor to it. However, the label is attractive, as the inner baby inside of you will, no doubt, be letting you know as your tongue and front teeth attempt to gnaw it off the jar.

Love Story (1970)
dir. Arthur Hiller

★★★★★
Where Do I Begin?

March 23, 2006

The picture holds up—that is, you may hate it but it hardly ever looks "'60s" or "'70s." Both O'Neal and MacGraw are rather good, I can't imagine what torment Arthur Hiller put Ali MacGraw through to get her to deliver those line readings which, by and large, are pretty appropriate and hardly ever wooden as she usually is in other vehicles. I remember years later watching the miniseries *The Winds of War* in which she plays Natalie Jastrow and thinking, in retrospect, that Arthur Hiller deserved an Oscar for making her seem like a human being in *Love Story*. There's one scene in which she opens an invitation for Oliver's father to his sixtieth birthday party, a sign she thinks that her father-in-law might be melting in his opposition to their marriage, and yet she can't make Oliver understand how much this means to her and how very much she wants to go to the party.

Instead he coldly forces her to RSVP and say that they won't go. Her frustration and pain while she's dialing the phone are palpable, real. *Plus* she's dressed exquisitely, in a khaki-green miniskirt with a metallic green-and-black belt that would look perfectly in vogue today. It's the kind of scene that sticks with you, especially in a movie so universally reviled, a movie that has millions of fans and yet, for others, it seems to have gone down in history as the sappiest and stupidest movie ever made.

What is with the actor Walker Daniels, who plays Ryan O'Neal's best friend and racquetball partner? He's like a blond, somewhat stockier Illya Kuryakin. The racquetball scenes with the two men in crazily tight white-cotton shorts and T-shirts are like something out of a Bruce Weber campaign, and their subsequent shower scene should be frozen forever as a certain kind of Abercrombie & Fitch porn. The actor is appealing and yet, apparently, never made another movie before or since. You wonder why he was even in the picture at all. (He plays Ray Stratton.) The focus of *Love Story* is almost entirely on one or the other of the two leads, and Jennifer appears to have no girlfriends at all. She exists in a cocoon first of forbidden love, and then in a hospital bed, after an interlude of watching Oliver skate in a white cable-knit sweater, then they go out for cocoa, and then he asks her what they should do for the rest of the day, she says, "Let's go to the hospital." The two of them stagger in a long shot out of Central Park into a cab. It really looks as though she's going to die in the snow, her legs crumbling in on themselves like Bambi trying to stand up. When she made it into the cab I was sighing real relief. I guess somewhere along the way I started to fall for the two lovers. Her snotty, tart, foul-mouthed "attitude" didn't bother me, though it remains startlingly unsaccharine, as though Ruth Gordon should have been playing the part.

One more scene deserves admiration, the one in which Ray Milland, having written a check for Ryan O'Neal for $5,000, money to secure an abortion for another girl (or so Milland thinks), sits there ruffling his checkbook after his son has left him with the unexpected words "Thank you, Father." The expressions which play across Milland's bemused, wrinkled old face are priceless. You can read his thoughts with a radical transparency, it's a tough acting job and he excels for a minute. Otherwise he's hampered by a script filled with Freudian clichés.

Song of the Loon
by Richard Amory

★★★★★
The Real Brokeback Mountain

March 28, 2006

Even if the book wasn't attached, Michael Bronski's introduction would be reason enough to buy this edition of *Song of the Loon* by the late "Richard Amory."

But this way you get the novel too, a groundbreaking, yet oddly ultratraditional, novel—really a romance, in Northrop Frye's terms—in which the white man and the Indian meet on a field of Eros rather than Thanatos. Yes, folks, this is the real *Brokeback Mountain* in which buckskinned pioneers meet up with and pursue Indian braves on the banks of the Umpqua in a territory of long ago. Thinking about the storyline, you realize how ridiculous the plot is, for there aren't very many people on the frontier and every last one of them is a man and every last one of them is either openly or secretly a member of the Loon brotherhood. Yes, it strains plausibility but Amory's power as a writer is such that while it is taking place you don't really quibble, Sybil.

He was a great poet as well, and the book gets a haunting resonance from Amory's descriptions of American nature, its flora and fauna, in the days before heavy industry moved in to shovel it into parking lots. The skies are an amazing blue, the rivers swift and clear. Over the great forests you can hear every animal's step in the fallen twigs, and the insects hum. "Darker green, the waters of the Umpqua fell in tiny crystals from the paddle—the waves from the canoe sighed in the shadows of white elders and lacy vine maples. A pair of jays screamed high in the treetops, then streaked far into the woods, crying hoarsely."

And because it is porn, it has men galore, all of them with heavily veined, vibrant, pulsating members under their loincloths. Ephraim is a white man on the run from a miserable relationship with Montgomery, a self-hating homosexual who could only have sex when he was drunk, who showed his naked form only to taunt the besotted Ephraim. Breaking free, Ephraim is on a long canoe ride into Indian territory where he meets one man after another, each more luscious than the last, and the members of the tribe teach him about polygamy and the joys of giving up your virginity in the scented wigwam rings. If it isn't Singing Heron, it's Bear-who-dreams—even an elderly medicine man, nice to see that old people have sex in the porn of the 1960s. And finally Ephraim meets his opposite number, the dreamy Cyrus, who is so big it takes three hands to hold all of him steady.

The book comes packaged with a dossier of contemporary reviews, interviews, photos, and other invaluable documents, just as though we were reading some "classic" by Dreiser or Balzac or Cather.

It is a wonderful version of time travel and comes highly recommended by thousands and thousands of one-handed readers. What a way to kick off this promising series from Vancouver's estimable Arsenal Pulp Press in tandem with the venerable Little Sister's bookstore of BC.

Chris Marker: Memories of the Future
by Catherine Lupton

Magic Marker

April 2, 2006

It's hard for a biographer to sink her teeth into an elusive figure like Chris Marker, for Marker is famous for not allowing himself to be interviewed, or even photographed, and when fans write to him asking for a signed photo, he sends back a picture of a cat, or sometimes an owl. He seems to see himself as an owl and made a great picture recently screened here in San Francisco called *The Owl's Legacy*. And by the way, Chris Marker isn't even his real name. And no one knows for sure if the legends about his early life are true. For example, people say he was the youngest member of the French Resistance. That would certainly be romantic if it were true. But what if his background wasn't exactly as PC as the myth?

Catherine Lupton explores all these quandaries and more in her new guide to Marker's life and work. Of course the work deserves the extended treatment that she gives it. His body of work is little known in the USA, for only a few of his films have gained purchase even in the "cinematheque" set, and if you tried something like Netflix I shudder to think what would turn up, they would probably send you Gilliam's *12 Monkeys*. Marker has a tortured relationship to his own films, and in recent years has taken on the extended project of reworking, reediting, and representing his earlier films in a new, gallery-based context which is quite site specific. It would probably be easy enough to catch a showing of *La Jetée*, and here in San Francisco the later *Sans Soleil* has a lot of cult appeal, for its beautiful shots of our wonderful city are as dazzling as any Richard Lester captured in *Petulia*. But the rest of the films are a terra incognita and we are lucky to have such a careful, scrupulous, and intelligent commentator as Catherine Lupton to narrativize them so skillfully.

Of the ones she describes, I am looking forward most to seeing *If I Had Four Camels* and *Remembrance of Things to Come* (codirected with Yannick Bellon). There is one sequence in *La Jetée*, otherwise composed—like *Camels* and *Remembrance*—of still photos, held in frame for slightly varying lengths of time, in which a flash of movement rips through the film and shakes the whole world of cinema to its foundation. It is like watching movies for the very first time. Marker is quite old now, I suppose, perhaps eighty-five, so maybe he wasn't the *youngest* member of the Resistance, just the most legendary. He still sounds as though he has plenty of tricks left in his bag. As the years go by his experiments with texture and "truth" seem more and more relevant, so that as Fellini (for example) seems less and less interesting as an artist, the balance tips the other way in the direction of "nonfiction" and Chris Marker.

They All Sang My Songs
by Jack Lawrence

★★★★★
Music, Masculinity, and That Ungrateful Sylvia Fine Kaye

April 3, 2006

Well, who'da thunk it. After reading William J. Mann's magnificent 2001 tome *Behind the Screen*, the story of how gay men and lesbians influenced production on both sides of the "silver screen" during Hollywood's Golden Age, I became intrigued by Mann's mention of Anderson Lawler, sort of the Anderson Cooper of his day. A part-time actor and full-time fun boy, Lawler was seen at all the right nightclubs, often glimpsed in photographs with more famous people, bringing up the rear as it were, most often as the roommate and putative boyfriend of Paramount contractee Gary Cooper, the multi-sexual Western and glamour star. Mann didn't get to speak to many people who had actually known Andy Lawler, but now it looks like he should have called Jack Lawrence, whose new memoir gives Lawler a big play. Lawrence had many run-ins with Lawler back in the day, sexual and otherwise.

He was the "master of oral sex," Lawrence reports, going so far as to have all of his teeth removed to facilitate said mastery. "He showed me a gold cigarette case given to him by some Scandinavian royalty and inscribed, 'To the greatest mouth in the world.'" Lawrence and Lawler lived in the same apartment building (in alphabetical order I assume) and Andy was often spotted with other Paramount stars such as Kay Francis and Marlene Dietrich, women whose sexual preferences were often gossiped about.

Lawrence was born back in 1912, which makes him nearly ninety-five years old, but he's still bright as a tack and continuing to add to a list of hit songs that includes "If I Didn't Care," "All or Nothing at All," "Tenderly," as well as the English words to "Beyond the Sea" by Charles Trenet. He even managed to outlive Linda McCartney, for whom he wrote "Linda" on the day she was born, and Rosemary Clooney, one of his very best friends, a woman whose tragic story he relates all over again in one of his very saddest chapters.

Lawrence managed to adopt one of his closest "friends," which is quite a trick if you know how to do it! His book is an inspiration to all, teaching us (a) never give up, (b) don't let the bastards grind you down, (c) keep striving for perfection, and (d) above all else, have fun while you're living this life, because at the end of the day, there's no alternative but death.

PS: He doesn't have much good to say about Sylvia, the wife of Danny Kaye. If you love her, skip chapter 27 of Jack's book!

Averno
by Louise Glück

★★★★★
Sorry Seems to Be the Hardest Word

April 3, 2006

As Louise Glück reminds us, Averno is a small lake, famous for being the entrance to the underworld. Her notoriety as a poet who will spare nothing to achieve perfection takes another corner here, as she jumps from angle to angle all the while drinking in the sad, almost preternaturally pertinent life (and afterlife) of the demigoddess Persephone who, as the daughter of Demeter, wound up sold down the river to pleasure Hades in return for allowing the eternal harvest to continue here on Earth.

Averno is not only a lake but a crater, and thus the cold darkness of the moon, beyond which Pink Floyd could only sniff the nitrate, penetrates into Glück's patented rhythms. She is cold here because her subject is cold. We all know the myth of Persephone, and perhaps it is an overworked subject, but Glück manages to give it a bit of a refresher course by showing us that the US incursion into Iraq is yet another byproduct of the ever-poignant power brokerage between the forces of Demeter and the forces of hellfire. As she grows older, she realizes she just doesn't care any more about the things that obsessed her as a young, lyric poet. And she must get tired of Anne Carson continually eclipsing her reputation with classical coverage all her own, with even more quirks than Glück. But if so, she only shows an icy hauteur, for the young and healthy (and stupid), not only the students of Yale, where she sometimes teaches, but all of us who lack her enviable distance from feeling. The sheer perfection of her syllabics is daunting, but many have endured and come to a place where her yearning to be loved meets with a corresponding affection. "I want to say—I'm just not interested anymore. // I wake up thinking / you have to prepare. / Soon the spirits will give up—all the chairs in the world won't help you." This is a brief medley of lines from "Averno" itself, a poem in which a bit of Glück's own personality squeaks through the rigidly constructed dramatic monologues she has created for Persephone to speak.

In "Archaic Fragment" (page 52 of my edition), syntax itself breaks down, as does the poet's unique ability to represent the obvious: "AIAIAIAI cried / the naked mirror." When she started so many years ago, the poet Ai was a rival. Now she is almost alone on Parnassus, except for pesky Anne Carson. "I want my heart back," she cries. "I want to feel everything again—" ("Blue Rotunda," one of several rotund pieces here). She is like Robert Browning, creating a social order out of a random, often violent, vision of anarchy. She wants to "see what you're saying goodbye to." Not for nothing is NO the last syllable of—*Averno*.

Brief Encounter (1945)
dir. David Lean

★★★★★
Bigger than Life

April 3, 2006

I read Richard Dyer's book on *Brief Encounter* years before actually seeing the movie, so I watched the picture in a Dyer frame of mind, and let me say he was actually spot on in nearly every frame and in every mood. Now that's a great book. Dyer is constantly pulling at each loose thread in David Lean's apparently small-scale film to show that it contains multitudes, and that it speaks for the entire human condition, not only adulterers but the whole politicized world. Thus when Alec announces that his brother is keeping a job open for him in South Africa, we are perhaps squeamishly reminded of British empire and the way in which the entire social structure in which Laura and Alec are conducting their "private affair" is already compromised by its dependence on Black slave labor, etc.

Everywhere, Dyer shows how the movie is constantly expanding its own borders. Its theme, after all, is travel, whether psychic or actual, and the device of laying most of the actual on the confines of a train station is a neat way of bringing in modernism (invented, you know, at the same time as the steam engine, so that a characteristic of both is speed) and to show the fractured, anguished inner workings of Laura's mind and heart. How about the clues of Laura's husband's crossword puzzle? Every little thing combines to create a picture of a society at war with itself. Laura and Alec are victims in a way, and we feel for them, crying buckets at a time, but they're also implicated in a complicated web of deception, political power, and the old droit du seigneur.

How about Laura's dreams of a life spent with Alec on the far corners of the world (in a gondola in Venice, on a paradise island in the South Seas)? Doesn't she look beautiful in her alternative, imaginary life, in which she finally goes to a hairdresser who makes her look good, and the gorgeous opera gown she gets to wear—just stunning. Otherwise Celia Johnson has to look almost stereotypically dowdy and suburban—respectable in a blah way. Thank God for montage sequences! She is a radiant actress and the shame is she made so few pictures. But perhaps we wouldn't think her so extraordinary in *Brief Encounter* if she made as many as, say, Lana Turner or Bette Davis. Trevor Howard is good but just not in her class, although he does have one great scene, the one in which he hustles Laura out of the borrowed apartment when his friend comes in unexpectedly, and then he has to deal with the man's smirking disappointment in him; this he carries off beautifully, as does the other actor.

Joyce Carey and Stanley Holloway, on the other hand, I could do without. They're like Ma and Pa Kettle without the country charm, just the bumptiousness.

The Girl Who Walked Home Alone: Bette Davis, a Personal Biography
by Charlotte Chandler

★★★★★
Home Alone

April 4, 2006

You have to admire Charlotte Chandler just for the way she prints a photo of herself with Bette Davis on the back cover, and in the photo she, Chandler, is wearing either the goofiest hat ever designed for a woman, or perhaps the worst haircut an author ever received. It is the kind of upswept hairdo we associate with Lillian Russell and the Gibson Girls, but different somehow, with the texture of a minor, pale fur like rabbit or nutria. In contrast Bette Davis, stroke and all, looks like she's got it all together. What a delightful book, compiled from hours and hours of taped conversations in which Davis details all of the movies she made (eighty-seven feature films, thirteen TV movies, one miniseries) as well as the men she made along the way. Yes, some of the material is familiar, such as Davis's worship of her mentor George Arliss, and her devotion to William Wyler who, for all I know, may indeed be America's greatest director but I doubt it. However, many of the comments Davis makes here are completely new to me. And in addition, Chandler interviews many of those who worked with Davis and solicited their opinions about "this 'n' that."

I enjoyed reading George Cukor's comments on Davis's appeal. Though he never directed her in a film, he was the man who picked her out to join his stock company while still working in the stage repertory system. "Even in Rochester as young as she was, Bette had star quality. 'Do you know what the secret of star quality is?' he asked me. 'It's being irritating. The great women stars have an irritating quality, each in her own way, individually irritating. It's a part of what makes them distinctive. … [Katharine] Hepburn, Garbo, Olivia [de Havilland], with all that sweetness of Melanie, each had that oh-so-irritating quality.'" I don't know whether this says more about Cukor or the women he finds irritating, but it's something to think about, and rarely so well expressed.

Another intriguing story is the one of the "film that got away," Irving Rapper's proposed biopic (from the 1947–48 period) of Mary

Todd Lincoln, in which Davis might have played the conspiracy-ridden first lady, committed to a mental hospital after her husband was assassinated and her son died. Todd Lincoln had an unusual friendship with a Black milliner which would have been part of the script too, at least as Rapper describes it—alas, a great part for someone like Ethel Waters or Marietta Canty lost to us forever due to lackluster studio response. Instead, Davis and Robert Montgomery made *June Bride*, a horse of a different color indeed.

Did you know Greer Garson was asked to play the part of *The Nanny*? I didn't, and there's an amusing story that goes along with that (pp. 245–46).

You have to give Chandler props as well for the bizarre collection of blurbs that decorates this volume! How on earth did she land Pavarotti, Liv Ullmann, and Michelangelo Antonioni to say things like "Formidable!" on the book jacket?

Most of the stars and studio personnel interviewed by Chandler give Bette Davis nothing but good marks; on the other hand, there's always Celeste Holm, who's been practicing a dill-pickle sourness for years now when it comes to the topic of *All about Eve*. She'll outlive us all, preserved in acid like a car battery.

Meet the Fockers (2004)
dir. Jay Roach

Love of the Loved

April 12, 2006

Dragooned into watching this one, what a mistake! Although, I do agree with others that the casting of Hoffman and Streisand is out of this world. They couldn't have been better, though whoever did Streisand's makeup should be taken out to the Everglades and shot like a croc. But the same catastrophe happens to youngish Teri Polo in this film. In the first one, she looked pretty; in this one, she looks harsh and garish, older than Blythe Danner. It's like they hate her.

It must have been madness on the set as for decades people have been saying that Dustin Hoffman and Barbra Streisand were the most demanding and difficult stars in Hollywood. Has time mellowed them, or have they finally woken up and smelled the coffee, that their careers have pretty much ended as stars, sure Barbra can still sing, but for the rest, are either of them ever going to get as simpatico a handmade part as the script of *Meet the Fockers* gives them? As Bernie and Roz Focker, they shine. Everyone's good, but the movie itself just sits there, nothing happens and nobody really cares. Ben Stiller gets himself in one embarrassing situation after another, but the actor has played this role so many times before we don't even feel for him any longer.

I liked that the Fockers cherished their son so much, never made him feel inadequate, smothered him with kisses, framed his jock and his ninth-place bowling ribbons and trophies. In their eyes he's the best male nurse in the world.

De Niro's CIA thing continues to be creepy. For the next Focker picture I'd like Jay Roach to step down and somebody like Ken Loach or George Clooney to take over the director's chair and show De Niro's character invading and decimating Ghana or Ecuador or somewhere. Find the laughs there, Focker.

Bugs & Critters I Have Known
by Ann Heiskell Rickey

★★★★★
A Neglected Master

April 16, 2006

Children might like this book, but I haven't been one for many years and still I enjoyed the homespun wisdom of Ann Heiskell Rickey, a poetic talent of the order of Emily Dickinson, only strangely concentrated on one subject only: insects. Why more criticism has not been done on the work of this seminal author, I have no idea. Maybe her fierce focus on the world of insects made people think of her as a children's author, though this hardly seems fair, either to children or adults. Maybe her salty, take-no-prisoners attitude, born of a colorful life that began in Memphis, Tennessee, like Kathy Bates, Shelby Foote, Aretha Franklin, Cybill Shepherd, and Morgan Freeman, made her seem like a "Southern" and therefore regional author. But for whatever reason, this poetry has been severely undervalued and it is good to see a whole book of it in print.

It may be that Rickey herself undervalued her work. We will have to see more biographical research done on this fascinating lyric poet before we know for sure. In the meantime, we ponder the mysteries of human life through an unusual prism, the tiniest among us, the bugs. Like the mystical "no-see-um," about whom she writes "They're either too small / Or ... they're not there at all." Like e e cummings, she plays with punctuation so that each of the three dots of the ellipsis may actually represent one of the mysterious "no-see-ums," of whom no man may say for sure that they even exist.

Is there a feminist consciousness at work in this material as well? There certainly is. Rickey's encounter with the praying mantis finds her, the mantis, delicately cleaning her teeth after feeding on her own husband. That's the way of the mantis and, after a bit, you begin to see that the poet has designed this as an allegory for women's lives. With a queer grimace of understanding across species lines, the poet tells the mantis "I salute your appetite. // You're very efficient at husbandry." Elsewhere there is an eco-consciousness that predicts modern movements in bringing back the land, and an awareness of the gentle and the elemental, words that not only rhyme, they go together in waves. I don't know whether I prefer the shorter verses here or the longer, more narrative pieces. The shorter ones are certainly more quotable. "To be turned on his back / To a beetle is hateful; // Turn him back over— / He'll be truly grateful."

The Golden Rule applied, not only to the lowly insect, but to poetry as well. The illustrations, by Ardeane Heiskell Smith (a relative perhaps of the author?), are cute, sort of, and children may like them, but they're not quite in tune with the poems, they make the poems seem whimsical which they are anything but. However, I would be happy to see more of the work of Smith in other contexts.

Who They Were: Inside the World Trade Center DNA Story;
The Unprecedented Effort to Identify the Missing
by Robert C. Shaler

★★★★★
Thenody for Bagpipes

April 17, 2006

Once again, stalwart Free Press comes through with another incredibly in-depth, in fact slightly overlong, inquiry into recent history. In fact, given the substance of the investigation, and its current limbo, this isn't really history at all, but rather current events of the most pressing nature. Who was it who said reading such and such a book was like holding lightning in your hands? Reading this book is like reading human blood.

Dr. Shaler gives us a no-holds-barred account of what it was like trying to deal with the innumerable scraps of human remains found at the site of the World Trade Center disaster on September 11, 2001, in New York, and in the days, weeks, and even months afterward. Scientists and doctors, some who had never spoken to each other before, strangers, and some who were outright enemies found themselves standing shoulder to shoulder trying to use forensics to fight back, fight against prejudice, fight against violence and terror and fight against the cloud of uncertainty by trying to match each scrap, be it of brain or liver, with an actual human being believed to have died in the attacks.

He even describes the chill with which his team came to understand that, even among the morass of human material, some of these body parts were probably those of the hijackers as well.

It's not all high science either. Dr. Shaler has the vocabulary of an average New Yorker, and he is given to a descriptive obscenity when the drama of his story calls for it. "'Don't tell me we f—ked up the identification!' I said" is a typical comeback from him. But in general, the science is paramount and it helps us understand the complexity of the work involved. By and by the forensics scientists found themselves invited to the funerals of the victims they had matched, through DNA or otherwise. The families were grateful. There must be a primitive urge to want to preserve the scraps of your own loved one's bodies, even miniscule ones, for there were funerals for mere fingers. Reminds me of the way Catholic churches in my youth were erected around mere "relics" embedded in the tabernacles. Dr. Shaler's writing is simple and moving on such occasions, as though Hemingway had willed his genes to a top scientist and bureaucrat:

"We stood around the grave site and waited. Soon, the bagpipers began playing and there was a short ceremony. The sun was shining and it was warm. I felt like I belonged."

The $64 Tomato: How One Man Nearly Lost His Sanity, Spent a Fortune, and Endured an Existential Crisis in the Quest for the Perfect Garden
by William Alexander

★★★★★
Garden of Eden

April 30, 2006

Working all day at a nearby research institute, sometimes Bill Alexander would have to gird his loins when he came home at sundown and still had all his gardening to do. He and his physician wife owned a patch of land neighboring boys used as a baseball field, but Alexander always had weekend dreams of turning it into a combination orchard and flower garden. Under the direction of a comically sketched land-scape designer, he made his dreams come true, despite the skepticism of his sitcom-like kids, a teen girl and a slacker boy named Zach, characterized as living in a dank room filled with unwashed laundry. The kids don't really care—on the outside; but inside their hearts swell with pride as their dear old dad tames a recalcitrant patch of land into a Robert Creeley–like garden of which Elizabeth Lawrence might have been proud.

His wife likes it too. Digging in the garden is like horticultural Viagra, and when he really gets going he rushes into the house and grabs her. "By the time I was done, I felt strangely, strongly aroused. That night, the smell of pollen still fresh in my nostrils, I made passionate, urgent love to my mystified (but appreciative) wife." When I was a teen, we called this "TMI"—too much information—but it's a nice reminder of the benefits of married life.

There's a sinister side to gardening as well, as befits a hobby so elemental, and Alexander meets a strange contractor with a bizarre resemblance to Christopher Walken. Elsewhere he characterizes his battle with squirrels as "like living in Hitchcock's *The Birds*, only with squirrels."

Alexander is not what you'd call an outstanding writer, and some of his sentences bunch themselves up like caterpillars, but at his best he provides an insight into the myriad reasons men like to garden, and as a bonus he has a graceful way of inserting potted history lessons into his anecdotes. Discussing how difficult it is to grow apples organically in the northeast, he manages to bring in both Johnny Appleseed and his own horticultural hero, Thomas Jefferson. Did you know that Saint Francis of Assisi was the one who first staged the now-popular nativity crèche scenes, and that he used actual animals to play the sheep, donkeys, and lambs? And Alexander also can turn a poetic phrase: the first apple trees to bloom become "a merry explosion of pink and white popcorn."

Finally, you'll laugh hearing about his father's ways with growing apples that bore little labels bleached into their skins, so that neighbors and relatives could have their own personalized apples, the "local community's version of being invited to Truman Capote's Black and White Ball."

The Hand That Rocks the Cradle (1992)
dir. Curtis Hanson

★★★★★
"Take Heart, Fair Days Will Shine"

May 10, 2006

Startlingly effective and bewildering, *The Hand That Rocks the Cradle* uses a variety of Seattle and Tacoma locations to great effect. Though isn't that the arboretum from San Francisco's Golden Gate Park standing in for Claire's workplace? We saw this when it first came out, and viewing it again you get sucked right back in, due to a potent combination of fine, horrid yet efficient writing and a handful of strong performances. Little Madeline Zima puts our present-day diva,

Dakota Fanning, to shame, with some quiet, subtle work worthy of the Juvenile Oscar—if only the Academy still issued them! Whatever happened to Madeline Zima? She must be twenty-one by now, I wonder if she's still working or did the trauma of working with Rebecca De Mornay drive her away from acting? With her big eyes and timid smile, Zima is outstanding as a child trapped in a manipulative relationship with a psychopathic nanny (Rebecca De Mornay). We see how easily Peyton, the nanny, is able to deflect the little girl's love away from her real mother, just by pushing the right buttons.

What to make of the Ernie Hudson character? Hudson is absolutely terrific, and has never again been used so well, but the whole "Black retarded friend who adores the white family" thing leaves a bad taste in the viewer's mouth. I don't really care for being politically correct, but the scene where the Bartel family gives him a new bicycle might well have been considered old hat even in the heyday of D. W. Griffith. At the end of the movie I wanted him to stand back and let Peyton destroy Annabella Sciorra, that would have served her right.

The music scoring I found very beautiful. The composer managed to find exactly the right aria, Arthur Sullivan's "Poor Wand'ring One" (from *The Pirates of Penzance*), to express something of Peyton's fragile mental state—and to let us discover that, beneath the malice, trembles a frightened and abandoned soul. Claire keeps playing this track over and over as though unaware that a real-life "wand'ring one" was under her roof. Later, at the very end, this music is used to underscore Ernie Hudson's last scene. You almost feel that the music knows more about the solitary and the traumatic than the director ever dreamed of.

Julianne Moore looks like an anorexic in her exquisite, chic, and expensive outfits. I wonder why the screenwriters didn't think of a plot in which she and Matt McCoy *are* actually having an affair, which Peyton finds out about and uses against them? As it stands the story rests on a mass of unconvincing coincidences. How on earth could Peyton arrange it so that Claire and Julianne Moore would go out on a girl date together on the very afternoon of the evening in which Moore and McCoy are planning a surprise birthday party? But without that, there's no way her plot could have worked. Oh well! And as another reviewer has noted, Annabella Sciorra, dimwitted throughout the whole first part of the movie, has a brilliant flash of deduction at the end which makes hash out of her characterization. Visiting Dr. Mott's house, she does more than put two and two together—she puts one together. Then she races home and slaps Rebecca De Mornay across the floor. Lawsuit, anyone?

Black Widow
by Patrick Quentin

★★★★★
Like *All about Eve* with Murder

May 10, 2006

Patrick Quentin was one of the finest US mystery writers of the twentieth century, although his influence doesn't seem particularly prevalent today. Maybe his most important development was the close, ugly examination of family relations he pioneered in the novels he wrote under the pseudonym Jonathan Stagge, which he then melded into the glitzy show business tales of his greatest sleuths, the producer-actress star couple Peter and Iris Duluth. Later in life, Hugh Wheeler, who wrote as Patrick Quentin, abandoned the field altogether and turned his talents to a series of Broadway libretti for Stephen Sondheim and others, thus ensuring his immortality among show queens, probably the only ones who really appreciated *Black Widow* in the first place. He wrote *A Little Night Music* and *Sweeney Todd*, and took on the complicated task of revising Lillian Hellman's book for *Candide*, among others.

Black Widow is a pip, and Peter and Iris emerge through the wringer of suspected adultery, recrimination, soul-destroying jealousy, and misogyny fit for a Strindberg play. We just finished watching the movie version, in which "Duluth" has been changed to "Denver" (maybe "Duluth" was judged too hard to pronounce?) but which otherwise follows Quentin's original pretty well. Van Heflin plays Peter and the incomparably beautiful, though here strangely muted, Gene Tierney is Iris. Peter gets involved with a pixie-like waif who dreams of being a writer called Nancy Ordway, here played by Peggy Ann Garner, all grown up and acting psycho underneath her Brillo-like blond blob. "Are you a good writer?" asks Peter, and Nancy considers, while spreading her palms down the balustrade of a fantastic NY penthouse with Central Park views to die for. "My professor said it's OK to write like Somerset Maugham, and OK to write like Truman Capote," she replies drily, "but just not both at the same time." Pretty slick for 1954! I can imagine audience members in the know shivering with sophistication.

Ginger Rogers is not especially suited for the part of Carlotta, a Helen Lawson type with a rapier-like wit and a sheer contempt for everyone not on her scale of joie de vivre, a star who keeps a mousy little husband man (Reginald Gardiner) as a badge of romantic success. She eats every scene she's in and otherwise lounges around in a succession of extremely bright New Look gowns and coats. Utterly amazing!

The movie loves New York and it shows. Most astonishing is a long scene with Hilda Simms, the amazing Black actress who played Joe Louis's wife in her one starring Hollywood role, a year or so before taking the part of Anne, a hatcheck girl at a darkened Manhattan lounge. What's odd is that the movie doesn't seem to notice her race. It's like total color-blind casting, twenty years or more before the notion took hold elsewhere. It's not that she sets the screen on fire, although she does, it's just that the production is so casual about giving her a role where she doesn't have to "represent" her race and can just be a knowing, sexy, reproving, hardworking woman with the key to the mystery up her sleeve.

Ministry of Fear (1944)
dir. Fritz Lang

★★★★★
Ding-Dong Bell

May 14, 2006

Maybe Graham Greene didn't like this movie, but he was like every other author and thought his every word was gold. The movie skips all the dreary insane-asylum scenes but one and goes straight to the heart of things, in the county fair, or fête, a concept of which people in the USA probably were saying, "What did he say? Fate?" No, it's a fête, and Milland walks in directly after having been let out of the asylum, hearing the music at the train station while buying a ticket out of Lembridge. He asks the station agent, "Where's the music coming from?" and when told it's the fête, he asks if he could leave his clothes and suitcases on a little bench outside the station while he investigates, has a little innocent fun after being cooped up for two years having killed his poor wife in a Dr. Death sort of provide-me-with-poison-please-darling murder case. In Graham Greene's novel, of course, the hero was headed for a brothel, not a funfair, but the movies of the 1940s had to sanitize things a bit.

Watching this scene, with the ticket agent saying "Oh sure, just leave all your earthly belongings on this bench, nobody will take them," we just gazed in astonishment. Those were different times! They may have had blitz bombings and Nazi spy rings and people pretending to be blind just to make off with your cake, but at least you could leave your bags on a bench and no one would steal them. In general, *Ministry of Fear* is an appealing blend of pastoral, not to say candy-box, innocence, with a moral squalor best conveyed by the decadent beauty of the male leads: Dan Duryea's Dorian Gray smirk; Ray Milland's poetic, nearly Rimbaud charm and effervescence, as though he were waiting for Jean Cocteau to take him out for some opium; and then the German-stud suavity of Carl Esmond, who plays Willi, the head of the charity Mothers of the Free Nations, the brother of the woman Milland comes to love.

Other points of interest include the fabulous apartment of Madame Bellane. Never seen anything like it. A painter herself apparently, she has a fantastic collection of surrealist art and primitive masks of African peoples. Even her doorbell is a work of art. I can't even describe it, but where most people have a doorbell she got Picasso to paint her door to conceal the bell as the nostril to one of his cubist-style multieyed profiles of a beautiful woman, I guess herself. When Milland presses the bell I thought the whole of London would blow up. It is extraordinary set design, hallucinatory like the best of Busby Berkeley.

And the low point has to be Marjorie Reynolds's Austrian accent. Weren't there any other actresses working at Paramount who could have at any rate dubbed it in for her? After a while, though, I gave up hooting at it and indeed developed a fondness for her. She kept slugging at it, as though eventually in twenty years she might get it right. She had courage, and that's really all you need in the movies.

Step
by George Albon

★★★★★
The Passion of George Albon

May 16, 2006

Step is an intriguing project in which the author of *Empire Life* and last year's prizewinning *Brief Capital of Disturbances* tries on a long poem. Each of its many stanzas has three lines, and he groups three stanzas together, setting each "poem" off from its brothers by an enlarged blank space. So that every page has two of these trios in it, and when you flip through the book like a deck of cards, you won't see a whole hell of a lot of variation in the way each page looks. Frankly, my heart sank when I saw this, because I was afraid I would forget where I was, in a landscape of identical trees or sign-posts. (There are page numbers, though, finally fulfilling the function for which primitive printers devised them—to help us tell apart the different pages from each other.) (This simple revelation of purpose is one of the things that make reading *Step* such a beatific experience.)

But I shouldn't have worried about confusion, much less bore-dom, for Albon really knows how to write. I saw him read from this work at City Lights Bookstore last month, really struck by how forceful he can be while reciting these apparent fragments, in which subject and verb are often curtailed afore, so that the object gets laminated, shines bright once you gaze on it. He really believes—not that there's no humor in the poetry. And he's not the sort of poet who depends on brand names, he's not pop per se, you won't find Jell-O and Kleenex in these lines. They've been scared out by Albon's passion! You don't find product placement in Carl Dreyer's films, do you, and just so the markers of the present are covered up, like cloths thrown over birdcages at night to shush the parrot's screech. There's Greek—I guess—"topos" and "derma," and there's a Hopkins-esque neologism here and there—"mothershape," for example, because the expressiveness of these little stanzas ensures that mere word is not enough. Even the letters of the alphabet appear almost as characters, "the vee," "the ess."

I've only read the book a few times (and listened to Albon read from it for about twenty minutes once) and the patterns are slow to come to the surface, but in the meantime it's the sort of poetry you could flip a penny into, make a wish, and it might come true. It has potential, it embodies the possible. It's actually just part of my life now.

The cover painting, with its arrows flipping every which way, its childlike figures like unbaked gingerbread boys, its hatch marks like the side of Archie Andrews's head, is like *Hellzapoppin'* compared to the somber pastoral within, so don't go judging this book by its cover and you'll be fine.

Elia Kazan: A Biography
by Richard Schickel

★★★☆☆
The Richard Schickel Story

June 4, 2006

Schickel adds nothing to the telling of Elia Kazan's story that wasn't already written up better by Kazan himself in his huge memoir *A Life*, except for constant interjections of Schickel's own opinions on everything under the sun. He (Schickel) thought that Juliette Binoche was great in *The Unbearable Lightness of Being*. He (Schickel) disapproved of the Oscars handed out to Roberto Benigni. Who on earth cares about these irrelevant opinions? Schickel is in love with the sound of his own voice, and somewhere in the shredded coleslaw of his prose, a decent book lies unavailable to us, about the real Elia Kazan.

Provocative? Yes, crazily so. The movies of Kazan you think are great Schickel finds overrated, and the "little" pictures you always forget are Schickel's masterpieces—*A Face in the Crowd*, for example. He compares it to Alexander Mackendrick's *Sweet Smell of Success* in favorable terms, telling us that *Sweet Smell* had a script "half-written by Clifford Odets." What do you think that means, "half-written"? He makes it sound worse than it is, but that's his *Time* magazine speak coming to the fore. Richard

Schickel can't write a sentence that doesn't sound like a picture caption.

And sure, he can make Elia Kazan sound like a hero for naming names to HUAC in January 1952, but that's just special pleading. "The scapegoats were all eventually welcomed back, often enough as heroes, while the committee's informers are the ones now scapegoated by polite, liberal-minded society." That's a cynical way of thinking about it, but why does Schickel say "often enough" instead of just plain "often" in the sentence above? Is it just plain hasty writing, or could he be even meaner spirited than he seems at first glance?

And why so nasty about Barbara Loden, Kazan's second wife? My God, you'd think she had started World War II. He's so unrelenting against her.

The whole book is about Richard Schickel and how he wrote Kazan's acceptance speech and assembled the clip show when the Academy gave him the special award. It's about how Schickel felt when the ceremony turned into an embarrassing dud. It's about how Schickel knew Raymond Massey pretty well and often heard him rage against James Dean. How old is Schickel anyway? He looks pretty good in the jacket photo, only the nose and the comb-over would betray he's got to be about ten zillion years old.

Always Magic in the Air: The Bomp and Brilliance of the Brill Building Era
by Ken Emerson

★★★★★
Crying in the Streets

June 6, 2006

His analysis of individual tunes is outstanding, and even when my ranking of certain songs differs from his, I find I learn something new from his talking me through them. I'm still not convinced about the majesty of Leiber and Stoller, and about Pomus and Shuman I'm still conflicted, but once the book gets into the slightly younger generation Emerson really gets into a groove, perhaps it's the Phil Spector touch. His descriptions of the making of "Then He

Kissed Me" and "Da Doo Ron Ron" rank with the best music writing ever, noting how Spector banished more grown-up voices for the nasal, childish sounds of La La Brooks, the Crystals' "baby" (only fifteen when she cut these tracks), to match what he calls the "adolescence" of these Greenwich-Barry numbers, in which gratification must be instant. And the nonsense syllables of "Da Doo Ron Ron," placeholders originally for lyrics never written, were frozen by Spector who told them don't bother finishing the lyric, it's fine just the way it is. Was he already in love with Veronica Bennett, whose nickname was echoed in these syllables?

At the end of the day we might prefer the insistent obsessions of the Barry-Greenwich tunes over the social realism of Barry Mann and Cynthia Weil, but there's always another day to change your mind on. Emerson writes, for the most part, with open-minded clarity that's closely linked to passion. These records are great, he just hopes you understand why, and better yet, how.

We see how pathetic Burt Bacharach's career was before he met Dionne Warwick, and I imagine this is a controversial thesis for Emerson to take, for hitherto he has always come to rock with a mantel of class, the "class" of having been Marlene Dietrich's arranger, conductor, love interest. Emerson pooh-poohs that notion, shows what a constrained and limited position he had worked himself into—actually I think he argues this too far, for his argument depends on arguing Dietrich's irrelevance, which just isn't the case. Surely working with Dietrich prepared him for recording "The Look of Love" with Dusty Springfield?

Howard Greenfield, the gay one, isn't given the full biographical treatment by Emerson. I wonder why? Of course he's been dead for many years, but he remains a shadowy player here next to the full-blown, vivid portraits Emerson paints of Cynthia Weil, Gerry Goffin, Ellie Greenwich, Mort Shuman, even minor figures like Tony Orlando or Neil Diamond. Why? Is there still some secret that he's not supposed to be telling us? Will we have to wait till after the death of Neil Sedaka to find out what sort of person, what sort of writer, Greenfield was? As is, it's the one part of the book that I feel Emerson is a little bit afraid of going there …

Vanished Act: The Life and Art of Weldon Kees
by James Reidel

★★★★★
Que Viva James Reidel

June 12, 2006

Last night at the Cinematheque here in San Francisco, we watched
a slew of Weldon Kees films. Guest curator Jenni Olson last year
turned an elegiac tribute to a dead friend, Mark Finch, into a feature documentary called *The Joy of Life*, which spoke in a spare and
moving way about people drawn to the Golden Gate Bridge, like
Finch, to take their own lives. She told us that in the course of her
research she came across the life, work, and of course the disappearance of Weldon Kees, whose car was found on the north end of
the bridge on July 18, 1955, and that she found herself drawn to
his work as both poet and filmmaker in the early San Francisco film
avant-garde. (Not much mention made of his painting.) Only
Olson, with her myriad connections to a hundred archives, could
have pulled together such a program, which was billed as the first
retrospective of Kees's fugitive film work.

Since he completed only one film, the program was supplemented by other shorts on which he had contributed his many
talents. James Broughton's classic *Adventures of Jimmy* began the
show, a nice print with Kees's barrelhouse piano score. Broughton
was in full Buster Keaton / Chaplin mode with this short, in which
he leaves a run-down cabin in the wilderness and goes to San Francisco to find a wife, or possibly a boyfriend, or one of each perhaps.
It's sort of coy, and Broughton's not a great silent-film actor, but it's
cute and the audience lapped it up. Olson followed this up with two
of Weldon Kees's "data" films, both from 1952, *Hand-Mouth Coor-
dination* and *Approaches and Leavetakings*, also silent, in grainy black
and white. Frankly, these left me a little mystified. Why on earth
were they made? In *HMC*, we see a harried blond mother go
through an entire day taking care of an adorable boy who looks to
be about fifteen months old—feeding him, bathing him, putting on
his diapers, while four older kids look on from the background and
attempt to steal scenes from the baby. Kees and Gregory Bateson are

sometimes shown in the corners of the apartment, cameras held up to their faces. But why? It seems so pointless and "Mass-Observation." The second "anthropological film" was lensed by Kees with a camera hidden in his valise, and documented ordinary Oakland and Berkeley citizens saying hello and goodbye. Kees (presumably) supplies some winsome captions for each brief scenelet, some of them lasting only a few seconds. In one of the scenes, laid in front of UC Berkeley's Wheeler Hall, an imposing professor walks across some steps with a brace of burly grad students, and a sharp-eyed member of our audience identified the faculty guy as George R. Stewart, the novelist (*Storm*) and author of the classic work on California's Loyalty Oath *The Year of the Oath* (1950).

Hotel Apex screened next, the only completed film Kees signed, a fascinating and beautiful poetic impression of a run-down boarding house badly in need of demolition. The camera glides and rises through the ruined space, stopping to dolly in here and there at odd-shaped remnants, a Dinah Washington poster, a scattering of beer caps, a soaked paperback copy of Phoebe Atwood Taylor's 1931 *The Cape Cod Mystery*. We wonder about the people who once lived in these broken spaces, how they came to run out on their old possessions; the Hotel Apex has some of the mystery of the *Marie Celeste*. Time heals everything, people say, but the displacement of the hotel remains, still, eerily vigorous, nearly a shriek.

Then we saw a color film, William Heick's *The Bridge*, on which Kees acted as a cameraman. Bizarrely it's a series of impressive "Wow!" shots of the Golden Gate Bridge, swamped in fog, glittering in the sun, viewed from a bird's eye view above, sometimes from the great steel pilings at its base, while a "movie voice" from the period recites, really skips through, a lot of Hart Crane's poem *The Bridge*. We see Kees scurrying down a steep slope balancing a tripod; it's spooky, the way he seems to risk tumbling into the rough white surf. I thought Hart Crane's verse really beautiful, but you could tell some people were having a hard time following it, especially the way it was enunciated, in these rapid-fire "You Are There" sub-Gielgudisms. Finally the lights came halfway up and we listened to a KPFA broadcast of Weldon Kees's own radio show, which he cohosted with a friend, Michael Grieg. This episode was recorded shortly after Kees's disappearance, and Grieg puzzles it out over the air, playing a song

("Daybreak Blues") that Kees wrote and reading one of Kees's longer, most interesting poems, "The Journey." Grieg's got a great voice, like Vincent Price crossed with sandpaper, and he made "The Journey" sound like a million bucks (funny thing, though, he pronounces "Formica" with a strange accent on the first syllable, as though along the lines of "fornicate.") And the grief and bewilderment of Kees's suicide you could eat with a spoon. It was very touching. Jenni Olson announced that she could never have begun compiling this program without the help of James Reidel's incredibly detailed 2003 biography, *Vanished Act*. I read *Vanished Act* shortly after its publication and to this day it remains, to my mind, the very model of a proper artistic biography. He makes huge claims for his man, but he's got the resources and the skills to back them up. You come away from his book thinking that, despite Dana Gioia, despite Donald Justice, whatever, Weldon Kees deserves all the scrutiny and commentary he's been getting. Maybe he wasn't the world's greatest filmmaker, but we have only these bits and pieces to ponder, like reading fortunes from tea leaves. Anything might have happened, and Reidel makes you feel that; he—Reidel—is a poet of endings and beginnings. Once you start reading it, be prepared to have it haunt you the rest of your born days.

The Delicate Prey, and Other Stories
by Paul Bowles

★★★★★
Postcolonial Blues

June 21, 2006

DP contains most of Bowles's classic gems, and it provides a good introduction to the kind of thing you will be encountering when you get old enough to take on *The Sheltering Sky* and *Let It Come Down*. A musician by training, he took on writing as a sort of hobby, then became obsessed with it to the neglect of his music, as he relates in his breezy, atypical memoir *Without Stopping*, written much later in life when he had attained a sort of Buddha-like, or Burroughs-like, I-don't-care attitude about the things that had troubled him earlier. When this book first appeared, it must have been one tremendous shock after another, and a few of the stories still carry an explosive charge.

One of the best tales seems to be an allegory of Bowles's progress from music to writing. In "A Distant Episode," a professor of music gets abducted by desert bandits who remove his tongue and "train" him into becoming a dancing clown, like a monkey owned by a hurdy-gurdy man. They exhibit him widely, and his brain is so badly damaged that he is content with his retardation, knowing only the blows of his captors, until one afternoon when he accidentally hears some bars of Western music. He starts to cry and bawl his head off, he knows not why. It is a thoroughly repulsive story, but it displays beautifully the ambiguity with which Bowles viewed his long-ago music career, which he must after a while have remembered only through a thousand veils.

"Pages from Cold Point" is pretty strong too, not to say ripe. In Belize in the Caribbean, a wealthy American gay man comes to stay in a seaside mansion with his sixteen-year-old son, Racky, the apple of his eye. What he doesn't know is that Racky is the bad seed incarnate, like a male Lolita, sex in dungarees. Racky enjoys going to every man and boy on the island, Black or white, and seducing them, for he is so lovely no one would say no to him. Eventually the elders and the women decide to put the hammer down and warn the dad to take his slutty boy off the island or trouble will ensue. You won't believe what happens next, but it is worthy of a great porn movie. Radley Metzger might have made you believe it, but for Paul Bowles it was just another day in the life.

Kate's Cake Decorating: Techniques and Tips for Fun and Fancy Cakes Baked with Love
by Kate Sullivan

★★★★★
Controversial Sampler

June 21, 2006

This is the book that has split the community of cake decorators right down the middle, from stem to stern. Half of us think that

Sullivan's craft, while passionate and inspiring, shows signs of sloppy, careless finish, while the other half holds her up as the exemplar of a new kind of fun styling that hasn't been seen in decades. I decided to make up my mind by ordering two copies of her book, one to give to my mother, one to keep for myself. We challenged each other to find the best and worst recipes and tips in Sullivan's opus.

Yes, the color photography is sometimes garish, nothing like the elegant Cecil Beaton–inspired photographs that sparkle and illuminate the "cake books" of her close contemporary Lindy Smith, whose brittle, icy designs have given her the reputation of a modern-day Klimt in frosting. And yet Smith could never have completed, nor even conceived of, some of Sullivan's neoexpressionistic "portrait cakes," such as the one of Elvis which is wiggy enough to have been featured permanently at Graceland, maybe sunk in intaglio form right into Elvis's tombstone. One responds to the sheer frivolity and nuttiness and, yes, the love that Sullivan exudes from every pore of her body. Even her somewhat portentous crush on fondant shows us that, deep underneath her smooth surface, great feelings roil up within.

Her tips are always helpful, and most of the recipes are rather good, very rich of course, but you don't spread gold dust over cream cheese filling and expect a low-calorie plate. This is cake, after all, and it's supposed to be bad for you! These cakes might have decorated the Technicolor visions of Maria Montez and Jon Hall in their Universal classics of the 1940s such as *Cobra Woman* and *Gypsy Wildcat*. My mother and I both agreed that there are no bad recipes, just bad critics.

1001 Beds: Performances, Essays, and Travels
by Tim Miller, ed. Glen Johnson

★★★★★
All about the Body

June 23, 2006

Editor Glen Johnson has done what I would have thought was just about impossible, between covers, and that is to bring the Tim Miller experience in extraordinary and full dimension. I've seen several of Miller's performances and despaired of finding a book that would adequately capture the range of his interests and imagination, let alone something of the fire of his person, his charisma perhaps. But here it is at last, the real, the unexpected, and the splendid thing. Cannily Johnson deploys a full spectrum of the different sorts of documents that make up a man, not only the texts of the performances, but occasional prose, some candid interviews, full-on essays, and a barrage of photographs, some of them very beautiful indeed, some just slapstick perhaps. Like Red Skelton, Tim Miller has always been about more than the tears of a clown, he's really all about the body, even the body of comedy. *1001 Beds*, as its title implies, is rooted in the body and its vain attempts to rest between taking on another, often agonizing day. The effort of living, particularly in the benighted political circumstances of our world today, exhausts the electorate, and Miller is honest and forthright about his attempts to harness energy to fight the combine. Some strategies work, some don't, but Miller's fearless and in the end that's what really matters.

He began in the golden age of performance artists (remember Daryl Hannah in *Legal Eagles*) with some spectacular and colorful, and very personal, work about growing up gay in Southern California, often with a partner, John Bernd, another very talented young fellow. Around him, like popcorn, issues began exploding in the heat. AIDS and ACT UP claimed his attention and his work became even more pointedly political, leading to the famous revocation of his NEA grant by right-wing forces marshaled in panic and cruelty. Freedom of expression, another huge issue, became the focus of subsequent work. Finally his meeting with the Australian artist and poet Alistair McCartney sparked a new avatar of the poet of gay immigration rights, for McCartney is still very much a victim of antiquated policy and lives and writes without security, homeland or otherwise.

These issues all come alive in the pages of the book. I asked some of my students, who had never seen Miller perform, to read one of his essays, and it electrified them. It soon became clear that, just like Arthur Miller, no relation I assume, was the "thinking man's playwright," now Tim Miller has assumed a similar status, the objective correlative for the images and emotions not only of gay men, but for a Kinsey-like spectrum of embodied world citizens.

Poems I Wrote While Watching TV
by Travis Jeppesen

★★★★★
"A Ticket to the Dream"

June 27, 2006

Physically a very handsome book, and the drawings and watercolor work by Jeremiah Palecek show an eccentric wit and a pallid dash, and yet the real revelation here will be Travis Jeppesen's poetry. Jeppesen lives in Prague, and writes in English, like an angel. Those who have read his critical writing, or his debut novel *Victims*, are in for yet another treat, but I should say first off that his poetry isn't quite what you'd expect, it's much more gestural and surrealist than his prose writing and for that reason alone sometimes a bewildering experience, like being thrown into a maelstrom without so much as a paddle's worth of context.

Was he watching TV when he wrote these poems? Maybe they exhibit some of the rapid-fire disconnect between image and line that you feel when zapping a remote from channel to channel, and yet paradoxically the suite of "TV Haiku," for sure the ones most obviously about the television experience, are the most placid and focused, like old-school haiku with the requisite number of syllables. It's elsewhere, away from the TV, that the madness rises to high intensity, as image upon image rains down from a mackerel sky upon the reader, like crockery from a high window, so that the experience of reading something like his "Pippi Longstocking" poem is like dodging a poisonous hailstorm. Keeps you on your mark, this writing does. If J. G. Ballard had turned to poetry while in the middle of writing *Crash* and *Atrocity Exhibition*, he still would have been lucky to have hit the heights of *PIWWWTV*.

I didn't cotton 100 percent to "The Bath," and yet it seems an experiment worth taking, perhaps a sort of cut-up of bygone diction, or applying prose breaks to an ornate, bourgeois prose? And if ever I meet Jeppesen I'll ask him why he doesn't get someone else to write the titles of his poems, for he is invariably bad at them, in the sense that none of his titles come anywhere near the quality of his best poems, and that's an unusual weakness in one otherwise so talented.

Outside of these picayune complaints, I bow down very low to this amazing, near-hallucinatory poetry. He makes me tremble. This past year we lost the surrealist master Philip Lamantia, but from far off in Czechoslovakia his spirit rises again in this new boy.

Straightening Boar Hair Brush (Teal)
by HAT

★★★★★
On the Straight and Narrow

July 1, 2006

Ever have one of those days when your alarm clock rings and you bound out of bed and even before you get to a mirror you know your hair is out of control? Some call it "bedhead," but on me it's like the enchanted broccoli forest. For years I've been looking for a cheap, elegant solution to the problem of overnight curl, and now thanks to the good people at HAT I think I've found it. Their straightening brush is one of the most well-designed products in my medicine cabinet, and the satisfying click you hear when you lock your hair into place with it reminds you of the high hat Charlie Watts used to set "Honky Tonk Women" roaring into the ether.

The color? Well, who doesn't like a bit of teal, and it's bright enough so you can find it, even when you're as hungover as I used to get—you know, when your ears are still ringing and the floor is still swaying and the last thing you want is something heavy, like a comb, passing over one's scalp. The HAT brush acts quickly, you grab a handful of hair, secure it in the provided ridge, click the brush closed, and then scrape away, and voila, within seconds even the most recalcitrant hank of hair (or cowlick) is tamed utterly. If you have naturally curly hair this would be even more useful. All right, I don't like to think that boars were killed to make this brush, but I keep thinking, "Maybe they just followed some boar trails in the Ardennes Forest and picked up the loose hair like pine needles."

Look me up sometime, I'll be the guy with the perfectly groomed head of hair thanks to the HAT Straightening Boar Hair Brush in teal.

Jane: A Murder
by Maggie Nelson

★★★★★
An "Orgy of Unthinkable Fire"

July 3, 2006

Jane's diaries are extraordinary; oh, maybe they're not but Maggie Nelson frames them in an extraordinarily telling manner, abstracting their most beautiful or witty parts so that often she comes across as a teenage Marquise du Deffand. Considering that Nelson had only two journals to work with, written many years apart, she mines them wonderfully, and part of the heartbreak is realizing how much Jane has grown in the gap of missing years between 1960 and 1966. Sometimes the older Jane strikes a note of spiritual exhaustion, like Françoise Sagan last year at Marienbad: "Cigarettes— one after the other; why?" And the 1966 Jane sometimes seems a little bit like the questioning heroine of the *Go Ask Alice* diaries, a far cry from her innocent days of youth, in which it was bliss to be alive.

And yet what Nelson does with this material is in the end a fitting memorial for a woman we feel we might almost know, except an evil spirit came down on Michigan and began stamping out its most beautiful citizens. Nelson has attained a niche in both true crime and poetry; has any other writer really been in this crazy space before? The life that she had, born in the wake of this terrible murder, has been a haunted one; for better or for worse poetry got a hold of her. *Jane: A Murder* is nearly a novel, for it has a strong subplot that culminates in the early death, revealed in "The Burn," of her father, described almost as an apple, strawberry, or rose. "I remember thinking he looked really, really red," a classmate tells Maggie. "Like he was about to burst."

The trope of bursting is everywhere in these plain and wonderfully turned poems. Ripeness is all, a surreal ripeness like the bright beating bead at the end of the thermometer. A friend recommended this book for its therapeutic value, as though Nelson had healed herself, or her family, through writing it all out, but I don't think that it's about rescue per se, it's more about noticing how vivid it all is, life, death, going away, coming back, the pulsating world.

*The Man Who Invented Rock Hudson: The Pretty Boys
and Dirty Deals of Henry Willson*
by Robert Hofler

★★★★★
Cuff Links, Plate Glass, Bran Muffin ...

July 6, 2006

Robert Hofler writes in strokes of bold lightning, like disco music mirrored on a spinning ball. What seems like disorganization is really only one facet appearing in a bright light, then another, then another, until an entire organization is exposed: in this case, the ways in which the major studios and the top talent agents of 1940s and 1950s Hollywood worked hand in glove to insure a Cold War gender balance that was fake from top to bottom.

You won't be able to make up your mind whether or not Henry Willson, Hofler's hero, really did sell Tab Hunter and Rory Cochrane down the river in order to protect the reputation of his greatest star, Rock Hudson—or was it the big boys at Universal who were behind this "dirty deal." Ironically, as Hofler demonstrates, leaking to *Confidential* the facts behind Rory Cochrane's juvenile delinquency made America warm up to the big bruiser a bit more—he became a "hero" after the facts came out and, like Robert Mitchum, his reputation as a colorful brawler was only accentuated by his prison record. And yet Tab Hunter, arrested for disorderly conduct at a pajama party for guys only, was shunned and demoted as soon as the studios found their use for him dimming.

Willson made up a lot of cool names! He should have been a poet, and indeed his names have the touch of poetry, even the failed names like "Race Gentry." Imitators thought of "Ty Hardin" and "Rip Torn," but they lacked the true Willson touch. *Variety* reporter Hofler notes that comedienne Kaye Ballard had a contemporary routine about those fabulous names, in which Willson would unveil his new lineup of beefcake—"Grid Iron, Cuff Links, Plate Glass, and Bran Muffin."

He seems to have gotten so many to speak with him, some of them candidly, some sort of candidly, some you know are lying! It's odd that most of the former Willson boys deny ever having had sex with their boss, the voracious monster of sex harassment. I can't blame them in a way, but don't you love the story in which one fellow refuses to bend over for Willson, and the agent flings him into a car and drives to an apartment building in Hollywood, thrusts him into the elevator, up the stairs, banging down an apartment door, past a puzzled roommate, saying to the recalcitrant stud "You're no prize, I'm going to show you something gorgeous." And they walk into a bedroom where Willson tears the bedsheets off the sleeping, seventeen-year-old, John Saxon. Nice story!

But the best story, as reviewer "Shinybear" points out, is about Connie Stevens and how Jack Warner led her to believe that she would be the one playing Eliza Doolittle in the *My Fair Lady* film and when she heard that Audrey Hepburn had landed the role, she led a twenty-four-hour walkout on the set of her current project, *Palm Springs Weekend*. Now I'm of the camp that likes *Palm Springs Weekend* more than *My Fair Lady*, and so why had I never heard this *Norma Rae*–like "strike" tale before? Maybe they're saving it for the DVD commentary on *Palm Springs Weekend*.

My Walk with Bob
by Bruce Boone

★★★★★
A Classic of New Narrative Writing

July 19, 2006

When I tried to summon up this book on Amazon through its search function, I got redirected to the memoirs of Rita Marley, widow of reggae king Bob; its title must be something close to *My Walk with Bob*, but it's sort of peculiar because it suggests, in retrospect, how actually white a book Bruce Boone's *My Walk with Bob* is. Maybe "apparently white" would be better, for the more I think about it, it's shaded by many different sorts of otherness—gayness just the tip of the iceberg—from its examination of Maoism to its retelling of the legend of Guadalupe, in which Bruce takes on the voices of the little shepherd girls and boys who claim to have seen this beautiful white lady hailing them from beyond, like Cortés appearing to the Aztecs.

It's worth noting that *My Walk with Bob*, when first published in 1979, was issued by a press called "Black Star," and that in intervening years, Boone has changed his nom de plume to the simple, brand-name-clean "Bruce X," with its powerful undertones of Malcolm X and Black nationalism.

When I first came to San Francisco, the whole New Narrative crowd was passing this book around with high recommendations. Copies were flying through the air with the hiss of daggers in a Hong Kong action movie. I read it, loved it, and put it firmly in my mind as the beau idéal of writing. My conviction of its superiority was so strong that it lasted a good twenty years without me really going back and rereading the darn thing again. Thank goodness that Ithuriel's Spear has brought the book back to print, it will give old fans, as well as new generations of curious readers, the chance to take a look and judge for themselves, Is this slim little book really the urbook of the whole postmodern movement? I had completely forgotten, for example, that besides its majestic and eponymous title piece, three little essays precede it, like three John the Baptists prophesying its brilliance in the desert.

In "Going Home," the first of these, Bruce goes back to a cold city to visit elderly parents and wonders how in the world he is going to make it through the next few days. We've all been there haven't we! "Dreams" is a different sort of story, a sketch really, something Italo Calvino might have written, a fleecy, yet steely, meditation on the way the dreams of the young first give them magic powers, then curse them with grim visions of the future, bringing the touch of Cassandra onto their tongues. It's a strain Boone never worked in very much, more's the pity; maybe it's my imagination, but his work in progress on Kurt Cobain seems to take up this surrealist strain once again, after a break of twenty years. In "Monsters," the last of the trio, Boone is on familiar ground. He surveys a group of then-current Hollywood films, *Saturday Night Fever*, *Coming Home*, and *Who'll Stop the Rain*, and delivers a cogent sociopolitical analysis of the moment, based on what he sees in the films, like you or I might read the leaves floating in our cups of tea. Boone has the great facility of seeing right through apparent dissimilarities in plot, character, genre, style, and finding something real, or essential, in even the most escapist fluff, though he makes a very ungay blooper here, ascribing Nick Nolte's breakthrough moment to

Spielberg's *Jaws*. Carelessness—or merely an understandable reluctance even to mention the name of the real Nolte vehicle, the indescribable sea adventure Peter Benchley called *The Deep*, a wretched film best known for Jackie Bisset's then-scandalous wet T-shirts?

Finally there is the title story itself. Bob and Bruce go for a walk, wander into Mission Dolores, of all accursed places, and drink in its beauty for about half a paragraph, and then they start gabbing about everything under the sun, especially the minutiae of their own lives. It isn't a long essay, or memoir: maybe ten thousand, twelve thousand words. But for some of you, it will carry more weight than all of Walter Benjamin's *Arcades Project*, in a slimline volume that won't distort your hip pocket as you carry it around town, miming the flaneur, creating your own world, dragging all of history with you as though it were tied by a fishline to the book on your tail. It is a kite to the rest of the universe. At first I was taken aback by the new edition and its lovely, romantic color photograph on the cover, by Gregg Chadwick, with its intimations of Maurice Prendergast or Edward Corbett. Those two boys climbing the steps on the cover are not the Bob and Bruce of my imagination. They're too jejune! Like twin Anthony Goicoleas on the bleachers of a boys' school from outer space. And yet after a while I readjusted; now everything is different.

Deluxe Vauxhall Freestanding Towel Warmer & Drying Rack
by Warmrails

★★★★★
European Luxury in a Modest American Apartment Building

July 20, 2006

I had frankly never thought of buying a towel warmer before. Is it me, or do they seem like you should be running a hotel if you have one? But the more I went to Europe, the more I noticed that even fairly modest households, even in the worst European slums, boasted warming towel racks, though I did see that in the worst neighborhoods the racks in question were nowhere near as lavish as the

Warmrails Vauxhall model Amazon sells. Some of them are really nothing more than old vacuum cleaner tubes crossed lengthwise, and they aren't always heated with electricity, some thrifty Edinburghers for example use Mentholatum smeared on the aluminum to warm it up a tad for their clans and guests. After my last such trip I decided to bring a little bit of European-style hotel grandeur to my own humble backside.

When you think about the cost, you think about the price of complete satisfaction. This rack holds at least twenty-five towels, or at least four of the superlarge towels you and your family deserve, the kind that are larger than the human body. Toss one, wet, onto the Warmrails Vauxhall and instantly a thousand intricate, diamond-shaped circuits go to work, producing the kind of kilowattage that you associate with the cigarette lighter in a standard sedan. In no time at all, those babies are warm! And dry! It's like stepping from a wet swimming pool into a mink coat, with a Euro twist.

Does it take up too much room in your bathroom? Well, for one thing, with the Warmrails firmly in place, you'll find yourself getting rid of a lot of bathroom furniture that you had cluttering up the place! You can also use it as a planteria, for it will hold enormous vases of flowers, or to stack up racks of neckties; however, it is advised that the manufacturer's instructions be followed down to the letter, as it is after all a highly skilled living machine, no matter how much it looks like a baby jungle gym. The rods maintain a comforting warmness that will not scald. One friend who has never been to Europe was startled in the bathroom, after a refreshing shower he brushed his genitals against the Warmrails and gave out a faint cry, but it was not a cry of pain. Believe me, it was a sigh of gratification I should think.

All ages can use it and, while I come from a large family and we use a lot of towels, now that my wife and I are by ourselves, we have received compliments from everyone in our low-security building. No one, but no one, on our block has the Warmrails Vauxhall brand of affordable luxury. This and the Dyson vacuum cleaner, and a small Keith Haring, might be the best purchases we've ever made home-wise.

Summer Crossing: A Novel
by Truman Capote

★★★★★
Trunk Music

August 1, 2006

Finally we find out why Chris Martin and Gwyneth Paltrow named their daughter "Apple," after the sister of the heroine of Truman Capote's masterful '40s novel *Summer Crossing*, discovered in a heap of trash by a fellow who moved into Capote's Brooklyn apartment after he vacated for Europe. The Berg Collection at New York's Public Library bought up the manuscript to add to their Capote archive when it presently became available through the trash-seeker's family (together with a whole heap of other manuscripts, letters, family papers, and one complete short story—a lot of unpublished material which makes a trip to the NYPL a must for the Capote fancier). And now his longtime publisher, Random House, has brought out the book to mixed reviews. Well, not everyone gets Truman Capote, and even I, his greatest fan of all time, vacillate like the ping-pong of radar between two states of adoration and cold hauteur. Sometimes he writes like the American Proust he said he was, and sometimes he writes like Maya Angelou on one of her greeting cards for Hallmark. Sometimes these disparate effects can be traced within the borders of one sentence. Maybe that's why I like him so much, because he cares about his writing, and yet he really doesn't care about taste.

Some people (like the publishers, for example) have said that the heroine of *Summer Crossing*, Grady McNeil, reminds them of Holly Golightly, that she's an early and inferior sketch for Holly Golightly, who charmed us all in Capote's later *Breakfast at Tiffany's*. If she's an early sketch for anything, she might be in the running for a proto–Kate McCloud. McCloud was to be the heroine of Capote's notorious unfinished novel *Answered Prayers*, and we all know what happened there. What's great about her passion in *Summer Crossing* is the sharply observed contretemps it gets her into. She knows it's ridiculous that she fell for Clyde's seedy charm. Something about his Jewishness got her where she lives, in the shadow of the Holocaust she finds his Jewish identity super sensual, with the darkness and profundity of a D. H. Lawrence hero. We haven't had this kind of direct equation lately—the Jewish under-class punk as the noble savage, the dangerous temptation to the "heiress of all the ages" whom Grady represents so beautifully. Some of the sex writing still takes one's breath away, it is so stark and unrelenting. Clyde may be an animal, but I'd do him in ten seconds if I were that kind of girl.

From sentence to sentence you haven't read a better book this year, but as a novel it's a little thin and undeveloped, or maybe it's a little bit confusing and Capote might have considered rewriting it from the POV of Peter Bell, the upper-class twit with the swimmer's bod who considers Grady his property, since they grew up together with the silver spoons. As it stands, Peter's just a sideshow for the main attraction. We see Grady going downhill irrevocably, but we don't believe it. She's too strong to be so weak—and yet that's the chief virtue of this creation.

Kay Francis: I Can't Wait to Be Forgotten; Her Life on Film & Stage
by Scott O'Brien

★★★★★
Speak, Memory

August 1, 2006

Scott O'Brien—you magnificent, astonishing fool, you! Imagine spending so many years of your life researching the life of a forgotten screen actress from the 1930s, a woman who is barely remembered nowadays! Why fling your undoubted energies after such a quixotic goal? If you must write about old Hollywood, why not write about someone people have heard of, like Joan Crawford, Garbo, Clark Gable? If you want to go obscure, how about Norma Shearer? But for goodness sake, Kay Francis!?! Scott O'Brien, you have labored in the vineyards where angels fear to tread!

As it turns out, *I Can't Wait to Be Forgotten* is starlore of a very high order, and if you want an engrossing examination of a great Hollywood personality, this is the book for you. Kay Francis may be little remembered today, but all that is about to change as succeeding generations pick up on the glory that is her screen presence. Born in Oklahoma City ("by mistake," she bitterly commented) in 1905, Francis dabbled in high society and became the social secretary to rich dowagers while pining for Broadway stardom in New York. Her own madcap ways were fueled by the great rush to sexual and economic freedom pursued by many women in the wake of World War I, in which they had been asked for so many sacrifices without even having the right to vote. Scott O'Brien is a sensitive cultural historian and writes with perception about this, the so-called Flapper Era, showing us that Kay Francis's fabled and open sexuality was part and parcel of the times in which she grew up.

After an interesting apprenticeship at Paramount Studios, Francis signed a long-term contract with Warner Bros., and for a time in the early 1930s she became the queen of the lot, eventually rising in salary and status to the absolute heights of success. She was the highest paid actor of them all, and therein lay her tragedy, for Jack Warner turned against her and forced her against her will to play out her contract in increasingly shabby B movies. Late in life, she and her Warner Bros. rival, Bette Davis, sat down and let down their hair about their disputes with Warner. "Why did you keep making those B movies?" Bette asked Kay. Because she was in it for the money, Kay replied. Bette said she walked away, because she was in it for the career.

Kay became a victim of public scrutiny, for her shabby studio treatment was the talk of the nation. Eventually she left Warners, and the films she made afterward, for other studios, are indeed, as O'Brien points out, among the best and most rewarding of her career, culminating in the Monogram Trilogy: *Divorce*, *Allotment Wives*, *Wife Wanted*, which sound like horrors but instead crackle with noir energy and a gritty raw realism miles removed from the somewhat grand products (like *The White Angel*, a biopic of Florence Nightingale) of Warners' A-list.

Despite love affairs with Fritz Lang, Otto Preminger, and even gay stars like Nils Asther, Kay's great love seems to have been a German nobleman who broke off their engagement, as the Second World War loomed, to go back and fight for Hitler. Although she never knew it, he killed himself shortly after Pearl Harbor, far away in Nazi Germany. It was like a scene from one of her great romantic movies, but twisted somehow, bizarre and bewildering.

It turns out that she wasn't even a lesbian, not really, though she had some passionate interludes with a woman here and there. That she was a lesbian, O'Brien traces back to a canard propagated by Phil Silvers, her costar in *Four Jills in a Jeep*.

When Kay Francis said "I can't wait to be forgotten," could she have somehow known that indeed the halls of memory would have been so thoroughly scrubbed clean? No matter now, for thanks to the incredible, noble efforts of author Scott O'Brien, and the hard work of the folks at BearManor Media, O'Brien's publisher, a new star has risen, and her name is Kay Francis. You can't keep genius down, even if it speaks with a lisp that turns all one's *r*'s to *w*'s.

Translating the Unspeakable: Poetry and the Innovative Necessity
by Kathleen Fraser

★★★★★
Without a Net

August 2, 2006

I turned once again to Kathleen Fraser's intriguing *Translating the Unspeakable* after a long hiatus, for I had seen a recent essay by her and it struck me once again that the older essays, collected here in this handsome volume from Alabama, had real qualities of composition and inspiration, though they perhaps struggle here and there for what she can now employ effortlessly, like Alec Guinness, that assured mastery of the form. Plunging right in, I felt the top of my head coming off as from every corner of (nearly) every page a rainbow of arrows hurled themselves at my brain. "What's messing up my tidy defense system, about to leave me open for attack?"

We go to Fraser first off for the inquiring turn of her mind, then for the activist spirit she has displayed in so many contexts, both in writing and in life. Often she returns to her own history, a story of a woman who got very lucky very early (having Frank O'Hara as a friend!) and who was also dismissed, neglected, and put on the shelf for gender reasons, and who managed to find a way to overcome this prejudice both theoretically and practically. Like Alex Haley's *Roots*, Fraser's *Translating* is a book of ancestor hunting, for like Haley she believes in the totemic power of those who came before, holding their lamps, shedding their light into our dim present and questionable future. In college she was taught a steady diet of marvelous male modernists, and it wasn't until later that she wondered why, except for Emily Dickinson, and a bit of Woolf, she was not introduced to any actual woman writers. The battle over the canon is just part of the texture of these essays, but it is always a stirring saga, one we return to with fascination like Civil War buffs.

Her studies of individual poets (Niedecker) are always to the point, and one essay here always catches my eye, her focus on the relationship between two very different writers, Mina Loy and Basil Bunting, which is among the best criticism I have seen of either poet. It is a book of keen observations, the poet Steve Benson for example sharing "the baffled seriousness of brilliant clowns such as Stan Laurel." And a book of prophecy, for it ends with a consideration of Charles Olson's "field" theory, embodied by feminist examples including Myung Mi Kim and Hannah Weiner, the page exploded à la Olson's poignant "rose" poem. Today, with Fraser leading the way into further realms of typographical bewilderment and wonder, I read "Olson's 'Field'" as perhaps her statement of intent, a map for what was to follow.

Alabama should have hired a copyeditor long ago. It's a shame that the book misspells the names of Daisy Aldan and Michael Amnasan—and that's just the *A*s!

Curse of the Narrows: The Halifax Disaster of 1917
by Laura M. Mac Donald

★★★★☆
The Winter's Tale

August 2, 2006

My great-grandparents were young people around the time of the First World War, and with the boys called away to service overseas, my great-grandmother and plenty of other "land girls" were called to man the plows of the little farms in upstate New York, where a struggling rutabaga truck farm kept all the neighboring women on the job morning, noon, and night, with time off only for Sunday school and church worship at the nearest community center, some twelve miles out. My great-grandmother heard the noise of the *Imo* explosion and never forgot it, for the mule she was behind got skeered and ran into the next man's acreage, a feat he never did again, that lazy gray mule they called Buster. The harvest was long gone, for this was the beginning of winter right after American Thanksgiving, but my great-grandmother was once again tearing up the ruts, a weekly chore even in a nor'easter or snowstorm.

"The sky was full of black dust," she swore to me, as a very old woman in the early 1970s. "Looked like a billion locusts. And then we sniffed the air and we knew, them was part of people!" Laura Mac Donald, a top-notch TV producer, has interviewed many survivors of that long-ago tragedy in Halifax, many of whom suffered permanent hearing loss as a result of the fiery explosion, the shock waves of which were heard not only in the Finger Lakes but, it is said, even in the Caribbean paradises of Cuba and Santo Domingo. In truth, it was a tsunami, and the producers of *The Day after Tomorrow* should hold on to their footage for when the day comes and the studios want to bring this Canadian tragedy to life.

As usual, the poor people paid the most, the people of the North End who couldn't get out in time. There were so many people killed and dying that they ran out of gravediggers. Why, they even ran out of preachers, and when did that ever occur before or since? My great-grandmother said the Catholics got it worst, and Mac Donald's figures show that in one parish alone, St. Joseph's, nearly five hundred members lost their lives in a single instant. "Some clergymen simply remained in or near the cemetery during the day," writes Mac Donald, "performing funerals until it got too dark to read."

And all of this in the days and weeks that should have been happy ones, the weeks before Christmas!

An inquest was held and Mac Donald somehow got hold of the complete transcript, which illuminates who was to blame and who was completely innocent. You have to know a lot about inter-coastal shipping to understand this material, it's dense, like the very thickest parts of the Warren Report. Otherwise the book grips you like three magnets.

———————

Everything I Have Is Blue: Short Fiction by Working-Class Men about More-or-Less Gay Life
by Wendell Ricketts

★★★★★
Workingman's Blues

August 4, 2006

I've never met Wendell Ricketts, but I have long admired his writing, and the tremendous power of his own writing in many genres he now brings to an editorial project which must have seemed daunting at the start, but which winds up, in his able hands, a terrifically rewarding anthology. It's not your typical book of working-class porn, where middle-class designers drool over the mechanics perched under their Mercedes. Nor is it precisely a book of agitprop urging the proletariat to armed revolution by any means necessary. James Barr's long story "The Bottom of the Cloud," which must have been written a good fifty years ago, has everything but period charm, thank God. It might have been written today, and only some of its circumlocutions tag it as the product of an era in which Henry James was widely read, even by John Fante types whose labor is of the dust. Barr's story (from his collection *Derricks*) is amazing on a sentence-by-sentence level, even if you don't know what exactly is happening to our hero, Robin, and his anguished pilgrimage through the gray areas of Central City. Barr was able to rewrite John Bunyan for our own time, and out of a fiery, almost blindsided gay sensibility. Torment, bruises, bondage, and pain abound, and he takes you there. Keith Banner's story "How to Get from This to This" shares some of Barr's bleakness of vision. Two gay brothers, Danny and Lucas, argue it out from either side of a tavern that might itself be mistaken for a class marker, and from either side of alcoholism itself. Lucas is pulling himself up by the bootstraps, edging himself into a higher class status, while Danny, at age thirty-three (Christ's age) is sinking deeper into a nickel-and-dime pit. "I see my apartment the way it truly is, a mouse-bit bag of bread, Old Crow bottles, old textbooks I never sold back to the bookstore. The magical couch with no cushions." He doesn't have much self-esteem, as we say here in California. But maybe that lack keeps us honest. Not all of the stories are as hard hitting as these, but in general there's a rock-solid thrust to them that feels good.

Ricketts has taken this material and made some hard sense out of it, in a long, engaging afterword that serves as a sort of apologia pro vita sua. Are there working-class people in gay literature? Or is working class "contragay"? Ricketts's thesis is a tough one, but he asserts that his own best experiences of bonding with men have occurred not in gay contexts, or even in the context of gay sexuality, but while working shoulder to shoulder in prisons and union-hiring halls with other working-class guys, even murderers. You may meet some dangerous scum there, but at least they're honest about it, unlike the coiffured and manicured men about whom, and by whom, so much of gay writing is being written. The working-class gay man receives nothing but confusion and shame when he attempts to enter the bougie world of "gay community."

He may say this, and he may believe this, but paradoxically enough, the stories he has collected here tweak his own definitions of what they portend. Fiction is volatile, like nitro. It doesn't do exactly what you think it will do, and it works differently on everyone who comes in contact with it. "Only connect!" E. M. Forster wrote, and the great thing about Ricketts's book is the attention he bears down, with his great brain and heart, onto proving and disproving that way-dated dictum.

Sap Moss Conditioning Detangler
by Aveda

★★★★★
Liquid Silk

August 4, 2006

I was watching *The Ring Two*, in which a heavily made-up Sissy Spacek appears as Evelyn, a patient in a mental asylum with extremely tangled black hair nearly obscuring her ghastly face, and it came to me that the conditioner I've been using lately hasn't really been working out.

What I really needed, I decided, flicking off *The Ring Two* just at the moment when, in flashback, a young Sissy Spacek was trying to drown her demon baby in a pool of holy water, was some of the new detangler made from the sap of moss which strong men had squeezed and worked into my hair at the barber shop on my last trip downtown.

Aveda's the brand name men and women swear by, for even if your hair has been bleached by the sun, or colored by cheap chemical processing, you will still be able to run a comb through it without undue pain. That scalp pain was what did me in most of all, and even wearing a hat grew uncomfortable. I'm a baseball-cap-wearing guy into thug style, but who wants urban chic if it hurts you to twist your hat from back to front on top of your head? "Aveda"—three syllables that go down like liquid silk, and guarantee ease of entry.

My cousin had a video for this product showing how they harvest the sap out of Norwegian, Swiss, and West German moss plants, to get that honey-colored sweetness into every drop of the conditioning detangler. When they pack it into plastic it's as good as sealed by pearl, and once again you'll have the kind of hair that boy who played Tadzio did in Visconti's *Death in Venice*. When the video was over, we just sat back on our heels and sighed a heartfelt moan of relief. Finally, a product made for men with "antler extensions."

Rocks on a Platter: Notes on Literature
by Barbara Guest

★★★★★
Salute to Rocks on a Platter

August 18, 2006

I liked this book better than the other fellow, but I can sympathize with his feeling that these poems make no sense. (I'm just guessing that the other reviewer is a guy, maybe because of the approving reference to August Kleinzahler, a poet unlike any other currently working.) *Rocks on a Platter: Notes on Literature* to me sounded like a great idea, for Barbara Guest was an infinitely patient reader and any of her opinions on the writing of others were always welcome, sometimes a little astringent, more often felt and generous. So even a book of her table talk à la Coleridge would have been a precious gift.

However, these "notes on literature" are something more and something less than the subtitle denotes. I believe that each page is her notes on a different text, but she has swept away most of the referents, like sand out of the foyer of her beach house, and so we come to them feeling the generosity and the asperity, but supplying our own texts. Like the *Publishers Weekly* reviewer who guesses that, if trees are in the first line of the poem, then they are probably the trees branded by John Ashbery in *Some Trees*. "No ideas but in trees." Thus a hundred texts propose themselves and disappear, like the same sands you're trying to hold back from the tide, running through your fingers. A feeling of "crewlessness," as she advises.

I misunderstood her and thought it was going to be about rock music, thinking of the way the '50s DJ in movies like *The Girl Can't Help It* refer to 45s as "platters." In her work you always hear the surf music, and the other great California invention, the Wall of Sound Phil Spector ran in Los Angeles. "Pockets jingle," she writes, "highly responsive place in the shelter / of those rocks at last the jingle of your pockets // HEARD ON THE PAGE." For her it became increasingly a question of punctuation, and indeed what alphabetical characters sat on top of others in the lines of a poem, the way John Cage would spell out the subject of his writing by enlarging one character and lining up the lines so you could read them vertically with greater ease than the horizontal. Must have driven the compositors mad! But then you get the wonderful tips, the tips of her hat to the poets and prose writers she loved. For example in "Shattered rocks," where the letters *D*, *H*, and *L* line up on top of each other like faces on a totem pole, to salute Lawrence and his animalist, inclusive poetics (and his modernity, of course). Like Guest, he was a painter too and thus deeply invested in the ethereal, yet scarily down-to-earth, quality they called "tonality."

All in all *Rocks* is a book that will repay dozens of readings. As I say, I was puzzled about it when it came out, and only now, in the silence of mid-August, do I start getting the beat.

Handheld Blender for Almond Milk, Soup, Purée
by Tribest

★★☆☆☆
A Mixed Bag

August 19, 2006

I wouldn't touch this thing, but my wife uses it all the time to grind flax seeds and to make smoothies. And she's loved it. Especially having a grinder that can be easily washed. When she travels, she even takes it to hotels with her and makes almond milk with it. She's had it fourteen months and the four-pronged blade assembly broke. Given the price of the unit, she feels it should have lasted longer than this. When she wrote to Tribest to complain, she was told that she was welcome to buy another blade unit. Bed 'n Bath sells a cheaper similar product.

Would I buy this again? Probably, but this time around I'd set myself a mental clock that would start ticking down the minute I unwrapped the unwieldy Amazon packaging. And I'd know it had only *X* amount of blending in it. Thank the Lord it's modular and I can buy her the pieces she needs even though they're more than twenty-five dollars a pop (if you count shipping), and in the end this may be your idea of a bargain though it is definitely not mine. However, this way you can have almond milk in your hotel room without paying those hefty room service fees, even if you should be lucky enough to check into a hotel that has almond milk on its menu.

It could be quieter, too. Sometimes I'm trying to sleep after a long, hard day at work at my regular job and after composing choice Amazon reviews to wake to the unearthly roar like the opening of the pit of Hell. It's just her trying to blend frozen blueberries with her ubiquitous almond milk. Who knows what the neighbors are thinking.

ABBA: In Concert (1979)
dir. Urban Lasson

★★★★☆
Hole in Your Soul

August 21, 2006

What's the best thing about this video? The big choral number "I Have a Dream" joined by what looks like eighty children at Wembley Stadium. Did ABBA find new children in every city in the 1979 tour and train them each briefly on the afternoon of the show? I don't think "I Have a Dream" is a very easy number for kids to sing, with that long held note on "I believeeeeeve," and yet these kids sail into it like pros. I wonder if any of the 1979 kids grew up and became pop stars themselves? The ones you see on the documentary all look as though spotlights are second nature to them; in the light they seem to grow into their full selves and find a brief happiness before being led off into the shadows of backstage. I wonder if a new documentary, rounding up these kids thirty years later, like that 7 Up Michael Apted series tracing London schoolchildren into their teens and beyond, could be commissioned by the BBC so that finally we could see what happened to the little angels. I wonder if they were orphans or maybe just professional child actors from some RADA of childhood. Anyway that's one of my great highlights from ABBA: in Concert, which must have been filmed, in my estimation, just as "Gimmie! Gimmie! Gimmie! (A Man after Midnight)" had been released as a single, and ABBA was in the process of seeking a harder, rockier sound.

Which really shows up in the best numbers here, among them the fiery, eclectically scored "Summer Night City," and perhaps only a little less successfully, "Hole in Your Soul," which borrows from old-school '50s US a cappella groups and the big Philles sound of Phil Specter and Jack Nitzsche to create a Möbius strip of sound in which big bursts of guitar alternate with an eerie blast of silence, then the angelic voices of Agnetha and Frida rising to a shout. It's at this period that people were really looking at ABBA and asking themselves, "Are they the strange ones, or are we?" Björn and Benny seem to be in constant control of their women, and yet they seem helpless, nearly stupefied, in the face of so much sex appeal, like the sailors on brave Ulysses's crew, urged to stuff their ears with wax so that they wouldn't hear the sirens' song.

Crashing America: A Novel
by Katia Noyes

★★★★★
"I Was Alive and Going to Stay Alive"

August 23, 2006

Wish there were a book like *Crashing America* when I was a boy. It's the kind of book they should issue to teens as soon as they get into middle school. Twice I had read it, but it wasn't until a recent trip crisscrossing America, "trying to find a way inside," in the footsteps of Noyes's implacable heroine Girl, not until I was tangled up with road maps, did I really understand it. For sometimes you have to be really young, or else really in tune with your feelings, to "get" a perfect work of art.

As everyone else will tell you, *Crashing America* is a powerful indictment of a society in which class injustice trumps every other factor in life, a system in which our children and our pets are our victims, brought into this world to amuse us and to provide a work-force, but otherwise to be ignored, molested, and put down at will. At seventeen, Girl already seems to have a political understanding that defies common sense—surely no seventeen-year-old ever had the writing ability that our narrator shows here—but such is the persuasiveness of Noyes's invention that I never bothered my head thinking about this until the long strange trip was over and, like Girl, I was walking up Market Street toward the Castro on a sad Sunday afternoon from the bus depot on Seventh Street, looking at the worker bees who weren't there, for they had vacated the space to the bums and the wounded. Reading *Crashing America*, I was reminded of similar scenes in Evelyn Lau's *Runaway* and some parts of Tom Spanbauer's second and third novels, but here the brew is different, more focused, more tragic, purer. Even the name "Girl," so reminiscent of a heroine from Erskine Caldwell's florid middle period, I got used to, as though it weren't so horribly symbolic.

After the tragic death of a girlfriend, Girl finds herself with literally nowhere to go. Her dad, Mistah White Socks, seems to despise her, and her mother committed suicide, her ghost clinging to the long reaches of Girl's memories. She heads midwest to get back to the farmland where the Clutter family got killed. That's the thing about Girl, you just want to shake her, for every decision she makes is a bad one! And yet you sympathize with her at every turn and you know why she makes all these wrong turns. Oh! There's one part of the book that you will just throw the book down on the floor, so horrifying is the life choice Girl decides to make. And yet then you will crawl back to the book just to find out what happens next. Katia Noyes, with whom I once took a writing workshop, has reader identification wired into every word she writes. And she can describe things so vividly it's like someone's waving them under your nose. A store detective wears a "surgically cut bob of red hair and a smug color of coral lipstick."

One caveat, and one spoiler—this book has a sequence in which a common house cat dies a tragic and painful death. It is not for the squeamish! The pages of my copy of *Crashing America* are stained with tears all over that chapter. I've never read anything like it.

Dream Dinners: Turn Dinnertime into Family Time with 100 Assemble-and-Freeze Meals
by Stephanie Allen and Tina Kuna

★★★★★
Something for Everybody

August 30, 2006

I've always toyed with the idea of making a little extra money by cooking some of my delicious recipes for upward of a hundred people. Alas, this is a fantasy that will never come true, given how much energy it would take, not to mention the high turnover in restaurants here in cosmopolitan San Francisco where a place will open one day, a waiting list three months in advance, and then in month four or five the "buzz" will depart, and a fickle public has found the next new place. Well, congratulations to Stephanie Allen and Tina Kuna for making it all work for them, and you know how they did it? The old-fashioned way—high quality and personalized attention—and oh, yes, it's not really a restaurant, it's a franchise. It's a whole new ballgame, so if you go, be prepared to come back with as many dinners as you can fit in your freezer. You may find yourself borrowing your neighbors' freezer just to fit in some of your favorites. As for cooking for one hundred? They've made it so anyone could do it, even me! And now, for the first time, a cookbook that shows you just how the expert chefs at Dream Dinners make haute cuisine food *au* bulk, you might say.

The book provides dozens of recipes that sound perfectly delicious. And some for every taste. And what's great is that, if you like how it sounds, you can follow column 1, and just make enough for yourself, or you can follow column 2, making enough for three meals. These three you could share with your family, or if you live alone, just put them in the freezer and save them for the next time you want, say, a reuben casserole.

What's handy about this is that, in the back of the book, Stephanie and Tina provide "Labels Times Three," so you won't forget what you put in that Tupperware over the weeks, perhaps months, before you defrost the reuben casserole you made yourself. These labels tell you not only what it is, but how to reheat it. For example, for Dream Dinners' famous Provençal flank steak, the label (which you may cut out with a pair of nail scissors, or a cutting knife—better keep some glue around to fasten the tiny piece of paper to the Tupperware!) will read: "Thaw completely. Preheat broiler or prepare a grill. Remove steak from marinade and sear on both sides, about 8 minutes per side." And then it gives further directions (I want to avoid spoilers here as much as possible, while still giving you a flavor of how marvelously the whole *Dream Dinners* cookbook project has been conceived).

The wild-rice salad was so good that I wound up not freezing any of it, but eating all three helpings in one sitting! Right now, I'm sampling a wee bit of the layered strawberry gelatin salad, which incorporates real strawberries, not just Jell-O (plus bananas which I didn't have, so I used tapioca pudding instead). That's the beauty of it, you'll feel like you're not only doing all the cooking yourself, but you're contributing to the invention of the recipes in a very postmodern, metafictional way. My wife likes "my" Parmesan green beans, but Grandma Killian prefers her Parmesan green beans without the Parmesan—cheese allergies—and so I have set aside one meal sans the cheese and frozen it for her next visit.

You know how when you have a Dream Dinners session yourself, and you go there with nothing but a large cooler for the ride home? You'll be stacking coolers on top of coolers, with the warm feeling that you made these meals yourself, hundreds of them, from the smallest thing like french toast to the more complicated chicken cordon bleu, which might stump you at first, but keep trying! At first I wound up missing the chicken breasts entirely when trying to spear them down properly with my toothpicks, and many a toothpick went the way of all flesh, but eventually I was able to secure each one, every time, and once the scallions were sprinkled on lightly, like a cloud of green rain, I had that rare burst of elation, the kind you get when people compliment you on your cooking, sort of as though the neurons in your brain were being confetti'd with endorphins.

Fresh Ideas in Dried Flowers
by Terry L. Rye

★★★★★
An Old Debate and a New Twist

September 4, 2006

When the postman delivered this book, I realized I had made a slight error and used my Amazon Prime account too hastily. I had wanted a similar book whose title I can't verify right now, but it was something like *Dried Ideas in Fresh Flowers*. Instead this book, *Fresh Ideas in Dried Flowers*, came and at first I was going to return it for credit, because I have never cared for dried flowers, and I'm a fresh-flowers boy all the way, one who often walks into the office with a fresh boutonniere newly snipped from my indoor terrarium. However, knowing the name Terry Rye from HGTV, I decided to open up the book and see what she had to say.

Hours later, my head caught up in a dream of dry flowers, I stood dizzily and made my way to the herb garden for a bit of meditation. Quickly I saw how, following Ms. Rye's tips, I could finally, after so many decades, do something about the tragedy that befalls nearly all fresh flowers—when they die, you pretty much have to throw them away. And after watching Al Gore's *An Inconvenient Truth*, a hit movie here in San Francisco at least, about the tragedy of global warming, I wanted to do something for my trash rather than just throw it away. What Terry Rye does is instill a new passion, "fresh ideas" is a perfect term for it, a new passion to recycle. And say you have some fresh roses, for example, that you want to last forever? Have you considered microwaving them, or perhaps ten minutes with your wife's hair dryer? I never had, and now I find myself drying flowers and hanging plants the instant they bloom (they can keep some of their polleny sheen on them if you head them off at the pass of life, as it were). My experiments with her methods have also led me to conclude that you can dry flowers in your washer-dryer, but you must leave them on a very low cycle, for they might burn.

In addition, she shows you how to make arrangements using some materials unique to dried flowers. Floral foam may not be good for the earth, but it is everywhere, and I don't see how we lived without it all these years. You can buy FF in many colors, not just camouflage green, and Rye's use of topiary foam establishes her as a pioneer in new ways to make fun three dimensional. A sunflower arrangement changes shape, like the sea god Proteus, halfway up the stems, and turns into a pair of balls studded with gorgeous, muted autumnal shades of color. I made one for my students' potluck and I got so many compliments I was blushing like a patch of heliotrope, and I'm not a modest man by nature.

Of course not every arrangement is to my own taste. I don't like the way she hangs Amaranthus sprigs, which look like peapods gone to mold, so that they fall in foot-long strands from the middle of your arrangement, and you can move it, willy-nilly for that casual "grew" effect, along the surface of the table or mantelpiece or windowsill on which your arrangement is resting. Maybe it's my modernism, but that just looks messy to me, as though you forgot to clean up even though you knew company was coming. But in general, this book will wake you up like a gentle slap across the face, and bring you into a new world of different things you can do with the dried parts of the vegetable world you had once thought too unmentionable to work with. Check out her "Palette of Color" in which you use an actual canvas, covered in mulberry paper, and you paste, pin, and glue little Linum blossoms and peonies to "paint your own van Gogh."

Little Miss Sunshine (2006)
dir. Jonathan Dayton and Valerie Faris

★★★★☆
Independent Smash

September 5, 2006

There aren't a lot of laughs in *Little Miss Sunshine*, and most of them involve mishaps to the van. Like when the door falls off, people in the theater laughed a little bit, perhaps startled by the noise of the door's clang on the parking lot asphalt. All in all it was a pretty glum affair, but a good one, sort of like the old-time New American Cinema movies of the 1970s like *The Long Goodbye* or *Five Easy Pieces*.

A family group tries to complete a road trip of one thousand miles west, mirroring an earlier voyage of discovery and colonial conquest by American empire builders and covered-wagon pioneers. And of course you can't take a road trip in the movies without learning a lot about yourself. For an independent film, *Little Miss Sunshine* hits practically all the three-act plot points Syd Field and his ilk recommend. Each of the actors undergoes his or her own trauma, revelation, and recovery. Most of them were pretty well done, like Greg Kinnear's encounter with Bryan Cranston at the Scottsdale hotel. It did seem a little coincidental that little Olive would happen to have brought with her a test for color blindness to use as a game. That was hard to swallow.

But what really threw me off was Steve Carell's encounter with the one person in the whole world he didn't want to see, at some kind of roadside 7-Eleven in the middle of nowhere. Did the screenwriters ever pause to ask themselves if an audience would believe this? It is to Carell's credit that he almost makes it work. And the rival Proust scholar who takes over Frank's title and his boyfriend? Isn't it the Canadian actor who used to play the gay son on *Dynasty*—Gordon Thomson? Maybe I'm getting mixed up and his character wasn't gay, just seemed like it. If so, it's great that Gordon Thomson has hooked himself onto a hit. It's been a long time between engagements for the man who once replaced Lane Davies as Mason Capwell on the NBC daytime drama *Santa Barbara*.

It is just little things that prevent me from awarding this film four stars instead of five. Little things like the revelation of the nature of Olive's number, which she has been practicing all through the film, at the close of the beauty pageant, is it supposed to signal that Alan Arkin's character has been molesting her during their nights together? I can't wait for the ten-years-later sequel, *Little Miss Sunshine 2: Monster, the Olive Wuornos Story*.

Absent in the Spring
by Mary Westmacott

★★★★★
"Nor Praise the Deep Vermilion in the Rose ..."
September 11, 2006

One of the most beautiful love stories ever told, *Absent in the Spring* takes Henry James's donnée about an unreliable narrator and brings it to a peak of perfection even James might have envied. Joan Scudamore, the unlikeable, ultimately tragic figure at the heart of the novel, is delayed coming home to England and stuck in a "rest house" in the desert outside Baghdad for what amounts to days on end, with nothing to read after finishing the life of Lady Catherine Dysart and John Buchan's *The Power-House*. With no one who speaks English to chat with, and not even a deck of cards, she finds herself thrown back on her own devices, which grow increasingly threadbare until she begins reflecting, at first smugly and then with more self-awareness, on her own life as a young bride, mother, and suburban wife to Rodney, a successful county solicitor.

It soon becomes apparent to the reader that, unbeknownst to Joan, everyone in her life either pities or despises her. Her grown children can't bear to see her around, and her husband feels sorry for her apparently sociopathic inability to care for anyone else but herself. And little by little we realize, as Joan does, that in fact Rodney once had an affair that was the kind of thing great songs are written for, an affair with a married woman in their little town, not an exotic beauty, in fact rather a dowdy, plain woman called Leslie Sherston. As Joan becomes more and more shocked at what the depths of the subconscious are telling her, her walks outside the rest house into the desert become more and more perilous, for so strong are her memories that she loses track of where she is and threatens to get lost in the desert sand, under the implacable, cruel sun.

She feels God has deserted her completely. In the words of one of Shakespeare's sonnets, "From you have I been absent in the spring." Joan was absent in her marriage, absent from Rodney, because she only believed in a certain limited bourgeois way of knowledge. He in turn absented himself from her by falling in love with the charming, if doomed, Leslie Sherston. Rodney and Leslie are too "fine" as human beings to have actually slept together, but like Trevor Howard and Celia Johnson in *Brief Encounter*, an erotic and romantic tension animates their every interchange.

Agatha Christie wrote six novels under the name of Mary Westmacott. At the end of this one, Joan's feverish memories begin to break down into sentence fragments.

Each paragraph is only a sentence long.

An emotional sentence.

A fragment, a piece of something.

"Oh, God," Joan prays, "make me a normal woman again!"

Some people can never get it straight and still, even in 2006, they doubt that Christie is one of the greatest modernist writers in the English language.

Fools!

They're blind, unseeing, fools, do you hear me?

69 Love Songs
by The Magnetic Fields

★★★★★
Battle Cry of a Generation

September 15, 2006

The lyrics are incredibly clever and persuasive, with some of the lilt and good humor of Ogden Nash, the poetaster of the '30s, '40s, and '50s who wrote *One Touch of Venus* with Kurt Weill. And Merritt's tunes, though some are rudimentary, occasionally reach for and pull down the high branches of Weillian angst and poisoned romance. To listen to the whole of *69 Love Songs* you'd have to have a big appetite for irony, and another whole set of immunity to purposely "corny" music, and if you didn't get your fill of banjo, Hawaiian, lounge, and Americana music from the last couple of Van Dyke Parks LPs you listened to, you might be hungry all over again for the nutty richness of this compilation.

It hasn't left my turntable in four years, for by the time I finish one of the three LPs, it's always time for the less familiar second one, and to gear up anticipation for the already-forgotten third.

One thing I don't like is the booklet that comes with the box set. It marks a platinum standard in self-aggrandization. Remember the *Rolling Stone* interviews that used to glorify even the most unlikely interview subject (say, Axl Rose or whomever). Imagine then if Axl Rose repackaged the interview some flunky did with him and tried to sell it to you with his LP, except a hugely expanded edition which tried to say that he was the best songwriter and in fact genius of all time. That gives you a taste of the booklet's effrontery. It's kind of not cool, but what do I know? I've seen it on the nightstands of a dozen young hipsters who have memorized all of the questions and all of the answers and whose mouths lip-synch the whole 28,000 words in their sleep.

The Voice of the Borderlands
by Drum Hadley

★★★★★
By the Edge of the Countries, by the Edge of All We Could Ever Know

September 25, 2006

My late friend Donald Allen used to say there was one poet at the Berkeley Poetry Conference (1965) he wished he hadn't let slip away, and that was Drummond Hadley. In Don's memory I picked up this enormous book, Hadley's account of thirty years and more in the poetry game, and opened it at the beginning, part one, "Cowboys and Horses." Two things became clear—one, that Hadley is a poet of enormous power and versatility, and two, that this was no mere collection of poetry, for there are accomplished pen-and-ink and watercolor sketches throughout of vegetation on the Sonoran Desert and elsewhere, and, right on page 1, bars of music to indicate what key we're supposed to be reading this writing in. "When you read these words slowly by the fire," Hadley promises us, "And your voice becomes the people, / The lions, the wildlife, and the land."

Do not go there if you are not willing to have your experience changed a little. In our day, the "borderlands" occupy a singularly charged political space, which Hadley both delineates and explodes. Cowboys and vaqueros speak the same tongue, and while there's a border between the US and Mexico, there is also one between night and dawn, the boot and the spur, between lines in a poem.

The book speaks through its characters, and by the end you will feel as though you have lived a whole life in the outdoors under a "blue, blazed-faced" sky and tucked under adobe walls. Past meets present, the future constantly in attendance. Cultures collide, with a puff of lazy smoke. "Roberto Avilez, my fine, mojado Mexican cowboy / Who's been on the trail for months and months / And who's ridden hundreds and hundreds of miles, / Who can rope and tie down a wild Brahma bull, / Is cleaning out the goat's ear / With the nozzle of an air compressor." Toward the end, Hadley acknowledges, bows, to the man who was his poetic mentor back in the day, the poet Charles Olson, and all comes clear. The epigraph to *The Borderlands*, taken from Olson's famous poem "The Kingfishers," says it all: "What does not change / is the will to change." The poem itself—Hadley's, that is—is impossibly lyrical and dry, liminal, like the dust of the region it settles on.

Selected Poems and Four Plays
by William Butler Yeats, ed. M. L. Rosenthal

Questions

September 26, 2006

During a recent fright when we were escaping our apartment down a ladder, I took two books with me, thinking that perhaps I would need something strong. Happily Yeats's *Selected Poems and Four Plays* was at hand, together with, well, something private. This book, edited by the late M. L. Rosenthal, is an expanded edition of a previous book by Rosenthal that had the same title except it was called *Selected Poems and Two Plays*. This present edition doubles the number of plays it prints in one stroke, adding the very late *The Death of Cuchulain* as well as the strange, feverish *The Words upon the Window-Pane*. Previously we had only the two plays *Purgatory* and *Calgary*. Did I say *Calgary*? I meant *Calvary*, and neither of them are worth the paper they're printed on. In college my professor used to tell us that Yeats, together with his patron Lady Gregory, invented the Abbey Theatre and kept it going by writing plays annually and encouraging their society friends not only to attend but to pledge money in exchange for participation in a community-based theater. However, according to Rosenthal, some of Yeats's plays were distinctly unpopular even with this subsidized theater and neither the actors nor the audience loved them to death.

As a boy, my dad used to quote Yeats on every occasion and he (Yeats) was a patron saint to many Irish folk. Today not so much, but as I made my way down the ladder, I was glad I had the Yeats book tucked into my pants. He is the epitome of the artist who keeps changing through circumstance, open to new influence, even partial to drugs, for many credit his late flowering to the monkey glands he took in Switzerland to rejuvenate his sex life, the precursor to today's Viagra. In his youth he became a member of a secret band called the Order of the Golden Dawn, and spiritualist interests fueled his poetry and politics both. On his honeymoon he discovered that his wife, Georgie, had mediumistic leanings, and they spent many nights holding seances and conversing with the spirits of the dead, all of whom, or so Yeats claimed, had arrived to dispense new metaphors for his poetry. He later wrote up these events in his book *A Vision*.

Rosenthal was a superb editor who went back and checked all of the original manuscripts and who could distinguish Yeats's handwriting in all its different avatars, and this helped him date the poems to within an inch of their lives. His task was made no easier by Yeats's habit of revision and by his need to provide an income for his sisters, who wound up producing elaborate limited private printings of much of his work to sell to collectors only at absurdly inflated prices. These books are beautiful but useless, like so many of the romantic Irish flourishes the poet's late work commemorates only to condemn. It is a poetry of questions, which always appeals to young people, those who know the answers. "What's water but the generated soul?" (That one always threw me.) "How can we know the dancer from the dance?" "Is every modern nation like the tower, / Half dead at the top?" (Makes you think about our nation, caught up in a senseless war against Iraq.) "Those masterful images because complete / Grew in pure mind but out of what began?" "What voice more sweet than hers / When, young and beautiful, / She rode to harriers?" Riding to harriers doesn't sound so fabulous now, but we've all got something we look back on and say "Everything's been changed, changed utterly."

Three Story Escape Ladder
by Plow & Hearth

★★★★★
Go Down to the Street in Style

September 26, 2006

You can't beat Plow & Hearth when it comes to quality, service, and imagination. And once you've had the occasion to use their Three Story Escape Ladder, it's no overstatement to say you'll be happy you have one. It packs up small, so you can stow it under one of the kids' beds or even in an ice chest or other storage unit. My friend Adam keeps his in the cabinet where he used to store his silver before the divorce.

But when it unfolds, it goes all the way to the ground and supports the weight of four or five grown men at one time. (Up to half a ton of rampaging beef.) About two weeks ago we thought we heard a prowler in the back of the apartment, and we felt trapped, insecure, and afraid. Thank goodness we remembered Plow & Hearth's Three Story Escape Ladder stuffed at the bottom of an armoire. We unrolled it, fastened the metal braces around the base of the windowsills, and each grabbed a cat while we silently slipped down the ladder into the night, calling the police once we were down by story 2.

At each step I found myself testing my own weight on the sturdy rungs, and seeing that it was pitch black (two nights before September's new moon) it was sort of scary and our two cats protested loudly, trying to wriggle back up the ladder toward the comfort of the apartment they had never known anything but! I looked up and thought I saw the intruder's face in a mask trying to dislodge the ladder's brace by prying it from the windowsill. My heart went rat-a-tat in my chest and my oaths rang out loud breaking the stillness of the alley. Whoever it was, faced with Plow & Hearth's magnificent craftsmanship, gave up and slunk away, ashamed even of trying. Later we weren't sure whether or not anyone had actually broken in while we were sleeping, or if maybe the TV was on—some heist movie with Cary Grant or Robert Wagner. I'm still confused. But grateful that we had our ladder nonetheless. The promo features a house on fire. Thank goodness we just had a phantom burglar. The moral is anything that gets you down to the ground in an emergency is a blessing in disguise.

Not without Love: Memoirs
by Constance Webb

★★★★★
Better than *Reds*

October 2, 2006

As a love story, this one's better than the movie *Reds* with Warren Beatty and Diane Keaton. As a book of memoirs, it's a little frustrating because it closes around 1960, right at the "first half of her life," as Constance Webb wrote. Perhaps she planned to write a sequel, but the recent announcement of her death makes us feel a great loss. She did manage to edit a book of her third husband's fairy stories for children, a wonderful boon for all those who enjoy great writing. Her third husband, after two inconsequential white pigs, was the Black, London-based cricketer turned economist and political theorist C. L. R. James, whom his intimates called "Nello," for one of his middle names was Lionel and "Nello" was a pet name for "Lionel."

On her side, she was a passionate labor activist and top model for the Conover agency. It's almost like a pulp novel, for during the day she's running around visiting California labor camps like Angelina Jolie in *Beyond Borders*, saving dying babies, and yet when night falls, she's a supermodel drinking in the sophisticated nightspots of '40s Manhattan like El Morocco and the Stork Club. In those days there were two top modeling agencies, one run by John Robert Powers, the other by Conover, who had the knack for renaming all of his discoveries with colorful names, rather like Andy Warhol did later on during the period of the Silver Factory. Conover's names were themselves lively and fun as the women who had to smile wearing them—including Choo Choo Johnson, Dusty Anderson, Jinx Falkenburg, Chili Williams, and Candy Jones. Conover didn't like "Constance" Webb as a name, so he called her "Frosty." And her career took off, but in the back of her mind she wondered how long she could continue as a supermodel while her Black friends, who included Chester Himes and Richard Wright, were suffering from pervasive race prejudice.

She took the plunge and fell in love with a kind friend, Nello, with whom she had a son, the unfortunate Nobbie. Later in life poor little Nobbie became a mentally ill street person. And many have wondered why Constance Webb refused to accompany her husband when McCarthy's henchmen had him deported back to London. Instead, she preferred to stay at home, raising little Nobbie, and corresponding with Nello by airmail, eventually divorcing him.

This book tells all! For anyone interested in Black participation in leftist causes of the 1930s, 1940s, and 1950s, this book is a natural, and also, of course, if you are curious about the political lives of supermodels. Fans of the comedian Jack Gilford will enjoy this book too, as well as those who want to read garish tales of Salvador Dalí's habit of licking his own sperm off the bodies of his love partners. And underneath all the gossip, you get a tragic love story.

Secret Anniversaries of the Heart: New & Selected Stories
by Lev Raphael

★★★★★
The Best of the Best

October 8, 2006

Ever since Yom Kippur I've been reading this book of stories as though my life depended on it, and strangers have gotten used to the sight of my walking down the street, boarding the cable car, and poking my way through the alleys of San Francisco with Lev Raphael's book propped up in front of my face. I might as well have a cane because I'm blind to everything else when I'm reading one of his books. And this one, I think, must be the best of them all, for as a collection of stories this improves on his earlier *Dancing on Tisha B'av* by abstracting the best of them and then adding as many more. The first book came out perhaps fifteen years ago, and since then he has only gotten even more into writing, and his wisdom about people has only grown, exponentially as it happens, so when you read one of his stories, it is like having a new life to live.

I don't know much about Jewish life so I don't know how accurate he is being about the mindset and customs of his characters (though I should say not all of them are Jewish) but even a gentile like me, who hardly ever has a religious thought in his head, comes to understand some of the conflicts shown by his people. In the title story, a writer living in Michigan with a successful and somewhat overbearing partner joins a writing group and encounters a Hungarian novelist with a mean streak who runs the group like a little Dick Cheney. To his chagrin, David can't speak up against this tyrant's ranting, even when it turns homophobic and a Bolivian newcomer is attacked for his poetry. Another workshop participant, Chase, reveals in rapid succession that not only is he Jewish, but he's on the down-low, a married man with a hankering for David. To his surprise, Jake (his boyfriend) and his accepting nature helps him realize that his paralysis during the workshop has everything to do with his now-dead mother, who was a survivor of a death camp and who just wasn't emotionally available to little David. She kept a suitcase under her bed just in case the Nazis, or their US equivalent, came again, and now David and Jake reflect that such a time may not be too far away. "She'd take it out and update the contents once or twice a year, always on the same date. Why those particular days? She never explained, but the bag was always ready, and so was she."

While our shelves groan with volumes of the American short story, we have a wealth of talent, but if I had a suitcase under my bed and wanted to take just a few books of the best, I would pack my Raymond Carver, my Grace Paley, and my book of Lev Raphael stories. He is beyond wonder, beyond guessing, his talent overflows like the gift of itself.

And plus, in "The Pathfinder," he has written possibly the sexiest story of all time. Check!

Stan Brakhage: Filmmaker
ed. David James

★★★★★
From a Wide Angle

October 9, 2006

What is the nature of art? What is its bottom line? At first when sent this book I was skeptical, thinking it would be a hagiography of a genuinely difficult artist about whom there are only shades of gray. But editor David E. James anticipated me there, and in his beautifully delineated preface goes right to the heart of the matter, the precipitous decline of Brakhage's reputation, a drop nearly unparalleled in contemporary art. Was he, as Annette Michelson or P. Adams Sitney once claimed, the sort of genius artist for whom whole eras used to be named? A filmmaker who combined a sincerity and authenticity with a true avant-garde spirit and actual hard-core discoveries that forever changed the medium? Or was he what his latter-day rep suggested, a driven, masculinist obsessive who was able to hide behind patriarchy the failures of an overdetermined use rule?

James makes it all sound so obvious, and yet he then comes around and suggests that even the haters might find something to cheer about with a new survey of Brakhage's voluminous output (four hundred films, of which it was sometimes said that even Brakhage himself had only seen maybe three quarters). Completists will sigh that James's compilation is too meager to do him justice, just as they balked at the recent Criterion release of twenty-seven films, with far too many from the last fifteen years of his life with those wild hand-painted strips of film. And not enough women writing about Brakhage, but that's one of the issues in the first place, isn't it, and this book merely reflects that. Even so, Carolee Schnee-mann and (especially) Abigail Child contribute two of the most cogent essays here. There are a few "poetic" pieces written by Brakhage's contemporaries, such as the essays by Bruce Baillie and Chick Strand, that not even their mothers could love.

As James points out, there are few notable artists about whom so little biographical information is available. I vote for James himself to give it a go. Not only does his introduction represent and con-dense a whale's load of original research, but one of his own pieces, "Amateurs in the Industry Town" (on Warhol and Brakhage wrestling with Los Angeles both as metropolis and conceptual free-domland), is a brilliant and focused article that sheds light not only on the supposed duality between the two filmmakers but on their mutual interests and fellowship.

Musee Mechanique
by Rodney Koeneke

★★★★★
The Search for Sexy Subforms on the Proust List

October 11, 2006

Now based in Portland, Oregon, the poet formerly of San Francisco is also an Amazon reviewer of long standing and has written a worthy follow-up to a prizewinning first volume, *Rouge State* (2003). Looks like a typo, doesn't it, and that I should have written *Rogue State*, but Koeneke's art is partly based on the sort of automatic mistakes Dr. Freud used to write about, and now in *Musee Mechanique* he tries to prove that on the internet, there are no accidents.

He reveals in the afterword here that since writing the poems of *Rouge State*, he enrolled in a poetic movement based in New York called "Flarf," named by the poet Gary Sullivan, who contributes a pen-and-ink portrait of Koeneke staring off into space, his lips pursed as though Apollo was prompting him to speak to memory. The idea of Flarf, Koeneke writes, was "to enter the most absurd or inappropriate search terms into Google and sculpt a poem from the results." Koeneke refers to Jack Spicer's concept of the poet as a radio, picking up transmissions from the outer reaches of the broadband, perhaps of the universe, and so the Flarf poet works with difficult, demotic, sometimes obscene materials—from whatever shows up on a Google search. Musée Méchanique itself is the tourist trap at Fisherman's Wharf here in San Francisco, which preserves primitive mechanical toys and coin-operated games from the nineteenth century onward. Put a penny in the slot, see what happens. Koeneke makes the conceptual jump from the museum of bygone toys (where, as it happens, he used to work in their gift shop) to the curious inner workings of postmodern poetry.

You might say that no "I" operates in this writing, since the poet as author has stepped back and let a host of anonymous, obstreperous voices do the actual writing for him (or her). Oddly enough, however, no matter how many chance operations the poet applies, something of a core personality still shines through and Koeneke emerges out the other end of the fun machine as pretty much the same curly-haired sprite he went in as. He hears the lamb's innocent call, and he hears the ewe's tender reply.

In four parts, like Eliot's *Four Quartets*, the book makes a religious pilgrimage out of the current junk culture of American commodity society (the Flarf writers, most often US citizens, cast a caustic eye on nationalism in general), and moves like a line in the sand from the hermetic magic of "Fire Water Burn" toward the musical iteration of "Verse. Chorus. Verse." One whole section, "On the Clamways," uses the humble bivalve everywhere you used to be able to imagine a noun, or verb. Does "On the Clamways" represent a revisioning of Clark Coolidge's jazz-influenced *On the Nameways* (2000)? There are similar salutes to the aleatory procedures of Jackson Mac Low, and to the perceived misanthropy of Lautréamont. The goofball lyrics of "Clamways" include "Houston, We Have a Clam Problem" as well as "That's Just the Clam Talking."

Is it just the clam talking? is what everybody always wants to know about Flarf, for how far does that line in the sand move and shift to erase, with the wind of technology, an artist's personal responsibility for what is being said? As the book draws to a close, Koeneke suggests that his poetry, and that of his colleagues, serves to reduce social tensions by miniaturizing and animating them like the coin-operated toys in his museum, thus robbing them of their threat, or perhaps their power to harm. In any case, he has written an engaging book that, for all its apparent insouciance, has a jewellike filigree of "work," and a sunny radiance that feels warm in your hands as you hold it to the light.

Creature From the Black Lagoon (1954)
dir. Jack Arnold

★★★★★
On a Tributary of the Amazon

October 15, 2006

We had the pleasure of seeing this the other night in San Francisco at the Castro Theatre, in dual-projection 3D against a silver screen. Flimsy little glasses were provided to help blend the images popped out onto the screen by the twin projectors. It must have cost a mint just to stage this show, but happily the event was packed with like-minded *Creature* lovers and everyone cheered, oohed and aahed as soon as the Brazilian diggers uncover, in a solid block of limestone, the skeletonized hand of a long-dead Creature, its webbed fingers beckoning right out over the audience's heads! It was a powerful punch to the solar plexus and a reminder that even archaeology has its thrills.

The 3D effects are more subtle than you'd think. There's nothing else, for example, as in your face as the Ping-Pong ball that jumps repeatedly off the screen in *House of Wax*. Here, director Jack Arnold seems to be trying really hard to give flesh and blood to his two protagonists, Richard Carlson and Richard Denning, showing them off as the brain and the emotions, while Julie Adams plays sensitively and sympathetically to both. Is she sort of trying to figure out which side of the bread her butter's on? The doctor tells her that she repaid any debt she owed Richard Carlson long ago—she doesn't owe him anything anymore, her playing Pygmalion to her untutored Galatea.

So in a way it's hard to tell up front which man she's going to wind up with. The Creature I found sympathetic in a way, but I think the performance must be docked a wee bit because of the different actors playing the part. Up on top, it's the sensitive, tortured Ben Chapman, while down below, Ricou Browning's frisky balletic style, like Harold Land underwater, makes him seem more fancy free.

To top it off Julie Adams and Ben Chapman were there, discussing the complex dynamic of the "beauty and the beast" scenario producer William Alland dreamed up on a South American jaunt with Orson Welles. Miss Adams has got to be in her seventies surely, and yet she is still heart-stoppingly gorgeous and lovely. She spoke to anyone who approached her, seemingly grateful to the fans who have kept the Creature from the Black Lagoon, and the woman he loved, alive in cultural memory for more than fifty years now. It was an enchanted evening—in dual-projection 3D, no less.

Velvet Goldmine (1998)
dir. Todd Haynes

★★★★★
Baby's on Fire

October 19, 2006

Fueled by a trio of brave performances by his leading men, Todd Haynes manages to pull off what could have been a disaster. His films have been hit and miss, and how dubious does that upcoming Bob Dylan biopic sound, and yet on the other hand *Velvet Goldmine* is a real achievement and actually makes me look forward to seeing Dylan played by Cate Blanchett or whoever it is Haynes has lured into it.

Jonathan Rhys Meyers has a tall order, he has to play someone with the charisma and good looks of David Bowie, someone who turns heads everywhere he goes and who's always the hottest guy in the room. By and large he makes it happen, although a few of his outfits are subpar and his performance at the Sombrero Club, while mimicking the *Hunky Dory* Bowie look to a T, just falls flat, you can't imagine anyone would listen to such a performance. Movie lovers are divided about Rhys Meyers, some of us love him, others wish he had never been born. This movie is probably his best part up to the present, and it's a keeper.

Ewan McGregor plays Curt Wild as though his life depends on it, and his ill-fated romance with Brian Slade becomes the center-piece of the film. When Rhys Meyers and McGregor are together, the movie comes alive, ludicrous and overwrought as it is, it has the furious kind of movie energy Pauline Kael always used to prize. She would have enjoyed Haynes's reinvention of movie tropes, the deep-focus Sternberg photography lavished on Brian Slade, the *Citizen Kane* / *Mr. Arkadin* style of multiple narrators, each with a different piece of the puzzle, the lurid redo of James Bidgood's *Pink Narcissus* Technicolor palette.

Christian Bale's reporter Arthur Stuart is the key to the movie, isn't it, from Bale acting a teenager in a stuffy London suburb at the beginning, hiding his love for Brian Slade under a bushel basket, to the later scenes where he interviews as many principals as he can dig up as an adult—a super skinny adult, looks like you could break him in two. When he approaches Toni Collette and mumbles "I'm Arthur Stuart," it sounds like he's introducing himself as "Martha Stewart," so everyone in the audience laughs nowadays, but Collette looks impressed, who wouldn't be?

Lessons in Becoming Myself
by Ellen Burstyn

★★★★★
Bigger than Life

October 24, 2006

Ellen's mother was always too busy for her and could never fully connect with her daughter's dreams. Ellen wound up spending much of her life in a vain effort to impress her mom, and not until full maturity was she blessed with the wisdom that some people are just unimpressable and don't really care very much, even perhaps about their own children. As for her father, much of the prepublication publicity about *Lessons in Becoming Myself* centered on her weird dad, and all I can say is you've never read anything like it. Jennifer Connelly, you thought you had it bad in *Requiem for a Dream*, but you should have asked Ellen Burstyn for tips on how to handle infinitely sleazy sex situations! Her father, whom she hadn't seen in years, came on to her in a very graphic way, jumping into her bed, when as a young adult she paid a visit to him and his new wife. He never gave up on his hope of bedding her, even on his deathbed! He's sickening and you can't believe she survived this incest trauma, but maybe it just gave her wisdom about men being pigs.

Even before she was famous, Ellen had the knack for attracting genius male artists, and some of the liveliest chapters of her book involve her encounters with the great. You get an extended glimpse of Jackie Gleason (Ellen was one of his dancers on his TV show in the 1950s), and in a very different direction, when she visited France, she was taken by two Texans to meet the elderly modernist painter Marc Chagall at his home in Saint-Paul-de-Vence. Chagall was so taken by her that he brought her out to the balcony and sat with her on his terraces, leaving poor Madame Chagall to deal with the other guests inside. Let's see, who else? She met the architect and futurist Buckminster Fuller and he wrote a lovely poem for her, bemoaning the fact that he was too old to make love to her, but their souls would always be intertwined. Oh, and Carlos Castaneda has dinner with her, then shows up the next day with the manuscript of his new book (*The Second Ring of Power*) asking her to make a movie of it! "Carlos Castaneda was very real, as were his experiences," she states flatly, but I don't know how she knows this for sure. It wasn't like she went to Mexico with him or anything. Maybe she picked it up from his aura.

She is super into the New Age, so if you get tetchy about New Age notions, you might as well skip this book. I guess you wouldn't be reading a book called *Lessons in Becoming Myself* if you were allergic to the way we think here in California!

By the time she hit it big, Ellen was already in her midthirties and more mature at handling stardom than some of her '70s cohorts. She gives unvarnished portraits of the camaraderie of movie sets, and details her adventures making *The Last Picture Show* in Texas, stuck at a motel for weeks and watching the inevitable romance between Bogdanovich and Cybill Shepherd. Cloris Leachman won the Oscar for the part, and behind her she overheard poor Ann-Margret whisper "I'm sorry, Daddy" (for she, Ann-Margret, had just lost the Oscar to Cloris). This resonated for Ellen Burstyn, who had spent far too much of her life trying to please others. It's a haunting anecdote, and Ellen tells the story well.

Making *The Exorcist* was a different kettle of fish, and the troupe was besieged by supernatural horror both on the screen and off. As Burstyn reports, nearly everyone involved in the film had something horrible happen to them, and Ellen did not escape the curse unscathed. Worse, she was drawn into an intellectual, then eventually romantic relationship with the film's troubled director Billy Friedkin, who ultimately jilted her to marry Jeanne Moreau (Ellen had to read about it in the papers)!

Her romantic life has been filled with trauma, and she is especially unsparing of her own conduct during some of these relationships. One husband, Neil Burstyn, was especially abusive, for due to a schizophrenic breakdown he began to think of himself as Jesus Christ and began stalking her, even after she had divorced him. He showed up in the audience of her Broadway play, *Same Time, Next Year*, and screamed out her name during a tender moment she shared onstage with Charles Grodin. I won't spoil what happens in the story, but it has a bittersweet ending.

There are tremendous accounts of making Bob Rafelson's *The King of Marvin Gardens*, nearly a forgotten film today but one of the glories of the so-called New American Cinema, and also regarding the making of Alain Resnais's *Providence*. Alas, she speaks very little about my own favorite of her films, Jules Dassin's *A Dream of Passion* with Melina Mercouri.

It is a book of grand ambitions and an inner voyage into the bottomless pit of self. One thing I was surprised about is Burstyn's insistence that she herself was responsible not only for all that great acting but for writing or otherwise creating many of her best lines in her very best work. She improvised parts of her role as Chris MacNeil in *The Exorcist*, huge sections of *Alice Doesn't Live Here Anymore* were her idea, the whole plotline of *Resurrection* she based on her own spiritual journey, and she even came up with the curtain line for *Same Time, Next Year* after it defeated dozens of script doctors. After a while Burstyn's propensity for claiming credit for everything good about any of her projects becomes a little amusing. I think it must stem from her inner insecurity about growing up in the Depression and having everything taken from her all her life.

Otherwise *Lessons in Becoming Myself* is a captivating book that will teach you plenty about acting, technique, style, the power of Sufi healing, magic in our lives, the genius of Lee Strasberg, and how to reinvent yourself and keep going on even when everything in your world collapses. I started reading this book after dinner on Friday night and spent the whole weekend on the edge of my seat, trying to contain my rising excitement. This should be a huge bestseller on the scale of Kay Graham's *Personal History* or Jane Fonda's *My Life So Far*.

American Movie Critics: An Anthology from the Silents until Now
ed. Phillip Lopate

★★★★★
Screen Tests

October 24, 2006

I wanted a book that would cover a wide array of reviews and struck gold with this one. Though now that I think of it, maybe I should have held out for one that included non-American writers in it. I'm such a dunce, I didn't see until too late that, on the title page, clearly marked, it reads "A special publication of the Library of America." No wonder it's so America-centric, but I picked up the book and opened it by happenstance to Penelope Gilliatt's scintillating review of Fassbinder's *Petra von Kant*, and naturally I took the book to be more international in scope than it actually is. In what universe do people think of Gilliatt as a US writer? It doesn't really matter because what remains deserves four stars.

Lopate doesn't go just for the simple no-brainer essays by each of the authors, but he actually spends time thinking of new ways to showcase their skills. Thus for James Agee we don't get the old silent-clowns piece, nor the one on *Monsieur Verdoux* or Val Lewton. He goes for the unfamiliar nearly every time, which is nice. (The only exception I can see offhand is Molly Haskell on "The Woman's Film," but that's nice in a quite different way since Haskell's essay is so lengthy and comprehensive that it is only occasionally reprinted anywhere, despite its historical significance.)

John Ashbery and bell hooks have certainly written better work elsewhere. But it is nice to see James Harvey and Stuart Klawans, both so underrated, here given pride of place. And having Libby Gelman-Waxner in a book of this kind is certainly a victory for gay incursion into the canon. James Baldwin on *Lady Sings the Blues* and Paul Schrader's "Notes on Film Noir" would alone make a great book, and there are literally dozens of others of equal quality. Gee, that Renata Adler could sure bite back, couldn't she? I don't remember her as so acerbic as she is here about Richard Brooks's film *In Cold Blood*. Talk about cold blooded, she's the kind of writer about whom I used to think, admiringly, "She's so New York," when I meant "acidic."

Everything Preserved: Poems 1955–2005
by Landis Everson, ed. Ben Mazer

★★★★★
Wanting Burning

October 25, 2006

By now everyone has heard of the story of Landis Everson, the golden boy of the Berkeley Renaissance of the immediate postwar era, whose poems were sought after by all the top poetry magazines of the mid-1950s (*Poetry, Kenyon, Hudson*, etc.); and then, after finishing up two extended serial poems ("Postcard from Eden" and "The Little Ghosts I Played With," both included here), he stopped writing abruptly just as the serial poem was bringing him into a new arena of intelligence and sensuality. Everson turned instead to painting, and people pretty much forgot he was a poet until a few years ago when the young scholar and poet Ben Mazer, based in Cambridge, Massachusetts, but researching a feature on the Berkeley poets, cast a net out to San Luis Obispo and found Everson still alive and ultra responsive—and perhaps looking for a challenge. Within a few months, Everson entered into a frenzy of new work, in which he was averaging nearly a poem a day.

The new material in *Everything Preserved* isn't as uneven as the *Publishers Weekly* review indicates; if anything, Everson's '50s material was the uneven corpus of work, and Mazer has whittled it down here to a mere handful of poems, whereas I could have stood to see a whole lot more from the '50s. Maybe they will appear in another volume. He definitely wrote more than nine worth preserving! But the newsflash is all about the seventy (or so) new poems written between 2003 and 2005 that Mazer chose for the heart of this volume. Some of the poems revive memories of long-ago lovers, friends, or colleagues (a few of the very best are written in homage to Jack Spicer and his theories of dictation and seriality); some are wry Ashberyan remixes of old movies from the glory days of Hollywood classic cinema—*Red Dust*, *My Favorite Blonde*.

Often Everson will pluck from the air a theme or two, entangle them like ribbons round a maypole within the first three or four lines of his poem, and then introduce a third, contra-contrapuntal theme in the second stanza, watching as these elements take on what almost seems like a life of their own in rondo. His is an elegant interchange of control and release, in which mistake, misunderstanding, the aleatory, and the interrupted are each given a place at the table. In "Another Look at the Garden" the images of fairies, food, fabric, furniture, and fire shift and interchange places like ceramic shepherdesses performing minuets inside a Fabergé egg, continually revealing new relationality. "They were not asked to share our sofas, / but once an idea is needed / it spreads like salt and sugar. They are / riding in our automobiles, / eating our dinners." What makes the poems so delicious is a limpid, sunny sexuality; you haven't seen a writing so filled with kissing, flirting, cuddling, stripping off since the "Goblin Market" of Christina Rossetti. Oh wait, that was kind of creepy wasn't it? Well, there's a fear factor here too. That's always the case when the fairy tale comes real.

The Heart to Artemis: A Writer's Memoir
by Bryher

★★★★★
It Ends at the Blitz

October 30, 2006

Her family had heaps of money, and some said her father was the richest man in England, though this is not immediately apparent in Bryher's account of her middle-class childhood and upbringing. Money couldn't save her from the old ennui, however, and she soon found, at age four, that the world seemed more real in books—books like her early favorite, Johann Wyss's *Swiss Family Robinson*, with its romantic reimagining of the nuclear family shipwrecked on a desert island yet still managing to maintain a happy structure. She was brought outside as a baby to watch the dark night sky light up for once during the Diamond Jubilee of Victoria. And yet she managed to throw herself into life and rubbing elbows with many of the modernist bigwigs, from Freud to Havelock Ellis. She married improvident men twice, and made her life with the poet H.D., who must have recently died when Bryher began her memoir, for much of the book's second half seems like an extended elegy to H.D.'s American elegance and sex appeal. For the times (first published in 1963), *The Heart to Artemis* is surprisingly frank about the relationship between herself and H.D.

The only weakness I see in the book is perhaps a fault only to the bourgeois; she literally tells about and neglects to show us—to use workshop jargon that she would have abhorred—how stifling it was to be a young woman in the prewar period. It's funny because she makes so many other things vivid and alive; the book is filled with specific smells, noises, colors, and the feel of fabric. But the utter restraint she so often moans about, and probably for good reason, remains uninhabited. Perhaps that's tied up with what it was: an absence. She has one funny part where she describes how even landscape gardening had its strict codes, and one of them was the absolute insistence on decoration, what would strike us now as an absurd number of plantings. "Everything at that time had to curl," she writes. "There ought to be some special term to describe the horror a blank space evoked in 1900."

Those of you puzzled by the title will find an explanation on page 111 in which, at age nine, she gave her heart to Artemis, her body to exploration. Social restrictions irked her; she despaired of succeeding as a novelist, for example, because "social taboos have cut me off from much of the material that I should have liked to use." She cites the case of a lumberman whose earthy chitchat she will never be able to overhear unguarded. At the same time, she is almost mystic about the power of the artist. "I have a profound contempt for the writer who speaks of making his work intelligible to the masses," she says. "He is not serving them but betraying their trust. Our job is to feel the movement of time as its direction is about to change and there can be no reward but the vision itself. It is natural that we should be both disliked and ignored."

A Bay of Blood (1971)
dir. Mario Bava

★★★★★
Bygone Beauty

October 31, 2006

Bava plays a Hitchcock-like trick at the beginning of *Bay of Blood*, using Isa Miranda precisely as Hitchcock used Janet Leigh in the first reels of *Psycho*. Surely once you had secured the services of one of the greatest international stars of all time, you weren't going to kill her off—and so quickly! But that is precisely Bava's strategy, and that's precisely what he does. The gesture of this shock effect is largely lost on contemporary audiences who don't remember Isa Miranda properly, but she was still a potent force in 1971 when *A Bay of Blood* (also known as *Twitch of the Death Nerve*) was produced. When you kill off your biggest star within the first fifteen minutes of the movie, in an especially brutal way, you are signaling your audience that all bets are off, no one is safe, and check your preconceptions about cinema and narrative structure at the door.

A shame in a way, because the movie sure could use a lot more of Miranda, though talented actors pop up every ten minutes or so like ducks in a shooting gallery. Isa Miranda was the great international sensation of Mussolini's Italy; even MGM got wind of her and imported her à la Garbo for a few unsuccessful American films right before the outbreak of World War II put a kibosh on her career in the States. Back in Italy she continued in her reign as a sort of Dolores del Río–slash-Nazimova tragedy queen, with huge dollops of sex thrown in for mass appeal. Thus in *La Ronde* (1950), Max Ophüls saves her perhaps the most delectable sequence of all, larding her into a sex sandwich between boyish Gérard Philipe (the Ryan Phillippe of his day!) and stalwart Jean-Louis Barrault from *Children of Paradise*. David Lean made her the earthy manageress of the *pensione* spinstery Katharine Hepburn stays at in Venice in *Summer Madness* (aka *Summertime*, 1955), using her magnificent, somewhat ravaged sensuality as a contrapuntal force, much as plain Deborah Kerr is confronted by wild Ava Gardner in John Huston's later film of *Night of the Iguana*. In *A Bay of Blood*, which begins with Miranda's countess rolling her wheelchair moodily past window after curtained window in her château over the bay, a mood of desolate and painful memory is instantly set up. It's as if she's thinking of all the "white telephone" movies she's ever played in, and ruing the day when her great beauty came to an end. Bava's photography is always top notch, but in the opening sequence of *A Bay of Blood* he puts it to memorial use: the color shimmers; the light radiates off of Miranda's hair, eyes, profile; and the wheels creak in protest as she forces them across the long gallery for one last look at her bay.

Multiple Orgasm Set II
by NARS Cosmetics

★★★★★
Multiple Choice

November 6, 2006

After reading twenty-five pages of reviews on a makeup-specific review site, and thumbing through the remainder I could see there were possibly over two thousand reviews, I was surprised to find no one has yet written about this product on Amazon. I'm not only the first man, I'm the first human being! Now, what I would like specifically to comment on today is the fact that you get not only one, not two, but three products packaged together with this product, and I think the combination may be cutting into sales instead of vice versa. The famous Orgasm blush, the color of pale, demure, Staffordshire pottery, is sitting next to the florid bronze tanner, like two squares in the old game show of *Hollywood Squares*. Never have two contestants seemed so disparate, so unlikely to get along. The golden shimmer of the blush versus the hard, cold, ersatz tan, like something worn by Gloria Grahame in Vincente Minnelli's *The Bad and the Beautiful*. It's almost as though the two beauty lines come from different planets, or families of Darwinian species. Surely when the blush on the left leans over and peers at its calculated, self-assured cousin the bronzer, it cries out a little in pure shock.

Some on Makeup Alley approve this experiment in contrast, others disdain it. One writer put it clumsily, and yet expressed in capital letters what most of us feel: "It's like apples and oranges and it will give your skin the consistency of a warm apple and the texture of rough orange peel." Translation: maybe if you want a blush, just go for simple NARS Orgasm, don't try to make yourself blush and tan at the same time.

Others compare the qualities, the innate qualities, of blush and bronzer by casting back to the nineteenth-century novelists: the icily beautiful and evil Lady Honoria Dedlock is the dark shadow in Dickens's *Bleak House*, while her daughter Esther Summerson is the younger, plain girl everyone adores for her winning simplicity.

The situation—as far as purchasers of the Nars Multiple Orgasm Set II—multiplies geometrically by the introduction of a daring lip gloss that seems to shout for attention, saying "Yes, you've been paying attention to your skin but in fact the lips need help immediately!" Thus putting a constraint over the user, asking the unnecessarily complicated question, What is the cost of beauty? If the house was on fire, should I take my gloss, bronzer, or blush? What kind of mood do I want to set in the minds of others? Does this blush make my face glow with apricot softness, or will the bronzer let me slip into a Hollywood wrap party unmolested? When you scrawl the inside of your arm with a swab of lip gloss, your arm starts to tingle with beauty. I started to write my name, and got out only the letters *K-E-V* before I couldn't write any longer, I was too overcome. People say that the bronzer has some of the qualities of baked earthenware pots from

Tucson, Arizona, and it has been suggested that one of its essential ingredients might be tumbleweed. Warm to the sun, or shy like a wet violet—or phallic as the lip-gloss tube that swivels in your fist like a slinky. If you had to reach for one, and only one, which would it be—a shrewd, if crude, psychological test.

---

35 Cents
by Matty Lee

★★★★★
Miami Vice

November 10, 2006

He was the victim of a horde of vultures who wouldn't leave him alone. "Everywhere I went they were there: at the bathrooms in the park, at the YMCA, at family gatherings, everywhere." He was molested so many times he began to think it was normal human discourse. There must have been something special about this boy, because he was tragically popular. He grew to hate being alone, for instantly they would ruffle their vulture wings, seeking a sacrifice. "Every time I was alone for five minutes or more, one of them would turn up." They played a game, pedophile and abandoned boy. "Always the same game, touch me, let me touch you." The wonder is that, in recounting these events thirty years on, Matty Lee is able to bring so much humor and clarity to his story. He brings to writing the gifts of a great comedian, the timing, the knowledge of human nature, and the capability for forgiveness and redemption.

Our narrator learns that "if you pretend to be something you aren't, sooner or later it will catch up with you." In Lee's own case, it wasn't so much pretense, it was an honest mistake. His abusive father taught him to solve his problems through alcohol and violence, and his termagant mother, who had him committed to the social services when he was still a little boy, just because she could, was no better. They set him up to try to please as many men as possible by offering his body, often for bargain prices and at least once for only thirty-five cents. The graphic designers who made a cover for this memoir, showing us the extreme mental poverty of thirty-five cents, bring it all back home.

Along the way he meets the pond scum of South Beach (Miami) and the detail is so disgusting that I hope never to find myself in Dade County ever again. And yet somewhere along the way young Matty learned lessons in resilience that help him even now. There were some good people, even among the men who bought his company. He buried his heterosexual desires under a cloud of heavy drugs, believing himself to be gay until he turned seventeen or eighteen. Amazingly he lived, when many of his *compadrinos* wound up dead, either from drugs, sexual predators, or heroin. Like a cat he wound up on all four feet, and after a difficult beginning with the mysteries of language (he goes to the library and asks for *Giorgio Armani's Room* by "James Baldron"), his verbal and imaginative skills skyrocketed. At the end of a long journey he has emerged from a dark and savage tunnel, the author of one of the best memoirs of our century.

The Most Beautiful Man in the World: Paul Swan,
from Wilde to Warhol
by Janis Londraville and Richard Londraville

★★★★★
A Poem for Trapped Things

November 12, 2006

I have a feeling this book will continue to draw acclaim as the months and years go by, for it must be the standard biography for some time to come. Drawing on a wealth of material from the artist's family, Janis Londraville and Richard Londraville have managed to animate a long-forgotten story, and it has made me completely interested in Paul Swan's works in all their guises. It's hard to imagine today the ease with which Paul Swan seems to have said to himself "Well, painting is only making me this famous, I think I'll add another string to my bow and become an interpretative dancer." How often does that happen, and how often does any artist excel in both wildly competitive fields?

Janis Londraville and Richard Londraville hint that Swan's good looks helped him along here and there. With so many photos of him spread throughout the book, a concordance of beauty begins to take shape in the reader's mind. Is he the "most beautiful man in the world," as his press agents claimed? It's a type of good looks you don't see very much today, or if you do, you see them in leading men who are just average looking—say, the Bill Pullman look. (Take a gander at the book jacket photo.) But Swan knew how to work his look, and he studied the Egyptian arts of presentation, so that his dances resembled early versions of Madonna's "Vogue" movements, with hand manipulations framing the face, the body, the long legs, and the cinched-in waist. He could have been a contender in the movies, but alas, he let the camera come close a little too late (he was already forty when he played a herald in *The Ten Commandments*, first version, by Cecil B. DeMille). In fact his age was always getting in his way, like a clumsy, ardent teenage boy stumbling over his erection. In old age he was still performing his "Grecian" and "classic" dances in which, apparently, he would dance off his seven veils and at the end reveal the original naked body Isadora Duncan had fondled way back in the day. In his prime, when he went to Greece, Greek newspapers claimed that their statuary had come to life and was walking in American clothes! "See him and then see our marbles! ... Is he not the Hermes of Praxiteles come to life again? Or is he Antinous?"

He was sort of a dramatic Paul Lynde sort of queen except without a sense of humor, and not much of a dad to his two long-suffering daughters. The authors luckily had his unpublished memoirs to draw on, and they are adept in art criticism to a scary extent, coming close to persuading me that Paul Swan's painting is necessary, like Thomas Hart Benton or Jackson Pollock. At any rate he is an American Rousseau, for good or bad, and I would love a companion volume with full-color plates of all his surviving work. And what a shame that the authors worked hard interviewing nearly every available witness who knew the old man, and in a touching vignette they report that one, the dancer Lisan Kaye, who posed as the Empress Theodora in 1944 for Swan, can't remember him at all, trapped as she is in her Alzheimer's disease. Something very Swan-like about that inability.

Do the authors cheat in subtitling their book "from Wilde to Warhol," considering that Swan actually never did meet Oscar Wilde? Yes, a little, I think, but it suits the carnival-barker aspect of their subject, for whom no publicity was bad publicity.

Elephant (2003)
dir. Gus Van Sant

★★★★★
Shadows Breaking over My Head
November 12, 2006

I think I was in the right space now for watching the film, for I found it beautifully filmed, well acted, and altogether insightful in its experimental approach to the violence underlying Western American culture in the present day. In the wake of Columbine and other high school shootings, today's kids live in an atmosphere of fear, and sudden death spares no one, not even the most beautiful and stylish. I guess high school has always been about fear (*Buffy the Vampire Slayer* had it right), but add guns to the mixture and you have a situation in which the bullied can finally strike back. Van Sant takes a measured approach to this quasi-revolutionary thesis, doubling back again and again from a crucial hallway confrontation (between Eli and John, as Eli takes what might be the very last photo ever taken of the lad) as if to prohibit us from deciding that "Aha, that's why they did it!"

So that we keep seeing this apparently simple scene more than once, not on a rote basis either, but the film returns to it at unexpected cadenzas, never when you might guess it was happening. Similarly the characters are "introduced" (by their names, in the sort of intertitles you'd see in silent films) at different lengths of time following their visual introductions. There's a free-jazz timing behind each production decision, and it's pretty exhilarating. Yes, there are some horrid, clichéd scenes in the script. The three girls all throwing up at the same time seem to have stepped out of a satire like *Mean Girls*; but up until that moment their interchange, and the agonistic byplay among the three, as one tries to break free of a slavish friendship, had been nearly lifelike and never boring (an extensive De Palma–esque continuous moving shot sees them warily circling the cafeteria like hummingbirds).

Van Sant begins the movie with a painful sequence in which John makes his dad pull over, too drunk to drive, and takes the wheel himself, and he casts the redoubtable US actor Timothy Bottoms to play the part of the dad, thus clearly signaling a tip of the hat to the 1970s New American Cinema in which Bottoms had played such a crucial part (*The Last Picture Show*, *Johnny Got His Gun*, *Love and Pain and the Whole Damn Thing*). All of a sudden, the opening tells us, a lineage shows itself, ancestry asserts itself. Youth grows old, despite what happens in the rest of the movie.

Donkey Skin (1970)
dir. Jacques Demy

★★★★★
Memories of an American Boy in France
November 15, 2006

You have to be able to give yourself to a movie without really understanding it, to appreciate the beautiful qualities of Jacques Demy's *Peau d'âne*. So much of the story doesn't make any sense to American viewers. Why, for example, does the prince sham illness in order to get Donkey Skin to bake him a cake? He knows who she is, why doesn't he just go for it? Why go through the rigmarole of getting every woman in the kingdom to try on the ring? How does he know that only Catherine Deneuve would be able to wear the ring? What if he got someone else instead? (We see a cute reaction shot when a very young princess, maybe four or five years old, tries on the ring and it's way too big for her.)

   Growing up in France, commercial TV played this movie every Christmas, just the way that here in the USA they were showing *It's a Wonderful Life*. For us American children trapped in Paris at Christmastime, there was one great treat, a showing of *Peau d'âne* every year to look forward to (this was in the days before DVD and even VHS). You'll see the special cake that Catherine Deneuve makes with her dirty twin, and you'll wonder why she makes such a flat cake for the prince—it's a visual reminder of our special Christmas cake, the galette, round and flat, into which a shoe, a baby, or other toy has been inserted. We would have a *bûche de Noël* every year, always a cause for general applause. (The princess slips a golden ring into the cake, and Prince Charming nearly chokes to death on it!) In many ways Demy puts in references to our charming French Christmas traditions. We would stay up late and have a midnight dinner the French servants called the *réveillon*, an enormous feast with chickens, geese, sausage, and sometimes quail. You'd think everyone would be fat, but even Santa Claus, or as we call him, Père Noël, although dressed in red like Prince Charming (Jacques Perrin) in this film, is always portrayed as thin, nearly emaciated: compare him to the enormously fat jolly man American kids call Santa Claus.

By the way, we put out shoes by the fireplace, whereas you American children hang up stockings on the mantelpiece! Then when we open our gifts, we settle in for the annual treat of seeing Jacques Demy's masterpiece, *Peau d'âne*. Now as an adult, I can see that Delphine Seyrig and Micheline Presle were still quite attractive in 1970, though to a child they seem quite elderly compared to how young Deneuve looks. We had gotten used to seeing Deneuve and Jacques Perrin together in Demy's previous film, *Les demoiselles de Rochefort*, but here they share even more charisma and sex appeal. Their number together doing backward somersaults and then gliding down a placid river on a painted barge, torches burning bright in daylight, is one of the best in the film.

At Home with Kate: Growing Up in Katharine Hepburn's Household
by Eileen Considine-Meara

★★★★★
Food, Famous Folks, and a Strange, Gruff, Charming Boss

November 16, 2006

As a child growing up in France, I had little contact with American films or TV, but my mother spoke often of her friendship with the US actress Katharine Hepburn, who had served as a spokeswoman for the international relief agency CARE when my mother worked there.

Now comes Eileen Considine-Meara's life of her mother, the chef Norah, who worked for Ms. Hepburn for many years and who, apparently, too shy to write a book herself (or perhaps enjoined from doing so by contractual agreement), has passed on many tall tales to her daughter. Young Eileen practically grew up in the household, and helped out as a waitress from time to time, or did other tasks at the behest of the aging, famously independent screen star. Neither Eileen nor Norah knew Spencer Tracy, of course, for he died in the 1960s and Hepburn didn't hire Norah until 1972. Yet his presence was everywhere in both the New York townhouse and the Connecticut country estate. One of the brief chapters involves a visit paid to Hepburn by Susie Tracy, the daughter of Spencer and his long-suffering wife. As grand as a movie star herself, Susie Tracy could have been an outstanding supermodel or politician, but she preferred to work quietly, in the shadows, helping deaf people the world over.

Yes, Norah and Eileen met hundreds of fascinating folk from all walks of life. Stephen Sondheim lived next door, kept a polite distance from Hepburn. Michael Jackson and Warren Beatty paid visits, not together. But Hepburn so craved adulation that she was not above inviting fans and plain old stalkers in off of the streets, like the parable of Dives and Lazarus in the Bible. And every year she let Norah have a huge Saint Patrick's Day party in her townhouse, vacating the space for a while.

Old friends Irene Mayer Selznick and Laura Harding make cameo appearances in this book. Harding, with whom other biographers have asserted Katharine Hepburn was involved sexually, seems like a nice enough soul in old age. She liked Norah's cooking and one dessert especially, Norah's famous lemon jello. In my test kitchen at home, I've tried to make several of Norah's recipes, feeling with some justice if they were good enough for Katharine Hepburn, they should be good enough for my own circle of theatrical friends. Alas, I just don't have the touch, for Norah's famous lace cookies that so entranced Sidney Poitier were a flop when I served them to Sidney Potrero of Daly City, and creamed chipped beef on toast, the dish Jack Larson demanded on each of his visits from Hollywood, proved a sensational failure in my South of Market kitchenette. I can't even describe what it looks like.

An exciting book with many nice touches, like a floor map of the Forty-Ninth Street townhouse and a photo of Eileen and her groom on their wedding day in which you can see exactly the Irish-spitfire charm that made her a favorite of her mother's Oscar-winning employer.

She Died a Lady
by John Dickson Carr

★★★★★
The Big Leap

November 16, 2006

As an American boy in France, I was often drawn to the cliffs of Normandy from which, if I stood on tiptoes, it seemed I could almost see the southeastern quadrant of England, the so-called hellfire corner which had borne the brunt of much of the V-2 activity during World War II. The cliffs themselves rose seventy feet in the air, yet during high tide the water rose a good thirty feet, so that a good swimmer might actually make a successful dive off the cliff. We played with white pebbles at its edge, tossing them at the white-water rafters at the edge of the sea. Grandfather told us that long ago, Victor Hugo had written about such brave, existentially challenged fishermen, calling them "the Toilers of the Sea." In *She Died a Lady*, one of Carr's famous "pronoun novels" (including *He Wouldn't Kill Patience* and *It Walks by Night*), Carr makes use of a similar dramatic cliff vista as the center of his chilling and somewhat far-fetched impossible-crime caper.

Elderly Alec Wainright (well, he's sixty, not so old, but beyond having sex with his wife) is apparently complaisant to the affair Canadian-born Rita is having with a boy actor, Barry Sullivan. Rita, a sort of Rita Hayworth type, full of animal fire, is thirty-eight, while young Barry, a mere stripling of perhaps twenty-five, cuts quite a figure in his trim British bathing trunks with a white belt. Everyone in the village knows they're having an affair, but our narrator (Dr. Luke Croxley, not in good health himself) may be the first to suspect they are plotting to kill Alec, à la the famous Edith Thompson case, or perhaps more to the point, the Stoner-Rattenbury affair about which Terence Rattigan wrote his underrated play *Cause Célèbre*. In both true-life true crime cases, an elderly husband was brutally struck down by a pair of adulterous lovers.

When one or more of the four characters disappear right off the edge of the cliff, we suspect a dramatic suicide. But is it murder hastily covered up? Anyone who has ever lived in France will agree, men have done strange things for love, and Sir Henry Merrivale knows this better than most men. At first you think this is going to be another *Murder of Roger Ackroyd*, and Carr seems to play with our expectations, teasing us into thinking we've got the correct solution taped, them all of a sudden he reveals all that Agatha Christie *chazerai* was just another way to *casser les couilles à quelqu'un*—the reader is warned.

Up Is Up, but So Is Down: New York's Downtown Literary Scene, 1974–1992
ed. Brandon Stosuy

★★★★★
Dark Allegory

November 17, 2006

(I love the way that when you search for this book on Amazon and ask for "Up Is Up," you get the insane Richard Pryor–Lonette McKee vehicle *Which Way Is Up?* and also *The Pop-Up Book of Celebrity Meltdowns* by "Melcher Media." That one I ordered!)

You don't have to be a New Yorker to fall for the grit, abandon, and passionate politics exhibited by the writers and poets Brandon Stosuy has collected in this jumbo book of unreason. You can skip the part where he explains why the book begins in 1974 and ends in 1992, though afterward you'll want to go back and follow up on these intriguing explanations, but first-time readers will want to just jump right in with a giant splash to the grimy, glamorous downtown swimming hole. The 1970s begin on a brash note with Kathy Acker, Ed Sanders, the debut of Patti Smith, "Blank Generation" by Richard Hell, the eternally underrated Constance DeJong, and a long, long, long piece by Laurie Anderson. In fact there's a power and cohesion about the writing in this section that the book afterward fails to recover. That's not to say that the rest of the book is dull, for the social issues of crime, poverty, and most of all the AIDS epidemic complicate the downtown aesthetic in totally interesting and provocative ways. I'm just saying ... if there was a time when "downtown" was fun, maybe the 1970s were it, and Stosuy cannily reprints (from the much-missed zine *Bikini Girl*) a hilarious three-way interview between editor Lisa Falour, novelist Lynne Tillman, and style icon slash photographer slash urban Narcissus Gerard Malanga that is a sort of mock salute to the old-style Factory school. Here you will also find a great poem, "I Missed Punk" from 1979 by Peter Schjeldahl. I'm indifferent to his work at the *New Yorker* and feel, "Couldn't he still have stayed a poet too, or did he have to give it all up when his muse took a powder?" In any case, "I Missed Punk" is super.

In general, the poetry isn't up to the silver standard of the prose work here, which is strange considering all the great poets who lived downtown in the period; but some of this must be assigned to Stosuy's apparent preference for prose, for he could have printed any number of poems by, for example, Eileen Myles or Dennis Cooper or Brad Gooch, opting instead for stories by each of them. That said, there are some beautiful poems here, by Tim Dlugos, Susie Timmons, David Trinidad, Bob Holman, Penny Arcade, among others; and even the duds exhibit a sort of snapshot realism about the period that brings it all to life like throwing sea monkeys into a glass of water. What happened to Susie Timmons? Is she still writing? I haven't mentioned yet the sheer churn of names, the wave of stars that flickered out into the night, people who stopped writing, who disappeared into drugs or drink, or just into mediocrity after brilliant beginnings ... But editor Stosuy has made this one of his themes, noting the contents of fugitive magazines, or big anthologies, in which the names we still know today mingle with the head-scratchers. Well, you know how time fades away.

The '80s is a much-huger section, as the commercial realities of *Bright Lights, Big City*, and *Slaves of New York* seemed to bear down on the more avant-garde, formalist work that preceded it, so that "downtown" began to market itself in numerous subtle, and subtly arrogant, ways. Heroically many artists took their economics realistically as a subject and began to whirl them around in Duchampian ways. The magazine *Between C & D* came right off those primitive computer printers on folded, pegged paper, and each copy was then stuffed into an elongated quart-sized baggie for immaculate consumption. Indeed this was the golden age of the *Between C & D* writers, their work highlights of Stosuy's volume. Lines blurred between genres, and New York's theatricality is rarely far away from the presentation of such texts as Karen Finley's "Baby Birds,"

Richard Prince's sublime "Practicing without a License," Sarah Schulman's *Girls, Visions and Everything*, Eric Bogosian's ponderous *In the Dark*. AIDS comes along and knocks everything into a cocked hat, and the graphics that often overpower these pages find themselves now shadowed by a fighting, communal spirit close in tone to the Revolutionary calendar. Though "downtown" apparently ends in 1992, with the death of the artist David Wojnarowicz, Stosuy still finds a hundred pages of 1990s material, a Jacobean flowering of excess and despair that includes Bruce Benderson, Mary Gaitskill, the late David Rattray, and the amazing Susan Daitch.

Physically the book weighs a ton and straphangers won't be folding it over their elbow like the *New York Post*. I wasn't crazy about how every page is a different color, most of them leaning toward the bleak or the Day-Glo. (The designer Angela Lidderdale's celebrated work on Benetton's *Colors* magazine has leached into her book design.) And after prolonged immersion in the book I found out that in fact I was wrong; many pages in a row are printed in standard black and white. I was just feeling cornea fatigue, I suppose. Stosuy, a fiction writer with an anthropologist's zest for reconstructing lost cultures, has found a wealth of material to support his thesis that the "downtown" writing scene of the post-Watergate Manhattan had energy and style to spare. I want him to come to San Francisco and I will show him around and persuade him that we did the same thing here only with less publicity, better weather, and cuter guys.

Ava Gardner: "Love Is Nothing"
by Lee Server

Ava Is Nothing

November 17, 2006

As an American child growing up in France, I combed the countryside hunting for truffles in early autumn and for yellow buttercups in spring. As Shakespeare wrote, in *The Winter's Tale*, "When daffodils begin to peer, / With heigh! the doxy over the dale, / Why, then comes in the sweet o' the year."

Europeans looked up to Ava Gardner as a sort of American flower of spring, and her sultry looks made her popular with bullfighters and ordinary French peasant boys. Often my family, encountering a single Frenchman, would be asked if we knew Ava Gardner back at home. She was sort of a one-woman Marshall Plan. Lee Server's biography is much better than his previous book on Robert Mitchum—better written, more convincing, less annoying. At the same time it feels less important, just as his subject, the dazzling MGM sex symbol Ava Gardner, pales in talent when compared to her RKO compatriot (her costar in the unfortunate *My Forbidden Past*).

"Tongue-tied by authority," and prevented from exercising her full sex appeal on the screen by a censorious Hays Office, and in any case, apparently not much interested in acting anyhow, Gardner had a pretty ho-hum career that ignited during the noir era in Robert Siodmak's *The Killers*, then went back to programmers. Mitchum's motto is said to have been "I Don't Care," but Ava really didn't care, and it shows on-screen I think. I'd rather watch Lana Turner any old day than try to take an interest in her brunette counterpart. At least Lana looked interested, and consequently her movies, no matter how bad they are by middlebrow standards, at least have some life in them. Was Ava ever very good? Lee Server claims that George Cukor made a great picture for Ava, called *Bhowani Junction*, but that MGM chopped and changed it around tragically out of fear of miscegenation charges (Gardner was ludicrously playing an Anglo-Indian Merle Oberon type).

Maybe one day we'll get to see this miracle. In the meantime her story is a sad one of wasted chances, an incongruous affair with Luis Miguel Dominguín, play marriages to Mickey Rooney, Artie Shaw, Frank Sinatra, and many, many martinis.

He points out that people loved to see her in public—a sighting of Ava could cause a riot—but they avoided her movies in droves (Sophia Loren was the same way, he writes). She was "popular" the way someone like Jessica Simpson is popular: people wanted to see how low she could go; eventually nuns took care of her.

She was the kind of actress David Thomson would like.

Native Moderns: American Indian Painting, 1940–1960
by Bill Anthes

★★★★★
Water Serpents

November 21, 2006

As an American boy growing up in rural France, I rarely saw an American Indian, except in the dubbed Westerns that showed up in our local cinema (*Un autre homme, une autre chance* or *Sérénade au Texas*). I had no idea that a vigorous postmodern painting revolution was shaking up the West seventy years after the death of Sitting Bull. Bill Anthes jumps in with both feet to a hotly contested area of debate, the state of American Indian painting during the period of American domination of the arts, World War II and the years leading up to Kennedy's inauguration in 1960. It was a time when, backed by the State Department, US art took the world by storm and the previous capitals, Paris, London, Rome, bowed to US supremacy and the apparent vitality of our modernist movement. Meanwhile even in the desert Southwest a handful of American Indian painters were getting tired of having to paint the prescriptive ways—deer as mascots in every painting—especially when the direct wisdom of the ancestors was becoming more and more a thing of the distant past, becoming only a shadowy memory and, some said, not a real thing at all but something dreamed up to please or put off the conquering white race.

The relation between Native American art and modernism has been a tortured one. In a race to shake up the very concepts of art, Picasso, Braque, and others had turned to African art, to realign themselves with the primitive before completing cubist operations. It didn't take modern artists long to latch onto Native art, so long as it embodied apparently traditional and ceremonial subjects. In this, the young contemporary Indians were encouraged by the white-run state schools, which thought that pandemic unemployment among the tribes might be alleviated if enough of them started producing old-fashioned artworks for the booming tourist market.

In addition, curious white patrons offered to underwrite the artistic careers of certain young painters if the latter would sneak into shamanic ceremonies forbidden to whites, and later recreate the wall paintings and other magical artworks produced in times of high ceremony.

Without these recreations, of course, we wouldn't have half the knowledge we have today, for the works themselves would have been lost to time, and yet there was still an element of cultural tourism when white money invaded the humble world of the reservation and the desert. As Anthes paraphrases, "many white-directed efforts on behalf of Native cultures were caught up in a funk of what anthropologist Renato Rosaldo has described as 'imperialist nostalgia.'" Meanwhile, young Indians painters caught up in abstract expressionism or whatever modern movement were told sternly that their work was "not Indian enough" and their funding or scholarships were withdrawn—back to drawing primitive deer with all four feet flying!

And there was another strain of illusion, embodied beautifully in Anthes's account of the career of the artist Yeffe Kimball, who was white but just told everyone she was an Indian because it was chic. Kimballl claimed Osage ancestry and began painting white buffalo. "Had Kimball actually been a Native American artist," Anthes tells us disarmingly, "she would have been a truly groundbreaking figure." Even as a liar, or self-inventor, he has decided, she was a pioneer of sorts in an "era of male privilege" which saw even as well-connected a painter as Lenore Krasner resort to calling herself "the more ambiguous 'Lee'" while signing her paintings with "gender-neutral initials." Anthes cleverly resituates Kimball in the general population of "counterfeit Indians"—men and women so fascinated by Indian alterity that they took the low road to arrive there, like the fellow who wrote *The Education of Little Tree*.

I don't have the time to praise this book as much as it deserves. Anthes seems to survey his subject from every imaginable angle and, just when you think there can't be anything left to surprise or illuminate, he stuns again.

In Search of Nella Larsen: A Biography of the Color Line
by George Hutchinson

★★★★☆
The Wrong Woman

December 2, 2006

I enjoyed Dr. Hutchinson's book on Nella Larsen, the enigmatic nurse who wrote two marvelous novels in midcareer and then took up her tents and wrote no more. Wow, does he lay into Larsen's two previous biographers! Sometimes it seems as though the whole purpose of him writing this book is to serve as a massive corrective to what he sees as their stupidity, their errors, their evasions, their sloppy thinking. This gives the book a lot of energy, and perhaps prompted Hutchinson to perform some brilliant feats of detective work. For example, he was able to prove that Nella Larsen actually did live in Denmark, for others had doubted her stories of a childhood in Copenhagen, seeing the purported fantasy as yet another manifestation of her self-hatred and the way she wanted to be white, not Black.

It is thrilling indeed to get the whole picture of this complex life, even at the expense of the two previous biographers who must now forever lay at Hutchinson's feat, their every inanity exposed to a sneering public. And yet, as he knows, without these two having done so much groundwork, such as locating and interviewing friends of Larsen's now lost to us through death, he wouldn't have been able to accomplish zilch. So his triumph is clouded by a blur of ironies, as I'm sure he appreciates, ironies worthy of a Larsen novel.

I enjoyed especially Hutchinson's calm treatment of Larsen's final years, which saw her leave literature and the "glitterati" of the Van Vechten circle behind, in favor of a nursing career, which most people have seen as a terrible tragic turn of fate, and now under Hutchinson's treatment, he's very persuasive that being a nurse isn't, perhaps, such a bad thing at all, for nurses help people nearly as much as, perhaps more than, we novelists do. He is occasionally over-given to speculation, such as his suggestion that "it is not unlikely" that Larsen chose night duty (while nursing) because she could "control and cover her drinking habit better that way." Why is it not unlikely? Does this mean that it is likely? How do you know, Dr. Hutchinson? And what about the part where, because one personage receives an unexpected visit on a Saturday, does that indicate that the visitor most likely worked on weekdays? Excuse me?

All in all, essential reading for anyone interested in either the Harlem Renaissance or in the life of American nurses in midcentury.

High School Musical: Remix
dir. Kenny Ortega

★★★★☆
Remix Reviewed

December 7, 2006

I've already written about HSM at length elsewhere, so shall limit my remarks to the brand-new "remix" edition. As everyone knows, the original DVD seemed rushed out, with hardly a bonus feature to be found anywhere on it, except for some sad excuses for music videos. What we need is a commentary track from director/chore-ographer Kenny Ortega, and perhaps from Broadway-music veteran Alyson Reed, who gives *High School Musical* the credibility it has from her years of showmanship and Fosse-like timing. But Disney is not going to let Ortega reflect on his achievement here, not while he had *High Scholl Musical 2* gearing up for production in February and release in July.

So what have we got? The chapter stops are lame, lame, lame, like some old K-tel DVD from the early days of technology. On the other hand, the video transfer is so crisp and clean that some of the CGI work shows its seams right through: never before has the opening shot of the ski lodge or wherever Troy and Gabriella are supposed to be meeting on New Year's Eve looked so fakey, obviously something made in the studio. Oh, but in the long run what does it matter? We who have watched the show twenty times or more have every one of Zac Efron's adorably tortured grimaces committed to memory and if we shut our eyes we could still see him torn between his loyalty to the East High Wildcats and to his father's love, versus his newfound desire to sing onstage. And those of us who took Vanessa Anne

Hudgens to our hearts the minute we saw her open up that book at the big-kid's party on New Year's Eve and sit down resolutely to read it, until the pale watery spotlight fell on her face, and she had to get up and sing karaoke, don't need a lot of chapter stops to tell us that she has the big soulful voice of Mariah Carey combined with the earthy glow of a young Claudia Cardinale.

The new remix of "Breaking Free," however, is just ghastly. Zac and Vanessa seem to be panting like racehorses in order to keep up with the new count of BPM. I felt like calling Child Protective Services after seeing them suffer like this! New footage shows them smiling at each other in the studio—and there's one great shot of Zac admiring his own reflection in the wall-to-wall *Chorus Line* mirror— but please, Disney, slow down, you didn't need to turn America's favorite power ballad into a disco stomper! This is the song that voiced all of our longing and yearning to be accepted for our real selves, and created a powerful dialectic between the accepted capitalist hegemony and a restless, nearly unnamable teenage angst: "You know the world can see us / In a way that's different than who we are." It's an indelible document of rage, persuasion, and hope. Now it just sounds like Alcazar trash with the Chipmunks.

Bell Stick
by Lark in the Morning

★★★★★
With My Bells and Velvet

December 8, 2006

As an American boy growing up in a run-down château along the Côte d'Azur, which is in France, I could wake up and smell the Alps in one nostril and the salty Mediterranean in the other. As Christmas approached, we would jostle each other at breakfast (steaming mugs of chocolate, large, leafy flaky *bricolettes*, and heaping bowls of Casino Boules Miel) in our rush to get out into the yard to the bayberry hedge abutting our property, where we would crouch like explorers waiting for a sign. "Hush," we would whisper to each other in choked excitement. "The Christmas Owl is approaching." Sooner or later we would spot the Christmas Owl—a fluffy, feathery white mass tottering along on the far side of the hedge. We would greet its arrival by spouting the mating calls of owls, the call children love: "Who? Who?" The French girl who took care of us would be giggling in the corner, sprawled on a hayrick, face half-buried in a volume of Françoise Sagan. "Silly children," she would reproach us, in French. "Bring a torch, Jeannette, Isabella." Eventually we were to learn that the mass of white feathers was not an owl at all, but rather one of Saint-Paul-de-Vence's most distinguished citizens, the painter Marc Chagall.

Chagall had been spending every Christmas in Saint-Paul-de-Vence for decades, known everywhere for his renderings of Jewish folklore and cows flying through the air and rapturous lovers jumping over rainbows. The local church, or as we called it, our *église*, was decorated with stained glass executed in Chagall's workshop. To local children he represented the eternal spirit of youth, and we liked to go to his seaside villa, with our jingle sticks, and sing him carols in English, a language with which he had little working knowledge. My parents were mum about the propriety of bothering our illustrious neighbor with our cracked and unmusical voices, but they worried about the possible implications of serenading such a famous Jewish man, with songs and bell-ringing explosions commemorating the birth of Christ. It seemed unkindly, to say the least. In our ignorance we just clutched our jingle sticks tighter and shook them without mercy. Have you ever really looked at your jingle stick? At Amazon you can order as many as you like, strapping them if desired to your arms and legs. They will ring out the Christmas season as loud as you want it to be, in whatever nation you find yourself, grown-up or not. And the velvet makes for a festive, warm touch. Its red is like the lustrous ruby red Russian-bred Chagall employed in *I and the Village* and other famous paintings. Oh well, it has been many a year since our elderly neighbor passed on to the great chamber in the sky, but I still think of him every time frost hits the air and my jingle sticks fall out of the top drawer of my treasured *directoire*, he who said so famously, his triangular mop of hair a cleaver of white owl feathers atop a jaunty head, "All colors are the friends of their neighbors and the lovers of their opposites."

What It Used to Be Like: A Portrait of My Marriage to Raymond Carver
by Maryann Burk Carver

★★★★★
Those Were the Days

December 21, 2006

Interesting that her book ran to 1,250 pages and took years and years to write, and that someone called John Stryker edited it down to its present lapidary form. Don't people say that Raymond Carver also wrote too long and that the notorious editor Gordon Lish cut and chopped as he saw fit in order to maintain that famous "minimalist" style we associate with Carver? Maybe he got it from his wife, as he got so much else. He's great and everything, but her book shows who was the real writer in the family. The first word of the book is "spud-nuts," did you ever hear of them? As she explains, they are the doughnuts of Washington State, made with potato flour and mar-keted as an Indigenous treat. She met Ray when she worked with his mom at a spudnut cafe in Union Gap, south of Yakima, and he was far and away the best-looking boy she had ever known. Though only fifteen, Maryann knew what she wanted already.

It was a sexist society which said it was all right for Ray to go to prostitutes and pay cold cash for an "around the world" (as MBC adds, if you don't know what that is, "don't ask") but that it was wrong for Maryann to want to go to college classes.

Most of the book is about her giving up her life to help Ray and his career, while raising their two beautiful children (by the time she was twenty, she was saddled with these two bundles of energy) in a series of run-down, crummy apartments.

It's all about how an ambitious girl of the working class suffers when her husband's a genius and naturally society makes her defer her own dreams so that he can become famous. And following the fame, Ray starts drinking even more heavily than before, while female groupies start prowling around, rubbing his legs, asking for more than auto-graphs, and spending weekends with him while Maryann stays at home, overwhelmed and doing a fair bit of drinking herself. She has a loyal and loving sister, who is quite talented too, in another field, someone to whom she can complain to, someone who will understand.

It's hard to believe that the Carver estate wouldn't allow MBC to quote from any of Carver's stories, not even from the love letters he wrote her. Who's in charge there and how deep does their vindictiveness run? Maryann is never nasty or confrontational, but she does paint an unpleasant portrait of Ray as a serial cheater, who couldn't keep it in his pants because he was too drunk to keep the pants up, and the coeds or whoever they were who wanted a taste of his fame have a special purdah all their own. A special golden spudnut goes out to Tess Gallagher, that talented poet who became Raymond Carver's widow, marrying him only a few months before his death and that's stretching it. She and Maryann apparently maintain cordial and amicable relations. God bless us all.

Breezy (1973)
dir. Clint Eastwood

★★★★★
Filling My Pockets with Peppermint and Thyme

December 22, 2006

Breezy beats most of Clint Eastwood's present-day output by a country mile, for it has no pretensions to being anything other than what it is, and plus in hindsight it is, oddly enough, one of the movies that best tells it like it was about hippie culture. The things that seemed "off" about it back in the day (Michel Legrand's "folk music" theme, for example, repeated endlessly, even in a sitar variation) have reached a pitch of resonance today. I, for one, got ready to weep every time the orchestra seemed about to launch into the nth variation on "Breezy's Song." Alan and Marilyn Bergman wrote many bad lyrics in the period, but their lyric for "Breezy's Song" perfectly encapsulates the hippie ethos that Kay Lenz's character is supposed to embody.

She is great, and another example of the strong roles for women that Eastwood seems drawn to even from the beginning. She is so young and beautiful, nearly flawless, that it seems odd her hair is always clean like a Breck Girl, even in the beginning scenes when she exclaims over William Holden's shower as though she's never seen one.

He plays Frank Harmon, a real estate agent in Laurel Canyon. That's the weak part of the picture, Eastwood never makes Holden believable as a salesman. He's not driven enough. He's more laid back than the hippies on the corner. Almost as great are the twists and turns that the screenplay makes. On the surface a placid little mood piece, *Breezy* has at least two great shocks, both taking place in hospitals, that will leave you with your jaw on the floor. Jo Heims, who did this screenplay, was also responsible for an earlier Eastwood vehicle, the thriller *Play Misty for Me*, and she knows how to throw a curveball. Shame that she is not more widely recognized among the great screenwriters, but perhaps her tragically early death has something to do with her current eclipse. For me, all the things people say Robert Towne does, Jo Heims really does, but backward and in high heels.

(She also wrote the Patty Duke thriller *You'll Like My Mother*.)

Holden is good, and manages to look younger as the movie rolls on and the love of Breezy reinvigorates him. Ultimately the movie depends on how much you can stand of Kay Lenz. Some think she's too intense for the movie. For others, she will seem too twee with her positivist philosophy of finding a bright spot in anything and counting on love to see her through. Her frequent nudity is unabashed and "natural," and it's great to see a woman on-screen whose breasts are so very different from each other, something you hardly ever see today in Hollywood! A wonderful bonus is the presence of Jamie Smith-Jackson as Breezy's best girlfriend, the miserably drug-addled hippie girl Marcy. Jamie Smith-Jackson! Cult legend of cult legends! Not only did she star in *Satan's School for Girls*, but she *was* Alice in *Go Ask Alice!*

220 More Crochet Stitches (The Harmony Guides, vol. 7)
by The Harmony Guides

★★★★★
For Those Who Think Irish

December 23, 2006

A kindly nephew, after hearing me at a family dinner announce how bored I was with my hobby and how I craved getting into a new one, thought of me this Christmas and bought me *220 More Crochet*

Stitches hoping I might find the world of, whatever it is, more exciting than my present hobby of rescuing abandoned pit bulls and training them to help the blind. Well, I'm torn. Of Irish descent myself, as is my nephew and pretty much my whole family, my eye was caught by the hefty section on Irish crocheting—oh, wait a second, "Irish style" crocheting, which is a horse of a different color, for never in any of my trips to Ireland have I seen such patterns as these. Lovely they are, some of them, and as I wrote my nephew, very dear, and yet I can't picture myself, even in the direst of straits, say I was reduced to penury and had to crochet my living so I could put a wee bit of a roof over my head, I can't imagine ever willingly picking up the crochet needles and having a go of it. Consider this, my friends, these are the first two steps of "Irish Style Crochet IV.16."

"1st round: 1ch, work 10dc into ring, sl st into first dc. 2nd round: 1ch, work 1dc into each dc, sl st into first dc." Not on my watch! Yes, after a bit I got into the sweet groove of it, as I imagine that "1ch" might stand for "one chain," by why not separate the numeral "1" from the initials "ch"? Why run them together as "1ch"? Looks like an "itch" to me! The finished product, in a watery green lace, resembles a leaf gone to seed in an old pool of grave water from a half-dug grave in County Derry. It's about the size of a doily, or perhaps a soup plate if you had such a thing in your house. Yes, I can see bringing in your needles when you're bored, perhaps if you're on a jury. (But will the judge or foreman allow you to bring the objects of steel backstage, as it were, onto an empaneled jury?) Yes, have a go if you must, but as I told my nephew, it's back to the pit bulls for me, for there's never a shortage of the blind wanting a good dog with a spirit in him.

In the City of Shy Hunters: A Novel
by Tom Spanbauer

★★★★★
The Chef-d'Oeuvre Inconnu

December 24, 2006

People say that Spanbauer, one of my favorite novelists, took so long writing this book because he planned it as his last testament, and that the manuscript mounted up to a magic mountain of pages, enough to dwarf a Thomas Pynchon or a David Foster Wallace. Cold heads at Grove Press prevailed and insisted on cutting the MS down to its present state, where it sort of just sits there, neither fish nor fowl, a sketch for a grander Balzacian social tragedy, like James McCourt's subsequent *Queer Street* but with an actual plot. What we have now is still pretty amazing, but don't you wish that novels were treated like movies and that we might someday hope for the "director's cut" of *ITCOSH*, with its lofty architectonics restored to us the way the writer wanted us to have it?

Perhaps in years to come a scholarly edition will be prepared, for Spanbauer probably has the missing sections somewhere? Can I do it? If there's a committee, count me in! I cried and cried all the way through the Will Parker story, and his hunt for Charlie the missing lost boy keeps the novel going through some dangerous backwaters. I didn't exactly fall in love with Rose, the glamorous transvestite character, I kept thinking of Angel, the one from the musical *Rent*; however, Rose is supposed to be more of an intellectual, a Dorothy Dean type yet with oodles of sex appeal and every trick in the book.

Many great novels have been written on the restaurant theme, and perhaps it's Spanbauer's concentration on this setting that, for me, evokes the glory days of Balzac and the nineteenth-century passion for knowing everything and educating one's readers in the process. This book takes place during the days when AIDS and HIV were still unfamiliar to most people, even to protosophisticated New Yorkers, when a man in the AIDS ward might not be able to count on his own parents visiting him (here, one of them is told that "my son died years ago"), and even one's own friends might draw back for fear of breath-drawn transmission. The heartbreak and the courage it took to go on in those days make for a stirring story, and even if the rumor isn't true, even if Spanbauer wanted his book to be exactly this size, he took a giant subject and smashed holes in it everywhere, like someone inside a pumpkin compelled to make a jack-o'-lantern—punching outward, and shining with a weird, eternal fire.

Little Children (2006)
dir. Todd Field

★★★★★
Let the Honors Roll In

January 4, 2007

Little Children turns on a couple of extraordinary performances that almost are enough to convince us it's a good movie. I guess it's OK, but not if you're expecting something special, and it ends with a disastrous one-two-three-four punch of narrative surprises, all four of which are dramatic duds. To be fair one woman was weeping her eyes out at the end, crying over the perfidy of men, but I asked her later in the lobby if she was OK, and she said that she found the movie overwhelmingly similar to her own life, for although she gave no details you could tell she had had an extramarital affair herself, with one of her own students in a college classroom. And this guy had really let her down. But really, has anything changed since the great days of Somerset Maugham and his story, "Rain," about the South Seas prostitute whom an evangelical missionary attempts to convert to the ways of the Lord?

If you'll remember, "Rain" ends triumphantly with Sadie Thompson crying in the middle of the monsoon "I tol' yas, men are nothin' but pigs!" Here the message is almost exactly the same. Whether you're Patrick Wilson, more interested in ogling the speed-boy skaters clattering up and down the ramp than you are in pursuing your affair; or you're Kate Winslet's husband, hooked on a jolly internet femme called Slutty Kay to the point of buying her underwear to wear on his face; or maybe you're Jackie Earle Haley, a pedophile with severe problems with women, no matter which man you are in this movie, you're a pig and you might as well admit it.

I almost forgot about Noah Emmerich, who plays Larry Hedges. He plays a disgraced cop who bullies an old lady and attacks an unarmed teen. He screams and yells his way all through the movie, acting out the vigilante impulses of his neighbors in the little town. Has there been any broader acting done this year? It's like the director had access to a blender into which he could stuff Jack Weston, Brian Dennehy, and Charles Durning, then slam it to ON, pump up the volume, and spill the boisterous bluster all over the screen and call it a "Noah Emmerich." What did I like? More than I should I found myself enjoying the scenes where Kate Winslet and Patrick Wilson have sex (on the washer-dryer, or under a closed attic window on a hot summer afternoon), Wilson almost loses that honey glaze he was born with as he stands thrusting, his enormous butt expanding and contracting like some sort of surrealistic crustacean, directly in the camera's eye. That butt does most of Wilson's acting for him and should accept any awards thrown his way, graciously, frankly, and with just a hint of its famous cracked smile.

14K Ruby and Diamond "Dynasty" Necklace
by Dynasty

★★★★★
Priceless Heirloom

January 5, 2007

As an American boy growing up in France, I became mesmerized by an enchanting painting of an ancestor that hung never very far from the hearth. The painting, smudged by smoke and damaged by Vichy occupation of the château, showed a very thin and angular woman, her face like something reflected in the bowl of a spoon, festooned in bright stones that gleamed out still bright after the passage of many decades. "Who is this woman?" I used to wonder out loud, until one evening, as my grandmother passed through the room looking for our vanished cat, Gateau, I noticed that she wore the same diamond and ruby necklace as the ancestor in the damaged old painting. I persuaded my grandmother to sit down and forget about her eternal hunt for a cat who had died long before I was born, when she was still a young woman not even married to my grandpapa yet, and to tell me about the necklace she wore. She took my little hands in hers and, in a low, breathy whisper, told me how she had stumbled across these precious stones in a valise once. Amazon's 14K Ruby and Diamond "Dynasty" Necklace looks a lot like my family jewels; the resemblance is shocking enough to have made me drop my cocoa while leafing through the jewel pages this morning in an attempt to bring back, madeleine-style, the vanished days of yesteryear.

These diamonds are perhaps a bit more brilliantly cut than the ones my grandmother used to sport, but as she mentioned, her diamonds predated modern mining methods so they seemed rough, scratchy, almost fungal in their savage brightness. You wouldn't want to wear them next to your skin, an aversion she averted by (normally) wearing a sort of wool ascot as a liner between her necklace and her body. The clarity here is superb, like drinking water from the nearby fountain at Lourdes when Our Lady wriggled her shepherdess's staff into the rocky ground on which Bernadette fed her sheep. I used to ask my grandmother what would happen to her diamonds and rubies when she died, and she said she would never die.

The rubies, in the Burmese style, have that distinctive pigeon's-blood shine that befits a country ironically wracked by civil war. Rubies and diamonds, "blood and water," my dad used to say—he had one of those great Irish voices, like a poet. I think I'll order one of these necklaces one of these days, for if nothing else, like all the other "Dynasty" jewelry I have ordered, worn, and stored away in a vault, it will be fit for a king. If only I had a JPEG of my grand-mother wearing this piece, darting after Gateau, half-consumed with anxiety and yet noblesse oblige always paramount in her fragile, gregarious mind, yet stopping for a minute to console a lonely and abandoned grandson who grew up without proper supervision in a country far from Long Island. I think I've come to a point in my life where I deserve the priceless luxury of a "Dynasty" heirloom.

Riot and Remembrance: The Tulsa Race War and Its Legacy
by James S. Hirsch

★★★★★
Legacy of Remembrance

January 23, 2007

I read Martha Southgate's novel of three generations of Black Tulsa women, each hiding a horrible tragedy. The name of the book is

Third Girl from the Left. The oldest woman, Mildred, has lived through the Tulsa race riots of 1921 and has kept her secrets well. After reading this accomplished novel I wanted to know more about the holocaust in Tulsa, and to find out why it was so underreported at the time and for the next fifty years. James Hirsch's book seems to be about the best of a new crop of revisionist history, and I read the whole thing in about two and a half hours.

At this late date there is no smoking gun, and a five-month search for rumored mass graves in the surrounding areas of Tulsa proper turned up nothing out of the ordinary. That will never stop people from assuming that more than the thirty-six victims of vigilante action were killed, their bodies disposed of summarily. Hirsch thinks that the figure is probably somewhere between seventy-five and three hundred. Thousands of people lost their homes, and acres of Greenwood, the so-called Black Wall Street, were burned to the ground. The famed historian John Hope Franklin came to Tulsa four years after the riots and bears witness today to the sense that in 1920 Black Oklahomans had made some definite progress, but after the catastrophe they lost their confidence and never could make up the backward steps. Of course trauma studies indicate that such a devastating blow can never be recuperated, not entirely. That is why the issue of reparations has come to the forefront of the debate in recent times, for it seems, following Freud, that money is the only thing that people really sit up and take notice of, and as such it is the only proper way of dissolving guilt from human relations. (One of Hirsch's chapters is called "Money, Negro," which is what Franklin told a Black politician who asked him what reparations represent.)

The latter half of the book is almost a personality parade as two men square off—the aforementioned pol, Don Ross, against the driven white liberal who wrote extensively about the forgotten tragedy as early as 1971, Scott Ellsworth. Neither of the two men care a fig about the other, it's plain to see, while elegant, courteous, and magisterial John Hope Franklin rises above it all with his superacuity and his refusal to bend principles.

The Living Unknown Soldier: A Story of Grief and the Great War
by Jean-Yves Le Naour

★★★★★
Beautiful Stranger

January 24, 2007

Anthelme Mangin wasn't even his real name, but the doctors had to call him something in order to fit him into their bureaucracy. In Jean-Yves Le Naour's research he found that many of the army records he needed to lay his hands on have mysteriously been "disappeared," but from press accounts and asylums he was able to piece together most of the story, though some details remain alarmingly vague. It didn't help him that the journalist who did the most to publicize M. Mangin's plight was himself a fabulist and made up picturesque details out of whole cloth if they helped him sell newspapers. (So there's a funny passage in Le Naour's book in which he enumerates how many fictions the journalist used in one piece, claiming that in the entire news release there was only one verifiable fact.)

I got puzzled too, because lost in the mist of history is the origin of Mangin's madness. Amnesia is now more properly understood as a secondary system of something else, and trauma studies have shown that war alone is able to induce amnesia (rather than postulating that the amnesiac is a "weak" person to begin with, or even more xenophobically, a foreigner). But so is the asylum and so is prison, so that Mangin's indisputably "nutty" symptoms might have cropped up later on in life when he began receiving wholescale public attention. (Jean Anouilh wrote a play about him, *Traveller without Luggage*, which premiered in 1937. Of course, Mangin was too "insane" to attend.)

Did you know that approximately 250,000 Frenchmen just disappeared during the First World War? Presumably most of them were killed in battle, buried in mass graves, but at least a dozen wound up with amnesia and remained unclaimed by their families. In Mangin's case the publicity brought him numerous surrogate families, and when he eventually died (during the Second World War) many lawsuits surrounding his identity clogged French courtrooms, as bereft wives and children and parents thought they recognized his mug from news photos and sued for a piece of his *cul*. An ironic way for the story to end, but it says something about our need to belong, and our need to make things tidy and recognizable. He was about five foot four, so asylum officials could dismiss the claims of families with missing six-foot-tall guys in them. His face was round, he had freckles, they could sort of figure out he had a high school education. Why, he even spoke some English! Maybe he was English, how would they know? He was found with a group of other French prisoners, but the numbers of his regiment, sewn to his greatcoat, had been ripped off by a bullet.

As an American boy growing up in rural France, I would pass by a secluded glade on my way to my lycée every day, and older boys whispered that deep in the forest was the grave of the famous living unknown soldier. It was cemented over, looked something like a sunken birdbath. Like the grave of Jim Morrison at Père Lachaise, it was marked up with savage and jubilant graffiti. I remember the famous tag from John Lennon: "I am he as you are he as you are me and we are all together / See how they run like pigs from a gun ..." Apropos for a man from whom war had blasted away an identity.

Cavalcade (1933)
dir. Frank Lloyd

★★★★★
Twentieth-Century Blues

January 24, 2007

We always think of Noël Coward as being this hip, ironic, sophisticated glibster, but at heart he was all mush and my, oh my, did he love England, everything about it, especially its aristocracy. *Cavalcade* the movie is a faithful recreation of his showstopping London hit, the one that made him a respectable man of the theater instead of just an angry young man. If you had a copy of his play in hand while following the movie, you would see how extraordinarily the screenplay follows the show, though director Frank Lloyd fails to make use of cinema techniques (like a split screen) that must have been available to him even in the early talkie days? However, it's not as clunky or static as some have made out, and scene after scene unrolls at a stately, but yet somehow hypnotic and indeed sometimes shocking, clip.

Diana Wynyard isn't to everyone's taste but if you like your Norma Shearer and wish that she had somehow surpassed her own levels of emotional hysteria, than Diana is the girl for you! She's like a manic Norma Shearer, her expressive eyes and quivering contralto like Shearer squared. Watch her long fleshy arms as she reaches down to hug her little boy. If she said any more with them, she'd have been arrested. Occasionally her servant counterpart, Una O'Connor, threatens to steal the show from Wynyard, but that don't happen, even in the fantastic scenes when the two women quarrel over their children's plan to marry.

William Cameron Menzies gave the screen some of its finest special effects and art design, and here the bombing of London during World War I, while Fanny and Joey watch from a nearby balcony, is magnificent and horrifying at the same time, like Thomas Pynchon's *Gravity's Rainbow*. The montage at the end of *Cavalcade* has got to be one of the most astounding sequences ever filmed, as Lloyd and Coward show us flashes of different responses to postwar "unfaith"— a Communist demagogue, a Christian priest (preaching to a near-empty congregation), an armament mogul, an atheist ("God is too crude a superstition to foist on our children"—cinema hasn't been so bold in seventy years since!), and finally a slow pan across a decadent '20s sex party in which every sort of sexuality is on display, a young girl frightened at the advances of a middle-aged woman, a pair of he-men swapping bracelets, one young vamp, bending slightly to adjust volume on an art deco radio cabinet, radiates sin with the movement of a single finger.

The Black Curtain
by Cornell Woolrich

Behind the Curtain

January 26, 2007

Gosh, what more do people want? This is only one of the most brilliant suspense novels ever created, and in some ways a more coherent piece of work than its celebrated predecessor, *The Bride Wore Black*. And yet the other reviews here would have you think it was merely so-so.

The Black Curtain is nicely excerpted in Jonathan Lethem's anthology *The Vintage Book of Amnesia*, and it's one of the very best amnesia stories going. Frank Townsend wakes up after years of being somebody else: three years that seem to have elapsed in minutes, but when he goes home his wife screams with relief and bewilderment. Who has he been all these years, and even more importantly, who is the intense man who is dogging his every footstep right now? Could it be that, in his other lost life, he did something bad, something his middle-class upbringing wouldn't countenance?

Could he really have committed a murder? Frank Townsend would never have done such a thing, but what does he really know about Dan Nearing, the man who's been accused of a murder honest witnesses saw him commit! Woolrich writes beautifully about spiritual defeat and about existential hope. "He sat there on the edge of the bed, a dejected, shadowy figure. And once, at some break in inner fortitude—like a split in a film running through a projection machine, quickly spliced together again and resuming its evenness in a moment—his head suddenly dropped into the coil of his arms.

Then he raised it again, and that didn't happen any more." What that man can do with a word as small as "that"!

Frank's wife, Virginia, bears with him through some tough times, but it's Dan's girlfriend who wins our affections, Ruth, a put-upon maid for a rich family; we see her totally, as in a Dreiser novel, a poor timid creature with a ferocious inner life and total dedication to her man.

Woolrich is a poet, and his novels are organized along the lines of poetry rather than cinema (contra the metaphor of film splicing in the quote above), each one a lesson in phenomenology, and *The Black Curtain* adds to all of this a human story of the pathetic, as well as a corking good page-turner of the best kind.

Ballets Russes (2005)
dir. Dayna Goldfine and Dan Geller

★★★★★
On Your Toes

January 26, 2007

People said it was good but I wasn't prepared for how good! I wonder what the talented directors will work on next. I fell in hook, line, and sinker the minute the narrator, Marian Seldes, opened her mouth. And I don't even know much about ballet, though everyone has heard something about Nijinsky and Diaghilev, which is where Dan Geller and Dayna Goldfine begin their story. It's a leisurely movie and, at 110 minutes, sort of on the long side, but its expert editing makes it a ride worth considering. I'd go anywhere to see Nathaniel Dorsky's work, and maybe I'm imagining things but either he was in charge of the introduction to Nina Novak or else the directors found another editor with the meringue-light "Dorsky touch."

Ballet must be a wonderful energizer, how else is it that so many of the film's principal characters are over eighty and apparently spry as spring chickens? I suppose that some of the principals died young, but there are no Tanaquil Le Clercq stories here, and half of the fun is seeing the people old then being flashed back to their youthful selves, so filled with manic energy, back and forth, back and forth, until one feels oscillated through time and space; by the end of the movie you feel you've known these people all your life, and the title card at the end that reveals that five of them died during the making of the picture is like a little stab in your heart. Among them, of course, was Dame Alicia Markova, the only one among them who had actually lived long enough to have served under the Diaghilev regime. The heart and soul of the picture is the happily acerbic Frederic Franklin, who puts everyone down with a charming simper. Indonesian-born Nini Theilade, so gorgeous in Max Reinhardt's *A Midsummer Night's Dream* (1935), still looks enchanting enough to make men mad.

The clips are amazing, the supertitles unobtrusive (and yet stylish, if that's not an oxymoron), perfectly chosen to make whatever point Geller and Goldfine feel like making. I did feel they must have been simplifying one or two points in *Ballets Russes*'s chronology, but it's a tangled tale they do their best to smooth out. Time has obscured the legacy of the Ballet Russe de Monte Carlo, and the movie's comical ending makes it seem as though Batgirl's leaps and jumps in the '60s TV version of *Batman*, and the porn films of Wakefield Poole (*Boys in the Sand*), are the leading examples of that legacy, but anyone who has been lucky enough to see this outstanding documentary will tell a different tale. It is a grand leap of the imagination, and makes you want to photograph everyone you know, especially the aged and the very young and beautiful.

Hair (1979)
dir. Miloš Forman

★★★★☆
Let the Sun Shine In

January 30, 2007

I remember seeing *Hair* in the movie theater when it first came out and disliking it, and I was in it, one of thousands of extras cajoled into spending days in the Sheep Meadow of Central Park and pretending it was still the 1960s. We were put into "cells" of about a hundred and taught various moves by different disaffected Tharp dancers. Mine didn't teach us any actual steps, just showed us how she wanted us to get from one patch of crabgrass to another about forty feet away. It looked like a Bollywood movie. Then in the theater I was upset I suppose because I couldn't see myself, well, duh, there were thousands of boys on-screen with long hair. With the miracle of DVD I suppose I could pause every frame of the Central Park bunch and see if I can see myself, or at least the guy, a fellow extra, whom I was in love with for thirty-six hours, for I will never forget what he looked like wearing a green-and-orange counterculture outfit, he was like a wonderful aquarium.

Also the new plot the screenwriters dreamed up, with its ridiculous "opposites attract" storyline, is as banal as anything ever put on the screen. It's like an old MGM programmer; you literally can't believe that they would risk a $50 million musical on such a tawdry storyline. *Xanadu* has a better plot. Andy Warhol's *Empire* and *Sleep* have better plots than Miloš Forman's *Hair*.

So I was disappointed for twenty years but recently the movie has been on again and each time I see it, I see something interesting and new. Maybe it's the sort of picture that discloses its secrets over time. Last night the scenes with Nicholas Ray transfixed me; the movie director as the army general who orders the whole PA system shot down on the Nevada desert base. Ray must have been, what, in his sixties at the time and must have been near death (the movie was released posthumously), but he delivers a ferocious, on-the-spot performance, bristling with fierce delight, once again showing his version of America for the benefit of all those European cinéastes like Miloš Forman. He should have been the one playing Kilgore in *Apocalypse Now*: "I love the smell of napalm in the morning. The smell, you know, that gasoline smell, the whole hill. Smelled like ... victory." Anyhow he's great here in a small role, but it's odd that the best roles in *Hair* are invariably the small ones (like Cheryl Barnes's) and that almost all of the main acting jobs have something terribly wrong with them. John Savage doesn't even pretend to try lip-synching on Wall Street singing "Where Do I Go?" He looks like he's being tortured just by having to observe movie conventions, as though nobody told him that *Hair* was a musical until he showed up on the set. Beverly D'Angelo is almost believable as a stuffed-shirt socialite whose love for Savage turns her into a hippie ally, and her parallel love for Treat Williams is nicely played; and yet, well, she's Beverly D'Angelo and the part really calls for someone regally beautiful like Grace Kelly. Treat Williams is too old to play Berger, and yet he gives the movie a lot of energy, and makes the end work. Though I don't understand how the tombstone in the very last scene bears the name it does?

Beyond a doubt it is the performance of Annie Golden that really separates the men from the boys. She's supposed to be adorable, like a poodle, like a Judy Holliday crossed with Giuletta Masina. Au contraire. Instead she comes across as the poor man's Bernadette Peters, and even regular Bernadette Peters would have found her part a tough row to hoe. When I think of the wealth of acting and singing talent available to Miloš Forman in 1979, and how he wound up casting Annie Golden, my mind, never too strong to begin with, slips into a dark crevice to bang its forehead against a wall, a poor, misbegotten thing, a pox on it.

Holiday (1938)
dir. George Cukor

★★★★★
"Just One Day out of Life"

January 31, 2007

I never really liked this movie much until my wife and I invested in one of those newfangled "Hepburninators" on TiVo, which allows you to watch a full-length Katharine Hepburn movie in half the time by eliminating all scenes in which she appears. Now, as I watch *Holiday* in relative comfort, freed from the worry that at any moment she may show up and spoil all the fun, I can relax, for like the old saying goes, an hour without Katharine Hepburn is like a month in the country. My posture improves, there's a bloom of youth on my cheeks, I've got that old joie de vivre again. There's a swing in my step even the neighbors have noticed and commented on. I think this Hepburninator is the greatest thing since sliced bread and it'll make 'em a mint.

In the meantime it's funny watching a *Holiday* in which Julia Seton, not Linda Seton, is the heroine. For one thing, since Julia never liked the childhood playroom in which most of the movie takes place, we don't spend much time there. Linda and her brother, the bibulous Neddy, played so beautifully by Lew Ayres, went there all the time whenever it got tough being the richest people in America. Julia prefers to stay downstairs. Doris Nolan isn't much of an actress, and most of her early scenes when she's engaged to Cary Grant involve her trying to maneuver an enormous mink muff or armpiece and keep it on her elbow. What is that thing, anyhow? It's triangular in shape, or really more like a conch shell, and sometimes it seems she can get her whole arm into it, up to one shoulder, and at other times it seems tiny, designed to cover a few fingers. Clearly it has the better of Doris Nolan. She's great and she can really stand up to Cary Grant for most of the movie. He plays Johnny Case, a former circus acrobat, who gets engaged to Julia in the Finger Lakes and never knew how rich she really was until given a tour through her mansion by one of those 1930s butlers, the kind who can't stand their own kind but don't like their bosses either.

Johnny Case uses his circus training by somersaulting his way through the vault-like depths of the Seton mansion. He stops in front of an imposing John Singer Sargent painting of an elderly statesman. It turns out to be Julia's grandfather. "Judas!" he cries out. "Julia, why didn't you tell me you were descended from *that* Seton?"

The best actors are probably Jean Dixon and Edward Everett Horton, who play Johnny's "gay parents," Nick Potter and Susan Elliott. They just love the way he scrambles over them, a young puppy in their tiny bohemian-village setup. He kisses them equally, calls them both "fellas," he's enthusiastic and wriggly as a kid. At first when he tells them he's engaged to Julia, they can only imagine that she must be some kind of gold digger and they plead with their "lad" not to let it get too far. Piles of books tremble on the floor and sheet music flies everywhere as the three collapse onto a couch, Nick and Susan sitting literally on top of Johnny to keep him single and out of Julia's clutches. Well, the last laugh belongs to them, of course. They have magnificent timing and Dixon especially has so much sapphic panache I wonder why I have never noticed her performance before. Once your Hepburninator has been installed, you too will be noticing all sorts of marvelous details about *Holiday* you never had the energy for before.

(After researching the matter, I see that oddly enough, this was Dixon's last role in the movies, though she lived another forty-three years! Who could she have pissed off with her performance here, I wonder!)

Torpor
by Chris Kraus

★★★★★
Twenty Questions for Chris Kraus

February 7, 2007

An American girl meets and marries a French boy who's carrying around an enormous number of paralyzing memories of the Holocaust, and she decides to adopt a baby from a Third World country.

If only I could ask Chris Kraus my twenty questions! Among them would be, "How would you describe the form you work in? It's very distinctive, very Chris Kraus, but what is it?" I've heard people refer to your books as "comic" books, not like Nancy and Sluggo but something more like a Jane Austen sense of social comedy.

Torpor conveys like very few novels the misery of a long-term relationship. You compare them to "hypothermia, giving yourself up in free and loose embrace into a dream state that turns out to be inertia." Do all relationships disintegrate into clownishness? You cite the comic French pairs, Mercier and Camier, Bouvard and Pécuchet, as models for your nagging lovers.

What's also so striking about your book is that you're not afraid to make a dog one of your main characters. I don't think any reader will forget the heroic dachshund Lily who gets carted around Europe in a sort of hideaway sack, nor that it's Lily's suffering that Sylvie and Jerome overlook in their picaresque adventure.

Sylvie is afraid that no one will ever take her seriously because she is untrained and has no MFA. And Jerome, who is a full professor at an Ivy League university, is always taunting her about this. Ms. Kraus, I read your book of essays, *Video Green*, and the title essay is pretty much about the same thing, only translated to the art world. Galleries are everything, and there is no entry into getting a gallery unless you have an MFA from a select school. The whole system seems hopeless.

Back to *Torpor*, we of the New Narrative movement want to claim you as one of our own for your amazing vulnerability and the frankness with which you paint Sylvie as basically a sort of loser doomed to fail at anything she takes up.

And the gossip level is fairly astounding. We feel like we're backstage with Nan Goldin, Félix Guattari, Kathy Acker, and so many more from the worlds of high art, French theory, transgressive literature. Of course, Ms. Kraus, everyone wants to know the identity of the few you have concealed in pseudonyms, especially "the writers Kenneth Broomfield and June Goodman." Sylvie can't even look at Kenneth Broomfield or even think about him without one unfortunate comment, which he may or may not have made, ringing in her head. We've all been there, haven't we?

If you were here, I would ask you, "Do you write for a particularly cultured audience?" And you would probably say something like "No, I write for a curious one, I want my books to be read by a girl just starting community college."

The problem with Europe, and Jerome by extension, is that people can't separate the present from the past of fifty years ago, or a thousand years ago. As Jerome is haunted and motivated by the events of his childhood, the Romanians seem to be trapped in a nightmare medievalism. In one city Jerome and Sylvie try to stay in, Brigitte Bardot appears to applaud the citizens who have let three hundred thousand wild dogs run feral in the streets. Meanwhile in LA, there's no past and there's no imperfection and everything is beautiful.

Kraus writes beautifully about sex, and there's a strong passage where Sylvie is transported back to earlier ages when she's experiencing orgasm, back to seventeen, fourteen, once to age five. It's very moving.

I don't know if I'll ever be able to ask these questions of the writer, but I can recommend *Torpor* to anyone interested in either happiness or despair, America or Europe, the new or the old.

Batman Returns (1992)
dir. Tim Burton

★★★★★
The Rip

February 12, 2007

Like the previous reviewer I saw this on TV last night also, but otherwise my experience was very different than his, because for me, Michelle Pfeiffer's fantastic performance as Catwoman / Selina Kyle *was* enough to hold the whole messy movie together. And a lot of the credit for her work must go to Tim Burton and his artists, who in every frame made her look attractive or demented or sympathetic or the reverse, every beat thought out ahead of time and then allowed for. The pink phone in Selina's apartment, the dollhouse she destroys with a can of black spray paint. Her sewing machine that she runs a Catwoman costume on, complete with claws she attaches to the fingertips. The rip in the left shoulder of her beige outfit when Christopher Walken attacks her and the cats bring her back to life in the snow.

Even the snow itself, so obviously fake, so beautifully flying around her face and body as she lies supine on her back while the cats crawl around her and, apparently, elicit sparks of movement from her, even that snow seems designed to make us feel, on some level, that it isn't really cold and it won't really be hurting the body of our beloved Michelle Pfeiffer, even when we think she's dead.

The way she pours the carton of milk over her cat's bowl and much more of it comes out than would if she were sane and had motor control. Then she brings the carton to her exquisite, bruised lips, and the white milk plunges like a facial all over her chin, throat, and lapels. "Honey, I'm home," she cries out, like one at the end of her tether, without a single drop of energy left, blood oozing from her forehead. Has abuse ever been so graphically felt in a movie before? The camera seems to know exactly where to land next in order to capture every nuance of her twitches and turns. Set design in excelsis. And yet, I wonder what would happen if I didn't know the backstory and that she would become Catwoman. Say it was some Persian or Andalusian story that wasn't as familiar to me as the back of my hand. Would I ever really think that Selina Kyle would transform herself into Catwoman? The development is supposed to shock, I think, and of course it fails to do that, it's too ingrained in our comic -book-reading subconscious. Still Pfeiffer manages to find some shocking elements in the particulars of the situation. She even makes Selina mousy, and rewinding and watching again and again exactly how she manages this (by holding her mouth in a special grimace, I believe aided by some sort of cotton-based prosthetic under her lower lip) is an education in great acting all by itself.

Even if Batman weren't in the movie at all it would still be a masterpiece. Crazy that Pfeiffer was nominated for an Oscar that year but not for this, instead for her work in the boring *Love Field*. No wonder Emma Thompson won, but she stole it from Selina Kyle.

Beautiful Enemies: Friendship and Postwar American Poetry
by Andrew Epstein

★★★★★
With Friends like These ...

February 17, 2007

I've got so many opinions about *Beautiful Enemies* that I will be misquoting its author for years, arguing about its contentions, red faced, drunken, at parties and conferences, watching with immense satisfaction as its truths eventually percolate through the strong soil of

O'Hara criticism. Andrew Epstein, himself an accomplished poet, wades into deep waters with his study of the friendships between O'Hara and Ashbery and between Baraka and O'Hara. I was enthralled throughout the entire book and think you might be too. Even the notes are beautifully written, compact, thorough, yet with Epsteinian touches of wit and spirit.

A contrarian, even controversialist bent animates Epstein here, and if you come away from *Beautiful Enemies* feeling your head is about to explode, don't say I didn't warn you. Seems that everything (well, all the obvious things) that we had ever been taught about the three poets were wrong, even the most basic of our assumptions. You thought Frank O'Hara the apostle of friendship and community? Wrong. Through a clever and conscientious use of letters, diaries, contemporary news items, interview material, and most of all through recourse to the poems themselves (including some "new" material that, for the most part, is wholly surprising and convincing), Epstein is able to shove O'Hara more toward the Jack Spicer school of contentious grump whose ideas of friendship included competition, division, testing, and a free-floating anxiety that manifests itself in unusual verbal tactics. "I hope," he writes, "to provide a corrective here to the usual sense that Frank O'Hara is a poet of 'sociability' whose work simply 'celebrates' his friends and his coterie." It's not just rhetoric, there's a genuinely original vision of O'Hara here that complicates the work immeasurably and makes him not so annoying— not that I ever really found him annoying, but thinking about the old, "received" version of O'Hara, the sunny Tom Hanks of poetry who's everybody's favorite pet, just makes my blood run cold. I like the new guy, and he's sexier to boot!

If you thought Ashbery cold or silent about the human condition, à la Mark Halliday, surprise, for Epstein reads Ashbery (particularly in *The Double Dream of Spring*, the book he wrote after O'Hara's death) as a poet very much concerned with personal relationships, particularly friendship and its ups and downs. The material here is thinner on the ground, but I suppose it's possible, and Epstein has won so much goodwill from his previous reading I could forgive him nearly anything. Plus he has unearthed a beautiful, witty, tender, collaborative poem written in alternate couplets by FO'H and JA that illustrates perfectly—as though fabricated for the occasion—how friendship is always a bag mixed to brimming with competition, adoration, a Wayne Koestenbaum sort of erotics, and a perfect period panache. (Maybe this balances out another undocumented poem by O'Hara that Epstein found in Kenneth Koch's papers, "Finding Leroi a Lawyer," which some may champion but others will find the single most dumbest poem O'Hara ever put to paper.)

If you thought, following all previous Baraka scholars, that Baraka's Beat period was but an inconsequential and negligible phase of what Epstein calls a "conversion narrative," then you are missing out on some intensely great work; Epstein reverses conventional thinking here, or comes close to it, by plumping for the early work (written before Malcolm's assassination in February 1965) as far superior to the later Black Arts poetry and, perhaps, as politically committed. In each case, Epstein just patiently plays his cards until what seemed shocking or just startling for its own sake when one began reading the chapter seems by the end of it a perfectly reasoned, exquisitely marshaled argument. Were O'Hara and Baraka romantically involved, perhaps sexually involved? Here Epstein wades right in where angels fear to tread, following the leads provided in Brad Gooch's criminally underrated biography of O'Hara, *City Poet*. It does seem as though the older, white, homosexual man, sometimes generous, sometimes threatening, always alluring, who pops up through much of Baraka's early prose, poetry, and drama must have worn O'Hara's face at least occasionally. Baraka's supposed to appear at City Lights on Monday, I'll have to go and ask him what he thinks of *Beautiful Enemies* and his new avatar as sort of the Billy Strayhorn of the New American Poetry.

All in all, a groundbreaking and even better, a gorgeously written and thought-out, book. Hooray for Andrew Epstein! Some caveats, I don't 100 percent buy this new John Ashbery, our greatest poet of love and friendship. No way. Well, maybe a little way. And also I OD'd a bit on how without Emersonian pragmatism nothing important would ever have been thought, written, or said. And I grimace when I see Epstein replaying Michael Davidson's effective yet rhetorical vision of the Spicer circle as a hellish hotbed of gay homophobia and "exclusion," in order for him, Epstein, to say "But our fellows didn't go that far." So there was no exclusion in the New York circles of O'Hara and Ashbery? Uh-huh, and I'm Tallulah Bankhead.

Edwin Arlington Robinson: A Poet's Life
by Scott Donaldson

★★★★★
First Crack

February 20, 2007

I've been reading three big jumbo biographies of literary figures all at the same time, this one and the new lives of William Empson and Kingsley Amis (the Amis one comes out in April), and this book, *A Poet's Life*, is the one I'd figured ahead of time I'd like the least. I went into it scoffing, but came out, if not a convert to Robinson, a convert to Scott Donaldson, who took a chance with this enigmatic figure and at least squeezed the scrotum of the sphinx hard enough to make him give up a few of his secrets.

Robinson's youth was joyful, his family close, but a series of interrelated family tragedies scarred his adolescence and delivered him into manhood an emotional wreck on many levels. Donaldson provides a table of these tragedies, that's the only possible way to keep them straight, but it's the cumulative effect that matters: when Mary died, the mother of the three boys, her diphtheria kept away every townsperson. "No one would come near Mary Robinson's body or set foot inside the house where she had died." The boys had to prepare her for burial themselves. Even the preacher kept a handkerchief over his face, and avoided facing the grave as he spoke. "It was snowing. There were no other mourners in attendance. During the funeral, one kind neighbor took the risk of hanging a bag of doughnuts on the front doorknob of the Robinson house." Shortly afterward, Edwin lost his two beloved brothers to addictions, and he himself became a poet—as Donaldson theorizes, an addiction like any other. Gardiner, Maine, was on the verge of a drastic reduction in status, as a city, as a trading center, as a place on the map, its mills and factories shortly to close. Robinson looked back a thousand times in his poetry, but in life he only rarely returned to the place of his shame, even though his closest relations still clung to their bourgeois gentility.

For himself, the life of a poet entailed living in Boston and New York, and the artists' colony of MacDowell, where he became the elder statesman. On his emotional life Donaldson is especially interesting. Robinson never married, and it is sometimes thought that he cherished a lifelong crush on the girl his doctor brother, Herman, married: Emma. I'm not so convinced, but Donaldson makes a good story out of it, pointing out that Robinson's numerous book-length poems frequently tell the same story, a woman who should have married a sensitive man, winding up with his prosperous counterpart, sometimes a brother.

Success came late. He compared his poetry to "rat poison to editors." For eleven years in a row no US magazine paid a penny for any of his contributions. He came of age in the same era as a few other now-forgotten poets (William Vaughn Moody and Ridgely Torrence, for example); of them all, today only Robert Frost is as read as Robinson. (Indeed many place him in a much-higher rank.) In *A Poet's Life*, Frost comes across as a selfish, conniving d—k, but that's no surprise, is it? However, Robinson's aborted Harvard career did eventually plow the way for his surprise success—never count out a Harvard man—and Theodore Roosevelt, of all people, made him a star of the first magnitude (for EAR was the tutor of Teddy's son, Kermit, at Harvard, and Kermit felt sorry for him). TR's review of Robinson's second volume, *The Children of the Night*, remains, Donaldson notes, the only piece of literary criticism ever published by a sitting US president. Can you imagine our president today turning his hand to such a task? Roosevelt found him a secured job with the US government, even though he had sworn to forego this corrupt practice, which had been the pleasure of every previous US head of state, finding jobs for one's cronies. Robinson was Roosevelt's poet guy, a badge of class, even of modernism.

Robinson seems never to have gone out on a date with any woman, much less lost his virginity, and his friendships with other men were of such intensity that some have suspected, well, maybe he was having sex with them (or drawn that way, at any rate). Any bit of evidence in this direction is immediately retracted by Donaldson. Mowry Saben, upon whose memoir Donaldson relies for a lot of this "evidence," isn't on second thought such a reliable witness, for he might have been bisexual himself. (We hear this a couple of times.) This gets my goat, for why does being bisexual mean that you're automatically untrustworthy? Perhaps the gay or bisexual would be more eager to ascribe their own condition to any prominent friend. I think it's the other way around, and Donaldson plays up the EAR-Emma "love affair" on evidence no less vague than Saben's, never adding the disclaimer "However, *Witness X* was a known heterosexual and may be prejudiced in that direction." All I can say is that Robinson seems to have left little old Maine for good reason, and he invariably turned up in homosexual hotbeds of the period, Manhattan's Greenwich Village and Chelsea, the back hills of Boston, and the MacDowell Colony, where the boys are, EAR was there. And yet we get this sort of thing, again and again: "Only Mowry Saben, among those who knew Robinson well, was moved to speculate that he had repressed homoerotic tendencies. And Saben, as we shall see, was an enthusiastic supporter of love and license in all their forms" (page 261). WTF, Scott Donaldson?

He was a tenant of Jimmie Moore's in NYC, the sybaritic gamesman who made his apartment building a Xanadu of fun and pleasure (even installing a bowling alley in the basement). Moore was the black sheep grandson of the divine Clement Clarke Moore, the one who gave us "'Twas the Night before Christmas." I think, if you've got the stamina to read this massive book, that you'll fall in love with the poet you meet in these generous and wise pages. And much of his poetry, which Donaldson quotes very aptly, rewards new attention, even a hundred years later. You get to know not only EAR but the bohemians and mandarins of a whole vanished culture—hundreds of them, from Amy Lowell and Algernon Blackwood to such "outsider artists" as Franklin Schenck, the painter, a student of Eakins, whom Robinson called the "modern St. Francis," who lived on an island outside East Northport, Long Island, on a "handkerchief of land." The "doctors told him he needed iron," writes Donaldson, "so he was boiling out an old horseshoe in a pot on his one-burner stove. He lacked the money to buy canvas, so he had painted birds and flowers and running streams on every window shade in his shack."

The Secret Life of Humphrey Bogart: The Early Years (1899–1931)
by Darwin Porter

★☆☆☆☆
Barrel, Bottom Of

February 21, 2007

I was given this book as a birthday treat from a wonderful young man who is a friend of recent standing. He is to be commended for knowing the kind of thing I like and supplying it under conditions of complete surprise. But alas, I come to bury Darwin Porter's book not to praise it.

I can't believe, first of all, that Porter thinks he is fulfilling the sacred wishes of Kenneth MacKenna (d. 1962) to have the whole truth about Bogart published. Why would that be anybody's dream? That's just hogwash. If MacKenna actually left diaries or journals or whatever, let's have them deposited in a place of public record, a university or industry library, for all to read. Porter then says that he supplemented the information MacKenna left with him, with a series of interviews with Joan Blondell, John Springer, Shirley Booth, Ruth Gordon, Louise Brooks, and Mae West—needless to say, not one of his sources is alive. He makes the often maligned Boze Hadleigh seem like he has the journalistic integrity of David Halberstam.

I am curious about George O'Brien and the care with which he polished, lubed, and prettified his amazing, man-eating orifice. Also the story of "Big Bill" Tilden having his way with Douglas Fairbanks Jr., when the latter was only thirteen. Truth can sometimes be stranger than fiction, but we're in never-never land here.

Chestnut Tree

★★★★★
The Spreading Chestnut

March 2, 2007

I bought one of these as a whimsical gift to myself for having stayed sober for over fourteen years, with only occasional slips. Two months later, it is still sitting in my front garden, like a soldier of Cerberus guarding off bad vibrations. My feng shui consultant said that in all the best Asian house-holds a chestnut tree is planted outside the door that serves the higher caste of people—he said, "In your case that means you, since you have no servants." It picks up on temptation and will not allow it to come into the door. Since the poor little tree is only a few feet high, a few tempta-tions have passed through its bare branches, and I have sometimes thought, in recent weeks, of taking a drink or two. But then I have only to crane my eyes down to the ground, and my cravings subside, for I think to myself, "How hard that little chestnut is trying to grow big, rotating its way out of hard dirt to find the sky and the sun and the rain!"

Why can't we all take a lesson from our trees and be ourselves, or perhaps more accurately, the "tree sort of people" they want us to be?

You will not regret your purchase, though some have said my tree was a bit puny and its colors don't really complement my eyes or face.

In ten years' time I expect to be eating chestnuts night and day, perhaps setting up shop selling the chestnuts I shall roast myself, like the vendors used to do at Rockefeller Center, but here in San Fran-cisco, it's almost as though the whole city hates the taste of the nut, for you see very few of us vendors, past, present, or future, on any sidewalk in any neighborhood. So I'll be on the cutting edge.

***

Zodiac (**2007**)
dir. David Fincher

★★★★★
An American Tale

March 12, 2007

First of all, I loved the multimillion dollar recreation of San Francisco in its days of hippie glory in the 1960s and 1970s. As though to show time changing, Fincher calls in all his CGI friends to build the Transamerica Pyramid (600 Montgomery Street) before our eyes, and eventually leaves it as another tall, lit-up silhouette on the famous horizon. Better than anything else, the Pyramid shows the difference between the new and the old city.

Anthony Edwards makes an amazing return (and his hair does too) playing Bill Armstrong, the lead detective on the case and the partner of

Dave Toschi, an outspoken Italian American cop played in colorful, John Garfield–in–*Tortilla Flat* style by Mark Ruffalo. I nearly didn't recognize Ruffalo without Reese Witherspoon or Jennifer Garner playing opposite him, but here he is as the man's man many think that "Dirty Harry" Callahan was based on, and he's almost convincing. As a pas de trois between three fabulously talented male stars (Ruffalo, Jake Gyllenhaal, and Robert Downey Jr.), *Zodiac* is never boring, and whenever Anthony Edwards comes on-screen, the movie rises up another notch.

Maybe the women don't do so well, though Clea DuVall is striking as the jailbird sister of one of the very first Zodiac victims. But whoever is playing Ruffalo's wife has almost nothing to do except cast knowing silhouettes, and Chloë Sevigny, as the love interest for Jake Gyllenhaal's character, looks sour throughout, like someone was feeding her lemon-flavored Epsom salts through a tube. Ciara Hughes makes an astounding screen debut as the mysterious Darlene Ferrin; you can believe that whoever committed the Zodiac murders knew her well and wanted to know her better. I expect this beautiful young actress will have a great career in Hollywood, if she wants one.

But basically you will want to know how creepy the show is—and the answer is plenty. The movie begins with a radio segue, from Three Dog Night singing "Easy to be Hard" into the acid-rock freak-out of John Paul Jones, Alan Parker, Jimmy Page, pre Led Zep, of Donovan's "Hurdy Gurdy Man" as the suspense and the darkness ratchet up. Outside the theater the marquee blinked on and off all evening: *Why did the killer stop killing? Is he still alive? Could he be sitting next to you?* You didn't even want to look up to see who was anywhere in the rows around you. If someone touched me, I would scream.

American Genius, a Comedy
by Lynne Tillman

★★★★★
"I Heard My Name ..."

March 20, 2007

American Genius draws you in with the dexterity of Scheherazade so don't plan on doing a lot of other things because hours will go by and you'll still be there hanging on every word of the mysterious yet utterly candid narrator, a woman who seems to be on a permanent vacation from the realities of her ordinary life, so that in a way, this is the updated, and very New York, version of *Monsieur Hulot's Holiday*. But is it a holiday entirely? Or has, perhaps, our narrator stepped outside the bonds of society and been incarcerated in this strange place, like *The Yellow Wallpaper* or *The Snake Pit*? Women have long written about being clapped into one sort of prison or another, but rarely so enigmatically. I dare you to work it out, indeed part of the miracle of the book is seeing, with such inflected pleasure, just how long Tillman can keep up the balancing act of keeping you guessing. For in other ways the world the narrator finds herself in is like one of those artists' colonies one always hears about, where they bring you lunch to the door of your cottage, then tiptoe away so as not to disturb the "genius" within.

Or it could be any sort of other place of temporary lodging, like the inn in Chaucer. "Flee flee this sad hotel," Anne Sexton wrote, but in many ways this place suits our narrator, and the other guests or inmates or whatever they are afford her (and us) endless hours of amusement and speculation, just as they did M. Hulot, or Henry James. "I'm not trapped here," she keeps telling us, or maybe she's trying to reassure herself.

Each "guest" has a turn in the sun, each a little lesson in characterization, just the way they share their communal meals, or turn away from each other, or form little alliances that may or may not include our long-suffering artist with the sensitive skin. And yet by the end of the book we may decide that all that characterization aside, only a very few figures remain with us, strong trees on which the spiderwebs have entangled themselves. There is our narrator herself, bemused, sophisticated, and yet nursing childhood hurts and ancestral memories that mark her out as different even to herself— her world defined by how thin her skin is, how tender and how untouched. There's her brilliant father, not so much rapacious as passionately interested in everything except for that which his daughter holds dear. "It was my father who first made me conscious of the cherry on the back of my upper thigh." Thanks, Dad! And there's the Polish cosmetologist, superbly assured, highly skilled, European servility turned on its head to wear the mask of the master.

She's great. Most strange of all, most touching, the real-life figure of "Manson Girl" Leslie Van Houten, imprisoned for real after umpteen appeals for parole, her memories of killing Sharon Tate and the rest fading away like spots on gold lamé, her personhood turning her into a ghost, an avatar of humiliation, guilt, shame, and yet otherness, the otherness our heroine seems to see as a sort of shadow to her own self, the moon to her sun. Who knows what we might have been capable of if we felt as strongly, or as vacantly, as Leslie Van Houten?

The back of the book compares *American Genius* to *Tristram Shandy*, *Moby-Dick*, *Gravity's Rainbow*. I don't think so, but I can see why George Saunders and Matthew Sharpe jumped overboard in exactly those ways. Like these classic novels, *American Genius* plays with time—slowing it down, making it jump hoops, negating it on the one hand while reifying it on the other—the way a prisoner does, marking the days scrawled in charcoal on the wall of his cave or cell. The long sentences with which our narrator marks time will resound in your head every time you try to put down this wonderfully achieved novel, and you'll be imitating Tillman next time you try to open your mouth and explain just what it is that happened that made you so strange and so bereft.

Dark Water (2005)
dir. Walter Salles

★★★★☆
Phenomena Revisited

March 20, 2007

Dark Water's a good horror film, if a bit overlong, and it's fueled by the passionate performance of Jennifer Connelly as Dahlia, a woman with mother problems of her own and a history of mental instability (or merely migraines)? Her intensity is mirrored by her little girl, Cecilia (Ariel Gade), who is like a little "Mini Me" version of Dahlia, and just as exquisite. I remember this little girl from *Invasion*, and I hope the poor thing doesn't grow up with hydrophobia after her exposure to dripping, ghoulish water in this film and in that ill-fated Everglades-based sci-fi series.

I kept flashing back to Connelly herself as the world's most beautiful little-girl actress, in Dario Argento's *giallo Phenomena*, where she had the strange power to talk to insects and make them obey her. Just as Dahlia and Cecilia seem to be haunted by the spirit of a little girl ghost turned malevolent by the trauma of being abandoned by her mother and father (and possibly murdered by a building super?), it seemed that Connelly's American schoolgirl in Italy in *Phenomena* was also "acting out" from being abandoned by her father, an American movie star on the order of Sylvester Stallone (or Al Pacino). Thus I think Walter Salles picked out the perfect actress to play the central part in *Dark Water*, for so many of his shots recall Jennifer Connelly as a young girl, so that the performance itself is haunted by an earlier performance, and we see like X-rays the bones that made this presence work.

I didn't understand if Dougray Scott, whom Dahlia spies talking to two evil teens who menace the building and its occupants, was in cahoots with them for real, perhaps paying them to drive his former wife crazy, or is Dahlia just paranoid? I'd be sort of paranoid myself, especially if I sat down for a nap and didn't wake up for twenty-four hours. Salles and his screenwriters lay on the agony a little thick, but how can they help themselves when they have one of the USA's most expressive actresses to bring their torments to life. One thing I don't understand about Japanese-based horror films: Don't the angry ghosts ever find a shred of happiness, or do they always just want revenge on the living? If so, why doesn't the little Russian girl go after Pete Postlethwaite?

Potato Salad (1 Pint)
by Kings BBQ

★★★★★
The Southern Way

March 26, 2007

I have loved potato salad ever since I was so young that I would scrawl on my Christmas list to Santa "Potatoe Salad." Well, my spelling has improved since then, but Santa keeps on delivering, for thanks to Amazon I now have a steady supply of Kings delivered to my door. It is the perfect side dish for any kind of meal, especially when I am barbecuing in the backyard in a long white apron with a beer in either hand. The best thing is when you order Kings Potato Salad, you get a mélange of flavors, the heartiness of potatoes and the piquancy of old-fashioned vinegar and apples, the bite of raw onion and the blandness of a long stalk of celery, chopped up into tiny nearly invisible morsels, no more of that deep-throat celery you might find at the other end of my picnic table.

Nor does Kings skimp on the pickles either. Nowadays, with a national trend demanding more and better pickling, health fanatics will turn to this brand of potato salad the way they might line up for free kimchi, I've had a table of vegetarians come by over the backyard fence, scorning my barbecue but curious about the distinctive yellow tint of my Kings Potato Salad. I just lob 'em some free samples and they're all over me offering up intimate favors for just a taste of my Kings. You know who you are, you're the people who are licking your lips and trying to hide the distinctive yellow tang of Kings from your wives and children and moms and dads. The handy one-pint tub you can use and reuse, but its chief purpose is to act as a container for pleasure. The Southern way.

Sorry, Tree
by Eileen Myles

★★★★★
Sorry, Haters

March 31, 2007

I've been a fan of Eileen Myles for decades, since I first saw her give a reading, with Michael Lally and Tim Dlugos, so you know it's got to have been a long time ago.

She would tip her hat to people like John Wieners and James Schuyler but she was always herself, people dubbed her the female this or that (like "the female Ted Berrigan") but that wasn't what she was about. Every time she was pegged, she shrugged her shoulders like Samson and brought down the pegs and the ropes around her, and the roofs and the ceilings of the master's stone buildings. Her line could sometimes be "Schuyler-esque" (and in the new book there's even a Schuyler-esque *title*, "April 5") but in the long body of history, I think, Schuyler will be seen to have forecast Myles, rather than have influenced her, because you can forecast the weather but how are you going to influence it—except with the evil global warming of which Jimmy S. would have been incapable even in metaphor.

"A book is / a web I suppose," writes Myles, in "Fifty-Three," but this isn't going to be one of those dreary poems about, What is a book? "A book is / a web I suppose / saying you come / here to go / out an / incessant / trembling bridge / which a tree / is / I imagine." At first I thought the book, with that title, *Sorry, Tree*, was going to be a wry apology for cutting down the tree to make the pulp onto which the book is spread, like jam. But hurray, that's not what the title is alluding to! (I read this part with the lyrics of that Serge Gainsbourg tune skipping through my brain: "Sorry angel / Sorry so.") Myles has often included, in her books of "poetry," some sort of prose essay, or manifesto, around which the poems accrete and gain meaning; maybe these prose pieces are also there to *détourné* the shape of the book, to make it not all poetry, for Myles is a well-known despiser of genre's segregations. In *Sorry, Tree* we get "Everyday Barf," which starts out as a simple tale of seasickness on a ferry to Provincetown and becomes, very quickly, an analysis of everything right and wrong in our world, and everything true and false about the individual in it. I heard Myles read "Everyday Barf" in a darkened performance hall in Los Angeles in the Gehry-designed Walt Disney Concert Hall three years back, at the "Séance" conference organized by CalArts. It was a day of extraordinary papers, from everyone from Shelley Jackson to Dennis Cooper to Madeline Gins, but this was the most exhilarating, a ship in a bottle she sent flying through wet and salty air—and we were in it like little people. Like the tiny leaves on the trees here in California.

Last time around, she published *Skies*, which deliberately limited its subject matter, like an Oulipo constraint, and found variety everywhere, but it wasn't my favorite by her. I almost said that *Sorry, Tree* is what I like, except its newness is still bewildering. In publishing *Sorry, Tree*, Wave Books has upped the ante on themselves, for one move, releasing a new book by one of the world's greatest poets, has put their previous books all in the shade. They have all of them been adequate, even fine, books, perfectly serviceable, but that's like saying a breeze has been perfectly serviceable but when a hurricane blows into town you don't notice the breeze any longer, does it even exist?

Black Rainproof Car Top Carrier and Duffel Bag (Pack of 2)
by Highland

★★★★★
Perfect Fit

March 31, 2007

We joke that our rolling duffel bags would be a good place to put Grandma in if, like in that classic Flannery O'Connor tale, Grandma were to die during one of our family trips. No one would ever suspect a thing and, as appropriate, the color Highland makes the thing in is a funeral black. We have transported no corpses (yet!) but we are pleased to report that, in general, all of our children's toys and masks made it without a scratch when we left San Francisco and headed for the World's Kids' Mask Championships in Memphis. Our load was considerably lightened on the road home, for we sold most of the masks and the toys, but to compensate we stopped at a big "box store" for masks and let the kids buy whatever they wanted.

Bumpy back roads and sudden downpours aside, our masks and toys had just as comfortable a trip as we did, the adults and children gathered in our roving SUV. We experienced a few problems reported by reviewer #2, including the flaking of the rubber interior surface, which must have been factory poured, for it began to flake as soon as we crossed the Pecos River and one of the kids wanted to bring out his "Hopi Warrior" mask and our little angel her "Christine in *Phantom of the Opera*" half mask. A little touch of rain made some of the feathers stick together but nothing a trip under the portable hair dryer wouldn't cure instantly. However, our stay was short and I wonder what would have happened if we had introduced any sort of mold culture into the twin duffle bags. After four days on the road, stopping at common Embassy Suites and bed and breakfasts from here to Tennessee, would the mold have spread, or would the tightened flakes of black rubber, so like stretchy masks themselves, have killed the culture with its simple, yet effective, airtight security? We each of us were very sober during the journey, reflecting on what life would have been like if one of our kittens was missing and she might have wound up in the duffel bag, only we counted them several times before pulling out of the driveway and everyone was accounted for in my chief purser's (that is, my wife's) list.

Can't say enough about the friendly service, nor about the admiring stares of envy from some of the other Okies who made the trip to Memphis by piling everything on their rooftops—without bags—just let it all sit out in the sun, which faded some of the delicate filigree on their kids' costly mask possessions. One little boy, could have been the twin of Opie (Ron Howard), burst into a crying bag when he done seen his mask blanched to a creepy white bone color where it had once been the color Crayola used to call "flesh." Needless to say, that boy won no prizes and his family hung their heads in mutual shame for him.

Hold On to Your N.U.T.s: The Relationship Manual for Men
by Wayne M. Levine

★★★★★
Man Oh Man!

April 3, 2007

For me, it's all about the masculinity, and that's why I was glad when a copy of Wayne Levine's "relationship manual for men" crossed my desk. The book is a sequel of sorts to a previous volume, *Finding Your N.U.T.s*, but at first I didn't know what these books were all about. I thought they were some kind of macho exercise tactics like Laozi. No one could have been more surprised than I when *Hold On to Your N.U.T.s* turned out to be a book for men who need to be gentler and softer! The *N* is for "nonnegotiable," but that's a misnomer, because Levine is very firm about if you're really a man, then you'll give in as much as possible. Well, he calls it "cooperate without compromising your N.U.T.s."

Levine leads workshops for men all over the nation, and brands them with eight practical steps, each one tipped with tools, that each man can use to have a happier life with his wife or girlfriend (or male lover, says Levine). And in fact when you subscribe to these policies (like "never argue with your wife"), you will find that you probably won't be arguing with anyone, even your boss, anymore. That's the beauty of it. And no, it doesn't mean that you're whipped, though Levine isn't good enough of a writer to make that distinction very successfully.

For example: "Warning! Don't expect being a good listener today will earn you a get-out-of-listening card tomorrow. This isn't a board game. Your job is to be a good listener every day." A lot of it is about this is your job or that is your job. It makes relationships sound like work and I expect that for some guys, they would rather lose their N.U.T.s than have to work as hard as the good doctor wants us to. People think I make these books up but every one is the gosh-awful truth. The cheeky squirrel that adorns the book jacket, and the silhouetted acorn, make a nice change from the pair of walnuts that testiculated the jacket of Levine's first how-to book for men.

Ladies in Lavender (2004)
dir. Charles Dance

★★★☆☆
Call It *Two Sisters*, That Would Have Brought In More Patrons

April 3, 2007

For a great actress, Dench has made more bad films than anyone since Helen Hayes, and this is pretty much the bottom of the barrel, but I can see that at Amazon it's immensely popular among a vocal claque of fans. What's up with that? My guess is that everybody loves the delicate, nuanced byplay between Janet (Maggie Smith) and Ursula (Dench) as the two elderly sisters who sleep side by side in their exquisite Cornwall house, and the fat maid, played by redoubtable ham Miriam Margolyes, is also a hit among the fans who like her being bawdy and Shakespearean toward the two sisters and the young male visitor, who "hasn't got anything she hasn't seen before."

People also seem to like movies set in the past, and 1936 smudges the edges into a faded romance. To me, this picture is exactly like *Notes on a Scandal*, in which Dench also falls in love with a young beauty decades her junior, except here it's played like something out of a fairy tale. The young man appears on the strand, near dead, they take him in, they play cavaliers to his sleeping beauty. *Notes on a Scandal*, however, at least took the time to establish the backstory of its characters. Here we know absolutely nothing about Andrea, the handsome young Pole, except that he's charming, roguish, and can play the violin very beautifully. (Wouldn't it have been a great casting coup if Charles Dance had let US violinist Joshua Bell, who provides the soundtrack, take the part? He's movie-star handsome and Andrea, after all, didn't have to be Polish, did he? He could have been shipwrecked from America too!) (Maybe deaf and dumb to provide the element of mystery Dance seems to require for Andrea's character!)

This movie did not do well, but that's probably because no man in his right mind would go to a multiplex and say "Umm, yes, two for *Ladies in Lavender*, please." I'd rather kill myself than utter those words. It would be easier to buy a case of Tampax at a busy Walmart. But on DVD perhaps some men will enjoy the picture. Poor Maggie Smith, I hope they paid her a lot of money because in every scene, Judi Dench reaches out her little paw and steals it.

I also think that Dance forgot to tell Natascha McWhatever-Her-Name-Is that the movie is set in the 1930s.

Tiger Traits: 9 Success Secrets You Can Discover from Tiger Woods to Be a Business Champion
by Nate Booth

★★★★☆
My Postbook Cooldown

April 6, 2007

Tiger Woods had to wait two years after winning his first big tournament to win a second one. Did he ever get discouraged? You bet, but he never let consistent losses kill his spirit. Dr. Nate Booth urges us to apply the principles of winning to our business problems, for the solutions that worked for Tiger might also help us earn more money and success. The traits of likability (it is said that Tiger never forgets a face and always remembers the names of the children and wives of everyone he meets) will put you in good stead when it comes to your career, and success will be a birdie in the hand.

Booth is an exciting and spirited writer. I would love to see him do a full-scale infomercial that would help us put the story of Tiger in perspective. He's got a nice balance of inflation and restraint, and he knows his facts. Most people know Tiger is of mixed race, but Booth has the eugenics at his fingertips. For the record, "his father is half African American, a quarter American Indian and a quarter Chinese, and his mother is half Thai, a quarter Chinese and a quarter white." Booth allows us to see Tiger's rise to fame as steps on a Joseph Campbell–like journey—the hero with a thousand faces, and here, a thousand races.

All the same, there's something a little crazy about this book, for although it says in big letters that Tiger Woods and the Tiger Woods Foundation have nothing whatsoever to do with *Tiger Traits*, it's selling largely on Woods's name, not on the name of Dr. Nate Booth, I presume. Isn't there a law against this kind of abuse? It would be like if I wrote, say, a cookbook and called it *Tiger's Recipes*, as long as I had a disclaimer saying "These recipes were not tasted nor tried by Tiger Woods, but they were inspired by his joie de vivre." I would call that cheating, but apparently in the world of business books and motivational speakers, anything not nailed down is fair game.

Divagations
by Stéphane Mallarmé

★★★★★
The Man of the Hour

April 12, 2007

I don't always think that the editors of *Bookforum* pick the right reviewers for most of the books they cover, but when they assigned Wayne Koestenbaum to review Mallarmé's *Divagations*, they struck gold, and it seems clear to me now that WK is a Mallarméan writer, or rather, of the school of Mallarmé, and yet I would never have thought so until I started dipping into Barbara Johnson's fantastic translations here. The wordplay and the love of digression, the little paragraphs and the long, lithe sentences, like Gina Lollobrigida stretched out on the beach, everything about Johnson's Mallarmé brings me back to the gifted critic and fiction writer of today. Then I was struck by how contemporary the whole of Mallarmé's *Divagations* enterprise seems. One piece, "Crisis of Verse," might have been written today, or at any rate the day before yesterday, and page after page of it, with its emphasis on the "white space" surrounding the word, anticipates Jabès, Barthes, all the most beautiful of twentieth-century critics. "What caused a medium extent of words, under the gaze's comprehension, to take on definitive traits, surrounded by silence?" (The entire paragraph—you see, they're brief enough, in general, to fit inside fortune cookies.)

I like the one where Mallarmé claims that, of all the French words for "shade," *ombre* is too "opaque" and *ténèbres* is "not very dark." "What a disappointment, in front of the perversity that makes *jour* and *nuit*, contradictorily, sound dark in the former and light in the latter. Hope for a resplendent word glowing, or being snuffed out, inversely, so far as simple light-dark alternatives are concerned." What a way to put it! As an American boy growing up in France, I too often pondered the way French people seemed to think of *jour* as a dour, creepy sort of time, while the *nuit* was full of radiance and fun. Well, now I know a little bit more about their ways, and it's no more Nabokov for me. We used to weave complicated fantasies about a group of little fairy people who came out at twilight, the border between night and day just as it seems, in retrospect, like the Maginot Line between life and death. In our language, *light* and *life* are next to each other on the tongue at any rate, and it was an irate schoolmaster who broke up our crepuscular reveries, urging us harshly to take up our cudgels and proceed home where Weetabix awaited us. I thought at first, before taking up Koestenbaum's review in *Bookforum*, that I would have to be considerably keener on Banville, Tailhade, Verlaine, Morisot, et al. (than I am) to get caught up with *Divagations*, but the truth is you don't have to know as much as you think you might to enjoy this book tremendously. You'll love the part where he theorizes that the slow, mournful syllables of "Lord Tennyson" account for the poet's popularity, and furthermore for "something serene, isolated, and complete; the proud withdrawal of physiognomy."

The Holy Forest: Collected Poems of Robin Blaser
by Robin Blaser, ed. Miriam Nichols

★★★★★
"Honey Wrapped in Intelligence"

April 18, 2007

You don't want to miss the new version of Robin Blaser's lifework *The Holy Forest*, now considerably larger than the version I remember when Talonbooks put it out back in 1993, by maybe another hundred pages or so. He, Blaser, is one of the poets the USA lost to Canada during a time of international turmoil, a time when crossing borders might have been a little bit easier than today and escape was still possible. He had been a slow starter, perhaps, in the days of the Berkeley Renaissance of the 1940s, and it might be that not until he moved to Boston to work in Harvard's Widener Library, and met Charles Olson and the US poets of the East Coast, could his particular genius truly blossom. (More than any other contemporary poet, it is Blaser who needs a proper biography written about him, and yet what a daunting challenge to try to tell the story of a life spent nosing down so many divagations and turning up so many splendors.) On his return to the Bay Area in the very late 1950s, he became an integral part of a then-lively San Francisco poetry scene, his friendships with the California poets Robert Duncan and Jack Spicer then productive to overflowing. In *The Holy Forest* you can see these concentric circles of poetic influence and Rauschenbergian "combine" expand and contract, expand and contract, within the first hundred pages of the book, like the movement of the glaciers that produced our islands and outcroppings. After that, and his move to Canada, a certain perfection is reached that never really drops off.

Underlying this achievement, Blaser moved in opposite directions at once, perhaps trusting his muse more than ever, a contradictory one for sure, one that was leading him to go more and more slangy, colloquial, partial, aphoristic, and playful—and then on what in a lesser poet you might call an opposite direction, he became the poet of lengthening odes and longer forms. You would ask him how a particular poem was shaping up, and with a mixture of marvel and abasement he might whisper "It's now over fifteen pages." "Just grew," he would add. And so we have the "Great Companions," and "Exody," and the rest, these intricate, phenomenal structures. If you could visualize the poems in *The Holy Forest* as real trees, spreading in visual space as they have in time, you might see toward the end of the range huge redwoods, where before you had had mere groves of oak, maple, and cherry. In our time he has been all things together the best kept secret of postmodern poetry; it's just fantastic that Cal has seen fit to issue this book—not only this, but a companion volume of collected essays (*The Fire*). May the saints preserve him, as my mother used to say, when she wanted to make sure someone most dear would stay safe and unafraid.

Pet Pawprint Hanging DIY Keepsake Ornament, Dog or Cat, Pet Owner Holiday Christmas Gift
by Pearhead

★★★★★
A Christmas Memory

April 21, 2007

When you think of baby presents, Pearhead is the name that comes to mind, for they have built up a repertoire, or should I say arsenal, of killer baby gifts, including a range of scrapbooks and photo albums that we thought Brent and Melissa's little girl might enjoy when she's older, and would like to see photos of herself as a baby. However, all the other Pearhead baby products are trumped by this one, which really is all about the donor as much as the baby.

For, strictly speaking, you may make a Christmas ornament out of your baby stepping in a thin bath of cement (or plaster, really), but as the other reviewer pointed out, if you have a dog or cat you can get the pet to place their delicate paw in the ring as well, and put it up on your Christmas tree much as my wife and I did this past December, for we have two cats, and no babies.

Then the fun really began as I was persuaded after a few cherry cordials and Manhattans and rum and cokes and a Ramos fizz, to commemorate my nose, like Cyrano, and run it up the Christmas tree like a flag. Bob Hope used to have nose-shaped ornaments, or so my mother used to tell me, and this was my tip of the hat to her and to Hope. Traditionalists with children can always dip their children's palms into the smooth, comfortable, lotioned solvent. But for me, invention is the mother of necessity. I wouldn't dip every part of my body into this sauce, but call me in the morning and I might have changed my mind.

In the meantime, I heartily recommend Pearhead to new parents, grandparents, uncles and aunts, big brothers and sisters, even twins might enjoy doing each other, if they aren't too mature. You know how at a certain age kids are embarrassed to be caught doing the childish fun things they used to long for when younger.

All Men Scrapbook Pages: Inventive Ideas for Masculine Layouts
ed. Emily Curry Hitchingham

★★★★★
Tying It All Together

April 23, 2007

My life's been a merry salad of male activities, and until recently I had just about given up hope of properly documenting it, but then I discovered Emily Curry Hitchingham and, even better, Hitchingham's books packed with scrapbooking tips for the newbie. I'd lived the complete life of a man—hardscrabble beginnings growing up as an American child, scared, isolated, and *désolé* in rural France, then early pangs of adolescent passions, a deep interest in American sports such as bowling, basketball, and college football, and then the typical career path of a US male, replete with wise mentors, obnoxious bosses, and toadying suck-ups. Now at the very top of my profession, and having found true love late in life with the novelist Dodie Bellamy, I found myself wondering, "How to get all of this wonderment down?" Hitchingham offered the glimmerings of a solution with her book *Pet Pages*, in which we found ourselves commemorating the loss of our two cats, Blanche and Stanley—one white, one black—through scrapbooking, the fastest-growing hobby for women in the USA.

Men should do more scrapbooking too! Men, you don't want to be like me, having attained maturity, with all your works around you, but suddenly feeling hollow, ill at ease with a world closing in on one like an old-time pup tent from Scouting days. My wife bought me a copy of *All Boys Scrapbook Pages*, and I blanketed an entire scrapbook with souvenirs of my bittersweet childhood years in France—postcards of Mont-Saint-Michel and Chartres, candid photos of Marc Chagall in repose, and Scouting badges from the American Boy Scouts in Exile. I did a page in rope since tying was my favorite sport. And yet by the end of the book I was only twelve or thirteen. I needed a book to show off my manhood, the Lawrentian way, the primal way, and *All Men* is it. Are you afraid of seeming feminine with pretty colors and coded allusions to domestic bliss? Then this may not be the book from you. But if you're man enough to take Emily Curry Hitchingham on her own terms, the way that Spencer Tracy always stood up to Kate Hepburn even at her most loquacious and mannered, then this book may be the answer to your dreams.

I've written many books, but never one as important as *The Kevin Killian Scrapbook of Being a Man*. And she helped.

Copper Fire Bowl

★★★★★
Creature Comforts

April 25, 2007

In my neighborhood lined with the hissing of busy backyards, over-the-fence gossip has it that the Copper Fire Bowl is overpriced, and that you might get similar results from using a concrete birdbath, but I have no such complaints about my purchase. Originally we planned to have one child stand there, at the entrance to the alley, lifting the fire bowl aloft to mark the opening of the South of Market (San Francisco) Spring Olympics, for what would an Olympics' opening ceremony be without a fire bowl swinging like an incense burner, held high by last year's champion athlete (in our case, speller)? Then our plans got scaled back some when some of our neighbors converted to condos and half the children on the block moved to another part of the world.

Bring your Copper Fire Bowl down to the beach at night, watch the ocean lit up through the seductive blue and orange flames of your safely contained campfire, throw on some chestnuts and marshmallows and you've got yourself a feast. And when you're done, pick up the handy metal stand (black, which sets off the pretty copper color nicely) and tuck it under your arm, head back to the car or bus. You could top it off with the Pebble Veranda Cover, sort of like a table-cloth of stone for your fire bowl, but I have found it not the easiest item in the world to clean, and though the dogs don't mind licking it off from time to time, I worry about their rough tongues somehow damaging or staining the pebble-like finish.

You could sit for hours watching the fire ebb and flame through the mesh-like screen attachment, which is like watching a movie in 3D, while feeling the heat on your face and along the long sweep of your legs as, cross-legged, you meditate on the sand or on the rugged crab-grass of your backyard barbeque area. Don't be surprised when nearby forest animals, such as squirrels or rabbits, approach cautiously, drawn by the spectacle and the concomitant promise of warmth. You'll see their eyes first, mindless blips among the hedges, and then you'll see their sharp noses come bounding out like little kangaroos. Keep some nuts and carrots on hand for such nocturnal animal visitations.

Next Life
by Rae Armantrout

Next

April 27, 2007

In the poems of *Next Life*, the natural world is taking a beating, not only from the rival attractions of the cinema and TV, but from the haste with which we have catapulted Earth's slide into eco-catastrophe. From the very first poem, "Tease," to the last, we see the natural order made to feel second rate, flowers turn into wallflowers. In "Tease," bare trees must be supplemented by their imagined resemblance to human skeletons to earn a place in the "provisional parts" of the world, while the poem works up a keen interest in a serial killer rapist movie—the eternal pair of cop versus serial killer. By the second poem, "Line," the speaker can no longer recall the origins of the term "rooting around."

Armantrout asserts that "Narrative prepares me / to see / whatever I see next," for one is always anticipating oneself, like the fellow Nicolas Cage plays in the new film *Next*—he can see everything two minutes into the future, thus it's hard to surprise him. In his case precognition itself foregrounds narrative's numinousness, to "produce a continuous present," as the poet reminds us in "As (2)." Three birds show up to stage a "framing gesture, // an inclusive sweep."

I have admired her writing for nearly twenty-five years, and last week I went to see her read from some of the poems in *Next Life* as she spoke on a bookstore panel here in San Francisco on "The Future of Poetry." It was the perfect topic for the theorist of *Next Life*, in which poetry's next two minutes seem always only as far away as the reach of one's hand. And she has a beautiful speaking voice too, her vowels pleasantly striated. If only I could have that voice of the operator eliminated from my phone system and have Rae Armantrout tell me that when I hear the tone, the time will be 10:49 a.m. and 50 seconds.

In the meantime her new book gives us flashes of another world, the *chazerai* of this one, and I find it telling that so much of it comes from an attempted rehabilitation of the flora and fauna that, dried and etiolated, we are losing every day. "Dry, white frazzle / in a blue vase—" (see Marlon Brando in *A Dry White Season*), "*beautiful*— // a frozen swarm / of incommensurate wishes" ("Close").

Liar
by Mike Amnasan

★★★★★
Double, Double

May 2, 2007

Joe is "no working class hero," but he lives a double life, by day a steward in the metal trades at a high-rise building going up in the San Francisco of, I don't know, 1990 or so, and at other times he suffers his way through the insular avant-garde writing circles of the L=A=N=G=U=A=G=E poets and their epigones. Similarly he's got two women as well, a long-term live-in relationship with the artistic, ambitious, and elegant Jane, and a dirty little affair with Ann, a married woman who can't get enough of Joe's big construction-worker thing. As befits a roman à clef of the San Francisco writing scene of twenty years back, the theoretical disputes between Ron Silliman and Leslie Scalapino form a convincing backdrop to Joe's intellectual disquisitions. Michael Amnasan's novel *Liar* works all these complications into one extremely rich and gritty piece of fiction that will have you thumbing through avidly to see how it all ends up.

Amnasan's prose style is insanely catchy; after you close this book you will inevitably wind up writing sentences like his—plain, severe, cryptic, and often laceratingly cruel, but yours won't be as unsparing or accomplished. He has a keen eye for the outfits his women wear, the way they pet their cats, and in fact he's all observation, like a Robbe-Grillet flaneur. *Liar* switches back and forth between paragraphs in the third person and a first person that seems to be Joe as well, or is he the author? Likewise we sometimes are presented with the present tense—particularly in his descriptions of sex play, and in the tedium of construction work and its hierarchies of union top-down organization—but then, after a tiny white space, we'll be in the past tense, a continuous past of entrapment and lack. He's jarring, but he wants to use the jangly, shifty surfaces of his prose to keep us feeling off balance, like Joe hanging upside down from the girders, high above the little people on the sidewalks of Market and Fremont Streets.

By now the story of how Amnasan lost track of his manuscript, only to have the only extant copy of it turn up, years later, in the collection of another New Narrative writer of the period (Camille Roy), has entered literary history as yet another example of how fragile is reputation and how random the ways art avoids oblivion. Spunky Ithuriel's Spear of San Francisco, which has already earned our gratitude for its sponsoring of the collection *Post War* by F. S. Rosa and the reprint of Bruce Boone's *My Walk with Bob*, has pulled another chestnut out of the fire with *Liar*, its most daring gamble yet.

Ready to Wear (1994)
dir. Robert Altman

★★★★★
A Crazy Quilt

May 2, 2007

Why all the hate for *Ready to Wear*? Like many of you, I was under-whelmed when it first came out but now thanks to constant showings on the Sundance Channel and all those channels in that narrow band of indie cable, it has been growing on me and now I can't stop watching it. Barbara Shulgasser's writing is wonderful, and if it has been chopped up like coleslaw by Altman's fitful direction, and by the generally impro-visatory style embodied by Kim Basinger's steamrolling fashion reporter, it is still Altman who gives the picture its life, its joie de vivre. And the fantastic outfits are to die for, each one crazier than the last.

Sophia Loren is so over the top in this one role that retrospectively her entire career takes on a veneer of camp Carlo Ponti could never have intended. If she were Elton John, her sunglasses couldn't get any vaster, like two TV screens perched on her nose, and her breasts bobbing like apples in the tub of her sausage-cased cleavage deserve equal billing with Mastroianni, who perhaps overdoes his sad-sack clown persona. Together they're not so much fun as you'd think, but she's great. Is there any black satin left in the world or was all of it used for her widow's wear!

My favorite, Anouk Aimée, gets all the drama parts. Why didn't Altman use Anouk Aimée more, she is simply the most striking and hawklike actress who ever lived! She and Rupert Everett as her avari-cious son are playing out whole three-decker Balzac novels with their back and forth, their mutual accusations of greed and contempt.

OK, there are some inanities to *Ready to Wear*, and I'm never sure if Forest Whitaker isn't laughing up his sleeve or revealing new, pre-viously unknown dimensions to his private life, but all in all it is a movie for the ages, and my favorite by Altman (except for *Nashville* and *A Wedding*). Maybe its angle about fashion being stupid is itself pretty banal, but you know, I just don't care anymore. If it's on, I'll watch it all the way through and I'll cry when it's over, just like Julia Roberts pretending her lost luggage hasn't yet been delivered to her closet.

Aalto 3.75-Inch Glass Vase, 2006 Anniversary (Petrol Blue)
by Iittala

★★★★★
Kind of Blue

May 3, 2007

What a bargain! If you had an original Alvar Aalto vase, you'd be a millionaire, but this one is reasonably priced from Finland, and now that price is slashed to rock bottom.

What you could do with this wonderful tribute to eccentric Finn design, as you ponder how the world's greatest visionaries always need to have a vase nearby. Trace with your fingers the many unusual surfaces of this vase and you will see, though it seems small, that the multifold shape of the glass actually means that it uses much more glass per cubic foot than even a very large US-made vase, with our straight modernist up-and-down lines. Now what would cause an architect designer like Aalto to go so wiggly? Some have laid the credit to the glacier-based farmland of his native country. For example, stand up, stand on a chair, and look down at this vase from a bird's eye view, you will see that from above it resembles roughly an air view of the shape of Finland.

Others have ascribed Aalto's quirkiness to the ups and downs of his emotional and spiritual life while here on earth. As his soul bubbled over, so did his glass blowing; compare to our contemporary Dale Chihuly, who has acknowledged this classic vase design in many recent commissions. To design in glass properly, you have to be very, very controlled, with an iron rod instead of a spine, and a mouth intuitively ripe for blowing, and yet you must be a romantic too. Anyone with a "petrol blue" vase at home will find Aalto's signature on the bottom (in replica on Amazon, of course), and those who know a thing or two about graphology will know the man from the way his hand trembled over the double *A* that began his name and which plunged him to the front of twentieth-century designers if you ranked them in alphabetical order. The conflict, you see, was always there, like a birthmark on his shoulder.

Jackass Number Two: Unrated (2006)
dir. Jeff Tremaine

★★★★☆
Good and Plenty

May 4, 2007

The movie is over before it's begun, but on the way to the end you'll be in pain you'll be laughing so hard. Then there will be the parts where vomit will rise up in your throat at some of the stunts and you'll be wondering if you can make it out of the theater before you throw up. That's a tribute to the stunt work here and the sense of danger. In "The Ice Horse," Brandon has to drop his pants (in chilly weather), douse his balls with Evian, then take a ride on a horse carved out of ice to see if his underside winds up freezing along with the horse. At first he's hesitant, his hand at his belt. Johnny Knoxville advises "Don't even think, just do it," and I guess that's the way they got through these new adventures, because if they gave any of them any thought they'd have backed off and called in sick that day.

Or there's the variety of stunts where, like *Candid Camera*, the boys are not told what's going to happen to them. A limo takes the crew to what they think will be a photo shoot but instead thousands of angry bees are pumped through the skylight. When they try to escape, first the locks are jammed, then when they finally fall out of the car, the lot is covered with what must be twenty thousand marbles and there's no way out except crawling on your hands and knees with glass under your kneecaps and the queen bee on your neck. Afterward you can't help thinking, "Is there a caste system on *Jackass*, so that the lower-paid guys have to suffer the most and the stars get put through a few showy stunts and that's it?"

In general everyone has aged pretty well but they could stand to pledge some new faces, for a few of our heroes are looking puffy, bloated, drugged out, or otherwise not as fresh as they looked in *Volume One* nor on the TV show, and because it's all about the butt, Chris Pontius should surrender his throne now and give it up to a boy who still has got a bit of jelly to him and not so much sag. Just my opinion, don't set the cobra on me!

Ordeal by Innocence
by Agatha Christie

★★★★★
Christie's *Waiting for Godot*

May 8, 2007

Ordeal by Innocence is one of the difficult Christies from her most controversial period, in which her novels grew longer and longer, while some argue her energies were primarily directed toward the stage, where she was amazingly successful and the Queen of the West End for a few years. The novels of the same time grow ponderous, as though overswollen with social and moral anxiety, and this is one of the touchstones of the era, cited by Christie herself in her *Autobiography* as among her own personal favorites.

Is it a plot she cooked up, then abandoned, for her contemporaneous drama *The Unexpected Guest*? It seems like it, right down to the gloomy, Stygian opening in which a mystery man crashes into the closed society of a wealthy family grieving over a recent loss.

As usual, Christie studs the novel with references to all sorts of high and low culture. As many have noticed, the character of Jacko Argyle seems borrowed from the real life "Let him have it" case of Derek Bentley and Christopher Craig, while she makes much of the famous line from Racine's *Phèdre* that goes "C'est Vénus tout entière à sa proie attachée" (She is Venus, now indistinguishable from her prey) and the beautiful Jean Ingelow ballad for which Arthur Sullivan wrote the music:

> *Ah, maid most dear, I am not here;*
> *I have no place—no part—*
> *No dwelling more by sea or shore,*
> *But only in thy heart.*
> *O fair dove! O fond dove!*
> *Till night rose over the bourne,*
> *The dove on the mast, as we sailed fast,*
> *Did mourn, and mourn, and mourn,*

Most curious of all, from our point of view, is Christie's reference to *Waiting for Godot*—Hester Argyle and Donald Craig are said to have attended an amateur production of the play in a tiny suburban town two years before the action of the novel proper begins. Indeed, seeing this play turns out to be Hester's alibi during the slaying of her mother! *Godot* was then a very new play in English, though it had premiered in French three or four years before the writing of *Ordeal by Innocence*. We don't expect to find Beckett in Agatha Christie, or vice versa, but a case might be made that the two playwrights and modernists had much more in common, and the bizarre comedy and overweening sadness of Vladimir and Estragon find weary analogues in the plight of the Argyle family, a collection of misfits who are all sitting around waiting for something to make their miserable lives meaningful. They don't know their salvation lies in the unlikely form of Arthur Calgary, a geophysicist whose temporary amnesia led to the crack-up of the strange, totally convincing plot behind Rachel Argyle's murder.

All the characters speak of the "calamity of the innocent," but Christie's theme here is really forgiveness. How do the children she adopted forgive Rachel Argyle for tearing them away from their blood kin? How does the polio-stricken air ace Philip Durrant forgive the fate that condemned him to a wheelchair? How does Calgary forgive himself for letting Jacko perish in prison? Though it has its longueurs and dead patches, *Ordeal by Innocence* is amazingly beautiful, reflective, yes, and suspenseful. It's not easy to see who did it, and the ending is a classic surprise. Christie's plots are Apollonian and worked out with a clinician's perfection, but her storytelling is surprisingly intuitive, moving sideways, working by allusion and rhyme.

The three love stories in the book, too, are all gracefully done. One forgets how much Christie knew about love (and betrayal). And how about that child ruining Tina's alibi by reporting the landing of a Sputnik! (That turns out to be Tina's much-bruited "bubble car," a sensation of the 1956–57 period that is the closest contemporary design has come to an actual spacecraft-inspired mass-produced car.)

Wake for the Angels: Paintings and Stories
by Mary Woronov

★★★★★
One of a Kind

May 9, 2007

Woronov is a brilliant fiction writer and memoirist as well as being a living legend in hip circles and a talented actress whose performance in *Scenes from the Class Struggle in Beverly Hills* is as good as anything Meryl Streep ever managed to put together—so nuanced, so heart-breaking, so sexual. As a painter, she has her ups and downs, and this huge collection of her work shows her at her very best and her very worst—and the two aren't that far apart, for what seems initially childish or clichéd in her work sometimes reveals itself, as you turn the pages, to show signs of divine fire. In her work, LA is the ultimate product of the Ashcan School, and her figures writhe in the bonfire of existential misery and obsession.

Wake for the Angels divides her corpus into thematic groups, and then she writes stories for each painting—sometimes turning a particular body of work into a graphic novel, kind of, with faces and bodies switching off and dictating the action or mood of the tale they inspire. Woronov's men and women and children all yearn to be good and to find a single bit of fun in the lousy prison sentence they tell us is human life, and they bang against each other like stick figures hoping to draw sparks. It's a strange, sometimes poisonous amalgam of artwork and fiction, but most of the time, to my surprise, it works like nothing else I've ever read. She is sort of a blend between the Hubert Selby Jr. of *Last Exit to Brooklyn* and the Jane Bowles who wrote "A Stick of Green Candy." The book is exquisitely produced with some foldout pages that do the work a reverent justice, as her harsh, hypnotic brush conjures up human life like the cats of Rousseau prowling king-like through jungle vines and brambles.

Every time you think you have her number, she surprises you by turning around the digits.

Ultimate Gay Erotica 2005
ed. Jesse Grant

★★★★★
Questions for Jesse Grant

May 14, 2007

Jesse Grant, who are you? How do you know so much about me, my deepest fantasies, my buried wishes? What is your secret? Do you come into my room at night while I lie deep asleep, reading my dreams with some sort of literary tickertape that measures not what I aspire to but the depth of the mud to which I hope to sink? I can't explain otherwise how you came to edit *Ultimate Gay Erotica 2005* and have gotten it all so right.

OK, there are one or two little numbers I could have done without, and one or two that wound up offending my dignity, spoiling my image of myself. And one or two which I stopped reading with one hand, because with one hand you can't flip through the pages quick enough to finish off the particular piece of tripe one wishes to skip. But outside of that, you had the genius to include not one but two stories by my favorite Thom Wolf, the British author of *The Chain* and *Words Made Flesh*, not only the top porn writer of the present era but one of the best writers I know period. "All I can do is sit back in awe of myself," you write in way of introduction, and for once such a boast is fully justified, since "The Ride In" by Thom Wolf is alone worth the price of admission, and Wolf's other story here, "Who Do You Love?"—its flip title drawn from Riva's epic 2001 single "Who Do You Love Now?" (featuring Dannii Minogue)—is just as provocative. What especially endeared me to this story was the way its hero, the anonymous pleasure seeker, on a pleasure trip to the Durham area in England, first notices Ben, the more aggressive of two beefy-top boyfriends, as Ben sits in a café "reading a collection of erotic stories by Kevin Killian."

There's something about reading one's own name in a porn story that speaks to many factors in the broader social network of reading. Do we read to discover something new about ourselves? The world outside? Or, in the case of *Ultimate*, to turn on and rub out? I still haven't made up my mind about these issues and Jesse Grant, that's why I want you to call me, I need your input, just the way that Ben and Will need to make ice cubes out of sperm in their lovely Durham-area freezer, so that they can upload them into the recti of visiting pig boys. "I moaned and tightened my muscle, keeping the load secure inside. The heat of my core melted the ice quickly. 'Can you handle another?' he challenged. I gasped again as the second cube was inserted. It felt so much harder and colder than the first, but the pain was sublime. As the spunk melted, I felt complete. 'More,' I hissed. I would have done anything for another of those potent little cubes."

The Lake House (**2006**)
dir. Alejandro Agresti

★★★★★
Back and Forth with *The Lake House*

May 14, 2007

Most of the questions that came to me during a recent screening of *The Lake House* had nothing to do with the "time travel" aspect of the movie which I knew going in would be over my head. But like everyone else, I respond viscerally to any movie that pairs Keanu Reeves with Sandra Bullock. The two of them should star in all movies, in any year—2004, 2006, or now. Think of how many films would have been much improved if only Reeves and Bullock had been available to take the title parts. I'm thinking of *Mulholland Drive*, *Million Dollar Baby*, *Ice Age*, even something like *Brokeback Mountain* could have used Sandra Bullock playing the part Anne Hathaway did and tempting Keanu Reeves with her knowledge of rodeo driving.

But my questions were more about, "What is with the strange brother of Keanu Reeves, Henry, and his leonine hairline which looks as though hair grows out of his head backward and gets crimped there? Where did they find this actor, or the woman who plays Sandra's mother?" For her part, the producers might have been turned down by Marsha Mason so they decided to get the "foreign" Marsha Mason, with her odd Dutch or Malaysian accent but all of Marsha Mason's Botox plumping out her face like a pin cushion.

(SPOILERS AHEAD)
It made me uncomfortable all the time she was around, even discounting the fact that I believe the mother (played by Willeke van Ammelrooy) made that bus run over Keanu Reeves as she sat with her daughter at Dealey Plaza and realized, when she lifted her gaze and saw Alex Wyler begin to approach, that this was the man who would once and for all take Sandra away from her at last. Did anyone else get this, or am I just reading into things? Notice that once Keanu and Sandra get together, you never see the mother again.

(END OF SPOILERS)
I believe that the movie calls out for a sequel in which Keanu's character, Alex Wyler, and his architect brother, Henry (played by Ebon Moss-Bachrach), would use their newfound time-travel powers to go back and save the life of their mother, the woman who broke Christopher Plummer's heart and who condemned her two boys to live lives of meaningless hedonism and avant-garde architecture. As for the misery Sandra Bullock's character causes Dylan Walsh from *Nip/Tuck*, if I were Dylan Walsh I would try to get another agent after making a fool out of me in *The Lake House*, period.

Niv: The Authorized Biography of David Niven
by Graham Lord

★★★☆☆
Twee Drivel?

May 21, 2007

After Niven's death the present owner of his chalet, Coco Wyers, went inside the house and surveyed Niven's murals of matadors in the dank basement of the prefab house. Psychic Coco knew something horrid had happened in the house, but what? "Oh my God," she thought, "what happened here? I felt that something was really not OK." Author Graham Lord has surveyed half a hundred of Niven's friends and associates and come up with the truth, that Niven could be charming and affable, some say generous, but he was a notorious womanizer and serial cheater. He always felt insecure, as most actors do, and he took himself seriously, cherishing the Oscar he had been awarded for his brilliant performance in *Separate Tables*.

At the same time, he and his monstrous second wife, Hjördis the drunk, adopted two little girls who grew up, Lord tells us, to be neurotic, quiet, detached from reality, and deeply unhappy. Well, Hjördis was a world-class monster. Betty Bacall is quoted often in *Niv* (she must have given the world's longest interview for she seems to be on every page) as calling Hjördis "cold." Bacall scoffs at Hjördis's acting ambitions, sniffing that she must have been crazy to think she could make it in Hollywood. Meanwhile Niven was playing with the girls. Naked, he encouraged the little girls, aged six and seven, to swing on his outsized member like Tarzan, telling a guest, the painter William Feilding, who witnessed this bizarre scene of fatherhood, "better get them used to a decent size at an early age." He thought more of his [...] than he did his family, that's for sure. At one point he was skiing with Robert Wagner and felt his [...] freezing within a too-thin ski ensemble. The two men raced down the slopes and into a bar where Niven plunged his "unit" into a snifter filled with brandy, to warm it up. Another guest went by and goggled, and Niven joked "I always give it a drink now and then."

But I felt sorry for those girls. Having that memory in your past must be a tricky thing. No wonder they're ultra reserved and lonely nowadays. They were always trying to please an oversexed dad, and a distant, cold, drunken mother, who was always impossibly gorgeous and never left the house without a full set of makeup. Many friends of Niv's thought Hjördis overdid it with the makeup. I have trouble spelling her name all the way to the end. I feel Lord did a hatchet job on a misunderstood woman whose failing, in the end, was neglecting to protect her two adopted girls from having to play jungle games on the thick vine sprouting from between her husband's legs.

However, Niv gave good performances in *Guns of Navarone*, *The Moon Is Blue*, *A Matter of Life and Death*, and *Casino Royale*. Docked one notch for disrespect to a great poet. Niven took the title of his memoir *The Moon's a Balloon* from a poem by E. E. Cummings. Graham Lord, said to have been the literary editor for the *Express* for twenty-three years (!), uses this as a springboard for an attack on Cummings nearly as rabid as his attack on Hjördis.

"The title was bewilderingly fey and came from a piece of dog-gerel by the pretentious E. E. Cummings. ... Why did Niv choose the title? Search me," Lord sneers. Elsewhere he calls the poem "twee drivel," which in England must be the worst insult you can give. To which I respond, "Please, Graham Lord, get over yourself! 'Bewilderingly fey'? *You're* the one who just wrote a 370-page ode to David Niven's [...]!"

The Life and Art of Elinor Wylie
by Judith Farr

★★★★★
"Murdered by Predestined Snow"

June 8, 2007

Due to recent interest in Elinor Wylie expressed by one of my favorite contemporary poets, I pulled this book off my shelves again and decided to give Wylie another think. For some, she has been the quintessential 1920s figure, her extravagant private life overshadowing her work, and for others, her work is just plain awful, phony and ornamented with coat after coat of bright "beauty" paint. Whereas her contemporary Amy Lowell idolized Keats, Wylie fell for Shelley in a big way, and seems to have believed herself a modern-day, female, Alastor. He was her "guardian spirit," her "archangel." "Poets," Shelley said, "are the unacknowledged legislators of the world," and Wylie lived her life copiously, as though exercising her right to law at every moment.

She had a glorious red-haired beauty, like Nicole Kidman, and everywhere she went she made heads turn. She married three times, loving them and leaving them, and had left her third husband by the time she died, throwing herself over the windmill in pursuit of a married British acquaintance. Shockingly for her time, when she left husband #1, she left behind her young three-year-old son, Philip, who sadly enough committed suicide a few years after Wylie's death. He showed up for her funeral, aged twenty-one, impressing all her friends with his lack of resentment and his curiosity. Cecil Beaton photographed Elinor Wylie, and Thomas Wolfe included an unkind sketch of her in *The Web and the Rock*. She felt personally hurt if anyone said anything nice about a third person, for that compliment belonged to her, to herself alone. She might have been difficult to deal with at times, but her presence was undeniable.

Elinor Wylie's poetry has its ups and downs, but the best of it is a remarkable reminder that the so-called freaks of literary history have a better chance of being appreciated today than a whole album full of well-crafted representatives. (Perhaps because of the tension that still clings, like Spanish moss, to every line.) Writing across history, Wylie wound up transcending it to a certain extent, though as I say, not everything she wrote is very good.

But even the bad stuff is interesting and Judith Farr makes a spirited case for Wylie as a Romantic novelist, going against the grain of the modernism of Dos Passos, Faulkner, Josephine Herbst. Like Isak Dinesen, her prose writing is studded with strange images, obsessed men and women, a sometimes treacly, sometimes trenchant vocabulary and diction. Virginia Woolf despised her, writing to Vita that Elinor was a "hatchet minded, cadaverous, acid voiced, bare-boned, spavined, patriotic, nasal, thick legged American." Hmmm, threatened much, Virginia Woolf?

Invasion of the Body Snatchers (**Collector's Edition**) (**1978**)
dir. Philip Kaufman

★★★★★
Invasion #2

June 8, 2007

Looking forward to the Collector's Edition, a recent review of the 1998 DVD got me to thinking about why this picture is so great! My wife says, "It's not because the guys are so good looking." Why on earth cast a movie with Sutherland Sr., Goldblum, and Nimoy? Well, it fits in with that New American Cinema vibe you get from the outset. San Francisco is a physically discombobulating city and director Phil Kaufman uses this well to underline how bizarre the events transpiring on-screen are. For example, when Nimoy leaves Sutherland's gorgeous apartment he has to walk a little pigeon toed to make it down the steep hill outside his house, and while he's walking on the level, the cars are parked at steep sixty- or seventy-degree angles between them, so it looks as though he's playing in space traffic. Elsewhere Kaufman seeks the unusual angle. There's one shot of Jeff Goldblum quietly crossing a threshold which Kaufman photographs from what looks like the position of the doorknob, an extremely low and tight angle so that his face emerges from the bottom of the screen, before a rapid rotation brings it into normal view.

All of this fits the rapidly shifting moods of the film. This time around I was struck at how much effort it takes for Brooke Adams to persuade Donald Sutherland of what's going on, and also how much times have changed. It seems in this version that if she doesn't convince Sutherland, she has absolutely no agency at all, she's incapable of response except by getting a man to see things her way. At least in the much-maligned Abel Ferrara version from the 1990s, Gabrielle Anwar, even if underage, knows how to get things done without waiting for the men in her life to kick in. And I expect in the next version coming up with Nicole Kidman that she'll give it her best college try at any rate. Brooke Adams here seems to be playing the same sort of affectless, drifting, mournful creature she already played in Terrence Malick's *Days of Heaven*. Of course she's wonderful in both pictures, it's just odd here how much the critical mass has shifted so that nowadays in a horror or sci-fi film, we sort of expect the women to lead the pack in terms of action.

From the San Francisco standpoint, as a native, Kaufman keeps the geography going pretty well, none of the bloopers that make something like *48 Hrs.* so painful (when Nolte and Murphy get out of the subway at "Castro," they emerge in—Chinatown?) to watch. Of course it seems a little overheated that when Brooke Adams leaves her job every day, she goes home to one of those quaint zillion-dollar Victorian "Painted Ladies" on Alamo Square—one of the most photographed houses of all time. One does giggle a bit at that, but hey, somebody lives in them, no? Why not a movie character?

I Married a Witch (1942)
dir. René Clair

★★★★★
Father and Daughter

June 29, 2007

Cecil Kellaway makes *I Married a Witch* a scary film indeed, and I suspect that John Huston must have recalled Kellaway's portrayal when he undertook the role of the evil, incest-driven patriarch in Roman Polanski's *Chinatown*. Against all odds, Kellaway has kept his daughter to himself for 270 years, thanks to the Puritans who have condemned him to live, as a ghost, in the form of smoke, under a giant oak tree on the ancestral property of the Wooley family. And in turn, Kellaway has cursed the Wooleys, ensuring that, in each generation, no man shall find happiness in love, all will be married to plain battle-axes.

Meanwhile Daniel (the warlock played by Kellaway) had Jennifer (his lovely daughter, played by the uniquely talented Veronica Lake) right where he wants her—he's the only man in her universe. When a lightning storm topples the tree, releasing father and daughter, it spells trouble for Daniel who risks losing the undivided love of his daughter, as, like Miranda in *The Tempest*, she discovers a brave new world of cute guys and sort of begins to neglect dear old Dad. Daniel's fury is right out of the *Chinatown* playbook, and he tries everything he knows to break up Jennifer and her new love interest, Wallace Wooley (Fredric March, looking pretty dumpy only a few years after his killer sex appeal in the Wellman version of *A Star Is Born*).

Some will love Veronica Lake, some will be puzzled, but everyone must admit that in her early scenes, before love makes her more "human," she makes some of the oddest acting choices ever captured on film (surrealist or otherwise). She employs a squeaky, oltrano voice, as though entrapment in an oak tree for centuries has blanched away her voice to mere oxygen. In her memoir, Lake told the story of how French director René Clair directed her from moment to moment, coaching and acting out her every phrase and expression, every mincing step. It is a performance more in bits and pieces than a whole, but it is extraordinary nonetheless. Readers of *Veronica*, Lake's memoir, will also recall that she got tired of Freddie March always feeling her up during their scenes together and she arranged a rocking chair scene in which she managed to steer the rocker part right into his most vulnerable area. See if you can spot it in the finished film and look for his momentary expression of ghastly testicular pain.

White Mint Box with Window

★★★★★
Sweet Bargain

July 5, 2007

I bought this box by mistake, thinking it would make a great window box for a patch of nasturtiums outside my bedroom window. Recently my wife and I came home to find scaffolding over our building, since our landlord had decided to paint the place as a surprise to his tenants. A window box would spruce things up, so I took myself off for a half-hour consult with my favorite place to shop, Amazon. I wanted a nice, white, mint window box, and so when I clicked on "White Mint Box with Window," I perked up considerably. When you see the picture, you say to yourself, "It's a slightly different sort of window box than the ones I'm used to, but it would be ever so cute under my window, forty feet up on the top of a busy alley in downtown San Francisco!"

And you cannot beat the price—five dollars and five cents! And with Amazon Prime, it was practically giving itself away. Later, my wife said that should have been the giveaway. Also, the little small print that said it weighs only eight ounces—hardly the proper weight for a box built to hold nasturtiums, to be packed with soil and regularly doused with water and sunlight!

Looks sort of like a Kleenex-box holder, doesn't it, but that's what wet my whistle for this strange White Mint Box with Window. That opening on the side of the box, long, with rounded edges, rounding the corner so it shows up on two sides of the box—two half sides, "demisides," you might call them. I pictured the flowers growing up through this hole and sort of crowding themselves out the front of the box, offering their fragrant scents to the air and the people passing by, and to our neighbors on the third floor across the pavement from us.

To which my wife gave a merciless bark of a laugh. It was not a window box at all, but what they call a "white mint box with window." It's tiny, the size of a box of mints, and the little demisides, in the phrase coined by me, Kevin Killian, open up only enough to let your finger slip through and pull out a single mint, maybe two. What kind of mints?—I know you're asking. Oh, any kind.

But check it out, an outstanding value, it's just not what you think, and if you're the type of guy (or girl) who hasn't learned to roll with the punches, then, as my grandad used to say—sailor beware. You may be left holding your nasturtiums by the roots, flakes of loam falling to the ground forty feet below, with nowhere to plant them.

A book of PROPHECIES
by John Wieners, ed. Michael Carr

★★★★★
"Just Perfect Now"

July 11, 2007

I think even those of us who love John Wieners's poetry have been taken aback, in fact bowled over by the greatness of his hitherto-unknown *book of PROPHECIES*, written in the 1970–72 period right after *Nerves* and preceding *Behind the State Capitol: Or Cincinnati Pike*, but whatever, we're all happy now. Halfway through the book you can trace the mark, so obvious it feels like an actual physical thing, perhaps a torso in marble missing an arm or two, where Wieners must have decided that the lyric style of *Nerves*, *Asylum Poems*, etc. just wasn't going to cut it for him anymore and it was time to move on to the "derangements" of his later style, the accent on language's materiality, the "cut-up" effects, the slide into a slippery first-person multiplicity. It's fascinating just from a biographical point of view, and in effect what you get is a whole mini anthology of two very different strains in Wieners's writing, and this *book of PROPHECIES* provides wonderful examples of both styles.

The other night there was a launch for this book at New College here in San Francisco, and as reader after reader took the stage to read from this book, we were struck by how many of these poems, which we had never heard before, had the force and the "click" of what amount to instant classics. They were new to us, and yet we felt we had known them forever. As it happens, a few poems will be already familiar to you from this book, as Wieners published them separately or in magazines and they wound up in the old Black Sparrow *Selected Poems*, only now in their full context they make sense and accrue a patina or luster of richness which they lacked before, appealing as they were in their abandoned state.

The book itself is physically beautiful, and the young Boston-based poet Michael Carr has done a fantastic service by providing this transcription of a "lost" Wieners notebook—replete with some scans of the actual holograph—with a fine sensitivity to Wieners's variegated methods of punctuation, spelling, line break, revision, and so forth. (At the end of 1991, the notebook itself was bought by Kent State Special Collections in Ohio, where Carr "discovered" it.) The poet Jim Dunn, who was close to Wieners in the final years of JW's life, has written an introduction that might be a model for this sort of thing, a memoir and an appreciation in one, in which he doesn't seek to shield the reader from the immense difficulties of reading Wieners, nor does he romanticize Wieners's psychological and physical ruin.

"I died no one / as [I once felt I [had / to be someone." He is the poet of heartbreak, and the shadow figure enslaved by the more vigorous and together figures in his life, like Olson or Creeley, feeling himself hardly human in his pale remnants of a life. Both shamed and inspired, as well, by the superhuman, glamorous Hollywood actresses and female artists he had glimpsed on-screen, or met in "real life," from Jean Seberg and Barbara Stanwyck to Nico and Nell Rice, Grace Hartigan, and Phyllis Webb. *A book of PROPHE-CIES* begins, eerily enough, with the single poem "2007," an ecstatic, Blakean prediction of a moment tragically removed from our own, his vision of Aquarius in "full flowers" and "music string and forms of verse controlled symbolism." The poems don't always work, and a couple of them dangle sadly into a ludic space, but the best of them are among the greatest poems Wieners ever wrote, and that's saying something. At the launch I read "Sexual Despair," nearly made myself cry out loud with repressed longing and hard-core sex tension. "I need you, my little son // to be beside me in bed / jerking your meat and / smoking hash-hish. // What will the future bring / this fear ling- / ers every day." Well, as you can see, all I am saying is this is a signal event for poetry and a rare opportunity to reassess the work of an authentic lyric genius.

Basic Instinct 2: Risk Addiction (2006)
dir. Michael Caton-Jones

★★★★★
Film of the Year

July 16, 2007

Like everybody else in the forum, I heard how rotten *Basic Instinct 2* was supposed to be when it hit the theaters last year, and acquiring the DVD seemed like an idiotic thing to do, though who could resist the premise? That haircut wasn't doing Sharon Stone any favors, though sometimes the asymmetrical cut of her fringe was intriguing and when the hairdressers parted it down the middle, it was annoying because she could have looked so much better. Oh well, she still looked great except for some scenes, like the climax, in which she looked rough as ten miles of badly paved road and leaning her head against Charlotte Rampling's, she still looked like the older woman in too many ways to count. And yet, and yet, when all is said and done, what a surprise! In many ways *BI2* has turned out to be the best movie of 2006, not the worst! And it's not only Sharon Stone who makes it good, although her brave, sizzling performance should have gotten her an Oscar nomination, not the Golden Raspberry or whatever it is. People who hate her just don't see the genius, I understand that much. Listen, I saw Meryl Streep in *Prairie Home Companion* and *Prada*, and she should have been awarded a place in the Raspberry Hall of Fame.

But enough about her, the point is that, as Walter Pater told us, all art aspires to the condition of *Basic Instinct 2: Risk Addiction*. We begin with the "inward world of thought and feeling, the whirlpool ... still more rapid, the flame more eager and devouring."

As the scenario plays out, we see Stone and David Morrissey move from couch (not that modern therapists use couches all that often nowadays) to the Jacuzzi whirlpool, where she offers herself to him and then performs an impromptu underwater ballet, her teeth angled upward, her grin looming larger through the colored water's prism, as though in a magnifying glass, death illuminating her beauty and her macabre eyes and stretched-out skin. This seems to turn him on more and more. "There it is no longer the gradual darkening of the eye, the gradual fading of colour from the wall—movements of the shore-side, where the water flows down indeed, though in apparent rest—but the race of the mid-stream, a drift of momentary acts of sight and passion," just as Pater predicted when, in the 1860s, he had his strange dream vision of *The Renaissance* that managed to suggest the "hard, gemlike flame" with which the eternally lovely and scary Sharon Stone would be burning in the present day.

I wouldn't kick David Morrissey out of bed either! How dare other reviewers suggest to judge him inferior to Michael Douglas in any way under the sun, much less in beauty and in the magnificent force of his thrusting ass extensions? I have seen a sight unrivaled in present-day cinema and, to top everything off, I was well and thoroughly gobsmacked by the surprise ending to the film. OK, *Basic Instinct* part one had Dorothy Malone, but I have it on good authority that she, like Bela Lugosi in *Plan 9 from Outer Space*, was then so out of it that she literally did not know she was being filmed and the footage to be used in a movie. Did anyone else hear that?

Finally, for the first time ever in DVD history, the deleted scenes actually contain something worth watching, the scenes in which Catherine Tramell reminisces about a hammock in Napa.

Also what's great is the way the makeup people have costumed and pomaded and teased the red hair of David Thewlis to make him exactly resemble our favorite British poet, the one and only Tom Raworth.

Beyond the Sea (2004)
dir. Kevin Spacey

★★★☆☆
Vanity, Thy Name Is Spacey

July 27, 2007

I usually have a soft spot for the "pet projects" of the stars, even when they fail spectacularly, like Marlon Brando's *One-Eyed Jacks* or Barbra Streisand's *Yentl*. Even when they're bad, you feel something's at stake, that passion is involved. John Wayne wore all his hats for *The Alamo* (1960) and when America didn't embrace it as enthusiastically as he had hoped, it broke his spirit, embittered him a little. And some stars never even have pet projects—do you think Elizabeth Taylor ever really cared about what movie she was making? It was the old factory mentality for Liz, punch in, punch out, bye, have a nice weekend. Thus I really wanted to like *Beyond the Sea* and when I didn't, I finally figured out the problem. It was the pet project of a star who isn't really a star, and inside this bright jewel box of a film is nobody you can really care about.

These projects are all about vanity and Spacey must never get bored with hearing how much he's like Bobby Darin, singing, dancing, acting, they even look alike with that fake little nose strip he's got pasted on his face in this film. Was turning the picture into a metafictional *8½* meditation on fame and disease the wise thing to do? Oh, who knows, it gives the movie a startling beginning and provides a "reason" for those spectacular sub–*All That Jazz* dance sequences that keep popping up every ten minutes or so ("Beyond the Sea," "Up a Lazy River," etc.), numbers without a lick of sense to them or even any real choreography. At least *All That Jazz* had Bob Fosse. *Beyond the Sea*'s got—Kevin Spacey, of course (and Rob Ashford, the Broadway choreographer whose dances for *Thoroughly Modern Millie* five years ago had everyone gasping in despair).

The truth is the Bobby Darin story was done much better in *Valley of the Dolls*, and the actor playing Tony Polar (the late lamented Tony Scotti) was more like Darin than Spacey will ever be. Darin's romance with brilliant and tragic Sandra Dee is already amply chronicled in the magnificent trilogy of Universal films they made together, *Come September*, *If a Man Answers*, and the superb *That Funny Feeling*. Watch any of these shows instead, they'll bring you more love.

Behind the Mask of the Mattachine: The Hal Call Chronicles and the Early Movement for Homosexual Emancipation
by James T. Sears

★★★★★
Behind the Mattachine Mask

July 30, 2007

I'm not sure what Sears thinks he is doing by lumping together pro-files of three generations of gay-rights activists into his enormous, authoritative study, but if you ask me, I could have done without those heaping helpings of Hirschfeld and Manuel BoyFrank.

Be that as it may, nothing will prepare you for the depth of research Sears has performed on the most interesting and still-controversial years of gay liberation, the Mattachine Society and its series of constitutional conventions in 1953. After all the scholar-ship in the last twenty years on the subject, you'd think there would be no more to say, and yet Sears has found a way to put a new spin on everything by approaching the controversy from a completely different angle. This book doesn't treat Harry Hay as a sacred cow or some kind of Joan of Arc angel; indeed as the subtitle shows, Sears is here placing front and center Harry Hay's worst nightmare, the San Francisco printer and porn impresario Hal Call, as the hidden master of the Mattachine.

It's an unconventional stance but it causes us to view anew our prejudices toward the original, "Communist" founders of the Matta-chine and to probe into a delicate area: To what extent did the "tainted" pasts of these leaders predoom the movement early on? Even to pose the question carries a thrill of transgression, and Sears winds up backing off from the implications of some of his answers. I had the funny feeling while reading the book that, as often as Sears speaks of Hal Call's heroic iconoclasm, his man's-man stance toward sex and war and everything in between, he (Sears) wound up not liking Call very much as a human being.

Much has been made of the unusual collage and enjambment methods Sears employed, almost like a novelist of the Dos Passos stripe, while putting together the multiple narratives of *Behind the Mask of the Mattachine*. The effect is as hard to describe as to analyze, but sometimes entire chapters are worked up out of people's letters in a way that looks like a two-character play, as though they are speaking back and forth; sometimes Sears takes these quotes from actual correspondence between two people, but just as often there is no direct link between the speakers, and Sears is using them as a sort of point-counterpoint way to make us scrunch up our scalps and sigh over the unreliability of any one person to tell the truth about a complex social event.

His notes are generous and detailed; the problem is that in at least the one collection I'm familiar with, the Hal Call Papers at Los Angeles's One Institute, the papers themselves are barely organized, rendering it impossible for Sears to actually be able to direct you to the right container, so it has been difficult for me to replicate all of his findings—the material is in what my dad used to call a shambles. Nevertheless, I must say that Sears has done amazing work making sense, for example, of the poet Jack Spicer's role in Bay Area Mattachine affairs, and he gives us example after example of the ways in which Spicer served in multiple capacities in the Oakland-area chapter, not just as a dilettante or looker-on, but getting his hands dirty in every conceivable way, far beyond what any of us had previously imagined.

Terrorist: A Novel
by John Updike

★★★☆☆
Timely Old Man

August 8, 2007

For those who had stopped reading John Updike, the publication of timely *Terrorist* was a warning shot fired into the night sky by an angry militia. By the time it was over I was drenched with admiration for the aging wunderkind who just wouldn't quit and instead delivered when challenged.

I had to keep putting the book down, tracing my thumbs across the cover, to convince myself it was really John Updike, for he is such a creature of the 1950s and 1960s he should be freeze-dried, shrink-wrapped, and thrust into a time capsule to represent a difficult time for

American letters. His publishers have never let him forget his origins, either, and keep producing his novels using the exact same format they did in 1959, which is touching in a way—their faith, his acquiescence. When I tore the jacket off the book, the reassuring Janson font greeted me like an old pensioner at a family reunion.

It was the one feeling of warmth I had reading this extraordinarily bleak and cool novel. It is one thing for Updike to say to himself "I think I'll write about Arab Americans now," and another to present his findings in fictional form and have them come out so stereotypical. Why does Ahmad talk the way he does, if he was born and bred in the hood and never opened the Qur'an till he was eleven? Now he's impersonating Peter Lorre in *The Maltese Falcon* with his inverted sentences and his calculatedly faux-polite speech, subaltern dialogue from a mandarin's POV. I can say nothing about Tylenol Jones and Joryleen that hasn't already been said by a dozen shocked readers, except that the spirit of D. W. Griffith lives on in John Updike and it's a wonder Al Sharpton hasn't invoked a boycott of Knopf, Inc. That said, I wound up concerned and anxious about the end of the book: What was going to happen, would Ahmad become a terrorist or go the other way? Would Jack Levy cheat on fat Beth with freckled Terry, the mother of Ahmad? (Well, adultery is a given, it's Updike's world and we're just co-respondents in it.) Until the last page I wasn't sure which way the chips would fall. That's suspense, and my caviling isn't worth a tinker's damn I guess, except, well, you know.

Beauty Talk & Monsters
by Masha Tupitsyn

★★★★★
Absorbed in Red

August 15, 2007

Marilyn Minter's garish and voluble cover photo, and the redoubtable design work of Hedi El Kholti, made me predisposed to like this book as soon as I flipped its pages. But that's just the beginning of the story.

I have never met Masha Tupitsyn, the young author of *Beauty Talk & Monsters*, but somehow I feel like we're on the same wavelength, and her writing exudes a magnetic force that pulls in a reader, renders him helpless and sprawling on his back like one of the butterflies of her beloved Nabokov. From Tupitsyn we learn how the movies of the '70s, from *Mean Streets* and *The Exorcist* through *Jaws* and *Suspiria*, shaped her consciousness, made her eternally receptive to a host of foreign influences, while '80s films, like *Top Gun*, *Pretty in Pink*, and *Dirty Dancing*, gave her agency and allowed her to become her own sexual object. In places this book, a collection of essays, memoirs, and stories, will remind you of an animated version of Nan Goldin's *Ballad of Sexual Dependency*, only it's not as druggy perhaps, for who needs heavy drugs when your mind jumps and quivers as Hitchcock's camera speeds down the sordid London alleys of 1972's *Frenzy* and melts with a reluctant empathy as poor Brenda Blaney, *Frenzy's* middle-aged matchmaker, meets her fate in a man she hardly knows? Though her stories are short on dialogue, and rely on a lot of "telling," her men and women are vivid creations, with minds of their own; you walk away from *Beauty Talk* feeling that Masha Tupitsyn has seen far too much of life and remembered everything worth relating in fiction.

She flits from city to city in search of—well, she admits she doesn't exactly know why. One story, "Proverbial," references the iconic 1930s lost-girl novel *Good Morning, Midnight* by Jean Rhys, a lovely tribute to one in whose footsteps she has been doomed to walk, a restless soul seeking meaning in a globalized world. Only the movies, and the touch of men, help her heroines situate themselves in an emptiness of loss and broken commitment. And like Kathy Acker, Tupitsyn is obsessed with violent death as a sourcebook for social change.

She is a poet of the short story, with a poet's resources, an eye, an ear, a sense of rhythm both internal and external. Her tales have the brevity of Isak Dinesen's, but seem somehow strategically cut off from the sense of the centuries with which we experience Dinesen's gothic world. Instead life, and love insofar as her heroines access it, is as Pat Benatar insisted, a battleground. I wonder where the money comes from sometimes—in Rhys you always worried with her narrators, though in Acker grand gestures replaced the anxieties of the pocketbook. In *Beauty Talk & Monsters* money's not an issue much, it's like "Meh, who cares."

The most brilliant story in the book, "Kleptomania," comes early on, so that succeeding stories, no matter how exciting or moving, have trouble living up to its fireworks, but that's OK. Any author would have given five years of his or her life to be able to say "I wrote 'Kleptomania,'" for it's a sensational disquisition on love, memory, Diane Keaton, celebrity, the mutant, and voyeurism, in multiple parts like a compilation film, and a sense of direction that shifts slightly from sentence to sentence but expands and grows in your hands like a water flower. Above all else, Masha Tupitsyn is a stylist and at her best a superb one.

PS: Pity about the typos and misspellings of the stars' names that litter her book! I always tell Semiotext(e), if you want to have a book filled with the names of stars, I'll vet it for nothing! Otherwise you get the same old violence against Liza Minnelli, for example—leaving one of the *n*'s out of her name, despite her signature song pleading with you not to forget it. That said, in another instance her name is spelled right, so it's hard to know whom to blame. Roy Scheider also—one time it's right, one time it's wrong. Or how about a simple sentence like "I am a thing that never let's [*sic*] go"?

Grab a Bag and a Crock Pot Cook Book: Bag It–Mix It–Set It–Forget It Great Recipes for All Ages; Saves Time-Turmoil-Trouble
by Frances Barrineau

★★★★★
Grab Bag of Crockpot Fun

Augusts 17, 2007

Frances Barrineau, one of the great home cooks of the East, comes back with another winner after her adventuresome *Grab a Bag* cookbooks, and here she has added a welcome twist, throwing a Crock-Pot into the mix instead of relying on mere bags as she did for her two previous best-sellers. As Barrineau points out, the Crock-Pot is not everyone's friend, but if your family is forgiving enough to grant you mercy for the Crock-Pot mistakes you're bound to make, then you're ahead of the game.

She warns that dairy products don't work well in the sturdy pot *du* crock, but otherwise you will be able to adapt freely your favorite recipes to fit the convenience of this modern, yet strangely ancient, appliance. My mother used to tell me, based on her studies in anthropology with Ruth Benedict and Margaret Mead, that if you take the average kitchen in the US, probably the most ancient and time-honored thing in it will be the humble Crock-Pot. Remember when they were made of terra-cotta and looked like flowerpots? My mother did, and Margaret Mead too.

Barrineau's recipes are tasty, nutritious, and so easy to make you'll be kicking yourself for having exiled your Crock-Pot to the dusty back of the kitchen shelves. College boys who have never done anything in the way of cooking will love this book, it's durable, takes a lot of abuse, and is written in simple, colorful English, and it gives a handy chart of spices and tells you ahead of time what they will taste like—everything from nutmeg and ginger to that mysterious "apple pie spice" that children love, coeds too. If you are in the dark about what "grab a bag" means, just think of going to the supermarket or the local produce mart, grabbing a bag, filling it with edibles, and then assembling the dry ingredients in your Crock-Pot, saving the wet ones until you're on your hike or camping trip, or perhaps an intimate supper for "the two of you." Afterward, you'll have enough for a lunch the next day with several friends, or just by yourself alone in the busy cafeteria.

My mother always said you're never alone when you've got your Crock-Pot nearby, and Barrineau will help you over the bumps of first cooking with it—of "first love," I almost said.

That other reviewer who disliked this book wasn't very kind! But ignore me at your peril, potential buyer (and Crock-Pot user).

But Darling, I'm Your Auntie Mame! The Amazing History of the World's Favorite Madcap Aunt
by Richard Tyler Jordan

★★★★★
The Best People at Their Worst

August 23, 2007

I enjoyed this compendium of backstage lore, but other reviewers are correct in saying that Jordan provides little context for the phenomenon of *Auntie Mame*. But who cares about that really when you have all these wonderful stories of difficult people and the tantrums they throw to get their own way?

Sumner Locke Elliott, the playwright and novelist originally hired to adapt Patrick Dennis's 1955 novel to the stage, gives a chiseled portrait of the late Rosalind Russell, depicting her as a sort of sacred monster who made sure everything went her way. Russell was never a great star but she knew how to adapt her act for changing times, and turned from comedy to drama to musical to farce to suspense to religion, whatever paid the rent. Her efforts at drama were pretty feeble, she was no Nazimova that's for sure, but in the annals of high comedy she will always have a shining place due to the sheer intensity of her performances in *His Girl Friday*, *The Women*, and of course *Auntie Mame*.

Jordan shows us how Hollywood got it wrong, casting Lucy as Mame when the cognoscenti wanted Lansbury in the musical version of Dennis's play. After reading this book I felt sorry for Lucy for the first time in my life, for reading the savage reviews attacking her physical appearance is actually painful, as though all the critics in the world had turned into John Simon for this one occasion. Lucy was sixty-one, is that really fifteen or twenty years too old to play Auntie Mame? Why? Not that Lucy was any good, I'm not standing up for her, but no one deserves the venom she got for playing in that one movie, shooting herself in both feet for her arrogance and pride and vanity.

Jerry Herman wrote the foreword to this book, but could he really have read it? He comes off like a spoiled princess, scuttling plans for a TV remake of *Mame* with Bette Midler for no good reason, then lacing into a great screenwriter for daring to pen an adaptation of *Mame* with the temerity to cut two horrible Herman numbers ("Saint Bridgette" and "That's How Young I Feel") which are, apparently, sacrosanct. Jerry Herman always seems so good natured and sweet, but now after reading this book I know he's a Teri Hatcher–style diva.

Harry Potter and the Order of the Phoenix (**2007**)
dir. David Yates

★★★★★
The Famous Five

August 24, 2007

We saw this in the IMAX 3D version so don't expect me to remember much about the ending, for the last twenty minutes produced nothing but gasps of terror and frowns of puzzlement from our row, since the editing is so rapid fire we couldn't really tell what was happening. I know they went to the ministry, and that's about it! I wish I had seen it the regular way without the 3D glasses, then I might have been able to understand it better. We take along Mark, an expert at *Harry Potter*, every time we go to one of these shows, and we are the irritating ones in the row ahead of yours who are always turning to the expert and asking, "Now who is that tall girl with the red hair? Was she in the movie before?"

The plot is so complicated now that ordinary notions of character development must have been the first thing the screenwriters chucked out. We know Harry is angry, angry, angry all the time, for not only is he in a funk through most of the movie but he even has a scene where he says, "I'm angry, angry all the time!" Everyone's trying to help, but Harry just can't see that. He's still traumatized, I think, by witnessing the death of Cedric Diggory in the previous movie. Pity in a way Cedric didn't stick around for book 5, isn't it, because he might have raised the beauty quotient a little. The producers must be fairly sick the way that they bet on a whole crew of child actors and now they have to watch them turn into awkward, plain galoofs of teens, barring Emma Watson, Dan Radcliffe, and one or two others (like that tall girl with the red hair). If Emma Watson loses one more ounce however, she is going to be able to squeeze through the eye of a needle no matter how much money she has. Rupert Grint? Well, there may be some who find him attractive, though director David Yates seems to be averting the camera every time it pans in Grint's direction—cut!

OK, so now can somebody tell me what was so great about that prophecy? I could have told you what it said and I've never read a

Potter book in my life. Couldn't it have been something a little bit more gripping? THAT'S the McGuffin of the whole movie? No, no, no, I must have missed something while in my 3D meltdown. Tell me that little ball thing said something interesting!

The Wind (1928)
dir. Victor Sjöström

★★★★☆
The Wind beneath My Wings

September 4, 2007

Lillian Gish evening last night when we had *Hambone and Hillie* on the one hand (late-period Gish where she was brought in like an old mailbox, kept on the corner for a scene or two, then hauled away back to her town house) and *The Wind* on the other. Of the two, we preferred the later film. I used to love Lillian Gish and I believed in her and I believed in the sanctity of silent film and all those wonderful sentiments Kevin Brownlow and Louise Brooks wrote about. But not anymore. It took me a few reels of old-style Lillian Gish to get over it. Everyone knows the story from the title alone, but what you may not understand is that Gish starts to go crazy the minute a breeze hits her face, and it doesn't get better.

SPOILERS. Finally she gets someone who says he will take her away to a place, a quiet place, where the wind doesn't blow. Should have been the looney bin, if you ask me. But in a way, she is still a remarkable actress even under the outdated conditions of film acting that seem so ludicrous to us today. (However, why is it that properly viewed in the proper number of frames per second, etc., most silent acting holds up today, Pickford, Swanson, Novarro, Fairbanks, Bow, etc., all remarkably naturalistic and real—and then there's Gish, acting acting ACTING with every quivering pore of her body—on a shelf all her own—the shelf of madness.) I liked the way instead of becoming more fluttery as she does in *Duel in the Sun*, her Letty in *The Wind* straightens her shoulders more and more, the way Bette Davis sort of acted with shoulders, so that by the time she's really mad she resembles one of the old straight-back chairs in my grandmother's parlor.

Her acting choices, while counterintuitive and madly different, are sometimes just meh. People say she was thrown out of MGM after just five pictures in a row, all flops, but they're not taking into account that audiences just didn't want to see her any more. They had had enough and they wanted her back on the New York stage or playing Ophelia in the real Danish castle of Elsinore, and then later on in life they enjoyed seeing her in *Snoop Sisters*–type vehicles. There was always Dorothy Gish for people to warm up to, while Lillian stood to one side, aloof and cold, and perhaps a little disapproving of Dorothy's mad, drunken passion for Louis Calhern, but never showing it—so she was capable of the kind of restraint Victor Sjöström insisted she check at the old corral during the filming of *The Wind*. Much has been made of the tragic ending the suits at MGM deleted, but I'll tell you, if it ever comes to light, and the ominous delay in the DVD release of *The Wind* might be a sign that it's in the wind (as it were), I will personally destroy every copy of the director's cut they issue, if it's the last thing I do.

Fracture (**2007**)
dir. Gregory Hoblit

★★★★★
Fractured Flickers

September 24, 2007

I knew my love for Ryan Gosling, already wavering at the brink after a few less than spectacular performances, was in deep trouble when he opened his mouth in the DA's office in *Fracture* and out poured this muddled-up, molasses-mouth Southern accent (I guess) filched in bits and pieces from Jude Law and Kevin Spacey in *Midnight in the Garden of Good and Evil*. They never exactly explained why Willy Beachum has attained a 97 percent conviction rate with this unintelligible Goober stammer, but you know what, after a half an hour or so Ryan just stopped talking in his soup and started speaking English like any other Angeleno. It's like his beginning to care about human values and other human beings brought on many changes, including adopting the standard "mid-American" speech patterns people on TV have. By the end of the movie he could have become a newscaster, and my love for him had returned, full strength, like an entire bottle of Excedrin. He's a fantastic actor and ranks right up there with his fellow new Mouseketeers of the period, Justin, Christina, and Britney, as far as star power goes. Didn't Anthony Hopkins win an Oscar or two? He should have brought them to the set of *Fracture* and gifted them to Ryan Gosling, as his successor, say on a break from filming, livened up the craft table or whatever it's called. For Gosling is the new Hopkins, and in fact when Hopkins was on the screen, the movie got unexpectedly dull—or if not dull, then incredibly obvious. It was like a successor to *Hannibal*—say Clarice got tired of being married to the ancient Hannibal Lecter and started cheating on him with a local detective, of course HL would seek his revenge, starting by shooting her point blank and leaving her for dead.

As Clarice Lecter—I mean, Jennifer Crawford—the lovely actress Embeth Davidtz who was so good in *Junebug* turns in an amazing performance here, and the odd thing about it is she's in a coma through most of it. Not since the poet John Giorno snoozed through five and a half hours of Andy Warhol's early feature *Sleep* (1963) has any leading player spent so much of a film out cold.

As for the plot, how on earth could Crawford make sure that his wife's boyfriend would be the one who came to his door after the shot was fired? If the whole basis of his plot rested on that happening, it's even more ludicrous than it seems at first glance. But Ryan Gosling whispered to me, "Kevin, just relax, don't think about tomorrow, just go with the flow and smile from every inch of your body." He's so good to me, I could forgive him anything.

Anthology of Apparitions
by Simon Liberati

★★★★☆
Pathology of the Pathaparitions

October 5, 2007

We don't go as far as our fellow reviewer Benjamin who has stated his opinion as greatest novel of five years, but on the other hand for us, and the men of our generation, *Anthology of Apparitions* is a kind of bible on how to behave when caught up in the meaningless revolving door we call existence in our forties.

Claude is just like us in so many ways! We've been there, in the great nightclubs of postwar Paris, New York, Berlin, London, and Tokyo. We too had a little sister, Marina, who disappeared under mysterious circumstances linked to the Heidi Fleiss scandal of some years ago. Simon Liberati, you are our hero for daring to speak through the murky truths of a forgotten echo, like the plink, plink, plink sound made by throwing three francs into the bottom of a deep well somewhere on the estate of the marquis, in France. As an American boy growing up in France, I knew many boys and girls like Claude and Marina, resourceful and gamin-like waifs who sullenly sold their bodies for a rind of cheese and a Gauloises, and who played aimlessly with needles—the hypodermic kind, the kind used at the millinery ateliers on the rue Sainte-Anne near the Palais-Royal, or the needle on the phonograph machine that, when applied to any of Françoise Hardy's or the Rolling Stones' numerous LPs, provided the yé-yé soundtrack to our lives.

Not since *Bonjour Tristesse* has a book come along that we could adopt with our hearts like Angelina Jolie adopting the needy of the world. Wherever I go now, whatever corridor of life I flaneur through, I seem to see the fleeting figure of young, sixteen-year-old debauchee Marina disappearing with a fleeting glance into the netherworld into which she vanished from Claude—not that he, or we, cared at the time.

We think we were all too busy with our own cares, our ceaseless need for cool, a need provoked by the extreme trauma brought on by French boyhood. For us, it was an existential thing; for the young readers of Liberati, for example Donal and Mike, who made us a present of this beautifully translated (by Paul Buck and Catherine Petit) book by London's noted Pushkin Press (and adorned with a remarkable, decadent photo by Thomas Nutzl), yea, for all of these, it is in the nature of a life-changing event for them. As Liberati so proudly states, it is the "humanist reader" who needs Marina to be alive, even if being dead is, in general, better, a happier state. Which camp are we in?

Puzzle for Pilgrims
by Patrick Quentin

★★★★★
To Be a Pilgrim

October 5, 2007

The longest, last, and saddest of Patrick Quentin's six *Puzzle* novels, though not the last of the mysteries he wrote featuring Peter and Iris Duluth, *Puzzle for Pilgrims* is nearly free of any fun. If you liked Malcolm Lowry's *Under the Volcano*, the horrid human-relationship hells of *Puzzle for Pilgrims* may entertain you. But otherwise, it's like a little stab in the heart for all of us who loved seeing Peter and Iris together, Peter the alcoholic theater producer who summoned the courage to sober up and face himself, and Iris the slumming Hollywood goddess who somehow shrugged and said "I take this jerk" etc., despite her being utterly gorgeous and alluring on the Gene Tierney / Hedy Lamarr model. We watched them struggle with their love for each other, finally overcome obstacles and marry, get through the war, even get through amnesia! And what do we get here? A couple more like Ingrid Bergman and George Sanders in Rossellini's weary, purgatorial *Voyage in Italy*, a couple no longer in love. In fact they've each found other, adulterous partners. Peter's gotten himself involved with brittle, English nympho Marietta Haven, while Iris is with Marietta's brother, UK expatriate novelist Martin Haven, a thatch of blond hair and a boyish appeal. Iris's problem? Martin is still married, to wealthy vengeful harridan Sally Haven.

All of our characters are living in Malcolm Lowry's savage, colorful Mexico, if you can call it living, for most of the book is spent with each of them wondering if they've made the right choice and what has led them to this corner of the world, depraved bohemians and artists and trust-fund babies whose very existences seem pointless. Into their lives a very special private eye comes to terrorize them, like Terence Stamp in Pasolini's *Teorema*—Jake, a man on the make if ever there was one. Little by little he insinuates himself into all of their lives, a big, blocky, stocky man who exudes testosterone, so much so that even Peter and Martin come under

Jake's spell. The ending isn't as fantastic as some of the previous Duluth masterworks: it's too much like some Ellery Queen novels of the period, *The Murderer Is a Fox* and *Calamity Town* among them. You'll see.

Patrick Quentin of course rivalled Ellery Queen for having the most homoerotics in a 1940s detective novel, but here the two collaborators Wheeler and Webb really go to town; it's as though they decided to write an X-rated scenario and just left out the explicit markers. There's Jake, stripping Martin of his pj's, reducing him to shivers, threatening to hunt for an expensive woman's bracelet up poor Martin's arse; there's Jake, easily outdoing tough narrator Peter in terms of manliness at every turn, so at ease with his masculinity he's always shedding his clothes whenever Peter's around, dropping his trousers on the floor and parading au naturel to stun Pete with his flopping, swaggering manhood; there's Jake wearing nothing but tight, bulgy white Jockey shorts, collapsing onto Peter and making "short convulsive jerks" with his body, toppling him to the carpet of the bedroom. You think Mexico's hot? It was ice cold till Patrick Quentin got there and worked out all the possibilities of love between brutal, film noir men.

Art and Sex in Greenwich Village: Gay Literary Life after Stonewall
by Felice Picano

★★★★★
Time after Time

October 11, 2007

Felice Picano is the man who was there and who did the work. He devised SeaHorse Press and built it up into a larger agglomeration called GPNY, with a pair of other like-minded publishers and dreamers. SeaHorse was responsible for some of the very best books of the 1980s, some authentic landmarks like Dennis Cooper's *Idols* and Safe, Bob Glück's *Jack the Modernist*, Brad Gooch's *Jailbait and Other Stories*. And plays like *Forty Deuce* by Alan Bowne and the book that put SeaHorse on the map, *Torch Song Trilogy*. Along the way, as Picano describes it, he encountered everyone from Robert Mapplethorpe to Nico and he lived to tell the tale.

The subtext of the book is survival, one man's survival through the worst of the AIDS crisis in Manhattan. No sooner do we come to know a writer, an artist, a lover, a friend, than he is carried off by the disease and that which he left behind becomes more precious. This terse threnody runs all along the underside of this delicately written book like the runner of a carpet; just when it seems to be all about publishing trivia and how many printings had this or that forgotten volume, Picano's novelistic sense surges forward and real human interest takes its place on center stage.

And the book has its own humor too! Gore Vidal averts Picano's overtures toward the republishing of *Myra Breckinridge* with his own King Charles's head, the alarming spread, even in youth, of American men's backsides, and how the Germans do these things so much better. Boyd McDonald, the notorious editor of *STH*, perplexed by a royalty statement; James Purdy, genius among plebes, equally baffled by niceties of copyright. SeaHorse and GPNY didn't last very long—not nearly long enough in my view—but the very compression of the period provides Picano with exactly the right amount of material for his project, a book which brings back all the glory days, and much of the terror, of a certain era in literary and artistic history.

I had a great editorial experience with him even though, in the end, SeaHorse passed on my book of memoirs, and the press was running down when I sent it in. He took the trouble to read the entire thing and made one enormously sweeping editorial suggestion which actually saved the whole thing and made it hang together, rather than the ragbag of half-assed New Narrative experiments it had previously been. I'm sure there are hundreds of younger writers who can attest also to Picano's generosity and, what would you call it, in Scotland it would be that he is a canny man. In the USA, he's a mensch.

Doing 70
by Hettie Jones

★★★★★
Age of Consent

October 15, 2007

I hope I have the drive to write poems when I turn seventy and I hope they're as frank and controlled as Hettie Jones's poems. I picked up this book having never read any poems by her, only her memoir of *How I Became Hettie Jones*. Knowing that book I had sort of a context to read the poems in, for in a way she comes across as a consummate New York insider, with a long memory and yet a forgiving nature, ready to do battle on behalf of the causes she believes in but otherwise relishing any scrap of life left to her.

Sometimes she writes as though a very young person, other times she sounds old as the "aged eagle" T. S. Eliot spoke in the voice of. And after all, jaded Tom Eliot wrote of himself as the aged eagle when he was about forty so in a way it's all in how you feel. Jones herself foregrounds the importance of her age by punning on it in her title, *Doing 70*, and she's got a great little sequence where she finds some of her own poems written from back in the day and then attaches her contemporary responses to them, and they might as well have been composed by different people ("Double Edges," pp. 16–17). The whole first section of the book is studded with references to age, from the first page, in which she asks herself, "are you lucky enough / to be breathing," to the title poem, a complex journey poem in which, when her car breaks down miles from New York, she accepts a ride from a flatbed driver who hauls it back from a Boston suburb even though he, Ryan, has only rarely driven to NYC before. Gamely, Jones joins him in a daylong adventure into their own questing spirits. She falls a little in love with the younger man, even "though doing seventy means / giving up the pretty boys // you lust you lose, you hear / the cry of the crows." Brrr! And yet every time they hit a bump in the road, and Ryan's glove compartment falls open to hit her in the lap, she gives a little shiver of Eros. It's a provocative, assured, and mysterious poem which could have been a story by the late Grace Paley, only it's a poem.

Other sections of the book describe the poet's encounters with world and local politics (progressive in nearly every case) and, in a grouping called "True Sisters," a lifelong affection for and attachment to women of every class, race, and age. I would say if I had to criticize, that a few of these poems were a little over the top for me, like watching home movies about somebody else's relatives and you still can't see what's so hilarious and/or cute about them. And also there's one poem about going to a farmer's market and oohing and aahing about how red the cherries are that might have been saved for *Hettie Jones's Cookbook*. However, the section contains some tip-top material as well, including a Beijing-based poem called "Women in Black," in which a scar at sunset becomes "a path, slick / in the glittering dark." About enjambment Hettie Jones is rarely wrong. She seems to know precisely where to break a line off to give it the most snap and brio, and sometimes it almost hurts it feels so good.

Sleeping with Bad Boys: A Juicy Tell-All of Literary New York in the Fifties and Sixties
by Alice Denham

★★★★★
Boys and Girls Together

October 19, 2007

If you love the AMC TV series *Mad Men*, with its highly stylized picture of Manhattan life circa 1960, you have to read this book! Alice Denham is a trip! "Manhattan was a river of men flowing past my door, and when I was thirsty I drank." I haven't read any of her novels, but she can certainly spin a juicy tale. You have to admire her chutzpah, setting off from Jacksonville to hit New York during an era in which women were seen as inferior, especially writing women, and in fact they were often "not seen" at all—Denham refers to herself and others as "invisible women," after Ralph Ellison's classic novel *Invisible Man*. In a sense they were invisible even to other women, taught that marriage is the ultimate act of love and that a woman's destiny is to become a supportive wife to her husband. Other women were competition. Alice Denham does, however, sketch a memorable portrait of one fellow woman writer, the much older Katherine Anne Porter, with whom she became drinking pals. "She was my literary guru, powerful as the ancient Aztec goddess of earth and fire, Coatlicue."

She has a long memory and never forgets a slight, nor has she forgotten the equipment of any man she ever knew. Somehow, fresh from college, Denham managed to find herself involved with many of the movers and shakers of New York culture of the period (roughly 1953 through 1965), when living in New York, she claims, was like Paris in the 1920s. I must correct an earlier reviewer of Denham's book. It was not James Dean who had the small "apparatus," no, his was perfectly average and OK—you're thinking of James Jones, whose tiny little thumb-like thing certainly did not send Miss Denham from here to eternity. (Though Jones made up for it in other ways!) The one bad boy who appears most often is Norman Mailer, whom oddly enough, Denham never did sleep with. She is utterly convincing as a portraitist, with a gift for the telling physical characteristic; among other things her book might be used to reconstruct the physical likenesses of all her leading figures, even if all photographs, paintings, and films of them were to vanish in an instant. Jones had "an abnormally long head front to back while, incomprehensibly, his features were bunched together in the squalling center of his face." Don't you love the touch of that "squalling"? She's a poet from top to toe. William Gaddis "looked New England gothic, slight, rail-thin with a highboned narrow face, bony hands, yet an insinuating air." Here it's the word "yet" that does all the work, gives us Gaddis to life. Naked, he's "only slightly muscled, but sporting a fine centerpiece"

Throughout all the bedroom hijinks (in what other modernist's memoir will you find out that the late film composer Leonard Rosenman had a fondness for—well, I can't even say it on this family-based website), she never loses her through line, which is her heartfelt attempt to write a great novel and then to get it published. Again and again she gets the rebuff from nasty male editors who just want her to continue with her career as a Playmate and/or to become a "hostess." Finally she gets somebody to believe in her wild vision and *My Darling from the Lions* gets published. In the meantime the guys she resents are often enough the ones who are great in bed. Evan S. Connell Jr. was the king stud, "tall, noble, with strong perfectly proportioned features and observant eyes, black as his hair. The royal bearing of an Indian chieftain. Was he descended from Sacajawea and Charbonneau?"

In her slightly ironic style, Denham is sometimes so anxious to avoid four-letter words that she gets a little cryptic, and some of her touches are sort of odd. "As he passed me, [Philip] Roth tried to tweak my mound by ramming his paw into my lap." But all in all *Sleeping with Bad Boys* is a masterpiece of wrath, tenderness, and compassion, and I predict it will someday outshine most of the "boy's books" that defined literature for Denham's generation.

Ellery Queen's 14th Mystery Annual: A Selection of New Stories from "Ellery Queen's Mystery Magazine"
ed. Ellery Queen

★★★★★
Winning Anthology

November 20, 2007

Ellery Queen had just written *The Finishing Stroke*, pretty much the last real Queen novel, when he turned his attention to what must have become an annual chore, selecting the best stories from the previous year's crop published in his magazine.

Queen would not publish another novel for years, and when he returned it was under slimy conditions in which hired-out hack authors would write his novels for him, a move which brought in some needed revenue but wound up sullying the brand name forever, and muddying what had been an honorable contribution to detective fiction with a number of not good, not bad books that fairly radiated question marks like wriggling worms.

In the meantime, however, he kept churning out these anthologies, and this one is one of his best. Stories by John Collier and Ray Bradbury remind us that *EQMM* was not all about who killed Colonel Mustard with a knife in the pantry; there was always room for fantasy, the baroquer the better. Clayton Rawson's "Miracles—All in a Day's Work" is sort of an average story, but who can resist the

Great Merlini once he starts with the mystification? Queen had a weakness for the literary so he made a big deal about having a story by *the* Somerset Maugham, yawn, and I never understood exactly why Stanley Ellin is supposed to be so great. (Maybe it was the austere "only one story a year" thing, very modernist.)

Queen saves the best for last, literally, and the final four stories are each fantastic. "Then They Come Running" is by the too little-remembered Herbert Brean, a thoroughly worked-up private eye story of a missing husband in a John Cheever cul-de-sac. William E. Barrett, who wrote *The Lilies of the Field*, here contributes a story called "The Lady, or the Murderer?" (sort of the stupid kind of title that busybody Queen often insisted on renaming the stories he bought). It's a tough little noir story of a Grace Kelly ice blond and the man she has her hooks in, the DA who tried her for murder but couldn't secure a conviction. Agatha Christie's famous late story "The Dressmaker's Doll" found its first book publication in *Ellery Queen's 14th Mystery Annual*. It's a story that still gives me shivers even to think of it. Finally, Rosemary Gibbons (who?) wrote the Best "First Story" of the Year and it is a genuine heartbreaker with a social twist, a reworking of the notorious Emmett Till case told from a child's point of view with a cold brutality and shock that would do credit to Stephen King. Whatever happened to Rosemary Gibbons? I'll have to look her up now. This one story is worth a hundred Stanley Ellins.

The New World (**2005**)
dir. Terrence Malick

★★★★☆
Don't Know Much about Geography ...

November 25, 2007

My wife says they should have called this treatment of the Jamestown story *Lolitahontas*, for the camera's interest in the young amateur actress playing the leading role is extreme, always playing at her lips like a smile or at the lower crescents of her huge eyes, like tears. Q'orianka Kilcher has a great part, a part made for a star, and she steps into it with a child's grace, while Colin Farrell and Christian

Bale walk over all sorts of tightropes not to look too lustfully upon her child's body, yet still express the mad passion each feels for her at different stages of her life.

It's clear than Captain John Smith is damaged goods from the minute you see him in a cage in the hold of the ship, trying to find a few drops of water to quench his thirst. His first act on Native shores is to stand with a noose around his neck, while Christopher Plummer very undramatically sighs and says, "Oh never mind, let's not hang him after all." I've been reading the new Library of America edition of John Smith's collected *Writings* and I can sense a discrepancy between the way he depicts himself in his memoirs and the way the movie treats him. But that's what the movies are all about, reinventing history, giving it room to breathe. They really should have a Pocahontas movie in which she is actually the queen of the colony—not just a young girl but a passionate and regal woman with a mind of her own—or maybe they did make the movie I have in mind a long time ago and they called it *Cobra Woman*.

The Poem of a Life: A Biography of Louis Zukofsky
by Mark Scroggins

★★★★★
Zukofsky Lives Again

December 6, 2007

Avant-garde poet Louis Zukofsky is the subject of a splendid new biography, one I scurried through, with barely a moment's pause for rest or water, over the past four and a half hours, and you shut the book exhilarated wanting nothing but more, more of this wonderful blend of exposition, narrative drive, and critical analysis all hand in hand like the heroic girls striding the battlefield in Henry Darger's painting. *The Poem of a Life: A Biography of Louis Zukofsky* is a masterwork of storytelling, and beyond that I expect it will do what any number of concentrated studies have done, open its subject wide to a mass audience, which may or may not have appealed to LZ, but if I read some passages in Scroggins carefully, I think he might very well be glad when his lifework *"A,"* for so long considered a book of grand difficulty, climbs the rungs of the bestseller list in this country and wherever high modernism is spoken.

Rich in character development as well as exegesis, *TPOAL* takes us from the crowded tenements of New York's Lower East Side, where Zukofsky was born in 1904, into the world of international poetry and art, a world he took to like duck soup, and finally through a teaching career of the highest interest to those wondering how to combine art and commerce. Along the way he was aided and abetted by a brilliant and scintillating wife, Celia Thaew, with whom he had a son, Paul, a violinist who was the apple of his father's eye. In the green arbors of Port Jefferson, Long Island, Celia and Louis retreated at the end of their lives, but LZ was never to rest for long, composing in late, late middle age a final full-length piece, *80 Flowers* (his "most private project," as Scroggins aptly dubs it), and when that was completed to his satisfaction, made notes for a "90 Trees" piece of which only a tantalizing fragment remains.

Only a life's work, that's all. Scroggins follows John Cage in pointing out that Zukofsky died in exactly the same way as did James Joyce—the "sort of coincidence in which each of them would have delighted." That may be stretching it a bit, but it is true that Joyce and Zukofsky were in correspondence, over a proposed film scenario of *Ulysses*. Film buff LZ was "bullish" on this plan, suggesting that Chaplin—or Charles Laughton maybe—would be a good Leopold Bloom. In such a way Scroggins is able to build up, bit by bit, a chain of associations which to my mind fully justify his reading of *"A"* as a poem deeply indebted to the cinema. Zukofsky like many other writers in the 1930s was polarized by social upheaval and strongly drawn to the Left; he worked for *New Masses* and wrote convincingly of the need to write poems that "everybody can understand." Scroggins points out that his bent was otherwise; while he urged poets "to confirm revolutionary theory in sensory values," it wasn't easy to practice what he preached, and yet on the third hand this tension goosed him into writing some of his memorable work between two masters as it were.

What of his much talked-about relationship with haunted, Hetty Sorrel look-alike Lorine Niedecker (1903–1970)? Did it really end in a squalid Dreiserian tragedy of betrayal and abandonment? The truth is, Scroggins argues, that no one today can know the truth about what really happened between the two geniuses. It was all too long ago. The book will be controversial in its picture of disgruntled schoolteacher Jerry Reisman and what Scroggins considers a tissue of misstatements made by Reisman and given credence by some late comments by addled or airy Mary and George Oppen, two Objectivist writers whom Zukofsky apparently didn't really care for and who probably knew nothing whatever about whatever it was that went down with Niedecker and Zukofsky back in the 1930s. Those of us who gave the pregnancy story any credence get a real slap of cold water in the face here, and expect tears in the days to come!

Otherwise, where Scroggins excels is in exploring the many ways in which Zukofsky took the materials of his own life—and when that failed, the materials of his reading—and turned them into *"A"* 1–24.

Frankly I thought I knew as much about Louis Zukofsky as any other ordinary, educated person, but as the pages of the biography melted in my hand, I realized I knew nothing, insofar as everything I thought I knew was dead wrong. I suppose there are still a few areas in which debate is possible, especially in the final Port Jefferson years, years in which Zukofsky seems to have been playing a sort of Cheshire cat game with his admirers, retreating into his own legend and letting Celia step up more and more. In the end, Scroggins's book becomes a sort of bewitched and sustained threnody on Celia's brilliance and loyalty, sort of the way biographies of Nabokov always have to paint a new picture of Véra in the days after VN's death. Sad to say, she outlived him for only a year or two; they both slipped out of life without really knowing how much their war on the world would affect the life of poetry in our time.

For strategic reasons Scroggins chooses to breach the gap between Zukofsky's era and our own by concentrating on three well-oiled hinges: the fact that poet Bob Grenier engineered one of LZ's last full-length readings (at Franconia); the Poets Theater reading at San Francisco's Poetry Center of the Celia/Louis *"A"-24* in the summer of 1978; and at greatest length the contretemps over Zukofsky's legacy fought by Barrett Watten and the late Robert Duncan at another Poetry Center event in the same time period. This makes Zukofsky relevant to today's readers is, I guess, the reasoning behind this move. It's elegant and simple and for me, it works, though I'm prejudiced.

I must say the book itself is a gorgeous physical object and David Bullen its designer is marvelous but he made one decision I hate, and that is placing the page numbers on the inside of each page, close to the spine, compact and neat but pretty much useless to those of us with opposable thumbs. You really have to dig in there with a pickax to find what page you're on, a shame in a book that's going to be thoroughly quoted and argued about for decades to come. Oh well, Post-it Notes might help and they come in cheery colors too.

Genie Headpiece with Veil
by Costume Express

★★★★★
Stylish and Retro

December 7, 2007

Ever have one of those days? I'm sure you too have felt like I did last month, when for a week or so it seemed nothing was going right. I was feeling a little headachy and feverish, people at work were looking at me weird, one of my students seemed to be staring at me with a look of hate across the seminar table … little things … we got two new cats and they weren't "blending" with our old two cats Ted and Sylvia … Like I say, little things, but add them up together and you start looking longingly at cute costumes in an enchanting *Princess Diaries* shade of blue with a large, outstanding blue rhinestone placed cunningly in the very middle of the sash, so that it looks like you have a third eye! I'm talking of course about Costume Express and their incredibly cunning Genie Headpiece with Veil.

I like blue, always have, so this baby was a no-brainer. You don't have to be a little girl to want to acquire, by any means necessary, something of the genie's power. He (or she, I suppose) lives in a brass lamp but it couldn't be any more squalid or overcrowded than our third-floor walk-up in a dingy alley in San Francisco; and yet he slash she has at [its] fingertips all of the powers of the Justice League of America rolled together, able to grant wishes, magically transport people like Hiro Nakamura from place to place, and to turn straw into gold. Yes, let me at that headpiece, and when I got it home and managed with a little help from Velcro to jam it down over my brow, arranging the flimsy blue veil over my hair, shoulders, and upper back, I felt kingly, like

Faisal in David Lean's *Lawrence of Arabia* my sunburnt face turned west toward the setting sun where, soon, night would fall and in the desert darkness one might spy stars like jewels flung up and pinned to the Arabian night, as I stood out on my landing on Minna Street and watched, forty feet below, a homeless lady cry out for seventy-five cents.

After continued use I did notice that the gorgeous rhinestone has a way of somehow imprinting itself on one's forehead if you forget to take off the genie headpiece and veil before turning in. I spent a restless night plagued with dreams and in the morning I had what looked like a scary bruise above my nose, but I could tell it was mere rhinestone dent. As Joni Mitchell used to sing, "Amelia … it was just a false alarm."

Madame de Staël
by Maria Fairweather

★★★★★
A Christmas Memory

December 22, 2007

As Christmas approaches nearer and nearer my mind strays to thoughts of Madame de Staël, who always kept a warm place for Christmas in her heart, even when persecuted by emperors and forced to live in alien lands, or when reeling from the tragic loss in her life, the death (by dueling sabre) of one of her sons while still a very young man, and she, though heavy in mind, insisted on Christmas as normal so as not to disappoint the little ones, nor her pensioners whom she gathered around her like old, well-loved blankets.

And her lovers, for she was a lover all her life. The poet George Stanley recommended this book to me, telling me that it seemed to him I knew nothing of de Staël and it was high time I learned. Immediately I ordered a copy of the recommended biography, but it looked a little dense, so I put it to one side, then wound up months later packing it hastily on my last-minute trip to Basel this past summer. Well, there I was in my single bed on top of a Basel garret, high summer and you could almost see the tops of the Jungfrau, and I opened the pages of the book and found out, to my utter surprise, that Madame de Staël was, in fact, from Basel! I swallowed this unbelievable coincidence with a twist of bottled water, and from there on in, I could see why George Stanley, whose own writing is filled with a boiling hunger for the human and a restless quest for the divine, why a writer like Stanley would be so taken with the peripatetic Madame de Stäel. She was everywhere and did everything, and she never stopped her love life. Maybe money helped. She was born Germaine Necker, the lively, bluestocking daughter of Jacques Necker, the man they called "the Croesus of Switzerland," and in thinking about her life I would have to say that she was usually able to summon up vast amounts of money and yet still, she had sympathies with all sides of the French Revolution in which she played a key part. She was friends with Marie Antoinette, sort of, and with Talleyrand (and with Napoleon Bonaparte until he took an uninformed dislike to her and to her novels and agitprop).

She wasn't the most beautiful woman in the world, not even in the top 50 percent, but she had something, didn't she, an intelligence that Coleridge said matched his own, and a joie de vivre that made men, women, children, and animals stop in the street and turn around and stare, drawn to her ebullience like honey. Maria Fairweather has a telling anecdote about Madame de Stäel attending the first French circus ever shown in snowy Moscow, in the company of famous Russians of all sorts, and the clowns and circus animals were all gazing in rapture at Madame de Stäel chatting in the royal box, trying to make out scraps of her witty conversation. Even the acrobats on their trapezes gradually stopped swinging, hoping for that perfect moment of silence in which one might hear her speak.

She was in love with many men, and many loved her; among them, Narbonne, the aristocratic white dandy whose plantation, Limonade, in Haiti was seized by his angry slaves and burnt to the ground in one of those famous anticolonialist demonstrations in 1792. Another problematic friend was the novelist Fanny (*Evelina*) Burney, who seemed simultaneously to admire and to despise her, like Mary Astor and Bette Davis in *The Great Lie* or *Old Acquaintance*. All of her life Germaine de Stäel suffered from the feeling that her mother hadn't much cared for her, while her true passion was for her father, the former Croesus of Switzerland, the man who saved France. The saddest day of her life was the day Jacques Necker expired in his chalet. Meanwhile she met and enchanted the weird Crispin Glover–like Benjamin Constant, and wound up traveling around Europe with him for what seemed like forever. Goethe translated her works into German, and years later, Jean Genet had them distributed to the Palestinian radicals he befriended in his later years. She was "the Empress of the Mind," Fairweather reminds us, but what makes her so interesting was perhaps her eternal curiosity—she was mad for knowledge and hardly ever minded changing her mind once the facts were in. People laughed at her rustic-peasant way of dressing, for it was a bit silly, as if Barbara Hutton dressed in the costume of Minnie Pearl, but she took the criticism with good grace and continued to cut her blouses down to here. She battled Bonaparte over his domineering methods and his forced alliance of church and state, using the public's fondness for ritual to shore up his own control. "Society cannot exist without inequality of wealth, and inequality of wealth cannot exist without religion," he argued, to which Germaine de Staël forthrightly replied, "Very well then, let us do without society!" "But never," she would say, clutching her harlequin-patterned satin blouses to her breast, "never let us give up Christmas, the season in which we remind ourselves, we are both animals and angels!" So *Joyeux Noël* to all who read these words, and who go on to imitate Madame de Staël in virtue and in vice.

Otto Preminger: The Man Who Would Be King
by Foster Hirsch

★★★★☆
A Valentine with Vitriol

December 23, 2007

When you deal with Otto Preminger, there's possibly too much story to possibly deal with in one volume. One might ask for a whole book just on the relationship between Preminger and his Marshalltown, Iowa, discovery, the late Jean Seberg, for their back-and-forth intimacy, the sense that they ruined each other in a way, is something Foster Hirsch works up perfectly, and for once he seems to have informants in all the right places and with the proper combination of critical judgment and insider information. One is encouraged to think of *Saint Joan* and *Bonjour Tristesse*—back-to-back flops for wounded Preminger—as two sides of a single coin, a coin with a profile of short-haired Seberg on each side. You're left thinking of her as a proto–Edie Sedgwick, Preminger as an irascible Warhol, and the *Saint Joan-Tristeese* one-two punch as their own *Outer and Inner Space*.

Preminger's affair with Dorothy Dandridge might equally well have been expanded. Hirsch credits Preminger as a sort of civil rights pioneer, pointing to Avon Long's often overlooked turn in *Centennial Summer* as just the sort of music number which Hollywood should be proud of, instead of apologizing for. For every step forward, however, that Preminger seemed to make—placing Duke Ellington on the piano bench alongside James Stewart, for example, in *Anatomy of a Murder*, or trying to hire Martin Luther King Jr. to play a senator in *Advise & Consent*—he takes two steps back. I suppose he should have encouraged Dandridge to take the part of Tuptim in Walter Lang's *The King and I*—it might have helped preserve her illusion of serious stardom for more than a minute. And speaking of which, how bad can *Porgy and Bess* be? Gershwin estate, release your shroud of silence over this film! It just isn't right to keep it from us, let us judge for ourselves how shrill and self-serving Sammy Davis Jr. can be, how miscast Sidney Poitier.

Big books could be written on so many chapters here—the supplanting of Lubitsch, the Gene Tierney spiral of madness and deceit, the Gypsy Rose Lee affair that led to the birth of their son, Erik Lee Preminger. The big, serious films of constitutional critique each need more pages than Hirsch can possibly give them, even in the deluxe sort of Knopf movie-bio glossy treatment he gets here. For goodness sake, for a Preminger fan, *The Cardinal* all by itself could use a complete encyclopedia, just for the way the man played up his little Viennese starling Romy Schneider, her quick-eyed grace so sumptuous and moving against Tom Tryon's need to be bigger, need to blow himself up. Though I must say this is the most complete treatment, in and out, that *The Cardinal* is ever likely to get.

What I dislike is Hirsch's need to have something to say about everyone in his path, and he is often vicious as Clifton Webb, which would be fine if you shared his bile and hated his targets as much as he must. Why the hate for the late Ira Levin (who worked with

Preminger on the screenplay for *Bunny Lake Is Missing*), why dismiss a great novelist as a "mediocre" hack? It's just gratuitous sniping, and it leaves you wondering why—perhaps an ill Levin refused the biographer an interview? Jackie Gleason is "humor-free" here, while Groucho Marx is "gross, uncouth, extremely unpleasant." Kim Cattrall will want to go into hiding after the full-scale attack Hirsch mounts on her. Not that I'm a great fan of Kim Cattrall, but still! Give the girl a break! As for Dyan Cannon, well, I wasn't there, but neither was Hirsch and he paints her as worse than Grendel's grandmother. And Romy Schneider? I refuse to believe that "Romy really was an awful person," "high-strung and arrogant," etc. and an impossible demon. No way Jose! Even Ursula Andress comes off as a shrew, and there's no evidence Preminger ever spoke to her, so it seems that Hirsch just delights in trashing all these women just because it's easy.

Friday Night Lights: Season 1
by Universal Studios

★★★★★
Can't Lose

January 10, 2008

I teach at an art school here in San Francisco and last semester one of my students (hi Kate) kept plugging this show, saying it was the best show on TV, she even wrote a paper analyzing it and in general propounding *Friday Night Lights* as one of the great art spectacles of our day and eventually, at Christmastime, I gave in and started watching the first season on DVD. Well, I had read the original nonfiction book back when it first came out and I admired it, but I was thinking a whole show based on that book would be depressing with a capital *D*. Suffice it to say that after the pilot I was hooked, and so was my wife (who hates sports and hates sports shows even more). It was like a Christmas miracle on Minna Street. Now that we have watched the whole of season 1, I can happily say that we are wondering how to contain our impatience until the second season gets boxed up. Especially with the writers' strike which seems to mean that season 2 will end at thirteen episodes.

Oh well, I forgot to mention that pundits claim that, like *Heroes*, *Friday Night Lights* took a dramatic and misjudged turn early on in season 2 which led to fans' outrage. I wonder what it could be! People said that melodrama had come to Dillon High School. Well, season 1 was entirely about melodrama so how bad could it be?

The hardest thing to believe in *FNL* is that Jason Street is in high school. The actor who plays him is talented, sort of, but he's got to be thirty if he's a day! I know that the Texas sun could age a person and that Lady Bird Johnson looked thirty when she was a mere girl, but come on, this guy is supposed to be seventeen and he could be playing a teacher at the school. Most of the other kids seem roughly of high school age, so Jason Street stands out for sure. In fact the girl who plays Julie seems sometimes as though she were eleven or twelve, when she decides she wants to explore her sexuality I felt like the show was moving into *Lolita* country here.

Everyone is fantastically beautiful. But that's probably exactly right. I have only been to Texas a few times but everyone *was* beautiful, though in a slightly different vein than the actors on *FNL*. Kyle Chandler and Connie Britton, come on! There isn't a better-looking couple on TV and Kyle in particular is like Tom Brady in looks, you just want to shut your eyes and capture that steel-jawed magnetism forever, especially when he's mad at a player. The one who's on the plain side is Grandma Saracen, but then the poor actress is hampered by having to play the part like she's just about to slide into Alzheimer's disease, and she's only forty-two. She's close to the real-life age of Jason Street, and you can tell she has no idea of how a real-life elderly woman would respond in the stupid situations they dream up for her.

That scene where Matt has to pretend he's his own grandfather and sing "Mr. Sandman" to his grandma to calm her down was just about the dumbest thing I've seen on TV in generations. But then why do I give it five stars? Because it has a fresh, handheld vigor that distinguishes itself immediately from most TV shows. The storylines aren't too byzantine, and if clichés pop up from time to time (whenever two cheaters kiss they are always immediately observed by the person who would get most upset), the honest dramatic acting sort of obscures these flaws. Clear eyes, full hearts, can't lose.

Autumn Leaves (1956)
dir. Robert Aldrich

★★★★★
Autumn Almanac

January 11, 2008

Cliff is a little wooden but the part he's playing would be a challenge to just about any actor. Aldrich tried luring Marlon Brando into the part and he would have been ideal perhaps, but few actors had the cojones in those days, the midfifties, of appearing so weak. Robertson spends much of the movie just lying down and crying like a little baby, as the process of infantilization takes its terrible toll on him. His sobs are real, it's just the other aspects of Hanson's character that he falls down on. You keep waiting to figure out why Joan is drawn to him. Can't she see there's something wrong there? That quickie Mexican marriage, with little Mexican children in sombreros, and donkeys in sombreros, why so sudden? I'm sure the contemporary audience would have read this plot as a retread of the earlier *Sudden Fear*, where Joan married a maniacal Jack Palance. Here as it turns out Cliff is no Jack Palance, he's just been turned into a boy by a trauma endured way before the movie begins.

[SPOILERS AHEAD]

When Virginia comes to visit Milly in the bungalow row, she's wearing a sweetly sophisticated sleeveless sundress and she looks all together. You immediately start wondering, "Who's she?" And so does Milly. Then Virginia reveals that she was once married to Burt Hanson, and that their divorce decree hasn't even been good for a month. For all Burt knows, says Virginia, she's still married to him! Joan shakes her head, she just can't believe it! Neither could I. But it's Vera Miles so she must be telling the truth. Then Lorne Greene shows up as Burt's dad, saying that even though he loves his boy, the way a man loves his only son, Burt can't be trusted and one shouldn't believe a single word Burt tells you. Also, he's a shoplifter!

I guess it could have been worse. I wonder why the movie didn't play it so that Burt and Virginia in fact were still married? Wouldn't that have made Burt more perfidious? Maybe it was against the code for him to then marry Milly in a bigamous relationship? It's all very dubious, especially when you find out that Vera Miles and Lorne Greene are committing, according to Joan, "the ugliest of all possible sins, so ugly that it drove him into the state he's in now!" I'll tell you, my heart flew into my mouth and it is still there! I always thought, "Vera Miles, nice but dull." Now I discover she's pure evil.

I always thought that *Vertigo* would have been a lousy film if Vera Miles, Hitchcock's favorite, hadn't gotten pregnant and had to drop out, leaving it for Kim Novak. I mean, who could believe that Jimmy Stewart would fall in love with Vera Miles even once, let alone twice! But *Autumn Leaves* must have been a good audition tape for Miles and she gives off a slow heat, like a leg of lamb. Is she still alive? All of a sudden I'm curious about her.

[SPOILERS NO MORE]

TV producers used to cast her in the pilots of all their favorite shows, for it was believed she was a good luck charm and that if Vera Miles was in your pilot as a guest star, the show would be picked up by the network. She was the Greg Grunberg of yesteryear. She's great and so is *Autumn Leaves*.

Novelty Lincoln Costume for Kids
by CostumeCraze

★★★★★
Glory, Glory, Hallelujah

January 17, 2008

With Lincoln's birthday right around the corner, the market is literally flooded with children's Lincoln costumes, so we took our time about ordering the best. Our little ones had each had bad experiences in the past with inferior costumes—some of the shoddy, garish trash they try to shuck off as quality materials will shock the living daylights out of you—and so our main concern was finding a fabric with enough denier, one might say, to take them through their vigorous school-mandated Lincoln-related tasks like splitting logs, pulling a tug-of-war rope across a pool of mud, and walking in the snow toward a one-room schoolhouse replica, also provided through the internet.

And so it came about that our first child, a boy, tested the sturdy polyester pants of this Abraham Lincoln costume, and lo! It was pronounced "keen" by him. We're mad about the boy and we like him even better in his new black bushy beard, for there is nothing cuter than the sight of a young man of late infancy decked out in a stovepipe hat of rusty black and crazy beard of Civil War days. I am buying the adult version of this very costume. I hope it comes with a similar bolo tie, the sort Lincoln is known to have worn in all those artistic Mathew Brady photos of battlefields bloody and serene.

Together, man and boy, we will walk barefoot to school on Lincoln's birthday, celebrated this year on February 18, preceded by others in our family band, one playing the flute, another a little drummer boy in rags, one with a patch on his eye to denote wounds of honor. My eyes have seen the glory in the coming of Costume-Craze's well-made and long-lasting child's costumes for year-round play, not just Halloween, also featuring Princess Jasmine, Darth Vader, Child Batman, Green Goblin, even Child Marilyn in her pink evening gown singing "Diamonds Are a Girl's Best Friend" in Howard Hawks's *Gentlemen Prefer Blondes*.

My Face for the World to See
by Liz Renay

★★★☆☆
Cult Classic

February 4, 2008

A young friend of mine (hi David!) gave me this book for Christmas and as soon as I saw its hot-pink cover, a wave of memories flooded my cortex like a wave of melting cotton candy. I remember getting the first edition, after a big push from the original publisher, the inventive Lyle Stuart, sort of the William Castle of publishing, who could take an ordinary book and, through the miracle of the modern publicity machine, make it a bestseller overnight. In this case he had *My Face for the World to See*, with its original cover photo with Ms. Renay looking angelic and very much like a more aristocratic version of Kim Novak. Very pretty but who on earth would buy, or publish, a memoir by a woman of whom literally nobody, except for a handful of inmates at Terminal Island, had ever heard? And even if you had heard of her, that was at least twenty years prior!

Well, it developed that in the intervening years Renay stayed busy mentoring her daughter, Brenda, to perform a mother-daughter striptease act with her, and also in writing this memoir, which is the longest celebrity memoir ever written.

It's not exactly interesting, but you can tell why John Waters wanted her to appear in his movie *Desperate Living*. I was a retail clerk in a midtown bookstore in Manhattan during the final months of 1971. Famous people used to come in every day and I got quite blasé. Wouldn't you know it, it was Liz Renay who blew my cool, just by showing up and rolling her top down in broad daylight nearby a pile of copies of her book, and a gang of press photographers arranged by Mr. Stuart were on her like flies on honey. They had still the old-fashioned box cameras back then and the cameras were clicking and bumping into each other, like child's toys, to get the perfect shot of this notorious décolletage. Brenda later killed herself and unfortunately Ms. Renay passed away this past year but I still cherish the photograph she signed for me years later, when I had recovered from the shock and she was at a low ebb in her career. We met at PALM, the Performing Arts Library and Museum here in San Francisco, both donating some of our memorabilia to their annual auction, and we swapped a few items.

The Notebooks of Raymond Chandler, and "English Summer: A Gothic Romance"
by Raymond Chandler, ed. Frank MacShane

★★★☆☆
Mean Streets

February 7, 2008

Poor Frank MacShane, the biographer and editor who died in 1999 after a lengthy bout with Alzheimer's disease. He did so much for Chandler's reputation, and really worked hard on his behalf, and now, in Harper Perennial's disastrous reprinting of MacShane's edition of Chandler's notebooks, he has been very nearly erased out of existence. He's not on the spine of the book. He's not on the front cover, not even on the back cover. They have his name on the title page, but it comes after Edward Gorey's, and he gets a tiny credit on the copyright entry. It's as if Harper Perennial wants us to believe these notebooks just got up off the shelf, edited themselves, and slipped into the display window a quality paperback pretends to be.

Then Harper Perennial prints the whole volume on—is it recycled paper? There's no other excuse, it's like your very worst nightmare of ugly, yellowed, tarnished cheap newsprint. What a disaster, especially when they're printing a selection of photographs which are now nearly totally unviewable, while Gorey's illustrations to *English Summer* seem to dissolve into the rag fiber as you're examining them. This is the kind of visual presentation you'd expect to see a publisher give a book by Pauly Shore, but it's Raymond Chandler for goodness sake!

OK, so he's not at his best here and his notebooks are far less interesting than one would think, but he deserves better treatment than what he's getting here, and as for MacShane it's a travesty of his work.

The Late Show: Poems
by David Trinidad

★★★★★
How Can I Meet Others like Myself?

February 14, 2008

Trying to remember the very first book by David Trinidad I read. Could it have been *Monday, Monday*, or perhaps one of the smaller chapbooks that preceded it? In any case, opening its pages, I felt like Pat Boone in *State Fair*: in the wonderful words of Rodgers and Hammerstein, "I know what I like, and I liked what I saw, / And I said to myself, 'That's for me.'" Ever since then I've been a sucker for this work, and as if to reward me for twenty-five years of fan devotion, David T. has come out with what is perhaps his best book yet, the most generous, the most expansive, and the one that shows, after all these years, that he is still a searcher, pounding out holes in the poetic universe with his fists and teeth and feet, the Bruce Lee of the transcendent poetic pop lyric.

The saddest, "Penelope," recounts the tragic tale of starlet Natalie Wood in rhymed quatrains as though she were one of Edward Lear's Jumblies, as indeed she was. While she (and Ann-Margret) will forever stand in cinematic memory as emblems of breathless youth, Trinidad explores the tragedy of what happens in Hollywood when a star gets a year too old and endures "three failures in a row." Without recourse, or psychological underpinning, "The movie star took to bed. / A steady diet of red pills / Numbed overwhelming dread." Identified for many years with the novel *Valley of the Dolls* and the epochal Mark Robson film based on it, Trinidad is always alert for further dollification trends, and in our modern world, dosed with heartbreak and disorientation, he finds them with regularity.

Into his vortex he brings the spirit of Oscar Wilde, children's toys reseen in the *Yellow Book* style of portentous doom, and another remakes a poem by Emily Dickinson, in a perfect pastiche involving lipstick, party dress, "costume" in its ancestral sense, the outward raiment anagogically disclosing the innermost soul of the wearer. Like Spenser and Shakespeare, Trinidad proceeds in a continual parade of metaphors and allegorical images, each one shading naturally into the one to follow. Whenever it's Chinese New Year here in San Francisco, and I watch the giant dragon move sinuously through the darkened streets around Kearny, I think of Trinidad's longer poems and how the pieces fit so beautifully together, and yet they become a whole greater than any individual part, a sometimes scary and threatening and glamorous whole, a "machine made of words," as W. C. Williams said.

The great set piece is called "A Poem under the Influence," in which the author moves from memory to memory in great splashing liquid sheets, as though on the set of *Flipper* or *Thunderball* in the Bahamas. One of the reasons I enjoy it so much is that it's so absolutely daring, a far cry from the perfect sestinas and haikus and the counting that characterize so many of his best and best-loved pieces. Trinidad has always had an autobiographical cast to his verse and in "Influence," you can feel the sheer relief and pleasure in bringing all of his obsessions to the surface all at once, in a masterful display of prosody and power, intertwined like the Yardley symbols that decorate the cover of this volume. Like the tiny "dancing men" of the Sherlock Holmes code story we all read as children, these tiny interlaced characters act as codes, or rebuses, for more complicated webs of emotion. Yardley "lace" activates complex formulas of '60s youth power, UK freshness, and an astringent nostalgia so potent it fuels the poem into overdrive. It's so capacious I found myself in it—literally. You probably will too.

The Exiles of Marcel Duchamp
by T. J. Demos

★★★★★
Troubled Sleep

February 22, 2008

I don't know much about Marcel Duchamp yet I'm always eager to learn more, as with every passing year he seems to become, more and more, the central art figure of the last century—well, he and Andy Warhol. That's just one man's opinion of course, but I take it from T. J. Demos and his absorbing new look at Duchamp that I'm not the only one who thinks so. To tell you the truth, I sort of bow down to Demos, whose book seems like a very model for cultural and visual criticism of a high order. It begins simply enough with a recitation, and little by little develops, with the stirring in of more material, and a careful sifting based on an ideological reading of history, into a complex and moving argument, responsive to change, responsive to our very moment. And incidentally it is another step in providing that comprehensive Duchamp biography we all hope is coming, for he examines in ways I haven't seen before some obscure alleys of Duchamp's life, and in doing so turns upside down some received wisdom that, until I read this book, I just accepted as a given, for that is my nature.

(There must be a connection between the conceit of "received wisdom" and the Duchampian "readymade" lurking under the surface, but I haven't worked it all out yet. My dad it was who pointed out to me that if one used Duchamp's famous *Fountain* piece as a urinal one would come a cropper, and the moral was one must lay on one's side, one knee lifted toward one's chest, if one hopes to avoid the gleeful, sardonic, sorrowful goose of the master.)

Anyhow, Demos explores at great length the aesthetic and sociopolitical strategies that lurk behind the creation of Duchamp's "portable museum," the "Dick in a Box" precursor subsequently developed by Justin Timberlake, our own great appropriator. Not only the nomadism of the twentieth century, but a resistance to Fascist and Nazi ideology, lay behind this work. I have never seen critical attention of much worth paid to Duchamp's participation in the 1938 *Surrealism Exposition*, but it's fascinating to see it read as Duchamp's saying no to a raft of opposing and delimiting political positions. The readymade, slick, new, and shiny, was hereafter to be rendered "dirty," to use one of Demos's key words; no steel shovel now, but a forest of burlap and cotton sacks still filthy from having had coal in them (the way the bad child might find coal in his stocking in US Christmas customs of the first half of the twentieth century)—real coal, and real coal dust choking the air like our modern sterile office suddenly made all Hogwarts when the temp drops the open tube of toner at the Xerox machine. Demos considers the ways in which Duchamp's suitcase served to accelerate existing trends within the art world toward miniaturization and compression, again, when you're on the run you want to gather no moss, only your diamonds. An admirable openness to phenomena of all types characterizes Demos's bold, yet careful, analyses. He sees what I imagine might be the big picture, some of the air in which our hero walked, something of the troubled sleep he longed to escape from.

The End of the World Book: A Novel
by Alistair McCartney

★★★★★
Under Two Flags

February 27, 2008

Alistair McCartney's first novel, *The End of the World Book*, might be the life's work of anyone else but for this superbly assured young

California novelist it is merely the beginning of a long career. Is it a novel at all? Not according to your grandfather who looked for a beginning, middle, and end as the alpha and omega of what should happen first, second, and third. Here McCartney cleverly enough goes back to the beginning, to the actual alphabet from whose shapely cuneiforms all stories are eventually told and molded. Thus the book pretends to be a sort of encyclopedia which, from A to Z, displays the definitions and what you might call feature articles on all sorts of topics which especially interest our protagonist, a young man very much like his creator, right down to the mysterious lock of dark hair dangling down his forehead à la Oscar Wilde of the late 1880s.

Though a Californian now, Alistair was raised in Perth, Western Australia, the home town of our dear departed Heath Ledger, and much of the interest in *The End of the World Book* lies in the implicit and explicit contrast between a fairly rugged, almost nineteenth-century part of the world and the Los Angeles of giant neon and towering klieg lights and the gang-related violence and terror of living there today. This is a novel of place, like the Wessex novels of Hardy, and as such the writing boils over when the particular scents and sounds and sights of each of McCartney's two dramatic continents are allowed to take center stage. And yet this is not to slight the cleverly written and often comic character passages, as the eccentrics and lovers who populate the boy's existence spring to life with fully developed hearts, minds, and bodies. At its best, this encyclopedia amazes with its range, and its depth too.

He certainly seems to know a lot about apocalypse, perhaps too much. At first I took the title to be a simple, somewhat childlike turn on the famous *World Book Encyclopedia* of my youth—*The End of the World Book* standing in for a state of affairs in which authority is invoked only to be revoked. But entry after entry alludes to a great darkness, a numen from which the texts themselves seem to shy away as though uncertain of its derivation, its very phenomenology. In a certain sense the modern world disappoints the hero-seeking Alistair of the novel: he laments that while Rimbaud and Baudelaire drank absinthe to derange their senses, their modern counterparts subsist on humble green NyQuil. Every bit of "fact" here is somewhat askew, like the lessons learned by Alice in Lewis Carroll's novels, so I would not be so sure that Praxiteles was the first and best of Greek porn directors, nor that in the eighteenth century Edmund Burke wrote about the porn star Kevin Williams who, in one scene, sodomized by one man, feels beautiful; in a second scene, sodomized by two simultaneously, becomes sublime. The double, or twin, haunts the author, who sees everything with a double consciousness, and might account for his living a double life of sorts—might even account for his love of stripes, for a field of one color might not be multifold enough for a man who sees everything twice, once as an Australian schoolboy in Catholic-school uniform, once as a gay grown-up in Venice, with a peach tree outside his front door so generous as to be scary. Fruit falls so fast it gets bruised unless the author's boyfriend, the imaginary performance artist Tim Miller, thoughtfully lays a woolen blanket on the lawn to prevent what one might call the "marks of the fall" from spoiling the face of the peach.

We Disappear: A Novel
by Scott Heim

★★★★★
Ghosts of Eternal Silence

March 7, 2008

For a mother and son, Donna and Scott's relationship is extremely close, almost too close, and from a certain angle *We Disappear* plays like a Midwestern version of an early Cocteau novella, for Heim is good at the suffocating tension that grips them both in the same strangler's noose, as well as the loneliness that dominates their lives. (I suppose that's why Scott has no friends or ties—except for Gavin, his drug dealer. For if he had someone else, anyone else, he wouldn't be so dependent on his mom, I guess.) In consequence mother and son both suffer from severe emotional problems. "Our world had narrowed," Scott explains. "There was only mother and son."

Scott is maintaining, but just barely, on a heavy diet of crystal meth that alleviates the boredom of a deadly writing job in Manhattan. Donna is, well, that's the mystery, one I don't want to give away, but the basic question is, WTF is wrong with Donna? One doesn't see Grace Zabriskie or Piper Laurie in the movies much anymore, what a pity since either of them could have played Donna back in the day and I kept seeing Zabriskie as I read the book, dreading what was going to happen next, plunging ahead with the courage that overtakes one close to death, where society's restrictions fail to apply. On another level the book may be Heim's mash-up of some elements in Stephen King's *Dolores Claiborne*, for here Donna's best friend is called Dolores and there's plenty of that salty "I'm a bitch because a woman needs to be a bitch" dialogue we remember from King. And there's the secret buried deep in the mother's past, the one she tries to repress, tries sometimes to recall, familiar not only from *Dolores Claiborne* but from a hundred other small-town melodramas like *Peyton Place* and *Kings Row*. What distinguishes Heim's book from its predecessors is the skill with which he deconstructs the melodramatic tropes and clichés, skinning them back until a point is reached when they cede their traditional importance in favor of a poetic ambience of language, texture, atmosphere, and broken signifiers.

Scott has always known of Donna's interest in vanished children, but for some reason never really made clear he has not known till now that this interest has stemmed from a shadowy episode of her own youth. (Heim does have some fun with the "recovered memory" narrative that dominated his first novel, *Mysterious Skin*.) Just when the back and forth begins to grow wearisome, for how many times can Scott try to guess which of the three contradictory backstories Donna gives out is correct?—just when this gets old, sly Heim unleashes a narrative move that will have you rubbing your eyes in shock. He is an ingenious story-teller: when his voice drops to a whisper, we just lean in closer. I was unable to stop touching the book even when circumstances prevented me from reading it. It has a weird, unearthly magic and his writing, from line to line, is inspired throughout. Heim is fearless in pursuit; he'll go just about anywhere for the mot juste, and most of the time his reach pays off. A boy sits eating peanut brittle, "the crunches from his mouth like a complicated argument." Even his clunkers have an atavistic spell to them: of missing children, Scott tells us "only the rare among them had ever returned alive." Only the rare among them? It's not a locution any English speaker has ever used, but it works, adding to the creepy Nabokovian vibe, reinforcing the connection between kidnapped children and rare specimens, like butterflies pinned to a wall.

Though there are no characters as appealing as the ruined boys of *Mysterious Skin*, this novel makes up for it by snaring the reader in an unexpectedly tender byplay of addiction and loss. Scott's meth addiction is rendered realistically; he's a collection of aches and manias, he can't even brush his teeth for his gums bleed, and the chemical smell that engulfs him at all times sends a sulfurous cloud on the page. And yet he's doing pretty good compared to his mother, whose final mission, we discover, has been undertaken for a totally different reason than we thought. I'm being vague here because, well, I don't want to spoil the developments of the plot, but also because I write through a veil of tears. I lost my own mother last year, and yet I couldn't deal with her death in reality. It takes a great novel to bring it all home and make you say "Yes, this was my life, this is life itself."

Hotel Size Soap Pads
by Brillo

★★★★★
Fantasia in Pink and Gray

March 10, 2008

I opted for the hotel size, even though I live in an efficiency apartment and even though someone else washes the dishes, because I have found through regular use that the ordinary (so-called biscuit) size just isn't enough, not when you want that extra sparkle of cleaning for your odds and ends.

We argued for several hours why Andy Warhol was so inspired by the Brillo pad that he offered to make a new box out of plywood and silk screens, a box that, as Arthur C. Danto has argued, marked the moment when art reached a pitch of self-consciousness from which it will never recover. For after all, Warhol created not only Brillo boxes but boxes of Heinz ketchup, Del Monte peaches, etc., etc., but when we think of his boxes, we think of the Brillo one, that seems to have achieved pole position in the popular mind. Why? Some say it is the familiar red, white, and blue logo of Brillo; others say the inanity of Brillo's name led to its hook in pop culture; my own idea is that the pinkish soap oozing through the gray metallic fibrous mass replicates some horrid Freudian primal scene we don't really wish to remember but we have no choice but to recall, and we prefer to do it through Brillo's displacement.

Anyhow hotel size is the way to go, especially if you are fond of squeezing them with gusto. Really, really making that pink film rise to the surface of the gray ganglia.

Buttmen 3: Erotic Stories and True Confessions by Gay Men Who Love Booty
ed. Alan Bell

★★★★★
Serendipitous Adventure

March 24, 2008

Webster's defines *serendipity* as "the aptitude for making desirable discoveries by accident," and traces its origins back to the (fictional) isle of Serendip in the British fantasist Horace Walpole's Gothic oeuvre. Myself, I illustrate *serendipity* by remembering the day I stumbled across *Buttmen 3*, a large collection of racy stories from diverse hands all with a common theme. I don't know why I found myself reading this one so carefully, jotting down my favorite plot points and strongly drawn characters, all while using one hand, but there I was, my cares and woes forgotten, nearly panting with sheer exhilaration, when I came across one story, "Collaboration," by the young UK writer Thom Wolf. Not the same Tom Wolfe who wrote about "the Right Stuff," nor yet the older modernist novelist who gave us Look *Homeward, Angel*, though he is an angel by an amazing coincidence. In "Collaboration," I, Kevin Killian, a middle-aged California novelist, travel across the seven seas to visit England for the very first time, and I make my way up to County Durham, where Thom Wolf lives. In the hours before my visit Thom takes his time, obsessing over his body and stripping before a mirror in order to survey, once again, the most attractive part of his anatomy. "He squatted over the mirror, opening the dark crack. He loved the look of it."

Indeed when I finally got a look at it, that color of dark honey entranced me like a wizard's spell. "Thom gazed at the reflection of his arse and wondered what Kevin would think. There was no reason for him not to like it. But would he love and cherish it? Kevin was getting on a bit. Was he still interested in men under thirty? What sane man isn't?—a straight one. Kevin's not straight—but he's married. I can take him," Thom boasts, trying to bolster his own self-confidence. I can't reveal any spoilers here but don't worry, you are reading *Buttmen 3* here and not a volume of Alice Munro stories. As I read the piece and remembered this perfect visit to England "collaborating" with Thom Wolf, I was glad to see it included in this volume as a sort of "aide-mémoire" to other, more private reflections. Bravo to editor Alan Bell for including Thom Wolf's fine work in your book.

High School Musical **Sharpay Doll**
by Mattel

Sort of OK

March 24, 2008

I bought this doll for one of my students who finds Ashley Tisdale tremendously attractive, but once I got it home and unwrapped it, I started liking it myself. I can see a problem looming ahead though, the problem being the durable and attractive doll doesn't really look much like Miss Tisdale. They even compound their error by featuring a photo of the actual actress toward the bottom of the doll's packaging, and a child would be able to tell that the doll is but a poor imitation, a generic version if you will, of Miss Tisdale's unique physiognomy and quirky features. Let's face it, Sharpay isn't as pretty as Gabriella and she is far from a nice person! However, she makes up for it in the films based on her life, by her high energy and her boundless self-esteem.

Recently Ryan from *High School Musical* was up here in San Francisco, filming the part of the young photographer Danny Nicoletta in Gus Van Sant's biopic *Milk*. I kept thinking, "Did the actor think that this was going to be a picture about milk like from cows?" If so, he must have been in for a shock. Actually there should be a Ryan doll for he is, if anything, even more outlandish than Sharpay, but until then I will keep my Sharpay doll in its box, staring out at me with an insouciant grin through the thin, clear layer of cellophane that separates her from me, my wife, and our cats. One thing you can't see in the thumbnail is how detailed the Mattel scientists have made Sharpay's clothes and jewels. She is literally sparkling from head to toe, and the patches on her pants pockets look like they are made of mini diamonds, while her halter top is pink with strawberry-colored sequins arranged in a psychedelic pattern that takes me right back to the appearance of the Strawberry Alarm Clock in Russ Meyer's epic fantasy *Beyond the Valley of the Dolls*. What will kids make out of this doll? Don't know—and I nearly added "don't care," but that would be a lie. Kids need to have a Sharpay figure in their lives to learn the value of niceness and fair play—not from her, but from the black hole of moral values in which she lives with Ryan.

Bunny Lake Is Missing (1965)
dir. Otto Preminger

★★★★★
Just out of Reach

March 31, 2008

Preminger always has something going on, though at the time of its release many of his fans were shocked at his decision to pull back from the big "superpictures" he had been making for years, each analyzing and recreating a different social structure (the Catholic Church in *The Cardinal*, the Zionist movement in *Exodus*, Congress in *Advise & Consent*, etc.), to make a black-and-white psycho thriller with a decidedly smaller budget and a trim cast. As I look at the picture now, however, I see it as roughly cut out of the same cloth, just a little bit further down the register. Certainly the best parts of the film are Preminger's imaginative, exuberant, and unsparing looks at the various social machines Carol Lynley is called on to negotiate. There's the "sanitarium" to which she is taken after a bad blow—you see the complete workings of the place in five or six minutes of incredibly well-chosen shots, and some wonderfully well-rehearsed "bit players," extras nearly, who carry forward the burden of exposition with just a few mumbles and disjointed comments. But we hardly even notice this deft background because of the high drama of the foregrounded situation, Lynley's attempts to escape the mental ward by hook or by crook. Watch the reptilian slither with which she extricates herself from her stretcher bed: she's there, and then with one ugly motion she's on the floor—nearly a whole Martha Graham dance in one little gesture.

Or how about the scene at the doll hospital? For some reason, Preminger constructs not just one set for the "doll surgery," but three—it's probably terribly symbolic, but he has made it have three floors, attic, basement, and main shop, where what looks like all the dolls in London have been lodged on row after row, shelf after shelf, their seeingless eyes meaningless holes onto a meaningless universe, while Lynley searches alertly for a particular doll that used to belong to the missing Bunny Lake. Despite her near breakdown, her search is deft and careful, as methodical as a princess in a fairy tale picking a needle from a haystack. This more than anything else convinces us that she's not as looney as the script wants us to think she may be. Yes, there are gaping holes in the plot, and critics who dubbed the movie *The Logic Is Missing* were right on the mark, and yet Preminger's minute examination of these weird English institutions has a fascination all its own. Best of all, I expect, is the Little People's Garden School that dominates the early reels of the film, the strange First Day Room, the "threes" and the "fours," Anna Massey's defiance and unhelpfulness dissolving into tears after Keir Dullea buzz-saws his way through her false front of propriety. Then the bizarre search up, up into a staircase that leads into the secret flat of ex-headmistress Ada Ford (Martita Hunt), with her collection of taped children's voices that would probably land her in prison today. There's not a wasted minute or word in *Bunny Lake Is Missing*, it is one of my favorite films of its era, and as an added plus the Zombies are outstanding! The fangirl in me screamed when I saw them on the pub TV. And among their three numbers, my favorite is "Just out of Reach," a telling comment on the narrative of *BLIM*, though I guess it could have been "She's Not There."

A Palpable Elysium: Portraits of Genius and Solitude
by Jonathan Williams

★★★★★
A Jubilant Thicket

April 2, 2008

I have had a soft spot for Jonathan Williams's photographs for many years, since I first saw one of his wonderful photos of poets' graves in a long-forgotten magazine. I was one of the lucky ones who got to "know" Williams in his later years, though only by correspondence, when I was researching a biography of one of the poets Williams had befriended and sponsored, and one day when I was least expecting it, the mailman brought me a heavily stiffened package that I just knew had something grand in it! I used a scissors to hack away at the duct tape surrounding all edges of the reinforced cardboard square, and soon my little studio was littered with bits of rubber, plastic, tape, and brown paper, and I was in hog heaven when the debris flew away and revealed a gorgeous print Williams had made for me of the man I was writing about. It was his way, he said, of encouraging me. I see this portrait reproduced in *A Palpable Elysium* on page 149, the poet Jack Spicer, casual and nearly unrecognizable in jeans and what looks like an Eisenhower jacket with padded shoulders, one flung back, his hands held awkwardly at different angles, one nearly hidden behind his butt. He's balancing on a huge hunk of felled timber, one of many massive trunks in the photo, a swatch of white sky like a flag poking through the timber at the top center of Williams's composition. The photo is from 1953 and had that eerie '50s quality peeking through it, I suppose a question of the color film stock JW used (and perhaps the particularly romantic gaze of the Rolleiflex with which it was taken).

Not all the photos in the book have this resonance for me, but many are remarkable in any light, and some have that archival quality of "Wow!" Lorine Niedecker, Mina Loy, who else but Williams has given both these writers the high-quality exposure their work deserved, or sat them down to give these uncompromising images for posterity. Actually there aren't many women in the book, and the "genius and solitude" subtitle might have been an indication that this was going to be a highly specialized, masculinist vision, but I couldn't help myself, I embraced this book as a memory of the late Jonathan Williams, for who could resist, in the captions that accompany each photograph, a man who tells us that in his youth Michael McClure was so beautiful that JW called him "Allure McClure," and once took advantage of an overnight trip to pilfer, for erotic purposes, a pair of Michael's boxer shorts ... God bless him.

Newcomer Can't Swim
by Renee Gladman

★★★★★
The Voice of Her Generation

April 3, 2008

Renee Gladman is one of our most interesting writers and artists, and Kelsey Street Press does her proud in a handsome edition of her slim, handcrafted stories, each one lavished by acres of white space all around the field of the page, and replete with one of those Jeff Clark Quemadura designs most poets would give their left sestina to have, lush and spare at the same time, huge diagonal capitals flying to the right as though pulled by blue kryptonite, as chic as you can get without actually being Samuel Beckett.

Gladman comes close though in some of her small-scale fictions and essays here, which extend and solidify the fragmented, scattered experiments of an earlier collection, *Juice* (2000), as well as the novel, *The Activist* (2003), for which she is best known. *Newcomer Can't Swim* describes well that fish-out-of-water feeling that Gladman is so great at exploring, and though she is a superb social satirist, she chooses her targets wisely. In "The Day, the Day" a group of bathers at a beach "out of the cold city" warm up while experiencing something of the shock of nature, a daylong series of tiny epiphanies, while the narrator focuses on two of them, Gus and Mona, in a previous story the center of a thriving city life filled with art making and flaneurism and friends, and now at the quiet beach Mona staring out I thought rather like her namesake Monica Vitti in some Antonioni narrative of postindustrial ennui. "Mona moves her head back, raises her hand from the sand. 'The day, the day,' she says with her eyes closed." Meanwhile, though she doesn't know it—or does she?—others are passing around a photograph of a woman who might be Mona; the mysteries of identity and the passing of time, as in Antonioni's *Blow-Up*, get a further workout, for Gladman is obsessed with event and whether or not such a thing might be said to have "happened," or whether, through the social agency of her writing, it might be successfully averted or ignored. "Ignore the leaves," Gladman advises, in the imagistic "Untitled, Park in City." "She must look beyond them, must not lie beneath them. The sun skins her. The shade makes her dumb."

Just as in Jeff Clark's evocative cover, sunlight and shadow play all over each other like practiced lovers, alternately skinning and silencing the heroine. At her best, Gladman's fiction is a powerful reminder of the need to keep speaking and acting out despite the twin oppressions of the system and the unthinkable body.

Tintin and Alph-Art
by Hergé

★★★☆☆
Elmyr de Hory's Treasure

April 12, 2008

I got into this book when I discovered, thanks to the Glasgow-based art critic Francis McKee, that it encompassed Hergé's own reflections on the Clifford Irving scandals of the early 1970s: Irving's book on the notorious forger Elmyr de Hory (*Fake!*) and his own attempted "autobiography" of the eccentric and reclusive millionaire Howard Hughes. Then came Orson Welles's film *F for Fake*, which ties in these hoaxes with earlier attempts at fooling a mass public, including his own radio broadcast of *The War of the Worlds*. It is plain that Hergé followed this case avidly, and it inspired the character of Ramó Nash, the great forger of this book. Instead of Ibiza, the island where de Hory moved in the early 1960s, Hergé places Ramó Nash in Ischia. "Oh! ... A Modigliani! [He accidentally touches the canvas; a little paint comes off on his fingers.] It's still wet! ... And here's a Léger ... a Renoir ... a Picasso ... a Gauguin ... a Manet ... A veritable factory for faking pictures, and perfect imitations, too!"

As a satire of a phony art world where everything is topsy-turvy in the name of money, and where the latest thing is but the insane reflection of the earliest thing (Castafiore enthuses about the invention of the wheel, of fire, of the first hard-boiled egg), it is a good satire, but for a *Tintin* book we look on it askance, for the drawings are nothing but placeholders and the characters of our heroes seem hardly to have moved on from *Tintin and the Picaros*.

I wonder if one of this kind of scrapbook could be worked up for every other of the *Tintin* books and we would then have a perfect knowledge of the way Hergé took popular culture and the social scandals of his day and turned them into authentic novels. I hate to think of this as our last glimpse at Tintin, turned into a living statue like a Charles Ray sculpture and shown in a museum as "Reporter." And no one suspecting he stands dead and agonized within like a sepulcher.

Include Me Out: My Life from Goldwyn to Broadway
by Farley Granger (with Robert Calhoun)

Bonanza Bound

April 14, 2008

I wonder what the backstory behind this book is, for didn't I hear that originally Eddie Muller was going to be the "as told to" in this book? Muller, who presides over the "Dark City" revivals of US noir films here in San Francisco, and whose voice is often heard as a commentator on the Fox Film Noir DVD releases, is thanked in the credits for Farley Granger's memoirs, but no more.

The book is, as some have lamented, a celebration of bisexuality rather than a straightforward account of a more or less "out" star who was engaged to Shelley Winters rather in the way that Malcolm Forbes was in love with Elizabeth Taylor. It's hard to understand why Granger wrote his life up in this way, but that's his decision, and from page to page the book has a lot going for it, he is very good at bringing to life both the famous and the infamous, and the half-forgotten, all of whom have another spark of life here, from Sam Goldwyn to the late, lamented Janice Rule, who deserves a whole book to herself. Granger admits he wasn't the world's best actor, but he does acquit himself well in the two Hitchcock films, in *They Live by Night*, and in *Senso*, a film so beautiful it more or less ended the careers of both Granger and Valli right then and there. Most of the book is about how his career fell off after walking out on Goldwyn and Fox (there was a blacklist for ingrates), and his later career in the theater and in soaps is nothing to brag of. Though who among us wouldn't have loved to see the live television drama in which Granger played Tchaikovsky and his romantic lead was Helen Hayes as Madame von Meck! Ah, for the glory days of live camp TV! They must have talked often among themselves of the late Robert Walker ...

OK, did I believe the stories of Farley G. in the arms of Ava Gardner, Rita Hayworth, Barbara Stanwyck, among others? Yes and no. I stopped actually believing him when he said his first Hollywood love was the young, vivacious Anne Baxter.

Mad Money (2008)
dir. Callie Khouri

★★★★★

Katie Holmes's Long-Deferred Return to the Screen a Cause for Rejoicing

April 14, 2008

Well, we got on the plane stoked because the lady at the counter said we were going to see *Enchanted!* And our hopes were dashed, like a pony piñata broken in many places bleeding candy on a coffee table and floor, when we found out through a helpful steward that the inflight movie *Enchanted* had been replaced with another entirely different show called *Mad Money*. Not one person on the plane had ever heard of it, but once the lights went down, you could hear the joy emanating from the audience, young and old, male and female, gays and straights, even people who were asleep, it didn't matter, when the titles revealed the name of Katie Holmes, all burst into spontaneous applause. "How long has it been?" we asked ourselves. It was an itch we didn't even know we had been missing, that fondness for a girl who is not only a hot paparazzi "get," but one who has been acclaimed around the globe for her stellar acting in such disparate roles as *Dawson's Creek*, *The Ice Storm*, *The Gift*, *Phone Booth*, *Abandon*, and *Pieces of April*.

The pilot broke through our reverie by announcing that below we could spot famous Lake Tahoe, but no one paid him a bit of mind. Instead we were all flashing back to Katie Holmes's last movie, *Batman Begins*, opposite Christian Bale, and how we didn't know it then, but that was to be the last time we would see her on-screen until—until now, three years later and a million gossip items later. The plot involved Katie Holmes starring as Jackie Truman, a loveable misfit who picks up trash at the Federal Reserve Bank, and who wears headphones and dances to her own private beat. Just like the real Katie, she harks to the sound of a different drum, but here Jackie Truman has larceny in mind—she develops a brilliant plan (which Diane Keaton, somewhat stereotypically, takes complete credit for) involving stealing millions of dollars destined for a shredder.

Due to her brilliant skills at improv, Katie Holmes brings us up against the bitter edge of the career criminal, how no amount of "mad money" is ever really enough, not when your blood is boiling and your heart is pounding against your chest like mad. With her own girl-next-door good looks, she vividly conveys the sexual excitement that fuels the addict's behavior, helping us understand that the unholy trinity of Diane Keaton, Queen Latifah, and Katie Holmes is not to be trifled with by mere goody-two-shoes rhetoric. These three live for the thrill of defying society, much as Artaud did in the France of his silent era, or perhaps the way the Marquis de Sade, a long-ago hero, defied provincial mores and brought pain into the repertoire of the bedroom. Keaton and Latifah have their own place in cinema (and in Latifah's case, in rap) history of course, but without Katie Holmes to inspire them, they would be flapping and floundering inside the inanities of Callie Khouri's lame script for *Mad Money*, like the dead fish they basically are. You'll laugh, you'll cry, and if you happen to be in a plane, the clapping that your hands will start at the end of the movie will be enough to be mistaken for sheer turbulence, and you will not be allowed to go and line up for the one bathroom at the very back of the plane. And you know what, that's all right, because now that Katie Holmes is back doing what she does best, all is right with the world and the sun and the moon and the stars are all in conjunction with Venus.

The Pear Is Ripe: A Memoir
by John Montague

★★★★☆
Ripeness Is All

April 24, 2008

I haven't read the preceding volume in this series, but from what I gather, at some time in his youth, Montague must have been mentored and befriended by an older Irish poet, the one and only Samuel Beckett, and there's a nice scene in *The Pear Is Ripe* in which a dying Beckett passes on his torch to Montague, in recognition of the younger man's great gifts as a poet and writer. In my country the USA, Bill Clinton had some video footage of himself as a boy shaking the hand of our then-president John F. Kennedy, and in Clinton's campaign speeches he often used to show this video clip, and the same heartwarming feeling permeates Montague's account of Beckett's compliments to him. You get the feeling that we're all little pygmies standing on the shoulders of giants, but seeing a little more just because of that, you know, time feeling.

I wound up enjoying *The Pear Is Ripe* no end, as much for its picture of Irish infighting as for its glimpses of San Francisco and Berkeley in the period around 1965, when Montague took a job at

UC Berkeley in the English Department and met a whole host of local bards, everyone from the white witch doctor Kenneth Rexroth to the love guru Gary Snyder. I hadn't previously read any accounts of Gary Snyder's life in this period, at least not in this much detail, nor written by a man who shared group sex scenes with the author of *Mountains and Rivers without End*. Snyder exhibited not a whit of shame about his body nor his drive for erotic release with every hippie chick in town. He comes across as a sort of John Galt of sex, good for him. Montague, who was married at the time to a somewhat complaisant Frenchwoman (whom he had left back at home in France), was the serial adulterer, but he convinces us that it was all fun and games and part of the cultural revolution.

In the book's second-best scene, he runs the dying poet Jack Spicer to his lair at Gino & Carlo, the working-class San Francisco bar where the poet made his second home. The experience of finally meeting his intellectual equal inspired Montague to write one of his best poems, "An Hour with Spicer." Later on, in Europe, Montague suffers the beginnings of his lifelong rivalry with up-and-coming Seamus Heaney, but this matter is treated with kid gloves amid the delicious gossip of *The Pear Is Ripe*.

---

260 Brass Sheet (Unpolished [Mill] Finish, H02 Temper, 36 × 12 × .016 in.)

★★★★★
Cut Just Right

April 24, 2008

My kids were asking why our apartment doesn't have its own brass sign outside unlike all the other apartments. We live in San Francisco's trendy South of Market district, where brass signs have become de rigueur in recent years. Signs with butterflies embossed on them that say "The Nabokovs." Signs with monocles engraved that read "Peter and Harriet." The lot. Yes, I know what it's like to be a kid and to be ashamed of one's parents for not providing one's family with something it seems all the other kids have. And so when I noticed that they were crying themselves to sleep over this issue, and that in the morning their pillowcases were wet with tears, I resolved to do something about it, so I ordered a few ultra slim 260 H02 sheets of brass from Amazon and decided to make myself a sign for "The Killians."

These brass sheets, less than .02 inches thick, are flexible enough for you, or your child, to wrap around a pole, massage into desired thickness, test for bugs, in any dimension you like. My kids wanted to paper the lintel with brass, and I let 'em. Might be hot on summer afternoons, but they'll learn. In the meantime you can hammer out the font characters you want, plus some amusing design (we had tulips) cut to $36'' \times 12''$ so you will have a nice plaque right next to your doorbell. Or should you discover someone famous once lived in your building, and your HOA approves, you could whip up a sign to commemorate the achievement right away. Like we discovered that Samuel Delany and Marilyn Hacker once lived in our building and staged a production of Genet's *The Maids* on the three-flight stairwell, so that spectators stood on the street and craned their necks up to see the fun. Blam! Another brass sign. At this price you'll be buying brass like there's no tomorrow.

Cléo from 5 to 7 (1962)
dir. Agnès Varda

★★★★★
Freaks of the Underworld

May 1, 2008

As Cléo stumbles through the streets of Paris, in shock over her prognosis, the ordinary sights and sounds of the streets attain a spectral radiance, in fact a disconnect from reality, that make her seem like the poor girl in *Carnival of Souls* (played by the incomparable Candace Hilligoss). The two films, *Cléo* and *Carnival*, were made right around the same time, 1962, otherwise it would be safe to say that Agnès Varda must have studied Herk Harvey's horror masterpiece for strategies on how to portray her heroine's gradual disintegration. Both films use subtle sound cues (as well as sound cues that hit you right over the head!) and both Hilligoss and

Corinne Marchand play musicians (Michel Legrand's churning, relentless score is all over the place, Marchand mouthing several numbers). As Cléo traipses through the boulevards, she comes across some pretty freakish sights that have been little commented on when people speak of Cléo's "charm" and "wit," as if to prove that flaneurs don't necessarily enjoy a Maurice Chevalier experience of life, not when they're delirious and that elegant b/w photography goes all Weegee on a person. Cléo's trying to keep it together when she sees the man who swallows frogs—big live frogs, one after the other, as the camera stares at him, hypnotized as she is. He's shown as the peasant type, the guy from the countryside whose class is so low he has made himself into a freak for public consumption. You wonder how he gets so many of those frogs down, it's totally disgusting. Then he performs the money shot: tipping slightly at the waist, he evacuates them all in a solid spray of projectile vomit, white and greenish like the cold waves lapping at the fishermen's boots in Victor Hugo's *Toilers of the Sea*. Cléo puts a fist over her own mouth and her eyelids flutter closed. I haven't seen anything as freakish since season 1 of *30 Rock*, the episode where Tracy Jordan is impersonating Star Jones on *TGS with Tracy Jordan*, stuffing his/her face with a thousand forbidden treats then throwing them all up like a vertical geyser across the studio kitchen, while Tina Fey and Alec Baldwin look on in what I now understand to be a subtle homage to Varda's nightmarish vision.

The other disturbing scene in *Cléo* occurs in a different neighborhood a few reels later, but Cléo's still reeling herself! There's a man running up to her proffering his bare forearm, through which he's worked what looks like two or three yards of waxed fishing line, which he pulls in and out of the suppurating flesh. It's like a burst of Grand Guignol still extant in the pop 1960s Cléo lives in, and again, she freaks out—anybody would. It's bad enough when you're walking around Paris and a flasher opens his raincoat, but these men are anticipating the body-modification movement of the 1980s and it's uncanny.

Experiment in Terror (1962)
dir. Blake Edwards

★★★★★
A Young Girl's Inner Soul

May 6, 2008

For those of you who are anxiously awaiting Éric Rohmer's next movie, or who have complained that the girls in Éric Rohmer's films aren't pretty enough, let me recommend Blake Edwards's *Experiment in Terror*, which stars Stefanie Powers (from *Hart to Hart*) as a sixteen-year-old American high school student in San Francisco around the time of the Kennedy administration. Stefanie's character is Toby Sherwood, an androgynous sort of name for her isn't it, considering she's extremely feminine, sweet, and obedient, and without too many thoughts in her head. The camera loves her as it follows her into the school swimming pool, on a date with her anonymous teen boyfriend, and fast asleep in her twin bed in her beautifully appointed home on Twin Peaks, the lovers' leap that towers above the Castro and the Mission here in San Francisco. Hope you're getting the "twin" references, for the movie is all about how many ways Blake Edwards can show mindless little Toby, as sensual and dumbed down as a fish, just being alive in her own female universe in perfect counterpart to her older, more neurotic sister Kelly (second-billed Lee Remick, in her second Blake Edwards part within a year), a bank teller. Anyone watching Stefanie Powers in this part will wonder if the screenwriters took her unusual name, "Toby," from Tobey Heydon, the heroine of a popular series of young adult books for girls by Rosamond du Jardin and extremely popular in the 1950s.

Toby's boy-and-girl love affair with Dave is fun enough, but nothing special, though Harvey Evans plays him with a nice dancer's grace. Audiences in the 1960s would have recognized Evans from his parts in the screen musicals *West Side Story*, *The Pajama Game*, and *Hold On to Your N.U.T.* he's supposed to be a heterosexual high school student? Only in San Francisco! Toby's not all sweetness and light, and somewhere out there in the noirish shadows is a man who's made it his mission to kidnap and torment her. Played by greasy screen genius

Ross Martin, Garland "Red" Lynch is totally weird and perverted, like Sal Mineo in the somewhat later *Who Killed Teddy Bear?* We see him wake in the morning, his asthmatic hiccups scaring himself awake, extreme close-up of the underside of his jaw, then the hair in his underarm, the long muscles of his ribcage, bare to the waist where his white, tight pajama pants, slick with sweat, are knotted in a crazy, ascetic way, as though he's been mortifying his flesh. When he finally meets up with sweet, virginal, confused Toby, the screen explodes into a lubricious madness. They couldn't film such a scene today and get away with it—well, maybe Rohmer could.

Greatest Hits!
by The Association

★★★★★
Overcoming Shame

May 15, 2008

Don't you hate those reviewers who complain about a greatest-hits album that one obvious song is missing, and yet I'm going to pull a facsimile of that exact review. Regarding the *Greatest Hits!* of the Association, I sent away for it just blindly, assuming without reading the fine print, and you know what they say about assuming? Well, it happened to me. I wanted one song, the theme from *Goodbye, Columbus*, and when the CD came I didn't even look for it, just thrust the disc into the player, and waited. And waited. And waited. Heard a bunch of nice songs, but you know, I said to my kids, I never did hear "Goodbye, Columbus." Us neither, Dad. "Gimme that sleeve," I swore. It's actually a beautiful image, of the six members of the Association grouped, some sitting or kneeling, on the rich green banks of some magnificent morning lake; they're all pushed to the right side in keeping with the Hudson River School, or some fantastic Turner painting like *Juliet and Her Nurse*, where it's the landscape, not the incidental human onlookers, that matters.

In tiny letters the names of the songs are listed in saffron—too small for me to read. "Kids," I cried out, "do you see the word *Columbus* anywhere?" No, Dad. The truth is that even in their heyday the

Association were hard to swallow, especially if you had an ounce of cool in you. I became fascinated with their minimalistic procedures toward language, almost on the Aram Saroyan level, they would focus in on one word at a time, *windy*, perhaps, or *cherish*, and each track would be this close, intense examination of how the word worked, its function in society. The blend of their voices was less jaunty than the Beach Boys, indeed it had something of the faceless piety of the Vienna Boys' Choir. Had they reached puberty? Hard to tell. I remember the guilty pleasure of hearing them boom out "Hello, life! Goodbye, Columbus!" on the radio waves and delighting in the misery that this iteration must be causing author Philip Roth *at that very moment*. It was like the Preston Sturges film *Sullivan's Travels*—he thought he was writing *O Brother, Where Art Thou?*, but the Association had rendered his sensitive novella into *Ants in the Pants*, 1969.

Or "Enter the Young," has there ever been anything more twee? And yet, and yet, when all is said and done, they had something—their very awkwardness and sincerity had a moral force like Luther pounding those proclamations into the cathedral door. I did love them, despite never knowing one from the other, despite the cloying sentiments of "Never My Love" or "Everything That Touches You." They weren't rock, not exactly, they were like looking at the US flag intently, then switch your gaze to a white wall and something like Jasper Johns's *Flag* pops out at you in yellow and green—yes, they were like listening to rock and then watching a white wall to see what might develop. A meditational exercise like tai chi. They're flawless really.

A Magick Life: A Biography of Aleister Crowley
by Martin Booth

The Master Therion

May 27, 2008

I was coming home from the library when a small child stopped me, tugged my hand, and asked me to step toward the boarding that covered an abandoned building on Eighth Street here in San Francisco. It seemed that a charitable agency was having a book sale for the wee ones of our city. A few adults stood prowling the street corners but otherwise the sale was entirely organized and manned by these children—none more than twelve years of age, and most barely out of kindergarten. I was a little surprised to see that their book offerings, propped up against the plywood walls of the abandoned shack, were largely books about the occult. Indeed I didn't know which way to look, it was all about black magic and how to hex one's enemies. Finally one child said, "What's the matter, dude, ain't you gonna buy nothin'? C'mon, it's all for the children." He looked ready to blow his tin whistle and summon the vague shadows of the adults on the corner and in the dark alley, so I took out my wallet, threw down a dollar bill, and came away with Martin Booth's 2000 biography of Aleister Crowley, who looked like a nasty sort on the cover with those large staring eyes and one side of his mouth drawn up in a gesture sort of like a smile, but probably a rictus.

It's taken me months to get through it, and in the interim I find that author Booth died on Lincoln's birthday, 2004. Since Booth gives us example after example of figures who, having angered Crowley in some manner, then passed on, no matter how many years later, insiders said that he had cursed them and caused their deaths magically, so naturally it makes me wonder if the shade of Master Therion, as AC called himself (he admitted in court to using literally "hundreds" of names), had perhaps been upset by this book, which calls a stone a stone most luridly. On the whole, it is one of the best books I have read in ages, and as a biography, I can't praise Booth enough for the way in which he continually manages to clear a space amid the rhetoric of Crowley's fans and enemies, in which his very real achievements can be appreciated for what they were. I do think he overrates Crowley's poetry, and his writing in general, but maybe I just haven't read enough of AC to make it resonate in my head.

Beyond everything else, *A Magick Life* is a book of eccentric characters. I loved reading about Oscar Eckenstein, for example, a mountaineer chum of Crowley's who suffered from a peculiar problem, throughout his life "he was periodically subjected to physical attacks by complete strangers, who tried to kill him: he assumed it was a case of mistaken identity." I liked when Crowley was living with Allan Bennett and keeping a human skeleton in the front room, to which they would try to restore human life by using toothbrushes to "feed" its bones a viscous mess of blood and sparrow meat. Elaine Simpson, one of Crowley's lady friends, was initiated into the Order of the Golden Dawn in top secret, and Crowley was later annoyed to visit Hong Kong and find out that Simpson was using the ceremonial golden robes of the forbidden rituals to enter and win "fancy dress party" competitions.

Booth is fairly broadminded about Crowley's erotic nature, his rampant desire for women on the one hand, and on the other for a younger acolyte who would mount him magically while he was on all fours high on ether. I mean, we've all been there, but Booth has an easy way with this dual nature, and never makes too big a fuss over it. When Crowley was a teen he was under the thumb of some religious relatives, one of whom wrote a moral story about the "two kings" who spoil young men's lives— "Smo King" and "Drin King," and impertinent Crowley wrote in that *he* knew two kings more popular among boys than Smo and Drin.

Even the saddest moments were marked by some comic incongruity. When Crowley's daughter died in infancy—she had been named Nuit Ma Ahathoor Hecate Sappho Jezebel Lilith—a catty acquaintance said she had been done in by "nomenclature."

It *is* a sad story of decay and decline, one that made me resolve anew to take better care of my own magical powers.

Alexis Smith
by Richard Armstrong

★★★★☆
From Another Generation

May 27, 2008

My goodness, this beautiful book drew venom from the reviewer at *Library Journal* back in 1992. Paula Frosch wrote: "The art seems less witty than clever, less creative than contrived, and the artist as brittle as the images. Along with the essay by Armstrong, the work contains a fictional biography, a patchwork of myth and jargon, an exhibition history, and a lengthy bibliography. As an example of self-promotion, this probably belongs on the shelves along with many other catalogs of a similar genre. However, it is by no means an essential purchase in times of budgetary cuts." Pretty harsh that part about an exercise in self-promotion. I can only imagine what she would say today of Alexis Smith!

In part this is because of Smith's deep-seated Californianess, and her job in the library at New York's Metropolitan Museum predisposed Ms. Frosch into thinking of Smith as a, well, poseur. The tradition of funk-collage-assemblage to which she belongs has its origins, perhaps, in the European-inspired surrealism of Joseph Cornell's "Utopia Parkway," and yet here in the West it has really taken shape, and many of the most inspired artists of Smith's generation have mixed conceptualism with humor with collage to create some interesting work. This large-scale book, the gift of a generous friend to me at Christmastime (hi Alvin!), is a perfect way to celebrate the career of an artist about whom you don't seem to hear quite as much as back in the day when the Whitney was doing this huge retrospective of her work and she was planning her *Snake Path* up the steep majestic hill at the University of California in San Diego, which leads to the steps of the Central Library there.

Like many artists, she has seized upon some common tropes and made them her own through skillful manipulation, rather like the poet Amy Gerstler with whom she has collaborated and who provides the biography of Smith at the back of this volume. In the case of Alexis Smith, we see playing cards all the time, playing cards and snakes, and also stars. When I think of her work, I think of an old-time Western, with gamblers playing poker in the front room of the saloon, and out on the range, a snake creeps toward the bound Gregory Peck spread-eagled in the sun. At night a blanket of stars covers the campground of the cowboys and ranch hands. One thing the book doesn't explain is how the actress Alexis Smith felt about this younger upstart who "appropriated" her name, and sometimes her image. (She was actually born Patti Smith, but I guess that wouldn't do either!) The statuesque Titian-haired Warner Bros. star was still alive, if just barely, when this book went into production, and we see one of the works labeled as being from the "collection of the actress Alexis Smith," so my guess is she didn't mind the implied flattery of having someone change their name to match your own, but I always think that's a little weird and would have liked more explanation.

Hitchcock and the Making of "Marnie"
by Tony Lee Moral

★★★★☆
"'Mumps,' Said the Doctor, 'Measles,' Said the Nurse"
June 1, 2008

We're all of us big *Marnie* fans on this site, though sometimes I think it would have been a better movie if there were more people in it! Tony Lee Moral provides us with an inside glimpse into the making of *Marnie* and shows that, at least as filmed, there were more scenes for Martin Gabel and especially for Diane Baker, who gives a gracious enough interview here but must still be fuming at the way her part was so truncated.

We get the impression that Alma Reville, though not technically credited as an editor on the film, was always Hitch's backstage editor and that she was responsible for many of the odd gaps in the film. (The credited editor, George Tomasini, died of a heart attack the year *Marnie* was finally released, worn out by the stress.) The Hitchcocks had wanted Grace Kelly—sort of—they didn't seem overly upset when she quit the project—and thus Hitchcock went back to Tippi Hedren, whom he had discovered on a TV commercial and who had made her debut in *The Birds*. The world knows the Tippi Hedren story and how Hitch put her into the deep freeze early in the shooting of *Marnie*, terribly sad, but he had made himself into a god and sometimes gods stumble and humans suffer. It was a little unnerving hearing Louise Latham, who played Marnie's mother, describe the way Hitch told her that he had Jessica Tandy in reserve if she, Latham, didn't shape up! As for Sean Connery, yes, perhaps *Marnie* is better because Rod Taylor isn't in it, but it's a close call, too close for me to make.

Does the book make sense? It is as close as we will ever get to discovering the truth about what happened to Grace, and what happened between Hitchcock and Tippi Hedren. What a shame that one of the screen's strongest and most powerful and lovely actresses was, for whatever reason, kept off the screen due to her owner's whims for many years, and when she came back, it was for the sort of parts that were beneath her. Apparently the higher-ups didn't want to offend Hitch by employing her, so she was on an unofficial graylist, broken only by

Chaplin who could have cared less what young Hitchcock thought, in *A Countess from Hong Kong*, itself a film of many mysteries and a controversial reputation. Mr. Moral has done his homework and has convinced me, at any rate, that that flattery of Truffaut, Godard, etc. had turned Hitchcock's head into believing that he was making some sort of nouvelle vague love-slash-art film in which the artificial was to attain a primacy hitherto reserved for suspense in his oeuvre. Does the movie work, oh my God of course, even with just a handful of characters and that red thing going on.

The Chris Farley Show: A Biography in Three Acts
by Tom Farley Jr. and Tanner Colby

★★★★☆
Fatty Falls Down

June 3, 2008

I never saw Chris Farley on TV when he was on *SNL* and only saw him in his movies, which weren't much (though Tom Farley and Tanner Colby valiantly make a case for the greatness of *Tommy Boy*), but now I'm a fan, thanks to this book. The oral history format is intrinsically flawed, but the authors do their best to balance out the variegated comments of Chris's friends with some solidly told narrative, so that we don't lose our bearings too often.

One thing I thought was interesting was that Chris was in so many rehabs, and kept them very private, that they were unable to find many details even from Chris's doctors about what clinic he was in on what date—the only way they were able to even get a vague idea about when he was in and when he was out was from contemporary diary notes made by his poor mother.

At first it seems like he's his own worst enemy, but then halfway through, you realize his father was his worst enemy, and he suffered from an Oedipal fixation which involved being a slave to his father and always needing the father's love. This involved ignoring what the surviving brothers call the "elephant in the room—literally," in that the father was four hundred pounds and drunk all the time, and yet because he was the breadwinner in the family they all acted as though he was Joe Normal. Chris was urged to lose weight, and he said that he couldn't, he had to be heavy to be like his father or his father would get hurt, spotting an implied rebuke. Oh, what a dilemma. But then finally you see how he spent upward of half a million dollars on rehab and nothing worked because, basically, the lure of cocaine, alcohol, and heroin is stronger than reason and eventually, stronger than money and love.

Sometimes the authors go too far, I think, in their breezy summations of history. It's tasteless to say, for example, that "in the comedy epidemic of the twentieth century, John Belushi was Patient Zero." What an insult to people with AIDS and the hundreds of thousands who have died of AIDS. I also wonder if they aren't overestimating Chris's place in culture. "That Saturday night," they write, "with one unforgettable performance, the phrase 'van down by the river' assumed its permanent place in the national lexicon." After reading this paragraph, I did a straw poll and asked twenty people if they knew what that phrase meant, and only one did. Then I watched the skit in question and it was funny, etc., and it made me a fan, but "permanent place in the national lexicon" is overkill. Now I sound like Scrooge, sorry fans!

The Seventh Sin
by Miklós Rózsa

★★★★★
Sin Is Splendid

June 6, 2008

We were watching the recent film *The Painted Veil* with Naomi Watts and Edward Norton, and I was savoring the movie except for its terrible soundtrack with that pseudo-Asian music in the background clanging and chittering. I wish Edward Said were alive, he could have written a sequel to his 1978 book *Orientalism*. Then it came to me that I had seen the movie before under the title *The Seventh Sin*, and that I had the soundtrack available to me.

We decided to start the movie over and watch it with the soundtrack to *The Seventh Sin* playing continuously. Back in the '90s people used to do this with a DVD of *The Wizard of Oz* and a CD of Pink Floyd's *The Dark Side of the Moon*, to amazing results. The results aren't quite as astounding when Miklós Rózsa's lovely score is placed on top of the current John Curran movie, and the "Rape" sequence comes far too soon to make much sense, but it makes you long for the days when composers like Rózsa ruled the music departments at studios. His score is a wonder of diverse orchestration and a romantic sweep which does much to alleviate the asperity of Ronald Neame's rather antiseptic and clinical look at a marriage in crisis. Eleanor Parker, as the errant wife who must learn to make amends to her bacteriologist husband, is superbly witty and alive, and she plays the thing as though it were Noël Coward. George Sanders as Waddington, the British consul next door to the Fanes, is so much better than Toby Jones in the modern remake that honestly if Jones watched Sanders play the corresponding scenes in *The Seventh Sin*, he would turn in his SAG card, just rip the thing up, they're not even in the same class. In the modern film, only Edward Norton and Diana Rigg can be said to have outacted their predecessors, and everyone looks better with *The Seventh Sin* score playing behind them, not the modern atrocity of fake Lou Harrison. Try it, you'll enjoy it!

Fame (1980)
dir. Alan Parker

★★★★★
To Live Forever

June 19, 2008

After reading a few pages of Richard Yates's celebrated novel *A Good School*, I tossed it onto the cushions of my bed, rebelliously thinking that if I wanted a disjunctive, multivalent account of four years of high school, the good times and the bad, I would rather be watching the DVD of *Fame*. Bruno Martelli, the hero, has a supportive father and uncle, a pair of colorful taxi drivers who cheer their boy's talent though they don't fully understand his drive to make music. And yet Bruno suffers from low self-esteem, thinking that he will never score with a girl, which seems sadly true, at least until his musical talent allows him to give Coco, his Puerto Rican muse, the sort of gift which a girl might really appreciate—a brace of pop tunes that might make people "remember her name."

Director Alan Parker struggles with his actors, especially with stolid Lee Curreri in the role of Bruno—he could really have used somebody mercurial or fiery, instead he wound up with a curly-haired pound cake. Coco has to do all the work, the impressive Irene Cara, good in both the tender moments and the hard ones, and very affecting in the scene in which she is tricked into taking off her clothes in front of the camera for a con man affecting a French accent and an acquaintance with the films of Jean-Luc "Goddard." The other young players are awfully good, though it is hard to believe that *Godspell*-like Barry Miller, as a would-be standup comic with a Freddie Prinze obsession, is magnetic enough to attract both Doris (Maureen Teefy) and Montgomery MacNeil (Paul McCrane), both of whom run quiet circles around the brash young Miller. *Fame* is sometimes decidedly hard edged and nasty, which is all to its credit and reflects its appearance at the tail end of the '70s, while the New American Cinema could still get a movie like this made, and the hopeful ending does not feel unjustified—these boys and girls have already lived life hard, and maybe they'll make some use out of all the pain in their lives. Though as Montgomery warns, it's a pie-in-the-face business and there are no guarantees.

What Is Sport?
by Roland Barthes

Barthes on Ice

June 30, 2008

I think Alyson Waters must have woken up on the wrong side of the bed when she wrote her blurb for *What Is Sport?* Yes, it is a little reactionary on Barthes's part to use the word *homme* so often when he could have used a more inclusive word, but if you listened to Waters you would think there was no feminine principle anywhere in the book and that's just wrong. In the Canada section (on ice hockey) Barthes goes out of his way to contrast the icy ranges of the prairies ("of all sports-loving countries, Canada is one of the most often frozen") with the warmth of the mother's gaze. Hockey players resemble children fighting on ice, for they are "merely learning to inhabit their country," while the eyes of their mothers watch their first adult gestures not as a mother would watch a war, but rather with the grim acceptance of losing a child to another order of life: in Barthesian terms, an initiation.

Richard Howard's translation is supple up to a certain degree, but you get the feeling he knows as much about organized sport as did Barthes himself, so it's helpful to a degree, and afterward it just goes to hell. Barthes's text stemmed from an invitation from a Montreal TV producer to write some voice-over for a *Wide World of Sports*–type show in the bellwether year of 1960. It was a given that Canada was going to be one of the nations celebrated in the documentary, while Barthes's involvement perhaps mandated a segment analyzing the Tour de France, its "water, flowers, kisses."

Even when he isn't really concentrating, Barthes is a fantastic writer, and when his formulas go stale, they still fill you up. "Speed," he writes, in the second episode, "is never anything but the recompense of extreme deliberation." Is this just in relation to the "2,500 gears" of the fast car, or is it applicable to all of life? It's the extreme ambiguity of his formations that make him so addictive. It's great that scholars unearthed this brief mythology from the archives of the University of Quebec.

Warm Springs: Traces of a Childhood at FDR's Polio Haven
by Susan Richards Shreve

★★★★☆
Life among the Polios

July 4, 2008

When I was a boy we had this lady come into my creative-writing class at school, and she read to us from one of her novels. Many of us fell in love with her at first sight, and especially when she began reading the pages of her book, for her voice, as many now know, is low and enchanting, the sort of voice that could launch a thousand ships. She was born a little too early to get into the phone-sex business but she could have cleaned up! Now comes the tragic story of her heart-warming travails back in the late '40s and early '50s, when she was one of the "polios," as they called themselves, installed among other children in the long, hot hospital they called Warm Springs.

In little Susan's day, the specter of Franklin Roosevelt, the most famous polio victim, was ever present. His photo was in the office of the main doctor, and the little children toasted to his memory (the president had died only five years before, keeping the extent of his paralysis a top state secret, but among the stricken, he was always eager to share).

She was a difficult child born to a wonderful mother who was a top chef and did everything perfectly. Stuck in Warm Springs, her fantasy life really took off and she was forced to be the roommate of sullen, disapproving Caroline, and also she found herself a little boyfriend called Joey Buckley, which made living in the enforced conditions of Warm Springs a bit more bearable. Her mother sent her many clippings to read, but only one book, oddly enough it was Shirley Jackson's *The Lottery*, which Susan didn't read but Caroline did.

She had a strange but understandable passion for Father James, the hospital padre, who could make any girl forget her vows. A charming man, James had what we would call today "charisma." I enjoyed this book but came to feel that she, Susan, was spinning out tale after tale based on tiny scraps of memory, for no one could remember all that, but embroidery is what the novelist does best: we learned that long ago at Ms. Shreve's knee back in the classroom at school.

Watchmen
by Alan Moore

★★★★☆
Ambitious and Addled

July 15, 2008

People told me that this would be the ultimate graphic novel experience and it was in a way, but dated Cold War elements have made this one a little top heavy. I wonder how the forthcoming movie version will play, or if the nuclear-threat plot has been toned down or something?

Time, or *AICN*, will tell, I suppose, but at the end of the day I found myself thinking, "When the ridiculously contrived superplot was revealed, how was this supposed to actually alter the course of history?" At any moment any number of its complicated twists and turns might have gone wrong. Just like the Roger Moore Bond films, the villain brags on and on for hours at the end, detailing every move he made for otherwise we would never be able to grasp the extent of his skullduggery. Well, this "bragging" scene happens in every action show or novel now, but Moore disappointed me, I thought he was above such showboating.

The storyline is great for the most part (till the last three or four comics) with the triangle of Silk Spectre, Nite Owl, Dr. Manhattan tantalizingly slow to resolve itself—though how did Laurie deal with that little blue nub of Dr. Manhattan's, bobbling above that ponderous sack of balls, that nubby nothing which looks so huge in the scenes where he stalks the earth as a giant? No wonder she fled to Dan's more normal size masculinity, even though he's fortyish and his body nothing much.

The minor characters are uniformly perverse, unsympathetic, nasty, and brutish—made it hard to care about the world's possible destruction. And Laurie crying about the pink and yellow rice spilled on the bodies of the scattered New Yorkers—it was an inspired and risky choice that just doesn't cut it, if you ask me. But for many the scene is probably one of the most wrenching and powerful in the whole of literature, so don't go by me. Same with the *Tales of the Black Freighter*—rigorously plotted allegorical masterpiece, or confusing sub–Knut Hamsun junk? Eye of the beholder, brother.

Nancy Drew (2007)
dir. Andrew Fleming

★★★★★
Tribute to David Lynch

July 21, 2008

Nancy Drew is a perfect film for kids, but adults will enjoy it too, especially those of us who rate David Lynch's *Mulholland Drive* highly and want to see it remade from a different angle.

On the surface, the story is one of those fish-out-of-water scenarios in which Nancy Drew is plucked out of pleasant, tiny River Heights and enrolled in a ritzy, snobby Beverly Hills school in which her ways make her a freak.

With the help of her heartthrob boyfriend from back home, Ned Nickerson, Nancy conquers the social world of Hollywood Hills, and the criminal world as well, solving a crime that happened right in the rented mansion that Carson Drew is renting. Thus tested by the oddballs of the Golden State, much like the original Nancy was forced to deal with California crime in *The Mystery of the Fire Dragon*, she returns home to Hannah Gruen's good home cooking and to her chums Bess Marvin and Georgie Fayne. However, viewers with long memories will glow with delight when they watch the saga of the murdered movie star, Dehlia Draycott, a thinly disguised version of Laura Elena Harring's turn as Rita in the David Lynch movie. Director Andrew Fleming spared no expense in his homage to Lynch, even going so far as to hire the lovely Rita herself. The plot, such as it is, rebounds with Lynchian mirrorings and twinships (former starlet Rachael Leigh Cook appears as a girl who may or may not share DNA with the long-gone Rita, who appears only in flashbacks), while Nancy Drew tries desperately to keep Cook's daughter from being deported by the state.

It's never easy for a love-addicted genre star to find happiness with the right man on Mulholland Drive. Dehlia Draycott made one wrong turn too many, and Andrew Fleming digs out all the right notes of compassion under the tinsel.

Murder in Mesopotamia
by Agatha Christie

Mesopotamian Madness

July 25, 2008

I read this book when I was just a boy, barely old enough to speak the word "Mesopotamia." In retrospect, I wonder why American publishers carried over Christie's British title unchanged, when they seemed to have so little faith in us so often that every other title was changed in some way—*Death in the Clouds* became *Death in the Air*, etc. The general idea must have been that we were dummies, and yet they let *Mesopotamia* slide in unchecked.

The book is a beautiful story about an enigmatic woman, Louise Leidner, definitely one of Christie's finest character studies. Biographers say that Christie based this character on an actual woman she knew in Nineveh and resented, a woman who called herself "the Queen of the Dig" and wouldn't give Christie the time of day. In fact this woman didn't like it much when Christie married her own pet boy toy, Max Mallowan. She was a married woman all right, but she was used to deference and she was used to every other man in the expedition falling in line as her love slave. Christie described this real-life woman, Katherine Woolley, in her memoirs, and I've always wondered how she managed to write such a scathing, searching roman à clef about Woolley and then, after 1936, when she knew Woolley must have read *Murder in Mesopotamia*, she coolly accepted her hostess's hospitality one more time when in Iraq. What nerve! But there was always sort of a cruel streak, or at any rate a pragmatic streak, about Christie. She honestly didn't seem to care whose feelings got hurt as long as their life made a good story. Check out the way she totally exposed Gene Tierney's feelings to the world when she wrote *The Mirror Crack'd from Side to Side*—or the Lindbergh family, for that matter, when she wrote the follow-up to *Mesopotamia* the same year in *Murder on the Orient Express*. She was a voracious tabloid reader, that seems clear, and it must have dated back to when she herself was in the tabloids every day and night due to her 1926 "amnesia" episode. Anyway Christie here creates not only Louise Leidner, the haunted "Katherine Woolley" figure, but Miss Amy Leatheran, a charming and engaging nurse with working-class roots.

Did Amy Leatheran come into being as a possible rival to the nurse/detective characters then in place created by Christie's American competitors, Mignon Eberhart and Mary Roberts Rinehart (among others)? Hard to say, but I do wish that Leatheran had featured in more than just this one novel. I would have loved to see more books with her in them and I always think that, with all Christie's many backgrounds, she missed a trick by not having a hospital story (or a theater story, for that matter, but that's another kettle of fish). The truth is that Christie's mind was so profligate she could afford to "throw away" a guaranteed long-running series of books and just dispose of their ingredients in a single novel, for she was blessed by a fecund imagination.

SPOILERS AHEAD! WARNING, WARNING, WARNING.

OK, so when I was a boy I drew back at the surprise revelation of who killed Louise Leidner, and I expect many will find it far fetched that she married the same man not once but twice, and didn't recognize him the second time. Christie explains it as best she can, without getting too graphic, and you could read the book trying to see through her euphemisms into thinking "Well, Louise either didn't have marital relations with the guy the first time around, or the second maybe—and that would explain why she didn't recognize his—well, his you-know-what," but as I've grown older and had more romantic experience myself, I can now totally subscribe to the theory that a woman will not necessarily recognize a previous lover. It's often the last thing on my mind when I have sex, either you've slept with them already or you haven't, and those bits of anatomy all tend to blur together, don't they, after the first few dozen. So I'm restoring the five-star rating *Murder in Mesopotamia* has always merited. It's one of Poirot's greatest cases and a marvelous showcase for Christie's unequalled creation of character.

Finnegans Wake
by James Joyce

Mean Girls

July 26, 2008

Haven't read *Finnegans Wake* in many years, probably not since grad school, but here it is again, everybody talking about it for some reason—it's resumed its place in the zeitgeist, the way Frank O'Hara's *Meditations in an Emergency*, featured on the season opener of *Mad Men*, is now rising up Amazon's bestseller list as we speak—has anyone noticed the boxed ad for *Mad Men* on AMC right on the page for *Meditations*? Merchandisers don't miss a trick. When I first read it, we really thought it was the greatest novel of all time and we aspired to be just like James Joyce. Then postmodernism set in and *Finnegans Wake* seemed valuable as a monstrous failure, one that moreover had everything in it, a capacious junkyard like the "golden" scrapheap at the center of Dickens's *Our Mutual Friend.* In any case I pulled it off the shelf last night at 7:30 p.m. and have just come to the end, feeling like I've just swum the English Channel.

The backstory has never been less obvious to me. OK, I can just about believe that the whole of the novel (bar some "real life" events impinging on the dreamers' consciousness—chimes, house noises, bladder pressure) takes place during a dream of a very sound sleeper, but how do they know for sure his name is Porter and that he actually has three children? I always liked the idea of "Kevin," my own name, being taken up by the great novelist James Joyce, and that Kevin was the golden boy of the family, but now I don't even remember how I knew his name was Kevin. In any case the dream of Humphrey Chimpden Earwicker shows the eternal return of man (and woman), the endless of cycle of history, exemplified by the legends of Swift, Parnell, Adam and Eve, Tristan and Iseult, even nursery rhyme characters like Humpty Dumpty and Little Boy Blue. The two boys are always in competition with each other, and physically different too, like Laurel and Hardy, except sexier, while the young daughter is the apple of daddy's eye, and sometimes he seems to be lusting after her in an incestuous way. The great set pieces remain hypnotic, but it is significant that they are the extracts that most respect genre conventions—the trial of HCE, the procession of ALP giving out treats for 111 "children" (or are they the witnesses in Porter's trial for—and what is it he did in Phoenix Park, showed off his "penrose" I expect?). The puns, anagrams, and blended languages keep one guessing, but I can see how they might grow wearying—just keep inhaling them, like weed, and you'll be able to ride the wild surf to the end.

I noticed on page 387 that there's a reference to "poor Merkin Cornyngwham, the official out of the castle on pension," and I wonder if this is where Merce Cunningham got his name from? Because it's such a grab bag, you can find everything in the book, and it's no wonder my professor used to say that Joyce had predicted events like the Berlin Wall going up, the assassination of JFK, and the war in Vietnam. Without even meaning to, I found Lindsay Lohan! You doubt me, punk? The extravagant exchange of the quarrelling washer-woman, in which every river of the world is named, yields the following: "The wee taste the water left. I'll raft it back, first thing in the marne. Merced mulde! Ay, and don't forget the reckitts I lohaned you." After that I knew I would find "Lindsay," too, quite close, even though her name might be muddled. Page 527 has "Linda, our seeyu," that sounds close, or how about page 492, where "Lindsay" becomes "Loonacied," as in "Loonacied! Marterdyed!! Madwakemi-herculossed!!! Judascessed!!!! Pairaskivvymenassed!!!!! Luredogged!!!!!! And, needatellye, faulscrescendied!!!!!!!" Why all the exclamation points? More acts of prediction, mirroring the way I feel about Lohan's relationship with Samantha Ronson. All in all, a five-star book with something for everybody.

Dennis Cooper: Writing at the Edge
ed. Paul Hegarty and Danny Kennedy

★★★★★
Dennis Cooper Démeublé

July 31, 2008

When I heard that there was another monograph devoted to my favorite writer, I ordered one immediately. Leora Lev's *Enter at Your Own Risk* (2006) set the bar pretty high; how would this new challenger stand up to the gold standard of Ms. Lev? When the book came, I was not disappointed. There's a lot of substance here and anyone interested in Mr. Cooper's work will find hours of enlightenment, amusement, provocation, and just plain brilliant work.

Well, there's one caveat perhaps, that the book suffers from using only men to write about Dennis Cooper's world. (Leora Lev is the one exception.) Perhaps diversity isn't an issue at Sussex Academic Press the way it would be in the USA? Otherwise editors Hegarty and Kennedy are chiefly interested in Mr. Cooper's novels, and the rest of his oeuvre is given decidedly short shrift. Does this reflect the emphasis of the recent Cork conference on Cooper, from which this volume is largely drawn? Wayne Koestenbaum does address the novels through their poetic qualities, making what seems in the larger context of this book the heretical observation that "his tempo has more in common with Robert Creeley's, Lorine Niedecker's, and George Oppen's, than with de Sade's, Bataille's, Genet's." I see I wrote "How true!" in the margin opposite this note. Elsewhere Leora Lev herself calls attention to Cooper's work as a delimited energy field of cross-genre experiment that includes poetry, art, the essay, his well-known weblog, indeed his life itself as a continual adventure in writing, and editor Kennedy conducts an interview with Mr. Cooper that ranges freely, like chicken in a Sonoma organic farm, over a wide variety of Cooperania from *Battlestar Galactica* to sculptor Charles Ray's interest in astrophysics—hmm, maybe not as wide ranging as it seems at first sight.

The essays themselves are sharply focused and largely convincing. Damon Young pulls the yarn of *My Loose Thread* through the needles of Kristeva and Roland Barthes. Martin Dines, theorist of the suburbs, proves conclusively that little Ziggy from *Try* rejects recent histories of suburbia to return to a previous, Forsterian "greenwood" impulse, "one that actually bears close resemblance to the ideal that inspired much of post-war American suburbia." Timothy Baker's remix of *The Sluts* with various limbs torn off screaming from the bodies of Blanchot, Hegel, and Adorno bears the weighty signs of gender-reassignment surgery, but since, as he argues, "the whole is untrue," it is rather like trying to stuff an oyster in a parking meter. We find that Polish genius Witold Gombrowicz exerted a similar planetary influence over his own field of readers as does Mr. Cooper in the present day, from editor Kennedy's article on Cooper's soi-disant "Ferdydurkism." And so on. You can see there's some interesting touchstones at work in this volume. Only once in a while will the layperson find some of the theory, mmm, uh, pretentious? I nearly couldn't get into Diarmuid Hester's exploration of Cooper's celebrated "blankness" in terms of Derrida's writings on mourning (though I'm glad I persevered), because I kept wincing through Hester's opening salvo, in which "I will not speak of 'mourning through Derrida' for, as I hope to show in what follows, mourning is always already Derridean and Derrida is always already mourning in advance." I never did work out if this wound up making any sense. To me, what would prevent such an essayist from writing an article which refused to speak of "eating rich French food and not gaining an ounce through Derrida" for similar reasons, that "eating rich food and not gaining an ounce" is already Derridean and Derrida is always already eating rich food and not gaining an ounce?

The homogeneity of the book, its emphasis on the novels, is broken by an opening selection of seven or eight brief prose poems by Cooper, and then even more radically by a center section, like a foldout of *Playgirl*, of poems (and lyrics?) by others, and a scattering of art inspired by Cooper. It's a charming idea, but in practice a little disastrous, chiefly because the poetry just isn't all that great. Sorry poets! But here you have allowed editors Kennedy and Hegarty to hoist you up against one of the greatest poets of our day, you were always going to come off as second-rankers surely. In another context I'm sure your work is splendid. In short, anyone interested in Dennis Cooper's novels, not to mention his thinking in general, should buy this book and prepare to get it dirty.

Screened Out: Playing Gay in Hollywood from Edison to Stonewall
by Richard Barrios

★★★★★
Everything in the Garden

August 1, 2008

This book deserves five stars just for its research alone, but it has to be said that Barrios grows steadily sourer as the present era starts riding in, like the tide. He doesn't like any show made after 1958 or so, and if you ask me, one of Doris Day's furry best friends must have escaped her palatial pet shelter in Carmel and bitten Richard Barrios on the ass, for there's no other explanation for his vitriol against the Doris Day–Rock Hudson movies of the early '60s. OK, OK, they were inane, but they did not cause cancer! And sometimes he seems unable to explain the results of his research, but unwilling to admit it, so he just blathers on covering his tracks. Maybe he spends too much time following market trends (and yet this proved such a fruitful field in his previous book, *A Song in the Dark*, about the early movie musicals of the late '20s and early '30s)? No one can really explain why so many of the big studio films of the *Children's Hour /Advise & Consent* period tanked at the box office, but Barrios just keeps doggedly analyzing and reanalyzing what went wrong.

In every other respect, the book is unforgettably brilliant and even when I disagree with his conclusions about this or that film, I respect his opinion and I admire the way he writes it up. (OK, except for Hitchcock's *Rope*, much more sympathetic a film than he gives it credit for.) Barrios's style, or banter, is generally persuasive and amusing, and he can summarize the plot of a bad film faster than an old-fashioned telegram by Gertrude Stein. And when it comes time for an aria, he really knows how to let go—such as his extended tribute to the "Naked Moon" scene in Cecil B. DeMille's *The Sign of the Cross*.

The book is punctuated by individual star portraits in prose, of Franklin Pangborn, Cecil Cunningham, Clifton Webb, and most hilariously, Bugs Bunny, whose manic androgyny and brattiness finally get their due here. He has gone through the files of the Breen Office, the Hays Office, every memo Geoffrey Shurlock ever wrote, and he has pored through multiple drafts of studio screenplays to find out how same-sex encodement was precensored by officious agencies. They still do this, only nowadays they call it "market research," and Barrios points out how it's the same old story watching Russell Crowe in *A Beautiful Mind*, the strands of gay sexuality in the original material as calculatedly snipped out as they were in *Night and Day* or *Words and Music*. Can't wait to see what Mr. Barrios writes next.

It's go in horizontal: Selected Poems, 1974–2006
by Leslie Scalapino

★★★★★
Come and See

August 1, 2008

Though she has had volumes of selected work before (I remember the Talisman House *Green and Black* with especial fondness), Leslie Scalapino's new book from University of California Press is very much a new starting out for the poet, a point of departure in which she seems to take delight in finding a pathway back—into the past, all the way through to the early '70s—and simultaneously in writing her way into the future with samples of new sequences not even finished yet. This is not the book of someone complacent nor braggy about what anyone else would consider a magnificent accomplishment. To me she has always had the attitude of (in this one way) a child, a child at the ocean who comes to you with her hands filled with seaweed dripping with shells and starfish, whispering "See all I have gathered for you!" And thus it is with *It's go in horizontal*, even the epigraph of which speaks of her work in poetry as both "minute" (à la Dickinson) and "voluptuous" (like Klimt or Marsden Hartley, or like Petah Coyne, whose voluptuous photos of flowers adorn the cover here). The blurbs speak of Scalapino as an original—well, that is an understatement—and yet what makes her work so valuable is the beautiful way she has of connecting with her audience, she is totally empathic, like the donkey in Bresson, we identify with her process completely, that of a human being struggling to stay true to consciousness in a century that wants to squash it flat for the sake of convenience.

And though she has left right out of the running some of my favorite books by her, including *Goya's L.A.*, *Defoe*, *The Pearl*, *R-hu*, what remains is a startlingly new and wonderfully realized voyage into the real, as well as a demonstration of just how many modes she has successfully worked in. If you have been lucky enough to hear her read her work, the excitement of being there as she seems to be writing it all on the spot, you don't have the chance to curl up with it as did, perhaps, the monks of medieval days, who illuminated the manuscripts as they read, work of remarkable slowness and attention. Here we have the serial poem, wedged up against the play, groove against groove. Next up, some of her work with visual images, often her own, and experimenting with the effect of handwriting, like her great predecessor Philip Whalen. We see also, spinning backward from the present, how her great prophetic voice, aligned with a sharply political jeremiad of shame and rebuke to present US-government policies, is not a new development in the work, that she has always been a poet of the social, of the political, of the word trembling in the hell of late capitalism. The selections seem ideally picked out to give the new reader a taste of the work in general, and to give the old hand—someone like me, who remembers the composition of many of these pieces—an exuberant sense of a life thoroughly lived in poetry, a fourth dimension (that of time) animating further the three dimensions I have always admired about her work and being.

Can You Ever Forgive Me? Memoirs of a Literary Forger
by Lee Israel

★★★★★
Out of the Depths

August 5, 2008

Once upon a time journalist Lee Israel was a well-connected Manhattan-based journalist with the world at her fingertips; her forte, well-researched biographies of what David Plante called "difficult women," gave her entrée into a glittering world of celebrity and real accomplishment. Her book on Tallulah Bankhead is really great, and her Kilgallen book is still the best single volume on the complicated reporter—one of the best biographies, in fact, of any midcentury journalist. The world was at Lee Israel's feet, but as she acknowledges now, a series of bad decisions and a horrifying addiction to alcohol laid her low in the 1980s; by the time the '90s began, the woman who had spent thousands a year in taxis and flowers alone was on welfare—when she could get it.

She began her "first trimester of crime" by stealing a clutch of Fanny Brice letters, then moved on to forgery by adding bogus postscripts to Brice's somewhat dull news, once she realized that the spicier the content, the more likely dealers would offer big bucks.

Then she began manufacturing letters wholesale, often starting with what she calls an "*ur*-letter," one from which she could extrapolate the general emotional tone of the writer, and above all else, one from which she could practice the signature to success by due diligence. (Her account of "inventing the lightbox" is surrealistic, unsettling.) Noël Coward, Louise Brooks, and Lillian Hellman were her cash cows, and with Edna Ferber—chosen for the extreme simplicity of her signature—and Dorothy Parker, she could milk her own caustic wit and alcoholic bonhomie.

Eventually she got caught—rather quickly, in fact—and the suspense of how she is going to get busted pervades the second half of the book. She was on probation for years, and is still persona non grata at many libraries and research centers, and of course, autograph dealers hate her to this day.

She is as blisteringly harsh on herself as Jean Rhys was, and like Rhys she casts a cold eye on the class structures embodied in late capitalism that condemn clever women to the dustheap of history. You ask yourself how a writer could abase herself so fearlessly, but maybe the alcohol burned off Lee Israel's shame long ago. How many people are making a living off of "signed" photos of Brad and Angelina on eBay as we speak? Do even authors write letters any more—those quaint piece-of-paper things? Israel's crime is site-specific—it couldn't have happened anywhere except ritzy, pricey Manhattan Island—and it's specific to a certain era as well. Her book is an extraordinary performance, a *De Profundis* for our times.

Monkey Smiling Italian Charm Bracelet Link
by Clearly Charming

★★★★★
Those Endearing Young Charms

August 8, 2008

When I got my first charm bracelet I was already a grown man. Yes, as a boy I had owned one or two charms—lucky amulets to protect me from the evil spirits known to haunt my childhood home in Smithtown (Long Island)—but I was too bashful to wear them on a bracelet, fearing taunts from bullies, fearing being considered a "sissy." So I kept my charms under my pillow, and when others found them I pretended I was hoarding them to give to an unspecified "girlfriend." Let's see, I had an angel, a piano, and a—what do you call those things graduates wear on their heads? Graduation caps? I also had a pewter rabbit, so cute, with onyxes for eyes and whiskers made out of actual rabbit whiskers. I acquired them by stealth, trading them for marbles, taking the SAT exams for others, and one, I'm ashamed to say, I took off the bracelet of a girl I knew who had passed away tragically of "the mastoid."

Boyish daydreams die hard, but by the time I was thirty I had utterly forgotten that I had wanted a charm bracelet my entire life. Isn't that funny how things work? Then a close friend and mentor showed me her Italian charm bracelet and all of a sudden, I was hooked again. There's a new, Italian way of doing these things, sharp and chic as a tattoo on Asia Argento's pelvis. These new Italian charm bracelets click right into each other, link by link, with the visionary synthesis of Ettore Sottsass (who pioneered these bracelets in the 1960s). See this cute charm of a smiling monkey? It protects me from the swirling influences of those jealous of my accomplishments as a literary author, as well as being the one I go to for a quick injection of cheer. Just as many who own GPS devices in their automobiles wind up naming the spirited female voice calculating their route for them, so I have named my little monkey.

"Sam," in case you're curious. The bracelet I wear on my right wrist has twenty links, most of them animals, but also licensed Disney characters such as Mickey Mouse, Winnie the Pooh, Snow White, and more. Other licensed charms include Red Hat Society, Elvis, Beatles, Barbie, Coca-Cola, Madeline, Garfield, Hello Kitty, Betty Boop, *Peanuts*, Archie Comics, and sports. And *Phantom of the Opera*.

King of Shadows
by Aaron Shurin

★★★★★
King and Country

August 25, 2008

Kings of Shadows shows that the "love child of Robert Duncan and Denise Levertov" hasn't lost any of his touch after decades of work as one of San Francisco's leading poets. His ease with prose is amazing, though it is not for everybody, and some of the measured, musical sentences are richer and slower than anything in the last ten or twenty City Lights books, but otherwise it is an inspired match of poet and publisher.

The brilliant title piece takes the form of an autobiographical collage which sees our hero trying out for a production of *A Midsummer Night's Dream* at Beverly Hills High in the spring of 1965; hoping to audition for Oberon, he is startled to find the director thinks of him as more the Puck type. In another panel he visits a newsstand and as casually as possible buys a few treasures: suggestive physique mags, posing straps strained to the last denier. What's startling is his description of himself as a seventeen-year-old, and how closely it resembles his look today. "If you look at me in photos of this period, my body is delicately thin, my impish nose turned-up, my cheekbones high, my

Mongol eyes slanted upwards mischievously, my small ears bat-like and similarly alert." Well, he must have a picture of himself in the Anne Frank annex of his home, a portrait aging and crackling with affect, for he is famous for looking exactly as he did twenty, thirty years ago.

It is a book of personal essays, in which various aspects of the first-person narrative are given a workout. Shurin has led such an interesting and diverse life that he can afford to shrink whole universes of experience into a single page, if that is the way the piece wants to go. In another writer's hands, the discovery that one's father has gambled away hundreds of thousands of dollars might have been swollen to a whole book; here it is the spur to a larger discovery about poetry's efficacy. No one has written better of the "sweet, communal" spirit that still abides in San Francisco, and no one has with more accuracy captured the horror of an era stabbed and mutilated by the spear of AIDS. And always he takes the long view, which is a gift beyond all others. Look at the beautiful cover of his book, all the glamour and electricity of a city teeming with mortals, and then above, the strange, older, haunted stars watching all our mistakes without judgment or moral.

Not the Girl Next Door: Joan Crawford, a Personal Biography
by Charlotte Chandler

★★★★☆
Not the Book You Wanted

September 12, 2008

Not the Girl Next Door is not the book we Crawford fans wanted, which is a pity because Charlotte Chandler has never before let me down. Her book on Bette Davis was astonishingly good! What happened with Crawford? Don't know. All I could think of was that she had this one new angle—that Crawford wasn't so bad—and she had to hold on to it despite all evidence to the contrary. She was able to interview a reclusive Crawford daughter, one who had never spoken before to the press, and their conclusions were that (a) Christopher was evil, and (b) Christina encouraged his weird behavior and alienated a loving, devoted Joan.

I agree with the other reviewer who was tempted to review the hair-do in the author photograph in this book. You can't see it from here, can you, but maybe there's a CharlotteChandler.com in which she displays her magnificent, Jeff Koons–like hair that occupies most of the photo space like a headdress by Carmen Miranda. She looks like a playing card, but not in a bad way, that hair makes one feel very affectionate toward her, plus it looks as though she could smuggle small cats and dogs in it, so it gives her some compassionate cachet.

The book comes alive in a lengthy description of the fairy-tale romance between Crawford and the young Douglas Fairbanks Jr., their attraction for each other and the thrill of being "young Hollywood" in the shadow of the two older players, her in-laws. Fairbanks's memories in old age of his "salad days" are warm and genial, but then the book grows faint and spotty and we never get an idea of who Franchot Tone was, Phillip Terry and Pepsi-Cola Guy blur in a haze. If this wonderful and gracious Joan is who she really was, then give me back my monster!

The Reality Street Book of Sonnets
ed. Jeff Hilson

★★★★★
Bumper Crop Bonanza

September 15, 2008

On the Poetics List the allegation was made that Jeff Hilson's book is too London-centric and that the talented poet publishes his friends at the expense of other British poetry circles. I always imagined that if I were making an anthology, I would first off canvass all my friends and see if they had something suitable, and if they had written any sonnets, and I was Jeff, I'd be all like "E-mail them to me as an attachment!" In fact every anthology I've worked on has operated this way. From California I can't tell if *The Reality Street Book of Sonnets* has too many people from London but I can tell you this, it seems padded down with people associated with Reality Street press and books, and sometimes this work doesn't seem of the highest quality. But again if I were the publisher of the book, I would want to see my lowliest author represented as well as, whomever, Harryette Mullen or John Ashbery and people who get published all the time anyway.

No matter, it is a big, expansive collection bursting at the seams with a richness and variety that surprised cynical old me. A friend had told me this was an excellent book, but I rolled my eyes, thinking "Sonnets?!?" For I'm of the opinion that even Jack Spicer, my specialty, wrote too many sonnets and what are we going to do with all of them. Adjusting my vision, I reviewed my friend as he sat opposite me at the bar, his repp tie, his trim lapels, the part in his hair so cleanly chiseled, and you know what, he did look like the sort of man who would enjoy roughly two thousand sonnets, the number Hilson has included. Well, I took a Kierkegaardian leap and wound up enjoying my time with this book immensely. Its handsome design ensures that there are never too many sonnets on any one page, while its chronological order (poets arranged by birth date) gives us a rough sense of the generations of sonneteers and how they think differently of themselves and their social practice. Are there many American writers here? Oh yes, he has done his spadework and flung the net far, including to my surprise the exquisite "Sketches for 13 Sonnets" written by the Black Mountain–inflected poet Ebbe Borregaard (one of many poets who, in these conceptual times, has in fact abandoned poetry entirely in recent decades). In fact the book begins with a nod to the US, as Edwin Denby and Bern Porter, Jackson Mac Low and Mary Ellen Solt, Borregaard, John Clarke, and Ted Berrigan make their presence known right away. There's a huge gap in time between the birth of Edwin Denby and the birth year of the first UK poet included here (Tom Raworth), and the editorial apparatus never really explains why; the book thus seems bottom heavy, as it were, with positive rafts and shoals of talented London-based poets all disinventing the sonnet wheel within what seems like months of each other. It's a terribly exciting time to be middle-aged or young in London and doing sonnets, and in the Americas one wonders what this book would look like had Jeff never read an issue of *Chicago Review* nor seen a catalog from Coffee House Press, because otherwise the pickings are slim.

I'm having all my students read this book and I look forward to a companion piece in which each of the poets—those still alive, that is—explain why they consider their poems sonnets, for what's missing is a theorizing poetics which would account for the development of the dismantling process, as well as the reaffirmation of form, embodied in such a volume, such a smart and luscious volume so ably edited by a practitioner with vision.

_____

1999
by Prince

★★★★★
The Place Where Your Horses Run Free
September 24, 2008

For some reason when I woke this morning, I had this tune in my head and couldn't rest till I traipsed down to the basement and found the old LP. What a difference from today when you can play all ten tracks on the CD without switching or changing the record, but back then I never heard the songs on side 2—and never played the second disc on the double LP, not ever, didn't see any point to changing up from the first two tracks. Why did artists make such long LPs, why not just collect a few perfect tracks? And thus it wasn't until today that I would up hearing "International Lover" and "Free" and the other songs (some of them not so great) on the second disc of the double LP—well, that dates me, but I expect at this time in Prince's career most of his fans are those who, like me, remember the 1980s as if they were yesterday and a time when 1999 seemed a zillion light years away, and when Wendy and Lisa puzzled us with their odd, superior androgyny like a pair of aloof Claude Cahuns, always nodding to the same beat, thrusting out their chins in unison, ten tons of hairspray making them look sort of feminine.

That's not to say that today's Prince fans love what used to be sides 1 and 2, 3 and 4 with equal fervor, how could they? They won't even remember the exquisitely perverse take on "Little Red Corvette" that Sandra Bernhard gave in her concert film _Without You I'm Nothing_, her unsuccessful attempt to divert '80s energy into '90s irony.

Vanity's on this CD too, which I did not realize in the 1980s, but that's because I never heard "Free," in which her vocals ring out loud and clear. That's not such a good thing.

Cherry 2000 (1987)
dir. Steve De Jarnatt

★★★★★
Red Melanie

September 25, 2008

My friend and I had a pact all through the 1970s and '80s, and we petered out in the 1990s when we realized that what we had was just a pie in the sky. Our mission was to artificially prolong the careers of our two favorite stars, Kim Basinger and Melanie Griffith, by actually showing up in the movie theaters for all their various releases.

This entailed sometimes a lot of loneliness, as often enough we were the only two paying customers in the theater, but one good thing is we hardly ever had to wait in line. At the multiplex there would be huge long lines for *Die Hard* or *Roger Rabbit*, but we'd be sitting pretty, able to slip into *Cherry 2000* hours ahead of time and stay for multiple shows if we liked (though this was actually cheating, as we needed our box office dollar to register in the far echoes of Hollywood's profit machine).

Cherry 2000 was actually one of Melanie's better vehicles of the period and she looked far younger than in her contemporary films—maybe a sign that the picture had been delayed? That was often the case with Melanie's movies, she'd make something and then it would just sit on the shelf till the studios sorted out how big a loss they were going to take that year. Sometimes four or five years would pass in this way but we hardly cared, all it meant was that her hair was just going to look more lustrous and beautiful and that she was going to be wearing some big outdated lips, but that's why we haunted these big empty movie theaters. Kim's pictures, for whatever reason, tended to find release soon after she completed them—no longer. And once in a while Kim wound up in a big fat hit, seemingly by accident, so we found ourselves in a perplexing fix when *Batman* (1989) came out and there were actually lines for a Kim Basinger movie and also, when we got in, I couldn't sit in the back row and him in the front row and still holler to each other about how beautiful she was. There were humans in between us—we hadn't counted on that, that had never happened before.

Cherry 2000 is not Melanie Griffith in any sense of the word, Cherry 2000 is a robot in the future, like a sex doll, owned by the hero, and when water seeps into her brain when they are making love, she stops responding and he has to find a replacement for her. He has to venture into the forbidden zone, and find an armed escort—who turns out to be Melanie Griffith, tough and taut in full Linda Hamilton mode with blazing red hair like a provocation. Their enemy, Lester, is played by Tim Thomerson in full '80s wack job form! He is the face of the '80s same as Nancy Reagan! Haven't seen him in years, but he used to be in every picture ever made like Wings Hauser! I'm sure that somewhere on this planet two boys roamed who had made it their mission in life to prolong Tim Thomerson's career by seeing every movie *he* made. Funny I never met those guys, especially on this one occasion so great for all four of us.

The Man Who Could Not Kill Enough: The Secret Murders of Milwaukee's Jeffrey Dahmer
by Anne E. Schwartz

★★★☆☆
Good Luck in Your New Career

September 26, 2008

I'm somehow not surprised that Anne E. Schwartz, in the years since she burst into fame by being the first reporter in Jeffrey Dahmer's sordid apartment, has first off stopped writing and secondly taken a job as PR woman for the Milwaukee Police Department. As a reporter, she had a big heart and lots of sympathy for overworked cops, but she wasn't too great at writing. And as a true-crime writer, her book is a bit of a mess. She was there, on the spot, but she never really learned much about Jeffrey Dahmer nor about any of his victims. She's not really able to give us much of that unexpected glimpse into the apartment, with the body parts littered around and the *Playgirl* photos of good-looking guys on the walls. Instead, a good chunk of her book takes up the theme of police tragedy, and what happens to you when you as a cop ignore a naked teenage boy running around on the street in shock, and you release him back into the hands of the guy who winds up killing him for good a few hours later.

Yes, that's what happened to Konerak Sinthasomphone, who escaped without his clothes from Dahmer's apartment, and because he couldn't speak much English, he was given back by several officers to the killer, who had a sort of plausible cover story. Afterward, when the story came to light, the officers in charge were fired for what seemed to the court to have been a shocking dereliction of duty, but to them at the time, they didn't see it that way. The *Milwaukee Journal* identified the cops; one of them cancelled his subscription to the paper in protest and lost twenty pounds. He was shocked that, after six years as a cop, people would think he was a racist. At least John Balcerzak had the support of a loving wife and some cute daughters. His partner, handsome, feather-cut Joe Gabrish, was not so lucky, being a bachelor with few social resources.

Their boss, Chief Arreola, was always smiling, sort of eerie! Anne E. Schwartz, in one of her few colorful passages, compared his constant unsettling smile to the Joker in *Batman*. Like his mouth was frozen that way into a smile that made no sense under the circumstances.

2001: A Space Odyssey (1968)
dir. Stanley Kubrick

★★★★★
Mercury Rising

September 26, 2008

People jeer at media-created celebrities of today like Paris Hilton, but things were worse in the 1950s and 1960s when we were always hearing about the ASTRONAUTS. Stuffed down our throats, nobodies like Scott Carpenter and Gordon Cooper became household names, even though (and maybe because of the fact that) what we knew about them was tightly controlled and protected by layers of government secrecy and PR. Even their wives were sort of famous, though they never really took as celebrities, none of them, no matter how many insipid articles in *McCall's* or *Good Housekeeping* on "Annie Glenn's Favorite Mincemeat Surprise" or "Cooking with Tang." There was Jackie Kennedy, then there were the astronauts, a group of highly trained men we all fell for, and I think Kubrick must have too, for he bases his astronaut heroes on the media representations of the original Mercury Seven US astronauts, wed to the plot of Arthur C. Clarke's story "The Sentinel," so that there would be a twist and the astronauts would seem soulful compared to the flat significations of HAL, their pet computer.

I assume that's why Kubrick selected some fairly colorless US actors to play their parts, although who knows, at the time Keir Dullea was regarded as a deep well of tangled and tragic emotion after starring in *David and Lisa* and *Bunny Lake Is Missing*, but Gary Lockwood had nothing on his résumé that would indicate any depth whatsoever, beyond his marriage to Stefanie Powers. Also in the cast, as Lockwood's mother, the swan song of wonderful Ann Gillis, once little Becky Thatcher in Selznick's version of *Tom Sawyer*, and also the voice of Faline, Bambi's love interest. She hadn't made a film in decades when Kubrick found her and cast her in this small but crucial role. She was the original "Little Orphan" Annie (1938) and her eternal sunny optimism is used ironically in the film. (Kubrick wanted the original Depression optimist, Shirley Temple, but her agents said no way was Temple going to relocate for the required London filming.)

That said, the acting in *2001* is terribly underrated, and the movie should have been nominated for Oscars in several acting categories. MGM built on the tech savvy of *Forbidden Planet*, with its similar mix of electronic music, beefcake spacemen, and uppity robot voices, and came out a winner all around. Kubrick had worked with MGM before (on *Lolita*), though *Dr. Strangelove* was for Columbia. After *2001*, Kubrick made a long-term pact with Warner Bros. which lasted until his death, but even though some love the photography of *Barry Lyndon* I don't think he was ever able to match the tech credits of *2001* ever again. (In fact some of his later pictures look very studio-bound and TV-like.)

2002 Holiday Celebration Barbie
by Mattel

★★★★★
Christmas Fire

September 26, 2008

I remember the disaster of Holiday Celebration Barbie 2001 and I bet you do too, people just couldn't get used to the sight of Barbie as an Austrian ice queen with fair, nearly colorless hair spread out from her face like the feeble rays of a setting sun. And the outfit they put her in was both garish and overstylized, like Bob Mackie without the charm. Fans speculated that Mattel was going for an otherworldly, elf-queen look, like Cate Blanchett as Galadriel in *The Fellowship of the Ring*, but on Barbie it just looked strange, though very pagan: one wondered what unearthly "holiday" such a Barbie could be celebrating—something from the cult of Cthulhu, perhaps?

The Holiday Celebration Barbies were, of course, intended as a sort of cut-rate or populist version of the traditional Holiday Barbies (no "celebration" in the name) that had been hits for years before the first HCB in 2000. Needless to say, the 2001 version nearly derailed this baby before she could properly be said to have left the station, so a lot of pressure was happening in the Big Doll House in relation to the 2002 model. And when she came out, we were relieved and pleased, and the piece sold in giant numbers. Though when I look at her now on my doll shelf, I realize that actually she isn't all that special, just a comforting step away from the dead-Valkyrie look of 2001.

HCB 2002, wrapped in a burgundy sort of tinfoil wrap, over a fuchsia gown embroidered with flowers and jewels, has a Paris Hilton look, doesn't she, but I think that's because Paris modeled her "evening look" after this very doll, complete with her extensions sticking right out the top of her head like a geyser. Like 2002, Paris parts her hair on the left and sweeps it severely from her shining brow so that the paparazzi must focus on her chiseled face and the great silver necklace she wears when she celebrates Christmas with the Hilton family. The packaging in this one is a further improvement over 2001, for you can see more of her all the way round (or nearly so) as compared to the restricted glimpse you had in the earlier model. One girl I know actually took hers out of the box to look at it, but we don't speak to her any more. I mean, really!

Bonjour Tristesse (1958)
dir. Otto Preminger

★★★★★
My Kiss Has No Caress

September 29, 2008

Juliette Gréco is perfection as the aging nightclub singer at a chic Paris boîte, who sings to strangers night after night of a "street with no address." Irretrievably ravaged by time and perfidious love, Gréco gives the part nearly everything she has; in her excellent Givenchy gown she bespeaks chic even as she allows emotion to tremble through her quack of a voice. As Gréco sings the haunting title track, Jean Seberg is twirling around on the dancefloor simultaneously drinking Gréco in and obsessing about her own memories of a colorful, blue-splashed summer on the French Riviera, the summer in which the mystic numbers 7 and 3 combined to form a summer of death and disaster.

Preminger is superbly understated here, his direction of Seberg assured and yet improvisatory. Some have criticized the way that Seberg, Niven, and Kerr never even try to sound like French people, and some say that the heavily accented English of the fourth lead, Mylène Demongeot, sounds like gobbledygook and makes her costars seem even flatter. None of them is actually convincing, and Niven and Kerr are oddly miscast, but all of them are great in their own lights. Kerr is believable as a dress designer, Niven sort of believable as a girl's-best-friend kind of dad, though neither of them seem sexy enough for their parts. Maybe in real life David Niven was some sort of super-playboy but I'm just not feeling it here. Why didn't they just hire Jimmy Stewart if they wanted a palsy kind of older actor to be Seberg's father? She seems like she's in love with him, or does she just feel responsible for his happiness since the mother's death? I kept waiting for the other shoe to drop and to discover that she had "accidentally" killed the mother, but we never get that story, maybe in the sequel?

What's great about the movie—beyond the main cast? Saul Bass's title design has got to be among his very best: the pattern of gold coins and crosses moving along a black screen like stars in the night sky, gradually being supplanted by red hearts and blue waves, and finally resolving themselves into the famous line drawing of Juliette Gréco's crying face—OMG, you will feel like you've died and woken up in France.

Geoffrey Horne as the boy next door, especially the scene where Cécile musters up all her courage and runs to his house, skips through the hallways like a thing possessed, and then pauses outside a door. She throws open the door and you see a dimly lit room and Geoffrey Horne asleep, face down, on a single bed, the whole room lit up by the eerie glowing white of his incredibly revealing under-wear. Va-va-voom, no wonder she jumps on that law student! Also the color design of the film, how the present is in black and white, but the flashbacks in color. The first, Juliette Gréco scene is especially impressive in this regard as Seberg, haunted by the past, is glimpsed dancing over the shoulder of her partner, until shards of color (blue) bombard her in triangles stripped into the negative (I guess) that finally overwhelm her and propel the film directly into the past, Must be taken from those *Jazz* cutouts of Matisse; this sequence is a direct ancestor of Kylie Minogue's Riviera-like videos for "Slow" and "On a Night like This." In fact the Kylie–Rutger Hauer relationship in the "On a Night like This" clip definitely smacks of the Seberg-Niven one here in *BT*. Maybe I'm overthinking this.

Gay Artists in Modern American Culture: An Imagined Conspiracy
by Michael S. Sherry

★★★★★
Remarkable

October 3, 2008

At first I was reading this book rather grudgingly due to what I per-ceived as its flaw, the almost total absence of West Coast–based artists among his case studies. In fact I still don't know why that would be, the book is about "modern American culture" not "modern

Upper East Side culture," nevertheless there it is, and what's here is almost bewilderingly good in all the best ways. It takes up a topic you thought you knew all about, and it brings to light the documents themselves that force you to see the whole "conspiracy" in a different light.

An Imagined Conspiracy shows us the intricate web of enemies any gay artist had to deal with in the 1940s and the 1950s, and perhaps in response the art of the men in question became more and more patriotic and American. Thornton Wilder's *Our Town* was praised for its universal qualities. Rock Hudson became the most manly and appealing of all movie stars, while Aaron Copland saw his composition *Fanfare for the Common Man* become a second national anthem. The most riveting and heterosexually erotic musical *West Side Story* was composed by an entire troupe of gay artists including Arthur Laurents, Leonard Bernstein, and Stephen Sondheim. Sherry shows us how the State Department and other proponents of American imperialism cynically pushed forward these cultural products as weapons in the Cold War with Russia and the hated Red Menace of Communism, and until such time as these tactics ceased to matter, the artists were protected to a certain extent from public exposure. Then in the '60s and '70s, all of their reputations collapsed: their Americanness had become too middlebrow, and besides the general public was now on to an idea of gay artists as being part of a homosexual conspiracy in which one hand was constantly washing the other or jerking the other off. *Hom* for "homosexual," *intern* for "international," and Samuel Barber perhaps got it worst, due to the international, or un-American, nature of his longtime relationship with the Italian composer Gian Carlo Menotti.

The book's climax occurs during the erection of the new Metropolitan Opera House in the mid-'60s and the opening-night performance of Barber's *Antony and Cleopatra* with Leontyne Price. The critics tore it apart, despite their previous acclaim for Barber's various works, and the thesis is that they felt free to attack him for his role in the so-called homintern. Going further, Professor Sherry explains that Susan Sontag sicced on the dogs by her treatment of Barber in her famous "Notes on 'Camp.'" You don't have to know anything about the private life of the creator, opined Sontag (ironically enough, since she went to such pains to keep her own so hidden), to know that Barber's *Vanessa* is a huge piece of camp from beginning to end. Indeed the theorization of camp proved to be something of a disaster for gay artists, for it gave scornful straight critics one more stone to fling at us; from now on anything could be dismissed as "campy."

There should be an anthology of the unbelievable articles that Sherry quotes from, by Gene Marine, Norman Podhoretz, Midge Decter, Anna Frankenheimer, Joseph Epstein ("If I had the power to do so," his famous *Harper's* essay starts off, "I would wish homosexuality off the face of this earth"). Of course it's still happening today, but now we just call it free speech.

Morphy's Games of Chess: Being a Selection of Three Hundred of His Games
ed. Philip W. Sergeant

★★★★★
Not Just for Chess Players

October 4, 2008

I got into this book first off by reading Frances Parkinson Keyes's novel *The Chess Players*, in which the game itself takes a back seat to the rather romanticized life and loves of Paul Morphy. And then when I was working my way through the papers of the American poet Jack Spicer, I found out that on his deathbed he kept a few books on chess, among them this book, in its 1957 incarnation which looks pretty much the same as this one except the chess pieces are all shadowed in a thick claret-like red instead of the cool blue we have now.

I decided to get a replica of Spicer's copy and see if I could follow it and somehow see how he (Spicer) used chess, and in particular the legend of Paul Morphy, in his extremely difficult poetry. He was attracted I think to Morphy in the same way as he found Rimbaud so intriguing: in both cases an exhibition of brilliance, nearly of genius, while both men were very young, teenagers I guess, and then only a few years later a renunciation so extreme it amounted to burnout, a psychic fatigue. Sergeant's annotations I find helpful, as well as his reasoned and well-argued account of Morphy's rise and fall as a grand master. What makes us turn away from the thing we do best, and go into trade? At least Rimbaud had reason to enter the mercantile world, for he was a poor boy and needed money for his family. But Morphy apparently was a scion of American aristocracy and would be counted a millionaire in today's money.

I found it interesting that they were annotating his games when he was a mere thirteen years of age! *And* that the games he played in blindfolds were among his best. If chess relies as much on memory as computers do, perhaps it would not matter to a clear brain like Morphy's how many games he was playing at once. In London he played five men simultaneously (two wins, two losses, one draw)—not exactly bukkake by the standards of today, but as Sergeant reminds us, he was playing the absolute top masters of his time. I love the idea of Game LXXIX, the opera house game, played in the royal box of the Duke of Brunswick at the Paris Opera House during a performance of Rossini! You can practically hear the triumphantly comic strains of *The Barber of Seville* in the air as you read the long columns of Morphy's assault. (He won, of course.)

The Lost One: A Life of Peter Lorre
by Stephen D. Youngkin

★★★★★
He Beat the Devil

October 6, 2008

Like all the other reviewers I'm staggered by Youngkin's accomplishment, which seems to me—perhaps profanely—even more impressive than Lorre's own. In a way, Lorre has found a biographer supreme, one beautifully blessed by all the gifts of sympathy and knowledge needed to translate an artist's work into contemporary times. How many of Lorre's peers have been given such a chance to live again? It's really shocking how few good biographies there have been of Hollywood stars, and even some of the most acclaimed (think of Gavin Lambert's *Norma Shearer*) have actually been among the most banal and simplistic.

Of course Lorre gave Youngkin a life really worth chronicling. If it wasn't the drug addiction, it was the dramatic life in Germany observing and protesting the rise of Hitler, till he and Celia Lovsky found their way out in a sequence right out of Shearer's *Escape*! The work with Fritz Lang, with Brecht, with Hitchcock, with Bogart, with Irwin Allen, with Roger Corman, each one of these phases could have made an interesting book, and Youngkin knows how to spread them out so that every angle is covered and yet our curiosity remains high. And the research and the interviewing is by itself amazing. Every time you turn around, Youngkin is eliciting revealing and wry comments from exactly the people you hope would comment on the particular situation he is writing about. Because the book has apparently been in motion for something like thirty years, his reach goes way back—he spoke with Frank Capra, with Hitchcock and Huston, with Broderick Crawford and Corinne Calvet, hundreds of actors, writers, directors, and behind-the-scenes personnel. This research gives the book a depth and richness of point of view that elevates it to the Mount Rushmore of biography.

I wasn't always persuaded by Youngkin's critical judgments, and would rather put a staple gun to my face than have to watch *Silk Stockings* again, for example—but now he's got me rethinking, "Maybe it is a great performance stuck within a lousy film." Youngkin pulls the camera way back and takes us through Rouben Mamoulian's whole career, his way of astonishing audiences by revealing unexpected sides to their favorite stars. I didn't actually need all of that to get the point, but I hope he gets to do the DVD commentary for *Silk Stockings*, for we need more enthusiasts and fewer haters. Why write a book about a man, even a drug-addled and morose one, unless you love him?

The Changing Light at Sandover, with the Stage Adaptation "Voices from Sandover"
by James Merrill, ed. J. D. McClatchy and Stephen Yenser

★★★★☆
Battlefield Sandover

October 13, 2008

I remember getting a copy of *Divine Comedies* for my birthday as a youngster and being intrigued by the story of Ephraim, and hearing about two people, JM and DJ, communicating with the dead through a Ouija board. The book has a list of dramatis personae that captivated me, for among them were some of my favorite artists like Maya Deren and W. H. Auden, together with some family relations and celebrities whom I did not know, enough to fill a whole novel. I suppose that Merrill knew he was onto a good thing, for he came back a few years later with a whole magnum opus about these characters and more ... then years later with a book, *Scripts for the Pageant*, really milking out the story for all it was worth, in beautiful cascades of verse both lyrical and coruscating—and much of it actual dictations from a heavenly place.

I wasn't sure how much to believe of the backstory, or how deeply to believe in the revelations of the divine that DJ and JM were getting through the Ouija. But at one point I was convinced that Merrill was the greatest poet writing in English. Today I think that he was the wealthiest poet writing in English, and all that implies. I know I wanted, like him, to have a fabulous life and know all these famous writers and legends, to move between Venice and Greece and Connecticut (later to Florida) with a different circle of adepts in each location—and to speak to the dead was the icing on the cake, a byproduct surely of charm and, you know, just being open to it. How many Ouija boards did my pals and I wear out, hardly ever getting anything except when I, well, cheated. Although one time this guy called Ray came on and claimed that Bobby Kennedy was going to be assassinated. But that had happened ten years before Ray's appearance, so we speculated that poor Ray was locked in a black hole or time warp like the characters in *Rocky Horror*, and that he, whom we suspected was the French writer "Ray" Radiguet, the beloved of Cocteau, could be set free if we all wrote poems about him.

I can't really separate the way I used to feel about Merrill's mastery of form and image from the picture of his money. Master anthologist J. D. McClatchy (and Stephen Yenser, a poet whom I have praised in the past) have produced a new edition of *Sandover*, free of the errors that had plagued previous editions. As the book proceeds, we get more and more of those small caps that signify dead people speaking—then it gets more tedious, though many will disagree, especially those who think the voices are bringing wisdom beyond the realm of the human. I often wonder what Scientologists make of James Merrill. Perhaps instead of making that ill-advised movie of L. Ron Hubbard's *Battlefield Earth* some years ago, John Travolta might have instead done a film version of *The Changing Light at Sandover*—would have been perfect when Merchant and Ivory were both still alive. I would have Travolta as JM, Tom Cruise as DJ, Priscilla Presley as Maya Deren, Angela Bassett as Erzulie, Sir Anthony Hopkins as Pythagoras, that guy from *The History Boys* as Auden, Penélope Cruz as Maria Mitsotaki, and Robert Morse (the actor) as Robert Morse, whoever he was in real life. I think a young Arnold Schwarzenegger might have done a fine, delicate job as Hans. Tom Wilkinson as Robert Lowell? Patti LuPone as Maria Callas? No—Katey Sagal.

Vancouver: A Poem
by George Stanley

★★★★★
The Lion in Winter

October 15, 2008

This summer at a poetry conference in British Columbia (Canada) I had the chance to meet up with the author of *Vancouver*, the 2006 recipient of the Shelley Memorial Award. He is a pleasant and complicated man with a bright-eyed gaze, George Stanley has spent years writing this sprawling poem about his adopted city, the one he came to after leaving San Francisco forty years back. The poem picks up almost literally from *Paterson*, William Carlos Williams's epic account of "a man and a city," as Stanley mockingly dubs it. This allusion highlights Stanley's struggle with an overwhelming literary influence, in the shadow of a revolving *W* that baffled me as I read on, not knowing what to make of it. Was this huge and officious and globalizing revolving *W* a reference to Williams himself?

Later I discover that the *W* is Woodward's beacon, a publicity gimmick for a local department store that "turned against life, against death, / against mortality, eternity, / turned, turned."

Vancouver (the poem) is piled high with aides-memoires, and it becomes clear early on that what is at stake here is a continual interrogation of description itself. "What to describe," "what not to describe" are affairs of the highest importance. Now in late middle age, George Stanley watches from the rear of the bus as its two facing rows up front fill up with elderly ladies in "coats & artificial flowers & 'permanents'" … They are silent but the poet sees them "batting thoughts back." The city is paradoxically the place where, amid a hundred thousand souls, you can feel most lonely (the handsome cover, from a photograph by Roy Arden, underlines this scary solitude as a long-haired man ambles off the edge of the book, nearly right out of existence). Stanley's solidarity is with the lower-middle-class people from whom he came, and the working class to which he is drawn politically, "the hungry people sitting in doorways."

He asks himself what is his relation to the "city I am not at home in"—for his attitude toward the place is so different than his attitude toward his hometown that I find *Vancouver* a dramatically different and more dynamic book than his earlier epic, "San Francisco's Gone." More dynamic, but darker too, darkened not only by age and the continual measuring of time between the moment of now and the moment of extinction. Is *Vancouver: A Poem* a return to travel writing, or architectural theory, à la Ruskin's *The Stones of Venice*? At times it has that melancholia, that sharply tamped anger. "And from what angle to expose it," he wonders, "so that maybe I could fall in love with it?" Instead of WCW's plan of a man and a city, why not the city as a man, "a man but not my man"?

A Song Flung Up to Heaven
by Maya Angelou

★★★★☆
From a Sister

October 18, 2008

This is one of my favorite books of the last two hundred years for the simple reason that my sister, Nancy, was walking down a street in New York and she heard a commotion from within a Manhattan bookstore, and when she poked her head in, who to her wondering eyes did appear but regal, imperious, humorous poet Maya Angelou reading from what was then (2004) her very latest autobiography.

With trepidation, Nancy entered the store and managed to strike up a brief conversation with the author, and when she told Dr. Angelou that her brother, Kevin, was a poet in the Bay Area, the good doctor grabbed a Sharpie and scrawled my name on the title page, with a special message just for me—"Joy." Later I found out that this was not the most joyful time (personally speaking) for Dr. Angelou and that private trials and tribulations were wracking her soul and conscience—but she had the show business stance of "give your audience what they deserve" and so she was able to impart her words of joy (or one word) to me once the book was wrapped and sitting underneath my Christmas tree. I shook it and held it to my ear, never guessing it was a book, never guessing that every word might have been written directly to be whispered into my ear.

I enjoyed finding out what Malcolm X and Dr. King were like, not as political figures per se, but as friends. We all know their history and the huge place they filled in the civil rights struggle here in America, but in this book, volume 6 of her autobiography, we find out how they (and also Nichelle Nichols from the original *Star Trek*) fit into the colorful and florid pattern of Dr. Angelou's voyage. We are present when she is trying to keep body and soul together by scraping out radio jingles and topical songs based on Philip Roth's *Portnoy's Complaint*. (By the way, when is that fugitive track going to appear on the long-awaited box set collection of Dr. Angelou's songwriting genius? We were promised this by Rhino over seven years ago!) She brings us to the intimate home life of the beautiful Abbey Lincoln and also Rosa Guy, both of them welcoming spirits who made a place in their homes for the wandering soul of rolling stone Maya Angelou. Is there any place that has not been blessed with a visit from the author?

At bottom the book is sad, because despite everything, she was in Ghana for much of the period exploring her African roots and the humid tendrils of her sexuality, and therefore she missed seeing firsthand what went down in the Audubon Ballroom, a story she has often told. You don't really get a good sense of her relationships with people here, other than Guy a little bit. I think she was too mournful and driven to write this book with the same care as her previous books, but subsequent work both in Hallmark cards and other forms of writing has seen a triumphant return. I wish her one word—"Joy." Thanks, Nancy!

A Unicorn Is Born: A Tale of Love & Magic
by Trinie Dalton

★★★★★
Powerful Reimagining of Ancient Love-Related Vitamins

October 25, 2008

I am not the target audience for this book and have never given any thought whatsoever to either unicorns nor rainbows, and when I saw this book I was just aghast. However, author Trinie Dalton knows exactly what she is doing and within a page or two I was hooked by her combination of narrative simplicity and the fantastic screen of illusion a unicorn embodies. Dalton is so specific about every last detail of her heroine's life. We get the names of the flowers, the exact length of each vibration, the heraldic symbols for the unicorn calendar, the stages of development of the unicorn language (Uniform), and the events of the annual unicorn mane-braiding festival (Honey Horn). I had never worried myself overmuch about how unicorns do manage to braid their manes with colorful crystals and flowers—I guess I always thought that the grooms in the stable did it for them, or young girls who liked to decorate their pets—but here you get a sense of the young unicorn learning to use her teeth to accomplish all sorts of physically dexterous things you would have thought impossible for an equine. Trinie Dalton made me believe!

Ursula, the mother who speaks to us, has a little bit of a biological-time clock working against her when the book begins, for she is over six hundred years old—in middle age for her species—and she is seriously considering adopting a young animal outside her peer group, perhaps a skunk or rabbit—when she meets Mr. Right at a Honey Horn gathering and on the sixth day of their acquaintance they make love— a magical love never seen by any humans so I can't describe it. The stud intrigues her with his tan-colored beard—oh Ursula, I know the feeling! But then when she winds up pregnant, I wonder what happens to male unicorns in the mother-daughter dyad Dalton so beautifully lays out here. Is there a place for a tan-bearded male unicorn after the love is gone? You never hear about the male of the species again, it's all about Ursula giving birth to Uma then teaching her life lessons.

I can't reveal any spoilers but you will learn the exact chemical process by which a young brown unicorn can, as a token to the power of female friendship, actually switch colors with her best friend while maintaining her own identity. As the story gets more involved, and Kathrin Ayer's evocative watercolors more impressionistic, Dalton perceptively grows the titles of her chapters—each one staggers on longer than the one before it, so that ultimately we get a blast of psychedelic-sounding chapters that hint at early Pink Floyd. I feel sure this book is probably a good handbook for girls (and boys too, I guess) who want to learn how to live in the woods year round in harmony with Mother Nature, her gifts, and her mushrooms, and for those of us who prefer four walls and a roof, it is a teasing reminder that not everything is solved by social realism, and that the world of fantasy and love can be as useful as a good dose of Žižek. Trinie Dalton is awesome and so is her book.

In the Time of Assignments
by Douglas A. Martin

★★★★★
House of Cards

November 4, 2008

I know Douglas Martin mostly through his prose writing, and among his many achievements are the two New Narrative masterworks *Outline of My Lover* and the collection *They Change the Subject.* Now here comes a bumper crop of poems, I mean really a big old book! In it Martin exchanges the extraordinary concision of his prose style—so crisp, so lapidary—for a discursive, generous, even eccentric verse line. I guess there are two Doug Martins, that's what. Brandon Stosuy's blurb hails this style as "expansive" and that's just the beginning.

I kept taking up this book and putting it down, because after every few pages my head was spinning with illuminations, as it does during a reading of *Leaves of Grass,* you just can't keep immersed in it, it will drown you. Luke Gerwe's innovative design splatters the front cover with discarded ID cards Martin kept as souvenirs—so there are at least ten Doug Martins that I can count, a telling comment on our current notion of "identity" as a costume to be picked up and discarded to suit one's convenience. These cards, however, also parallel the narrative the poetry unfolds inside, from a red-state obscurity, in which "all there seemed to be / was the endless war on TV," to the present moment of *nel mezzo del cammin di nostra vita*, when we "saw what was killing us coming," when "we were asking for it, with our white asses." The life of the poet climaxes in assorted revelations, not a few of them chilling, but also a few moments of a magnificent redemption, one that could hardly have been predicted.

I, Afterlife: Essay in Mourning Time
by Kristin Prevallet

★★★★★
Don't Leave Me This Way

November 22, 2008

A kind friend, knowing that I was having a bit of trouble dealing with the deaths of my father and mother, sent me Kristin Prevallet's book *I, Afterlife* and recommended that I read it in the course of coming to terms with my feelings of grief and abandonment (if that's what they were). "In any case," he said, "it's a beautiful book, how can you lose?" Prevallet's book is striking with its beautiful cover photograph that I came to understand was representing the ordinary sort of parking lot in which the central action takes place, and a numinous orange stain—the reflection in rain of a traffic cone? The inscription of a traditional sunbeam?—glowing downward from the top right-hand corner. We seek to make sense of whatever events befall us, that's just human nature, even when they are inexplicable.

In a sense, *I, Afterlife* is a kind of detective story, as Prevallet struggles to account for her father's suicide. She creates an eerie cut-up poetry out of fragments of the police reports that accompany violent death, and one section is made up of photographs over which the naked eye travels looking for a clue. Why did he go to a doctor in the first place? Did prescribed antidepressants lead to a downward spiral? Who bought that gun, who drove that car to its fatal destination—the man or the pills inside him? He pulled into the parking lot of an athletic field in Colorado, then papered the car windows from inside with newspaper—presumably to prevent the car from being splattered? Or to save the sensibilities of those who would inevitably find him? Prevallet's verse fractures and insinuates to match the twists of the living trying to get inside the head of the dead man, but remains remarkably supple and inventive. I never could tell, from page to page, what discovery she was going to make next, but the poetry keeps you going like a house afire. Stylistically the book leaps from mode to mode, almost as if the poet is jumping from hummock to hummock in a swamp that threatens to submerge her at any moment. Essay gives way to lyric which gives way to proscription, parable, warning, as the story keeps moving westward, like the sun. (This book is from Ohio's worthy Essay Press, a project of the editors Eula Biss, Stephen Cope, and Catherine Taylor to explore and irrigate traditional essay form with the strong waters of poetry.)

Eventually memories of the father's entire span of years emerge, so that a more rounded picture appears. In one powerful scene the poet and her father take a hike in the Rockies and encounter a figure she comes to understand as a ghost—an old man so dedicated to the mountain he has slipped into an identity vortex, he has become the "spirit of the mountain," and yet the extraordinary thing about this Walter Scott–like character is that, as the poet compares her father to this specter, she realizes something she had not known about him, that he was "walking ahead of me with a pace not at all suited for the terrain." His questions, she sees, are unrelated to his experience—there's a disconnect, a troubling removal from the real. After his death these disparities assume the heightened density of poetry. "Afterlife" itself is a comforting fiction, which elegy heuristically contradicts.

"Afterlife is a tidy package that presents a simple truth," writes Prevallet. "Elegy is the complexity of what is actually left behind." The book has a furious energy that takes us, emotionally and intellectually, to a place where we understand why the brochure the police give to a suicide's survivors advises not to make shrines, at the same time we understand why the shrine-making impulse must be obeyed and given living space. The ineffability of suicide, the porous membrane between life and death, becomes a scratch in the surface of reality. Even social questions seem to lose their edge—so strange and moving to see Prevallet, the most socially conscious of poets, try to grapple with this loss, this disappearing certainty. It is a terribly affecting and beautiful book—just like my friend said—she is a genius, pure and simple.

So Many Ways to Sleep Badly
by Mattilda Bernstein Sycamore

★★★★★
News That Stays News

November 25, 2008

People sometimes ask me, "Who are the novelists of today that really matter?" The truth is I like all sorts of books, and I throw around the five-star rating pretty frequently, and yet "what matters" is a different breed of cat. *So Many Ways to Sleep Badly* isn't for everyone, but those of you who read it all the way through will have been through a life-changing experience. It is in Mattilda Bernstein Sycamore, and a few others like him, that the future of New Narrative lies.

As the title suggests, Sycamore brings the body into the story right up front. His cranky, chatty, utopian narrator makes his money as a rent boy, and meanwhile pays the price of city living by calculating every atom of food that goes into his body and enduring endless sessions of strenuous yoga, and still chronic pain keeps him awake all night in his rented and rat-infested apartment in some Tenderloin tenement. Life is grim no matter what way you slice it, yet elements of heaven creep in sideways, like light through a venetian blind. Friends see our hero through a swirling cast of multiracial misfits and activists whose antics the speaker reports with the same naturalistic fascination he gives his food allergies.

Sycamore updates Armistead Maupin's *Tales of the City* "gay central consciousness + kooky friends" formula but he also inverts it, blows it up as it were, with refreshing results. While Maupin's finest moments confront his characters with the political issues shaping their lives, Sycamore approaches politics at a cellular level—the sociopolitical forms the language he has to work with, and at every turn he's reading and quoting from some appalling misuse of words. If our hero knows "so many ways to sleep badly," it's largely because we are living during Goya's sleep of reason, and the nightmare of unrest stalks the land. Few other American novels have been able to penetrate so deeply into the psychic underbelly of a nation turned into wrath by an unjust war. As I read on, I kept flashing back to an earlier period of English-language writing, before irony took over, when it was to the novelists that ordinary citizens turned for our news, when we read Norman Mailer's *American Dream* or *Why Are We in Vietnam?*, or Doris Lessing's *Golden Notebook*, or James Baldwin's *Another Country*, to find out something we couldn't see on TV. As I say, *So Many Ways* is a perplexing book in some ways, and every page has something to offend, but its rewards are serious and many, and at his best Mattilda Bernstein Sycamore has an electrifying prose style, like eels on acid.

Words to Be Looked At: Language in 1960s Art
by Liz Kotz

★★★★★
Enter the Word

November 26, 2008

I've been reading Liz Kotz's book for many months and I still haven't plumbed its depths all the way to the bottom, however what I have made of it, I love. In its range and in the brilliance of its insights it reminds me a bit of Pamela Lee's *Chronophobia* book, which likewise was always coming and throwing delightful curves at the reader, though Kotz goes beyond Lee, or so I feel, in the arcane angles from which she pursues her subjects. She also has a lot more humor than Lee, which is all to the good. Kotz's thesis is—well, I can't boil it down here on Amazon since her arguments, like the mythical Hydra, are multiheaded, but she takes on the donnée of much contemporary art writing, that in the 1950s and 1960s language made enormous and telling inroads into the world of visual art, and she tries to account for this "turn toward language" by pursuing various cultural and historical markers. Simultaneously she shows that the process itself (the "turn") devolved into a "re-turn," and the art became conscious of itself as being embroiled in a genre-churning mash-up. So there's all this activity, and some of it looks inward—and coupled with the social revolutions of the 1960s, there's a lot of ways in which anyone trying to make sense of all this material could go wrong, and Kotz evades every trap. You feel like cheering for her to succeed the way one cheered on D. B. Cooper's getaway after that hijack caper.

The book begins with a consideration of John Cage's enigmatic *4'33"* and its three scores. Kotz has a lot of fun about which one of the three is most canonical; in the end, we are led to agreeing with her that it doesn't matter, but that the resistance of critics to the so-called 1960 version is largely due to the fact that it is represented not in conventional musical terms, nor even by the familiar plunging graphics, but in words—humble but actual words (this is the one with the "tacet"/silence interchange that always strikes me as monastic). In any case working her way through conflicting claims, Kotz arrives at one of her most striking points, that after 1952, duration becomes one of the building blocks of art. Soon, Sol LeWitt is claiming to see that the idea becomes the machine that makes art, so that torques a little to reveal that the event is the machine that makes art. She tracks the progress of artists as different as Ashbery and Acconci through the 1960s, and winds up with a dazzling look at Warhol's novel *a* as the ultimate '60s durational work, a "project that must be undergone to be understood." Along the way she has a ball with the contemporary critics of *a*, and I always love reading that sort of thing—Michael Sherry performed a similar analysis of contemporary reviews of Samuel Barber's *Vanessa* and *Antony and Cleopatra* in last year's *Gay Artists in Modern American Culture: An Imagined Conspiracy*. Really some of the same knuckleheads were involved in tearing apart both *a* and the "empty-minded" operas of Barber. Hmm, makes me afraid that forty years from now, the scholars of the future will be pouncing on all the one-star reviews I've written for Amazon, and showing that the works of art I hated will be universally held up in 2049 as works of genius and I'm a fool. I know it's going to happen, and knowing I'll be dead by the time that happens doesn't make me less afraid for myself!

Twilight (2008)
dir. Catherine Hardwicke

★★★★☆
My Little Spider Monkey!

November 29, 2008

I keep hearing that if you haven't read the book, it wouldn't make sense, but we saw this one last night and everything did make crashing sense. If they had showed one more time how clumsy and uncoordinated Bella is, audiences would have started hooting. Based on what I saw last night, ideal casting for Bella might have been Joan Davis, and Edward could have been Eddie Cantor.

I started reading the book but abandoned it after about a hundred pages, so I was ahead of the game you might say, though everything that happened after that fateful biology-class meeting was new to me. I liked seeing Edward with angel's wings behind him as he sat there retching and throwing up in his mouth when he first saw Bella. I guess they were the wings of some statue behind him but the director, Hit You over the Head Catherine Hardwicke, lined up the camera angle perfectly so it looked as if he were an angel. Well, he was in a way. Both Robert Pattinson and Kristen Stewart looked great in their parts—though Kristen's dye job was pretty bad, I could just about let it pass as probably the dye jobs a teenager in Phoenix and then Forks could afford are probably pretty bad. I forget, does the book explain why every gay teenager in all of Forks High School comes on to Bella the first day of class? Does she give off some special hag essence? Because she doesn't seem like she really wants her popularity—isn't that always the way, the popular girls are always the ones who would rather be far away up a three hundred-foot tree with a boy with red-velvet lips.

Pattinson looks a lot like James Dean—maybe James Franco as James Dean? And when Bella and Edward are up in that tree and he's horizontal, Hardwicke seems to be referencing that famous photo of Dean up in a tree that Keith Mayerson used as the basis for his 2007 painting *Love Triumphant*. Without transgressing the boundaries of good taste, Hardwicke loves to eroticize her characters through fabric, color, makeup, contrapuntal textures (Edward's pale fleshy

fingertips against the broken metal of the truck he saves Bella from).
OK, but those of you who have read the book can maybe tell me,
why does Meyer have it so that vampires can read minds? Does it
come with being dead? Or have they sold their souls to get to this
mind-reading phase? It's sort of like *True Blood*, but in that case the
mind-reading girl, Sookie, *isn't* a vampire, so this confused me. Does
the mind-reading thing give them an advantage over their human
prey? Can they read the minds of animals too?

I liked how the animals for *Twilight* were supplied by a firm that
humbly calls itself "Talented Animals."

Vital Signs: Essential AIDS Fiction
ed. Richard Canning

★★★★★
Never Ever

December 4, 2008

Richard Canning's anthology of AIDS fiction includes many of the
best-remembered stories from the 1980s and 1990s, when AIDS was
essentially a death sentence and those who came down with it were
shunned and essentially quarantined. Edmund White's canonical
novella *An Oracle* stages its age-old drama on the Greek islands where
Ray, a youngish New Yorker, mourns the death of his older friend
George, and learns how to step outside his shadow while simultaneously fielding questions of colonial privilege as he makes his way
around Marco, a delicious native gigolo. Ray's not a complicated person by any means, and White relates his story without an ounce of
condescension or amusement. Andrew Holleran's "Friends at
Evening" announced itself as the harbinger of a new kind of writing,
a faceless and multivalent babel of voices all talking about the same
drastic subject, the panic of AIDS-related illness against the glittering
social world of New York in the early 1980s.

At the same time as these established writers were adapting traditional styles to new, apocalyptic realities, a bumper crop of younger
writers were jumping in with new experiments. Matias Viegener's tale
"Twilight of the Gods" caught the attention of many with its new

wave fabulation of Rock Hudson, Michel Foucault, and Roy Cohn all being treated for AIDS at the same time in a Paris hospital, in a ragtime-style imaginarium of history, desire, and glamour. Carole Maso's novel *The Art Lover* included a strong AIDS subplot, in which the heroine visits a childhood friend, Stephen, in a forbidding NY hospital, back in the early days when the signs on the ward windows read "Enter at Your Own Risk." "Stay away at your own risk," responds our angry narrator, and you want to cheer.

David Wojnarowicz and Robert Glück take up New Narrative positions on either end of the spectrum, but they share common techniques, especially the blurring of fiction/nonfiction and the abdication of the traditional bourgeois narrative posture in favor of a more essayistic, even agitprop voice, the '30s voice of social activism and what was once known as "special pleading." I wonder why Canning didn't think of something like "Nobody Ever Just Disappears" by Sam D'Allesandro, another innovative remix of the procedural and diaristic. But considering he lives in England he does give us an awful lot of American fiction—in fact, is there a single non-US story in the bunch? I must have missed why, since Canning in his introduction (and Dale Peck in his foreword) is at pains to foreground AIDS' status as an international disease with innumerable cultural manifestations. *Vital Signs* is an immensely satisfying collection, and when one has put it down, one wonders how it was that so many fiction writers lived right through the era in question (roughly 1986–94) without apparently ever thinking once about AIDS, like P. G. Wodehouse never writing a word about the Nazis while their prisoner in Berlin. I'll never figure that out, never ever.

SS United States: *Lady in Waiting* (2008)
dir. Robert Radler

★★★★★
The Grandest Ship Ever Christened

December 15, 2008

One memory I have of my dad is him taking me to see the SS *United States*, the subject of Robert Radler's new documentary, when it came to dock in New York Harbor. I would sit on his shoulders and he would point out, from the dock, the various features of the great ship. "There are many liners," he said, "but this one's the grandest ship ever christened." He and my mom never went anywhere, they were too busy raising a passel of kids out on Long Island, but I remember one time his old wartime buddy and the friend's wife were setting sail on a voyage to Europe, and they invited my parents to a shipboard party before the sail—and I got to go too—course, I was only a tadpole and remember hardly anything except the clouds of confetti that enveloped us everywhere we walked on the huge, wide sundeck of the *United States*. A sundeck big as a supermarket!

When I saw the documentary *Lady in Waiting*, all these floods of memory came rolling in, but I think the film will work even if you have never heard to the ship before; it is designed to appeal to any-one who has ever sailed anywhere—or ever wanted to—and its clever combination of vintage, newsreel, and originally shot footage and contemporary interviews mimics somewhat the easy, almost hypnotic motion of a great craft on the water.

And passion! The people you will hear and see speaking of their love of the SS *US* love the old "lady in waiting" (now biding its time in Philadelphia, where it has become part of the scenery), and that love shines through every frame of this stirring documentary. At times you have to pinch yourself and say, "And this isn't a made-up story, dramatic and inspirational as it is. By golly, this is real!"

New material supplements well-chosen clips so the feeling throughout is a delicate balance between past and present—the two worlds collide in an eerie, romantic way. All right, the ship is seven hundred thousand tons of steel but it comes alive as a living, breathing presence, both in mothballs and in period footage of her glory days.

The whole doc goes by in what seems like minutes. I can't wait to see what happens with the preservation campaign, more power to the conservancy. Let it shine as it did for my late father, whose dream it always was to sail away on it. Sadly, by the time he could raise enough money to take himself and my mom to Europe, the ship he loved had been decommissioned! Everyone who has ever had a dream should be able to identify with the warm hearts and high hopes of the makers of *SS United States: Lady in Waiting*.

Milk (2008)
dir. Gus Van Sant

★★★★★
Good for Gus

December 26, 2008

We sat in the Castro Theatre in San Francisco during the week before Christmas, while the organist rose from out of the floor playing "I Saw Mommy Kissing Santa Claus." Every seat was filled up and the beautiful old theater grew warm with anticipation. I was a little skeptical, as perhaps others in the crowd, all thinking "Sean Penn as Harvey?" And yet by the end of the movie our palms were raw from clapping so hard. We clapped for every actor, we clapped for every real-life person they were playing, even the ones we disliked in real life! We clapped for the young screenwriter who put it all together (Dustin Lance Black), but most of all we clapped for Gus Van Sant, whose legendary stamp is all over every frame of the picture. Black's script, and Van Sant's reputation, lured in some of the cinema's brightest talent, and the effort paid off mightily.

We loved the filmmakers' efforts to show us the old San Francisco, before cell phones and computers, when Dianne Feinstein always wore that curious hat that looked like a baby bat, but peach colored. The Castro Theatre itself was restored to its garish '70s look, and the costumes were great. Some have criticized Diego Luna's shambles of a performance, but I thought he was great and really the only one to carry off the '70s look without blushing. Oh, that hair! It was interesting seeing the different ways the straight actors decided to play gay. Emile Hirsch? Just imitating Alicia Silverstone in *Clueless*. James Franco? Just played it like he was super high all the time with a huge stoner grin. Ryan from *High School Musical*? Just playing himself except with a strawberry-blond wig.

I don't know if Sean Penn will win the Oscar, or even if he should, but I bow to him for simply disappearing into his part. You forget it's him, and that's how good he is. You don't forget all the time, but from time to time you forget it's him and how amazing is that!

Dead Silence (2007)
dir. James Wan

★★☆☆☆
Speechless

December 29, 2008

Looked forward to seeing this movie ever since we made the acquaintance of star Ryan Kwanten on *True Blood*, the HBO-scripted series in which he plays the heroine's dumb brother. He's great in that, but now that I've seen him in *Dead Silence*, I can only surmise that on *True Blood* it's his buttocks that do all his acting for him, and they should be awarded the Emmy for the superlative work he puts them through on that show. Here they are continually hidden underneath an unsavory pair of jeans, and thus poor Ryan has literally nothing to work with. In a way this acting theory matches the premise of *Dead Silence*, a film that asks us to believe that an entire town, Raven's Fair, has only a few residents in it, and all of them are controlled by the vengeful spirit of Mary Shaw, an amateur ventrilo-quist of the early 1950s who loved both children and dolls until one snippy little rich boy spoiled her show by exclaiming loudly that he could see her lips moving.

In consequence, everything starts going wrong for both Mary Shaw and everyone she knows.

The film suffers from an extremely low budget. They could only afford to hire about four actors, to represent not only the populace of the godforsaken town but also the entire population of NYC. They could only afford three colors also, so everything is drenched in deep blue, except when Jamie gets into a red car or a horrible ghost tears out red tongues from people's mouths. And there's black as the third color, but how cheap can you get? But they really could have saved money, as well as improving the film by about 1,000 percent, by leaving the pants off Ryan Kwanten and his unforgettable assets. Oh, what a waste.

Cinema Stories
by Alexander Kluge

El Dorado

January 5, 2009

Kluge is now the grand old man of German cinema as well as one of Germany's most distinguished fiction writers. For his seventy-fifth birthday (February 14, 2007), New Directions issues a book of his aphorisms and notes on the byways of the movies. "We don't perceive a contradiction between writing books, making films, or producing a television program," he told Hans Ulrich Obrist in a 1998 interview. "These days you can't choose how you want to express yourself anymore." *Cinema Stories* isn't exactly fiction, it's a collection of his thoughts about films, filmmaking, and most of all the experience of the audience, though some employ elements garnered from fiction, or poetry, so that the book is a close cousin of the late Barbara Guest's 1999 volume of "Hollywood stories," *The Confetti Trees.*

Kluge's chief interest is in time, in deconstructing conventional notions of time's workings. In his little tales, both here and elsewhere, many less than a page long, he reveals himself capable of viewing time in vast chunks. The whole history of the cinema, for example, is no older than his maternal grandmother. *Cinema Stories* proceeds more or less chronologically, with the earliest cinema pioneers, Méliès and the Lumière brothers, and beyond particular innovators the "cinema of the attractions," as Tom Gunning has called the earliest, "primitive" cinema. What was this certain something that cinema possessed, which other art forms before it lacked? Again and again, Kluge's book seeks to encapsulate that enigmatic essence.

Kluge's detours are as intriguing as his main currents of thought. In a footnote he suggests that traditional grand opera appealed to European capitals because in its purest form opera raises the "possibility of total abandon without anything left behind afterwards," of the gallant renunciations of *Madame Butterfly* or *Carmen*. Then he suggests that it was this impulse, toward what he calls "exodus," that leads toward world war.

In the present we have returned to the earliest days of slot machines, again the "primitive cinema." The book opens up with an account of a bombed-out theater, ironically the "Eldorado" in Beirut, in which the proprietors still show movies under a tent, and spectators sit in folding chairs and enjoy whatever movies can be scrounged up ("Cinema in a State of Emergency"). The cinema brings a cartography of the social: "In times of danger they [the poor] liked to sit together sociably (not possessing the means to flee available to the rich)."

He's not all superintellect either, and doesn't mind traipsing into Kenneth Anger *Hollywood Babylon* territory, when it pleases him; and he is farsighted enough to envision the end of cinema, for "No one will want to watch the old acts forever more, since, after all, contemporary events offer sensations surpassing any circus act" (90).

Cinema Stories is a provocative and lively collection of fragments on the cinema. Kluge's book should appeal to an audience larger than film specialists alone, for his observations seem to extend themselves laterally to many of the arts, as well as to the progressive politics of the past fifty years or more.

Destry Rides Again (1939)
dir. George Marshall

★★★★★
You've Got the Look

February 10, 2009

We watched this particular DVD and I have to say, this film needs restoration badly. When Dietrich gets on stage to sing "The Boys in the Back Room," you can barely distinguish her from the gauze curtain behind her. (Or was she photographed with a piece of gauze hung between her and the camera?) Universal did her no favors in the hair or makeup department either; when wet, her hair looks great, but dry, it looks like a Shirley Temple doll with shiny cellophane instead of human hair, and the cellophane is constantly winking and glittering in the camera's lens, like the jewels or sequins in her corsets and showgirl outfits. Now I know where Kylie Minogue got her total-showgirl look.

It is a strange Western without Indians, though we hear them referred to in the dialogue, stories of how the elder Destry faced down a whole Comanche tribe, etc. Otherwise the conflict is between corrupt municipal bosses, allied with gamblers, who scheme to monopolize ownership of all surrounding land—that is, anywhere that could be used as a cattle trail. Wonder if the movie was inspired by current events in Europe; James Stewart, reluctant to strap on the guns and live as his father did, has to make up his mind in the face of escalating and evil violence—an allegory for the isolationism of the US when Hitler was taking over Europe? Everything fits, but if so, it makes the presence of Dietrich (and Mischa Auer) in the movie fit even more … Still you'd think there'd be Indians, or would that be a distraction from the anti-isolationist politics of the film?

Needless to say, we loved it. We devised a drinking game where we would take a shot every time the flustered sheriff pulled his shirt out of the front of his pants, and we took two shots every time Jimmy Stewart slowly and lovingly tucked it back in for him … We cried the last time he did this … In fact I'm still drunk.

Viniyoga Therapy for the Low Back, Sacrum and Hips with Gary Kraftsow
dir. Ian Albert and Mark Holmes

★★★★★
Ask the Answer; Grow the Question

February 17, 2009

I wanted to get a good viniyoga tape ever since the early '70s when, as a boy, I suffered a lower-back injury in France, when I was pushed out of a slowly moving bus by some schoolmates.

Ever since then I have moved more slowly than my contemporaries, but just like the tortoise overtaking the hare, I have found Gary Kraftsow's slow, deliberate yoga teaching a clear case of therapy. I wasn't looking for an instant cure! Just a way for me to intake the knowledge of the viniyoga into my sacrum and lower back, let alone my hips, just as once I looked up at the low-hanging French sky, on my back, in a crowded avenue, while my school bus shot off without me, and French boys were laughing at me through the still-flapping backdoor of the bus, and my whole body radiated with pain. Kraftsow isn't a comedian like so many other yoga "entertainers" and he seems to want to educate the viewer into going along with a slow-paced regimen, nothing flashy, just good old-fashioned poses and a l-o-t of stretching of tight tendons. Deep in the sacrum, where a bewildering variety of muscles come together in confusing interstitial junctions, the pain gremlins shriek in fright when they hear Gary Kraftsow's relaxing voice boom out changes with his trademark conviction. The guy really believes in what he's doing, and when I'm watching this on my wide-screen TV in my sunroom, I occasionally take a break and write him a little personal note of thanks, mailing it off to his atelier with name and address attached. In France my teachers at the lycée, when I confronted them with evidence of anti-US bullying, told me to ask not the question, but to ask instead the answer. I didn't understand their wisdom, their *bon sens sagesse*, but now I've got an inkling.

Advil Tablets (Ibuprofen, 200 mg, 300 Tablets)

★★★★★
Feels So Good

March 19, 2009

Ordinarily I agree with James Koenig's reviews 1,000 per cent. Not for nothing is he one of Amazon's Top 100 reviewers. And yet, when he tells us we might as well just get the generic version of ibuprofen, instead of brand name Advil, I demur sharply.

Other reviewers recommend Advil for its ease of use, but I'm here to tell you the main reason to buy it is that it is tasty and sweet, rather like a cherry. If common sense and doctors' warnings didn't preclude it, I would be popping Advils all day just to get that delicious taste in my mouth, like a kid in a candy store.

First week of January I had an industrial accident at my office when a large box of heavy paper stock tumbled down onto my foot from a great height. Rushed to the hospital, I found myself weak and faint, and when the doctor told me that I should be having an Advil every four hours for the next three months, to reduce swelling and to heal the fracture, I perked up considerably. Now in front of me as I type is a king-size dispenser of Advil, used to be an oversized Pez dispenser in black and gold, wearing Tim Lincecum's uniform, which some friends had bought me on a trip to the SF Giants' stadium here. Now it dispenses Advil and I find myself looking at the clock wishing it were four hours later already. I'm hooked I guess, and a little piece of me wishes I could return to the days of youth when I needed nothing, no poppy or mandragora as Shakespeare says, but in the meantime I do enjoy a nice Advil every four hours, and as a side benefit, its healing atoms have sped the recovery of my swollen foot inside its sturdy surgical boot.

Scrapmetal
by Ammiel Alcalay

★★★★★
Individual Lives vs. Historical Contingency

March 20, 2009

I first came across this book when a short excerpt caught my eye, and I liked what I read so I ordered the whole thing from Amazon.com. The excerpt involved a letter by the poet, Ammiel Alcalay, constructing a parallel history in which he writes to a poet of a previous generation, Jack Spicer, regarding the positions on political poetry Spicer staked out in his 1965 lectures transcribed, annotated, and edited by Peter Gizzi in the 1998 compilation *The House That Jack Built*. To Alcalay's way of thinking, physical and intellectual labor are not only mirrors of each other, but pretty much the same thing, and Spicer himself, though a mandarin of sorts, took plenty of odd jobs to make ends meet in the California landscape of the late 1930s, through the '40s and '50s, a list which Alcalay seems to recapitulate in brief paragraphs of his own work history. He suggests that the painter Jay DeFeo's work on a single heroic picture, *The Rose*, which took the better part of six years, contains as much sweat equity as a dockyard trawler or a migrant farmer.

Scrapmetal gathers luster in the face of today's brutal economic climate, in which it is estimated that auto-part stores will soon become patronized only by the upper class, like antique stores, since more and more manufacturers of spare parts are going under. Studded with "historical interludes" that frame his own thinking in terms of government and societal repression and control, Alcalay makes an urgent plea to take heed of the lessons of the past, otherwise our freedom to think and feel will be inexorably stripped from us. Will poetry survive? Is it already on the scrap heap? In the middle of a prolonged fast from poetry, having written almost none since 2001, Alcalay discovers a new freshness in his engagement with the poetry (and, it seems, the jazz) he first encountered when he was young and impressionable, way back when. I'm tempted to read this as an escape almost from what he terms the false or surrogate debates that have engulfed our intellectual life in a miasma of mud. What winds up happening in his book is that different forms rise up, take shape, reconfigure almost in the way of the golem, to rise up and pull into one being such disparate historical— and what might nearly be called "unhistorical"—events as the World Trade Center attack on the one hand, the death of poet John Wieners on the other, into the form of a diary that seems to describe not only today but yesterday and tomorrow as well.

Message to Love: The Isle of Wight Festival 1968 – 1969 – 1970
by Brian Hinton

★★★★☆
A Poet's View of the Festival World

March 24, 2009

I was having a reaction to the hyperbrilliant and fully theorized rock criticism of the present era, having read one too many of those 33 1/3 books, and I needed something with a mindless, laidback feel. Did I ever get it in this, Brian Hinton's guide to the first three Isle of Wight festivals of the 1960s, titled, like Murray Lerner's documentary film of the 1970 festival, after a Jimi Hendrix number played during his set. "Well, I travel at the speed of a reborn man. / I got a lot to love to give / From the mirrors of my mind, / I sent a message to love." Hinton expands on Hendrix's lyrics to show the appeal of these enormous rock festivals to the youth of the 1960s, and how that love went geometric over the course of the three years in question. The first festival was a homegrown affair that boasted the first UK appearance of the then red-hot Jefferson Airplane in its *Surrealistic Pillow* days—and the first light show seen over there. UK bands included the brilliant folk-based Fairport Convention and the *S. F. Sorrow*–era Pretty Things. The second festival exploded after the three knucklehead brothers who ran things for the festival corporation had the bright idea to ask Bob Dylan, sidelined since a mysterious motorcycle accident in the summer of 1966, to return to the stage at the Isle of Wight, and oddly he agreed.

The Beatles came to stay with him in his rented IOW HQ, and the attention of the world press hovered over the quiet island to see what was happening. The actual concert was, for Dylan, a muted affair, even with the *Big Pink* Band, but Hinton gives it his best shot and makes the reader wish he had been there. The third festival was the death knell, but what a way to go! It was the final appearance for both Jim Morrison and Jimi Hendrix, and so many hippies refused to pay the entrance fee that the organizers were forced to declare the proceedings a free festival. There would never be another week like it, for all of its crazy misguided eclecticism. Concertgoers were supposed to appreciate Ian Anderson, Joan Baez, Miles Davis, Alvin Lee, and Melanie—that's a tall order. But somehow Brian Hinton's book makes it all seem not only possible, but idyllic. He is a poet and reminds us often that the Isle of Wight was Alfred Lord Tennyson's home, and notes that when Dylan was asked at the press conference "Why the Isle of Wight?" he actually cited Tennyson. Cool or what!

Les Girls (1957)
dir. George Cukor

Ladies in Waiting

March 30, 2009

Cukor was tempting fate giving his stylish musical a polyglot title like *Les Girls*, for half the audience isn't going to know what *les* means, unless they thought it was short for "lesbians." In fact it's a sort of sapphic fantasy in which Taina Elg and Kay Kendall are suing each other with the sort of venom that only ex-lovers can feel for each other, their husbands clearly accessories in their battle of the court-room. Weaving a London sandwich-board man in and out of the present-day action, wearing a sign that reads "What is Truth?" under-lines what is apparently the intellectual point, but the movie has a built-in weakness in that we can never really figure out what did happen, it just isn't possible on film. Was Kay Kendall an alcoholic in all three versions of the story? In none of them is she really amusing, but I'll just pretend that her performance must have cracked them up in the mid-1950s.

She is exactly the sort of actor Cukor loved, all style and elegance and yet human and imperfect, and her sharp little chin and huge eyes and those sharp cheekbones always make her worth watching, even if in some shots she's made up so much one loses track of what her face might actually look like. But if you ask me, Minnelli gave her a little more to work with in *The Reluctant Debutante*, not to mention all those British movies people loved her in like the car one. Taina Elg looks great too, especially in her audition costume, if you'll remember it's an audacious two-piece number in which it looks as though her body parts are falling out of flower baskets, very surreal. You can't even imagine how her dressers got it onto her! Finally Mitzi Gaynor is, well, I used to think she was the definition of mediocre, as maybe a third-rate Doris Day, but in this movie I was really struck by how alert she was, and how subtle (I can't believe I'm saying these things about, oh my goodness, Mitzi Gaynor!!!). Shall I give her another chance? Maybe in her other movies, but I can't make myself see *South Pacific* again, not in this lifetime. Gene Kelly? Mixed feelings, but whoever said that he was emotionally unavailable hit the nail on the head. Cukor gets five stars for his setups and his theatrical backstagery, and more stars for the bumpy multilevel charm of *Les Girls'* ramshackle flat, but the picture drags and we have to wait too long for the big payoff scene between Elg and Kendall. But they are hot stuff and this film should be required viewing for a course in Lesbianism in the Movies.

Chasing Darkness
by Robert Crais

★★★★★
His Best in Years

April 5, 2009

I completely had lost track of Crais after reading too much about Carol Starkey and about Joe Pike, a great sidekick but not a good hero, and then I was on my way to Buffalo, got to the airport late, and had ninety seconds to pick something schlocky out of the ever-reliable SFO newsstand, and when I saw *Chasing Darkness*, I said to myself, "Well, even if it isn't a good Crais, it's going to be appreciably better than anything else on this shelf," so I went for it.

Yeah, I'm a happy boy now because I'm here to tell you, it may be long and drawn out, but *Chasing Darkness* has action and thrills to spare, and more bite than Robbie Dewhurst's kitten Winston! The only thing I didn't exactly buy was that after a lifetime of private eye work, Elvis would be so shocked by the album of Polaroids he's confronted with early on in the novel's action. Yes, they're ghastly, but I still don't know why they compel him so. I know he chases darkness to bring more light into the room, but still, he has seen a lot worse and I could quote chapter and verse. Nor did I buy that Carol would endanger her career for Elvis in the precise way she did. She was always a little nuts but this is just crazy! Anyhow the book delivers, and there are some great shocks implanted in the action, one around page 220, another around 280, and the greatest of all when Elvis picks up someone else's cell phone and says hello.

Oh my goodness, I nearly jumped out of my seat (16C on a horrible Northwest flight for which they made me pay fifteen dollars to check a bag), and my head was going to bump the overhead compartment and contents would have shifted for sure—contents of my brain, that is! Crais forever! Never rule him out, he's not even down!

This Is the Army (1943)
dir. Michael Curtiz

★★★★★
If You Love Dada ...

April 23, 2009

George Murphy puts on a show in Yaphank to cheer up troops about to leave for France in World War I. We see him come back without a leg, hobbling around on the primitive prosthesis of the 1918 period. Ronald Reagan plays his son, rather a chip off the old block. Murphy's story is rather tragic though, since he had been a talented dancer and now has to sit on the sidelines while other, less talented soldiers get to strut their stuff. Suddenly it's World War II and Murphy gets the idea to reboot his old show for a new generation of soldiers. This movie does bring it home how weird it must have been to have another giant war with Germany just twenty years after the "War to End All Wars." In the new musical, *This Is the Army*, Reagan is a stage manager whose offstage plots are two, attempting to cheer up his dad and also to evade having to propose to the girl he loves, Joan Leslie, since it just wouldn't be fair since he is going off to war.

This Is the Army is probably the strangest musical I've seen in many years, and I recommend it to anyone interested in floating gender zones. From what I understand, the Warner Bros. producers who brought the long-running show to the screen tried to get rid of the drag numbers (at least a dozen in the original show), but Berlin put his foot down and so a lot of them remain. This movie definitely rivals *Paris Is Burning* for extravagance of drag invention and for a wild queer spirit running all the way through it from beginning to end. You can see Berlin's mind churning out numbers for every conceivable racial or ethnic group, and Sergeant Joe Louis, the heavyweight champion of the world, performs in a specialty act in one of the best—OK, he's not very graceful perhaps, but he seems like he's trying. LeRoy Prinz's choreography is stunning—not only the individual specialty numbers, but the massive formations of hundreds of GIs gathered onstage in synchronized movements. Shows back then employed jugglers, midgets, gymnasts, opera singers, every sort of showbiz performer was drafted by Uncle Sam, then apparently released to Warner Bros. to get this movie made. And Kate Smith sings "God Bless America."

The comedy bits aren't funny as they used to be, but that's fine, they can now better be appreciated as bizarre performances of anxiety being played out on an international screen. Strong powerful men portray Lynn Fontanne and Alfred Lunt, then the king and queen of the serious Broadway stage, as self-absorbed and superannuated hams—what could the real-life couple have thought about their portrayals? (The guy who plays Lynn is exactly like Dolores Gray!) They claimed to have been honored, but these impersonators were going for the jugular. In any case, when I heard about the Amazon dustup or glitch in which hundreds of gay and lesbian titles were deranked earlier this month, this was the first item I checked up on because it is definitely the gayest thing on sale in all of Amazon. I was glad to see it remained available right through the whole fracas, vibrating with the lavender vibrations of a genuinely revolutionary object.

Parish Krewes
by Micah Ballard

★★★★★
Bringing It Back Home

May 23, 2009

Of all the poems in this book, a new collection by San Francisco–based poet Micah Ballard, I keep going back to one of the plainest, the aptly named "First Conjure." It is a simple poem in four couplets; the first line of each couplet is a single verb, an imperative, and the second line adds both an object and objective to the commands it responds to. Finally, a brief ninth line: "Wait, listen & call." That might well be young Ballard's lesson learned from life, for he has an enormous patience and what strikes this reader as the sort of ear a medium might envy. What he doesn't pick up through waiting, he apprehends through the call. Way down in Louisiana folks both fear and depend on the conjure, a supernatural spell or entreaty. *Parish Krewes* is that faculty motion. It waits, listens, and calls.

I didn't think it was possible to hear something new about New Orleans, but Ballard has hit upon a whole medley of methods for bringing it all back home. For one thing he does not shy away from the direct: if a hurricane hits the city, then a poem comes about to speak of it. (His social embouchure is keen.) That said, he is not averse to misdirection either, like the movie *The Prestige*, and many of his most enchanting poems reveal their secrets only after repeated readings. A lit cigarette flung from an open window tziganes into a pentagram. Magic appears on street corners, in coffins, in the dark eyes of the beloved.

I see a parallel between the way Micah Ballard's poems flow and tumble into one another, and the structures of language itself, and you could open *Parish Krewes* at random to any page to discover illustrations of what I can only hint at here. There's a strange willed concision to the thing, as though the poet has worked his voodoo and has signed the ashes with a single finger. Even the title seems to embody, in the space of twelve letters, as much local color as two nouns can handle. When he first started out writing, he seemed very much in the service of John Wieners, Robert Creeley, even Keats and Shelley, what you might call Eastern masters. And now that he is his own man, he is "vast & seeks also // foreign bellows."

Salvation Army
by Abdellah Taïa

★★★★☆
"Where Does It Come From, the Darkness of This World?"

May 26, 2009

I came to this book under the spell of Alistair McCartney's persuasive review in a recent issue of *Lambda Book Report*. (Part of it is reproduced above.) He had me all excited. And then when I got the book, I turned to Edmund White's enthusiastic preface and it was even more enthusiastic than what Alistair had written. But nevertheless, when I finally turned to Taïa's text, I found a different book entirely than the one the two great novelists had described to me. Were we all blind men, and *Salvation Army* the elephant in the parable? Yea, I think we are.

McCartney looks at the book as a version of the coming-out novel that was once a staple of gay writing, given new freshness by its unique setting and, perhaps, by the extreme subject position of its main character. White views it partly as a jeremiad against Western sex tourism. I kept reading through the whole thing and couldn't find either of those books; what I saw was the astonishingly frank story of a young boy who knows his feelings are an offense to society, but who persists in them anyhow. His incestuous love for an older brother—a brother much, much older, a brother old enough nearly to be the boy's father, his delight in the brother's company, in his fruity cologne, his body—is the book's core, and then there's another story tacked onto it about having two affairs with Swiss men, and how cold the Swiss guys are compared to the hot, passionate men of Morocco. But whole sections of the novel seem to have slid off the sides of the page, so that I close the book feeling a hunger for what has been left unsaid, unwritten, or censored, perhaps by the same self that has been so eager to detail the intricacies of Abdelkabir's butt in and out of those sexy black underpants.

Frank Stock's translation is pretty amazing, and you feel like you are right there, in Geneva's cold capital, on the hot beaches of North Africa, or wherever Taïa chooses to bring you. For me, *Salvation Army* just needed one more thing, can't tell you what exactly, in order to recommend it to you without reservation.

Doubt (2008)
dir. John Patrick Shanley

★★★★☆
III Wind

June 1, 2009

Saw this one under duress, since it looked kind of dumb in the trailer, and also the play had such a good performance in it by Cherry Jones I couldn't imagine anyone else playing Sister Aloysius. Well, the movie is slightly better than I had hoped. It is awful in a way, but sticks in your mind even weeks after seeing it, so it must have something, right?

It doesn't have subtlety, that's for sure. The scenes of Meryl Streep battling the wind are more laugh inducing than the combined efforts of Jim Carrey and Steve Carell, and you can throw in the Marx Brothers too. They must have suggested to Streep that she watch the silent classic *The Wind* with Lillian Gish and then ordered her to out-Gish Gish, with some Marcel Marceau thrown in too. I'm surprised she didn't pluck a flower and smell it, she is so hammy you have to love her. That, and the lights going out, are movie devices you hardly ever see today, more's the pity. In fact we don't have enough symbolism about Vatican II in general. I lived through the whole era, and in fact had an inappropriate relationship with a priest, without any of the wind coming down and whipping our garments around our faces. And it just gets worse and worse. At least Streep and Hoffman look like they're having fun, as does Viola Davis, much more pragmatic about letting her son carry on with an older man than my mom ever was, God rest her soul. Amy Adams on the other hand does more moral suffering than all the actresses in *Cries and Whispers* combined. Why she ever took the part I don't know, but it's lousy and so is she.

Don't hate me, *Doubt* lovers. I just call them like I see them. And remember, that was my T-shirt the priest put in my locker, and I've got a right to give my opinion of what was basically the story of my life if I were Black and teased.

The Gleaners and I (2000)
dir. Agnès Varda

Winsome

June 9, 2009

Agnès Varda could have gone the other route and turned up in her own films as an icy, chilling presence—all regal and pope-like, but instead she has made a name for herself as the world's most loveable, clownish senior. While they were alive, this was the title that was contested for decades by the previous contenders, Giulietta Masina of France and Ruth Gordon of the USA, but now it belongs solely to Varda, the magnificent scavenger of cinema.

The DVD of *The Gleaners and I* has some awesome special features, among them yet another great documentary: *The Gleaners and I: Two Years Later*, in which Varda-mania reaches its zenith. *2YL* is largely Varda's follow-up with some of the people she covered in part 1, but large sections of it focus on her fan mail and the way people love her. She has changed the lives of millions, and this pleases her no end. Varda shows us one anagrammatic-mash note in which the writer points out that the French words for *gleaner* and *angelic* are anagrams and both are about her. I expect this adulation helps soothe the psychic wounds to which she often returns in her documentaries, of aging and the disintegration of the body. I wonder, Does no one use a computer in France or Japan, or do they only send fan letters in the exaggerated handwriting that we in the US know best from the signature of John Hancock?

I Know Who Killed Me (2007)
dir. Chris Sivertson

★★★☆☆
Split Decision

July 24, 2009

Well, it took me eons to get through the whole thing, but I wound up admiring the style with which director Chris Sivertson challenges Lindsay Lohan to give it everything she's got in scene after scene of staged contempt, erotic display, and graphic takes of dismemberment and torture.

It's just hard to watch, that's all. Maybe in ten years it will seem like child's play, but as of 2009 the violence against women this film trades in is deeply disturbing, and if you ask me, probably pushed La Lohan closer over the edge when she had her famous breakdown. Whether she's playing Dakota or Aubrey, she's the same, but she has some good moments opposite Neal McDonough and Julia Ormond, who play her concerned parents, though McDonough himself evidently knew no one would be watching him anyhow. Ormond on the other hand does exemplary work as the mother, though apparently nobody told her she was in a horror film and she plays out the confused identities Lindsay Lohan performs as though the late Harold Pinter had written it just for her.

Would I watch it again? No way. And how she figured out who killed her, I'll never know, but life's too short.

Advanced Elvis Course
by CAConrad

★★★★★
As I Said Many Years Ago (Counting in Elvis Years)

August 3, 2009

Until I read this book, I too was afraid of the vibration of Elvis, but CAConrad is such a good Virgil he makes one feel safe, adored, and capable of feats of great spiritual power.

Advanced Elvis Course first travels to Graceland and then in a big sweep of daring brings the lessons of Graceland back home, to Philadelphia in this case, a city healed and renewed in that merciful glare.

Meanwhile the car radio soars with the final anthemic choruses of "It's Now or Never" and "Surrender."

Conrad has an open, Whitmanian optimism and sunniness and he's a sucker for kitsch, again like Whitman, but he's got a sense of humor about it, and all those who cross his path will find themselves laughing their way right through the lower chakras and beyond.

Is his tongue in his cheek? I hope—for the sake of American poetry, for our nation's tremulous soul—not.

The Happening (2008)
dir. M. Night Shyamalan

★★☆☆☆
The Wind Cried Mary

August 11, 2009

From the reviews I knew the movie was going to be a letdown, but we had fun watching it and got suckered in by the spooky, melancholy sound of the wind stirring the grass and the leaves at the top of the incredibly tall trees. From that standpoint the film's technical credits get high marks. I even liked James Newton Howard's score, but I have a weakness for overemphatic film music—at least I thought that Howard understood the plot of the film, possibly better than MNS himself.

TIRAMISU SPOILER AHEAD!

The movie made us examine our own lives as Plato urges us to do. We walked a mile in the other man's moccasins thinking that if a rare virus sprung up on the wind and made us try to kill ourselves, how would we do it? It's not as easy as it sounds! Sure, you could slide a hatpin out of your long hair and stab yourself in the throat with it, but most of us don't have that sort of hair ornament. You saw what happened when Philadelphia comes to a standstill and an armed cop falls to the ground, his pistol clattering on the cobblestones, and a woman picks it up, then the gun falls again, well, that gun gets a lot of use, it's because people are literally starving for ways to kill themselves. First off, I decided, I would smoke a carton of cigarettes and enjoy a pitcher of margaritas … then see what happened. Maybe a heroin overdose? In the movie we marveled how the characters managed to off themselves using just the tools at hand, like MacGyvers in reverse—I never would have thought of lying down on the lawn and letting a mower tear me to shreds … though jumping out of a building is a natural. Mark Wahlberg, John Leguizamo, Zooey Deschanel were all uniformly terrible, and Betty Buckley brought back memories of *Carrie*, where she played the girls' understanding gym teacher … Does she ever survive till the end credits in any of her movies?

Most of all I thought M. Night misplayed Zooey Deschanel's secret. We knew she was harboring a guilty secret, but why did it have to be something as banal as sharing a tiramisu dessert with Joey? Why couldn't they have had sex like most guilty lovers? Did he die for this dessert sin? Or is he still alive at the end of the movie? We were all ready for the twist ending in which it would be revealed that Alma's pregnancy was the result not of that one dessert date but of a long campaign to drive Mark Wahlberg mad with their deceit—so the twist ending would be "You told me you had dessert with him and now I found out you're having his baby!" "But you seemed stressed, otherwise I would have told you sooner, I just made up that part about the tiramisu."

I Went Looking for You
by Ruth Lepson

★★★★☆
Red Rose in the Back of the Mind—Bonnard Red
August 28, 2009

A writer new to me with a very simpatico view of the world, so that I sink into this work as if she were an old friend, catching up on shared points of interest on the best phone connection ever established. How does Ruth Lepson manage her effects, for whenever I was a boy and went to a magic act, that's what I asked my dad, pulling his sleeve till he gave me a hasty answer. And now that I'm a man, I respond in a similar way. Ruth Lepson speaks in the ordinary language of an American, with nothing difficult in her vocabulary. Even Anne Sexton and Sylvia Plath used vocabularies more elegant and Latinate. "I'm turning and floating," writes Lepson, in her new collection from feisty little BlazeVOX [books]. "My body tells me things. / But something in me says / the water's amorphous, deceptive, / I can't leave behind anyone who loves me." This is the final stanza of a four-stanza poem ("Reunion Dream," and if you knew how I hated dream poems ordinarily you would be surprised to see how far I made it in this one), and I see the line width stretch out, George Herbert–like, as the stanza progresses. There's a charming sort of docility about the final line, as though love itself made it stretch as long as it is, love or an eagerness to please. "My body tells me things." The body, haunted by revenants, assumes the stance of the other, and when the other speaks, even the water listens, "amorphous, deceptive." Meanwhile the original, sanctioned "I" of the lyric turns and floats, turns and floats, the way Tennyson used to on the Isle of Wight.

Later, "your mind must be turning," so I take it that the turn itself is integral to Lepson's poetics—turn of the earth, or the slow, eternal return of time and space? Maybe both, but she is committed to the detail of the very present moment, in all its luminosity. That involves a particular courtesy to the gerund—there's even one in the title of the book, a tip of the hat to the early Patti Smith and her "Redondo Beach"? ("I went looking for you / Are you gone, gone?") Later still she goes "looking for you" in a poem addressed to the departed spirit of Sexton—

there are also remarkable elegies, if that's not too strong a word, for Levertov and Robert Creeley. In "Clark Park" (Philadelphia? Detroit? Somewhere with trolleys), Lepson remarks, "I know if you touched me / I could relax. / I went looking for you, angry / at myself for that." The humble inward turning to the consonants, between "relax" and "angry," denotes a typical jump in Lepson's thought, where sound is always in the service of sense and here, oddly, all the better for it.

The Meaning of Matthew: My Son's Murder in Laramie,
and a World Transformed
by Judy Shepard

★★★★★
A World Transformed

September 18, 2009

He was very small, looked like he was thirteen or fourteen, and when eighteen-year-old Aaron Kreifels saw his body propped up against a fence, his mountain bike skidded across the road for it looked like a scarecrow, a "Halloween guy," Kreifels remembered. A tiny body, but soaked in blood, most of it under his head. By this time Matthew Shepard had been hung on that fence for nearly eighteen hours, his lungs gradually pooling with blood. How any mother could cope with the Laramie Police's findings I don't know, but it was up to Judy Shepard to take it all in without fainting, and she has written a book to try to find the meaning of Matthew—the meaning of his death, but also the meaning of his life, how did this all come to happen.

It is a disturbing and chilling account, but it's human. We come to wonder about the killers and their girlfriends and their families, and how drugs and poverty have chipped away at their moral sense. One of the killers robbed a Kentucky Fried Chicken of $2,500 (and "some desserts," adds Mrs. Shepard) and hid away in Florida to avoid the heat, then sneaked back when he thought it would be OK. Judy Shepard isn't what you'd call a natural writer, but she has given us something of a different order, the thoughts and feelings of a person devastated, and on top of it a person strong enough to pick up the pieces and do something that will mean something.

There's always a through line of something resembling guilt giving her narrative an edge of real feeling and conflicting pressures. The book opens up that way, herself living with her husband in the Middle East—so far away from Laramie that it takes her days to get back to her son's bedside. There was the puzzling and horrifying earlier incident when Matt was assaulted by several men in North Africa—again she asks herself, "Where was I?" Matt was complicated, too, and like a bird he couldn't be contained by parental worry. He had to do what he wanted to do, and he had to go where he wanted to go. In that one way, he was just like his mother.

Eloise in Paris
by Kay Thompson

★★★★☆
Memories of a Golden Youth

October 10, 2009

As an American boy growing up in rural France, there wasn't much for us kids to do, so we farmed a lot, played with the local *jeunesse*, and caught up on reading our American books a faithful family friend made sure we had plenty of. This woman, a sort of "good fairy" to a foreign-based US family, made sure that we each had our own copy of *Eloise in Paris*, and I have often wondered why my parents cut off contact with our benefactor shortly afterward. One by one all copies of this book were confiscated, though when I saw what was happening, I hid mine in a hollow hole in a large fig tree, where it sat until nature eventually made away with it.

In the meantime we gathered around at twilight and once again drank in the old story of Eloise, accompanied by her turtle and dog, and Nanny, go to meet Koki in Paris. Koki is the chauffeur of the *avocat* employed by Eloise and her mother. I always liked Koki, a scamp of a chauffeur with no fixed morals and a taste for cowboy movies. We kids determined that somehow we would get to glamorous Paris like Eloise, and see the Renault Dauphines whizzing like tops around the place de la Concorde, but somehow we never did.

However, Eloise made us feel like we had been there. She has a lust for life that still, after all these years, communicates itself to the reader. Will kids like these books today? I don't know. Eloise's attention to the high points of French cooking is "rawther" exaggerated for a little girl; it is like an issue of *Gourmet* magazine in a six-year-old's body, and look what happened to *Gourmet* magazine. Those were the days, my friend, we thought they'd never end, but they did.

Deflowered: My Life in Pansy Division
by Jon Ginoli

★★★★★
Crowd Pleaser

October 10, 2009

Jon Ginoli may not have been the best-looking guy in rock 'n' roll, nor the most talented musician, but he was cute and aggressive and a fantastic lyricist, and the success of Pansy Division never spoiled his basically right-on attitude. Nowadays it's hard to recreate all the handicaps an openly gay rock band faced in the late '80s, early '90s when Pansy Division was playing local shows like crazy. Even in San Francisco, straight kids were sometimes hostile and, when they were "tricked" into listening to the band at a show, could get upset and show it. For Ginoli & Co. were nothing if not in your face.

His memoir, *Deflowered*, accelerates this Rabelaisian mode, showing us that he was a late bloomer in a way: late to act on his nascent sexual feelings, late to leave the area where he had grown up, late to put together a band that would serve his vision. But once he had it all together, that pent-up energy found expression, and at the exact time that would be most propitious for him, during the so-called homocore days when, in the wake of ACT UP and Queer Nation, it really seemed as though a new gay and lesbian culture was being born and even better, conquering the world.

It might not have always been easy dealing with Ginoli (and his right-hand man, guitarist Chris Freeman), since the narrative arc in *Deflowered* is consistently bad-mouthing every drummer they play with. But he's so great one forgives him all the things he leaves out of this otherwise hard-hitting and fascinating tour through your pants.

The Mama Cass Television Program (1969)
dir. Sid Smith

★★★☆☆
Great Outfits and Costumes, but Cass Seems Nervous

October 28, 2009

Cass's TV variety pilot is great fun to watch, but in some ways also painful.

When Cass and Buddy Hackett were together, the camera cuts in close on the hands in her lap, and she seems like she's pulling her fingers apart, out of nervousness I expect, though she keeps her eyes on Hackett's. She seems like she must have been a wonderful listener; when she listens to Mary Travers sing, or Joni Mitchell play the guitar, she looks as if she is in awe. (Well, she had displayed this lovely quality in the *Monterey Pop* movie, where the camera catches her mouthing the word "wow" like a mantra.) I never liked Buddy Hackett, but he is excellent here, and don't fast forward through his scenes, he has that sort of broken-down Chaplin appeal that people misguidedly ascribed to Jackie Gleason. Maybe it was a little gauche of him to boast to Cass about how much weight he's lost in recent years: Does she look a little wounded, or fatigued, during this part of their interchange?

Bizarre also to see Cass, Mary Travers, and John Sebastian all in the same show. Each had been a significant part of a great pop group, but going solo is always fraught with peril, and you might say that none of them were ever as good alone as they were when they were in their groups. But you can see they each had style! Joni seems too smart and eccentric for TV, doesn't she, though she still thought of herself at least in part as an entertainer. She and Cass share a sequined, designer-hippie sense of style, while Mary Travers, with her long blond processed hair and her minidress of blue zirconium, looks like Nico in the days of the Silver Factory. Mary Travers's bangs were also copied from Nico. Goodness knows Joni had bangs, but Mary's continue right past her eyelashes! When it's her turn to sing, she rises up from her chair as though "I just gotta dance while I sing." Well, it's not really dancing but it is really '60s and you got to love it.

Another unfortunate note, Mama Cass's backing band is brilliant and soul inflected and all that, but it's weird that they were called "Hamfat." You know why.

And Party Every Day: The Inside Story of Casablanca Records
by Larry Harris (with Curt Gooch and Jeff Suhs)

★★★★★
The Party

October 31, 2009

No one in this book gets out alive, or so it seems, for Larry Harris and his cowriters have the scoop on everyone whether high or low, and most of them were quite high during the Casablanca years.

From a business point of view, the revelations here are mainly about how the company never was successful, despite a million-dollar promo campaign and a lot of money juggling on Harris's part. he was ordered to cook the sales figures for PolyGram to show many more sales of Casablanca products than actually occurred—this despite the fact that the returns would be coming in constantly to contradict his lies. Harris seems to think this is a standard business practice, but for his sake I hope the statute of limitations on fraud will prevent them from carting his butt to jail like Bernie Madoff! Neil Bogart characterized the Casablanca years as a time of "profitless prosperity," and that seems apt.

I enjoyed hearing how a group of Brooklyn-born salesmen with great ears for what would sell turned the industry on its ear by making a commitment to disco, of all things. The discovery of Giorgio Moroder and Donna Summer is an amazing story, but even the flops of Casablanca have their charm. Take for example the signing of Stallion. Ever heard of them? They were going to be Casablanca's answer to the Eagles, but when Harris asked their Svengali to make them sound more like the Eagles, he should have known right away it wasn't going to fly, since the producer, genuinely puzzled, asked, "Who are the Eagles?"

The Village People and Kiss are the other big names here, but every page has a good story about someone, usually revolving around "blow." "Blow" allowed Larry Harris, one of the plainest men in show business, to live the Hugh Hefner lifestyle with a revolving cast of available and beautiful Hollywood starlets. Thus he was living every man's dream, and never had to look at a mirror throughout the entire '70s. Go, Larry, go!

Marvelous Melba: The Extraordinary Life of a Great Diva
by Ann Blainey

★★★★☆
I Am Melba!

November 9, 2009

Nellie Melba became the first internationally known opera singer from Australia, and when she hit the top, she stayed there for forty years. Ann Blainey's biography is what they used to call compulsively readable, and will provide even those who thought they knew Melba with many new insights. Perhaps it might have reached five-star level had we learned more about Melba's music itself, but Blainey is not a musicologist per se and seems more interested in aspects of nineteenth- and twentieth-century performance style, and of course the progress of a flamboyant woman through the world, than she does about what made Melba so special as a singer.

That's OK, there is still plenty left to admire about this book. Melba was born Nellie Mitchell and even from birth seems to have been headstrong and willful, not content to stay on the farm and stay married to good old Charlie. Her treatment of her son, George, was even more cold, you might say—basically she just abandoned him and went on to Europe and England to further her career, though in later years, as Blainey shows, she became fairly obsessed with reconnecting with the boy she had left behind, and he did indeed come back to her in middle age. Melbourne, the town where she was born (as was Ann Blainey), was of two minds about her, pride and scorn mixed together. She was in some ways the victim of Australia's "tall poppy syndrome," wherein those who stand a little taller than the run-of-the-mill populace are put down and pilloried. But Melba loved Melbourne and, indeed, changed her name to remind people of where she was from. Her name was her way of keeping herself real, even when she went on to live the life of an international diva and take on more affectations than most opera stars before and since. People loved her though, because she never forgot her roots. She costarred with Caruso, with John McCormack, with her favorite Jean de Reszke, and in some of the most glittering productions of her day, but she always went home when she could, back to Melbourne. In this way she reminds me of my favorite pop singer, Kylie Minogue, whose career followed a similar path, back and forth from Melbourne. Well, Kylie is very different of course—excuse me, opera buffs.

Kings and princes adored Melba, and musicians loved her too. Early on she became a particular favorite of a generation of French composers whose works she triumphed in—Gounod, Ambroise Thomas, Delibes, many more. Saint-Saëns created an opera for her, *Hélène*. She tried singing Wagner though her heart wasn't into it, primarily because shifting markets wanted a singing actress in their opera now, following Wagner's conception of opera as total theater, a totalizing art form that would combine all arts into one. And oh how she loved her jewels! And yet we see that Melba fetishized her love of jewels and made it a prominent part of her press releases in part to imitate the earlier diva Adelina Patti.

Valiantly fighting rumors of facelifts, Melba met her maker in 1931. Thanks to Ann Blainey, something of her spirit is still alive, just as she herself predicted many years ago now. She shines.

Carnival: An Original Cast Recording

★★★★★
Cirque de Paris

November 11, 2009

When I was in high school, our drama department put on a musical every year, and this was the first of them I remember. Rival schools would stage famous musicals—*West Side Story*, *Oklahoma!*, *Guys and Dolls*—but the ones our teacher produced were musicals of—what?—the second rank—or third rank? Well, it strikes me only now that maybe he was paying less for shows like *Carnival* than his rivals were paying for *West Side Story*. But he told us he wanted to put on "fresh shows," shows that hadn't been spoiled by seeing them so many times. (In subsequent years we did *Take Me Along*, *Where's Charley?*, etc.)

But despite everything *Carnival* will always have a special place in my heart! It was the first time I was on stage, scared to death, playing some sort of circus freak way in the shadows, but I sang my heart out in the big opening number, "Direct from Vienna," swaying in quasi-Gypsy costume and acting giddy and crazy with performing excitement. The show itself, of course, is quite dark, but when you're fourteen, that's just the sort of thing one likes. The love story between Paul and Lili, I thought, could scarcely be improved on. (Liner notes in the new CD tell us that the novella *Love of Seven Dolls* is even darker, nearly Sadean in its weird, cruel enslavement plot.) I loved the puppets almost as much as Lili did. We had a leading lady without any of Anna Maria Alberghetti's charm and/or ethnicness. But she was great, and our Paul had a thrilling voice half the time, and the puppets were so cute! "Her Face" was to me the most beautiful love song ever written. OMG, what Mel Tormé does to it on one of the extra bonus tracks included here—he "swings" it to death, you just want it to be over.

After our show closed—well, it was only for two performances— our drama-teacher guy took us to New York to see the City Center revival with Victoria Mallory as Lili (and Karen Morrow as the Incomparable Rosalie). We all agreed, our high school had done it better.

Topic Sentence: A Writer's Education
by Stan Persky

★★★★★
A Cup Filled with Pencils

November 26, 2009

I bow down to Stan Persky in general, and my admiration for his work both in poetry and in prose has been a constant in my reading life for twenty years or so. *Topic Sentence* is just the sort of book I wanted from him: a big book, capacious, wide ranging, with an assortment of intellectual pursuits tempered, always tempered, by the inimitable personality. Which I can't really explain except to describe it as Socratic and humorous. The book seems like it's been cobbled together from articles written here, there, and everywhere, but the through line, as they call it in writers' programs, is often about the education of one man and by extension the ways in which we ourselves are invited to learn, by the culture, by the politics, and by the raw materials of nature and life that are handed to us.

He is always at the center, and charmingly so, the "topic sentence" of his own life. His memory for the strange circumstances attending it is strong, vivid, always filled with sensual detail and the ring of the truth. I don't know where Persky would be without it! History has left its track in his back, but I find that the more you read from *Topic Sentence*, the stronger your wonderment will be, for like the old saying goes, he brings history right up into the present moment in a way few educators can seem to manage. His account, for example, of the life and trials of Oscar Wilde ("Feasting with Oscar"), takes the very long view. We are with him as he manages to pry out of hiding the real story behind Wilde's double life, his ping-ponging back and forth between classes, that was at heart the real "trouble" that got him into Gaol. We learn that Wilde was seriously in love with Bosie, while Bosie was too much of a child, or too selfish a lad, to give Wilde back what he got. We learn how Wilde got trapped by his own pride (and by his nascent politics) into bringing the disastrous suit that pretty much ended his charmed life. But then what we don't expect is that Persky takes all this "historical" material and brings it still quick and panting right into our present situation, like one of Burroughs's "Wild Boys" tossing a still-beating heart onto the campfire of the guerrilla tribes halfway up the Atlas Mountains. "Not so much to propose a political agenda as to understand where we are," he writes. It is a Wilde, and a GLBT, struggle, transformed by Marxian theories of the law of uneven development.

2012 (2009)
dir. Roland Emmerich

★★★★★
End of Days

November 28, 2009

How did the Mayans know that the world would end in 2012? What made them so smart? These questions remain unanswered, on-screen just as in life, but for goodness sake, what does it take to make you guys give up five stars to a movie? This picture has everything, and then it has everything else piled on top of it like a big yummy sundae dripping with chocolate sauce and nuts. We went on Thanksgiving Day, traditionally the one time in the year when 50 percent of the audience is sleeping off a gigantic meal, yet this time around, people were screaming in terror and wonderment. Screaming and pounding their fists on their seats and clutching their neighbors even if you didn't know them from Adam. At that point none of us were worried about the likelihood of a Mayan prediction. The screen told us what was happening … The world was suffering from Earth Displacement … The inside of the earth became a microwave … Yellowstone Park turned into a volcano. There haven't been too many good movies set in Yellowstone Park, but let me tell you, those scenes there are unbelievably tense. I wonder if Yellowstone will suffer a dip in tourism because after seeing *2012*, you'd have to be crazy to visit there, just in case the Mayans were right!

John Cusack stars as a novelist whose book *Farewell Atlantis* has some eerie parallels with what's happening right underneath his feet. They never do explain why his book is so similar to the events of *2012*, but I figured that maybe he had a little Mayan predictory blood in him. What happened to Cusack? He was never an Adonis, but now it looks as though someone had punched him in the mouth at birth. What a mug, and yet, he underacts his way through a part which another actor might have botched utterly. There are scenes where he and Amanda Peet are trying to comfort each other and give the other one strength that are really beautifully done, but what's weird is that Peet, who has gone through the same ordeals as Cusack or nearly, still has every mg of her makeup on and her expensive haircut is still lovingly teased into just the right suggestion of earth-ending anguish, while Cusack just looks like hell. Maybe the audience wouldn't stand for it to see him with a plain woman, or even an average woman. Well, more power to the star system! On the Black side of things, we have Thandie Newton utterly exquisite as the art-consultant daughter, Laura, of the US president, Danny Glover, and she meets cute with a top geologist called Adrian (Chiwetel Ejio-for), and they are pretty evenly matched according to looks. Glover plays the US president as though he were shell-shocked going into the movie, with touches of Reagan's last days of dementia.

Apocryphal Lorca: Translation, Parody, Kitsch
by Jonathan Mayhew

★★★★★
Enhorabuena, Mayhew!

December 26, 2009

I bought this book to help me in ongoing research into Lorca's influence on US poets of the Cold War generation. It has repaid my investment many times over. Thank you, Professor Mayhew, for your invaluable guide through the myriad pathways of Lorca's influence.

Mayhew, alert as a caterpillar, knows where, when, and who was borrowing from Lorca's style during a dark and dangerous period of US history, plus he has a sense of humor about how awful some of this borrowing turned out to be. If translation is a two-way street, then there have been many head-on collisions in the name of love. But in general, we get a measured sense of how all of a sudden many of the New Americans were talking about "duende" without really knowing what it was. I understand that I myself, for example, will also never know what it is, as that knowledge is vouchsafed only one in every two million US citizens. It is the one thing that most people will never be able to understand. Even in Spain they don't really get it either. I have been working with a Spanish scholar, David Menéndez-Álvarez, who has steered me toward the instances in which Jack Spicer translated directly from Lorca's poetry, and Menéndez-Álvarez advised me, "Why not skip the whole duende thing." But Mayhew shows us how, for one reason or another, and for reasons not entirely divorced from the ongoing crisis of masculinity of the 1950s, the concept of duende became extremely important to this group of poets—mostly men, though Mayhew points out that Denise Levertov, Diane Wakoski, and Hilda Morley wrote with at least a glancing awareness of Lorca.

His list is a long one, but perhaps the most intriguing chapter of Mayhew is the coda, in which he acknowledges that Lorca's influence on US poetics appears to be drawing to a close. Where once everyone from Langston Hughes to Creeley to Frank O'Hara used him as their personal MFA program, today very few poets of note bother with the man. Is this a testament to the never-to-be-underestimated shallowness of our gene pool? Or is there a way in which, once more generally understood, a cult figure's mojo ceases to shine or vibrate? I have also thought that it might be a result of narrowcasting: now that there are actual experts on Lorca in the United States, people who actually know what duende is, the rest of us are just left feeling pretty inadequate. Until that moment, Mayhew has written a book that will stand the test of time, an authoritative survey on a controversial and protean subject, one infinitely twisty like a snake on the Andalusian plain.

Thank Heaven: A Memoir
by Leslie Caron

★★★★★
The Glass Slipper of Hollywood Fame

December 28, 2009

My friend the novelist Bruce Benderson author of *Pacific Agony* has been trumpeting this book far and wide, and he has never steered me wrong yet, so I opened my Amazon account and ordered it pronto. I have to say that it is one of the most evocative movie-star memoirs I have ever read.

Growing up during World War II in a middle-class family left open to the privations of war, little Leslie learned how to dance as a way of escaping the strange dreams of her mother, one of the oddest characters in all of nonfiction. The mother seemed to want to live Leslie's life for her: brother Aimery seemed to escape Maman's iron will due to his gender. Caron brings us backstage into her life of early stardom as one of Roland Petit's principal dancers: it is here that Gene Kelly apparently saw her and clapped his hands and voila! Caron and Maman were in Hollywood as the "guests" of MGM. As always, memoirs of the final days of Louis B. Mayer's MGM are always welcome, they are so bizarre and the men and women who passed through his rule came out the other end utterly changed (some for the better, of course). The collapse of the studio system took its toll on their identities, and Caron seemed to want to put away her toe shoes and study heavy dramatics under the tutelage of Jean and Dido Renoir, Christopher Isherwood, and the British wunderkind Peter Hall, whom she eventually married.

Mistake! Well, not so bad a mistake as her first husband, a wealthy eccentric from the Hormel family. Cultural differences and Hormel pride prevented Leslie until too late from discovering that her handsome bridegroom was a grade A nut! Peter Hall just comes across as small minded, jealous, and cruel, and yet now Caron can say she did love him and he did give her two wonderful children. Outside of that—pfui! She made a huge impression in the early '60s reinventing herself as the unmarried mother in a "kitchen sink" drama, *The L-Shaped Room*, and then she met Warren Beatty and it was "Peter Hall who?" Beatty brought her back to Hollywood and for a brief period they were the most glamorous couple in town. He poured cold water over her dreams, however, by laying stress on the fact that she could not be Bonnie to his Clyde (in the 1967 Arthur Penn movie)—not because she was French, but because she was so old! Tut-tut, and the next thing she knew he had replaced her with a Bolshoi ballerina, then Julie Christie.

Throughout, Caron's natural delicacy and humor battles with a newfound urge to tell her life the way it was really lived. Every page has some La Rochefoucauldian pensée on love, on death; and yet every page has some hot gossip about some star of the past one has just barely heard of. I never wanted it to end! Thank you, Bruce Benderson! And thanks, Leslie Caron.

Theatre Experiment: An Anthology of American Plays
ed. Michael Benedikt

★★★★★
Exciting Manifesto

December 28, 2009

Possibly the best anthology of American poets-theater work ever done, Michael Benedikt's *Theatre Experiment* has it all. Its focus is including an absolutely up-to-the moment panorama of the scripts that were interesting actors, audiences, and directors at what seemed to be a crucial juncture for the American stage—the birth of off-Broadway and off-off-Broadway (1967). It was a time when Broadway itself seemed in danger of losing its hold on the populace due to escalating costs and a star system gone berserk (and a drying up of traditional sources of new material), but at the other end of the economic spectrum, a whole world of experimental theater was making itself heard.

This anthology follows the call of the great US modernist Thornton Wilder, still alive and productive in the mid-'60s but a man who, like Jeremiah, had been preaching change for decades. The theater he had in mind would, he said, "capture not verisimilitude but reality." Benedikt goes back to Wilder, and his poetic contemporaries like Gertrude Stein and Wallace Stevens, and includes some of their best work here, but then goes on through the decades all the way back to Ring Lardner's parodies of European surrealist and expressionist tendencies, E. E. Cummings's *Santa Claus* from 1946, Paul Goodman's *Birthday* play from 1940, and on to the off-Broadway sensations of the moment like Jack Richardson and Rosalyn Drexler. Performance work is not neglected either, so Allan Kaprow's happenings and Carolee Schneemann's notorious *Meat Joy* find their way into these pages. Some of the work will be familiar to you (Robert Lowell and Kenneth Koch deliver what amount to anthology set pieces) and some will definitely not, or at any rate works like Robert Whitman's *Flower* and the "poem plays" of Ruth Krauss were delightful surprises to me.

Tiresias: The Collected Poems of Leland Hickman
by Leland Hickman, ed. Stephen Motika

★★★★★
Cd Shed Rage Shd Love Come

December 31, 2009

Nightboat Books got together with Otis Books / Seismicity Editions to produce this handsome volume of Leland Hickman's collected poems, and you know, I can't really believe this is happening! Two years back, at the Orono Conference in Maine, editor Stephen Motika spoke of his plans to edit a complete Hickman book; he, Motika, certainly is too young to have known Hickman personally or to have participated in the network of Southern California–based magazines Hickman edited. Perhaps he was the perfect person to take on this task then, but I wondered how he had stumbled onto Hickman's writing at all. As the poet and scholar Bill Mohr explains in an informative afterword, the difficulty of establishing Hickman's reputation lies chiefly in the very fugitive publication of his work, small presses, small editions, a circle of influence that was more interested in his editing projects than in his poetry perhaps. Timothy Liu printed "Yellowknife Bay" in an important anthology of gay experimental poetry, *Word of Mouth*, but that was about all of Hickman that was easily accessible.

As we discover, other reasons caused Hickman to put his own work on the back burner, and it sounds as though while we were all waiting for a successor to the one book, the *Great Slave Lake Suite*, Hickman was actually not writing much of anything at all. Editing *Temblor* and maintaining, in the days before email, a vast correspondence with many of the world's most innovative poets ate up his time, and of course so did AIDS. Motika produces a few "new" pieces (of very high quality), but don't go looking to this new collection for lots and lots of new material; instead, the value of the book is twofold, it returns to print the major work of an interesting poet, and in addition it simplifies and makes legible, by rearrangement, the order and the valences of this work.

It is a prophetic, shamanic work fueled by rage, grief, and sudden bursts of homosexual feeling. Hickman lived in a dangerous age in dangerous cities, and he was punished, imprisoned, institutionalized for his penchant for public sex. A private story makes itself felt through the densest and most lyrical parts of his poems, something to do with his dad, an intense Oedipal love-hate thing like Raymond Massey slapping James Dean in Kazan's film of *East of Eden*. In one excruciating passage the father strips the son to douse him with a burning liquid to rid him of crabs, souvenirs of the teenager's uncontrollable need for sex with strangers. Hickman's poetry often seemed to me to be a queer amalgam of Ginsberg, Charles Olson, and something of Swinburne in him, a masochistic drive that spits the words out over the page (many lines begin with the single word "o," not the uppercase "O" of Keats, but just a tiny little mouth remembering) and creates a portrait etched in acid. And like William Burroughs's *Wild Boys*, his memories seem to reach back to a prewar paradise of roadsters, red-tiled public toilets, outhouses with rattlers twisting in the Pasadena sun. The speaker derives power from the scopophilia that makes him anxious to see, to watch, the forbidden accidentally exposed, in a dramatic rehearsal of his own early abuse.

That makes *Tiresias* sound sensational, and Mohr advises us not to think of Hickman's writing as "confessional" in any shape or form. Hickman's sophisticated, alienated use of language allows him to revisit American trauma, by endowing the primal with a series of complicating screens and taxonomies. I don't know, it still seems confessional to me, why there are even scenes of the child Lee Jr. going to confession, confessing the sins of the child. "Absolve, absolve him." This new book invites us into a dark wet cave where all the most exciting and painful things are happening all the time, awake and in dreams. Somewhere there's a whisper, "Sonny, hush, stop dwelling on it," but the roar in one's ears drowns out that quiet voice.

5198 Ferrara Latin Brief
by Clever Underwear

★★★★★
Clever Isn't the Word for It!

January 1, 2010

Top scientists collaborated on the design for this product in two teams, meeting daily for three weeks. One team worked on the crotch and pouch fabric, producing a cotton-spandex blend that was more or less like some other sort of underwear you might buy, but for the huge tentlike monolith in the front of the underwear molded to show off your package. The other team took responsibility for the remainder of the underwear, the sheer nylon and spandex blend that will remind you of an old-time nurse's white stockings. Thin slips of a hardier material are sewn in (or perhaps pressed in with nuclear tape) to form the natural ends of the leg openings. And the waistband tells you "Clever," in appealing black letters. Should you manage to get someone to give you these for Christmas, thank them kindly and then make your own way to the dressing room, for it will take you a good fifteen minutes for your eyes to stop popping out of your head.

Once again, scientific underwear design brings us a future in which you seem to be wearing two things at once, neither of them very flattering, but together they create a wily, synchronic lilt that as you rub your thighs together, will insure a cottony susurration audible from the building next door. Sort of a white noise, very much à Lou Reed's *Metal Machine Music*.

To get them off your hips, you really have only to wear them until you're tired of them. In public and semipublic places, whether it be a beach in Malaysia or the penthouse roof of a hot Madrid nightclub, they will be your tickets to success, if not happiness. Somewhere, a lone Lycra molecule will be smiling.

30-Inch Teardrop Christmas Swag with Apples, Holly, and German Ivy
by Good Tidings

★★★★★
When in Doubt, Go with the Swag

January 1, 2010

I wanted to get the kids some swag for the holidays and thank goodness didn't look for the reviews that accompany Good Tidings! I might have gotten so discouraged it would have been a terrible Christmas for all of us in our group, kids and adults alike. Goodness knows 2009 has been a terrible year, what with economic foreclosure, broken promises, worry about jobs and careers: I feel sorry for the children is what. My kids have a thing for swag, always have, maybe comes from a special place in their hearts and a time when, as itinerant festive merrymakers, we would take them from town to town at Christmastime to sing carols in front of happy and well-off familes' town houses in the nicer parts of town. Sometimes the snow would be falling and the kids, who had seen snow only on TV, would watch like angels in wonderment as the cold white flakes covered the holly and the ivy.

Now here it comes back again in swag form. For those of you who have missed out on the joy of swag, it is an agricultural product made from living firs and other decorations. I have seen them threaded with miniature gold horns and harps, but here it is just Mother Nature speaking—holly, ivy, and a few apples for good measure.

The kids have always enjoyed a nice apple. Many a Christmas morning they would rub the sleep from their eyes and then plunge a greedy little hand into the very bottom of the Christmas stocking hung from the dinette with care, to find the prettiest apple available in stores. Now all this goodness is available in season no matter what part of the country you're from (we're in San Francisco). It's shaped like a teardrop and may indeed bring a tear to your eye if you have any heart at all, and remember, Christmas is for the children. When in doubt, go with the swag.

For the Thrill of It: Leopold, Loeb, and the Murder That Shocked Jazz Age Chicago
by Simon Baatz

★★★★★
Chicago Summer

January 4, 2010

I remember my great-grandfather telling us what it was like to live in Chicago in the period between the death of little Bobby Franks and the arrest of the two killers. This tense period fortunately lasted only a week or so (maybe ten days), based on some forensics work involving the glasses Leopold had left behind him in the marshy grasses of the culvert. The air, my grandfather said, was still like glass, you could barely breathe, even at night, and everyone seemed to be looking over their shoulder. There was an outpouring of offers to help from the Gentile community to the hard-hit Jews of the Chicago area, and then once the arrests were made, and the Christians learned that two Jewish boys had murdered "one of their own," tensions blew sky-high. Simon Baatz discusses in detail how an ecumenical policy wasn't going to be working. Why, he asks, did this murder hit people where they lived? How did it become the crime of the century?

The killers were wealthy young men who did not need the $10,000 demanded in ransom, and thus the "motiveless malignity" perceived in the brutal slaying was itself a factor in the horror. The senselessness of the crime seemed to rhyme, Baatz argues, with the general loosening up of moral and social structures that the "Roaring '20s" ushered in. In general Baatz works from a journalist's precision and accuracy toward a deeper historical and cultural analysis.

Like Tom Kalin's film *Swoon*, or *Rope* for that matter, Baatz's book doesn't hesitate to "go there" in terms of the two young killers' sexual relationship. It would be hard to say who was the dominant one, so intertwined were their fantasies and their needs (and their privileges, as far as that goes). Sometimes you'd think it was Loeb—the ostensibly cuter, more popular one—but sometimes Leopold emerges as a true "power bottom," manipulating the S/M drives of his partner for his own satisfaction. Leopold told court-appointed shrinks that he envied every scrap of food or swig of water that Loeb took in, for food and water were getting closer to Loeb's wonderful body than he, Babe Leopold, ever could. What I hadn't known until reading this book is that the murderous pair were also suspected of a slew of other heinous crimes. Oddly, Baatz doesn't seem to take a stand on their involvement one way or another with any of these crimes. But I'm thinking yes, at least one of them can be pinned to Leopold and Loeb. It just follows.

The Girl on a Motorcycle (1968)
dir. Jack Cardiff

★★★★☆
Almost Forgot *le* Skiing!!!

March 15, 2010

Marianne Faithfull is exquisite, but as other reviewers have hinted she does not take easily to a motorcycle. She gets better as the movie goes along, but until then her voice-over is way, way embarrassing when she speaks of her passion for the motorbike and how it makes her free and how her husband, the sap, would never understand her. At times the v-o reaches heights and depths Marguerite Duras might have envied, and that's not entirely a compliment. Faithfull is always wonderful to look at, and Jack Cardiff must have been physically enamored of her, he makes her look so sexy. I loved seeing her in that 360-degree pan and I wondered how this was accomplished in the age before computer-generated effects, likewise for the opening circus nightmare in which Faithfull, as the unfaithful bride Rebecca, is shown standing on the back of a cantering horse parading around a one-ring circus, while Alain Delon in ringmaster garb snaps the leather off of her body piece by piece. I'm like "How is this happening?"

I don't remember where Marianne Faithfull's ancestors came from, but this is one international coproduction where you're thinking "Too bad she has to pretend to be French in this—or is she English? Or German, or Swiss?" She doesn't really try to be anything other than Marianne Faithfull in leather. Her husband wasn't too bad, except modern orthodontics would have given him perhaps a half an inch more gum: when he pulls up his lip you see no gum at all, just teeth the length of piano keys. Alain Delon, as the professor Rebecca falls for, is charming when he wants to be, callous when he wants to be, and always cute as a Beatle. His looks would be popular all over again today. He could play on *Gossip Girl* with that remarkable face. No wonder Romy Schneider broke her heart over him, Nico too, Visconti as well. Is he still alive? We know that Marianne roughened up her image to gain critical viability, did he have to do the same?

Cardiff died within the last few months, aged ninety-four. (The new issue of *Cinema Retro* has a cool interview with him regarding his work with Errol Flynn on the never-finished *William Tell* film.) The movies he directed, those of them I've seen, are a mixed bag, but in *The Girl with a Motorcycle* he brings to the project the same passion for gorgeous women that distinguished his contributions to others' films, including *The Red Shoes*, Marilyn Monroe in *The Prince and the Showgirl*, Leslie Caron in *Fanny*, and of course Ava Gardner in *The Barefoot Contessa* and *Pandora and the Flying Dutchman*. *The Girl on a Motorcycle* isn't perhaps very dramatically satisfying, but it is a great showcase for his star.

Oh, the ski-chalet scene—ten stars! And Faithfull's Lanvin wardrobe—a knockout!

John Wayne: American
by Randy Roberts and James S. Olson

★★★★★
Outstanding Achievement

March 30, 2010

A few years back I reviewed an inferior book on John Wayne and lamented publicly why one of the greatest Hollywood stars had never received proper biographical attention. To my delight, a helpful reader wrote in and recommended this book so strongly that I rushed out and bought it. I'm no conservative by any means, and this book is very up front about its conservative politics, but I can recommend it without question to anyone, no matter what their political stripe.

In fact to me it seems only the gung-ho preface really makes a case for conservatism. You could read the whole book without detecting an ideological message of any sort. It's puzzling. In fact, I had a moment of liberal guilt when I imagined a scenario in which authors Roberts and Olson constructed a well-nigh perfect biography, then perhaps failed to find a regular publisher, resorting only at the end to hooking up with a conservative press that required them to concoct a flag-waving preface. Is it really true, as they claimed, that a liberal cultural elite has "marginalized John Wayne, the brightest star in the pop culture firmament"? Gee, I hope not! Roberts and Olson go the whole distance with Wayne, showing how he responded to the shifting cultural changes in the US, showing for example how Wayne turned against Jane Fonda when she went to Hanoi, but forgave her only a few years later, going so far as to bestow her the Golden Apple Award voted her by the Foreign Press Association. So he was never a cultural monolith and was often capable of surprising turns, both ideologically as well as on the screen.

Roberts and Olson give us a man bafflingly devoted to John Ford, who seemed to think he had the right to abuse the Duke just because he had discovered him way back when. There was something a little masochistic going on in John Wayne's soul, he seemed not only to suffer but to welcome Ford's abuse, losing countless poker games to him, never once letting the old man know he was acting the fool. The Ford-Wayne relationship has been covered dozens of times, of course, but Roberts and Olson make it new all over again, with a savvy combination of candid interviews and trenchant analysis. They shine a powerful light on all aspects of Duke's career, from his three marriages to his guilt over his deferment during World War II to his slump in the late 1950s, a period when it seemed he just didn't care anymore. Struggles with studio bosses, with critics and audiences, everything looks brand new again under this cool, steady, biographical focus. They don't make Wayne a plaster saint; at the same time, the multidimensional profiling gives us the illusion of a 360-degree pan, as though we could reach out and touch the man.

I saw only one little section that left a bad taste; in their section on the production of *Hondo*, they see fit to carve up poor Geraldine Page like few actresses have ever been carved up. According to Roberts and Olson (largely following the memories of Mary St. John, Wayne's personal secretary), Page slept around, drank heavily, smelled like nothing on earth—and she was a liberal too, of course. In this account Page was so blowsy "even Ward Bond wouldn't take advantage of her availability." After burning her at the stake for four pages, suddenly the authors switch to Page's point of view in a personal interview which reveals her in a bizarrely different light, as a charming, affectionate, sober, insightful witness. Roberts and Olson, have you treated the late Geraldine Page with the good faith anybody deserves? No, I think not—one shoddy episode in what is otherwise a biographical triumph.

Petals of Zero Petals of One
by Andrew Zawacki

★★★★★
"Unevensong" as Delimited Space

April 1, 2010

I've been reading the three poems of *Petals of Zero* for nearly a year now, and I still haven't plumbed their depths, I know. I'm beginning to think that for me *Petals* is going to be a lifelong project, for something about them resists the limpid, surface dipping-into that I take away from most modern works of poetry, even my own. At first when I started to read the book, which opens with a long poem in honor of Georgia—the state—I was all prepared for a Johnny Mercer experience, a reassuring and pleasurable nostalgia. I get that a little, but right away my anticipations were blunted by a call of something deeper and more perdurable, like a man falling down into a pit of ashes and coal. A salutary wake-up call, and as I read it, a lesson in civics and economics from one who, like the old masters, has thought hard about such things and found a progressive line through them. "All things that are unlit Georgia / black like lapis in a quitted room / the feedback Georgia / the anvil's hymnal / a dial tone looped in a flophouse Georgia." You can see just from these five lines that Zawacki is not content with one time or place, for his vocabulary flip-flops almost painfully between a King James sort of diction and a Britney/Janet/Kylie fascination with modern technology (like "dial tone" and "feedback") (come on, wasn't "Feedback" the last great Janet Jackson single?). And beyond the wide spectrum of allusion (and register), a subtle music knits all this empty space together. Listen, you can hear it in the gnarled prosodics of "lapis in a quitted room" versus "looped in a flophouse Georgia."

When you call a book *Petals of Zero Petals of One*, even a dolt like me knows it's something about digital vs. analog, but binaries appear along the trellis of Zawacki's poems like bright blossoms, always in pairs. "The empress and the outcast." "Oar stroke, key stroke." "Gauntwater and brittlewhite." "Talcum code & piston." Let me study up on this some more; in the meantime, I can safely say that Zawacki is among the more interesting poets published by the unpredictable Talisman House of New Jersey.

223 Multipurpose Duct Tape (Dark Green, 3 in. × 60 yd.)
by Polyken

★★★★★
Duct Tape Special

April 21, 2010

I was impressed by the manufacturer's claim that "this product's actual size is 72 mm × 55 m. This tape is typically cut to width from log rolls so most sizes ship on a plain white core." I've used enough duct tape in the past to know that although many manufacturers claim they're cutting to width from log rolls, it's not always the case. Duct tape's a funny thing, isn't it? No matter what you're using it for. I like Polyken as a brand and I always like products cut from logs ... When I was in shop class in high school, they used to call me "the Log Lady," and one time it was my birthday they brought me an ice cream cake shaped like a log! So I ordered several rolls of the dark-green 223, as you see here, and when it came I went a little crazy with the back of my refrigerator ...

And also I had the common problem of having three cats (of my wife's) who run around the kitchen sometimes knocking down the upright broom and dust mop much to my annoyance. Problem licked with Polyken! I just applied a few inches of that thick, log-derived polymer on either side of the broom handle, basically taping it to the wall. Mop too. One caveat, but this is something all duct tape users know, if you are actually taping yourself, or another human being, watch out, that tape stings when you peel it off, so save the bare skin by inserting strips of linen or cotton underneath, and save yourself some swearing down the line.

It has a nice aroma just sitting in my shop cellar. I keep thinking it wouldn't be inappropriate in my top dresser drawer, if I ever run out of potpourri—again, a nice mixture of clean, sweet, unearthed log, and maybe something a little chemical like air freshener.

Just Kids
by Patti Smith

★★★★★
Dancing Barefoot

April 22, 2010

A very kind young friend knew I was going to New York and pressed this book on me. Stephen said that he hadn't planned to like it as much as he did. I too felt ambivalent and probably wouldn't have read the book, only he was so adamant that I would like it, so I tossed it in my carry-on and spent the next five and a half hours high in the sky, sinking into Patti Smith's memories like a warm bath.

I suppose she must have a certain amount of survivor's guilt, and it was strange to find out that as a child she had another little girlfriend who had polio, with an enormous pile of comic books and other beautiful things, and Patti kept something precious after the girl died, by just never giving it back. Similarly she treasures the things that Robert Mapplethorpe left her—or that she wound up with. She seems to have a wonderfully vivid memory for details— all the tchotchkes she and Robert accumulated, the details of every item of clothing, hats, shoes each wore. I thought of them as a pair of magpies, picking up (or picking up on) everything bright and sparkly—or dirty and dangerous, in Robert's case. Smith presents herself as a totally postmodern simulacrum of an artist, an amalgam of Rimbaud, Jagger, Joplin, Genet, every romantic artist she ever read about or sniffed out. I guess she might have turned out awful, but somehow this combination of borrowed traits produced a uniquely arresting musician and songwriter, many of whose songs still sound fresh today.

Finally we find out the truth about her love affairs with Sam Shepard, Todd Rundgren, Jim Carroll, Allen Lanier, and with Mapplethorpe himself. In this touching memoir she writes with both gravity and humor about her hard times, and when Robert gets AIDS, she is genuinely startled, as if finally in the presence of the great mystery she had chased for thirty years or more.

I hope she writes a follow-up book that explains the other great lacunae of her life, why she quit at the top and retired to become a married lady. It's none of our business I suppose, but her disappearance into Detroit doomed thousands and thousands of fans into a whole decade of head-scratching and lamentation. (And when she came back, she wasn't really herself again.)

The Collected Poems of Theodore Roethke
by Theodore Roethke

★★★★☆
High Spirits

April 27, 2010

A friend loaned me *The Collected Poems of Theodore Roethke* when I was trying to compile a program of poems related to the painter Morris Graves, who is having a centenary exhibition of his work this year in San Francisco. I had never really studied up on Roethke, even though my teachers in graduate school were keen on him, but they were keen in a certain way that left one thinking "He may be great, but Robert Lowell is miles ahead of him." Or, "Between them Lowell and Elizabeth Bishop are doing everything poor Roethke tried to do, but with a solid East Coast grounding of reality." It was still an age when the suicide of poets meant something. Lowell and Bishop were both still alive and working, and every time Lowell came by our campus (I never met Bishop), you could see him growing nuttier and nuttier, and that was the way things were in the 1970s.

Anyhow, Roethke was relegated to a lower, West Coast brand of confessionalism that hadn't the classical rigor of his Eastern counterparts. He was about to do some good work—when he died—was the general feeling. Now, as I read the work, much of it for the first time, I wind up thinking that maybe the naysayers were partially right. Roethke's diction seems clotted and strange, a byproduct of his attempt to "do" Yeats and Blake and Hopkins in American accents. Sylvia Plath does it too, but from her it sounds vaguely natural, like she thought in metaphysics. Roethke's "Praise to the End!" is emblematic of the problems a reader encounters while trying to love the guy. "It's dark in this wood, soft mocker," it begins. "For whom have I swelled like a seed?" You can almost hear "Daddy" coming around the corner. "Bumpkin, he can dance alone. // Ooh, ooh, I'm a duke of eels. / Arch my back, pretty-bones, I'm dead at both ends. / Softly softly, you'll wake the clams. / I'll feed the ghost alone. / Father, forgive my hands." As a matter of fact, you can get used to this kind of thing, and in fact positively savor the whole stew of infelicities, the raw and the cooked heated together like a tuna melt. The humble and the grand, the high and low. It's sort of an absolute binary that TR seems hellbent to break out of, but he always takes the high road eventually.

"Where are you now, my bonny beating gristle, / My blue original dandy, numb with sugar?" At moments like this I pause, feeling irritated, like Travis Bickle. "You talking to me?" Nevertheless, it is a book of great historical interest, and maybe you too will feel a little intoxicated by the end of it.

The Black Automaton
by Douglas Kearney

★★★★★
Hard to Breathe Nights

April 28, 2010

I went to a recent reading in Oakland in which Douglas Kearney read from his new book, *The Black Automaton*. Wow! What a show-man, he came in and tore the place up with his exciting readings—well, really performance showcases—that made full use of his many voices. In fact he was so fine it made me wonder, "Yeah, but what about reading the book, will the book still be good without this tremendous theatrical energy pushing it alive like a fire lit under the stage?"

It is a book fueled by music and by sight, and these elements speak freely within Kearney's pages which, he told us, he had designed himself. He is like the Orson Welles of poets, starring in, writing, directing, producing, composing the score, and here drawing and detailing the entire thing. Good going, for even if one or two details look askew, the book profits from the organicity of its concept and the polish with which the tiniest detail is buffed up. On racial matters, about which experimental poetry has had a checkered history, we turn to Kearney for a brilliant new viewpoint. Folk tale, fairy tale, hip-hop, legendary materials from a huge swath of cultures and coteries he has brought together, like a master weaver, all the colors of the night and day, but this metaphor suggests an easy silken road, and the actual experience of "reading" the book (including deciphering some of the concrete-poetry sections in which, for example, there's a page on which the words "blowing down" look to be repeated, stamped on each other, superimposed dozens of times, with little tributaries of other words floating away from the general explosion) isn't always so easy. I felt a little twinge going in, not knowing my early-'80s rap lyrics as I should, nor the contemporary Saturday-morning cartoons out of which some of this diamantine music has been mined. Here it is, and I wonder what it looked like when the judge for the National Poetry Series, Cathy Wagner, picked it out of the pile on her desk, of all the other semifinalists she had to read.

Oh, what was that Keats poem about first seeing something great? And the subject feels like a conquistador? Somehow in the midst of reading *The Black Automaton* one will tingle with that similar sensation, reprovable or not. Let me conclude by saying that you don't need the man himself to make his book a sensational event in your life.

Tau, and "Journey to the End"
by Philip Lamantia and John Hoffman, ed. Garrett Caples

★★★★★
"Blueness of Crows"

May 1, 2010

Invited to read at the Six Gallery reading of October 1955, surrealist Philip Lamantia declined to read any of his own poems, and instead read, from an onionskin manuscript, pages of an unpublished collection that his late friend, John Hoffman, had left behind. Editor Garrett Caples, who knew Lamantia in his final years, and who shepherded his papers into the archives of the Bancroft Library at UC Berkeley, posits that the decision to read Hoffman might have been the lucky byproduct of another decision Lamantia made—to reject the poetry of *Tau*, his then-recent project, in the face of a volcanic conversion (or reconversion) to Catholicism. This has the effect, for me at least, of showing Lamantia's human side, one prone to snap judgments and error just like anyone else.

Of course it was an accident, or nearly so, that made the Six Gallery reading a famous event in poetry history, thus pinning, like a fixative, John Hoffman's name into position, and yet it has been a curious immortality, hasn't it, since no one has actually seen any of the poems in question until now. This City Lights Pocket Poets edition reunites the young men who bonded together in the late 1940s in North Beach with such passion and vigor, by printing all of Hoffman's extant poems with the manuscript that Lamantia was working on in the mid-1950s, poems he recanted but, tellingly, never actually destroyed. *Tau* turns out to be one of Lamantia's most interesting achievements. From the moment it begins, it plunges us into the mind of one who saw the way Tanguy painted, in a poetry of edges, splinters, riven landscapes still crackling with dead energies. I read these poems while the TV showed us the footage of Eyjafjallajökull, the volcano in Iceland, and I clutched the book harder. Half horror, half sublimity, the features of *Tau* take a long time to emerge from the smoke cloud. "His color is green green, / to distend him from the earth," writes Lamantia in "The Owl." "He does not fly. / You meet him while walking." I wonder if Lamantia knew Hawthorne and Melville well—it feels like it to me.

As for John Hoffman, he isn't as dazzling and his metrics aren't as menacing, but he has a great sadness to him, the sadness of youth (he died at age twenty-three, far away from home, in Mexico under disputed circumstances). "Do, re, mi, fa—how lugubrious!" is the refrain of one piece. The enormous pleasure of seeing this work arrive after so many years in shadowland, for now, makes it hard for me to feel very glum, but I can always go back once the initial high has subsided, right?

The Lottery, and Other Stories
by Shirley Jackson

★★★★☆
A Crusader against Racism

May 12, 2010

None of my students had ever read, or even heard of, Shirley Jackson nor her famous story "The Lottery" when I taught a fiction workshop in a prestigious MFA writing program eighteen months ago, so I have to believe that, with the proliferation of newer models, Shirley Jackson doesn't have the cachet she once had. Maybe Shelley Jackson has taken her place in the minds and hearts of young writers today. (Both writers grew up in the Bay Area and we are proud of them both!) Anyhow "The Lottery" was a big hit and many said that it reminded them of a film project that would be a good fit for disgraced movie director M. Night Shyamalan (*The Sixth Sense, The Village*). "Professor Killian, are there other Shirley Jackson stories as chilling as 'The Lottery'?" My brow furrowed. "Not exactly," I admitted. "She wrote some scary novels, but I can tell you're not interested in those."

Finally one student slapped down a well-worn paperback copy of *The Lottery, and Other Stories* onto the seminar table. "Talk about a one-hit wonder!" he snorted. It was up to me to stand up for the other stories in the volume which, though none of them are exactly as perfect as the title piece, still carry a certain amount of resonance even sixty years later. We noticed that much of the work was written during World War II, with the consequence that men play small parts in general in these stories. It's mostly a woman's world, and the women are really messed up. In "The Tooth," a housewife from upstate takes the bus down to Manhattan to get a tooth seen to, and somewhere along the way she loses her mind and thinks that she has a demon lover. By the end of the tale a sordid amnesia has set in. In "Pillar of Salt," another married woman goes to Manhattan and has a breakdown just from the noise and bustle of city life. You'd think an editor would have spoken to Miss Jackson, pointing out the similarity between the two stories. But maybe it's a systemic failure she's pointing to—the way in which society has both denigrated women and put them up on a pedestal. And in many of the stories, it's another woman who's the enemy. Jackson attacks the casual racism and anti-Semitism of the period in that forthright 1947 fashion that we loved so much in *Gentleman's Agreement* and *Intruder in the Dust*, but on other issues, like that of identity, she seems curiously muted, perhaps convinced that human beings are constitutionally drawn toward evil and malice. So it's not a cheerful book by any means.

Neither is it a particularly compelling one. For some reason the *New Yorker* was encouraging vague markers of identification, for everyone in the book seems to have the same name and the same futile tags. This one wears a housedress, that one carries a pug dog, and that's about it, they're all pretty shadowy and prejudiced. And lost! Lost in the broken dreams of post-Fordist America.

Letters to Jackie: Condolences from a Grieving Nation
by Ellen Fitzpatrick

★★★★★
Get Out Your Handkerchiefs

May 20, 2010

Letters to Jackie is an impressive book, and I like the way that editor Ellen Fitzpatrick plays up the transparency behind her decision to make the book one that would appeal to a broader audience than the specialized audience of fellow historians she had originally envisioned. Likewise, she steps out of her academic robes to reveal that she, too, was one of those affected deeply by Kennedy's death, and her memories are touching indeed. She is just my age and, like me, was in the sixth grade when Kennedy was shot.

On the one hand it's disturbing that the National Archives cleared out miles and miles of letters by pulping them in a cleaning tizzy some years back, but given their mandate to reduce the collection to manageable size, they seem to have done so thoughtfully. They attempted to allow for any foreseeable scholarly need in the future, so that, for example, all letters from celebrities were preserved, as well as a nice sampling of letters from various groups all well represented in the present collection: immigrants, Holocaust survivors, people who knew Kennedy even slightly, the retarded, the blind, the minority cultures of the day, US soldiers serving overseas, those who had been, like Jackie, suddenly widowed themselves, the very young, the sailors who had been on *PT-109* with Kennedy, teens, the very old (there are letters here from people who remembered the assassination of Lincoln). These letters will bring tears to one's eyes, some of them. And some of them will make you scratch your head with how greedy the writers were—imagine asking Mrs. Kennedy could you have her late husband's trademark rocking chair to remember him by? Maybe it's human nature to want a souvenir of someone dead, particularly one as loved as JFK. Many seem to ask for autographed photos of JFK, Jackie, or the kids, Caroline and John-John.

I'd like to see two books next, one would be celebrity letters only. The letters here from Douglas MacArthur and Langston Hughes are just samples. And I wonder if Fitzpatrick could compile a book of letters Jackie wrote back—she was a persuasive and fluid correspondent. What I'm getting from Fitzpatrick's analysis is a little bit contradictory. She places the phenomenon of these letters in a time predating our own celebrity culture, thus making the outpouring of two million letters even more extraordinary. It was also an age, she argues, when people kept their emotions bottled up and there wasn't the rage for self-expression that fuels the internet. And it was an age of letter writing, far more than today, people wrote and received letters regularly. So what was so extraordinary really? Fitzpatrick provides few historical parallels, but I wonder if the outbreak of grief was more or less in the case of Diana Spencer's death in a Paris tunnel—how many letters did her death inspire? (And who received them? Her children, I guess.)

Masculine Domination
by Pierre Bourdieu

★★★★★
Was My Face Red

June 2, 2010

A local fraternal organization was presenting Anthony Bourdain in person, speaking about his career and showing clips of his shows, to benefit charity. I got a premium ticket, being such a fan of Bourdain and the original TV series of *Kitchen Confidential*. After the presentation he was to do a signing, so I thought I'd surprise my partner with a signed copy of Bourdain's latest book, which I ordered ahead of time (from Amazon, of course). It sounded like vintage Bourdain, *Masculine Domination*. Some of the funniest moments in *KC* the series were when Bradley Cooper wouldn't let any female chefs on the "line" as they call it, whereas even the worst male chef he'd give the nod to. This drove the restaurant manager (female) crazy and eventually Bradley Cooper gave in a little, rolling his eyes and heaving great sighs.

The lecture and clips were first rate, but I made a fool of myself when, after waiting in line a good fifteen minutes, I asked the famous TV chef to autograph *Masculine Domination*! He looked at it in disgust, curling his lip and letting loose with some salty language, and his handlers whispered "This is not by Bourdain, it is by Pierre Bourdieu." Were there two of them? I asked, but then they escorted me back to my table where some of the other attendees and I discussed the situation. Was my face red! He wouldn't stop grimacing at me, even in the midst of chatting up the remaining people standing in line with their proper books. The man has written more than his share of books, but it appears that this is not among them.

That said, even though *Masculine Domination* fails the grade as a Bourdain book about bad kitchens, it's not a bad read. Bourdieu has this concept of "symbolic violence," basically saying that the forces of power no longer need to exert actual violence on the little people to keep the status quo of capitalism going; things have reached a perfect melting point of image and reality, so that now mere "symbolic violence" is frightening enough. In particular, for women, who are "subjected to a labour of socialization which tends to diminish and deny them," so that they reach instinctively for the positions men want them to take—namely, "self-denial, resignation and silence." Bourdieu sees this syndrome as a total one, in operation everywhere around the world, in all nations, rich and poor. Historically speaking, masculine domination has been but one way, argues Bourdieu, to propagate what he refers to as "the masculine vision," and the chief agents have been the family (far and away the leader in ideology), the church, and the educational system. Paradoxically as bourgeois women leave the workforce, they become mainstays of the church, so that from Victorian times onward, for all practical purposes, men have ceded membership in the church to the women otherwise disenfranchised from agency. But men "continue to dominate" both the public sphere and the field of power (particularly "economic power—over production"). You can see how reading Bourdieu and Bourdain is but either side of the same coin, and how the hyperselection of women occurs even in the kitchens of the chicest restaurants in New York, Paris, and London, and the bistros surrounding them like barnacles at the bottom of a submarine. So I was wrong, but I was right at the same time.

Persistent Voices: Poetry by Writers Lost to AIDS
ed. Philip Clark and David Groff

★★★★★
Uncanny

June 6, 2010

It's natural I suppose that AIDS has disappeared from public consciousness, and that the present generation of young people are living in an artificial white light concerning the recent past. The era was too painful for us, too painful for anyone to have to think about. In the twentieth century this phenomenon happened again and again, a trauma followed by a period immediately afterward of complete and benign dissociation, and then a third period where the original trauma can return to the brain, modulated by the twin effects of time and sobriety. *Persistent Voices*, the new anthology of poetry edited by Philip Clark and David Groff, thus comes along at a time that is not likely to make it a bestseller, and yet it is the sort of book that is worth reading for that reason alone.

We all knew that having AIDS did not automatically make you a good writer, and yet I found something of value in just about every poem here. Messrs. Clark and Groff did a fair amount of cherry-picking here and there to find perhaps the two or three only good poems written by a few bad poets, but that's what editing is all about, and why not look at these guys in the best light honor can provide? An air of respect and yet a fine discrimination soars through the pages of this book like birds through the windows of a lighted mead-house. Then there were the writers who, no matter how sick they got, notoriously denied having AIDS: How to represent their contributions? Everywhere, you see, there were traps and pitfalls for our editors, and yet by and large *Persistent Voices* is just the book we all hoped it would be. Out of the writers in this book, I knew two quite well (the New Narrative boys, Sam D'Allesandro and Steve Abbott), eight or nine others well enough to cry when they left us, and some I knew not at all. (Anyone my age will have the weird experience of reading through the book and murmuring "Hmmm, didn't know he was gay," "Hmmm, didn't know he was dead.")

In *Chroma*, UK writer and editor Richard Canning published a characteristically thoughtful review of *Persistent Voices*, though he controversially asked two pressing questions. "Why select poets simply according to their medical condition, unless that condition became the governing subject around which the poems are based? And—churlish as it may be—if you do use this criterion, why then bend the rules, to accommodate poets who, suffering from ill health, committed suicide?" At this point I depart from Canning's line, though it served him well for his own, outstanding, AIDS-themed anthology of the best short stories written about AIDS a few years back (*Vital Signs*, 2008). In fact I can't even figure out what his reasoning is. Why all this talk of "rules" in the face of the most devastating epidemic in our time? Why go all neoformalist on us at this juncture? It is the very unruliness of *Persistent Voices* that best reflects the tragedy it memorializes. I don't want a book of poems about AIDS written by the poets Canning finds sorely absent from this collection: "great poets who either escaped HIV infection themselves, or have not died of AIDS: Thom Gunn, perhaps, most famously (*The Man with Night Sweats* collection), but also Olga Broumas, Rafael Campo, Mark Doty, Marilyn Hacker, Rachel Hadas, Richard Howard, Richard McCann, J. D. McClatchy, David Trinidad and Gregory Woods." That's your book, but this is not that and I'm glad.

A Star Is Born (1954)
dir. George Cukor

★★★★★
Lose That Long Footage

June 23, 2010

I love *A Star Is Born* and I have ever since I saw it first, on TV. I couldn't figure out how Judy Garland was so old looking, and my father said, "It's because she's been around the mill," so I thought until a recent viewing that she was a millworker while financing her musical career with Danny's band. Seeing it again, it seems fine that she's not a young girl just starting out, what kind of story would that be? We want someone who's been hurt by life and who has unexplained traumas in her past (watch closely now, as Garland's face darkens as she remembers waiting tables. "I'll never do that again," she vows, and I'm thinking, "I was a waiter, it wasn't that bad!") ... we don't want a Lola Lavery to be the center of the movie. Well, *Lost in Translation* by Sofia Coppola was a little bit like an *A Star Is Born* remake, wasn't it? The mistake of that movie was in assuming we'd find the heroine enchanting because of Scarlett Johansson's unlived-in face and attitude. Well, enough about that, I just wanted to reiterate that, for the most part, Robert Osborne, Judy Garland was not fifteen years too old to play the part.

The movie progresses in infinitely small, naturalistic bumps between one scene and the next, so that we get an almost novelistic drenching in textures and atmospheres, all in the service of character development. And yet the movie seems "written" only in its set pieces, the scenes we all remember, where the characters are more eloquent than we imagine they would actually be in "real life." I noticed last night how the film progresses by revelation, and everything moving the plot forward is something overheard by the protagonists that shatters their views of reality. Norman's all content after Esther performs her big "production number to end all production numbers," but then he signs for the delivery boy who calls him "Mr. Lester." Norman at the race track, Libby making a hash of his face and hearing people whisper (no, not even whisper, shout) "He's drunk ... He's been drunk for years."

Finally the big, and satisfying, shock, when Norman overhears Oliver's real opinion of his acting. The scene should have won James Mason an Oscar, but Charles Bickford is also supremely skillful at delivering the speech in question. Tom Noonan's big speech bucking up Esther is well done too ... You can't believe she's going to fall for such hokum, and then when she does, you realize her character has changed and she has "gone Hollywood" in a real, and terrible, way.

Loved the dressing room at Oliver Niles Studio, and the seaside house Norman builds for Esther, but actually I liked the Oleander Arms the best, I think. It is the most glamorous and evocative motel I've ever seen in the movies or out of them.

But it is a long movie, that's for sure. At the intermission credit I seriously considered pressing "Exit," under the belief that all the succeeding scenes had been scarred into my memory ever since my mill-working days. But I'm glad I stayed! I cried, but even when I was crying, I thought how vain of Esther to tell Norman "Oh, I'll sing to you from the kitchen window, my soft, wondering number 'It's a New World,' and yet you'll hear me over the pounding Malibu surf."

Sterling Silver Fish Bone Earrings
by Old Glory

★★★★★
Bony Memories

July 24, 2010

Not the highest-ranked jewelry on Amazon, Old Glory Sterling Silver Fish Bone Earrings are a delightful gift for a special anniversary, or to wear on your own. I first saw them at a popular seafood place nearby at the Wharf in San Francisco, but the price was artificially hiked to attract tourists, and I knew I could do better using my Amazon Prime account.

My wife liked getting these earrings, as they constantly recall for her a transition from not eating fish at all, to once in a while, on the advice of her doctor, trying a salmon or trout, perhaps once a month, for protein reasons if nothing else. At first, the bones made her feel grisly but then she realized, it's all nature. And as it turns out, it is not silver plate covering actual fishbones, but each earring is 100 percent solid sterling silver without a trace of the original bone, now lost to history and the artist's imagination. Our three cats totally ignore them, which they would not do if even one cell's worth of fish remained in their makeup. We can leave them out on the dinner table or even in the cat's dish, and they will remain untouched, still gleaming with the traditional heartiness of fine silver.

You will always be getting smiles from neighbors and strangers when you leave your apartment wearing earrings from Old Glory. This is my fourth pair and it won't be the last. They are unisex, though perhaps they look better on someone with a smaller lobe than mine. I wish Old Glory would consider making a longer pair, with five or six pairs of lateral bones, instead of the present, skimpy four. But such are the dreams of an impossible princess.

---

9 to 5 (Sexist, Egotistical, Lying Hypocritical Bigot Edition – Widescreen) (1980)
dir. Colin Higgins

★★★★★
Labor Day Special

September 7, 2010

I want to raise a glass to *9 to 5*, a movie I didn't love love love when it first came out, thirty years ago, but now it looks brilliant. And despite all the changes in the world, the world of work is still just as grim as the movie suggests. How well the three stars interact! Many have commented on how Jane Fonda, the movie's producer and the biggest star present, seems to enjoy playing a dowdy-type nebbish and taking a back seat to the bigger personalities of Tomlin and Parton, but she has got some wonderful scenes on her own. Just to contrast, there's the pathetic scene when she comes home from her first horrible day at work and finds her husband at the apartment door. It's all in her face, the momentary hope that he's back, and then the disillusionment when instead he hands her the divorce papers, while his new girlfriend sits out front by the curb in his sports car. Her absurd little corsage doesn't wilt, but her spirit does, though she tries to keep her cool.

Joan Fontaine in *Letter to an Unknown Woman* didn't do that kind of acting any better than Fonda here. But Jane also shines in the all-out Lucy Ricardo comedy when the monstrous Xerox machine goes out of control, spitting all colors of paper out at her and all she can do is keep shuffling them and trying to match their corners. In fact it's a scene worthy of Chaplin. Lily Tomlin has the fiery part, but her best scenes are at home, accepting a joint from her teenage son while she fixes the garage door opener on a stepladder. Ditto with Dolly complaining to her husband that the other girls treat her like she's trash, and she doesn't know why. "It's because you're so pretty," he tells her, and she protests, but she likes to hear that, doesn't she? I guess I like the movie because of its incisive picture of office life, and because of the spirit that its leading players (and even its supporting actors—like, is that Marian Mercer as Hart's wife?) give to the show. It's a comedy, so the first half is better than the second half, but it's got the right stuff all the way through.

Air Transmigra
by John Norton

★★★★★
Burnt Norton? *Norton Anthology*? A Bit of Both.

November 1, 2010

Norton is one of the original writers of the New Narrative, at least the branch of it that opened in Bob Glück's writing workshops, given for free courtesy of the California Arts Council, in the 1970s and 1980s. He was already then a practicing poet, one who worked as a teen boy with poet Jack Spicer as a page at the Boston Public Library.

Like Spicer, he is fascinated by media and mediation, and his experiences maneuvering through the phenomenological system make up some of his most interesting poems. His new collection, *Air Transmigra*, is just out from the admirable San Francisco artist-run press Ithuriel's Spear. I admire Norton's poetic stance, and in his best work he is a remarkable writer, as adept at bringing to the foreground the romantic yeses and nos among lovers as he is showing the political and social dimension behind every human choice, ethical, poetic, or otherwise.

He is among our chief poets of work, the daily grind in which capitalism maintains complete control for forty hours a week and even when we think we're "off the clock." The opening section of *Air Transmigra* is called "Rules of the Road" and is made up of a solid suite of positions, a jeremiad breaking like waves into individual whitecaps of passion and outrage (and analysis). "Black street lights positioned like / upended quarter notes / stacks of green and red containers / tankers full of Coke / heaps of disassembled dream / shredded to resupply Toyota."

At the other end of the book a different register of "brand names" takes center stage, and these are the painters and other artists whom Norton invokes in a group of ekphrastic poems inspired by artworks: *The Skater* of Gilbert Stuart, Jan Steen's *Marriage at Cana*, et cetera. Like Jack Spicer, Norton names a poem after the Cézanne master-work *The Card Players*, but Norton is more precise and narrative than Spicer, for his focus is different. In her blurb Beverly Dahlen gets the matter of Norton exactly right: if his themes seem grim, "that would be misleading: this poetry is witty and ironic." Norton won the American Book Award for his first book of poetry, and if they have a rule against repeats, it might be time to break it.

Burlesque (2010)
dir. Steve Antin

★★★★★
One Shock after Another

November 30, 2010

In *Burlesque*, the actress Kristen Bell, whom I remember from TV's *Veronica Mars*, does the sort of total reinvention, bordering on scarification, that won Charlize Theron an Oscar when she tried it in *Monster*. After the movie we were all sitting there, saying "That was Kristen Bell?" The film has her playing Nikki, a dancer with enormous talent and charisma who's hobbled by two nasty problems— megalomania and alcoholism. Something's a little wonky with the script, which seems to be playing on two time scales at once … one in which Nikki is roughly the contemporary of Christina Aguilera's character, maybe a bit older (in fact Bell is five months older than Aguilera), and the other in which Nikki was around when, together, she and Cher started the burlesque dance palace around which the movie, and their lives, revolve. I'm sure I wasn't the only one who was scratching his head when the big parking lot scene took place and Nikki started giving Cher (I mean Tess) a guilt trip for preferring the new girl Ali! That's the part where Cher says, "What about all the years I held your hair up out of the toilet bowl while you were vomiting everything but your memories?"

It almost seems that their memories changed and transformed as the decades passed. Both Nikki and Tess look pretty ageless, but Nikki actually seems younger than Tess because at least she can still move her body. Cher parades through the movie as though she had no feet and is being wheeled about on casters by invisible unions whose members are all field mice. On the minus side, there is perhaps one spectacular musical number too many, but outside of that, *Burlesque* is perfect.

Black Christmas (1974)
dir. Bob Clark

★★★★★
Canadian Chiller

December 23, 2010

At Christmas time I like to watch *White Christmas* and I like to watch *Black Christmas*. Actors Andrea Martin, Olivia Hussey, and Margot Kidder really do interact like a trio of sorority sisters, and when Hussey ignores the policeman on the phone and begins to mount the stairs toward the end of the picture, for once you don't start shouting at her, you understand why she would be reluctant to walk out of a house without her two friends. (Irony!) I don't know how much they paid Olivia Hussey to make this film, and from what Bob Clark said she only did it on the advice of a psychic, but they didn't pay her enough—she is far from the greatest actress in the world, but she really holds the movie together. Her quiet strength and her compassion give the movie more warmth than its algebraic plot (one character disappears every ten minutes) actually has room for. I always love the scene when carolers come and sing "Adeste Fidelis," and Olivia Hussey looks entranced throughout the whole thing, and then, even in the middle of the panic about the murders, she remembers to run out to the kids and give the female coach some money (as a tip?)—now, that's classy!

She looks genuinely moved at the music. I relate this to the fact that Olivia Hussey also was later to play the Virgin Mary in the Zeffirelli version of *Jesus of Nazareth*. Altogether she has had a much more varied screen career than her detractors would have one believe. She has to do a lot of heavy lifting, as it were, to make her scenes with Peter work. They just don't seem like they were ever a good couple, she's annoyed with him from the get-go and he's a mess, although he gets to wear a splendid green, yellow, gray, black, and brown houndstooth jacket when he gives his all-important piano recital. Keir Dullea is of course a legendary presence in the '60s and '70s cinema, and every time he comes on-screen he brings with him the rags and tatters of all his famous roles. Did you know he could really play the piano, and was a favorite student of Glenn Gould's (the two spent the off hours of *Black Christmas* hanging out in Toronto and attempting to rehearse Peter's shattering solo), and that the jacket in question was actually borrowed from Gould as a good luck charm? Well, it worked. Today listening to Peter's recital, it is probably the most impressive segment of a really great score … Keir Dullea grimaces when he hits a note by mistake … or is that what his face is saying, because it sounds killer to me.

Until the Collector's Edition DVD, I never really understood the disconnect between what Billy says on the phone and the expressions on the actresses' faces when they react. He says the most vile things and they just stand there po-faced, and then when he says something innocuous they let him have it! Well, apparently the actual Billy dialogue was recorded later and during the time of filming, Hussey, Kidder, and Martin were just listening to a silent phone and prompted to react at different moments of the clock. Although I don't know how they worked this out during the infamous "wart" phone call that upsets our heroine so. Maybe that was one time in which she actually knew what was being said on the other end of the conversation.

Is *Black Christmas* actually better than *White Christmas*? Well, neither are high-art-type pictures, are they, but watched in rapid succession you might convince yourself that this really is the "most wonderful time of the year."

Black Swan (2010)
dir. Darren Aronofsky

★★★★★
Swan's Way

December 30, 2010

We went expecting the absolute worst, having been fully briefed ahead of time about the film's misogyny and the plain blank ridiculousness of its plot and its various setups.

All ballet movies are somewhat silly, though this one makes something like *Center Stage* seem like a hard-hitting documentary; and yet I wouldn't hesitate to recommend *Black Swan* even to Moira Shearer herself if she rose up from her grave and asked what was playing at the movies. It has something, perhaps the tremendous conviction of the director and his lead actress, that makes it watchable at all times, even when the sheer level of camp rises to over your head, which is often, believe me. Someone said that Natalie Portman, as Nina Sayers, wears one expression on her face through the whole movie—that's not quite true, but *BS* veterans will know which expression my catty friend was speaking of. She is extraordinarily disciplined in the part, and it looks crazy difficult, so I predict that she will get the award for this that Catherine Deneuve should have gotten for *Repulsion*, the movie this mimics in many ways. Some have compared *BS* to *Showgirls*, except while that Gina Gershon is miles better than Mila Kunis at playing the sensual, careless rival, Portman seems really to believe in Nina in a way that Elizabeth Berkley always seemed too timid to really go there. Plus, the costumes and the hair and the makeup (in *BS*) are all astonishing, probably as good as the ones in the original *Red Shoes*.

The problem with *Black Swan*, finally, is that the cards seem stacked from the beginning against poor Nina. She has nothing from the beginning of the movie, and never gets anything (except briefly, she gets to replace Beth Macintyre)—(and Winona Ryder makes sure Nina never gets to enjoy a moment of that victory). She has no men, no friends, no fun, a horrible mother, and a lousy life. She has Portman's beauty and grace, but not fifteen minutes into the picture she has that rash on her back where it almost seems wings are going to grow. The movie makes sure that Nina suffers with an almost obscene glory. In casting Barbara Hershey and Winona Ryder as look-alike avatars for Nina, Aronofsky insures that we will (perhaps subconsciously) pity Portman for her present-day good looks (so like Audrey Hepburn's in some shots), because we see what happened to Hershey and Ryder and conclude that time eats away at beauty just like the garbage can opening up its yawning mouth to accept the whole giant cake Hershey orders for Portman in the film's cruelest scene.

Looking for Mr. Preston
ed. Laura Antoniou

★★★★☆
Not Robert Preston

January 15, 2011

A recent article online by Philip Clark led me to recall distant memories of the late John Preston, once a bestselling writer of gay porn and later an anthologist whose appeal crossed all borders. He was indefatigable till AIDS struck him down at the height of his powers.

I ordered a copy of this book thinking that it would bring me into his world, and I'm glad I did. I met him a few times in life and, like many, I was attracted by his gaze, the gray eyes with black irises that are described so often in this Festschrift. A writer myself, I envied Preston his work habits, his popularity, his ease with images, his connection with a wide variety of readers. I don't suppose he knew anything of my own work, and now that I have been reading Laura Antoniou's collection of memoirs of the man, it doesn't seem really as if anyone knew him very well. I keep turning the pages, looking for the ultimate insight. And though many of the essays and memoirs are well crafted, I got the feeling that Preston himself must have been elusive. Many of the memoirs are about regret. Scott O'Hara wishes that he had let Preston spank him, and William Mann similarly looks back to a half-[…] response to Preston's overtures, with a feeling of having missed out on something extraordinary. In fact I don't think any of the people who wrote for the book actually had sex with him, and since his sexual power was part of Preston's charisma, it sort of leaves a hole in the book. Maybe the guys who subbed for Preston, none of them were writers? It's strange! I'm still reeling thinking that none of Preston's famous "three protégés" ever had sex with him?

Strange also is the decision of editor Antoniou, a well-known writer of "erotica" herself, to let the book trail off into a welter of confusing fictional or semifictional pieces "inspired" by one or another aspect of Preston's life, work, and thought. None of the latter are any good, and yet trying to put my mind back to the mid-1990s, maybe it might have seemed a good idea at the time, I'll give her that.

Will we get a biography of John Preston similar to the rescue job biographer Justin Spring performed on the late Samuel Steward (who knew Preston)? Anything could happen I suppose, but what are the odds?

Where the Action Is! Los Angeles Nuggets 1965–1968
ed. Andrew Sandoval

Vintage Pop

February 6, 2011

As many have noted, Southern California was a land of its own during the mid-'60s era of these recordings and for some it was home, while others thought of it as the "Golden Land" William Faulkner had written about a generation before: "California Dreamin'," as John Phillips and Michelle Gilliam dubbed it. For decades creative people had come west to enjoy the sunshine and to yearn for the money, and musicians had always been a part of this migratory process. Phil Spector's relocation from New York to Los Angeles was the way to go, producing an amplified and reworked version of what had worked before in the Brill Building, but now there was so much space and people were so—*groovy* was one word for it—that the sound of the music changed in some easily identifiable ways. The clangy jarring guitar sounds the Byrds made famous really jump out on every other track here. Maybe also the extreme play with language sounds and the voices needed to act out this new sort of lyric ("Come to the Sunshine" by Van Dyke Parks, "Darlin' You Can Count on Me" by the Everpresent Fullness) also helps to unify this set. Yes, there was a world of difference between the quaint folk rock of the 1965 tracks, the pop ambitions of the Association and the Beach Boys, and whatever amalgam Arthur Lee and Brian MacLean were working out with the Love LPs. But a highly worked theatricality—the shadow of the big studios—lay under them all. There could have been no Jim Morrison without James Dean—in fact, without Warner Bros.

Not all of the songs here are great and some are downright lousy, but dozens of them are revelations to me! I'll cite but one example. I'd never really understood what fans saw in Nino Tempo & April Stevens, but their cover of Spector's "I Love How You Love Me" can take the paint off of cars, with its bagpipe played like Hendrix playing fuzz feedback. It's an insane song to begin with, but this arrangement, both vocally and instrumentally, adds to the agony and the ecstasy, listening to it I know I'm alive!

Scream 4 (**2011**)
dir. Wes Craven

★★★★★
Best of All the *Screams*

April 25, 2011

One scene is badly filmed, or maybe just awkwardly filmed, the reading Sidney gives at the Woodsboro bookstore to promote her bestselling self-help book, *Out of Darkness*. Not sure what makes it look so phony, but it's almost as if the filmmakers have never actually been to a bookstore in their lives, or at any rate gone to a reading. Sidney is forced to read in a shadowy corner of the store, attended by a few extras dressed as booklovers, all of them standing, none seated. When she finishes the reading the five fans clap. Five sales right there—really a lousy turnout for poor Sidney. Her publicist (Alison Brie from *Mad Men* and *Community*) must be tearing her hair out. Why even bring Sidney back to Woodsboro on her book tour if only five people are going to buy books? Then the Q&A portion of the event is interrupted by Sheriff Dewey (David Arquette) and Deputy Judy (Marley Shelton) who have somehow triangulated the missing cell phone to the general vicinity of the bookstore. It's a calamity as far as commerce goes, but it is the only false step in *Scream 4*, by far the best sequel in ages and, I would say, one of those rare movies that transcends even the original.

OK, Emma Roberts (playing Jill, Sidney's young niece of high school age) is pretty much a washout in a pivotal role, but it's not really her fault, is it? Jill's ambiguous and charged feelings toward her famous aunt perhaps parallel young Emma's feelings about her own famous aunt, the better-known actress Julia Roberts. It's strange that Emma Roberts has to play Jill Roberts—isn't there any other last name they might have picked? The phone rings in her house, she picks it up, "Roberts residence," she chirps brightly, just as though she were in her own home in Hollywood or wherever teen stars live nowadays. Writer Kevin Williamson brings on the jokes and scares so quickly that the movie moves from beginning to end on an adrenaline high, the rush of confidence you get when a top writer gets to do pretty much exactly as he pleases, and Wes Craven responds by giving all of his players the shading and the humor they need to make it work. Hayden Panettiere has never impressed me, but here she gives the performance of a natural movie star, while the central trio of Campbell, Arquette, and Cox keep a very steady lead against a troupe of energetic youngsters in the new cast. Wasn't Lauren Graham supposed to be in this thing? Is she playing the part that Mary McDonnell is now playing? Poor Mary McDonnell, her newest facelift was so raw and red that it looks painful to touch. Her brow and chin almost meet, like old-time silhouettes of the crescent moon. I think that Lauren Graham upped and left the production and they had to wake up Mary McDonnell by giving her smelling salts right on the operating table and summoning her to the set without taking out the stitches first. That said, she is fine in the movie and those of us who loved her as White Woman Raised by Sioux in *Dances with Wolves* will be happy to see her triumph again in this latest box office semihit.

Critical reaction among Amazon reviewers has been sharply divided, perhaps along the same lines as critics in general. Some think the movie played out, ridiculous, overlong, and poorly motivated. Some praise it as the best since the original *Scream*. But I go further and salute it as the best of all the *Scream*s, precisely because its motivation is so delicious and so obvious. I could kick myself for not getting it, whereas the killers in all the other movies were just "Oh, who cares why they did it." When the movie was over, my wife turned to me and said, "This is better than *The King's Speech*, and better, in fact, than all ten of last year's Best Picture nominations." Pity social satire rarely wins awards, much less slasher films!

Mildred Pierce (2011)
dir. Todd Haynes

★★★★★
Piercing Glances

April 29, 2011

It didn't sound like a good idea when I read about this project in *THR*, for I was one who looked forward to Todd Haynes's Sirk pastiche *Far from Heaven* with great expectations, shattered by the limp results. And *Mildred Pierce* was to last for five hours! It was my wife who made me watch the show, but you know what, afterward I was glad she did, for thinking it over, I find Mildred Pierce by far the best thing Haynes has done. And yes, I am counting *Safe* and *Poison* and that *Karen Carpenter* show.

The story is supposedly more faithful to the book than the old Joan Crawford vehicle, which is both good and bad. Cain's story, I think, was improved by the liberties Jerry Wald's screenwriters took with it, the framing device of the murder of Zachary Scott, which gave the tale an urgency and indeed a gravity that ultimately Haynes perhaps isn't very interested in—that's OK too. Haynes is working in a cinema of gesture and hair color and costume and sound. And of the ordinary lives of women, I guess. Though hiring Melissa Leo and Mare Winningham as hags doesn't exactly strike the "ordinary" note, but they're so bizarre Kate Winslet actually seems, in relief, like an everyday person, only fabulously beautiful even when she's vomiting in disgust for having to turn to waitressing to raise money after Bert leaves them. We spent five hours wondering what was going to happen, and the answer is, about halfway through, cute little Morgan Turner, as the young Veda, goes away and comes back as Evan Rachel Wood and ruins the picture. Well, that's too strong. Evan Rachel Wood just isn't as nasty as the first little girl, that's all. She's not a very good actress, and yet you can't take your eyes off of her, and if that's her voice they're using as Veda's singing voice, then she's pretty astounding.

I mean, she was good in that Beatles film (at singing) but here she sounds like a young Kiri Te Kanawa, except sexier. Indeed the movie could have lost half an hour if they had limited her singing numbers to maybe one or two. I didn't realize this was going to be a musical, and imagine what's on the cutting-room floor. The deluxe version of the DVD is said to contain audio versions of omitted arias by Delibes and Gounod and others. And she looks great with her clothes off, so does Kate, so does Guy Pearce. "Why Guy Pearce?" we wondered. Was he the first name the producers thought of when they heard the show was *Mildred Pierce*? "And we need a hot guy ..." Eureka! It gets kind of funny when Kate Winslet and Guy Pearce are supposed to be this all-American California golden couple, but that's OK. I don't want to spoil the plot for you, so I have no time to tell you what I think about chicken and waffles as a plot point, nor how odd it seems that no one knows Veda is a great singer until they hear her on the radio, but so be it. In any case, from what I understand, not a single frame of *Mildred Pierce* was filmed in California? All those ocean scenes—Long Island Sound? Glendale and Pasadena? Astoria, in Queens, or Scarsdale maybe? Thus there's a queer left-and-right mirroring to the show, reflecting the bemused political ideology Haynes and Company have served up, warm and honey colored, in this reiteration of Depression desperation and hope.

Unknown Halsman
by Philippe Halsman, ed. Oliver Halsman Rosenberg

★★★★★
The Lion King

May 2, 2011

Reconsidering an artist can be an exhausting experience, and therefore one is especially glad when a latter-day artist marshals the
evidence like a great defense attorney. In this case, our contemporary
the young San Francisco–based artist Oliver Halsman Rosenberg
spent several years working on the archives of his late grandfather, the
once celebrated portrait and fashion photographer Philippe Halsman, and published this very grand and visually exciting book as a
brief. I remember Halsman's photographs, the most famous of which
appeared in the old *Life* magazine. There was something heavy and
European about his style, even when he wore his joker mask.
American photographers made less of a fuss, one felt, and Halsman
was like the Roberto Benigni of his day, always living large, leaping
from chair to chair, exuding geniality like a madman. His collaborations with Salvador Dalí's mustache, and people like the Duke and
Duchess of Windsor jumping into the air expressing careful exulta-
tion, furthered this impression of Halsman as a showman pure and
simple, a man for whom statement was understatement: well, he wasn't
cool like William Eggleston or whomever.

But now, through OHR's ingenuity, I've changed my mind
180 degrees. The archive has proven a bounty of unusual and
sometimes stirring surprises, and most of all I see now that not all
of Halsman's photographs were about being goofy (or super
somber, like his pictures of Einstein and the like). Dalí is still all
over the volume, but his effect has been relegated to the second
tier, so that their collaborative work reveals a Dalí influenced by
Halsman; it's this new perception of Halsman as top banana that's
nothing short of a wake-up call. How about that photo of Mia Farrow, her long hair frizzed in front of her face, resembling nothing
so much as a board of knotty pine wood (which she happens to be
holding next to her, or peeking from beyond). Visual grammars
combine, assert themselves, retreat, while Rosenberg's deliberate

confusion of chronology shores up the body of Halsman as a body of infinite gradations.

Rosenberg also brings forward what one might call the camp element. Cocteau in a 1949 *Life* magazine spread makes all his actual work look silly as he himself parades through a corridor of human arms, here sans candelabra but distorted into the hands of little boys pretending to be firing guns. On the flip page, Edward Albee in 1961, and over the top of his skull Halsman slaps on a smorgasbord of tiny actors playing out the most shocking scenes of all of Albee's early one-acts. His work is possibly the pivot point where camp turns over and becomes true horror, or at any rate true abjection, the photos of Tippi Hedren and Alfred Hitchcock literalize the dreamy imagery of *The Birds* into a point of no return, beyond ordinary categories of the sane and the unsane. Rosenberg reminds us of his grandfather's horrible early life, of how he was condemned to solitary confinement for the murder of his own father—a crime of which he was totally innocent, and a punishment meted out by anti-Semitic state forces afraid of the young Latvian and his Jewish convictions. Remember how Dostoevsky was hauled out before a firing squad and saved only by something completely arbitrary? That's how Halsman lived his whole life, in a state of posttraumatic stress. No wonder he gravitated toward the impossible glamour of Martha Graham, Sharon Tate, and the international conceptualisms of Marcel Duchamp, Isamu Noguchi, Sid Caesar, and Cantinflas. That mash-up of Mao and Marilyn Monroe stands for me, right now, as his most emblematic work of art.

Heat Wave: The Life and Career of Ethel Waters
by Donald Bogle

★★★★★
A Life of Dramatic Ups and Downs

June 9, 2011

How far is too far? might be the underlying theme of Bogle's outstanding life of Ethel Waters, and he plays out this theme with variations in nearly every chapter. How far did racist American society have to push the gifted young Ethel Waters before she blossomed into a fully-formed "race woman" (WWI-era slang signifying a political activist)? Her truculence and rage at the white man was, heaven knows, fully justified, but she wound up cutting off her nose to spite the white faces of others. And that's the rub. Alcohol and great lashings of food helped to stave the pain, but they ruined the sexy figure of a great star once dubbed "Sweet Mama Stringbean." Painful stories about how, in later life, she needed to have extra accommodations made for her. Though her talent never failed her, at some point she began going over to the right wing, and in this case it seemed pretty incredible that a race pioneer would have embraced Nixon and others the way she did. Other entertainers shunned her for her politics, but let's face it, had she been a different sort of person, they might have remained admirers her whole life long.

How far is too far? I'm not crazy about Lena Horne, but Waters was vicious to Horne on the set of *Stormy Weather*, terrorizing the younger soubrette and provoking a huge backlash among studio executives, effectively crippling her own career. Waters was twice the singer Horne was, but she wound up steaming when Horne robbed her of her signature song, "Stormy Weather," effectively making it her own number. Yes, I'd be annoyed too, but Waters just came off looking bad. Waters's talent was vast, and she could act the great tragic parts too, making an enormous personal success out of a brutish part in the Heyward's *Mamba's Daughters* (1939) and later, in the fifties, creating indelible portrayals in new plays by Carson McCullers and Thornton Wilder. (In a rare slipup, biographer Bogle seems not to have read Wilder's *Bernice*, one of the dramatist's masterpieces, and only mentions it in passing, as though it were nothing.)

Otherwise, he is well up to the challenge, and has used his vast knowledge of Black show business to present us with a dazzling panoply of perspectives on Waters, even those who have been dead for years and years. Sometimes he is a little too measured; I can't figure out if he really believes that Clifton Webb and Marilyn Miller treated Waters shabbily during the run of *As Thousands Cheer*. He's so evenhanded I found myself doubting the hotheaded Waters. C'mon, Bogle, come out and say it—were they (and Bea Lillie, and Eleanor Powell, in a later show) guilty or innocent? Bogle makes me want to run and see Waters's portrayal of Dilsey in the film version of Faulkner's *The Sound and the*

Fury, released in 1959 … But really, he should have just used the same title for his life of Ethel Waters, for if anyone was rich with sound, and loud with fury, it was she.

Manhandled: Gripping Tales of Gay Erotic Fiction
ed. Austin Foxxe

★★★★★
Tagged

June 13, 2011

A friend who sort of knew what I like sent me a copy of this old book with a note: "They don't make 'em the way they used to." This was a guy who had read the edition of the *Best Gay Erotica 2011* that I helped to edit, and noted the number of stories in which, well, there was a forced sex element. This book has it and nothing but it. So yeah, I loved it. Not everything is great, but all the authors are in there really trying and, let's face it, it's not an easy subject to make palatable, look at the reviews here, one guy is saying "I don't like this sort of thing, I'd rather have a love story where people feel good about each other."

I guess I like that too, but when I'm reading with one hand, send me *Manhandled*, and if editor Austin Foxxe has compiled any sequels in the years since the first one came out, throw them my way too, I'll catch them with my one hand still left empty. In this volume there was a story called "Cherry Pops" that was so strange I wish I had written it myself! It was a class-warfare story in which a gay executive is somehow lured back home from a bar by a rough-trade carpenter who does a lot of construction work in his office. Yeah, it didn't make a lot of sense, but you get the picture that in the past our narrator has pulled rank over the handyman guy, and now that the handyman has the big boss back in his apartment tied to an enormous coffee table and kissing the carpet, and has snipped off the boss's pants and underwear and started spanking him rhythmically, a lot of payback is going to take place. I just didn't expect the insertion of one, two, three, I lost track of how many, cherry popsicles into the bent-over boss and it made me shiver! Good work, Dan Kelly, and please let me know when you're going to be on Minna Street next.

A lot of good stories, including one by my favorite, Thom Wolf ("Hunger Takes Over"), in which a simple autograph request turns into a bus ride of exhaustive physical passion, and there was one I thought I would never like, "Hostage" by Barry Alexander, sort of like if *Game of Thrones* had been filmed by Fred Halsted, and that's not a bad thing.

So yes sir, send me the sequels too, thanks so much.

Lost Boys
by Slava Mogutin

★★★★★
Lost and Found

July 25, 2011

Others have said it better than I, but Russian-born, New York–based photographer Slava Mogutin is one of the best around, for his work captures some of the sheer zest of being alive that I'm afraid too often gets filtered out of our day-to-day existence by the pressures of the quotidian. The book *Lost Boys* seems to take us on a long journey, from the dreary and gray suburbs of Russia, where hideous brutalist architecture lies half-hidden under the eternal snows and mists, to the back rooms and bedrooms of a shrinking bohemia—often New York, but in other photos it looks like Berlin or maybe Prague, Frankfurt, Florida. Critic Dominic Johnson overreaches a little, I think, comparing Mogutin's worldview to that of Godard, Sade, Rimbaud, Buñuel, etc., but his is a useful direction toward articulating a politics behind Mogutin's often garish photographs of boys, often barefoot or in their stocking feet, on the make. And how does politics work within photography? Johnson reaches out toward Mogutin's other art practices, installation work, poetry, video, collage, and so on, to show how our auteur ultimately is not content to produce these remarkable prints, instead he is slowly and steadily punching holes in the paper bag of capitalism every which way he can.

I don't see that these models are as "emotionally unsatisfied" or "transient" as Johnson claims. Most of them seem remarkably secure and open, though the fetishes some practice leave them open to charges of pathology or neurosis. I don't feel the darkness within

Mogutin's work as stemming from the individual—though his title, *Lost Boys*, has that Joan Didion note of pity—rather he suggests that in our world of neoliberal globalism, who isn't lost?

Breast Cancer Awareness Pushpins (Pink, 200 per Tub)
by Officemate

★★★★★
Think Pink

August 27, 2011

If you are worried that having these pink pushpins on your desk at home or at the office will somehow brand you as a softie, well, worry no more, just enjoy. First off, this is a product with true quality. I have bought six packs of these pins and have never experienced so much as a jab or a defect. It is almost as good as it gets! Then, the color pink is not as feminine as you might suppose. Indeed, as you can see from the illustration, no two pushpins have the same exact tint of pink. And their colors change depending on the light. At morning, spill out the jar of Officemate Pushpins across your blotter in the morning sunlight. You'll see a soothing, almost angelic pink on their tips, as friendly as a dog's tongue licking your face. At noon, under the white-hot sun, spill them again, the pink nearly disappears, almost burnt off by the summer heat. You'll think you're looking at little white dots of loose-leaf clipped from a pad of white paper, instead of the backs of sharp pins. Seeing them pushed into corkboards, you wonder, "How'd that pink get so pallid?" like an old formal your former wife wore to her high school prom and for some unaccountable reason kept hung and wrapped on the back of her closet door for years. Miss Havisham, anybody?

Then, at evening, when the breezes pour in through the veranda, and it's time for a nice planter's punch, knock over your container of pushpins once again and see the difference! The pink has turned red, lobstery red, as though engorged by blood, and the pins seem sharper than ever. Take your thumbs and plunge these pinheads through paper and cork, feel the satisfying crunch going in, the press and release. Tell me this ain't the way pushpins should be—like small, personalized power tools of the mind.

Under the Dome: A Novel
by Stephen King

★★★★★
My Solution

October 31, 2011

OK, I figured out what I am going to do should faraway space-alien children ever set their eyes to Earth once again, deciding to spotlight "our little lives" with a glass dome around my city. In my case it's San Francisco, and at every drugstore downtown, souvenir stands sell glass domes with San Francisco looking pretty groovy. So it isn't that I haven't thought about the cute thing already. But Stephen King's novel, which I've been reading for eighteen months without any sort of break whatsoever, hammered it into my mind. In a little town in Maine, things fall apart pretty quickly, and anarchy and hatred and oppression are each unleashed after only one day with a dome on. We never do find out why, not exactly. Another thing we don't find out about is why the children start having visions of Halloween and pink stars! Are the alien children implanting the human children with visions? Why only them? I never did figure this out. It would have been bad enough if the whole *Lord of the Flies* scenario played itself out, with human beings revealing themselves to be monsters once they realize no one is around to stop them, but to add the child-vision thing in was too much for me, I think King just wanted to forecast an apocalyptic ending.

So what am I going to do when the dome comes down? Well, for one thing, this is a city of peace and love, so I'm assuming the cops aren't totally inhuman right-wing creeps, led by a used-car dealer, although after the events of OccupySF I have to wonder! Even if they were, I'm assuming that there are enough protestors right here to give them holy hell. Then I would start looking around for some air, especially in tires. I would also experiment with digging under the dome, maybe a tunnel would do some good. I'd look for the meth labs within the seven-by-seven-square-mile radius of the city and I would siphon off the methane peacefully, instead of leaving it to be blown up by a stray bullet. I have to say that while I never understood the appeal of meth addiction, I'm

understanding it now, for King describes the meth high so delight-
fully it made me want to try some pronto. And I'd try to look on
the bright side of things, unlike the glum Julias and Barbies and
Rustys of Chester's Mill, Maine. A thick dome around San Francisco
would protect us from tropical storms and earthquakes too, I guess,
and the occasional ocean breezes I feel sometimes here South of
Market wouldn't mess up my new emo look and my carefully insouciant haircut. For a few days, at any rate, there would be dancing in
the streets. I think it was only when the air started to run out would
things get bad for San Francisco. So I'm happy I have stockpiled,
over the past twenty years, a huge cabinet at my office filled with
drawers holding those sheets of packing material that come with
big balloons filled with air protecting whatever you're wrapping
from breaking en route. I always knew they would come in handy
one day, though actually I was thinking of using them as an air
mattress should unexpected guests arrive. But now that I know
you could just keep chomping into tablet after tablet, releasing an
energy-filled puff of oxygen directly into your mouth, I have to say
I'm glad I have more of these scraps than, I don't know, practically
anybody else in my office.

*Full Service: My Adventures in Hollywood
and the Secret Sex Lives of the Stars*
by Scotty Bowers (with Lionel Friedberg)

★★★★☆
The Oldest Man Alive

February 13, 2012

I wouldn't give this one five stars, because it was pretty "badly written," but we live in an age of contingency and I don't really care
about what's good or bad in that sense. Obviously the autobiography of Scotty Bowers, or any eighty-eight year old, is going to be
uphill sledding, but I come away from it liking the man and envying
him his exciting life at the top of the heap, procuring for and tricking
the stars (and not only the stars but people like J. Edgar Hoover
and the Windsors).

Once or twice I started to doubt the accuracy of his memories. Not the Spencer Tracy story, the one that has so many of my fellow reviewers hollering, but just little things. For example, Scotty attests that he procured young girls for Katharine Hepburn, the Duchess of Windsor, and Phyllis Gates, once the wife of Rock Hudson. Is it a coincidence that, as he remembers them, all three preferred "slim, small, dark-haired, trim-figured girls"? Or was it just that he couldn't remember and dragged out the same tag any time his "as told to" guy asked him for a preference. On the other hand, I was impressed that the first star we hear of him having sex with was not someone super famous or legendary like James Dean, but instead the sort of forgotten Walter Pidgeon. Come on, if you were making the whole thing up, wouldn't you start chapter 1 with somebody people remember, instead of gentlemanly, intellectualish Pidge? It had the ring of truth to me, just because Pidgeon's fame is so nondescript.

I was also impressed that unlike every other star autobiography, Scotty didn't claim to have had sex with Marilyn Monroe. I have new respect for Desi Arnaz as well, a man so generous that he gave his girls two hundred or three hundred dollars a throw when the standard price was twenty bucks. Sad, sad, sad was the story of Scotty and Betty's precious daughter Donna. I just didn't see it coming! I had no idea how bad Katharine Hepburn's complexion was; at any rate, Bowers describes it here as a cross between old burlap and brand-new steel wool. She always looks so good in the movies! Oh, and I wish I were a fly on the wall of the closet into which Scotty sneaked in order to watch Bob Hope have sex with the superglamorous starlet slash tart Barbara Payton! I never thought of Bob Hope as sexy before, but Scotty saw the man in action and it wasn't just a ski nose on Hope! I don't suppose he ever got any sleep, but Scotty Bowers remembers a lot of risqué '30s slang, some of which was totally new to me, the acronyms "BLC" and "PTM," and also his peculiar use of the verb *to trick*. My own sex life hasn't been as long as Scotty's, but I never heard of *trick* as a transitive verb: "We both tricked Spencer Tracy," rather than, as I would say, "We both tricked with." Well, name your own more modern-day closeted star.

Barbara Stanwyck: The Miracle Woman
by Dan Callahan

★★★★★
Them There Eyes

June 13, 2012

If you go to a biography of Barbara Stanwyck and expect to find the conventional pieties of a movie star, you are apt to be disappointed. For better or worse, she wasn't that kind of actress. Great stars work according to their own rules, subject to the whims of an ever-changing mass audience, and great biographers similarly play by the seat of their pants, shredding the rule book as they go along. Dan Callahan's critical biography is a true work of art, and I suspect that Stanwyck herself, if puzzled, would be proud of being its subject.

Born Ruby Stevens in a lower-class Brooklyn tenement, Stanwyck suffered deeply from abandonment issues stemming from early death and an unsettled extended family. It takes a village to raise a child, Hillary Clinton used to say, but in Stanwyck's case it's clear she came through the process scarred and essentially unraised. Something was missing and, hints Callahan, something unnatural happened as well, and the father seems especially shady. The subsequent screen image, the brassy, vibrant tough girl who could take good care of herself, was molded in this molten crucible and proved durable, one might say immutable, in any genre, comedy, melodrama, Western, thriller, musical (Stanwyck started as a showgirl and married up; she was always wonderful dancing and moving across the floor, though her singing wasn't all that).

Somehow—well, through her first husband, the domestic tyrant Frank Fay—she arrived at Columbia Studio, not quite a poverty-row film factory but not quite a major either, at exactly the right time, the frenzied days of the early talkies, the moment when the old stars died and new ones were born every day, many of them from the New York stage. Frank Capra offered her new roles, new expressions of vitality, new personae, and these stuck to her, she could work with them. Callahan has drawn some fire for sticking so adhesively to the auteur theory, and skips all over chronology telling you all about Stanwyck and Wilder, Stanwyck and Sirk, etc., but for me, I saw nothing to fault, and the approach makes it easier for the patterns to register in what otherwise looks, to the eye untrained, like a messy career. It was the age of the studio system, and yet once done with Columbia and Harry Cohn, Stanwyck refused to sign with another studio; she would not be an indentured servant. The upside of this policy is that she got to work opposite every major male star, but the downside of this independence was that the studios had little investment in helping her maintain a long-term career. She made crews love her with her salty populism, so she nearly always looked good, but sometimes it was touch and go, and as she got older she became more stolid and robust. When I was a boy and she was still making pictures, she always looked angry, like the mean old lady you didn't want to ring the bell of at Halloween.

Her private life remains a mystery, despite years of sapphic rumors and a (beard?) marriage to screen idol Robert Taylor. Callahan encourages us to believe the tales told by Robert Wagner, of a May–December romance fostered by Fox. She adopted a son in a shabby episode that made her look nasty, for though no star treats his or her children well, no one has ever had a youth as neglected and *désolé* as Dion Fay. The cycle of abuse! Callahan takes the long view. He's no idolater, and indeed is sometimes brutal, often about Stanwyck's work in what I consider some of her very best pictures. (He doesn't like *The Night Walker*.) (Neither does he care for *The Colbys*.) But he is such a compelling writer I rush from sentence to sentence, drinking it all in, thirsty for more wisdom and love.

I even grew fond of his King Charles's head, his bit about Stanwyck's tiny eyes, which occurs roughly once every six pages. At first this slur had me jumping up and running to a mirror to check to see if I have tiny eyes myself. How would a person know? I never noticed anything small about Stanwyck's eyes, did you? And yet it is one of the two central facts of Callahan's book, that and the notion that she, Barbara Stanwyck, is the single greatest actor in American movies. Hear, hear!

The Chocolate War
by Robert Cormier

★★★★★
Frightening as *1984*

September 7, 2012

I absolutely worshiped this book as a kid, perhaps because kids take the broad point of view and are willing to see, much more than adults, that life is basically a horrible rat race and most everyone falls into its trap at the end. What some have seen as the cynicism of the book kids see as a virtue, and what made this book special in 1974 (the era of Watergate) was that Cormier stood pretty much alone in his absolute negativity, while everyone else, from your school counselors on up, was encouraging you to look on the bright side always. Today, perhaps, the bright side isn't strictly enforced the way it once was. A general aura of gloom and doom prevails, in everything from TV to the news to comic books and social media. The increase in school shootings has given kids another reason to be afraid of their peers, but in 1974 we went to school, saw the evil, and couldn't see it reflected anywhere else but in *The Chocolate War.*

It was enough to put me off chocolate, and anyone who knows me knows I love the stuff! We raised money at our high school (another Catholic boys' school) to help the legal defenses of one of our own who was unjustly imprisoned for smuggling drugs across international borders. In this book, Jerry Renault stands alone against a tide of evil greater than any ever amassed in history, and several have read the book as an allegory for the conquering wave of Hitler and the Nazi party across Europe in the 1930s, while Brother Leon and Archie Costello stand in for Hitler and Mussolini. The book's title has these echoes, and also those of the Vietnam War, still raging while Cormier labored on his novel. Others have contrasted the world of Archie (the "assigner" of Trinity's secret society, the Vigils) with the world of Archie and Jughead at Riverdale High, and suggested that maybe private school, for all its cachet, isn't as good an education as the one meted out by Principal Weatherbee and Miss Grundy.

The Chocolate War is also thick with sexuality and violence. Some of its action was taken by Cormier from the existing school classics

To Sir, with Love and *The Blackboard Jungle* (for example, the famous "destruction of room 19" in *The Chocolate War* has its beginnings back in *To Sir, with Love,* when the teacher on his first day of school leans on his desk and finds it collapsing under his touch) and those books had dark elements, but in none of them was a student photographed whacking off in the boys' room and blackmailed about it, the linchpin of the action in the Cormier book. Jerry starts throwing up in his mouth when assailed as a "fairy" by Emile, ironically enough one who finds himself getting aroused when wrestling or tackling an opponent. Everyone's sort of dissociated from his feelings. Adolescence is a time to flex one's mental and physical muscles and there's a lot of flexing going on, and it never stops being grim. Maybe the book might have improved had there been one little ray of light, if only for contrast's sake, so if someone asked me for a good book to read about a private boys' school, I might suggest instead the superlative *A Good School* by Richard Yates, but this one isn't to be sneered at, even its silly parts.

Contagion (**2011**)
dir. Steven Soderbergh

★★★★☆
Nothing to Sneeze At

September 14, 2012

I watched *Contagion* with my wife and we both agreed that Steven Soderbergh has an eye for pretty women. Four of them star in the movie in question, but we watched in dismay as two of them wound up grotesquely disfigured and abused. One of them winds up with the skin pulled right off her face à la a memorable horror scene in the 1991 Michele Soavi import *La Setta*, produced by Dario Argento. I don't want to spoil any surprises so I won't tell you who's who, but another beautiful woman winds up kidnapped and forced to teach Chinese schoolchildren in a remote province of China, and yet she manages to stay as drop-dead gorgeous and coiffed as if she had Anouk Aimée's hairdresser combing her up after every class. I never did figure that one out, but the implication, my wife said, is that she didn't really mind being taken hostage at all; we thought maybe she had fallen for her principal captor, or at any rate she believed him when he said he wanted only health for his village and would seize it by any means necessary. She had beautiful sweaters and pearls for a schoolteacher, but that made sense because she was actually not a teacher at all but a—oh, mustn't say, that would be a giveaway about which of Soderbergh's four stars it was. Three of them are Oscar winners, and the one who isn't should have won for this!

Did Matt Damon and Jude Law win any Oscars? Weren't they in love in *The Talented Mr. Ripley* a few years back? Now they look considerably past their prime, but wouldn't you, if one of you were a blogger with a fierce conviction that the common forsythia, like the bush my grandma used to have in her side yard, could cure the outbreak, stop it cold, only the Centers for Disease Control in Atlanta wasn't letting the truth be known, and the other of you were this glum mournful widower who has to put on his own prom for his teenage daughter because of the quarantine? I won't say which is which, but let me tell you, there were many creepy scenes but none so creepy as our widower trying to turn his living room into prom night with yards and yards of white-satin ribbon and a weird prom gown delivered in a plastic bag. My wife and I were surprised to find that he wasn't supposed to be unnaturally involved with his daughter, it was just supposed to be a cute thing he was doing to make her feel better about the disease ravaging Minneapolis. I have to say that the movie was filled with surprises and I felt that the blog thing was right up to the minute two years ago or whenever this movie came out.

A Man and a Woman (1966)
dir. Claude Lelouch

★★★★★
Spinout

September 18, 2012

We had recorded a whole sheaf of movies off of Turner on our DVR and there they were, stacked in alphabetical order, and by chance the first two listed were both '60s French new wave films, *A Man and a*

Woman and *Band of Outsiders*. We started with the first. Oh, what a show! At first it's slow and shaky, and it's hard to get used to the idea that basically we are going to have to watch a whole movie about what amounts to the French NASCAR. I was rolling my eyes, and you know, that part of the movie never got much better. Were race cars just coming into their own in the 1960s? We were switching back and forth between this picture and Elvis in *Spinout* (with Shelley Fabares and Deborah Walley), and again and again, we saw a little car make a big circle around a track, dust hitting the camera lens, and a handsome man presumably behind the wheel. Seemed like race cars were the thing in the '60s! After a while we just shrugged and decided to have a drink every time Jean-Louis Trintignant emerges from a tiny car, and so by reel three or four we were feeling no pain! We got giggly and started ordering only French drinks, like the Sazerac, and for the rest of the movie we laughed and laughed, until we got morose watching Anouk Aimée's big tragic black eyes and her wonderful hair. Has anyone ever hugged a man and used his ear to hide a depressed stare into empty space even half as subtly and effectively as Anouk Aimée? I don't think so.

She's haunted by the stunt death of her perfect husband, and trying to find love again with a race car driver, well, I can see why she's getting jitters. And his first wife went nuts worrying about the danger he constantly puts himself in. Maybe the race car thing was about the existentialism French people cultivated back in the 1960s. It wasn't perverse per se, it was just the obvious way to assert one's personal freedom against a backdrop of individual loss and social malaise. God, those scenes when the lovers get together with their children—Trintignant has a little boy, and Aimée a little girl—and you see the little boy talking a mile a minute, totally dominating the conversation, and effectively shutting up the little girl entirely—that was spooky, but the adults seemed to take it for granted. We loved the color and the b/w footage alternating, apparently at random—that is, once we ascertained that we were both seeing the same thing, in our altered state. "Are you seeing what I'm seeing?" I mumbled. "Yes," said my wife slowly. "The color went away." "Banished," I said sadly. "Abdicated," she said, "in the face of a great love and that catchy, frisky French music." "Wait," I said, after a few more laps round the track, "I think the color is back!" We sat there, breathless, before turning the channel to Elvis in *Spinout*—so strange that Shelley Fabares's millionaire dad is played by Carl Betz, the very actor who played her dad in *The Donna Reed Show*! Did they think audiences wouldn't accept her without Carl Betz?

Robert Duncan in San Francisco
by Michael Rumaker

★★★★★
Robert Duncan in San Francisco

November 20, 2012

Michael Rumaker is one of the last Black Mountain students still alive and active with memories of the fabled alternative institution at which Anni Albers, Mary Callery, M. C. Richards, Ruth Asawa, Hilda Morley, and Trude Guermonprez all taught. When the college collapsed, many of the students wound up in San Francisco, where a thriving art and poetry culture awaited them, in the wake of the *Howl* trial of 1957. Rumaker's memories center on Robert Duncan, the poet and artist who had served briefly at Black Mountain with his partner, the one-named painter Jess, and befriended Rumaker there, and later in Philadelphia, where Rumaker hailed from. They were both young men; well, Duncan was in his midthirties and seemed endlessly professional and together to the floundering Rumaker.

Not only that, but Duncan was openly gay, while Rumaker, though highly sexed, found himself a prisoner of the "city of night" that was homosexual life for most men in the 1950s. It was a time of cruising, blind determination, and often terrible luck (Rumaker was "once raped, twice almost murdered" at Rittenhouse Square). This covert sexuality was the product of a confused postwar nation which had caught a glimpse of homosexual activity from the Kinsey Report and now seemed determined to stamp it out altogether. Complicating relations between the older and younger man were several factors. Duncan painted one scenario in which he and Jess enacted the sort of domestic happiness and mutual love that was the mainstay of mass-culture magazines of the period like *Good*

Housekeeping and *Ladies' Home Journal,* but on the other hand flaunted traditional gay promiscuity much as had Baron de Charlus before him. In addition, callow Rumaker was both attracted to and afraid of Duncan's sensuous face, twitchy fingers, and his crossed eyes, which could look at you in both directions. (Rumaker calls him the "bountiful looker," a lovely way to put it.) And then there was the fact that they looked at each other across a very wide genre gap, for Duncan was the king of poetry, and Rumaker's forte was the short story, was prose in fact.

Duncan was the locus, but many were the attractions of the new-old city of San Francisco to a young man bristling with sensitivity and an eye for good-looking guys of every stripe. Rumaker arrived in San Francisco, having hitchhiked from the east with thirty bucks in his pocket and his clothes jammed into a battered old suitcase of his mother's, and tried to find a job uncompromised by his 4-F draft status. But living was cheap and easy, and friends like Paul Alexander, John Wieners, Joanne Kyger, and Tom Field helped him through the nights and days of high bohemia.

The original text of *Robert Duncan in San Francisco* was composed in the late 1970s while Duncan was still alive, and published in 2001 safely after his death. City Lights will shortly issue an edition swollen to twice its length by appendices, introductions, an interview with the author, and contemporary documents such as letters to and from Rumaker, and some readers will find this material as interesting as the slight memoir itself.

Collected Poems
by Naomi Replansky

Out of the Darkness

November 29, 2012

Recently I compiled a list for the online blog *Band of Thebes* of my favorite GLBT books of 2012, and I named this book, remembering only then that I hadn't written about it on Amazon, nor about the mix of complicated feelings that came about when I picked up this book at an independent store and saw its cover—markedly different from the one Amazon pictures above. It's a cover hard to describe, but it's two profiles both facing off toward their left, I thought at first two women of different races, but probably the same woman once when young, the other with sun-darkened skin and the snow-white hair of extreme old age. I take it that Naomi Replansky is still alive, for there are recent poems collected in this book, and she must have been quite handsome in her youth, if the short dark hair and the long neck and the exquisite long lashes of "youth" on the cover are any indication. And she's still pretty amazing looking, though a bit like Ossie Davis in his last days, but this might be the overenthusiasm of Black Sparrow's designer.

As befits an author who mourns Grace Paley and George Oppen in her acknowledgments, Replansky gives us back a nearly forgotten world of radical enthusiasms and controversies from the mid-1930s (*Discrete Series* time!) and I cannot be alone in finding these some of the most beautiful poems in the book. We can hear Auden in them, the committed Auden, and I think of the dynamic Hollywood films of William Wellman from his *Wild Boys of the Road* period; a poetry of the people, and yet perhaps a little bit removed. One brief series is called "Sideshow," and the characters, like the ones Bob Cummings and Priscilla Lane run into in Hitchcock's contemporary *Saboteur*, are traveling entertainers in a circus, the "Half-Man Half Woman" ("She must shun what he pursues / Down divided avenues"), the "Mammoth Man" (who stares "from wintry acres of despair"), the "Quick-Change Artist" (who "takes his shape and size / From the image in your eyes"), and the "Tattooed Lady." Wry, angry self-portraits, or perhaps portraits of conflicted intellectuals in the American Communist Party of a certain period? The Tattooed Lady has her heart and her life written on her skin, making her "public," Replansky asserts, and I wonder how much radical politics allowed her, and prevented her, from living out a life of committed same-sex affections and rejections.

I don't know as much as some about American poetry, but I was surprised indeed to discover in this remarkable book the life's work of a poet as fine as Auden or Oppen or any of her contemporaries, and yet I never heard of her! That's always a great feeling, isn't it, and yet brings its own disquiet, because I thought I was educated!

Anyhow here's to Black Sparrow, thanks for another must-have book. Maybe this, the first review of Replansky's *Collected Poems* to appear on Amazon, will be only the first of many.

German Potato Salad Can (15 oz., Pack of 12)
by Read

★★★★★
Holiday Seasonal Salad

November 30, 2012

Now that the holidays are here my wife and I attend many parties at church functions and social media events in San Francisco. Oddly enough the one food you see at both types of affairs is the so-called German potato salad. Recently we were at a party celebrating the arrival of young Twitter folks to our block. It's nice to see young people digging into the foods we had long ago as children in another time, predigital culture, when basically you went to the deli and asked for one of two different kinds of potato salad, or some wise old neighbors made it themselves, adding crumbling bacon and diced pickle chips to their golden hoard of spuds.

I asked the corporate hostess who had made the delicious potato salad we were wolfing down and she replied, "Alice Waters of Chez Panisse." It was worthy of Chef Waters, but as it turned out, later that evening the hostess sought me out and said she had been misinformed, and the Chez Panisse potato salad had been reserved for the Twitter VIPS, while we latecomers made do with fancy Read German Potato Salad. Nice of her to let us know, she was all apologetic and so forth, but Twitter had nothing to be ashamed of. In the backroom of the kitchen, we found empty cans of Read stacked high in the dumpster, easily seen even by fading eyes due to the distinctive red, yellow, and black packaging, like the flag of Germany, so simple it is like the red, white, and blue of the USA. The caterers had spiked up the Read canned salad with some extra potatoes, bacon, parsley, and some sagacious slices of fresh strawberry as a splash of garnish.

I compliment the Read people for making a product that not only baby boomers and the foreign born can enjoy, but something that new grads and new Twitter hires take to with the reckless abandon and élan of their generation. My wife who knows about such things whispered that, in addition, it is probably cheaper than ordering from Berkeley's Chez Panisse, where California cuisine was born, so if you had to pay off a student loan, it was probably going to be Read for you, at least till your start-up took off in a big way and all of a sudden the Rolling Stones were playing your company's Christmas party.

Sweet Judy Blue Eyes: My Life in Music
by Judy Collins

★★★★★
Ravaged by Addictions but Still Going Strong

December 31, 2012

We went to see Judy Collins singing Christmas songs with the San Francisco Symphony the other night and she wasn't that great at hitting notes, opening with a surprise, a crazy swing version of "Chelsea Morning" that had all of us gasping in despair. But as the evening wore on we warmed right up to her, forgiving her just about anything, and I do believe her voice improved as she kept singing, or else it was her between-song banter. So many amusing and touching stories that I said to my wife, "She should write a book!" Little did I realize she had written three memoirs until I got one for Christmas— this one, the most recent. She tells so much in this I wonder what she had to say in memoir #1 and memoir #2.

In later life psychiatrists suggested to Judy that her father, a famous musician himself, had committed "emotional incest" with her by confiding to the child Judy the graphic details of his extramarital affairs, perhaps as a way to separate the young girl from her mother's influence. Collins tells us that she rejected such diagnoses, preferring to think that her father was merely treating her as one adult friend might treat another, as a confidante. It's hard to know what to believe, especially because Judy seems never to have met a quack she didn't spend thousands of dollars on, and some of her counselors, especially those influenced by Harry Stack Sullivan, acted like a cult trying to lure her in and make her sleep with more men than even she wanted to sleep with, and that was a high figure to begin with. "Emotional incest" is a strong term, and yet to me it would seem to explain some of Collins's subsequent difficulties with food, alcohol, and self-esteem addictions. Obviously she was looking for love just like her father was. It was a different era too, when people drank all the time, at the drop of a hat, even in the swinging 1960s circles in which Judy moved, where drugs were the drug of choice so to speak, when she began recording the first of her thirty-eight LPs. She gives us details on the making of the first sixteen of them, and that's the very best part of the book. I don't think she gives herself enough credit for her break (around the time of *In My Life*) with strict trad-folk music, into the highly orchestrated and Brechtian song-cycle material she produced during a five-year superstreak, during which time she made Joni Mitchell and Leonard Cohen into stars.

The story of her romance with Stephen Stills has been told before, but now Judy admits that even though she was the older one in the relationship, she acted less maturely than Stills. He was not such a heartthrob if you ask me, but her taste in men was never traditional. Did she sleep with Richard Fariña? I think so, but she's not going to admit it until the death of her second great frenemy, Joan Baez. (I'm thinking that distant, elusive, snickering Joni Mitchell is obviously #1.) What I didn't expect was how beautifully Collins writes. She is a much better discursive writer than she is a songwriter. As the critics mention again and again, she brings people to life, even passing strangers, with a few words of brilliant description, and she has also the power of making people whom we thought we knew well (like JFK, for example) seem like newly minted, living beings for the first time.

As for the death of her son, I do not blame her for his suicide, unlike others who have written in this spot. Poor thing! The only false note in the book, or so I felt, was when she denied being bitter that she was not asked to sing at Woodstock, telling us instead that going to see Olympia Dukakis in a play was much more satisfying than singing would have been. Sorry, Judy, but that rang hollow, hollow as the Marabar Caves!

Long Island Modernism, 1930–1980
by Caroline Rob Zaleski

★★★★★
Not Only a Nest of Ninnies

January 12, 2013

I grabbed this book for a reason: I'm from Long Island myself and as an adult in California I'm haunted by the memories of the houses I saw and visited as a child, a teen, a young adult on the North Shore of Suffolk County. I wonder whose houses I was in, I wonder if they're still standing, and the evocative cover of *Long Island Modernism, 1930–1980* promised the exact answers to many of my idlest daydreams. Caroline Rob Zaleski's history is, for the most part, exceedingly well researched and imaginative; she has a huge sympathy for modernism in this era in which it has been reviled and, we see in the text, continually defaced and overbuilt. In some cases, like the famous Frank Lloyd Wright houses, the owners came to realize they were living more in a cathedral setting than anything homey, and covertly added toilets and the like, and central heating. The earliest house in the book had only a water pump outside the main structure to provide water for all of its residents. And we see that some modernist architects called for vast rooms impossible to heat in Long Island's frigid winters, though they must have been lovely in early October and mid-to-late April.

Long Island in this period was a strange combination of farm and beach land, and growing suburban kitsch and sprawl. Wealthy people came to live right next to the poor settlers, and often the latter turned to serving the former, like the society pictured in the 1960s sitcom *Green Acres*. (Or its converse, *The Pruitts of Southampton* with Phyllis Diller.) As Zaleski shows, the great architects came and saw and conquered, more or less, though neighborhood associations and the like sometimes vetoed innovative plans because they were just too weird. My town, Smithtown, prided itself on its colonial atmosphere, having been founded in 1664 by a man who made a wager against Native peoples that he could ride around huge chunks of forest on the back of a wild bull, and whatever land he traversed would belong henceforward to him and his descendants. A giant statue of a bull greets visitors to Smithtown at the junction of Routes 25 and 25A, anatomically correct, and in my day it was the sport of the high school kids to paint its genitalia red and green at Christmastime, orange and black at Halloween, green for Saint Patrick's Day, etc. Most of the houses and buildings were generic split-level "shingle style" cookie-cutter schlock, those that were not three-hundred-year-old former blacksmith shops, but now and again we would be greeted by something authentically deco or Bauhaus in our midst, a quiet home, sprawling at one end or the other, with nothing cute about it, nor ornamental. I remember one house in my neighborhood, on Eckernkamp Drive between River Heights and Landing Avenue, nearby Sweetbriar Park and the Nissequogue River, that was just amazing, as if Mies van der Rohe lived there, and of course he didn't, but who did? Since no kids were ever seen entering or exiting the house, we had no plausible way of finding out.

Zaleski has organized her survey according to architect, and each chapter gives us the accomplishments of a great visionary, so that perhaps individuals who made only one cool house might get lost in the shuffle a bit; at any rate, it's an effective method of getting the reader through vast quantities of social history. In architecture as perhaps in no other art, one sees the power of money, vast quantities of it, to make a change. Perhaps it took less money to build the Conger Goodyear House in Old Westbury than it did to construct Versailles, and perhaps the Goodyear house is a bit less fussy, but both exude the solidity of state power and perhaps something of its woeful playfulness. A prewar photo of the Goodyear shows us the "long gallery," with its barrage of then-contemporary pictures lining the wall as seen from the lanai, a splendid Picasso guitar, a Matisse, a Segonzac, Cézanne's *Peasant in a Blue Smock*, winding up with a Salvador Dalí so new it must have been still wet. Zaleski takes her vocabulary for discussion of each house from the terms the architect or the family used, so a sentence studded with quotations appears quite often, there's one on page 140 in which we are told we are "looking through the 'long gallery' toward the 'sunroom.'" It took me awhile to understand the reason for all this internal quotation, but "now" it's quite "comprehensible."

Many of the families remain colorless, perhaps because they have watchful descendants, but Zaleski is capable of *Answered Prayers*–like innuendo which spices up her style from time to time.

Her pages on Villa Riele (Rielle Hunter, anyone?), the cozy mansion of the playgirl baroness Gabriele Lagerwall in Lloyd Harbor, speak volumes about the dissolute lifestyle of the very rich and those who invent perfumes like "White Shoulders." These people often knew exactly what they wanted and their architects struggled to take care of their demands. Richard Neutra added a hydraulic contraption to one side of the bed in John Nicholas and Anne Brown's Fishers Island home, because Anne loved to smoke in bed and wanted an ashtray-type thing that would descend into the servants' quarters so they could clean it and return it to their mistress's bedside table. Other colorful clients included a Westhampton hotelier who had Charles Addams come in and create a large mural over the bar in which the *Addams Family* characters went fishing and swimming in the ocean outside the Dune Club, and a Hempstead theater mogul who built a grand modernist movie palace at exactly the wrong time, commercially, to do such a thing, but who managed to scare up Edward Steichen and Carl Sandburg to attend the opening. By the end of the book these architects are working on large, somewhat brutalist state universities and other public buildings, and some of the fun goes out of the writing, but all in all this is a fantastic read, and even better, the book benefits from the services of a fantastic photo editor. Simply put, everything you want to see that's mentioned in the text is right there, in a gorgeous period photo. It beats the internet!

Finally, the book intrigues in its several accounts of the US sculptor Mary Callery—I've heard of many artists but never of this one—and Zaleski makes a case that she is dreadfully underrecognized today, whereas sixty years ago she was one of the leading (I was about to say "female," but strike that) artists in the USA and what we see of her work is fantastically period and more. What gives, when someone mentioned in the same breath as Calder, Noguchi, Brâncuşi, not once but all of the time in the 1950s, gets completely forgotten?

The house I was looking for is not in this book, sadly enough, so if any of my readers know Smithtown, and know the house on Eckernkamp between River Heights and Landing Avenue, right before that curve onto the bridge over the Nissequogue, and perhaps you have kids and the present owners have kids, have them mingle and get back to me with, Who was the architect and how did he come to build that house in Smithtown, of all places? I looked it up on Google Earth and I swear I saw some kids playing in the shadows.

———————

Gone Girl
by Gillian Flynn

★★★★☆
What Was That Movie Called ...

January 15, 2013

What was that movie called, with Michael Douglas and Kathleen Turner, and Danny DeVito was in it somehow, where they were a couple getting a divorce and there was nothing too low for either of them to wish on the other? *The War of the Roses*, wasn't it? The movie played on the good feelings, the chemistry, the stars had exhibited in earlier teamings (like *Romancing the Stone*) and then bludgeoned everything nice the audience felt for either by a sick, twisted, heaping helping of absurd malice and overkill. Well, perhaps you know where I'm going with this, but if you saw *The War of the Roses*, there's really no need to read *Gone Girl*. I will say that *GG* is wonderfully written, and Gillian Flynn hasn't lost her knack for gothic suspense built up on lonely settings populated by demented people with a thrill for blood.

I was ready to hate Nick from the moment I heard him call his sister, Margo, "Go." Pardon me, I beg you, if any readers are called "Go," but in a book overteeming with coincidence and farfetchedness, I found the use of "Go" as a diminutive of "Margo" the hardest to swallow. I would love to see what the original Margo (Margo Channing in *All about Eve*) would have made of Nick if he were her brother and he came up with one of his trademark banter-bordering-on-incest lines like "Go, you're just like me if I had a dick." He would be mincemeat. It's plain above all else that Missouri really is an awful place to grow up in and an even worse one to return to. The burghers of Missouri must have photos of Gillian Flynn posted next to every cash register reading simply "Shoot on Sight."

I did think that the device of a successful series of children's books based on an "Amazing Amy" character was very believable and I hope

Flynn grants a deserving young writer the franchise rights to flesh out the series, continue the brand. Flynn has seen the very worst of men and women and she is leaving no stones unturned in her effort to permanently deter a nation from heterosexual intercourse.

Lincoln (**2012**)
dir. Steven Spielberg

★★★★★
Like the *Lord of the Rings*, Sort Of

January 29, 2013

We plunged into *Lincoln*, four of us, each with a different relationship to Spielberg, Sally Field, and Daniel Day-Lewis, and so when we filed out again to John Williams's credits music, there were at least 16 and probably 256 mixtures of feeling, all told. We climbed into the car, parked several blocks away from the busy downtown San Francisco movie palace we were at, and avidly discussed the movie until night fell and the stars broke through the low-lying clouds on a warm January night. The main topic of conversation: how lucky for Abe Lincoln to have Adam Driver to turn to on those cold Washington nights when the war was keeping him up, not to mention the madness of Mary Todd.

Adam Driver, who plays Adam on HBO's *Girls*, plays Samuel Beckwith, the lead White House telegraph operator, in Spielberg's *Lincoln*. We wondered first of all why screenwriter Tony Kushner hadn't just called his character "Adam" too, as his other writers do. Poor Adam must have had a disconnect when he realized he was going to have to answer to somebody else's name. Thus when Lincoln brushes his hair fondly, mumbles "Good night, Sam," you can see it in Adam's eyes, he doesn't really know why Lincoln is calling him "Sam," it's not registering, his beautiful eyes fill up with puzzlement, just like on *Girls* when Hannah won't answer his calls. One of our party denied it was Adam at all, citing the blond highlights in Sam's hair that glisten in the thousands of gas lamps and sexy candles that brighten up Lincoln's private telegraph office, complete with bed. "Adam isn't blond," our friend argued. "Well, in the nineteenth century he was. Samuel was blond," I countered, believing at the time that Samuel Beckwith was a real-life nineteenth-century communicator (perhaps the inventor of the telegram?), not knowing then what I know now, that Kushner and Spielberg had made up the appealing character of Sam, to use him as a sort of yes man slash devoted friend, like Sam in *The Lord of the Rings*, willing to do anything to get his Frodo-like master out of a jam. "Substitute Lincoln for Frodo," I continued, "Sam for Sam, and the war against slavery for the war against Mordor or whatever it was called, and it's working for me."

My wife happened to be in the ladies' room during Adam's big scene, and we kept waiting for him to come in at the end, but alas no. His simple act, however, of

[SPOILER ALERT]

telling someone in Virginia to stash the peace delegation in a shack somewhere,

[SPOILERS CONCLUDED]

changed the whole course of the war—no, not the war, but he caused the Thirteenth Amendment to be signed and slavery abolished forever more. It was the kind of miracle that Adam Driver fans expect of their idol. That bravery, that competence with machinery, and otherwise the dumb look of a man who can't keep it in his pants for very long, and maybe that's why, we speculated (except for the one of us who denied that it was Adam at all), maybe that's why Daniel Day-Lewis kept him within arm's reach, to warm his pallet and to bring back the simple joys of boyhood.

The Redgraves: A Family Epic
by Donald Spoto

★★★★★
A Surprise

March 11, 2013

I bought this book basically because of pressure from Amazon, or maybe "pressure" isn't the mot juste, but you know when it tells you that "People Who Bought This Book Also Bought," and it shows you four photos of other book jackets? Well, this one had pictures of the recent biographies of Henry Fonda, Dana Andrews, and Elizabeth Montgomery from *Bewitched*, and since I owned all of them, I figured why not join the other "people" in question and get this book too. The funny thing is that, despite all expectations, this book was actually the best, by far, of the four biographies.

I have to agree with the other reviewer who praised Spoto for his restraint here. Yes, Rachel Kempson married Michael Redgrave even after he told her up front he would always be gay and would always be looking for outside affairs with men. And yes, Vanessa went and did the same thing with her first husband Tony Richardson, who wound up tragically dying of AIDS long after Vanessa had gone off him. The previous reviewer praised Spoto's refusal to speculate on the connection between these two marriages, but of course it is exactly the heart of the family narrative that we are given, like a hinge. It all seems to be about, Well, did Vanessa know about her dad, or know about Tony? Spoto can't say. That's all right. It is a puzzling coincidence perhaps, and makes me look closer into the private lives of Liam Neeson and whoever it is that Joely married because three times is the charm. Be that as it may, one wishes that Rachel and Michael, who are so big in this story, were better represented in the movies than they appear to be. We hear much about how great Rachel was as Volumnia and Dorcas and in other minor Shakespeare parts, and how towering a Lear and Macbeth was Michael, but without a filmed record, it's hard to judge. I did love Rachel Kempson in *The Jewel in the Crown*, but I get her mixed up in my mind with that UK actress who often plays Emma Thompson's mother because, well, because she *is* Emma Thompson's mother.

The financials are given here, frankly, and they give a through line to a complicated story: how Michael and Rachel had no equity really, because even when they were momentarily rich, people wouldn't give them credit because as actors they had no fixed source of income. I hope Liam Neeson is managing better than his in-laws' family, otherwise the next step is invariably a theatrical boarding house where you have to share the kidneys and mash with a table teeming with ambitious understudies and faded has-beens still looking for their spotlight.

A Bundle of Time: The Memoirs of Harriet Cohen
by Harriet Cohen

★★★★★
The *Just Kids* of a Bygone Generation

March 27, 2013

Like many readers today, I was hooked by Patti Smith's memoir of a few years back, very moved by its razor-sharp recall and the generosity with which she was able to look back at a very distant time, acknowledging the heartbreak and the pain of some of the scenes she found herself in, but in general compassionate enough to see the beauty even in the darkness. And I kept thinking as I was reading *Just Kids*, "What old-time book does this remind me of?" Finally, after a two-hour hunt through my bookcases, I remembered this book, *A Bundle of Time: The Memoirs of Harriet Cohen*. A friend had pressed it on me some years back when I told him I had never heard of Harriet Cohen, and now she has become a watchword to me, a sign of utter sympathy and high culture, like the code of recognition between strangers that E. M. Forster writes about in *Two Cheers for Democracy*. "I believe in aristocracy … if that is the right word, and if a democrat may use it," he averred. "Not an aristocracy of power … but an aristocracy of the sensitive, the considerate. … Its members are to be found in all nations and classes, and all through the ages, and there is a secret understanding between them when they meet."

For me that's what connects Smith and Cohen, but I should back up and explain that she was a British pianist, quite beautiful, who knew all the great modernists in England and abroad, in the '20s and '30s at least, which is the period she managed to write about fullest in this book, published posthumously and cobbled together from scraps by the publishers shortly after her untimely death in 1967. You can hear her piano playing on YouTube, and it will not be to everybody's taste; she has little power and often seems like a dilettante or a ghost, preferring lovely little things with too many or too few notes. But if you are in the mood, she is completely convincing and you can see why many of the great artists of her day wanted her to premiere their new works. And she can write like a dream! And she was movie-star beautiful, there is not a photo in existence which shows her as anything but a goddess. Her career was stalled by anti-Semitism, or "racialism" as it was then called; in the period between the wars she comes to realize the dangers of Nazi ideology years before the dopey politicians of England and France. She was an activist even though her life seems otherwise comfortable and wealthy from the start—oh, and I forgot to say that her gender probably also hindered her from full acclaim, for many of the conductors for whom she might have worked dismissed her as a sort of musical Anaïs Nin with wrists too fragile to play her instrument properly.

Her best trait in writing is her ability to draw the reader into the innumerable social and aesthetic scenes of the day. She knew Elgar, Vaughan Williams, Bax, Holst, and scores of British musicians—the book jumps forward in time a little to present accounts of her friendships with (and letters from) the somewhat younger Britten and Tippett. She traveled widely and met Manuel de Falla, Sibelius, Stravinsky, Ravel, Richard Strauss, musicians of dozens of lands. And she knew the writers too. She was a particular pet of Arnold Bennett, H. G. Wells, Somerset Maugham, George Bernard Shaw, and she spills dozens of anecdotes about them, not just charming but really incisive. She is the sort of voice, like Patti Smith, that you want to hear about everybody from—she inspires trust in the reader. I learned more about Einstein (yes, Einstein!) from this book than in the multivolume biographies on the man. In a way, a cynic could find this penchant for famous names amusing, like the second-act number Judy Holliday sang in *Bells Are Ringing* ("Drop That Name"), but Cohen was there, and invariably she saw the tiny things that make each human soul memorable, unique. Karsavina, Horowitz, Busoni, Ethel Smyth, they swim through these pages like beautiful jeweled fish.

Nobody, not even Patti Smith, can give us a complex cameo like Harriet Cohen can. Here's one taken more or less at random, plunging my finger into the book as one might consult the *I Ching*: "Lytton Strachey had wanted me to meet Ottoline Morrell almost as soon as we became acquainted, and I was anxious to do so, having seen this astonishing creature only from a distance. In her enormous hats, swathed in pale, floating chiffons—the tinkling of jewels at her ears like sounds of pagodas—somehow she called up unimaginable delights even if the beholder were only a woman. She had a proud head that reared like that of some wild creature in a forest, one awaited a neigh. When she gave her hands in greeting, she gave herself. I adored her on sight."

Gershwin wrote "Oh, Lady Be Good!" for Cohen. Rilke seems like he was in love with her. Thornton Wilder told her that she was the true "woman of Andros." But one reads *A Bundle of Time* for Cohen's writing, its firm yet delicate tracery of the varieties of human experience. "Talking of Bartók," she will write, "Gray once described him to me as 'completely inhuman.'" (It is like Cohen to remember and credit those friends of hers who came up with striking remarks.) "It is true that his very appearance suggested pure spirit, the intensity of his gaze, that slender, later-attenuated form—'like gold to aery thinness beaten' as Donne had it—gave him an almost diaphanous quality. But the reserve, the aloofness that I had expected was simply not there, as he sat laughing at the small supper party after the concert." The reference to Donne is so Harriet! As is the twist, the narrative surprise of the slender beaten-gold apparition becoming full human through the power of laughter. My copy of the book is marked now with dozens of colorful Post-its marking her wise and witty remarks, but I could sit here till 2014 and not get them all down. You must read this book and let it change your way of seeing.

Center Square: The Paul Lynde Story
by Steve Wilson and Joe Florenski

★★★★☆
In Memory of Bing Davidson

April 18, 2013

I remember seeing Paul Lynde on TV game and variety shows when I was a boy, and then seeing him in George Sidney's version of *Bye Bye Birdie*. What an astonishing dad he made, with that somewhat handsome face that crumpled at the drop of a phone call or a sign from Ann-Margret that she was growing up. He was great at reacting, and that's rather rare in screen acting, but you could watch the whole movie if Christian Marclay–like Photoshop interns blacked out 90 percent of it, cut out the soundtrack, and just left his expressive face reacting to his daughter's confusing combination of daughterly pampering and siren-like keening. She—Ann-Margret—embodies life, or youth, as no other star ever could, and Lynde watching her seems like an old man, though he was what, thirty-three when the movie was filmed? His is the gaze of death, puzzled death, death mystified that life goes on without him, life has got another life to lead, outside of the family structures Dad embodies.

Of course the authors make clear how ironic this setup is, since Lynde was himself running headlong from the disaster of his own nuclear family (and the line of individual deaths it entailed), and his own drive for pleasure was no less pure and driven than Ann-Margret's. Now that I think of it, funny how neither star had any children themselves? I'm not saying there was a curse on *Bye Bye Birdie*, but—

In fact, how could there be when Janet Leigh, playing the Spanish songwriter Rosie so memorably with the black wig, was already the mother of two lovely daughters?

This is all prelude to my concise description of *Center Square* as a biography of a great showman who used alcohol as a crutch to make his way through a difficult, if charmed, life. The authors have apparently interviewed a number of players in Lynde's life, though unfortunately the editing of the book obscures their original research, making it seem as though they surrounded themselves with twenty years of *TV Guides* and let the chips fall where they may. But a vivid picture of a legend shines through. He had his own cadres of celebrity fans, if we can believe authors Steve Wilson and Joe Florenski— including Garbo, who sent him a fan letter (where is it now?), Alfred Lunt and Lynn Fontanne, Harry S. Truman, an unlikely bunch all around. *Hollywood Squares*, of course, propelled him into superstardom, and eventually he clawed his way into the center square, sometimes attaining a political edge that made remaining in the closet a moot issue. "According to the old song, what's 'breaking up that old gang of mine'?" he was asked, and after a pause he ventured "Anita Bryant?" You tell 'em Paul Lynde! I came away from the book thoroughly impressed by Lynde's durability as a star, and his sex, drug, and alcohol problems I chalked up to the perils of fame, but I wasn't prepared for the incident of July 1965 that occurred here in San Francisco, on the eighth floor of the famed Sir Francis Drake Hotel here on Powell Street, coincidentally enough right around the time famed San Francisco poet Jack Spicer was writing his final poems very close by.

That was the night that Paul Lynde checked in with a bartender boyfriend, and before the wild party was over, the younger man was dead. Bing Davidson plunged to death after lowering himself out of the window ledge and clinging by his fingertips. The last thing he saw was Paul Lynde's leering face hovering above him and one by one his fingers slipped. Bye, bye, Birdie! Kenneth Anger left this lurid story out of his book *Hollywood Babylon*. Was he paid off, I wonder? Kenneth Anger: we thought you had integrity! Anyhow I can't walk up Powell Street now without thinking of the poor man, Bing Davidson, cute, smushed-up victim of a comic's lust.

"Viva Miscegenation"
by Brian Kim Stefans

★★★★★
A Neuropathic Catullus

April 23, 2013

Brian Kim Stefans hasn't had the normal career of a poet, but instead the zigzags of his life and leanings gave him access into fields of inquiry that most of us were ignorant of until he opened the way. His latest book, *"Viva Miscegenation,"* comes already titled with the quotation marks Louis Zukofsky took to distinguish his *"A"* from other *As*—or should I have written "'other *As*'"? *Miscegenation* itself is a cold, distant, and cruel word, so one wonders why anyone would wish it long life, especially a poet of mixed racial heritage as rehearsed in his own name (for he is Brian, the emperor of the Irish, then Kim, Polish like Kim Novak, and somewhere back in his ancestry his family belonged to the Stefans). There's a lot to unpack just on the cover of the book, and I'm not discounting the glittery, shiny silver-on-white tiny stripes that roll vertically across its recto and verso—like an ornate present in a 1950s society wedding.

I trace the movement of the book from a measured, mannered New York School pastiche to the somewhat scattered and tangential vibrations one picks up in Southern California. It is not immediately easy for poets such as BKS or Aaron Kunin (who writes a blurb for this book and to whom one of the very best poems is dedicated) to subject the keen ice of their intelligence, that bristling wit, to the torporous history of La Brea's famed tar pits, but in each case the operation has been a success, both poets writing as never before, with an ease new to them, a contingent glow of imperfection, almost a Cheshire cat's smile evaporating from the pages as quickly as one reads them. There's a distinct luxuriance in mouthing the words, those that Brian Wilson whispered in Glen Campbell's ear during Campbell's 1965 solo recording sessions: "I guess I'm dumb, but I don't care." (See the end to "Metro," on page 123: "Why are you never asking / or putting your arms around me when you see, I'm dumb?" Such a beautiful heaping of the tropes of abled vs. disabled, question vs. sentence, first vs. second person, all come tumbling down like the perfect endless wave.) The impression is of a beloved genius somewhat happy at last, like he would even kiss a sunset pig, to quote another unlikely transplant from colder climes.

This Ain't No Holiday Inn: Down and Out at the Chelsea Hotel 1980–1995
by James Lough

★★★★★
A Gritty, Grotesque, Vanished World

June 25, 2013

I met author James Lough on the rooftop garden of the old San Francisco Museum of Modern Art, introduced by a mutual friend. Perhaps he knew of my interest in the '80s (about which I have often written), for he told me that he'd be soon publishing a book on the Chelsea Hotel during that period. Not exactly the glory days for the hotel, but I told him I'd look out for his book and now that it is under my belt, I'd like to recommend it to those of my readers who can look a gritty subject in its face and not shrink away, for *This Ain't No Holiday Inn* is bold with a capital *B*. Quickly Lough sketches the bygone days when Thomas Wolfe and O. Henry lived in the place, when Sarah Bernhardt built her own exotic pyramid in her apartment with which to restore her energies. The '60s (Dylan, Joni Mitchell, Nico, Patti Smith, Leonard Cohen, Joplin) made the hotel a synonym for raffish sleaze, but by the time Sid killed Nancy, it was all downhill.

Lough has assembled a team of talkative Chelsea habitués, I think all but one or two former residents of the hotel, to spill their most intimate stories. I hadn't heard of any of the witnesses, so in terms of star power this is no *Edie* or *Reds*, but each has his or her own charm and the stories that come tumbling out of them are like some lost Pasolini film like *Mamma Roma* or whatever, the drive, the lust for life, the passion for drugs, the rebellion, and the ennui. These witnesses describe the last days of Beat legends Huncke and Corso, the birth of the love affair between Viva Superstar and William Eggleston, the conflicted post-Ramones musical career of Dee Dee Ramone, and the mess that was Jaco Pastorius, in his twenties one of the most talented bassists of jazz, in his thirties a corpse self-medicated to death. Dee Dee Ramone is quoted as having said "all you need for a good punk rock song is three chords and a grudge." Most of the action takes place on the hotel's second and third floors, where most of the lowlifes were housed, and we hear very little of the upper floors of the hotel, where wealthy aristocrats passed their days on oysters and ormolu furniture, little guessing about the human misery groveling below their parquet floors. Yes, five or six stories below men and women were turning tricks for one hit of crack cocaine, and that was on a good day! *Last Exit to Brooklyn* move over, *This Ain't No Holiday Inn* is the new benchmark in squalor and broken minds. I take 1980–95 as the era during which AIDS ravaged New York City and the world, and the Chelsea, of course, was not spared. Some affecting AIDS stories give the book its depth, its compassion, its courage.

Lough can write (his analysis of Eggleston's photos is astute and provocative) and he seems to enjoy the perfect confidence of these blind creatures of the night. (One was his brother-in-law.) Witnesses describe the painter and poet Rene Ricard as autocratic and sometimes withering (he appears in a subchapter titled "Scary Poet Rene Ricard"), but he is given his proper due as a Leonardo-like Renaissance man—one guy tells Lough that "if you're an intellectual, Rene Ricard is a blast. It's like sitting with someone like Shelley or Milton." And he refers not to Shelley Winters or Milton Berle; he means to place Ricard in the very pantheon of human genius, so yeah!

It is too bad they couldn't afford a proofreader down there, so that Virgil Thomson's name appears as "Thomson" some of the time, as "Thompson" the rest of the time—Thomson and Thompson, like the twin detectives in the *Tintin* books. Is Peter Brook alive? After hearing himself referred to as "Brooks," he may not make it to eighty-nine. Nevertheless, anybody who's ever had a cockroach crawl over their shoe will warm to this book as I did. It's got vitality.

Rin Tin Tin: The Life and the Legend
by Susan Orlean

★★★★☆
Almost Excellent

July 7, 2013

I came to Rin Tin Tin through my study of the works of contemporary poet John Ashbery, who early in his career wrote a trio of poets-theater plays, and one of them was said to have been lifted from the intertitles of *Where the North Begins*, a very early Rin Tin Tin silent. Watching the movie over seventy times to transcribe all the intertitles (and indeed pinning down quite a few Ashbery borrowings), I began to feel first admiration, then respect, then downright awe for the star dog's acting range. One of the suggestive parts in Susan Orlean's massive biography of Rin Tin Tin is her continual assertion that possibly more than one dog was used in any one film, and that Lee Duncan's own German shepherd, discovered as if in a miracle in war-torn France and just about smuggled back to the States against all military regulations, got the credit that might have been shared by dozens of look-alikes. Indeed can one call Orlean's book a "biography," since its hero dies pretty early on in the book and we hear about this and that of his inferior sons and grandsons, etc.? I suppose she would say that she is writing instead about the "idea" of Rin Tin Tin and so anything goes.

Anything certainly gets into this giant book. As many reviewers have noted, Orlean could have used an editor or two, or is she too powerful to have to submit to one, like Stephen King must be? There are so many extraneous bits of material here; you follow a tangent expecting it will amount to something, or have at least a tiny connection to Rinty, and it just doesn't. What was the point, Susan Orlean, of that long chapter about the crypto-lesbian poodle trainers who put poodles on the map in America in the 1930s and 1940s? It was fun to read that a halftime show of trained poodles at Yankee Stadium got more cheers than Joe DiMaggio, but then the story just peters out and it's back to more glum moments with Lee Duncan's charmless daughter. BTW, the daughter seems like a reasonable woman somewhat beat down by life, but one comes away feeling that Orlean had something of a grudge against her for some reason, because she's painted as though her whole life were a disappointment orchestrated by Theodore Dreiser or Michael Haneke or some other misery-meister.

Nevertheless, I forgive all the flaws of the book for the power of the scenes in which Orlean discovers Rin Tin Tin's grave in a Parisian animal cemetery … and for the ending of the book, actually about ten endings, a multitude of riches, for it seems she wasn't sure which poignant moment to end on so she puts all of them in over the last forty pages of the book, finally the kitchen-sink strategy pays off big time!

Until They Sail (1957)
dir. Robert Wise

★★★★★
Wise Virgins

August 27, 2013

I watched this picture the day that Eydie Gormé died, so I was thunderstruck when the credits rolled and David Raksin's theme music started playing and Eydie's distinctive voice started singing the theme song! It was the last thing I expected to hear, but so welcome on a day of national mourning. Eydie sings a phrase or two, and a man who must have won the National Whistling Contest whistles either the same phrase or a phrase that ascends instead of descending, etc. In this way the song parallels the central movement of Robert Wise's film, a series of insinuative statements and ironic, sometimes bittersweet counterstatements. (I've since found out that the whistler in question is none other than Muzzy Marcellino, the man who whistled the themes from *The High and the Mighty* and [later on] The Good, *The Bad and the Ugly*!)

Anyhow the movie itself is in black and white, and if only they had spent a little bit more on color, then I'd be ready to declare this a masterpiece on the level of John Sturges's *By Love Possessed* or Douglas Sirk's *Magnificent Obsession*. The black and white makes the New Zealand settings look tacky, cheap, though perhaps in the 1950s people oohed and aahed when they saw Christchurch on the screen. Wise's darting camera does its best to give the movie the sweep and motion of a historical epic, but we don't feel the grandeur. In a way it hardly matters, what with all the human emotions roiling on the screen, any time Piper Laurie pipes up, with her sluttishly tight sweaters and her eyes on the glittering sheaf of American GI wealth and chocolates, the movie takes off with its own sizzle. It's not that Piper Laurie is a great actress or anything like that, but Robert Wise gives her the signal to just tear up the narrative as the bad sister, Delia. "Dee," they call her in times of kinder reminiscence. They never know what last name to give to her, as she uses the name of whatever man has the most money.

This is one of those home front movies that details not only the four sisters losing every man they had—a husband, a brother, a boyfriend, a father—but gaining back replacements for them via the steady supply of new American blood to replace their own, depleted, Kiwi energy. A Cold War movie in many ways, *Until They Sail* shows us an American army in fine fettle, fighting trim, guaranteed to win the war for the frail females—though to be fair, it does show us some foul soldiers, fully capable of Abu Ghraib–style atrocities; it's like the Ernest Borgnine character in *From Here to Eternity* multiplied by hundreds. But it shows us good men too, like Charles Drake and Paul Newman, men with needs but who don't abuse hospitality. Joan Fontaine learns this lesson best of all, and the extreme arc of her character must have intrigued the flighty, sensitive actress, but it's still hard to swallow that she of all people would go off to Nowhere, USA, based on a grim telegram which any sensible person would shudder at. But that's enough spoilers for me. Suffice it to say that Fontaine and Laurie give performances equal to their more celebrated roles, and Jean Simmons and Sandra Dee are not far behind. For once, Jean Simmons is playing a heroine untrammeled by Freudian traumas, while Dee is weirdly cast as a young girl totally devoted to the opposite sex, and she was what, twelve when she made this? You'd think they'd have tried to cast some-body a little bit older, but perhaps this was the era of *Lolita*, and Robert Wise was dipping a toe into that piquant, pellucid water of potential.

Vertigo (1958)
dir. Alfred Hitchcock

★★★★★
Vertigo Challenges

September 2, 2013

It's the greatest movie of all time, at least I think so in certain moods. Tonight we saw this one at the Castro in 70 mm and it looked pretty convincing, almost as though it might have been made yester-day. But it's long, I had forgotten how long! Maybe because the movie breaks off into two more or less equal parts, it's like watching a double feature, a movie that carries its own sequel in its tail. This evening I decided to give myself up to the Bernard Herrmann music—since it's so insistent you listen to it, I decided to put my other senses on dull and just go for that total immersion … the way that Barbara Bel Geddes recommends that James Stewart immerse himself in Mozart ("Mozart is the boy for you," she says, rather infan-tilizing Mozart if such a thing were actually possible, but that sort of remark reminds me of why Scotty doesn't really appreciate Midge's good qualities, because she's so much like a mother!)—in other words, I let the Herrmann score wash all over me like the high tide that splashes behind the lovers in the climactic kiss scene in *Vertigo*.

So what happened? I started wondering, "That one theme is so dominant and seductive in the score, was it ever made into a pop tune with lyrics, sung by Nat King Cole or Julie London or some-one?" Help me out there, soundtrack geeks! It's gorgeous indeed, and yet I remember when I was a kid seeing *Vertigo* for the first time, I didn't like the music, it felt dissonant and distracting. There's that one section of music when Scottie follows Madeleine Elster into the Mission Dolores and he turns a corner and finds himself in the grave-yard where the music goes sort of "religious" in a really rote way that just wasn't working for me, it made me giggle to myself like "Didn't anybody else in the theater get the joke?" The Castro crowd was certainly giggling when Midge tells Scottie, "Oh, you want the kind of guy who knows about the gay old times in San Francisco back when everything was gay!" But when this mock-religious bell-tinkle music began, I heard nothing from the audience, just awe perhaps.

SPOILER ALERT. Now for my own challenges with the movie.

I was struck by Ellen Corby here as perhaps never before, the hotel manager who wipes her rubber plant leaves with olive oil. How is it that Madeleine is in her room, above their heads, and yet Corby swears that she never came today and points to the key dangling from the hook? We have seen her with our own eyes, and it looks like she's undressing, and yet when Corby calls down the stairs "Mister Detective, do you want to take a look yourself?" Scottie manages to run up the stairs like a trooper and no, she's not there. But why? Corby must be lying, perhaps she is in on the plot, but if so, why the mystification here? Why doesn't she just say "Yes, she's upstairs," and Scottie can wait for her to leave? I wonder if there wasn't some extra plot line being developed here that was eventually cut back from the finished film, in which dematerialization itself would have been used by the criminal cohort? But for those who think that Gavin Elster will get off scot-free at the end because Scottie has no living witness for the substitution plot at the heart of the film, I foresee a crazy Scottie going back to the McKittrick and rubbing Ellen Corby with olive oil until she too confesses her involvement (whatever it is), and voila, Elster is led off in handcuffs and Corby is sobbing and dripping with emollient.

And also, has anyone thought much about Midge as a possible accomplice to the murder? I thought about it during the Argosy Bookshop scene, where Midge first assures Scottie "Oh, Pop Leibel the bookseller, sure, he's a great friend of mine!" But when they go to the store, Pop seems only vaguely aware of Midge at best. He calls her "ma'am" or "miss" as though he's never met her before. When Midge goes back into the store and taps Pop's knee, affectionately saying "Aw thanks, Pop!" a little ping went off in my head and I thought, "She's lying!" It seemed she was lying all through the movie, and once you see it, you can't miss it for the rest of the movie, she just seems guilty of everything! Maybe some of it can be blamed on a certain blatant quality of the exposition. "Midge, we were engaged for three weeks, weren't we? Or am I remembering wrong?" Her pencil snaps, her eyes narrow, female rage threatens to boil over the lens, but she's already part of the plot, or so I gather. I wish Midge could write out a letter to Scottie apologizing for framing him, the way that Judy Barton does, such a handy device for telling us what went on while we were just grooving with the brooding music and wondering why San Francisco has so many white people in it! There's that one beautiful, tall Asian woman sitting in a corner at Ernie's—just representing, I guess. And maybe a Spanish man or two among the jury panel at San Juan Bautista during the inquest into Madeleine's death. However, the Chinese presence in San Francisco is also "represented" by Jimmy Stewart telling Kim Novak about the "Chinese saying" that if you save someone's life, you are forever after responsible for them. My student Leo, from China, says that in the real China that is not an actual belief anyone he knows has ever heard of. Meanwhile, the Spanish and Mexican feeling in *Vertigo* is quite palpable.

How about James Stewart's nightmare? We see him and Gavin Elster triangulating over a beautiful woman dressed as Carlotta in the painting, and we see it's not Kim Novak at all, it's the original of the painting. Is the actress supposed to be playing the actual Madeleine who by this time has been killed? And Scottie's subconscious is somehow pointing this up to him so that he wakes up sweating? What is the name of that actress, I wonder? *Regal* isn't the word for her. Is she Vera Miles? No, I think she's too old to be Vera Miles. (Kind informants have told me that this actress, whose eyes can be seen close up in the opening title sequence, with spirals coming out of them, is called Joanne Genthon, who never made another picture!)

So I don't have time to read all 493 other reviews of *Vertigo* to see if others have established the guilt of Barbara Bel Geddes, but I did see that one reviewer (at least one) has applied the Alison Bechdel test to *Vertigo* and seen it fail, since the two female leads seem never to be in the same frame—though we do see Midge driving by Scottie's apartment at the exact same moment that Madeleine steps out of his door, and Midge starts muttering behind the wheel and drives away, apparently upset. But perhaps not upset at all, since she has engineered the whole thing? Maybe there's a reason in the plot, and not so much in the psychosexual atmosphere, why Judy must not see

Midge at this point in time—or at any point, since doing so would make Elster's and Midge's plot collapse in of itself? Does the key to the mystery lie back in Salina, Kansas? I think so. If someone gave me one hundred dollars, I'd find out the truth and tell the world.

Vertigo is also a film in which women show men representations of more than one woman (as though to hint at a "monstrous regiment of women" that might one day bring down the oligarchy). We have Midge, of course, gleefully jamming her own face into her version of the Legion of Honor portrait of Carlotta (as though to say "I did it"), and we also have Judy showing Scottie her proofs of identity—her dad in one old photo, and herself and her mother in another. Check out that photo of Judy and her mother, what are we really looking at? Was Judy to have been kept away from Midge because she might recognize the face of her own mother? I know it sounds preposterous, but really, when Scottie asks Midge if she remembers Gavin Elster from when they were all in college together before the war, and she shakes her head no, maintaining her quizzical smile—frankly I don't believe her! The screenwriters link her to Elster, then encourage you to forget about their college days together. Scottie and Elster seem about a million years older than Midge, but if she was in school with them, is she also supposed to be fiftyish—in other words, plenty old enough to be Judy's mother? And in that case, is it too far removed to name Scottie as Judy's father, perhaps conceived during the famous three-week engagement?!?! I don't think so. Watch *Vertigo* again with my theory in mind and watch the jigsaw puzzle click together.

Let me add my interpretation of Pop Leibel's "Carlotta story" as a clue. As we hear, the nineteenth-century Carlotta had a child and then the child was taken from her and she was driven to living off the streets and going mad and painfully asking passersby, "Where is my little girl?" Maybe that is the link between Midge and Judy. That hidden link, but maybe Judy is now living in San Francisco because her real mother (Midge) has gotten her there as part of her secret plan to destroy Jimmy Stewart?

I have now watched and rewatched the so-called alternate ending to *Vertigo*, an extra to the DVD (and also readily available on YouTube). What do you think? For me it is proof positive of Midge's guilt, as she hears the radio announcer report that Gavin Elster has been captured and prosecuted in Europe, and her face grows bleak as she realizes, in my mind, that Gavin will turn state's evidence on her or whatever the equivalent term is in the courts of Italy. She will never get her Scottie, who stands a broken man next to her even if she's cleaned out nearly every trace of herself as an artist. And how about the announcer's report on the three Berkeley students arrested for trying to smuggle a cow up a staircase? Three Berkeley students? Gavin, Midge, Scottie. Staircase? Well, we know what that is. "Cow"? At Columbia, that's what Harry Cohn called Kim Novak when he was mad at her or trying to taunt her. An allegory for the secrets of *Vertigo*?

Read My Lips: Stories of a Hollywood Life
by Sally Kellerman

★★★★★
The Girl with Two Mothers

October 1, 2013

Sally Kellerman's life story, *Read My Lips*, evokes the Hollywood of the New American Cinema of the late '60s and '70s in a way few other books have managed to. As a public personality, Kellerman had it all—a unique look, instantly memorable, an enchanting voice with which she could have essayed Shakespeare's Cleopatra, comic timing, an adequate singing voice, and most of all, she was there, born in LA, a product from childhood of its streets, schools, diners, bars, clubs, and acting classes. She was a waitress at Chez Paulette when she first encountered Brando, McQueen, Beatty, the actors whose advocacy of the Actors Studio and a new, European-inflected directorial style led to the experimental Hollywood in which she could flourish, for in the '50s she would have been too tall, too mannish, too kooky, too coterie. In Altman's movies she fit in like a giraffe in a birdcage and she became famous because of them (*Nashville, Brewster McCloud*).

Unfortunately stardom went to her head and she began acting out in big ways, and she said no to the parts that might have continued her brief stay at the top. She had Neil Simon removed from the set of *Last of the Red Hot Lovers* because he laughed when her costar said his lines but stayed grim whenever she spoke. She was temperamental, and it showed in her face. So she took loveable dreck like *Lost Horizon* and quickly slipped from leading lady status to that of "mother of Diane Lane" and "mother of Jodie Foster." Drugs, depression, alcohol, bad taste in men, none of these helped, and I don't think dating Henry Kissinger was supersmart, and meanwhile she had a mother feeding her Christian Science maxims about illness being a construct of the mind and a sister who fled heterosexual life, and her own daughter, and left childless Sally to take poor Claire under her wing and eventually to adopt her.

Happily she also found her way into an older social circle, the A-List of Hollywood stars, and her second mother, she affirms, was the eternally glamorous and mysterious Jennifer Jones, who, ending her career just as Sally was beginning hers, helped her in innumerable ways, and introduced her to all the screen legends—Ingrid Bergman, Deborah Kerr, John Wayne, Simone Signoret and Yves Montand, Louis Jourdan, many more. Perhaps she couldn't have attained the natural style she was to master if she hadn't encountered this glamour set to play off of, as it were. Her descriptions of Jennifer Jones herself are sublime.

So is her account of cutting a track with Quincy Jones and Harold Robbins for the soundtrack of Lewis Gilbert's *The Adventurers*, a song slyly called "Coming and Going" in which Sally was asked to simulate moaning orgasms against an orchestral background à la "Je t'aime … moi non plus" of Jane Birkin and Serge Gainsbourg.

Eventually she made a comeback of sorts as "Queen of the Voice-Overs," a transition for which membership in a very exclusive Hollywood group therapy chapter helped her no end. Frank Gehry and his wife are in the group apparently! And Blake Edwards, who gave her parts. And Milton, the top therapist, is always there to give her profane, pithy advice about how to handle whatever life gives you. She stands in distinction to the starlets she loved the best, her girlfriends she grew up with, women like Luana Anders and Anjanette Comer, whose lives, whether tragic or fulfilled, just don't have the oomph you need for a book as big and sprawling as *Read My Lips*.

Rebuilding the Player Piano
by Larry Givens

★★★★★
Dangerous Is All in Your Mind

October 3, 2013

Perhaps you are one of those who participated in the Kickstarter campaign to buy Kevin a dilapidated old player piano that was on Craigslist, and then haul it to his apartment in the South of Market district of San Francisco and shove it up the three flights of steps and into the front room of our flat. I'll be the first to confess that I'm new to the automatic-player hobby, and basically know little about rebuilding the player piano, so obtaining a copy of Larry Givens's classic 1963 handbook was a personal triumph. Score! Now when you come by our Minna Street pad, you'll see only the soles of my boots, the rest of me has pretty much set up shop inside the World War I–era beauty, trying to make the damaged pneumatics pump again and trying to do something about the lost motion and wear in the bushings, the clicking noises that plague the hammer softeners (so reminiscent of a boyfriend I once had who, when I used to drink too much, made these disapproving tch-tch sounds in the back of his throat that just drove me up the wall!), and sundry other problems with my new investment. The problem is, as Givens explains lucidly, you don't know how bad or good the sound will be without you completely fixing the pneumatic system, and I didn't know that going in!

I thought all you needed were the player piano rolls, and I have four of them, but I totally failed to grasp the concept that you must keep pumping the bottom lever and that's what introduces the air into the system, with a system of miniature bellows that looks so cute, perhaps, when they're not torn or worn out like mine are. My bivalves are worn out and weak like the earlobes of the modern-primitive kids who've stretched them so they hang lower than their shoulder blades. Givens's explanations are succinct and precise: so succinct, indeed, that sometimes I just scratch my head and wonder what he's on about! Too bad he's not here anymore to explain at length for the ADD generation I belong to.

I think a lot of guys my age want a new living project, and for me, it's the automatic-player hobby, as I have learned to call it. They exhibited four of them on the playa at Burning Man about a month ago, and I went green with envy. Some guys turn to nickelodeons (that is, a player piano with a coin-slot attachment that can actually make you some money if you ever get it going), and some prefer the so-called reproducing pianos, which instead of pumping your foot and running the roll at whatever speed you like, they are designed to rearticulate the exact style of some famous pianist of the 1900s era—there are some recordings of George Gershwin playing for the "reproducing piano." And other fans of the automatic-player hobby might like the orchestra in a box, or the player violin, but give me the old-fashioned Ampico eighty-eight-keyer any day. My cats like it too. You have to pry off the front panels totally, and the result is something like a three-tiered shelf stuffed with keys and valves and yet still room for three overfed cats who think they're somewhat smaller than they are. It'll be a sad day when I finally peg this sucker back together, my cats will feel the pitiful sting of exile, but for now they're living the dream. In the meantime, don't believe the reviewers who put down Givens for giving bad information. He's not going to destroy your automatic player by any means, even if you goof up, San Francisco style.

Martial Arts Dummy Full Size with Hands
by C4L

★★★★★
Used Again and Again

November 23, 2013

Like most of the other reviewers, I first bought this dummy in 2011 as a prop for a haunted house my mates and I were operating in Oakland, just across the Bay Bridge from San Francisco. We run a nonprofit artist-run space that hosts poetry readings and meetings of like-minded people into poetry and the verbal arts. For years, ever since the shut-down of government support for poetry, Halloween has been a big money-making time for us, but in 2011 as I recall we were especially wary of other competition breathing down our necks, because a good spooky house is something every artist wants to have at his disposal this time of year. With increased competition everybody has got to boast more gore, more carnage, more fake blood, and most of all, more corpses, and realistic-looking ones particularly, otherwise a jaded audience gets weary and bored easy, just as if we were presenting two Language poets, say, while the other guy down the street could boast Mary Oliver and Billy Collins. Thus in 2011, we were totally up against it, and we wound up going wholesale and buying dummies, where once we could count on our friends acting crazy in homemade costumes— Jack the Ripper, the Human Blockhead, the Spider with Ten Legs, the Hypnotic Eye, Jayne Mansfield without her head, Tarzan, and many more.

Alas, those once unemployed poets had landed good tech jobs at Twitter and Google and were no longer amused by nor available for the long hours and unpaid lifestyle of a spooky-house volunteer for poetry. Amazon came to the rescue so I bought one of these guys as a treat. We planned to employ Dummy Full Size with Hands as a mummy, sort of a Frankenstein mummy with a meat knife sticking out of his chest, a mummy that would greet the terrified pilgrim who opened the door to the back room with a maniacal recorded cackle easily downloadable from numerous sources on Spotify or iTunes. And it worked.

It worked so well that our competitors from other poetry groups protested that we were stealing all of their thunder. They didn't realize we were trying to raise the money to start off 2012 with a bang and we needed the extra dough to be able to afford Christian Bök and Dottie Lasky to come together onstage for our Valentine Ball. The only question was what to do with our dummy till the next year, Halloween 2012? None of our members had an extra bedroom for the fellow, so even though he was fairly heavy and nearly my own height, I wound up taking him home back to my place where he remains today. My cats love him, they sit in his lap all day and shroud his crotch with hair (I should say, it's not really anatomically a crotch). He went back to work just this past Halloween in a new cos- tume—Manson! And when I'm feeling lonely and my wife has gone out of town on business or pleasure, I hate sleeping alone, so I shoo the cats away and drag my guy into the bed with me to spoon with. You know, he's stuffed, and his spine comes with extra holes into which you can feed more stuffing, be it grain, acorns, or Styrofoam, and I like to move my fingers up and down his spine looking for the holes and sealing them up if necessary. His hands are fully operable and will wrap themselves around any elongated object.

Billy Rose's Jumbo (1962)
dir. Charles Walters

★★★★☆
Doris Day's Finest Moment?

December 21, 2013

I'm reviewing just *Billy Rose's Jumbo* and not the multi-DVD set many are talking about here, they must have arrived to the review arena through another channel. For some reason, though I consider myself a great Doris Day fan, I must have subconsciously avoided seeing *Billy Rose's Jumbo* until late last week, when I watched it over several days so as not to overdose with pleasure if I stayed with it too long. Mostly I'd get to a big musical number and then I'd pause and everyone in the room watching it with me would have to stand, at my invitation, and applaud the players—and the director, Charles Walters, beyond a doubt one of the greatest musical directors of all time. Was he buried at MGM? I think so. He certainly stood in the shadow of the big players like Minnelli and Donen, tsk-tsk, but here he outdoes himself.

So why was it so unappealing for so long? Well, I'm old enough to remember my grandparents coming back from an evening showing of *Billy Rose's Jumbo* at the Smithtown Senior Center, late in the 1980s, and their lips were locked, as if stricken by terror or contempt, and Mom said that as far as she knew, they never spoke of their evening out, ever again, but she too remembered they looked terrified, as though they'd seen something awful. That, and the idea of Martha Raye, and Jimmy Durante, and Jumbo himself, and the old-time period setting, and Doris Day dressed as a clown, well, they all seemed awful ideas, visually and otherwise, and maybe I didn't like the idea of the title itself! Why call it *Billy Rose's Jumbo*? Even in 1961, was Billy Rose still a thing? He couldn't have been bringing in too many customers if so. Was it in his contract, that if ever they made a film of Jumbo it had to have his name in it somewhere, like *National Lampoon's Van Wilder* or *Lee Daniels' the Butler*?

'Whatever! I began watching with enormous resistance, but as soon as ten minutes in, I realized I was seeing perhaps the last film of Doris Day's great, and bizarre, drama period. Paralleling her real life to an eerie degree, the films of this period have her suffering because of a man, and no one, ever, in real life or in the movies, suffers like Doris Day. Remember *Julie* with Louis Jourdan? *Midnight Lace* with Rex Harrison? *Love Me or Leave Me* with Cagney? Well, you get the picture, but here she is, in shock as it turns out over and over that her beloved rogue of a father (Jimmy Durante) has a secret shadow side: he's addicted to gambling and puts their livelihood, and that of dozens of other humans and animals, at risk while he goes and gambles away the night's takings, and in the morning it's Doris who has to deal with the disaster. "Oh, Pop, not again, you didn't!" she wails, having to face the contempt and the misery on the faces of everyone in the circus they have let down. In a way I read this as Doris Day's take on the old legend of *Dr. Jekyll and Mr. Hyde*, where Hyde goes out, gets drunk, gets high, carouses with whores, and kills people, and in the morning it's Jekyll who must pay the price. (Or the other way around, now I can't remember.) Anyhow this aspect of the movie is as compelling as anything Cassavetes ever had Gena Rowlands do, and yet they get all the credit while it was Doris and Chuck Walters who did the spade-work a good ten years or more, and on a tightrope literally, and trapezes, and in clown makeup! As if that isn't bad enough,

[SPOILERS AHEAD]

Doris is forced to suffer the loss of her beloved pet Jumbo, and these scenes alone should have won her the Oscar she has been denied for over sixty years. She is magnificent, touching, strong, desperate, loving, and fearful all at once as she attempts to console the lachrymose 22,000-pound beast, who doesn't want to go onto the truck and leave the only humans who have ever been kind to him. And if that isn't enough,

[MORE SPOILERS]

Stephen Boyd, as Doris's love interest, has a terrible secret all his own. This part of the picture reminds me very much of a Minnelli picture of the same vintage called *Home from the Hill*. He is the son of a tyrannical circus potentate determined to use Durante's gambling addiction to wrest control of the circus and Jumbo and amalgamate them into their own supercircus, the way that the

Ringling Bros. took over Barnum & Bailey and boasted about it! It is sheer colonialism and to its credit the movie, *Billy Rose's Jumbo*, emerges with a sane and throughout-Marxist approach to the brawling America of unregulated and unleashed capitalism raging at the period (the movie must take place before the First World War, I would think?) and also at the time of its making, the zenith of Cold War fears of the other, exploited by the masters of war to create a giant spectacle under which they could consolidate their holdings in, well, everything. At the end of the movie we understand that an arte povera is needed to restore art to its correct place in society. The film accomplishes all this so beautifully that one takes it as a bittersweet goodbye to a corrupt and venal studio system, but it is as if Walters and company are out on a limb, sawing it off of the dead tree, and yet they know they have nowhere themselves to land except into thin air. It is an effective and long goodbye.

I liked Stephen Boyd in this—he should have played in more dramas like this one, tough and gritty as a mouthful of Kansas dirt. Martha Raye, whose shtick was that of the plain, lascivious woman, looks beautiful here once in a while, a flicker of magic, while Doris gets to sing "Little Girl Blue" by Rodgers and Hart and then to stop singing it and instead act it out with the full-bodied passion of the great Balanchine dancers like Maria Tallchief or Gelsey Kirkland. Impressive, and yet did it win her any awards? My grandfather was especially harsh about this movie. Even though they saw it for free, he said it was the worst night of his life, he would have paid money not to have to see Raye and Day in their final clown sequence.

Love Actually (2003)
dir. Richard Curtis

★★★★☆
Christmas Classic or Antifat Diatribe?

December 27, 2013

Both! Nothing says Christmas to me like *Love Actually*, with its all-important children's Christmas pageant, and its race to find out which pop star will land the coveted Christmas #1, and Rowan Atkinson at the jewelry counter creating an extravagant paper turkey of a wrapped present. This time, however, watching it at Christmas on Wednesday, I noticed for the first time all the many gibes about fat people that writer-director Richard Curtis puts in just about everywhere. I guess you'd call it a leitmotif! With its ten storylines, there's room for all sorts of social commentary. It's a two-hours-and-fifteen-minutes movie, the longest rom-com ever, but if you took out the antifat jokes and agit-prop, it would be maybe one hundred minutes tops.

The movie begins with Bill Nighy's worn-out rock star Billy Mack trying to remember the new lyrics to "Christmas Is All Around," watched over by his seen-it-all, tolerant-to-a-fault manager Joe, who stays with him even though he's a joke to everyone else in the show. We all love this story because we like watching an under-dog comeback, and right away we see the fattest person in the movie, as though to clue us in this is going to be a picture in which people's physical frailties are going to be relentlessly mocked.

In succeeding scenes we see normal-sized people being dismissed by the skinny as too fat, and even the thin ones are fretting about their weight. Perhaps a seasonal touch, for when the holidays come we all have to worry about rich food. But *Love Actually* gets nasty, particularly when Hugh Grant, as Prime Minister David, meets his new assistant Natalie, from the wrong side of the tracks, and instantly the chief of staff apologizes to David for saddling him with a fat assistant. Martine McCutcheon isn't violently slim like Kate Moss, but she's attractive (in a weird way, almost as though she didn't have enough features in her face) and she dresses in red often, as though to show she's spirited and full of life, the way we know Maureen Stapleton embodies life in Woody Allen's *Interiors*, whereas Geraldine Page embodies death, since Stapleton wears scarlet and Page beige. Anyhow it takes Hugh Grant a long time to work out how he feels about Martine McCutcheon because of the social opprobrium she creates wherever she treads. "If she was so scandalously fat," I wondered, "how did she get the job of handing out the chocolate biscuits anyhow, at Number Ten Downing Street, which seems like a foul place in this movie. Except for that one large pre-Raphaelite painting in the hall."

OK then, same thing happens to Alan Rickman, attracted to Mia at his office and yet saddled with Karen and her fondness for Joni Mitchell, who taught her how to feel. I didn't really think Emma

Thompson was fat either, but Richard Curtis gives her this scene where she has to try to wriggle into a dress that's too small for her now, though once she fit into it handily when she was Mia's age and wore a size 0. It's a complicated role that Emma Thompson doesn't make any easier by not having gained weight for the part. She's a thin woman who's acting as though she's too large to fit into a dress—extraordinary work, yet watching this scene I wonder how well it reflects ordinary society of today where if you're just a little bit heavy you're cast into perdition, and have things gotten better in the past ten years, since when *Love Actually* was filmed? I doubt it. Today, Martine McCutcheon would not be giving out scotch to the US president and wearing red, she'd be in jail.

And the antifat theme even reaches out to beyond the borders of the UK, as Colin Firth, in love with a thin Portuguese waitress, learns her language and comes unannounced at Christmastime to ask her father for her "hands in marriage," and the father calls for his daughter and it's not Aurelia at all, but Sophia, the fat one! She's not only fat but mean and jealous and plain. Even Aurelia fears gaining weight and becoming like Sophia. Sophia gets some good laughs in her final moments, but it's pretty gross of Richard Curtis to play the fat card one more time just when you thought it was going to be a feel-good ending.

MacKenzies Smelling Salts (17 ml)
by MacKenzies

★★★★★
The Answer to Deep Grief

December 31, 2013

My Irish grandfather used to keep a bottle of MacKenzies smelling salts next to his desk. He was the principal at Bushwick High School (in Brooklyn, NY) in the 1930s and 1940s, before it became a dangerous place to live in, and way before Bushwick regained its current state of desirable area for new gentrification. And he kept one at home as well, in case of a sudden shock. At school, he would press the saturated cotton under the nostrils of poor girls who realized they were pregnant in health class, before he expelled them. Or when the policy of corporal punishment had allowed him rather too much paddling of the sophomore boys, he would apply smelling salts to their faces till they recovered from passing out.

For me, 2013's a new era, and the salts themselves seem way more organic than they used to when first I sampled them in the '70s. I was a typical teen raiding my grandparents' medicine cabinet, trying a little of this, a little of that, you know ... I took a whiff of the MacKenzies and I was like "Whoa!" It was the feeling when your face has been "stuffed up," and reality has blurred your vision, your passages clogged, the doors of perception jammed shut. And one infusion of this magic ointment opens all of them up within a fraction of an instant, you can't even get a syllable out, you're just yourself again, your very best self.

Nowadays, with my ongoing heart problems, I use them only when I'm in a deep grief or have had a shock. I was so sad when Paul Walker died. And then again one day I came staggering down the stairs, having been passed over for inclusion in the 2014 Whitney Biennial by a troika of careless curators, I simply collapsed out of grief, and it took my wife a minute or two to locate the MacKenzies, but passing it under my nose, as though she were my grandfather ministering to the pregnant girls of yore, or the sore-bottomed "tough guys," suddenly I snorted and came awake, shot to my feet, still grieving for my disappointment but at least able to function and go back to making my art, feeding the cats, etc., being a man. In time of deep mourning thank goodness for small miracles!

Kylie Fashion
by Kylie Minogue

Gift of a Lifetime

January 4, 2014

Hail to my friends David and Sara for bringing me this book for my birthday! They are beyond-belief sensitive to a fellow's needs and wants.

I had my eye on this book from the beginning. It's not that every book on Kylie is good, though I never read one I didn't enjoy. For me the first and still the best was, oh, I don't know what they call it but it's known as *Kylie Evidence*, from the late '90s? Came in a box?

That book showed off the extent of Kylie's collaborations not only with top designers but with the crème de la crème of British and international artists, from Pierre et Gilles to Wolfgang Tillmans to, ah, what's her name, she made that film about a teenage John Lennon and then married its teenage star? Well, the anagram for "Kylie Minogue" is "I like 'em young," and this woman artist underlined that in red! I know, I'll google her name—oh, here you go, Sam Taylor-Wood, the one who's directing *Fifty Shades of Grey*. Anyway, *Kylie Fashion* is pretty cool. At first I thought, "They're not giving enough space to the pre–*Light Years* era," but that was heavily covered in *Evidence,* and perhaps in the splashy, vacuous *La La La*, and though I feel that the '90s were the decade in which Kylie was the most glamorous, there is still enough greatness in the 2000s, the cancer years and the *Aphrodite* rollout, to make the act of reading *Fashion* a pleasure from cover to cover.

As other reviewers have noted, there's not too much of Kylie's longtime stylist William Baker in this one, and for that we can all be grateful. I don't know about you, but I was sick of him from the minute I saw the videos for "Please Stay" and "Your Disco Needs You." Now and then he lets Kylie wear something suitable for her, but so often he brings her to the ateliers of the world's greatest designers and then picks out their worst costumes for her, *cough* Dolce&Gabbana. I only like him because he stuck with her through the cancer period, but even Olivier did that, who would desert her in her time of need. Why make a movie about what a good friend you were, William Baker, with her all hugging you and crying on your shoulder? On the third hand, there's no denying the greatness of the *Body Language* campaign, nor the way you dressed Kylie at the BRIT Awards when she did "Can't Get You Out of my Head" with tiny braids and a robot dress. Nor the videos for "Slow," "CGY-OOMH," "Get Outta My Way," "Wow," "All the Lovers," or "Santa Baby," so I'm still rooting for you to a certain degree. On the fourth hand, it was a great idea to have sidebars through *Fashion* consisting of interviews of the designers to show how they first met Kylie. I could read them all day. Gaultier seems like Wittgenstein, he's so acute. On the fifth hand, those hot pants were not your idea and I'm glad you're finally admitting as much.

David Park: A Painter's Life
by Nancy Boas

★★★★★
One of the Best Biographies I've Read in Ages

February 1, 2014

A biographer myself, I haven't been so taken by a biography in a long time, and my hat is off to Nancy Boas and her incredible life of the Boston-born, Bay Area–based painter David Park, who died in 1960.

First off, this author has done her research. I couldn't believe I was reading the life of a man born in 1911, and she had interviewed many of his contemporaries—people who would be over a hundred today! She even interviewed David Park's *aunt*, an artist herself who perhaps inspired her young nephew with the love of art and more, a vision of how to create it oneself. Nancy Boas has been working on this book for so long that many of her witnesses have themselves passed on, but her ability to quote them so freshly keeps them alive and kicking, speaking frankly as though to a trusted friend. She is really good at a difficult art, isolating quotations in a way that characterizes the speaker too, so *David Park: A Painter's Life* reads like a novel with a bevy of interesting characters for good and bad.

Park hailed from a comfortable and socially well-connected clerical family and his father, a noted minister, never thought that his son would become a painter. Early on, Park fled the East and his family to go to California, as far as he possibly could from the lot of them, though we see him warming up to his brothers little by little, particularly after one of them is stricken by polio in the air force and suffers physical reverses.

What impresses most about Park is how much he himself suffered in order to find time to paint, and the interesting part of the story is how long he waited to find success. He was forty-four before he had a real job, hired as professor at UC Berkeley, and it was about that time that everything started happening for him: selling his work, finding a supportive dealer, vindication after many years of struggle.

And then, before you know it, bang, a diagnosis of lung and hip cancer that killed him before his fiftieth birthday. In the meantime, an epochal battle with abstract expressionist Clyfford Still, Park's nemesis at CSFA, as they called the San Francisco Art Institute in the exciting postwar years when visionary curator Douglas MacAgy ran the place. Boas finds ways to show us the odious egotism of Still, but we also see through her narrative powers that Still came from a place of pure poverty in Canada, and that where he came from, you either lay down in the snow and died, or you stood up and lived, so that survival was a class thing for him and if it meant browbeating the mild-mannered middle-class figurative guys like Park, then so be it. Still does come close to stealing every scene he's in. "Imperious and defiant," writes Boas on page 108, "he was prone to self-dramatizing statements like the description of his career as 'one of the great stories of all time, far more meaningful and infinitely more intense and enduring than the wars of the bullring and the battlefield.'" You got to love someone who can speak with such Ted Baxter vanity!

Boas delicately narrates the marriage of David Park to the beautiful, energetic, and yet strangely depressed and dissatisfied Lydia, whom he called "Deedee" or "Deed." I don't know, I felt that she was watching her step when it came to Park's domestic life, pulling her punches a bit, and maybe if the daughters of David and Lydia who are still alive, weren't, she might be more forthcoming. There are certainly hints that Lydia was rarely home because she was spending many boozy afternoons with the neighbor couple, and basically that Mr. Neighbor and she had some sort of romantic attachment to each other? Did David mind being a cuckold, if that's what he was? We never see him involved with other women. His penchant for painting nudes gave him access to many gorgeous women—and men, but Boas is not interested in "queering" Park the way another biographer might be tempted to. When she notes the "explicit frontal nudity" of Park's paintings, she sees it in terms of tone and scale, nothing more.

The exceptional brilliance of Park's many friends (mostly heterosexual couples, though Jess and Duncan, and Brown and Wonner make appearances) leaves the reader envious for a time when people had party after party, drank and smoked like crazy, all the while participating in a postwar Beat-era avant-garde that was not quite Beat, but fellow travelers, you might say. Rents were cheap—they had to be, since the hardscrabble jobs David and Lydia worked at paid so little. For years they lived in an old house high on a Berkeley hill that eventually collapsed all around them while they ran out with the kids under their arms. We also get to hear quite a lot about Howard and Dorothy Baker, who were sort of the Paul and Jane Bowles of the West Coast. Nancy Boas also shows considerable erudition and knows how to write briefly about every one of Park's hundreds of finished and unfinished works in order to illuminate just what about him was so special, and what made him better than his confreres Bischoff and Diebenkorn. Imogen Cunningham's photo of Park on the cover gives him the charisma of a rock star or of an Old West lawman—did any succeeding generation know how to rock a T-shirt like the painters of Park's cohort? I don't think so! All in all a book of enduring value, a masterpiece of hunting and gathering information and a fascinating portrait of a good man and an intriguing artist.

Payard Desserts
by François Payard (with Tish Boyle)

★★★★★
My Mother's Pudding, My Children's Braised-Rhubarb Napoleon

February 3 ,2014

Our kids were always sort of pudgy, and for years we wondered if it was because we did not know how to fix them proper desserts.

My father was an absent-minded scientist and would eat iron filings if you put them on his plate. My mom was a busy professional, and her idea of dessert was making chocolate or tapioca pudding, from the same mix Bill Cosby advertised on TV. She also liked to bake molasses cookies, and sometimes she walked to the corner store and bought the old-fashioned boxes of ice cream, in which chocolate, vanilla, and strawberry ice cream was molded together in stripes. As kids we could never figure out how they did that, or why, for you had to cut away every molecule of strawberry before the chocolate ice cream wasn't gonna taste all "stwawbewwy," we complained in that annoying Long Island lisp we sported as kids, influenced by the late Pee Wee Herman's *Playhouse* show I'm sure, and Johnny Depp in *Edward Scissorhands*.

Naturally as the years passed we took cues from the way our parents cooked, and also by the food revolution that has taken over here in San Francisco, but when I took up *Payard Desserts* on publication day—Halloween 2013—I felt like a lucky son of a gun. The message is largely about "Don't even try to make a dish in the wrong season, instead go for the ingredients not only if they happen to be available, but do like Payard and buy them only at their peak, and base your dishes on that one factor." Well, what's at its peak on Halloween? Candy corn, of course, and Red Vines, Reese's Peanut Butter Cups, and other trick-or-treat nonsense, but also pumpkin, squash, apples, beets, kale, broccoli, scallions, lemons and oranges, passion fruit, persimmon, cranberries, so I decided to concentrate on Payard's November recipes, starting with citrus terrine, in gelatin, with its secret surprise of a whole white peppercorn crushed with the bottom of a pan. My wife suggested, to save the pan, use instead a small metallic kettledrum that my grandfather Doyle left me and which I use as a paperweight in the study. The sugar and the star anise build up an intoxicating aroma somewhat tempered by the jolt of the single white peppercorn, now in pieces due to the brass kettledrum's dense, explosive shrapnel-action effect.

In San Francisco there aren't many trees whose leaves fall, red and brown, onto the ground, and the other traditional signs of November are likewise AWOL, but we make do just fine at the Ferry Building Farmers Market, where we asked what leaves were edible and extant—at their peak. "At their peak," I asserted, speaking in firm tones to the Romanian poultry farmer from Gilroy, whose simple stall was festooned with peak strands of garlic cloves, gray doves lustrous as coral, deciduous branches of young white pine, and baby pumpkins tied together in a net of crisp Romanian sugar. The orange tuiles, one of Payard's singular attractions, ruled at the PTA potluck we attended with our teens. This forms part of a complex feta cheesecake which Payard pairs with wine-soaked dates and white-pepper ice cream. He has a sort of thing about white pepper, white peppercorns, the way Julia Child had a thing for butter, and some of the younger children in the PTA potluck made ghastly faces when they got to the ice cream portion of the dessert.

I look forward to February when chocolate is said to be at its peak, so I can make some of Payard's chocolate-based desserts, such as his cubes not of Kobe beef but of chocolate mousse, painted with chocolate down the sides into which the first entry of a fork tine will pierce to release a gushing blaze of salted caramel. Has Payard realized how hard it is to escape in today's market from sea-salted caramel? I think I will try the *fleur de sel* right now, without waiting for the other elements to kick in. My mother, who loved to make chocolate pudding the Bill Cosby way, is possibly rolling in her grave, and I'm not sure how much my own kids are going to enjoy working their way with me through *Payard Desserts*, but I plan to roll with it all year round. Plus, you can freeze the four-hour baked apple napoleon (what Payard calls his version of American "comfort food") and it will stay fresh and lively for as many as ten weeks, we discovered, during the recent drought here in California that slightly cut down on apple production. And each of the kids has lost on the average of two pounds per foot.

Changing
by Liv Ullmann

★★★★★
Can I Handle the Seasons of My Life? One Woman's Poignant Reflections in Snow-Covered Hills.

May 14, 2014

In Liv Ullmann's memoir *Changing*, only a few colors stain the crystal radiance of the skies above Norway, gray, pink, white, black; someone holds the great Norwegian star for a few minutes, then lets her fall back to the rocks of Fårö Island, and yet even though it hurts to be so deeply in love, and you're betraying your husband, you still feel like life is worth living. All your allegiances are to the theater, and then to the cinema of Ingmar Bergman. All the phones are rotary, yet she longs to work on stage because that is one place in which you don't hear the phone, she says. How different from today, where you can stay in touch with your daughter even if you are onstage playing one of your signature parts. In Liv Ullmann's case, she became famous, as she tells us, at nineteen, in a Scandinavian town beginning with a *S* (I just looked it up, it was Stavanger), playing Anne Frank; and later there was her sensational success as Nora in Ibsen's *A Doll's House*, which she takes on a long straw-hat-circuit trail in the Sweden of the 1960s, and Norway in the 1970s, entertaining farmers and forest rangers in run-down dinner theaters that had not seen a single play for over thirty and in some cases over one hundred years.

Everywhere the weather haunts her. The sun breaking through the snowcaps, the threat of the ground shifting beneath your feet, that moment between autumn and winter when you can see your refection in the snow-covered hills. When this book came out during America's Bicentennial, it made an enormous impression on young California feminists and hedonists, who took the message of perpetual cosmic and personal shift to heart. The young Stevie Nicks took the emotional and wintry landscape of Ullmann's difficult Scandinavia and condensed this book into her signature song. Like "Landslide," Ullmann's memoir is haunted by the puckish spirits of a girl child, her own child self, orphaned by a WWII accident and a beautiful, willful mother, and by her own daughter Linn, whom she gave birth to during her five-year-long affair with director Bergman. One or the other of the two little girls appears on nearly every page. As Stevie sings, "I've been afraid of changing, 'cause I've built my life around you." Bergman was so jealous that he was the source of all of her fears and joys. He was like Lindsey Buckingham, the way Stevie writes about him in "Silver Springs." Then little Linn broke the ice and made Liv see she was living in what had turned into an emotional nightmare.

When she left, Liv fled to Southern California, as Stevie did. "Time makes us bolder," said the latter. "Even children get older." Eternal changing, but one thing that did not change is Liv's penchant for human depravity. She dated Henry Kissinger, and apparently thought this behavior sort of cute. She had the opportunity many times to poison the world's most evil living man, and yet she stayed her hand. The only star who comes off looking bad in this "landslide" of an autobiography is Vanessa Redgrave, like Liv a stranger in Hollywood, but otherwise an inhuman freak who is interested in Liv only if she will write her a huge check to support the cause of violent Trotskyite revolution. It was a strange era in Hollywood, one never to be repeated, a time in which these two weird, beautiful, Nordic powerhouses could each be asked to anchor a huge Hollywood musical: Redgrave, the box office disappointment *Camelot*; Ullmann, the total disaster of the legendary *Lost Horizon* musical. I guess there was also Jean Seberg, weird like them, European sort of, sort of respected for her acting, and so perplexingly cast as the lead both men wanted in *Paint Your Wagon*. But she at any rate was from America, like our own songwriting virtuoso, the one and only Stevie Nicks. I can only say that *Camelot*, *Lost Horizon*, and *Paint Your Wagon* would have all been improved with the casting of Nicks, who has never been given her due in American movies, nor those of any other country or planet!

Wild West Hero: A Gay Erotic Novella
by Thom Wolf

★★★★★
The Rocking of the Trailer, the Burning Sun of Spain

November 29, 2014

Thom Wolf takes pen in hand to bring us the thrilling story of what actually happens on the set of the spaghetti Westerns of the 1960s and '70s. A film scholar as well as one of today's most acclaimed erotic novelists and short-story writers, Wolf combines the critical acumen of the reviewer with the raw passion of one who fell in love with the good-looking stars of these "Westerns *all'italiana*" as much as with their violence, suspense, and revolutionary underpinnings. The (fictional) movie he chronicles is called *Dollars in the Dust* (1969) and his protagonist and narrator, young Eddie Drake, is new to film, though hardly to the casting couch, when he arrives in the remote Spanish location used for so many of the Italian coproductions of the period. He knows little Spanish or Italian, so he's lonely, but buoyed by knowing that the great Hollywood Western star Hank Kinney is due on set for the last two weeks of shooting.

Wolf writes well of Eddie's loneliness and self-doubt, and about how he has to negotiate his hidden sexuality in the mazes of Hollywood and international film production. There were then no "out" stars, or even "out" extras for that matter, but among those in the know there have been, for twenty years or more, whispers about the great superstar Hank Kinney, now down on his luck and reduced to playing in the sort of films he hopes will never reach America. Eddie is all excited to meet his costar, but when the famous actor arrives he disappears into his trailer and won't respond to the director's entreaties. In despair, director Benito (sort of a Sergio Leone character, trying to make a masterpiece out of hackneyed materials and a tiny budget) sends Eddie in to lure out Hank Kinney. In the heat of the Spanish noon, all of Eddie's dreams come true, but first, pure pain.

Not only the pain of fearing that your dreams of stardom will evaporate like dollars in the dust, but the pain of being invaded by the titanic male members first of insatiable Italian bit player Sandro, and then another one for whom the huge encroachment of Sandro will have only been a loosening up. Like many of Wolf's most memorable characters, Eddie experiences life through the sensitive membranes that make up his hot, molten, stretchable core, and between these two guys he's often left too sore to sit comfortably on his palomino. That feeling, and the endless plains of Pamplona, and the unforgiving sun of Spain, are the things I will take away from *Wild West Hero* long after I stop reading it with one hand, longing for Eddie to find the happiness he deserves. It is a book to treasure, to inflame, and you will never look at *Django* or *Once upon a Time in America* in quite the same way after reading about the secret lives of their Wild West heroes.

Dear Alain
by Katy Bohinc

★★★★★
One Plus One

January 3, 2015

We are presented with an audacious epistolary: a young American poet, based in New York, writes in English to the eminent French theorist Alain Badiou (born in Rabat, Morocco, in 1937), and writes him love letters of astonishing honesty and passion. Echoes of Max Ophüls fill my mind as I read through the first fifty pages, letter after letter from Katy, no response from *le philosophe*—you've seen Joan Fontaine write pages and pages to Louis Jourdan, filling the screen with impassioned hand, in *Letters from an Unknown Woman*, right? It's the saddest picture in movie history, so my first instinct is to say that young Bohinc has set her sights too high, and that he, "dear

Alain," won't even remember her if shown a picture of her after her death. But then finally I get it, that what she is proposing is no ordinary love affair, but rather a test of love, a test to be played out according to her understanding of his writing, and the main action of the book turns into an interrogation, then a subversion, of his tenets, of the monstrances in which his words are displayed: his books and articles and public statements. As she writes, she changes his writing—at least its import, perhaps its meaning.

Tender Buttons has published many books that demonstrate this sort of twisty, suspense-driven turnabout, so I expect that whenever I pick up one of their books it is not going to be what I expect. Into this tradition Bohinc fits beautifully, but even so, the surprises are earned. The reader must bring a lot of attention and empathy to meet her on the page, and to be wise enough to distinguish lover from writer from artist, melancholic from joker. I'm sure I stumbled a couple of times across this lengthy book, but there was always something beckoning, a pennant faintly flapping upon Mont Blanc, to keep me murmuring "Excelsior" and going forward. Well, for one thing she's witty as hell, and for another she has a gift for extravagant metaphor, perhaps from hip-hop roots, that delights in transforming into every variant of itself imaginable. Maybe that's what love does—love with a capital *L*, as she insists you spell it—creates a hall of mirrors around the loved one that produces infinite lights and angles.

The lovers live parallel lives on either side of fame; they experience the same events, like the resignation of Egypt's Mubarak, and she reads his reaction to Egypt in the papers and he reads hers in these letters. They are either end of the spectrum of age, and of gender, but ungodly connections bring them together. And she can sometimes boast that she knows more than he about this or that—not only matters of the heart, but cold facts, like math. "I suppose you've mapped sociality like a chessboard. But I'm mercurial, at best." In the next life, she recalls, the philosopher is going to reincarnate as a dancer; but as the poet will turn into a janitor, will he still want her? Cocteau or Demy sort of transformation turns the old Ophüls plot into something more like a sun-warmed fairy tale, but *Dear Alain* convinces me, and will you too, that miracles can happen even in the most blighted of social circumstances and broken civic systems. I enjoyed it very much, and it spurred me to direct action, and to going back to the basic arithmetic I abandoned as a teen, and one can ask no more of a book or a friend.

The Despairs
by Cid Corman

★★★★★
West Gone East

March 20, 2015

The Despairs might be the best of all of Cid Corman's many books of poetry. (He is said to have written over seventy of them.) In later life, he lived in Kyoto for decades at a time and his poetry became inflected by Japanese syntax and form, so that most of his poems are short. He wrote haikus in the style of the great old five-seven-five masters of his home country and his adopted land, for example "The Wanderer Theme," which reads "Coming back after / all this time only to have / to find yourself gone." He showed us that many of his poems could fit on one page of a then-traditional brand of Japanese composition book, small enough to fit into a hip pocket, for example. Life wasn't luxurious for Corman and his long-suffering wife, particularly in Corman's final years when Japan found itself in a recession and prices rose, for everything had to be imported and the little island, so inventive, began charging for everything, as did we in America at the time. Corman was visited by a continual procession of American and Canadian admirers, maybe as many as five or six a year, the kindest among them bringing treats like cans of Campbell's soup, or maybe fresh vegetables like artichokes, things unavailable in Kyoto except among the superrich. In return, Corman always had a little book he had printed himself and he might give you one on your way home.

    The Despairs has a gloomy title, but we come to understand that nothing will get the poet down, not seriously, though he flirts with foul temper and, like other expatriates, sometimes regrets having left his homeland. A host of old American friends are invoked— George Oppen and William Bronk among them, Bronk in filthy, Rabelaisian terms as though there was bad blood between the two.

And there's a note of whining about old age, though not despair as we know it philosophically, but even a bleak poem might wear a sprightly title like "Acme." Here's the poem, aired out with blank lines and plenty of blank space all around the page: "Isn't it // obvious / you are as // good as dead / already? And it wont / get better." (He abhorred the apostrophe as a form of punctuation, arguing that it detracted from the look of the word and called attention to that which is not there, just as his fellow Black Mountain–influenced poets made a fetish of the word *yr* for "your.")

When he returned to the US for a brief fundraising visit, I saw him in the second-floor gallery of a Market Street emporium on an engagement for the San Francisco Poets Theater. He was going to fill the bill solo, he announced, for in the years since he was away he had written over five thousand poems. That night, as the fog rappelled down Market Street as if in the pathetic fallacy of parkour, and as the hours of the Western clock told us it was 7:00 p.m., then 7:15, then 7:20, and finally midnight, he read them all, none smoother nor truer nor more packed with old-man defiance than the magnificent poems of *The Despairs*.

Hi-Tec-C Maica 0.4 mm Extra Fine Point Ballpoint Pen (12-Color Set)
by Pilot

★★★★★
A Breath of '60s Air

June 9, 2015

As an American boy growing up in France, I got used to the French way of doing things very quickly—so quickly that my dad worried that French ways were taking away some essential kernel of "Americanness" from me. It wasn't overnight, of course, for French ways are so different than those my parents had taught us on Long Island—but after a while I began to think of every French product as better than the ones I had left behind in Smithtown. The game of Risk, for example, I preferred infinitely to the bourgeois American Monopoly with its sordid focus on capital. The Risk we played at home, of course, was itself a bastardized version of Albert Lamorisse's

French original. Luckily we could play both versions often on one bureau, sweeping our pieces madly in the French style and being more sedate and mannered when we went back to the American board. Anyhow, Dad was glad that there was at least one American staple I found superior to its French avatar, and that was the simple ballpoint pen. Though many of my classmates *à l'école* had, of course, beautiful pens that were almost family heirlooms, and many carried the Montblanc pen like it was a badge of cultural superiority, I was always so glad when cousins and merchants back home airmailed me *et ma soeur* the latest round of Pilot pens—the beautiful Pilot with its jaunty cap and its slim, yet strong, plastic encasement. "Encasement"—is that how you would say it in the US?

They had to be strong, for I was a rough-and-tumble athletic teen, always ready for a gang fight or a rigorous round of pétanque, and the pens in my back pocket sometimes broke—if they were Montblanc pens—and a sharp collision with turf, or another *garçon*'s foot, might leave *mon cul* a hideous mess of blue or black ink. I ordered the twelve-pack of Pilot Hi-Tec-C Maica pens recently through Amazon Prime, and as soon as I unwrapped the brown paper of the box, my years in de Gaulle's France came back to me like the madeleine that made Marcel swoon back to an earlier, simpler time, in Proust's seven-volume novel *Remembrance of Things Past*. Of course with today's sleek Japanese influence the pens themselves are rather different, and kind of clunky, wouldn't you say, their encasements encumbered with useless protrusions—though the glittering jewel cameo laid into each pen top is charming, like a diamond almost in its brightness. Like other owners, I too am perplexed about the color range Pilot is giving us in the Hi-Tec-C twelve-pack. There are something like three or four oranges—from gold to apricot to a pale root beer—why so many, I wonder? It's not like many people of any age or gender do much writing in orange shades, do they? Oh, maybe they do in Japan. I brought out some old French stationery that I kept, a stone blue, and when I tried writing a note to *ma soeur* with the "apricot orange" pen, I couldn't even see any marks on it! Looked like invisible ink. Similarly there is a scarlet and two pinks, and I can't tell them apart.

The caps are constantly being mixed up, but maybe that's just me. Each twelve-pack should be issued with a separate, extra assortment of tops, just in case they slip onto the carpet while writing. My wife said, "Why not use the orange and black pens you complain about every day and every *nuit*, and make a pen-and-ink drawing of the San Francisco Giants' stadium?"—our uniforms, you see, are orange and black. I think I will. She is *toujours* the one with the best ideas and knows her colors well, having had them "done" herself by a certified New Age color consultant. Boasting all those orange shades, the Pilot twelve-pack is what we in the New Age would call an "autumn" set. "They write beautifully," my wife says, "and I love them." She keeps stealing them to grade student papers with. We are bringing this pen set to our four-year annual color-palette review, and seeing if it makes the grade with our Franco-American style. However, I will never lose my memories, not so long as these pens stay on my desk like beautiful reminders of the land of my birth.

David Carradine: The Eye of My Tornado
by Marina Anderson

★★★★☆
In a Tornado of Genital Jewelry

July 28, 2015

I wish I had the new edition that is supposed to have new information in it, but I hesitate before buying it when I already have this one and it comes with almost more information than I can actually take in! I wonder if the new edition solves his murder and releases his name from the implication that he died in a typical Hollywood autoasphyxiation sex accident. But who would have wanted to murder him?

Marina Anderson's book suggests that maybe it was "X." X is some relative of David Carradine who entered into a long-term sexual relationship with him, but we don't know the person's name, nor their exact relationship with Carradine. Marina seems to indicate that if any of you is thinking that the person is one of Carradine's own children, she wants you to abandon that ugly thought, and still the word "incest" is whispered on many pages. After a few hundred pages of *The Eye of My Tornado*, I realized that no gender is ever given for X. Marina never says "she" when referring to X, and this made me wonder if X, the sexually abused young relative, is a guy. David tells her that he was once in love with X, and this made her sick. Naturally because of the incest theme, I wondered if David had any younger brothers, or nephews.

Marina actually gives short shrift to those of us, like myself, who don't know much about Carradine's life or career. She never tells us who his parents were, nor very much about how he became a household name. We don't even hear about Barbara Hershey except at the very end of the book, when the beloved Oscar-nominated actress appears at a vernissage in honor of Free, her son with Carradine. This is incidentally the last time that Marina sees David Carradine, and the passion is still reigning like a flame between them, but he is married to the new wife, the lovely widow, Annie.

Small-world department, as I was finishing up the last gruesome chapters, I turned on the TV and there was Frank Darabont's film of Stephen King's *The Mist*. "Wait," I said, "There's that girl in it who was in *The Walking Dead* and she was married to the Governor and she was Michonne's girlfriend?" Laurie Holden. Anyhow it turns out that Laurie Holden's parents split up and the father married Marina Anderson! This was before Marina entered the third marriage that was to make her famous. Michael Anderson Jr. was, I think, Marina's second husband. Cute, too.

I enjoyed finding out about all the genital piercings Carradine sported and the jewelry he used to adorn his private parts. The story grew grim, however, when after a few years of passion, Marina determined that he was trying to hurt her when they had sex by wearing all those adornments on what she calls his "genital wand." All in all she was a good wife to him and put up with an extraordinary number of sex quirks. As a male reader I was a little ill at ease when she describes herself submitting to his demand that she bite his genital wand "harder, harder, harder," he couldn't be satisfied until she could feel the sides of the jaw close in a viselike grip. No wonder she was gagging. But he seemed pretty out there from the beginning. What happened to him to make him so freaky? (Abused as a child, thinks Marina, and she was too.) I thought I was a freak but then I read this book and I'm off the hook, baby!

Jagged Edge (1985)
dir. Richard Marquand

★★★★☆
The Horrors Hidden by History Slice Through

September 13, 2015

We saw this movie when it first came out, right here in San Francisco, a city now so changed that watching *Jagged Edge* today is like watching Stroheim's *Greed* or something from another age entirely. There is the usual '80s feeling about "If only she'd had her cell phone on her, all her problems would be simplified vastly"—but also there is a belief in the daily-newspaper system that doesn't exist today. There are two San Francisco newspapers in the movie, the *Dispatch* and the *Times*, and each is prominently displayed; not only that, but Jeff Bridges's character Jack Forrester is the publisher of the *Dispatch*, and there are scenes of him looking very baronial in his grand office suite. When the curtains are pulled back, we see the walls are made of glass and look down into a giant production room for the newspaper being printed and folded and wrapped— impressive, but gone the way of vintage radio at this point. New technologies were, of course, abloom in the mid-1980s Bay Area, but it's telling that here the key piece of evidence is a series of anonymous letters composed from an old office Corona of what looks like the '30s, in which the *t* is wonky and jumps up higher than the other characters. Thus the movie sits in a sort of no-man's-land of time, but that's why people like San Francisco maybe. Screenwriter Joe Eszterhas kept going back to the well of San Francisco high society, didn't he, what with this and *Jade* and *Basic Instinct*? The movie opens up like some Brian De Palma classic sequence from the killer's POV, in which doors open as the killer touches them, and finally the woman is revealed and the screams begin, while a magnificent terror theme pounds suspense into every frame—it's got to be John Barry and it is!

Barry stays "on" throughout the whole picture, and when Jeff Bridges and Glenn Close grow intimate with each other, the pounding plangent repeated chords modulate into pleasant romantic-melody time—I had almost thought Sheena Easton might appear to croon, at a Trader Vic's sequence, "You, my love, are the jagged edge / Loving you is a priv-i-lege." Close and Bridges look alike, don't they, though he towers above her, but their faces in profile line up with each other in such a way we might believe that they belong together—he's more in her league than her dumpy ex-husband who understands her kids better than she does. Loved seeing young Brandon Call as Teddy's son, only a few years after he broke into TV-soap stardom as the disputed toddler in *Santa Barbara*, stealing every scene he was in. Is he still alive? He's the best actor here by a long shot, and in fact it's filled with good acting, battling with Eszterhas's trademark vulgarities—they say his lines, crude as they are, with nearly straight faces, though Robert Loggia and John Dehner don't even care, for director Richard Marquand has instructed them both to play their parts loudly and broadly as possible, "Have fun with it." I think if this movie were made today, Loggia's character would be killed off in the penultimate scene, to give the audience something to get upset about. But here, they just want the Loggia smirk, as familiar from a dozen Blake Edwards films, to last as long as the movie does. Instead Marquand has directed Leigh Taylor-Young, who appears in but a couple of places, to give the kind of performance that once won Oscar nominations for the likes of Ina Claire and Fay Bainter. And she's very worthy. This role should have catapulted her into Susan Sarandon territory. What happened?

Elsewhere, I'm assuming that the Black angle of the movie might be well made the center of a *Fruitvale Station* sort of protest movie about how Black lives matter. The film ends, or nearly ends, with a haunting shot of a silent Black woman staring down Glenn Close at an impromptu press conference and, apparently, shaming her into an act of reparation that needs to be made today on a national scale, with actual financial reparations made to those done wrong by racism and American capitalism and state-controlled slavery of Black men farmed into the penal system because white supremacists find it convenient to hold them there till they break. Only a few fragments of this backstory remain in the finished film, but enough to suggest that the movie, which seems like a white person's romantic suspense thriller, is really a *J'Accuse* of racist San Francisco, and that's never going to go away.

The Toaster Oven Cookbook
by David DiResta and Joanne Foran

★★★★★
Looks Faded, but It Was This Way Brand New

September 21, 2015

It took me only a few minutes to plug in my new toaster oven and perhaps twenty to read the revised edition of David DiResta and Joanne Foran's *The Toaster Oven Cookbook*. Ever have half an hour in your life where you had nothing to do but do the thing you always wanted to do? I was getting ready for the monthly meeting of my Bicoastal Mask group, and thought to myself, "I'll just make something out of *The Toaster Oven Cookbook*," the way I had always wanted to do.

For too long this book has lain on my Formica counter, handy to my cooking station, but somehow the time never seemed right. Now, with the meeting coming on, I flipped open the cookbook and tried to find some of the recipes I had salivated over during previous reads. There was one with shrimp and broccoli that sounded right. (Why is it, I ask parenthetically, that I find the word *broccoli* so hard to spell? Early childhood aversion to green, wiry, tough vegetables?) I grabbed the book and looked at it guiltily, it had lain in the sun so long that the cover looked all faded, even the hot-orange cylinders of the toast filaments seemed dim, like candy corn. But now as I compare it to the illustration on the book cover, I can see it hadn't faded, it was just printed with a sort of sepia finish. The very first recipe was what I wanted (and indeed it is the one on the book cover), shrimp and broccoli pizza. While the authors advise the readers to get little pizza pans, and even tile ramekins, on which to place your pizza slices, not me. I was willing to risk the inevitable disappearance of some of the crumbs, dropping off into the hot hell of the lower levels of my toaster over— i.e., the drip tray, what my wife calls the "crumb tray." Some of your food is going to be lost, that's a given. That's toaster oven cooking, you might even say, that's the heartbreak of toaster oven cooking.

But there are many rewards. The smiles on the faces of your friends in the Bicoastal Mask group when you bring out tray after tray of toaster oven pizza, with that shrimp and broc combo spiced with oregano and store-bought pizza sauce! The curious, envious questions your guests will be peppering you with. The sheer joy of the heavy, viscous scent of the pizza, bringing back memories to all of days spent eating heartier fare at Domino's or Little Caesars. Each page in the cookbook contains one recipe, and by the time you've finished one, you want to try the next one, which is just perfect for one- or two-person meals. It's intense, this craving to go on, turning the pages, dialing up the fun.

Frozen (**2013**)
dir. Jennifer Lee and Chris Buck

★★★★★
Do You Want to Build a Lesbian Masterpiece?

September 29, 2015

Disney's *Frozen* has some magical sequences and tuneful numbers, but mostly people respond to it because of its story of sisters who can't live with each other, can't live without each other. The simple plot must hold a deeply felt Marion Woodman appeal to a variety of audiences—the largest of which, apparently, is girls under ten, millions of whom have made home videos of themselves singing "Let It Go" and released them on YouTube in cute outfits and with (sometimes) bewilderingly sophisticated, perhaps parent-supplied backgrounds and props.

Idina Menzel can be imperious in real life, but in *Frozen* she seems deeply sorry for having offended anyone and for having turned all of Arendelle into a winter hell without a single flower. And also for hurting her sister Anna (once again!) with her magical power of coldness. The ingenious screenwriters have simplified the plot of Hans Christian Andersen's "Snow Queen" story of the Danish Romantic period, so that now instead of an evil snow queen menacing a brother and sister (Kay the brother and Gerda the sister), the siblings are both female—perhaps they took their cue from the way "Kay" never sounded like a boy's name anyhow … Instead of three characters, they reduced them to two by making the evil queen and the devoted sister the same person!

Kristen Bell employs a beautiful, strong voice as Anna, and she is so funny your sides will hurt at some of her byplay with Kristoff and Olaf, yet halfway through she becomes increasingly out of her game, for a reason I can't disclose—

[SPOILERS AHEAD]

OK, because Elsa has shot a chip of ice into her heart, the way the Snow Queen did to Kay in the old Andersen story—

[SPOILERS CONCLUDED]

As she grows weaker and weaker, she has to undergo some dramatic suffering rather beyond Bell's own Veronica Mars comic charm. Well, even tragedy queens like Angelina Jolie might not have been able to handle the depths of the part, so I would give Kristen Bell a good B for doing her best ... If Billie Whitelaw were still alive, she could have given Anna that precipitous *Camille*-like decline and tragic illness inherent in the part. And having Jonathan Groff as Kristoff doesn't help the situation much. Luckily here the little snowman and the big reindeer come in and steal the show with their heroics. That snowman, Olaf, is the most original cartoon character in eons, and his big oblivious number "In Summer" is more surreal than anything Man Ray ever made in or out of Hollywood. Suffice it to say, my wife and I were like two seven-year-old girls watching this film and for the first time in forever we burst out into applause and clapped until our palms grew raw and chapped. I wouldn't say that the cold never bothered me anyway, but I felt pretty heroic after watching *Frozen* and look forward to at least fourteen other sequels—fingers crossed!

Dear Darwish
by Morani Kornberg-Weiss

★★★★★
The Unintention of Living

October 2, 2015

Buffalo's doughty little BlazeVOX [books], publisher of many recent landmarks in contemporary poetry, has issued a volume of political poetry from Morani Kornberg-Weiss, a name new to me, with a title invoking the great Palestinian poet Mahmoud Darwish—an epistolary collection like Katy Bohinc's recent Tender Buttons book *Dear Alain*. Kornberg-Weiss cites Jack Spicer's landmark 1957 volume *After Lorca* as a source of inspiration and as a parallel, since like Spicer's letters to Lorca, Kornberg-Weiss is writing letters and poems to a poet deceased (Darwish died in 2008 in Houston, Texas), whereas philosopher Alain Badiou, addressed and wooed by Bohinc, is happily very much alive. And yet in a way the gendered thrust of *Dear Darwish* aligns it with Bohinc's cheeky-were-it-not-so-oracular mode of address, since Kornberg-Weiss is female, addressing a famous male, in a culture that "prefers that women keep their gentle hands clean."

Spicer too was a bit cheeky in addressing, and even manufacturing replies from, Federico García Lorca, but because they were both male subjects the playing field was more even, and the writers' politics similar. I take it that *Dear Darwish* has been criticized for its imaginative rethink of idealized "ally" strategy. She, Morani Kornberg-Weiss, is an Israeli dissident poet firmly opposed to the actions of her nation, and living in voluntary exile in the United States. She has read Spicer thoroughly and has applied his theories of "correspondence" to the facts of a conflict soaked red with blood, scrubbing with words "until this body / becomes nothing. // I am a skeleton walking among poets." She renders well the brutalities of prison, of torture, of the systemic withholding of what Darwish called his "id," the loss of the ID badges in "the blind spot of the mid-century."

Beyond Spicer, this poetry reminds me also of Plath, and her insistence on speaking of the ravages of war and abuse even within the supposed privilege of domestic life. Critics saw an overkill, an unseemliness, in such Plath poems as "Daddy," or in the yoking together of the deaths of the Rosenbergs into the breakdown melodrama of *The Bell Jar*. What can poetry do in the face of such stalemate? "Life, initially," Morani Kornberg-Weiss tells us, "is about unintention." Hers is a poetry so unruly that one keeps landing on lines that the mind keeps trying to parse into gentility, but as the poet reminds us, "What is mild to one person may be terrible to another." That is the risk of all political action, including the action of writing and reading poetry. *Dear Darwish* is a serial poem to ponder at length, to read and reread, as I have done during the past eleven months. She quotes Robert Duncan as having said "We cannot rid ourselves of the form to which we now belong," and yet she unclenches her fists to reveal the lines in her hands, which indicate, mmm, maybe we can.

It Started in Naples (1960)
dir. Melville Shavelson

★★★★★
For Better or for Worse

October 6, 2015

I walked into the living room and the TV was on but suddenly my wife, sitting near the remote, snapped it off as though it was something she didn't want me to see, her face nearly expressionless except for a gleam of worry in her eye, the sort of look one wears when one's keeping a secret. But we are both New Narrative writers and usually there are no secrets between us! When I picked up the remote and switched it to reverse, I could see that she was watching some kind of highly colored vintage melodrama set on the Island of Capri. Eventually she broke down in giggles and admitted hysterically that she was watching Sophia Loren and Clark Gable in Melville Shavelson's *It Started in Naples* (1960).

This is really my kind of picture and not hers, so I must have infected her with rom-com fever! "Well, rewind it, I'll watch it with you," I offered, but she wouldn't hear of it, she was too caught up in the action. She said she would just recap things for me. "Previously, on *It Started in Naples*," she began, and quickly ran through how this little eight-year-old boy was the center of a custody war not between two divorcing people (perhaps there was no divorce in Italy in 1960, we guessed) but between Sophia Loren, whose sister had married a bohemian American expat called—we never did find out what he was called, but he was the younger brother of important US corporation lawyer Clark Gable. And her sister and his brother had perished in a Fiat crash, or perhaps the car had gone off the narrow, twisty mountain roads above Capri's beautiful blue waters—leaving behind a son whom aunt Sophia Loren, a second-rate cabaret entertainer with little talent but a fabulous figure, was trying to bring up, when she thought of it. Eventually they were going to get together, but not before a lot of *neorealismo* hijinks and a lot of vino and cheese and grapes went down, and sexy dancing and captivating photography. Many on IMDb claim that this is their favorite movie of all time. Well, for one thing, it is a blistering anti-American satire of imperialist business and law practices, the whole "ugly American" thing Clark Gable embodies. This is harsh pseudo–Billy Wilder stuff! It's like *A Foreign Affair* with Loren in the Dietrich role, and Gable in the Jean Arthur role. Gable is incredibly withered and shrunken, but still magnetic, and game for anything. In this role it's almost tragic that his American sophistication and wariness of being "played" almost loses him his chance to find the one boy he had never even known he wanted, his eight-year-old self, half-American, half-pleasure-mad-Italian.

The little boy is like nothing on earth I've ever seen in the movies. With long arms and legs, and tiny playsuits, his face often dirty, he gets drunk, sneaks cigarettes, just wants to have a good time in Capri. His English is rusty, and we could barely make out what he was saying half the time, but he's learning American slang ("I'm a tough guy, see?") as fast as Gable can dish it out. Often in his underwear—a weird Italian pair of ur–Jockey shorts you'd never find on an American boy—he stays out all night, steals trinkets and things he thinks his aunt might like, knows far too much about sin and gambling, and avoids the hated schoolhouse. His mouth is always running, his bare feet stirring up a continuous whirligig cloud of dust, like the old Road Runner cartoons, or Pigpen from *Peanuts*. He's thoroughly criminal, like little Jackie Earle Haley from *The Bad News Bears*, or actually like a boy from an earlier Italian strain of cinema, like the boy in De Sica's *Bicycle Thief*. De Sica is in the movie too, playing Gable's lawyer, super tall and handsome and expansive and a double-crosser, like everyone else on this tourism-driven island.

Loren is gorgeous, but more slovenly than usual in her US films, often wearing one weird blue ensemble with green underpinnings that doesn't know if it's a house dress or a cocktail dress. It's like the producers forgot to buy her any more outfits. This one factor allows the movie to go into overdrive, insisting on its status as "neorealistic," that she should keep wearing the same dress every day like an ordinary housewife of Italy. And the sunny criminality of the boy (the child actor Marietto, who actually was about thirteen when he played the role), and De Sica's practiced vamping, it's practically a potted history of postwar Italian cinema. But in bright color, brighter than anything Visconti or Bava ever achieved. It's like the cinematographers and set designers here were practicing for upcoming Jacques Demy movies, for not until *The Umbrellas of Cherbourg* would there be a movie where you really didn't care what was happening on the screen, everything was so luscious like flowers blooming before your eyes. When Gable and Loren slip out of a motorboat and into the velvety waters of Capri's Blue Grotto, part of your brain knows it's not them, but you don't care, they're svelte silhouettes at play in all the moonlit waters of the earth.

Gephyromania
by TC Tolbert

★★★★★
Running Up That Hill

October 10, 2015

Gephyromania indicates a keen interest in bridges. I'm sure I'm not the only one who didn't know what this word meant before turning to TC Tolbert's brightly colored Ahsahta book. I knew the opposite, gephyrophobia, a fear of crossing bridges, for it is a fear that has possessed me since I was a child. But for the trans person there may be both: a fear of the bridge, and yet a compulsion to build and cross, and cross back. I met the author earlier this year, after several years of hearing about her/him from mutual friends, most of them poets, as one of the most charming, attractive, and talented poets in the West. It didn't take me long to connect the work I had read in *Gephyromania* with the bridge-building of the trim, sharp subject before me. Instantly we fell into one of those talks where two people finish each other's sentences. Or three people, for we had an old friend, the poet Samuel Ace, with us too. In *Gephyromania* the speaker announces, from within parentheses, that "I am the least brave person that I know." I understood this as a reaction from one who has been called "brave" for the gender and poetic choices s/he has made for so long it is like breathing out and breathing in, and perhaps a nod to other forms of courage.

"What," I asked myself, "is the symbolic function of parentheses within Tolbert's text?" They form a version of fort, like Freud's construction of "fort/da," a forested space in which to hide or protect one's body from attack. Perhaps a confessional booth—must find out if Tolbert was raised Catholic, as I was—a ceilinged space in which one can speak truth with the hope of forgiveness, or to announce oneself without fear of contradiction. That this place that is a revelation of fear is a space in which one can deny being brave—indeed, in which one can declare one to be the least brave person—that's paradoxical, like something from an unfinished Bataille story.

We always hear that in Italian, *stanza* means "room," and here, on page 84, the little room of parentheses is the only thing you can see on the page—besides the page number itself—two words in parentheses: "(and still)." Here the phrase lies hobbled to the left edge of the page, but because of the horizontal, Doug Powell–like orientation of the poem vis-à-vis the book, what one might think of as the left turns out to be on the right (close to the book's spine) like some Elizabethan alchemy performed by John Dee. What I'm suggesting is that Tolbert is harnessing the shapes and rhythms of the poem to mirror the disconcerting trials, trails, and exhilarations of trans subjectivity? I wish I knew more, but reading and rereading this marvelous book will keep me firmly on the take for as long as I can hold on. John Wieners told me he had to stay "on the take" to find all the poems he wound up writing, and through the sometimes difficult patches of his life, there was this one tendency that allowed him to live—the habit of acquisition. Tolbert's breakthrough is to add to this habit the one of, not diminution, but of walking away from, of rolling one's box up a hill till its shape changes to something one can recognize as one's own. Like Kate Bush used to say, "If I only could, I'd be running up that hill."

Charles M. Schulz: Conversations
ed. M. Thomas Inge

★★★★☆
Theater of Cruelty

October 12, 2015

Charles Monroe Schulz was a household name even in France, where I as an American boy growing up in French provinces had my own subscription to the *International Herald Tribune* from ages six to ten. In this remarkable book of conversations, we discover much about the lure that held Schultz a prisoner of French thought, feeling, and culture, including his service in WWII as an American GI. Professor Inge, who published this book within a few months of Schulz's lamentable passing in the year 2000, reproduces the notorious *Peanuts* strip that Schulz created for the Sunday comics on the forty-ninth anniversary of D-Day, in which the skies are filled with white foamy clouds, American soldiers huddle in prayer on long benches built into hulls of airplanes, and then they are dropped in chutes onto the bloody beaches of Normandy on June 6, with those huge crucifix-like objects the Vichy government erected in the sand to prevent invasion. One Charlie Brown–like boy in a huge checked cap rocks in the surf, only his face visible—is he drowning? Underneath, a box caption: "June 6, 1944, 'To Remember.'" The Sunday strip puzzled *Peanuts* readers back then and continues to act as an anomalous reminder that for Schlulz, like William Faulkner, the past was not dead—it's not even past.

The continual return to childhood is treated again and again in these interviews, which span a good forty-five years. As they go on, they get more ponderous, but so does Schulz, while many of the interviewers seek to find out why *Peanuts* lost so much of its punch in later years. Few will now remember that it was part of the "sick comedy" movement that changed American laughter in the volatile 1950s, like Lenny Bruce, Nichols and May, Albee plays like *Who's Afraid of Virginia Woolf?* But childhood is cruelty and that's where *Peanuts* excelled—with the existential nightmare of Lucy always grabbing the ball before Charlie Brown can kick it, or the cloud of dust that attends the eternal outsider Pigpen. "I couldn't do that now," Schulz says, examining some old, cruel comic strips. Even the expression "good grief" had too sadistic a connotation for the aged Schulz. Did he live a lifetime of regret? Seems like it. Modernism played hell with one's values, and devils like Lucy masquerade as psychiatrists for five cents a session. Anarchic Snoopy flips into air and barks at the planes flying overhead, and in one of them Schulz kneels, praying over the Norman coast, among a group of boys he will never see again.

Finishing School (1934)
dir. Wanda Tuchock and George Nicholls Jr.

★★★★★
Bird on a Wire

October 16, 2015

Finishing School has the sort of raw edge of the pre-Code films, the sort that shocks you a little because you pause and ask yourself, "Did she really say that?" There's the one sequence where the girls are in a taxi looking forward to a weekend of gin and sin, and the youngest girl decides she wants to experience the weekend without her braces. It's like something from a John Waters film, the way that they actually reach into her mouth and grasp at the metal wire until it's wrenched out—just not all the way, so that the poor girl is stuck there with three or four inches of mousetrap steel sticking out of the left side of her face. She doesn't even blink an eye, she's like an animal who just wants to maximize pleasure. The shocking thing is that among the girls egging her on is Frances Dee, who until now has been the goody-two-shoes girl who is from the highest of American aristocracy, shocked by the casual drinking and sex play of her classmates. Now she reveals herself as just as amoral as the rest of them. That picture of the girl with her braces wedged into one side of her mouth is as disturbing as anything Man Ray or Luis Buñuel was making around the same time. Can we credit the presence of Wanda Tuchock behind the camera, a Hollywood screenwriter credited here as codirector, for the picture's deeply unsettling picture of women together on a spree?

The film benefits from a raft of astonishing performances, from Frances Dee herself; to Ginger Rogers as her roommate Pony; to

Billie Burke as the vain, selfish mother (like Gladys Cooper in the later *Now, Voyager*); to Beulah Bondi, who could often go sentimental but here is a hard case operator, cold as they come, and always watching and lurking like a cobra. And then there's Bruce Cabot from *King Kong* who is a total love god in this picture, handsome as they come, and more understanding than Dee has any right to ask of him. He's like a big, elongated version of the present-day literary critic Kaplan Page Harris, with the same knowing grin. Tuchock seems to know how to make the most of Cabot's limited acting abilities—just train the spotlights on his cheekbones and let shadows rest on the bones of his forehead and he will seem to be irresistible enough to make even the goodest girl go "bad." He's a waiter in the hotel where Rogers and Dee go to have sex with frat boys—then he's an intern at a children's hospital fighting disease—then he's a crusader in the war against stuffy finishing schools—and he comes down the chimney at Christmas Eve like a lithe, dark, wet-eyed Santa Claus with a big gift for the poor little rich girl. The thing with the pre-Code movies is you have to be more adult than it's possible actually to be nowadays to understand what is actually happening in them. And this movie, as you can tell by the various reviewers' wildly differing synopses, is not easy to follow—to say the least. But it is magnificent, for all its cruelty, like an early Pasolini film.

The Big Builders (**A Whitman Learn About Book**)
by E. Joseph Dreany

★★★★★
And I Loved Seeing Things Go Down

October 19, 2015

The Big Builders came out the year I started the fourth grade, and it became an important book to me. As an adult I can see what appears to be an ideological message I never really understood as a kid. But what kid would? Or do I mean, What boy would? I still don't understand why I was so fascinated with builders and junkers both, could stand for hours watching construction crews erect even the smallest of buildings, and I loved seeing things go down, too, as they often were in the Robert Moses–dominated Long Island of my youth. I hear from my grandchildren (now grown themselves, starting families of their own) that their own kids love videos involving big trucks and that they are the best babysitters around, these videos. You can leave the house for hours and your kids will literally not know you are gone.

That's how I was with this Whitman Learn About Book by the utterly strange and compelling immigrant figure, E. Joseph Dreany. The back of my tattered copy of *The Big Builders* reads: "In that part of northern Canada where log cabins and tar-paper shacks are still plentiful, and where winters mean deep snow, long icicles, and temperatures that tickle the sub-zero mark—that's where E. JOSEPH DREANY, author and artist, was born and raised." I wish I could show you some of his illustrations but they are quite fanciful and cinematic. On the front cover a crew of four hard hats reach out to each other from opposing red-gold girders as they lasso the Golden Gate Bridge, above the raging waters of Hoover Dam, while above soars the then-new United Nations Building. It turns out these workers are Mohawk Indians, who have the "iron nerve" it takes to stand without safety belts with only a steel beam to stand on in heavy winds. "Once they came from an Indian reservation in Canada. Now they live in Brooklyn." Dreany doesn't talk down to kids, exactly, and it was from this book that I found out that the iconic Lever Building was the first NYC building to be erected without setbacks, from the third floor up, a giant slab on its end, like the UN Building that followed it. Now we see these buildings and don't even appreciate the power of the Mohawk Indians that made them—like the artisans who created Mont-Saint-Michel and Chartres, they are forgotten balancers.

The chapter on the building of Hoover Dam likewise is written and illustrated with real force. My total knowledge of Hoover Dam comes from a gay amalgam of Dreany's *The Big Builders* with memories of Elvis and Ann-Margret touring the dam for kicks in the splenetic dreamworld of George Sidney's *Viva Las Vegas*. It was from Dreany that I learned that the construction of Hoover Dam was larger and more difficult than the building of the Great Pyramid of Cheops, or to look at it in another way, imagine a grand pyramid erected upside down within the walls of a Western canyon, and then flooded with water, and you can see how the "chariots of the gods" isn't just a fanciful Canadian idea, it may be a real thing, and that is why this extraneous scene of Elvis and Ann-Margret was inserted into the film in question, to announce the endorsement of the thing by actual twentieth-century gods of music, beauty, and dance—a "dam that tamed a wild mustang of a western river," to be colorful about it. The book also answers the questions "What is a 'gismo'?"—"Can you bounce a Ping-Pong ball on water?"—"Who eats 'woodburgers'?"—and many more attractive propositions that every child yearns to know.

This cover shows just half of the visual excitement that the legendary Dreany brought to us in Whitman Learn About Books. You'll learn about colors and capitalism in *The Big Builders*.

Eye on the Struggle: Ethel Payne, the First Lady of the Black Press
by James McGrath Morris

★★★★☆
A "Window Seat on the World"

November 29, 2015

A friend told me I knew too little about the Black press of the twentieth century and, with my interest in mass media, that it was silly of me to be so ill informed. He recommended a forthcoming book which is now on my bookshelf, the life of Ethel Payne, the Queen of American Journalism. Folks called her the "Queen of Black Journalism," but after reading even a few chapters she jumps across racial boundaries and takes on the title from her white counterparts. Yet she is hardly celebrated at all. Is there a reason for this? McGrath Morris does his best to make us understand what it might have been like for the young Ethel Payne, growing up in a racist society and struggling for every meal, yet driven by parents who believed fervently in education as the way out for an embattled race.

Payne herself was sometimes—not her worst enemy, that's a cliché—but sometimes she was not her own best advocate, and time after time in the book McGrath Morris shows her getting tired or frustrated with this or that plum job and then moving on, sometimes without a clear vision of what she wanted to do next. Periods of joblessness ensued, but like a cat she always managed to use her extensive network of friends and business contacts to find something worthy of her talents. She was a journalist who learned quickly, and she could put away scruples when she had to, and best of all she stood up for what she believed in, and risked the ire of many powerful forces of evil. Her personal life? Well, it isn't easy at the top, especially for a successful woman, and especially, or so she believed, for a Black woman. The contretemps in which she criticized Vernon Jordan in 1980, when he survived an assassin's bullet only to be told by Payne in her nationally circulated column that he had no right being out late at night with a white woman not his wife—this story alone could make a whole movie, and yet we see Ethel Payne as acting perhaps without knowledge of the facts and, at the least, uncharitably, but again, she was not afraid to chew up and spit out even Black men if she thought they were making fools of themselves.

The dramatic moment of McGrath Morris's story is his account of the 1955 Bandung Conference, an episode of world history very little covered today. This was an international conference for representatives of five Asian nations and five African nations, no white powers invited, and the first time in modern history such an event occurred. Indonesia was the country selected to host this amazing meeting of minds, and all around the world far-seeing Blacks saw and celebrated that something new had come into being—a conference in which white nations were treated as not the majority of the peoples of this earth. US emigre novelist Richard Wright wrote, "Only brown, black and yellow men who had long been made agonizingly self-conscious, under the rigors of colonial rule, of their race and their religion could have felt the need for such a meeting." Great minds fought like tigers to get to Bandung, but in the end, many leftist intellectuals like Paul Robeson and W. E. B. DuBois found their entrance denied via the machinations of the State Department. McGrath Morris points out that of nearly eight hundred delegates, not a single one was female, and in general very few women managed to get into the conference at all. But Ethel Payne went! And her coverage made her a household name, angering Eisenhower but sealing her reputation among the Black readers of the Black press. (Adam Clayton Powell, the controversial Black Harlem congressman, also went to Bandung, but ironically he was so fair skinned that security refused to give him Black status, preventing him from entering some assemblies, so he clung to Payne, claiming to be as Black as she. [I can't really repeat his exact words here.]) The biographer digs in and brings us an hour-by-hour account of the riveting, surreal congress, and Payne's strategies to give her American audiences a sense of what was going on without censorship from either the right or left. She was present at, and wrote about, nearly every important civil rights initiative. And while she pioneered the rights of Black women, she refused to write the "women's pages" pap her editors sometimes asked her to. Very few figures from the entertainment world, for example, make it into the pages of McGrath Morris's book—perhaps they were judged too peripheral or self-aggrandizing.

Can a white biographer write an adequate biography of a Black subject? Can a male biographer write successfully, thoroughly, of a woman's life? I'm glad this isn't a test case for biography, because there are more than a few places in which McGrath Morris's race and his gender show themselves all too painfully. And yet he has written an exciting, provocative book that makes one stand up and cheer for Ethel Payne, while shaking one's head at the vicious racial climate through which she had to pass and which prevails today. I don't know.

Guide of the Thyssen Bornemisza Museum
by Fundación Colección Thyssen-Bornemisza

★★★★★
Farewell to the "Misza"

April 4, 2016

The last time I was in Madrid I stopped in, as so often before, to the privately held Thyssen Bornemisza Museum, but for the first time, foreseeing my retirement and how soon I would no longer be able to afford an annual jaunt to Iberia, I did something I never thought I would do, I accepted the museum's proffered gift of a hard copy of their guide.

Actually, had I known I could get it off Amazon for one cent, I wouldn't have made such an impulsive buy on such a sad occasion. But now I'm glad I own this handsome book, for it reminds me of many long Madrid afternoons spent wandering from the first floor to the second floor, and back again, and dipping down into the basement cafeteria for a quick-fixed meal, and looking at the North

American pop art which is so well represented here. Aficionados of "el pop" know that the collection of "Tita" ranks high among all collections of pop art in the world, makes the collection of New York's Museum of Modern Art, or the Whitney, look puny in comparison.

In fact, I'm old enough to remember the days before there was a Warhol Museum in Pittsburgh, so if you wanted to see a slew of Warhols, best thing to do was to get a good seat on the Concorde (the legendary transatlantic "bird of choice," on which there were literally no bad seats) and hie thee to the Thyssen Bornemisza—what the poets called "El Misza," or simply "Tita's Place"—and see the Warhols larger than life there. It was Tita's famous definition of "el pop" that gave us its shape, its contour. There were three key elements: it must quote from existing cultural tropes, like a can of soup; it works on free association, like the great Rauschenberg combine *Express*, seen here since the '60s and the model for David Fincher's video for Madonna's later international hit "Express Yourself"; and finally, it is extrovert (see page 162 of the English translation of this guide).

Tita's cocktails were a bit like that too. She had the pop on the ground floor and the Renaissance on the floor above, so she would pour in a few dashes of Coca-Cola then top it off with guava or grenadine. Refreshing, like Schwitters with a twist of Merz.

Alas, those days are no more and I am glad now that I accepted guide Pablo's kind gift of this shiny, gaudy catalogue. In my dotage now, I can open it at every page and remember my annual jaunts to Madrid and how hard people worked for their money, but I could relax, peel some olives, and sip me a Tita.

500 Capp Street: David Ireland's House
by Constance M. Lewallen

★★★★★
Houseful of Brooms and Dooms

April 11, 2016

Constance M. Lewallen's delightful guide to 500 Capp Street is now the book I give to newcomers to San Francisco who would like a taste of the past, a taste of the present, a good tip for the perfect date night, and also, writing at the top of her form, one of the most erudite, yet readable, art historians and critics of our day—a true treasure of San Francisco.

Since the book came out, a few months back, the philanthropic trust has reopened to the public after serious refurbishment, an opening timed perhaps to the reopening of the Berkeley Art Museum and that of the San Francisco Museum of Modern Art. These will all be destination sites for visiting art lovers, and perhaps a kooky, private citizen's home might seem a strange point of triangulation for the uninitiated, but once you read Lewallen's book you will see, maybe there's something to this—maybe David Ireland (1930–2009) is in fact the quintessential Bay Area artist.

Even if you can't come to San Francisco, this lovely little book will leave you feeling that you've been there. The color photographs are exquisitely reproduced, right down to Ireland's distinctive amber-tinged walls, they actually do possess that yellow drench, like an Argento film, the saturation accomplished with numerous, even countless, coats of paint. A young art student I know called it a "piss-soaked look," and yeah, kind of. Lewallen speaks knowledgeably of 500 Capp Street in the tradition of the "house as 'total work of art,'" the *Gesamtkunstwerk*, and that seems right. It's inspiring to consider a place in which the owner has treated every surface, every piece of furniture as handcraft and perhaps has an eccentric devotion to the smoothness and antiqueness of things. It's on a block in San Francisco which John Ashbery, writing in 1983, describes as "unremarkable" and "rundown," but with the recent tech-fueled gentrification of the city, bohemian friends have been evicted and left, and right on that block, driven away by insane rent prices, so that the restoration of 500 Capp has an awkward side to it, though maybe its instant anachronism will heighten its numerous charms.

Lewallen describes Ireland's slow movement into the world of conceptual art, for he was not a young artist ever, it seems, and his house is a monument to many strange careers. He conducted African safaris for wealthy white tourists in the '50s, and really the board might consider posting a "trigger warning" at the doorbell telling how many parts of wild beasts will be on view in different rooms, like the home of an old planter in *White Mischief*—so it's disconcerting and a little foul. However, there are many splendid rooms, vistas, head-scratching moments, and sighs of wonder, both in the house and in the book under review. It is truly a one-of-a kind experience, and as Lewallen hints, it will make you forever question the shifting lines between sculpture and architecture.

Lewallen is also adept at putting this house into a lineage of other houses and structures worked on by Ireland during his lifetime, and this one does seem the best, though now I'm curious to go back to 65 Capp Street and to the "Rodeo Room" at the Headlands Center for the Arts across the Golden Gate Bridge from my apartment. In the photo of the Rodeo Room here, the walls gleam the color of spun gold, but brighter, like the oleomargarine of the '40s, like they have been rubbed with the pollen of a billion marigolds.

Jeepster (2003 Remaster)
by T. Rex

★★★★★
Cars and Girls and the Future

June 11, 2016

Now that I get unlimited streaming of this song with my Prime membership, it has been playing again and again to weird effect. I found myself living, after my fourth playing, in two eras at once. Back when I was eighteen or nineteen, I thought Marc Bolan the beginning and end of everything. Must have driven my family and friends crazy with blasting out *Electric Warrior* all over the place and for the infrequent visits of T. Rex to Long Island, where I lived in my parents' basement one long, hot summer.

He was an enormously appealing little guy; David Bowie called him "the Prettiest Star," though that wasn't really true, he wasn't all that handsome, but he had a wonderful smile and seemed to take to the switch from folk-acoustic occult-trance music to basic rock 'n' roll with great aplomb, as though to say "If Dylan could do it, so can I." And for three or four LPs in a row, he released the catchiest material: not every song was memorable, but many of them got under your skin so that one wondered, "This is so primal, why hasn't it been written before by somebody else?" *Jeepster* was among this group.

Bolan's lyrics could sometimes veer on the Orientalist, to fetishize colonial cultures, and that makes them fishy viewed today, but he also had the knack, shared with Bowie, of seeming to predict the future and to be able to peer into technological and philosophic developments that hadn't yet occurred. The concept, corny as it was, of the "electric warrior" might be emblematic of Bolan's interest in what we would today call cyborg culture—that a pretty, sweet girl could turn him into a "jeepster" spoke to a world in which boy + machine could merge and, once combined, become something even cuter than either apart.

"Just like a car, you're pleasing to behold. I'll call you Jaguar, if I may be so bold." The sentiments were so dumb and yet so outlandish they allowed him to get away with murder. The famous punchline of "Jeepster," in which he calls out "I'm gonna suck you," went without editorial challenge from upstairs at my folks' house in Smithtown—maybe Mom and Dad couldn't understand his British accent.

Oh, and the other thing is in how many ways he anticipated Prince! Watching Prince live was like watching T. Rex live, I wonder if the relation between the two little guys will become clearer as time passes on. So that was the second phase of my life that comes back to me as I listen to "Jeepster," the early 1980s when I first saw Prince and heard "Little Red Corvette."

In the Empire of the Air: The Poems of Donald Britton
by Donald Britton, ed. Reginald Shepherd and Philip Clark

★★★★★
A Treasure Returned to Us

June 19, 2016

One of the most piquant developments in poetry this spring is the revival of a little-read, out-of-print poet few among us have heard of. I belong to an even tinier subset, among those who never met the poet in real life but own a copy of his only book, *Italy*, so we think we know more about him than we do. He was handsome, talented, well educated, and knew many of the movers and shakers of New York City poetry in the mid-'80s. I've been in love with him since

1986, when I saw his picture in a monograph of paintings and drawings by the late Larry Stanton, from Twelvetrees Books. Why, then, is he so little known? His name is Donald Britton, and AIDS killed him. Now we are privy to much more of his work and, almost as good, a contextualization of his career besides, thanks to NYC poetry press Nightboat Books and the work of a pair of editors who have spent a dozen years or more putting him together and bringing him back to the brink of life in the new volume *In the Empire of the Air: The Poems of Donald Britton*.

We have followed this recovery project for ages, and in itself it has dramatic aspects. The work was originally undertaken by the late, and beloved, prize-winning poet Reginald Shepherd, whose passion project this was. And when Shepherd died in 2008, all too soon, of cancer, it looked as though Britton would remain unknown, and with him a fascinating tale of intersectionality as well. Why was Shepherd so all on fire for the poems of a man he had never known? Through the editorial apparatuses of the new edition, we find out at last a little bit more about the shifting identifications of writership and readership. In the end it was another attractive young man, Philip Clark, who took on the process of coming to terms with Shepherd's manuscript.

As a lagniappe, MacArthur "Genius Grant"–winner Douglas Crase appends a beautiful portrait of Donald Britton as a prism for his time, his dual sense of "spectacle and diminishment" emblematic of the trying voyage many were encountering in the gay world—the AIDS crisis which was claiming so many of Britton's friends and which would shipwreck many lives and many careers. Crase's memoir is so terrific you might buy the book just to read his piece, but beyond that there are fifty-five poems by Britton, and they will prove a revelation to some—brilliant vehicles of passion in repose, witty as Congreve and wily as Isak Dinesen. I have new favorites every day, and yet there is no denying that Britton is an acquired taste and easily dismissed as "Ashbery lite." The frothy design of the late John Button's painting used for the cover, the very "airiness" Britton seemed to prefer, I find charming, delightful, "amusing" as the "amusing notion" Britton writes about, in "Here and Now," the notion that "life might someday / Not be confusing," and that this notion "coordinates / Our award-winning sentiments these past days." No one, after all, has been more "award-winning" than Ashbery, but Britton leaves it up in the air whether or not "award-winning" is an ironic slam or a glamorous bouquet with which to award our sentiments.

He is capable of astounding metaphors—"Living and Bleeding" is one long continuous ribbon of metaphor, "like hair folding over / A valley." "The spokes / of our bikes" are "as invisible as the momentum / Bringing us here to be mounted on the air / Like TV ghosts." That's a trail that needs much unpacking, and yet the music carries us through any amount of this intensive doubling and redoubling. "We're the front and back of the same page" (isn't that terrific?), "unknown to each other, but identical." I think those of us who take to Donald Britton find in him something of that two-sided page, though maybe we're kinder about his poems—no two are identical, and yet in each one all of his readers will find something of their own hearts that has been occluded by despair and regret. There's freshness here, like the days of Eden ashore.

An Attempt at Exhausting a Place in Paris
by Georges Perec

★★★★★
Timeline of Clayton's *Gatsby* Reception in Paris
July 29, 2016

Georges Perec published *Tentative d'épuisement d'un lieu parisien* in 1975, only a matter of months after the October weekend he spent observing traffic patterns and tourism in the place Saint-Sulpice in Paris and writing down everything he saw. Sometimes his account feels rigorous and strict—for example, if someone walks too far to the right, he tells us he is not describing nothing that takes place in his peripheral vision—but then we realize he's constantly moving his head to the left, right, up and down, like a drone, and we wonder, "What's the point?" And sometimes he seems to make use of outside information—like his friends are telling him where they are going or where they have been as they pass by, whereas if he relied only on his eyes we wouldn't find out, say, that philosopher Paul Virilio was on his way to see *The Great Gatsby* at the Bonaparte.

Perec refers to the movie as *The Lousy Gatsby*, perhaps reflecting his own low opinion of the movie, but one wonders, "Had he already seen it?" This Virilio sighting takes place on Saturday, October 19, but what the translator doesn't make clear is that although the notorious Mia Farrow–Robert Redford star vehicle had made its debut in the spring in America, it opened in Paris only three days before Virilio is spotted hurrying to see something Perec refers to as "lousy." Hmm, portrait of Virilio as crowd-following trendoid? We all know people who have to see movies on opening week, even those with middling word of mouth. On paper Jack Clayton's *Gatsby* looked like a sure thing, with Redford's unstoppable golden-boy appeal paired with Mia Farrow's still-potent haunted-poor-little-rich-girl act. But when the movie came out, French people approved only of the look of the divine Lois Chiles as Jordan, and the approved American harpy-slut routines of New American Cinema favorite Karen Black as Myrtle.

But these speculations are necessarily far removed from the chess problem Perec sets for us. What would you see if your gaze were confined to one of the busiest intersections on earth, one with dozens of buses every half hour, and carloads of Japanese tourists snapping cameras at signposts? It's like that Tati movie where you see through a see-through apartment building into the mime-like silent lives of the tenants and visitors, but Perec cheats so much the payoff suffers. And were Japanese camera bugs and English schoolboys the only foreigners walking the place Saint-Sulpice that weekend? Perhaps so, otherwise he might have mentioned a few others, here and there. A general exhaustion pervades the piece. He's tired frequently. Perhaps the onset of the illness that did him in far too early? He's just sitting there in cafés writing down snatches of "in the distance, two boys with red anoraks" and "a bird settles atop a lamppost," together with snippets of the old color-chase game the Situationists used to play, following a snarl of green paper blowing through the wind tunnel caused by the appearance of so many silent, snapping Japanese people staring aimlessly at French sights. The puzzle of mass tourism persists, decades after the horror nostalgia of *Hiroshima mon amour*, but here the Japanese are staring back on one's own place.

The Invitation (2015)
dir. Karyn Kusama

★★★☆☆
We Just Disagree

July 29, 2016

We sat down to view *The Invitation* in a second-hand rush of excitement, the kind born of having heard a lot of excited chatter about it from horror-fan friends. People said you couldn't believe what was going to happen, that it started like a normal movie and then whammo! It took you to a place unrecognizable as human existence. Well, that did happen to me while watching *Glitter* starring Mariah Carey and Terrence Howard, but that was back in 2001 and I was ripe to repeat that experience. Pauline Kael used to say that the best American movies managed just that feat, a clever combination of several genres of film so that, in say *McCabe & Mrs. Miller*, you were watching a Western on the one hand and a nouvelle vague film on the other (and a musical with all those dour Leonard Cohen songs thrown in). Anyhow, *The Invitation*, directed by talented Karyn Kusama of *Girlfight* fame, was exactly what we were looking for, and I was all nestled in with my popcorn expecting something really great when I noticed the name of Michiel Huisman in it.

That instantly shifted the mood. My wife really likes him, me not so much. He was OK playing Liam when *Nashville* was on ABC—the Irish rock 'n' roller who threatened to give Rayna Jaymes the Bono treatment—but in over his head, or so I maintain, when they hired him to be the new love interest for the *khaleesi*. I can't even pronounce his name but I always recognize him on *GOT* when he's naked, for he has the tiniest butt God ever gave to a man, what my friend Dan's girlfriend referred to as "ass negative." Anyway he's just lost next to the blond powers of the *khaleesi*, not to mention all the other colorful characters in her storyline, the one who's turning to stone but still loves her, the Grey Worm, the Imp, her handmaiden who's so beautiful, her first husband Aquaman, et cetera. Now he appears in *The Invitation* as a mysterious cult leader with a haggard, yet luscious, alcoholic wife, who looked strangely to me like the young Judy Garland, but old. We soon determined that the wife indeed was the young Judy Garland—at least she had played the part in the docudrama about Judy Garland, and then when Garland grew up she was Judy Davis (*Me and My Shadows*, 2001—also the year of *Glitter*, in fact). Well, Huisman underacts and Blanchard overacts, but otherwise than that, they seem like they're evil from the start. If you don't get that within the first ten minutes, you haven't been to "understanding overacting" school very long.

The setup has a little bit more backstory built into it, and that may have helped the positive buzz about the movie, that it's a B or C movie with A-level rewards, the way Val Lewton in the '40s at RKO had only ten thousand dollars, no budget for special effects, so he had a bus emit compressed air and everyone jumped out of their seats thinking it was the cat woman attacking. Basically the evil couple has invited the previous husband of the Judy Garland character and his new, Black, girlfriend, and the previous husband is wary as hell of these new advances. So they go to the party expecting the worst and you think it is going to have some Cassavetes realness about it. It also seems like Michiel Huisman is living large, they are in some fabulous Benedict Canyon–like section of LA in a designer home living the lifestyle of the rich and famous. Logan Marshall-Green, who actually looks so much like Michiel Huisman that I may have confused them, gets drunk and belligerent right away, and rightfully so, for he feels as if his first wife left him only to marry a doppelgänger of himself only one slightly more good looking and with hella more in the bank. The spoilers which I will not reveal are of the sort that used to happen in slasher movies all the time where the minority characters get murdered first—but here Karyn Kusama seems to be both conscious and unconscious of her narrative choices in this regard. However, I won't say any more, only to say that by the end of the movie (which is very short, not even as long as an episode of *Sherlock*), one of us was applauding and raving about *The Invitation*, and the other of us was tapping his fingernails sharply against a deco Formica coaster from the '40s, wishing that he had had the cojones to insist on watching *Crossroads*, with reliable Britney Spears, for the fifteenth time.

Nelly Sachs, Flight and Metamorphosis: An Illustrated Biography
by Aris Fioretos

★★★★★
Life as a Series of Scares

August 25, 2016

Today I returned to a book I've been too disturbed to read for very long at a time, the life of Nelly Sachs, the Jewish poet who fled Hitler's Germany in 1940 for a life of mental illness, poverty, and high drama in Sweden. She and her mother literally got out one week before they were due to be hauled off to a concentration camp. The book, *Flight and Metamorphosis: An Illustrated Bibliography*, is by Aris Fioretos and was translated by Tomas Tranæus. I don't exactly know who did what, but *F&M* is somewhat of a mess on a sentence-by-sentence level: it might take you, as it has taken me, several attempts to understand the English of any one paragraph, but it's fascinating nonetheless.

The basics of Sachs's story are terrifying and banal in a familiar, twentieth-century way. She was a nomad, she was half-mad (when she heard German speech she grew afraid, even though it was her own language). Paul Celan was her friend and the two bonded out of a mutual paranoia, but it was she who won the Nobel Prize (1966), another of those writers that surprisingly one has never heard of, so one feels that the Nobel people are charlatans—and years later one realizes that one wasn't savvy as one had thought. I kept thinking, "1966—the year of 'Eleanor Rigby,'" and she was sort of the Eleanor Rigby of poetry.

The Diary of a Teenage Girl (**2015**)
dir. Marielle Heller

★★★★★
The Wrong Cat

August 25, 2016

Bel Powley has pillow lips and enormous eyes, wide and nicely spaced; her eyes do her acting for her the way that, back in Hollywood's Golden Age, Bette Davis's eyes worked for her: slightly protruding, always alert, they register the slightest emotion like a thunderbolt has hit the screen, the nervous system jumping into a system of visual shows and tells that can get fatiguing after a while—at least people got tired of Bette Davis, and refused her Oscars for *All about Eve* and *The Night of the Iguana*, but Bel Powley doesn't have to worry about middle age yet, she has it all over Kristen Wiig, who plays her mother in *Diary of a Teenage Girl*, the new feature based on Phoebe Gloeckner's renowned 2002 graphic novel and laid, like *Tales of the City*, in the San Francisco of the bicentennial years: fern bars, promiscuous sex, and young people living by their wits while confronting the slightly sinister charms of their more seasoned love partners.

Powley plays Minnie, a schoolgirl attending what looks like the Harvey Milk Photo Center on Scott Street, but must be a private prep school like the one Alysia Abbott attends in *Fairyland*, her own memoir of growing up fast as the daughter of a flighty, drug-addled parent. Wiig is perfectly fine playing the mother, but the screenplay gives her only one scene (sort of like the Bechdel test) in which she's not interacting either with Minnie or with Monroe, her adorable boyfriend (Alexander Skarsgård). Well, he's sort of adorable, but the movie opens with Minnie, who looks like she's fifteen or so—a Bette Davis sort of fifteen—announcing that she's just had sex for the first time, with her mom's boyfriend. I actually think they fudge Minnie's age a little bit in the movie, while they make Monroe more sympathetic than he is in the book, and the drug and sex scenes, while hypnotic and well handled, are nowhere near as existential as in Gloeckner's original. There's a Hitchcock-type appearance by Gloeckner who appears seated at a fern bar, shocked by what she overhears from Wiig, Powley, and Skarsgård having one of their showdown scenes, but she might almost be registering, "What happened to my monsters?"

I was enchanted by the way the movie made San Francisco look as if forty years of development had been shaved off like a bad perm. I spent the summer in San Francisco in 1976, the summer Elvis died, I was here, and the filmmakers have it almost exactly the way I remember. I didn't like the cat, Domino, much. But Domino, like Kristen Wiig, gets sort of shortchanged in the movie. He has one big scene within the first minutes of the picture, when Minnie asks him, "Do I look different today now that I've had sex than I did yesterday?" and he makes a revolted face—the only piece of CGI in the movie that doesn't succeed. And then you never see him again. Most of the time cats in movies just get bigger and better feels every time they appear. The movie is a triumph for the actors and director, it hurts but not too much, and it looks fantastic, but that darn cat must belong to someone on the set who has an overinflated opinion of his beauty and talent. It's like Darryl F. Zanuck trying to persuade the public that Irina Demick or Genevieve Gilles is a great actress. Just doesn't fly.

Games (1967)
dir. Curtis Harrington

★★★★★
Scared of Signoret

August 25, 2016

When I was an American boy growing up in France, the actress Simone Signoret, still in her forties, popped up continually on French TV, while the feature pages of *Paris Match* were always writing up tragedies suffered by the talented, Oscar-winning star. We children were deathly afraid of her. We would scream when we saw her visage, with a sick pleasure, for just as Catherine Deneuve was the face of Marianne in France, Signoret represented a scary-monster type of evil. Our nanny encouraged our fear by telling us matter-of-factly that if we did not behave, Simone Signoret was going to come to our rooms at night and eat us. One look at that smeary, sad, voracious face would make a wise man believe she had teeth, and in *Games* (1967) she uses them in what is perhaps her best Hollywood part. Director Curtis Harrington had originally written the part of Lisa Schindler for Marlene Dietrich, but then producers told him Dietrich was box office poison at Universal, nix on Dietrich. What a shame, but at least now we have the spectacle of Simone Signoret giving a long, detailed, extended Marlene Dietrich impression. And much else besides! I look at the movie now, years removed from my TV terror at Signoret in *Games*, and I see how beautifully Harrington shows us a glossy, moody Upper East Side New York—constructed solely from standing sets on the Universal lot—in a time of changing morals and an "exploding plastic inevitable." Partygoers snicker at the op and pop art glaring at them from the old brownstone interiors. "Paul picks it out," says one dryly, "then Jenny pays for it."

They're bored and rich and kinky. How kinky? She peels off his fake mustache after he kisses her, and applies it herself, returning his kiss and making him feel the way a woman feels—shades of Rusty and Myra in *Myra Breckinridge*, more subdued than the rape of Rusty, true, but anticipating something of its gender-bending swagger. The interior decor makes me swoon: its hasty but full-hearted embrace (pastiche?) of Lichtenstein, George Segal, Bridget Riley, Paul Thek, Stella and Warhol, Yves Klein, this hurriedly copied décor (almost as if they sent Elaine Sturtevant into Leo Castelli for an hour, then twitched her out and had her copy everything she saw all over the walls of a brownstone), overlaid with primitive brass masks and panniers, and vintage pinball machines à la Jack Spicer, dates this picture precisely in 1967, though period music cues are strangely absent. (Maybe Curtis Harrington didn't care that much about music, although one knows from his later work he loved child stars tap dancing.) But in *Games* the nonrock soundtrack makes it all the easier to take in one fabulous wig after another on Katharine Ross's lovely head and to marvel at how tiny James Caan's eyes are. How cute he is, like a small doll. Next to him the hunky grocery boy played by Don Stroud comes off as a top—looks like Fred Halsted, in fact, with his sulky gaze, enormous lips, big nipples like shell casings. One strange thing about *Games* is that usually when movies are laid in Manhattan, scriptwriters take pains to avoid giving exact addresses (*Rosemary's Baby*, for example, is set at the fictional "Bramford Apartments," though it sure looks like the actual Dakota!), but Paul and Jenny Montgomery live at 11 East Sixty-Fourth Street, and maybe some of you do too, it's a real address right off the park, cozy between Fifth and Madison. You can look it up on Google Maps or Google Earth, and wonder! To sum it up, *Games* is like *Wait until Dark* with Audrey Hepburn blind, except Katharine Ross isn't blind, or if *Who's Afraid of Virginia Woolf* were played with a pair of antique dueling pistols. It's about the silly, kinky, addictive love games that Foucault told us were the first new sex acts invented in over 2,500 years. With Ross,

Caan and Signoret, totally disguised in wax-doll masks, prepare an elaborate human sacrifice to shock the family attorney, it's like some sort of grim but chic sitcom set in Thelema Abbey.

In My Room
by Guillaume Dustan

★★★★★
As Kylie Said, "Get Me into the Shade!"

September 19, 2016

A young writer, Parker Bruce, recommended *Dans ma chambre* to me as an example of a short, sexy novel that doesn't run scared of the sexual and the medical in contemporary French gay relationships. This is the first book of the late French author to be published in English. Or was he French? At the back of the book it says that "Guillaume Dustan was the pseudonym for an Australian judge." It's hard to work that one out, but all I could think of was if he was a judge for real, I wouldn't want to have him adjudicating any case I had a stake in, and no more did he seem Australian at all. Nobody in the book ever mentions anything to him about "You have a great French accent for an Australian, Guillaume," or "What part of Australia do you hail from?" Nor do any of the hundreds of men who meet Guillaume in the sex clubs seem to belong to any Aussie-chaser fetish, so that's unusual, for everyone else is shrewdly assessed to disclose that they are top or bottom, S/M classic or fetish, into pain or pleasure, or just plain versatile.

In fact in France the men of *In My Room* are all bewilderingly versatile. They'll play the stud one night and present pert posteriors the next. They seem liberal, undecided, agreeable to trying something new. One will call the other up from work and say, "When I get home from the office, will you penetrate me?" With the right sort of drugs they can stay up all night even after trying a legal case, or working for a society couturier. We learn that one fashion designer, a Karl Lagerfeld type, keeps a stable of hot boys all between the ages of eighteen and twenty-two, none of whom work except at the gym, but all of them given a "salary." They are "sponsored," Dustan explains, though he fails to tell us what happens when they turn twenty-three. "Are they murdered?" one wonders. They must all know too much and their precarity makes them expendable, for there will always be new studs being hatched right now in the provinces, the outer arrondissements. In short, lean chapters we learn much about the nightlife of gay Paris, and particularly what happens when men taken each other home and open up their wardrobe doors, revealing their range of sex toys and lubricants.

The larger question is, How evil is he? Edmund White's blurb introduces this question, which I had never thought of till I looked at the back cover where the blurb appears. Is Guillaume evil because of his addiction to sex? Because he will bareback when he can? Because he cares so little about his partners once he's done with them? He reminds me of the Duchesse de Guermantes, I think it was, in Proust's novel, a woman caught up so much in the world's vanities that when a poor relation comes to call, begging for financial help, she cannot even listen to the supplicant's appeal, she wants so bad to get to the party where she can show off her new red shoes. Thus Guillaume is always anxious to hit the new bar and find someone hotter he and his boyfriend can take home with them. So he's careless maybe, but evil? White introduces a theological complication that the novel, scary as it is, cannot entertain, but I don't know—it's stimulating. The late Rex Ray, the American artist, created a lovely M. C. Escher–inspired design of interlocking butt plugs in pastel colors like those little French candies you gobble between rounds of pétanque. I give the book an extra star if you can find it in this edition.

Intersecting Film, Music, and Queerness
by Jack Curtis Dubowsky

★★★★★
Under the Midnight Sun

September 24, 2016

Jack Curtis Dubowsky reminds us that even in the days of silent cinema, moviegoing was not a silent experience. He might well add, in the name of intersectionality, that even when the movies were being censored for gay reference, there has never been a straight cinema. My, can this fellow write. He's convincing at every intersection in his argument, and it's a doozy, centering on texts in which film and music interact, texts which to establish another constraint, must suggest a queer subtext.

Dubowsky can always back up his opinions with savvy research, and a knack for the perfect quote. He goes back to the contemporary notes of film editor Helen van Dongen, who worked with director Robert Flaherty on his famous documentary *Louisiana Story* (1948). Van Dongen noted the director's strange attraction to his twelve-year-old male star. "Though he has a beautiful face, should not be reason to have all sequences same." Flaherty is a funny case, isn't he? Supposedly straight, a dedicated husband and father, he stuffed his documentaries with good-looking young guys. And when he had Virgil Thomson doing the music for *Louisiana Story*, and applying his own pointedly romantic music for a Bayou boy searching for a lost raccoon, he won the Pulitzer Prize (the only time a film score has been awarded the prestigious music award), but this is a move that perhaps crystallizes "straight" Flaherty as perhaps the gayest of American filmmakers.

There are amusing typos ("hoards of gay men" on page 101, rather than "hordes"), but it seems as though scholarly books suffer most from typos nowadays, having no budget to use the copyeditors they once employed on staff. That said, the book is certainly worth the hundred dollars it may cost you to get your paws on it. As Susan Stryker hints in her blurb, it is an expansive and multitudinous book with valuable, if dense, theory, broken up by gossip and scandal of all sorts, like a Derrida under the influence of Kenneth Anger. (This is my own radical paraphrase of Stryker, of course.)

The "hoards of gay men" typo comes toward the peroration of Dubowsky's set piece, on the "failure" of the much-beloved *Brokeback Mountain* (2005). This is perhaps Dubowsky's most bristly argument, but it persuaded me, and partly because of his musical analysis of the themes composed by the Brazilian composer Gustavo Santaolalla, and the somehow retro feel of what we think of as the "love theme" from the movie, which has lyrics too and they call it "The Wings." I remember in 2005 going to a dance club here in San Francisco and hearing a seventeen-minute disco version of this plaintive, homo-pessimist tune. "The music in *Brokeback Mountain*," argues Dubowsky, "reveals a conservative perspective that allows the male couple little joy, happiness, or fulfillment in their sexuality, relationship, or life." The men I saw at the Midnight Sun were dancing riotously but each had tears bright in his eyes, a little bit of crystal flash.

Dear Yeats, Dear Pound, Dear Ford: Jeanne Robert Foster and Her Circle of Friends
by Richard Londraville and Janis Londraville

★★★★★
The Female Zelig ... the Real Zelig ... Jeanne Foster

September 28, 2016

Dear Yeats, Dear Pound, Dear Ford: Jeanne Robert Foster and Her Circle of Friends (2001) is an older book by the authors of the fabulous Paul Swan life, *The Most Beautiful Man in the World*. The Swan book has become such a favorite of mine that I wondered, like a good reader, if there were other books by its authors, and although I had never heard of Jeanne Robert Foster, I ordered the book sent to me post haste, so greedy was I for the kind of intimate, imaginative, and authentic bio experience the Londravilles have perfected. The book came instantly and it has kept me enthralled ever since.

It is not easy to sum up the sort of woman Jeanne Robert Foster was—unlike Paul Swan, who had "The Most Beautiful Man in the World" on his CV, she had no publicity tagline and, outside of her intimates, most of whom she outlived, she left little profile. Richard Londraville tells the story of coming across her name while researching the plays of William Butler Yeats in 1965, and then realizing she was his neighbor, in the Adirondacks of all places, and that indeed she worked for the Schenectady Municipal Housing Authority—not exactly a poetic sort of place by any means. Could she possibly be the same woman who had known not only William Butler Yeats, but his father too, Jack the painter? And John Quinn, the millionaire patron of Joyce, the man who bought the Ulysses MS? Yes, indeed she was, and she made herself known to Professor Londraville little by little.

It is always amazing to find an artist in one's backyard. As an American boy growing up in France, I remember my parents' consternation to discover that the painter Marc Chagall was our neighbor over the hedge—as the French say, our "voisin sur la haie." Richard Londraville describes her as turning up on the fringes of, or sometimes in the center of, so many artistic and modernist circles she reminded him of "Zelig in Woody Allen's film, a mysterious figure smiling and at ease with the great men and women of the early twentieth century." Together the Londravilles sketch a portrait of mountain life in the 1880s and 1890s that makes it clear that even total obscurity and clouded social relations could not keep an ambitious, beautiful, and friendly young woman down. The family was so poor she never had a Christmas tree as a child, and only one rag doll called Peggy to play with. No wonder she retreated, like many gifted children, into her imagination and dreams of France ... I did, and I wasn't cooped up by blizzards all winter long. She was doomed to live out life as a hired girl, but instead by luck and pluck turned herself into a schoolteacher.

Married to an old man, Jeanne Foster found this a mixed blessing. Marriage freed her up to travel to places denied to a spinster, but she wound up childless. Even her great affair with John Quinn turned out to be an adultery performed too late, in that Quinn also was too old to cut the mustard, or so she later claimed, though her contemporaries assumed they were lovers. At eighteen, she married a man older than her father to protect herself, she claimed later, from "real life." Isn't that haunting? He was so old and sickly that he gave up working and the Fosters started going to New York for pleasure trips, and during one such trip Jeanne Foster became the "Harrison Fisher girl," the subject of many fashion illustrations by the influential American photographer Harrison Fisher. And after that, Jeanne began all of her numerous careers in one fell swoop, and became the intimate friend of many writers, playwrights, novelists, and poets—three of them appear in the title of the book. I thought maybe it was going to be Henry Ford at first—the "Dear Ford" of the title—and Foster got around so much and lived so long that my wife joked that it was probably Harrison Ford of *Star Wars* fame, but no, it was Ford Madox Ford.

Foster's intimate friendships with the other women on the scene are also wonderfully parsed. A deep sadness underlies this book, but it was a full and unexpected life in so many ways, of a woman who, though perhaps not a pathbreaking figure of genius like Joyce or Jan

Masaryk, had a genius of her own, didn't she, for friendship and for "go with," as we called it in France, in the long-ago days of Saint-Paul-de-Vence in the Côte d'Azur. As I approach middle age myself, I think longingly of finding work in some municipal housing authority and then, late in life, letting some professors discover that I was, in fact, the Kevin Killian.

Amnesia: Somebody's Memoir
by Eileen R. Tabios

★★★★★
A Calculus of Experience

January 17, 2017

Eileen Tabios has been a grand force in US poetry for twenty-five years or more, and it's difficult to think of our own time without acknowledging what a large psychic space she has made for us. The sheer volume of her writing is impressive, like the rivers of Tigris and Euphrates; among postwar Americans, maybe only Leslie Scalapino, Steve Jonas, Alice Notley, and Lew Ellingham have written so much with such assurance and endless, difficult-made-easy experimentation.

There are many veins to Tabios's work, but one of the most fruitful has been the list poem, and of those, we have grown especially fond of the sort of poem she collects here in *Amnesia*—a reversal of the famous "I remember" form of Joe Brainard. In this form the forgetful poet tells us, line by line, of all the things she has forgotten. And not just "I forgot where I left my car keys," but forgettings which, by the very nature of her recalling them, prove that they're as much recovery work as expressions of loss. They're dynamic for that reason, and each page crackles with alchemical energy— somewhere John Dee is opening a gold compact and the makeup mirror inside is staring at him to scry to him of legends present and old.

The "forgets" are often tender as well as candid, and it would take a hard heart not to be moved by Tabios's vision of life as a pageant of feeling and vision, unrolling before us on crystalline rods oiled perfectly with WD-40. Has anything happened to anyone anywhere that this book does not prophesy forgetting? I doubt it.

"I forgot the young hugging the ground, their damp faces eagerly turning here, eagerly turning there, searching their surroundings for treasures invisible but I also believed existed when I still shared their innocence." The form is capable of infinite variety in Tabios's hands, so that one never gets bored. One of the poems is like a babaylan version of David Markson's *Wittgenstein's Mistress*, or Steve Abbott's *Lives of the Poets*—a poem in which all the dumb trivia one associates with the great masters of modernist art and poetry unlodge from their hiding places and escape the steel traps of memory. In the Poetry Foundation blog for today, New York poet Stacy Szymaszek quotes the painter Agnes Martin as saying "I can look into my mind and see it empty." What an extraordinary thing, like opening a hatbox and finding no hat there but, on the other hand, such a bliss of nothing.

Another poem is notably shorter, in both line and weight, almost an erasure of a poem. "I forgot magenta," "I forgot ivory," "I forgot molasses / I forgot bonhomie." But it's not only abbreviation, for sometimes a line like "I forgot persimmons" will be followed by an associative, expansive (but also narrowing in the sense of specifying) line like "I forgot the pulse pulsing among persimmons."

That's what *Amnesia* is like—a calculus of experience, as well as a continuously staged battle and retreat. For those trying to emulate such knowledge, Eileen Tabios gives us an instructive epilogue, "Babaylan Poetics & the MDR Poetry Generator," which will give much pleasure all year round, from January through December.

Minimalist Wallet for Men – RFID-Blocking Credit Card Holder (3K Carbon Fiber, 3.6 × 2.25 in.)
by Fidelo

★★★★★
State Surveillance Overcome—for Now

April 8, 2017

When I bought this little carbon wallet I didn't realize that what I wanted was more simplicity in my life. I looked around my apartment in the South of Market section of San Francisco—on a spring morning with a hint of freesia in the air—and what I saw was a mess, the mess of lived struggle against the capitalist machine choking our lives. I have barricaded myself in, I realized, keeping my head close to the ground. Well, close to the ground as you can get in a third-floor walk-up.

When we moved in, it was after the big earthquake of 1989, and tenants had left this building in droves because of the rocking and rolling the building underwent during the revenge of Loma Prieta—and if you weren't on the somewhat more stable ground floor, you moved your kit and caboodle back to Kansas or wherever you had come from. But rents were cheap then. Now we pile up our books and pictures as though they could keep us alive, though it's fairly obvious they can't.

That's why the minimalist slim-front carbon fiber wallet is the one for me now. You can't put a roll of bills in it, but I don't have much of a roll anyhow. This is the sort of wallet that I have considered tucking underneath my skin like a Scarlett Johansson sci-fi thriller. It's not all fantasy! After the earthquake when our cat Stanley ran away, we were urged to embed a chip under his skin so we could always keep track of him. He did come back, but we never did that implant and maybe if we had he would not have died the crummy death he did.

But the best part is that since acquiring this wallet, I have not been troubled by any state agency or criminal organization (and they are basically two ways of saying the same thing) employing drone technology to read my credit card numbers through the skin of previous wallets and gaining access to all of my capital and to my info as a person, which is more valuable today, apparently, than my own body. Something about the carbon fibers is preventing surveillance cameras from gaining access to my digits. We live in a comic book world now and I live a little easier knowing that one bit of it has been deferred at least for a few weeks, until *they* come up with a way to see through carbon!

I Loved Her in the Movies: Memories of Hollywood's Legendary Actresses
by Robert J. Wagner (with Scott Eyman)

★★★★☆

The Carl Andre of American Pop Cinema

April 29, 2017

Robert Wagner strikes me as a nice guy, though I know there are many who suspect the worst of the man and to tell you the truth, the events that took place that night on the *Splendor* have cast a long shadow over the past thirty years, not only for me but for every Natalie Wood fan. But I came to this book hoping to start a new page clean.

He tells us at the beginning that the book will be free of negativity, but has to eat his words over and over again, especially when thoughts of Betty Hutton cross his mind. Or Raquel Welch, of whom he says that the eight weeks they spent together shooting *The Biggest Bundle of Them All* chafed more than "an eight-week-long proctology exam."

It's hard to believe he's still up and at 'em having been around so long. He worked for Carmel Myers, for goodness' sake. OK, he's eighty-eight now and still active thanks to the ministrations of the beloved Jill St. John. When he appeared on TV to roast Robert Osborne on a *This Is Your Life* segment, he looked fit as a forty-year-old man (maybe because Osborne was sinking in front of our eyes, poor guy).

Wagner still has plenty of insight into Natalie as a woman and an artist, as Carl Andre probably has plenty of insight into Ana Mendieta. Wagner tells us that she won the role of Deanie in Elia Kazan's *Splendor in the Grass* due to a strange Wood quirk. Jane Fonda had the inside edge, but Kazan chose her over Jane Fonda because "Natalie admitted to him that she was ambitious, and Fonda wouldn't. Kazan wanted an actress who wasn't afraid to be great. Natalie wanted to be great, so she was."

When Natalie was alive, she had Wagner wanting to be great too, though they made rather a botch out of playing Brick and Maggie in that awful version of *Cat on a Hot Tin Roof.* Now he is playing lackluster comedy parts, like the poor man's Leslie Nielsen.

Wagner's good at both inductive and deductive reasoning. For example, he followed his friend Ida Lupino through her acting career and her pioneering work as the 1950s' premiere female director. When she made the transition into TV roles, she was able to get good gigs directing "tough" shows like *The Fugitive* and *Have Gun – Will Travel*, and he says this was lucky for her because the few women who had their own shows like Donna Reed and Loretta Young wouldn't hire Lupino to direct them. It's all "ironic," Wagner claims, but he makes connections between this behavior and the male-dominated Hollywood world in which every woman had to fight for herself. Even the greatest female star had at most a ten-year run of box office gold—then she was yesterday's dog's dinner. Who else would know the tawdry details of the feud that split apart Hollywood's oddest friendship, that of Barbara Hutton and Rosalind Russell? Only R. J. Wagner, who was there when it all happened.

He knows who had the greatest jewelry collection in Hollywood. No, not Liz Taylor, but a three-way tie between Merle Oberon, Paulette Goddard, and ice-skating goddess Sonja Henie. Why them? Because they cared about jewels, seeing them as objective tokens of the love men gave them. "Jewelry *mattered* to them—it was a way of keeping score." Rosalind Russell's obnoxious husband was called behind his back "the Lizard of Roz." Why? Wagner asks. "How to put this delicately?" he muses. "Because he was an arrogant a$$h0le." Amazon won't even let me print the things R. J. gets away with, because he's so cute that even Barbara Stanwyck wanted him, when she was forty-four and he was nineteen—and she got him.

The Wolves That Live in Skin and Space: A Novel
by Christopher Zeischegg

★★★★★
"With a Taste of a Poison Paradise"

August 21, 2017

The Wolves That Live in Skin and Space is an impressive novel by LA-based artist Christopher Zeischegg. His name isn't on the cover, and that should have alerted me, maybe, to the decentering aims and methods of his book, which straddles the line between novel and memoir in troubling ways. I was about to say that this book is set in the porn world, but mostly it is set in the run-down, crummy underworld of poor white people in Los Angeles in the present day. It's a proletarian novel like those of John Fante and Chester Himes, and yes, there's a porn storyline which has removed some of the rainbows and unicorns off my adolescent fascination with porn as a thing.

It certainly seems to be the most difficult and painful career in the world, to hear Zeischegg tell it. His narrator starts out feeling increasingly alienated from a world which used to treat him well, but neoliberal economic policies have created a situation in which oligarchs eat up the smaller studios so that everyone is working for the same Man, and the product suffers correspondingly. It's claustrophobic on the set, and not only because there are three or four techs running your every move. Readers will get the feeling that only damaged people would work in porn, and that the damaged seek each other out to have often thrilling sex, but it is in no way therapeutic or liberatory. Chris (known on-screen as Danny Wylde) identifies as straight, or lets the readers suppose he is, but he also keeps up an active webcam practice to supplement his faltering income from his screen work, and it is the webcam world, with its promise of uniting patrons with their idols in "private shows," that proves the fatal door.

A terrible escorting gig goes even wronger when Chris meets a demented Ernest Brown, whose therapist wife no longer satisfies him, whose son Joseph has become the object of his erotic desires. When Ernest asks Chris to perform sex on the teenage son, we begin to think, "Well is that really fair, the boy is in a coma after all," but as we understand, Chris's sense of right and wrong, much less his sense of propriety, has been damaged by both his porn-star popularity and its rapid unraveling. So he does it and by doing so opens another can of worms, but I dare not divulge anything else beyond general vague remarks about the book's second half. In this section Chris falls for Joseph, the young son of crazy Ernest Brown, and the two begin an unlikely romance. Zeischegg is terrific writing about obsession, and he is also persuasive at showing us Chris's attraction to the perfections of Joseph's hungry, pliable frame and face. *The Wolves* takes up a storyline something like an adult-film-industry *Star Is Born*—

always a captivating plot in which one party rises while the other falls, as potent today as when E. M. Forster outlined the *Thaïs/*"hourglass" plot in his 1927 Cambridge lectures, published as *Aspects of the Novel.* As a novelist, I myself envy Zeischegg for his considerable skill. I'd like to get him to work on a project with me, but I doubt if, after the cathartic final scenes of his book, he will ever want anything to do with sex again. A stunning achievement.

Fortuny: His Life and Work
by Guillermo de Osma

★★★★★
A Brilliant Spanish Eye

September 30, 2017

What to say about the genius of Fortuny? From the perspective of 2017, some of his soundest ideas seem dated and gimcrackery, while others retain the dazzle that so impressed the soulful moderns of a hundred years ago. Yet even his silliest creations illuminate for us something about the age of modernism that the study of other artists obscures, and that might be his interest in science. Guillermo de Osma has "owned" Fortuny for forty years or more, and his first book on the topic was published in 1980. I'm sure many Fortuny fans still treasure their original Osma biography, which added Fortuny's first name to the title—nowadays, I suppose he's one who doesn't need a first name anymore—there is only one designer, and we call him Fortuny.

As an American boy growing up in France, my mother used to take me to visit an elderly lady in a neighboring arrondissement, one who had fallen on hard times like the "bachelors" of Henry de Montherlant's novel. And like those bachelors, this lady still treasured a few outfits from days way in the past, and whenever *ma mère* and I would visit, there she would be, resplendent in a Fortuny Delphos gown. "Oh Marie-Louise," Mom used to say, "who did you get to do all those pleats?" The senior lady would smile and wave her hand as if to allude to a host of servants now dismissed, who had done such ironing. That was one of Fortuny's key inventions, of course, a system of treating silk so that permanent pleats could be embedded in it—unlike his contemporary Coco Chanel, who disdained science and believed that women should be employed to iron such garments, all the time. The gown itself was a rich copper color, weighted down with an array of seed pearls that kept the garment's shape as it neared the floor. This old lady, nearing eighty I suppose at the time, had herself shrunken with age, yet she still looked magnificent, a tigress, like a French Lauren Bacall in a tall copper vase. "Remember her, Kevin," my mother would say, "for she is the spirit of France." Reading the new Osma biography I was surprised to find out how much of his life was spent outside of France. In fact he was of the Catalan people of Spain, and spent much of his life in his studio in Venice (Italy).

Osma prides himself on being the first modern biographer of the great Fortuny, and even if *après* him, *le déluge*, he can always say, and he will always say, he was there ahead of everyone else. He started his research so long ago that you could pick up a Fortuny stage curtain in the thrift stores of Trullo or Corviale, and he could interview people like silent star Lillian Gish, one of the earliest American customers of Fortuny's salon in Venice. Since 1980, there has been a veritable monsoon of Fortuny books, but Osma basically says "I fathered them all" and shrugs in delight. The thing you will remember about the first book in 1980 is how the illustrations were largely in black and white, of no use whatsoever for showing off the work of one with so rarefied a sense of color that Anni Albers herself sought private lessons from him in his old age. But the pictures in the newly updated *Fortuny: His Life and Work* book are almost all in color. A rich, thrilling color! When things were pitiful for Fortuny, for after the stock market crash of 1929 he always had to scramble, his famous face, as distinctive as those of Picasso, Chaplin, Dietrich, could be seen in magazine advertisements for cars, handkerchiefs, champagne, a sad comedown, and meanwhile his couture customers had either killed themselves or moved on to newer and trendier designers. Osma reminds us that things were so bad that in 1936 Fortuny sold his entire collection of Goya drawings to the Metropolitan Museum of Art in New York. Sad, sad, sad! He did not live to see the triumph of the New Look but he would have laughed, for what was it, after all, but a trimming down of many of his ingenious ideas of the 1910s and 1920s. Today, as screen stars like Alicia Vikander and Kristen Stewart continue to proclaim Fortuny as their designer of choice at the Met Gala, you will also see Fortuny lamps imitated in such ersatz shops as Design Within Reach and even IKEA. Oh, how the mighty have fallen! Check out the glorious black-and-white photos of mezzo Gladys Swarthout (1900–1969) in enough Fortuny fabric to fill an opera trunk on pages 284–85.

A Toast in the House of Friends: Poems
by Akilah Oliver

★★★★★
Shattering Grief

March 19, 2018

I felt desolate entering this book, searching for some traces of its author, of the wise, witty, empathetic woman she was in life. Hers is a presence gone too long from American poetry, and perhaps forgotten too soon. My students don't seem to know her name, that's for sure. But only a page or two into the book, and traces of Akilah Oliver already seemed to stir and wake in me both the great tragedies of her life and the great gifts with which she was so amply endowed. Many poets have the knack for creative, memorable chains of words across the page, and many poets can shape those lines to impressive "open field" structures. And many poets, if fewer, have mastered the verse forms of white folk and Black, and a few have created their own language to talk to us in, as God is said to have done when he came whispering to Adam in Eden. And many of us have lived through sorrow and have tried to embrace it while repelling it in apotropaic forms.

But Akilah's achievement is pretty well unparalleled. She had lost her son, and she brings him back through the pages of "Toast," Oluchi McDonald, not only as he was when he died, an adult, far away, and not only as a child, a boy in her arms, a baby, but seemingly through every stage of life. The poems of *A Toast in the House of Friends*, in ninety-eight exquisitely etiolated pages, are like panels in a graphic novel, each presents a pictogram which, flipped through one's fingers, produces not only tears but great shouts of joy and freedom, as she has managed to conquer death, to find the past in the present, and to allow us to drink both of consolation and rage. Ghosts are "wearied world things, / always in return," yet "sumptuous"— "as if all things had origins in delight."

Because his name was McDonald, she parses for us the old folk song of "McDonald's Farm," with its squeal of vowels, *e-i-e-i-o*, some have said a death chant of the days when slaves worked plantations and looked to the animals for their cruel masters, but also a song of profusion that will never end, that will always intrigue the child just discovering how many different sorts of things there are, and always a new one more fabulous than the rest. Akilah Oliver was a singer of songs and a teller of riddles. She dared speak to the dead (one of the final poems extends her keen and wise seeing to the dead white Laramie student, Matthew Shepard) and sees that those who die before us leave us their gifts as well as their bodies, and if we listen hard enough, we are possessed of their brains and souls. "I have been an exiled orphan in the bright world for too long."

Motherhood
by Sheila Heti

★★★★★
Motherhood an Admirable Sequel to Its Toronto-Centric Predecessor

May 9, 2018

Canadian novelist Sheila Heti has a new book, *Motherhood*, from Henry Holt, just in time for Mother's Day. Six years ago Ms. Heti made a huge hit six years ago with another novel, *How Should a Person Be?*, which came out in 2012 to rapturous praise. The American conceptualist Kenny Goldsmith called it the "most candid fictionalized memoir ever written," while the London journal *Prospect* called it "last year's most polarizing and widely discussed novel in the United States." These are large, reckless statements, of course, designed to make people paranoid or to feel ignorant, or to remember 2012 as a year in which *How Should a Person Be?* polarized nobody in America—at least, all the people I know who read it loved it, took it to their hearts, the way they did the HBO series *Girls*, which also came out in the spring of 2012.

Charts comparing *How Should a Person Be?* to Lena Dunham's *Girls* are common as the lists contrasting the assassination of JFK to the assassination of Lincoln here in the States, but what was wonderful about Heti's novel was its actualized sense of Toronto itself as a North American city. This was a phenomenon with few precedents, for such is the strength of the so-called nylon curtain that separates Canada from the US that the great novelists who have penetrated through to US audiences have been famously international, or universal, rather than Canadian—Margaret Atwood, Leonard Cohen, Michael Ondaatje, so that the ordinary life of one living from hand to mouth as an aspiring artist in the actual city of Toronto has never really been seen nor felt here in America, whereas the conceit of *Girls'* four main characters carrying on in Brooklyn felt old as soon as it was made. I loved in *How Should a Person Be?* when Sheila walks out on a street she calls the "longest street in the world" and starts to cry—anyone who's been to Toronto might identify it as Yonge Street just from that brief phrase, but it's nailed down completely as Sheila passes by the crummy jewelry shops and sad coffee bars that fill block after block.

How Should a Person Be? is filled with angst and grand delusions and the hell of being a young artist in a world with nothing much to offer someone who can't make up her mind about how to live. Sheila works as a hairdresser in a rackety and personality-driven salon, though we don't see her at work much, it's more of a stage set where flamboyant stylists reign and rage. She is one who has lived her whole life through men, and enters the novel wondering what she has missed by never before having had a woman for a friend. She meets Margaux, a talented and charismatic painter, and is drawn into her world of feeling and thinking deeply, a bohemia with a goal at the end of the rainbow. Refreshingly enough, the principal relationship is with Margaux, and it passes the Bechdel test, though she also falls passionately in love with Israel, the long, lean, tousle-haired sex god who makes everything sexy, rather like Adam Driver did for Lena Dunham in *Girls*. In her books we see Toronto as one of the world's great art capitals, and Sheila must learn that living in such a city doesn't make it easier for any individual artist. Ha, that's a lesson we could never learn in a city like San Francisco.

Instead of copied-down conversations, Heti's new novel leans heavily on the device of its heroine asking some coins for the answers to her questions. She just has to phrase the question (usually about herself) in a way that will yield a yes-or-no answer, then roll the coins, and the coins will read yes or no. Sort of like a Ouija board, but with the money, the currency factor, put way up front. Sheila has a nice boyfriend called Miles who's been married before, had a son by mistake. And her main dilemma through the book is whether or not it would be moral for her to have a baby. She is always conscious of a heritage of mothers and grandmothers and a curse that was placed on the women of the family. Both novels depend on a lot of knowledge of Jewish mythology and history and culture, so I fell behind in some of its pages. *Motherhood* is a more somber book than the earlier book, in which Sheila was then always crying about Margaux or whatever, but she also had fun times like a week spent partying at Art Basel Miami Beach. Here Sheila, now a grown woman nearing forty, traipses on a book tour from one European city to another, gathering testimony from women about what motherhood has changed them into. It is hypnotic, glittering, hypnagogic, and as finely pointed as those pins and needles the Jewish mystics once carved the name of God onto.

Much of the public's fascination with Sheila Heti has revolved around the question of how much of this writing is fictional, and how much is her life story. Critics invented the word "autofiction" to simplify the delicious dilemma of not knowing, of being unable to distinguish true from embellished, or the degrees that it takes up and sets down. This weekend I felt I was having a true Sheila Heti moment. I was in LA, reading the end of *Motherhood* everywhere I went (as you will see, once begun you just can't abandon Sheila in her intellectual worrying about what is the right thing to do). Anyhow there I was at this dinner, book in hand, and our guests said, "If you drive us back to our place, we can show you something you will appreciate." And we drove back—a moonless night, still hot at midnight, on quiet roads with a car here and there—to the midcentury house, promising we would only stay for five minutes. Our host pointed to a rough-hewn wooden bench with a backrest nailed into it, a backrest with a big hole carved out of its center like a guitar. It was painted gray and black and off-white, country colors. "There's that painter in Sheila's book? The one who makes a whole show of work and the police confiscate every painting as child pornography?" I did remember the sad, handsome, guiltless artist, faced with state obloquy, who left Toronto for LA and yet everyone remembered him, the way we here in San Francisco might remember, oh, I don't know, Robin Williams, or those two twin sisters who dressed just alike and were always walking together downtown. Mothers used to tell their children "Go up to Robin Williams and ask him to talk like Mork," "Go up to those two old ladies dressed alike in their matching fur jackets and say how pretty they are, for it will bring you good luck." "That chair was made by Eli Langer. My best friend," said our host. He said that Eli went through a phase where he made all his clothes by hand. "We came to your reading," he said to Dodie, "and Eli was in a homemade sailor suit. I wish you had seen the underwear he made for himself. Such luxury, to make one's own underwear." Neither of us remembered him exactly but I almost thought I could, for Sheila Heti has made the life of art and thought in Toronto almost as vivid as life itself.

Gold Dust Woman: The Biography of Stevie Nicks
by Stephen Davis

★★★★☆
A Long Life with Spots of Great Accomplishment
May 24, 2018

After reading the life of Harry Nilsson, I wanted to travel further in the choppy waters of late twentieth-century American pop music and drug addiction, and right next to each other in alphabetical order next to Nilsson I found the life of Stevie Nicks. Despite their propinquity in the phone book of the Betty Ford Clinic, Nicks and Nilsson don't seem to have made many overlaps in real life, which I find rather odd. Between the two of them they burned enough bridges to shore up a tottering empire of rock. Nicks married once, but only for three months, whereas Nilsson married three times and had more children than his idol, Johann Sabastian Bach, so they had different ideas about propagation, but made about the same number of LPs.

Davis, who penned the scabrous story of Led Zep in *Hammer of the Gods* many years ago, covers all the bases, and in a lot of ways his recounting of the Fleetwood Mac story opens it up in a way unusual for previous journalists. We see the close-knit family from which Nicks sprang, and we see why her meeting with Lindsey Buckingham was able to change her life forever. Two crazy kids in love, both festering with talent, and yet somehow they couldn't catch a break, but thanks to Keith Olsen they found themselves in the floundering blues-rock band Fleetwood Mac, which had a curse on it right from the very beginning. And somehow Stevie's ritualistic shamanism gave the tired old band a new shine, putting them onto the cutting edge of soft rock. Davis is sympathetic to Stevie throughout, even at her worst he finds something kind to say about her, but if there's one fault it's an unwavering antipathy toward Lindsey. I think the book would have found more balance if Lindsey wasn't painted as a monster without talent. How many times does Davis describe a Fleetwood Mac show by saying audiences were spellbound when Stevie came on, but when Lindsey took the stage to do one of his own numbers, that's when they visited the beer concession or the urinals? But repetition is built right into the saga of Fleetwood Mac, and it stops being interesting when Stevie turns thirty-two or so.

I did appreciate the verification of something I had always suspected, that it's Stevie providing background vocals to Kenny Loggins's hit track "Whenever I Call You 'Friend.'" Really she sings more of the song than he does—"I know forever we'll be doing it, doing it." It's insane but so catchy.

The through line in *Gold Dust Woman* might well be Stevie's attempt to get her mother royalties from the gift of her song "Silver Springs." Rejected from *Rumours*, "Silver Springs" became the B-side to Lindsey's "Go Your Own Way," but if it had been on *Rumours*, then Stevie's mother would have been a wealthy woman from 1977 on. It wasn't until fifteen years later that "Silver Springs" became a hit and allowed the mother her own financial freedom. Davis sets this up as another of the egregious slights that Lindsey, jealous of his girlfriend's appeal to crowds, dealt her again and again. He's still doing it, we understand. But now she's risen above it. I found it very elegant the way that Stevie could write two songs,

"Gold Dust Woman" and "Silver Springs," contrasting gold and silver like Hugh Grant singing "PoP! Goes My Heart": "You are gold and silver." For that matter, for the Fleetwood Mac comeback album *Tango in the Night*, Lindsey wrote "Big Love" and Christine "Little Lies," and the dynamism of the big-little split haunts that record to this day.

Stevie wasn't a lesbian exactly, but has any man had such beautiful girlfriends as Stevie? Stephen Davis is always referring to her entourage as though it were a floating seraglio, and of course, Stevie was so involved with Robin Anderson that when Robin died so tragically after giving birth, Stevie married her widower (Kim) and started to raise her son with him, but after three months she had a crystal vision and realized she was doing the wrong karmic thing. It's confusing, and part of that is the buzzy drive that brought Robin and Kim to marriage in the first place, since "Kim" could be a man's name or a woman's, and "Robin" too.

The Comics of Hergé: When the Lines Are Not So Clear
ed. Joe Sutliff Sanders

★★★★★
The Baddest Boy

June 8, 2018

I have been reading *Tintin* all my life, well, from the early '60s on, when we moved to Smithtown and I befriended the Galinsky brothers across the street who had at least four or five of the *Tintin* books which I had never heard of. The first one I remember was *The Castafiore Emerald*. Perhaps not everybody's favorite but I thought it peachy. So that's fifty years of reading Hergé and I never understood the critical terms for the appreciation of his work, at least according to editor Joe Sutliff Sanders, who maintains that Hergé is but one of a number of other cartoonists bonded under the sign of the "clear line," or in Dutch the *klare lijn*, defined by Sutliff Sanders as a set of "carefully selected, meticulously researched, and scrupulously copied details drawn in precise, well-defined lines," emphasized by a "lack of shadow." Generations of subsequent cartoonists have followed Hergé's lead here, to the point that another Hergé scholar, Pierre Assouline, has pooh-poohed the very existence of such a "hergémony."

At the same time as praising his hero's triumph in the world of pure art, Sutliff Sanders is more than happy to discuss what he calls the murky sides of his character. Did Hergé collaborate with Fascists during World War II? Did he cheat on his wife, the long-suffering Germaine Kieckens? What about the racism many have found in Tintin's adventures among the Congolese and Tibetan peoples of the world? The once clear lines grow spotty and muddy—is there a way out of our modern-day compulsion to consider the work of art only after a judgment of its maker's sins?

Individual essays in the book are by and large fascinating, both because the material is new to me and also because individual books (or "albums") by Hergé are so familiar to me, yet I see them still through the eyes of the child and now these scholars help me read them anew. I enjoyed Sutlif Sanders's account of Hergé's wartime experience as "making a deal with the devil" in which he dirtied his hands—as a collaborator of sorts—but became progressively better at layout, except for the execrable and mysterious results of turning *Red Rackham's Treasure* from strip to album. Andrei Molotiu reads *The Castafiore Emerald* as Hergé's response to Flaubert's call to modernism as the place where "nothing happens"—his own *Madame Bovary*, in which the subject is "almost invisible." "With it, Hergé brings (albeit belatedly) full-blown modernist formalism into the Tintin canon." Vanessa Meikle Schulman gives a marvelous approach to the sometimes painful-to-read, and unfinished, last *Tintin* album, *Tintin and Alph-Art*, laid in the world of contemporary artistic practice (begun in 1978, *T and A-A* seems familiar with such developments as minimalism, conceptualism, land art, and so much more).

If I had one complaint, it's that there's too much about inferior and subsequent comics and artists, and maybe there could have been a bit more about the series Hergé invented with Jo, Zette, and Jocko in them. Of course, no one is as charismatic as Tintin—in real life or in the studio.

*On the Road and off the Record with Leonard Bernstein: My Years
with the Exasperating Genius*
by Charlie Harmon

★★★★★
Four Years of Hell, and Some Fun Added

August 9, 2018

I like Charlie Harmon. In his memoir of four years employed by the
not so magnificent Amberson Enterprises to assist Leonard Bernstein, he displays an astonishing memory for every fun moment he
shared with Leonard and other gay men during a difficult time (when
AIDS became a thing, and grew and grew until it seemed that all
would die from it), and he also remembers every slight that people
gave him because of his job as "the toilet paper man."

One chapter of this is fun, but at length it grows tedious and one
longs for Bernstein and his complicated crew to get rid of the sad
sack. He always complains of overwork, of feeling tired, of being
underpaid, of having to pay for things that Amberson should have
supplied him. He persuades us that Bernstein was getting away with
murder during the years in question (1982–86, roughly).

Harmon tells us that it was Bernstein's practice to hit on his assis-
tants three months after he hired them. It seems as though the
Maestro was what we would call today a sex addict, but then again,
in the days before AIDS, it had become the practice among a certain
class of man to have as much sex as possible, sometimes with several
people a day, and Bernstein was just doing what others would do had
they the chance. He was known for traveling the world and conducting orchestras and then relaxing with drugs, alcohol, and fine
food, and sooner or later the all-male parties would get naked and
jump into the swimming pool and do laps. This was also a way of
freshening Lenny up because he rarely bathed and smelled like a
Russian wolfhound, sweating continually and planning more social
occasions in which he might shine. He was immensely popular all
his life, perhaps especially at this period when he was striving to
complete his first full-length grand opera, *A Quiet Place*, with an
inexperienced librettist called Stephen Wadsworth, soon to soar to
fame as an opera director and academic at Juilliard. None of this

impresses Charlie Harmon. The only people he really likes are Bernstein's servants, like Ann the cook, who gets fired, and Julia the housekeeper of Bernstein's haunted Dakota apartment, where his late wife appears regularly to his newer friends, so real they think she's a living, glamorous woman. *On the Road and off the Record* is best when Charlie tries to find out more about the enigmatic Felicia who, like Rebecca in Daphne du Maurier's novel of the 1930s, was chic and charismatic and funny and glamorous and no one could live up to her. But he should really write a book about her, because even with all his sleuthing, he doesn't tell us enough about her. Did she mind that Bernstein was cheating on her with marines and midshipmen, or was it just part of her theater training? Did she even know? We never find out. Was there an element of mystery in her death? Possibly.

In the meantime Charlie vividly recalls not only slights and snubs but meeting many of the world's most famous celebrities, including Boy George, at the height of his fame and dressed like a geisha girl, asking Lenny to autograph his menu. Lenny responds very politely, I thought, with a quote from his famous *Candide* song "Glitter and Be Gay," and Charlie wonders (rather snidely, I thought) whether or not Boy George "gets it." Well, what's to get, really?

A Great Unrecorded History: A New Life of E. M. Forster
by Wendy Moffat

★★★★★
The Man Who Wrote "Only Connect!" and the Connections He Made in Underground Gay Life

September 11, 2018

Wendy Moffat taught for thirty years at Dickinson College before publishing her life of English novelist E. M. Forster, and she must often have thought of the coincidence that Forster admired a Cambridge don and friend, philosopher Goldsworthy Lowes Dickinson, whom his intimates called "Goldie," presumably because "Goldsworthy" wasn't a real first name, not in the social circles in which Forster, almost a charity boy, grew up with his widowed mother Lily. In the spring we went to Cambridge to visit the grave of Goldie, and the porter was almost embarrassingly glad to see us, for nowadays the grave people want to see there is that of Wittgenstein, whom Forster thought little of. The graveyard also has the grave of James Frazer, once famous for writing *The Golden Bough* but now as easily dismissed as Goldie, who once in the day, especially after Forster's work on his life, was on his way to becoming a hot topic, but then the craze for Wittgenstein took over the peaceful, vine-and-bracken-covered English landscape, and it was "Goldie who?" Forster himself, not a believer of any sort, except in gay liberation and the secret understanding between liberal men and women, had himself cremated after his death in 1970, having long seen his contemporaries like D. H. Lawrence and Virginia Woolf die much younger and more romantic deaths.

Moffat begins her story in the dramatic days after Forster's death when Christopher Isherwood and John Lehmann lifted the lid in Santa Monica on the multiple manuscripts of Forster's novel *Maurice*, which he wrote after *Howards End* but found himself unable to publish it due to its Whitmanian gay themes. It was his fifth novel, but the world knew nothing of it, except for a tiny handful—well, maybe about thirty people, a cocktail party's worth—of gay men and their female allies, to whom he had entrusted it over the years. T. E. Lawrence refused to read it, but everyone else loved it. As the Wolfenden report came out and the laws against buggery were lifted in England, Forster added a late postscript imagining what would have happened to his beloved characters had they lived under today's more open society (more open for some, that is).

I enjoyed the book all the way through. Just when it looked as though Forster would die a virgin, he went to Egypt and met Cavafy and some sparks flew between them, and a compliant railroad conductor had sex with him and then, well, I'll tell you, in middle age he began to have sex like crazy. I'm sure he wound up having more sex than I, when you count up all his conquests and just the ones we know about! It was the age of cottaging and John Gielgud arrested and public ignominy, but Forster as an older man was the object of much adulation among the young creative set, and his new young friends either offered themselves or introduced him at studio parties to willing, compliant trade. Cops or robbers made no real difference to Forster, and that was refreshing. Auden and Isherwood, Benjamin Britten, J.

R. Ackerley all took him up, and then he went to America where even more hip and worldly artists made him the toast of their dinners and socials, people like Paul Cadmus, Glenway Wescott, George Platt Lynes, Donald Windham, and Sandy Campbell. Moffat perks up every time a new crew of gay supporters shows their hero the sort of good time one thinks of in Paul Cadmus paintings like *The Fleet's In!*, or in *What I Believe*, in which Forster himself, a nude old man, stands tall in a garden filled with windblown acolytes and worshippers. Of course he loved America! England was drab, no cakes anywhere, rationing still on, and snobbery against the police career of Forster's long-term boyfriend, Bob Buckingham.

The camaraderie he found among these young guys did inspire him to write a series of short stories more or less homoerotic all of them, some of them quite frank, which like *Maurice* also were published after his death. Since then Merchant and Ivory filmed all of his books, or just about, so in a way we still live in his world, as distant as it seems today from the moment when the little boy Edward Morgan Forster was sexually interfered with as a child at boarding school, which forever left him in a frenzy of PTSD, fear, and blackmail. It was not altogether a happy life, but Wendy Moffat encourages us to feel that lucky breaks gave Morgan the last laugh, perhaps. Highly recommended.

A Taste of Broadway: Food in Musical Theater
by Jennifer Packard

★★★★★
It Was Like My Brain Died and Went to Heaven
October 27, 2018

Jennifer Packard's book caught my attention in a Venn diagram of new books about vintage Broadway shows and another section of books about food (including cookbooks), and this book teeters on the edge of both. I was surprised and shocked to find out that so many of our classic musicals apparently use food in one or more of seven distinct ways, and often it advances the plot but sometimes is just there to highlight the texture of the musical in question.

She has me persuaded even before she gets to Lionel Bart's *Oliver!* and its paean to "Food, Glorious Food." Packard has done a great job researching the personal food foibles of some great songwriters and librettists—there's a whole chapter about what Oscar Hammerstein II liked to eat and how this showed up, or didn't, in the musicals he did with Richard Rodgers, whereas Lorenz Hart had little interest in food perhaps and you don't hear much about food lyrics in Hart. In Hammerstein the cattle are standing like statues and corn is as high as an elephant's eye, then at the state fair people sing "On Ioway corn I'm fed," then there was a real good clambake, and believe me there's lots and lots about chop suey in the controversial *Flower Drum Song* (1958). Packard doesn't mention The *Sound of Music*, but by now a Packardite, I can cite the "crisp apple strudels" of "My Favorite Things," rhymed cleverly with "schnitzel with noodles," though the nonfood terms "doorbells" and "sleigh bells" separate them.

Packard can come down harshly on those who use good terms in the wrong way, or for syllabic reasons—that's you, Frank Loesser, you who wanted *The Most Happy Fella* to resound with Italian good cheer and pathos in the Napa wine country, but apparently ignored the facts that mozzarella is not a very smelly cheese at all (or if it was, it means that it went bad) and that "Malaga, Malaga red" is not the right kind of wine to mention in the situation in which it finds its foul self. Everywhere Packard provides recipes, too. Discussing an early Irving Berlin–Moss Hart collaboration, *Face the Music*, Packard goes all social history on us to explain what the Horn & Hardart Automat was and how it thrived in the era of mechanical reproduction but closed when I was a teenager, but from somewhere she unveils the formerly secret recipe for the Automat's wonderful pumpkin pie.

It gets tiring after a while, but she always has some amusing things to say about how often women are compared to "tomatoes" et cetera, how all the characters in *Fiddler on the Roof* are in one food industry or the other, how both mother and daughter in *Hairspray* use food as solace for problems of low self-esteem, how *Waitress* makes you hungry for the heroine to find happiness through food allusions, how people the world round love vanilla ice cream, how *Hello, Dolly!* finds its climax in the expensive Harmonia Gardens with its cadre of dancing and singing waiters. (Dolly is on the book's cover, Carol Channing spearing her lower lip with a fork, Horace giving her that glare.) It made me long for a Broadway musical without food in it.

Devotion
by Patti Smith

★★★★★
A dream from the past come to life

November 11, 2018

Patti always seems so on top of things that her new book begins with a startling twist, that one day she's invited to France to speak for a week to writers and wannabe writers, and yet when she picks up her own notebook, she realizes anew that she's written nothing. How ironic, she thinks! A nonwriter traveling a thousand miles to lecture French people into writing.

She seems like such an excellent person, it is no wonder that she's meeting the family of Camus and using his place as an Airbnb hell, I would let her come into my place any old time! Her photograph of the gun with which Verlaine shot Rimbaud twice in the wrist is a classic, and who on earth could get access to that thing, why no one but Patti Smith. (It has since come on the open market at auction, in 2016.) Smith was both appalled by and empathized with Verlaine's decision to wound Rimbaud's wrist, for it was his way of expressing his disapproval of what he considered Rimbaud's excessive masturbation. (As though there were any real way of preventing a sixteen-year-old boy from pleasuring himself!) Patti understands the basis of sexuality as a game of potlatch and denial, and delves deeply into this question in the fairy tale with which she proves "Yes, I am a writer, and if you don't like it, Windham-Campbell Prizes, future generations will uphold me." Since the '60s or '70s she has shown herself to be a great devotional writer, almost a priest, a servant of the bright and divine string with which we are all knotted by the master jeweler above.

I can also recommend *Devotion* as a study, like Henry James's novels, of the differences between American and French society, even today. She has a fascination with the Belle Époque, but also the underclass of the prewar Jean Genet has met with her ultimate regard. The parable of the empty notebook, the one that must be filled, is a Jamesian conceit, but it was also the itch that kept scratching Flaubert who hated blank white paper. I wish that she would put aside for now her tendency to look back at her life and write the full-length novel her fans dream of—her answer to Bob Dylan's fabled *Tarantula*. Until she does, *Devotion* will please her old fans and win her some new ones. In the early '80s, when I moved to San Francisco, I met a noted psychic, a lovely woman called Sylvia who was often on TV. I got the chance to ask her a question during a TV taping, and this was in the period where all Patti's fans were distraught and agonized over the long silence that followed the release of *Wave* and her marriage to Fred "Sonic" Smith. So naturally I asked Sylvia Browne if Patti Smith would ever return to the stage or release another single. Sylvia didn't bat an eyelash, she replied instantly, "Yes, but first she will come out with a novel that will knock your socks off." When *Dream of Life* appeared (was it in 1988?), I chuckled and thought, "This is one time when Sylvia Browne spoke too soon." But for all we know, she did write that novel during that mysterious Michigan period of childbirth and gestation. For all we know, *Devotion* is part of it.

The Crime of Art
by Kota Ezawa

★★★★★
If Wilde Could Trace

November 13, 2018

With that title (*The Artist as Critic* meets *Lord Arthur Savile's Crime?*) sounds like Oscar Wilde wrote it, but this book is the work of the accomplished German-born, Oakland-based artist Kota Ezawa. I've been a fan of his for ages, ever since he was a student here in San Francisco working on his MFA for the Art Institute and volunteering at what was then SF's most interesting exhibition and lecture space, the late New Langton Arts. Then, his thick German accent slowed many down, and I remember years later saying to him, "I hope I wasn't one of those who patronized you," and him replying drily, "You were."

The Crime of Art is exquisitely bound and printed by Bortolazzi-Stei in Verona, Italy, and boasts a factor one rarely sees in California printing, each plate is laid in (by hand, I assume) and glued correctly—that is, none of the plates I examined seemed to deviate from the ninety-degree angle I assume they were looking for. Are they robots or *ragazzi* in Italy, or neither, but exquisitely skilled craftsmen like, say, Ettore Sottsass, taking the time to lower the perfectly printed slip onto its exact position and then holding open the pages to let the glue dry? How many hours would it take to produce the book? Crime fascinates Ezawa, who grew up in a country in which the Far Left action group the Baader-Meinhof Gang inflamed the social sores left over from denazification. Then there was the effect on young Ezawa of Gerhard Richter who, no matter what else he did, began in 1977 to construct remarkable, claustrophobic paintings of captured moments in the Gang's multivaried career of crime and punishment. Jordan Kantor's touching catalog essay describes the two of them, himself and Ezawa, as studio mates in Dogpatch years ago, working in very different valences, but in enough agreement on methods of reproduction and display to continue indefinitely and productively.

Ezawa's first great success, the video work *The Simpson Verdict* (of which we see a few stills here), captured a strangely cartoonized O. J. Simpson at the moment when the jury foreman reads the verdict of not guilty, as lawyers and their staff embrace in joy. It was shocking in its concept and even more in its effect, for as the murder of Nicole Brown threw the always-tender racial tensions of California into sharp relief, so it seemed that big money could produce any verdict its bankers saw reason to pay for. It was brief and flickering, hypnotic as the best TV. Newer projects here include a more elaborate restaging of the still-unsolved theft of thirteen artworks from Boston's Isabella Stewart Gardner Museum. In a utopian touch of the wand, Ezawa recreated all the missing objects in his fluid but clarified hand, and hung them back up on the walls. Vermeer's *The Concert*? Restored. A book is only a compendium of dreams, and I could sit, lie, and die in Kota Ezawa's dreams happy throughout.

In Part: Writings
by Julie Ault, ed. Julie Ault and Nicolas Linnert

★★★★★
Stunning Writing; Frustrating Presentation (Which Some May Really Dig I'm Sure)

December 6, 2018

In Part is my first exposure to a collection of Julie Ault's writing and I have to say, she's terrific, but her essays are so much better than the selection of pages and single paragraphs clipped from essays or reviews or interviews. Next time, do a whole book of your long pieces, Ms. Ault! I know that would be a book to cherish. Don't get me wrong, here in *In Part*, the briefer pieces are OK too, but they seem selected to say "And here's the good part, don't bother reading the context!"

So it seems like a constant stream of congratulation, and this is not helped by the worshipful introduction by critic Lucy Lippard. The introduction does perform the work of telling us who Julie Ault is, why we should love her, why we should revere her particular practice of always searching for the bigger picture.

It's neither writer's fault that the very opening sections of the book take us through the entirety of the AIDS crisis (well, ending in 1997, not that AIDS did really), and that some of the material after that just isn't as vital. Ault's description of her rediscovery of Sister Corita Kent, as outlined in the essay "Archives in Practice," is the best writing in the post-AIDS decades, like Linda Nochlin writing about Florine Stettheimer, without the flowery metaphors Nochlin relied on. Like many of Ault's memories, she makes it clear right away how once she knew little about its subject ("In 1995 I had only a vague awareness of Corita Kent") and then comes the clincher, "But now I'm the world's leading authority." Well, she doesn't say that exactly. Corita found meaning in different forms of graphic expression and so does Ault of course, and so I am sympathetic in a way to the patchwork assemblage of *In Part*. It's not gimmicky per se, it just isn't doing what the author thinks it's doing.

The early parts of the book still have the power to shock. When Larry Rinder asks Group Material to put together a MATRIX show at the Berkeley Art Museum, they all assume that talking to the students will reveal an already-politicized body angry at leaving their own. Their surprise came when, after interviewing dozens of Berkeley students, not one admitted having AIDS or HIV and none of them knew anybody who did. These "people's unawareness is part of the policy," Doug Ashford argues, and that floored me today as much as it did back in 1990, when Maria Porges published her Group Material interview in *Shift* #4. All in all a marvelous book and if it repeats itself from time to time, well, so does Martin Wong, right?

The Zanzibar Shirt Mystery, and Other Stories
by James Holding

★★★★★

Glad These Stories from My Childhood Have Been Reassembled by a Master Editor

December 30, 2018

I came to this book after a refresher in James Holding while reading the wonderful Pachter-Andrews anthology from earlier this year, *The Misadventures of Ellery Queen* (Wildside Press, 2018). As a boy with a gift subscription to *EQMM* from a loving, if strict, uncle, I waited every month for *EQMM* to slide into my mail slot, and you know something, I didn't much care for Holding's version of the Ellery Queen quandary so I skipped them, looking for more exciting stuff. I guess I was a square kid in some ways, and the biggest thrill that came with *EQMM* was when they published Agatha Christie's insane "The Harlequin Tea Set," do any of you remember that?

I always wanted to be a writer but never had any idea of writing a detective story. I rarely could invent a plot, much less go to the elaborate ruses involved in covering one up. Oh well, I went my own way—a way that has now led me to reconsider the stories James Holding told about two heterosexual white guys who collaborate on a successful single identity, "Leroy King," and the vacation they and their lovely wives take around the world on the SS *Valhalla*. From reading between the lines we see that Holding came late to the writing game, making a fortune off the stock market as a broker and taking to world travel in his retirement and probably going to all the out-of-the-way places he sets his stories in on one cruise or another. He started too late in the writing game to establish a fair share of the market, and by the time these Leroy King stories came to him there was little market for his kind of writing in the "slicks" any longer, and the last part of his life found him sans agent or publisher. Sad! At the Boston College archives, it was sad following a similar journey taken by Charlotte Armstrong, and her distress as market after market dried up in front of her eyes. But at least she had begun early enough to reap the bonanza of lucrative magazine work—and television work—and movie rights and so much more.

No one could say that Holding had anything like Armstrong's gift for character, but some of the stories here are splendid puzzles, worked out in arguments between the two writers, King Danforth and Martin Leroy, and then their wives. One of the men is described as lanky and as taller than his sidekick, but despite all my notes I can't remember which one it is. You'd think the tall one would be "King," and maybe that's right. I'm sorry, but I can't visualize the men with anything like the precision I can their wives. I do forget if Carol is married to King or to Martin, but I do know her look, which is a sexy lady with black hair, dark and passionate, while Helen is blond and insouciant with flawless skin. This took me aback because I always associate "Carol" with blondness, perhaps due to too-early exposure to Carol Channing in *Hello, Dolly!*, Carroll Baker as Harlow, and assorted Carols like Lynley, White, Landis, Lombard, and the ill-fated Carol Wayne, who appeared on the Johnny Carson show forty-two times and then died a mysterious death on a cruise to Manzanillo, Mexico—exactly like a story from *The Zanzibar Shirt Mystery*. Blonds all of them, and yet here the blond is not Carol, but Helen, and beg pardon, isn't Helen a sultry brunette name like, well, Helen of Troy? Or Polly Bergen as Helen Morgan? Or Helen Lawson in *Valley of the Dolls*? It's rough being one of the wives in a Holding story: they're—if not exactly independent—at any rate feisty to the point of ball busting, but in every story they get exposed as brainless and every one of their guesses is wrong, like, idiotically wrong. (If Carol is married to King in this book, my mnemonic will be the popular '70s singer-songwriter Carole King, but again, I can't work out from my notes who was married to whom.) Carol and Helen do add an element of femininity to the plots and the boys gossip as much as the girls, but it's the boys who, working together, not only solve a crime in every country they visit, but also have sold (figures vary) between 80 million and 125 million copies of their Leroy King books.

The cases themselves are also rather sketchy. [SPOILERS AHEAD.] Often the boys will declare the case solved without exactly pinning down one criminal, but saying for example that they have successfully narrowed down the shipboard thief who made away with Carol and Helen's jewels to "one of fifty Chinese ship painters swarming over the liner that day," in "The Hong Kong Jewel Mystery." And I love a dying-message story as much as any EQ fan ever but I have to say that the message worked out in "The Italian Tile Mystery" is one of the stupidest I've ever read in a long life of wasted time, and (a) I don't believe the words that the husbands and wives assign to each pictorial tile, and (b) I don't believe that saying them in order would make a poem, and (c) the poem would not tell me that the tile table must be opened to find the dopey solution within. And when you find out what it is, and what the beneficiary does with her treasure, you'll just sigh. [SPOILERS HAVE ENDED.] Holding improves after these lousy stories, I will say that. I wound up enjoying this book very much, it just takes a while to get into this Johnny-one-note approach of something happens / boys declare there must be a mystery plot in it / girls scoff / boys prove themselves right, at least to their own satisfaction. But some of the stories achieve that postmodern pinnacle of perfection of being woven out of nothing at all, and finish with gossamer banks of invisible glory.

Never Mind the Moon: My Time at the Royal Opera House
by Jeremy Isaacs

★★★★☆
The Most Important Bloke of the Royal Opera House, and a Brash, Cultured Thackeray Too

May 23, 2019

So firmly shut is the back door to the twentieth century that it is now difficult to remember a time, mere decades ago, when Jeremy Isaacs ruled it over the Royal Opera House in London. He was not even then a young man but a salt-and-pepper daddy type, with a tough background in the Gorbals, a mountain range in Glasgow from which many wild cries would emerge and some of the best musicianship was available, for cheap, to the sons of the district nurse—she who would spend her days curing smallpox among miners, then she'd make sure her own boys were scrubbed down well before taking them to see and hear the avant-garde music of their day—we're talking about the days right after World War II, proud days for Scots musicianship and for dedicated, tough-talking nurses and doctors who had seen the worst casualties of WWII in foul old, dear old Glasgow, and yet they had come away with a new determination to make sure that British musicians, singers, choreographers, and dancers found the light too.

Peter Pears and Benjamin Britten spent many a late-night romp in Scotland and Aldeburgh, spreading Forsterian gay omertà all over the surrounding countryside, not that they weren't disdained by some, including Isaacs himself, who describes to a frost the glittering pubic hair of the enchanting soprano Maria Ewing (mother of the current-day actress Rebecca Hall) who captivated all men and many ladies by appearing full frontal in the title role of Bizet's *Carmen*—well, in any role really.

Isaacs was no pushover and in fact came late to Covent Garden, first making a name for himself in the high-stakes world of UK television, where he was the chairman of the board. Married for decades to a lovely, tragic woman, he lost her to disease when she was rather young, and many of his stories involved the now lost-to-time Tamara. He married again, to a harsh and beloved taskmistress, who is credited with helping him edit his memoirs by holding him to a severe standard, always enlightened by the rough-and-tumble casual obscenity of the Glaswegian people. You will immediately find out why Isaacs's memoir is called *Never Mind the Moon*, and never will you forget its ribald rejoinder. His favorite British composer of all time? Surprisingly, Purcell.

He was known as a tough business man, and many of his toppers involve him "easing out" signed-up talent whom he found too, too tedious and boring. His removal of the conductor Gennady Rozhdestvensky, whom Isaacs found too lightweight for Massenet, is a classic of the *Sweet Smell of Success* school. He was lazy, according to

Albery, and missed far too many rehearsals, and so found himself kilt pulled up over his head and flat on his sporran in Shame Alley, like some period Guy Ritchie crime drama when he was still happily married to the US pop singer Madonna. "Before you could say Machiavelli, we were able to whistle in another conductor, Mario Bernardi, who actually knew the piece," and he brought in the divine Susan Graham. "Tosh perhaps, but enjoyable tosh."

.

BOTH/AND

I begin this piece on the anniversary of Kevin's death, writing in my spiral-bound notebook with a fountain pen that occasionally lets out a glob of ink due to the cabin pressure. I'm on a plane home after spending a week with my brother in the intensive care unit of the U Chicago Medical Center. My brother almost died. It feels like a cosmic joke that five years ago on this same week—#24 in the Gregorian calendar—I sat in another ICU in San Francisco, holding Kevin's hand and slowly giving up hope—a coincidence too perfect, too corny to make the cut in any movie or novel that has a right to hold up its head. Yet here I am, once again getting all intense. When you touch the boundary to the Other Side, it's hard to return to the realm of the living. Ordinary existence no longer makes sense. What is a writer to do with that? Derek McCormack once told me that after he survived a bout of cancer and its grueling medical interventions, he could no longer write the way he was accustomed to. He had to figure out a new way. Five years after Kevin's death I have no clue what writing means to me. Kevin credited an earlier brush with death—his 2003 heart attack—as being the catalyst for his Amazon-reviews project.

For three days Kevin kept complaining of heartburn and guzzling Pepto-Bismol. When he mentioned pain down his left arm, I urged him to call the Kaiser advice nurse. She told him to come in first thing the next morning. (Telling him to wait was horrible, dangerous advice.) The next day when Kevin arrived at the clinic (via public transportation), his condition was so alarming they immediately put him in an ambulance and drove him across the street to the hospital.

Kevin was hospitalized for a week and a half, going crazy with nicotine and caffeine withdrawal, waiting around for something to happen. The doctors couldn't decide what to do with him—stents or open-heart surgery. Plus, it was Thanksgiving week, and not much happens in hospitals during holidays. Kevin was freaking out because he was under deadline to turn in a catalog essay for a Wattis Institute exhibit on portraiture, but he was too fucked up to write. So I helped finish it, not knowing anything about the work in question, not even having seen images of it. *The portrait emanates anxiety*, wrote he/I, *its aura a menace of malevolent will.* Kevin would tell me what he had intended to say, and I'd type an interpretation of what I heard, adding my own flourishes. *"There is something fatal about a portrait," says Dorian Gray*, wrote he/I. Then I'd read it back to Kevin and he'd refine and I'd type some more. It was an arduous though entertaining process. *To the eye*, wrote he/I, *what difference between life and death?* When we finished, we had to figure out how to get the piece to the Wattis. Wi-Fi was still in its infancy, so I plugged the phone line in Kevin's room into my clamshell iBook—the same model that Reese Witherspoon carries to her college classes in *Legally Blonde*—and managed to dial up the internet. On Thanksgiving Day the nurses gave Kevin a reprieve from his tasteless cardiac diet, so Marcus Ewert and I brought take-out turkey dinners, and the three of us feasted on the white cardboard boxes of yum. We had fun.

When Bruce Boone visited, he pointed out that this period of waiting for the medical powers to decide Kevin's fate was a liminal space between life and death. This was the realm of the seer—and Kevin was in it. Kevin perked up and took that idea and ran with it. From then on, his own mortality was a recurring theme in his poetry. Consider his 2005 poem "Cat Scan" (from his series *The Cats*, a riff on T. S. Eliot's *Old Possum's Book of Practical Cats*):

> What's a cat scan, anyway?
> You lie on your back, flimsy gown of paper,
> and a cat walks down your body,
> your forehead, your throat, sternum, stomach
> and so forth, til the tiptoeing creature stares
> back at you over his shoulder.
> Kevin, plan to die.

Sixteen years later, when Kevin was in the ICU struggling to breathe, and things weren't looking good, Bruce is the one person he asked to see. At the time I found this surprising since he and Bruce weren't all that close, but now it's so clear he had internalized Bruce as a guide.

Finally, the doctors returned from turkey weekend. They had a big meeting about Kevin's situation and decided on a stent. After the procedure he had to lie absolutely still so he wouldn't bleed out. To pass the time we watched a VHS tape of *Finding Nemo*. Two others on his floor did bleed out. One of them died. "Just keep swimming," said Dory in *Finding Nemo*.

Physical and emotional trauma, as well as his intense medication regimen, impaired Kevin's cognitive abilities. In a 2006 email to poet James Wagner, he said it was like the drugs had removed his mind. The upside to not being able to find his way to the end of a sentence was that he was continuously happy, as in "a warm heroin or mescaline high." He saw no point in writing. Months later, as he adjusted to the meds, "an urge to write began to creep around, underneath my skin, like the red ants in that *Night Gallery* episode." To find his way back he needed to take baby steps, and thus he began his "assiduous" project of writing Amazon reviews. Kevin compared himself to the Greek prophet Tiresias. "So I have been that person who no longer cared to write, and that person driven to it, both—like the Tiresias of this particular set of parameters."[1] Kevin's references can be oblique to those of us who do not share his encyclopedic knowledge base, so I start googling.

When I studied feminist poetics in the early 1980s, around the same time I met Kevin, I was taught that while the patriarchy has an Either/Or mindset, a feminist paradigm is Both/And. Tiresias is a Both/And figure on two accounts. He was born a man but when he angered a couple of mating snakes, they turned him into a woman; and then seven years later when she again encountered the copulating snakes, they transformed her back into a man. Sometime after that

1. Kevin Killian, "To James Wagner (2006)," in *Five Stars*, ed. Ted Rees and David Buuck, vol. 4, *Selected Amazon Reviews* (Oakland: Tripwire, 2022). This chapbook, published in the pamphlet series from *Tripwire: A Journal of Poetics*, includes this email to Wagner as well as the interviews by John Fran and Cam Scott quoted below.

he angered a goddess, who struck him blind. As a sort of consolation prize, he was given the gift of prophecy. "Tiresias," Google reminds me, is a central figure in *The Waste Land*. "What Tiresias sees," wrote T. S. Eliot, "in fact, is the substance of the poem." Abrupt change propels Tiresias into radically altered perception, granting him the ability to see beyond the duality of the world of appearances.

Kevin started with brief reviews, no longer than a sentence or two. Within a few months he was "writing away, often twice a day, commenting on this, that, or the other, whatever book I was reading, whatever DVD was in the machine. It's surprising how many texts you can actually experience in a lifetime, or say, in the span of a year. This was my regimen, therapy, if you will."[2] It took "maybe two or three years" for him to regain his full strength as a writer, when he again could "do those theoretical-critical essays I used to write before my collapse."[3] Kevin typed his reviews directly onto the Amazon website. He didn't save copies. He wrote them swiftly, as if he were channeling Jack Spicer's poetics of dictation, furiously trying to catch the voices that were moving through him. The amount of typos in the unedited manuscript of this collection is a testament to his urgency. He rejoiced in the not-useful ratings his reviews received. Kevin's Both/And mindset resisted hierarchies. To rank cultural production according to its use value deflates its mystery. A work of glorious surplus is treated like an oppressed laborer, cowering before its performance evaluation. In public, Kevin would perform a burlesque of the torment he felt from all those not-useful ratings, and he would urge others to help him out and boost his ratings. It became a thing for poets to log on to Amazon and give Kevin some thumbs-ups. For him, writing was never "useful." It was a practice, a calling, a compulsion, quirky love vibes let loose on anybody willing to receive them.

As a sort of method-acting approach to Kevin's process, I scroll through the list of my Amazon orders and randomly choose "Necoichi Cat Scratcher Tower." I type into a thinly lined box, "Do

---

2. Killian, "With John Fran (2013)," in *Five Stars*.
3. Killian, "With Cam Scott (2017)," in *Five Stars*.

we need this? No. Do we want this? Yes, yes, yes." The outline turns vermillion with a golden halo, and the text area turns a pale sky blue. My words are up on a marquee. It's Prime Day, and Amazon has programmed the reviewing experience to celebrate that. I hadn't planned on posting my review, but when I click the Submit button there is an explosion of happy, sparking colors. My dopamine surges and I feel like a Skinnerian rat in a cage, compelled to push that lever/click that button over and over.

I failed at Prime Day this year. I thought I snatched up a four-pack of Apple AirTags for seventy-five dollars—a steal—but somehow I never completed the transaction. By the time I discovered them still in my shopping cart, the deal was no longer available, and I had to pay eighty-nine dollars. I tried to focus on the positive—I still got them for ten dollars less than Apple's list price—but in truth my consumer incompetence is still driving me crazy. If Kevin were alive, I'm sure he would have tossed off a review of the AirTags, only half understanding the point of them. Or perhaps understanding their point too well—our terror of loss. We stick the AirTags on things, telling ourselves we're efficient consumers, protecting our valuable stuff. But the misplacement of keys is never just about keys. What does it mean to tag the air? Half-black, half-white like a pared-down yin-yang symbol, the Apple AirTag is a fetish, warding off the precipitous void we could at any moment find ourselves tottering before. When Kevin's health started to decline I secretly began to track his iPhone. I wasn't suspicious or anything—I didn't care what he did—but if he was ten minutes late coming home from work, I would panic, fearing I'd never see him again. Then I'd locate him on my Find My Friends app and breathe a sigh of relief. Apple gets me.

I imagine some instinctual, and perhaps inaccessible, part of Kevin, prodding him on, whispering that if he wrote frantically enough he might ward off death. In the Amazon reviews, Kevin enacts a ritualistic, disciplined quest through the wasteland of rabid consumption. T. S. Eliot: *These fragments I have shored against my ruins.* Kevin never criticizes Amazon in his reviews. He's not interested in a simple fuck you to capitalism. Kevin queered capitalism like he queered everything else, but he was concerned he was opening himself for criticism.

"The obvious philosophical problem," Kevin told Cam Scott, "is that I was doing this without being paid, in the service of a huge multinational corporation that was killing bookstores and perhaps writing itself. But some defended me and said, 'He's torquing the system from within; they're not actually reviews, they're poems,' so it was a poetic project."[4] The Amazon reviews are an archive of the vastness of Kevin's intellectual universe and the tragedy of its/his evanescence. Every word—all 1,087,107 of them—trembles with mortality. This writing brought him back to meaningful life.

4. Ibid.

Hedi El Kholti and Robert Dewhurst

EDITORS' NOTE

Making this book has been an intense and rewarding experience. Kevin Killian left his readers, and his unsuspecting audience on Amazon, with an embarrassment of riches: nearly 2,400 product reviews, totaling over 1,000,000 words. We have endeavored to shape a book worthy of this astonishing archive, reflective of its monumental scale, extreme range, and infectious enthusiasm.

Our selection criteria have been guided by our sense of Killian's own priorities. Reading the entirety of the reviews, some patterns and purposes emerge. In these texts Killian conducted a seemingly infinite conversation with himself, and with anyone out there, in which he mapped his massive love affair with culture—his obsessions with cinema and literature, fascination by history, concern for social politics, and delight in the absurd. Sometimes separately, often all at once, his reviews are acts of reading, viewing, invention, parody, friendship, fandom, gossip, self-portraiture, and more. A review might be a love letter to an author or a remembrance for a recently departed actor, a message in a bottle tossed to the literary community, a retrieval from history of a startling aesthetic choice (a hairdo, a costume), an improvisation on the inanity and/or irresistibility of a commodity, a lucid engagement with current scholarship, an expression of adoration or arousal. As Killian once understated it, "I get a lot of my kinks out there, on Amazon."

Here we present the most vivid exemplars of Killian's many modes, and highlight both his capaciousness and compulsions. Like any aesthete, he had clear favorites, genres which "entranced" him "like a wizard's spell": avant-garde poetry and literary fiction, biography and memoir, cinephilia and "starlore," erotica and murder mystery, anomalous home goods and accessories. As our hefty selection began to push the physical constraints of this book, and our decisions grew more difficult, we deferred to Killian's own estimation of what was important. Often, thrillingly, that estimation would be at odds with the wider culture's, as when he would champion a small-press book unlikely to be widely noticed, or revalue a schlocky film as a lost or contemporary classic. At the same time, he reveled in mass culture. Killian "queered everything," as Dodie Bellamy writes in her afterword. A phone call with Wayne Kostenbaum early in our editorial process—Wayne's tossed-off phrase "gay hermeneutics"—became a beacon for us as we waded deep into the waters of these words.

One of our greatest pleasures while editing *Selected Amazon Reviews* was the effect of collage and disjunction generated by the sheer variety of Killian's subjects. We initially considered organizing this book by category, perhaps according to Amazon's long drop-down list of "departments." But we quickly abandoned that idea in favor of the chronological order found here, which conserves this effect of "wild combination" (to borrow a phrase from Arthur Russell) for the reader. As a bonus, the resultant timeline brings to light a diaristic aspect of the project as a whole. Clearly, Killian did not set out to appraise a perceived canon, nor to propose his own: many "significant" works (even *Who Killed Teddy Bear?*, one of his favorite movies) are missing from his reviews. Rather than a syllabus, the reviews seem to amount to something like a "diary of consumption." Many entries are in-the-moment reports wherein Killian processes *whatever* text he has experienced on a given day, without inhibition or concern for its cultural status.

We are indebted to Will Hall, who in 2021, prompted by David Buuck, scraped all of Killian's reviews from Amazon's servers, rescuing them from the flux of the internet and establishing the archive which made this book possible. We would also like to acknowledge the editors of Killian's *Selected Amazon Reviews* chapbooks, volumes 1 through 4 (2006, 2011, 2017, 2022), where we ourselves first encountered some of this material: Brent Cunningham, Jason Morris, Dia Felix, and Ted Rees and David Buuck. Special thanks is also due to Michael Malone, who conscientiously assisted us in manuscript preparation. Finally, we are supremely grateful to Dodie Bellamy, for her trust and support as we worked on this project.

As Bellamy narrates in her afterword, Killian composed his reviews in a happy rush, self-publishing to Amazon with typos aplenty. We have lightly edited the text for spelling, grammar, and obvious slips/omissions, but have otherwise preserved his many flourishes and freedoms of style.

Index

Clinton, Bill, 29, 400
Clinton, Hillary, 538
Clooney, George, 194
Clooney, Rosemary, 188
Close, Glenn, 597, 598
Clouzot, Henri-Georges, 32
Cobain, Kurt, 218
Cochrane, Rory, 216
Cocteau, Jean, 171, 202, 387, 445, 530, 591
Cody, Iron Eyes, 172
Cohen, Harriet, 557–559
Cohen, Leonard, 549, 562, 621, 642
Cohn, Harry, 538, 571
Cohn, Roy, 458
Colbert, Claudette, 93
Colby, Tanner, 411
Cole, Nat King, 567
Coleridge, Samuel Taylor, 230, 373
Colette, 117, 118
Collette, Toni, 253
Collins, Billy, 21, 575
Collins, Jackie, 168
Collins, Judy, 548, 549
Comer, Anjanette, 572
Condon, Bill, 46, 47
Congleton, Angelique, 96
Congreve, William, 145, 618
Connell Jr., Evan, S., 366
Connelly, Jennifer, 254, 311, 312
Conner, Bruce, 37
Connery, Sean, 410
Conover, Harry, 246
Conradi, Peter, 162
Considine-Meara, Eileen, 268
Constant, Benjamin, 374
Cook, Rachael Leigh, 418
Coolidge, Clark, 250
Coon, Darwin E., 172
Cooper, Anderson, 188
Cooper, Ben, 115, 116
Cooper, Bradley, 512
Cooper, D. B., 455
Cooper, Dennis, 272, 314, 361, 422–424
Cooper, Gary, 76, 182, 188
Cooper, Gladys, 116, 117, 609
Cooper, Gordon, 436
Cope, Stephen, 452
Copland, Aaron, 112, 441
Coppola, Francis Ford, 40

Coppola, Sofia, 515
Corbett, Edward, 219
Corby, Ellen, 568
Corman, Cid, 592
Corman, Roger, 444
Cormier, Robert, 540, 541
Cornell, Joseph, 409
Corso, Gregory, 563
Cortázar, Julio, 43
Cortés, Hernán, 217
Cosby, Bill, 585, 587
Cotten, Joseph, 52, 53, 74
Coward, Noël, 28, 120, 291, 292, 413, 427
Cox, Courteney, 526
Coyne, Petah, 426
Craig, Christopher, 331
Crais, Robert, 470
Crane, Hart, 208
Cranston, Bryan, 238
Crase, Douglas, 618
Craven, Wes, 525, 526
Crawford, Broderick, 444
Crawford, Joan, 135, 222, 430, 431, 527
Creeley, Robert, 197, 344, 423, 473, 480, 491
Crosby, Bing, 94, 95, 107
Crowe, Russell, 425
Crowley, Aleister, 15, 406–408
Cruise, Tom, 446
Cruz, Penélope, 446
Cukor, George, 74, 75, 192, 274, 297, 468, 469, 515
Cummings, E. E., 140, 141, 337, 338, 493
Cummings, Robert, 546
Cunliffe, Juliette, 56
Cunningham, Cecil, 425
Cunningham, Imogen, 585
Cunningham, Merce, 421
Curran, John, 413
Curreri, Lee, 414
Currie, Cherie, 167
Curtis, Jamie Lee, 24
Curtis, Richard, 578–580
Curtiz, Michael, 155, 471
Cusack, John, 124, 125, 489, 490

D'Allesandro, Sam, 458, 514
D'Angelo, Beverly, 296

Harvey, Herk, 402
Harvey, James, 257
Harvey, PJ, 59
Haskell, Molly, 257
Hathaway, Anne, 335
Hauer, Rutger, 440
Hauser, Wings, 435
Hawke, Ethan, 128
Hawkins, Richard, 139
Hawks, Howard, 380
Hawn, Goldie, 145
Hawthorne, Nathaniel, 508
Hay, Harry, 348
Hayden, Sterling, 39, 41, 115
Hayes, Billy, 126
Hayes, Helen, 94, 317, 398
Haynes, Todd, 252, 253, 527, 528
Hayworth, Rita, 116, 163, 270, 398
Hazzard, Shirley, 170, 171
Heaney, Seamus, 401
Hearst, William Randolph, 178
Heckart, Eileen, 144
Hedren, Tippi, 410, 530
Hedrick, Wally, 38, 57
Heffron, Richard T., 164
Heflin, Van, 200
Hefner, Hugh, 485
Hegarty, Paul, 422, 424
Hegel, Georg Wilhelm Friedrich, 423
Heick, William, 208
Heim, Scott, 387, 388
Heims, Jo, 283
Heisler, Stuart, 161
Heiss, Carol, 106, 107
Hell, Richard, 271
Heller, Marielle, 623
Hellman, Lillian, 52, 64, 120, 171, 173,
    200, 427
Hemingway, Ernest, 31, 149, 197
Hemingway, Margaux, 87
Hendrix, Jimi, 467, 468, 525
Henie, Sonja, 636
Henry, Justin, 136
Hepburn, Audrey, 88, 217, 523, 626
Hepburn, Katharine, 55, 128, 159,
    192, 261, 268, 269, 297, 324, 537
Herbert, George, 479
Herbst, Josephine, 339
Hergé, 396, 397, 646, 647
Herman, Jerry, 354

Herrmann, Bernard, 567
Hershey, Barbara, 523, 596
Hesse, Eva, 38
Hester, Diarmuid, 423
Heti, Sheila, 641–644
Hickman, Leland, 494, 495
Hicks, Bill, 34
Higgins, Colin, 517
Hiller, Arthur, 183, 184
Hiller, Wendy, 116, 117, 122, 123
Hilligoss, Candace, 402
Hilson, Jeff, 431, 432
Hilton, Paris, 28, 436, 438
Himes, Chester, 246, 637
Hindley, Myra, 54, 55
Hinton, Brian, 467, 468
Hirsch, Emile, 460
Hirsch, Foster, 374–376
Hirsch, James S., 288, 289
Hirschfeld, Magnus, 348
Hirst, Damien, 37
Hitchcock, Alfred, 23, 52, 53, 57, 64,
    74, 81, 112, 113, 198, 260, 351,
    379, 398, 410, 411, 425, 444, 530,
    567, 624,
Hitchingham, Emily Curry, 323, 324
Hitler, Adolf, 97, 162, 223, 443, 464,
    540, 623
Hoblit, Gregory, 357
Hockney, David, 41
Hodiak, John, 81, 82
Hoffman, Dustin, 124, 137, 193, 475
Hoffman, John, 507, 508
Hofler, Robert, 216
Holden, Laurie, 596
Holden, William, 54, 282, 283
Holding, James, 657–659
Holleran, Andrew, 457
Holliday, Judy, 296, 558
Holloway, Stanley, 191
Holm, Celeste, 193
Holman, Bob, 272
Holmes, Katie, 398–400
Holst, Gustav, 558
hooks, bell, 257
Hoover, J. Edgar, 536
Hope, Bob, 323, 537
Hopkins, Anthony, 33, 87, 358, 446
Hopkins, Gerard Manley, 505
Hopkins, Miriam, 111, 112

Jones, Quincy, 572
Jones, Shirley, 83
Jones, Tennessee, 43
Jones, Toby, 413
Joplin, Janis, 504, 562
Jordan, Richard Tyler, 353, 354
Jordan, Robert, 91
Jordan, Vernon, 612
Jourdan, Louis, 572, 577, 590
Joyce, James, 369, 420, 421, 630, 631
Justice, Donald, 209

Kael, Pauline, 253, 621
Kahlo, Frida, 169
Kalin, Tom, 498
Kantor, Jordan, 655
Kaprow, Allan, 493
Karsavina, Tamara, 558
Karvoski Jr., Ed, 55
Kaufman, Philip, 339, 340
Kaye, Danny, 189
Kaye, Lisan, 265
Kazan, Elia, 67, 204, 205, 495, 635
Kearney, Douglas, 506
Keaton, Buster, 207
Keaton, Diane, 245, 352, 399, 400
Keats, John, 338, 473, 495, 507
Kees, Weldon, 207–209
Kellaway, Cecil, 341
Kellerman, Sally, 24, 167, 571
Kelly, Daniel, 532
Kelly, Gene, 469, 492
Kelly, Grace, 107, 296, 367, 410
Kelly, Nancy, 143, 144
Kempson, Rachel, 556
Kendall, Kay, 469
Kendall, Suzy, 160
Kennedy Jr., John F., 511
Kennedy, Arthur, 62
Kennedy, Caroline, 511
Kennedy, Danny, 422–424
Kennedy, John F., 275, 400, 421, 445,
    510, 511, 549, 642
Kennedy, Robert F., 445
Kent, Corita, 656
Kerouac, Jack, 34, 38, 39, 70
Kerr, Deborah, 117, 146, 261, 439, 572
Kerr, Jean, 98
Keyes, Frances Parkinson, 442
Khan, Aly, 116

Khouri, Callie, 398, 400
Kidder, Margot, 124, 420, 421
Kidman, Nicole, 338, 340
Kieckens, Germaine, 647
Kilcher, Q'orianka, 367
Kilgallen, Dorothy, 427
Kilmer, Val, 33
Kim, Myung Mi, 225
Kimball, Yeffe, 276
King Jr., Martin Luther, 375, 448
King, Carole, 658
King, Hayward Ellis, 57
King, Stephen, 367, 388, 535, 536,
    564, 596
Kinison, Sam, 24
Kinnear, Greg, 238
Kipling, Rudyard, 169
Kirk, Tommy, 176
Kirkland, Gelsey, 578
Kissinger, Henry, 572, 588
Klawans, Stuart, 257
Klein, Yves, 626
Kleinzahler, August, 230
Klimt, Gustav, 211, 426
Kluge, Alexander, 462, 463
Knott, Bill, 34
Knoxville, Johnny, 330
Koch, Kenneth, 303, 493
Koeneke, Rodney, 249–251
Koenig, James, 465
Koestenbaum, Wayne, 303, 319, 320,
    422
Kohner, Susan, 94
Koons, Jeff, 431
Kornberg-Weiss, Morani, 601, 602
Kors, Michael, 79
Kotz, Liz, 454, 455
Kraftsow, Gary, 464, 465
Kramer, Stanley, 119
Krasner, Lenore, 276
Kraus, Chris, 298–300
Krauss, Ruth, 493
Kreifels, Aaron, 480
Kristeva, Julia, 423
Kubrick, Stanley, 40, 436, 437
Kucinich, Dennis, 127
Kuna, Tina, 234
Kundera, Milan, 168
Kunin, Aaron, 561
Kunis, Mila, 522

Meyer, Stephenie, 457
Meyers, Jonathan Rhys, 252, 253
Michelson, Annette, 248
Midler, Bette, 354
Mies van der Rohe, Ludwig, 551
Miles, Vera, 378, 379, 569
Milk, Harvey, 392, 460
Milland, Ray, 71, 114, 115, 184, 185,
    201, 201
Miller Sr., Percy Robert,
Miller, Ann, 152
Miller, Arthur, 212
Miller, Barry, 414
Miller, Dorothy C., 38
Miller, Marilyn, 531
Mills, Hayley, 136
Milner, Martin, 181
Milosevich, Karla, 172
Mineo, Sal, 405
Minnelli, Liza, 352
Minnelli, Vincente, 262, 469, 576, 577
Minogue, Dannii, 334
Minogue, Kylie, 44, 440, 463, 486,
    581, 582
Minter, Marilyn, 350
Miracle, Irene, 126
Miranda, Carmen, 431
Miranda, Isa, 260, 261
Mitchell, Joni, 372, 483, 549, 562, 579
Mitchum, Robert, 53, 216, 274
Moffat, Ivan, 92
Moffat, Wendy, 649–651
Mogutin, Slava, 533, 534
Mohr, Bill, 494, 495
Molotiu, Andrei, 647
Monroe, Marilyn, 75, 148, 155, 500,
    530, 537
Montague, John, 400, 401
Montaigne, Michel de, 173
Montand, Yves, 572
Montandon, Patricia, 57
Montherlant, Henry de, 638
Montez, Maria, 52, 211
Montgomery, Elizabeth, 82, 83, 556
Montgomery, Robert, 83, 194
Moody, William Vaughn, 305
Moon, Larry, 57
Moore, Alan, 416, 417
Moore, Clement Clarke, 306
Moore, Honor, 25

Moore, Jimmie, 306
Moore, Julianne, 159
Moore, Marianne, 63
Moore, Roger, 417
Moore, Terry, 62
Moral, Tony Lee, 410, 411
Moreau, Jeanne, 51, 255
Morehouse, Bill, 57
Morisot, Berthe, 320
Morley, Hilda, 491, 544
Moroder, Giorgio, 126, 484
Morphy, Paul, 442, 443
Morrell, Ottoline, 558
Morricone, Ennio, 22
Morris, James McGrath, 611–613
Morrison, Jim, 291, 468, 525
Morrissey, David, 346
Morrow, Karen, 487
Morse, Robert, 446
Moses, Robert, 609
Moss-Bachrach, Ebon, 336
Moss, Kate, 579
Motika, Stephen, 494
Mozart, Wolfgang Amadeus, 567
Mubarak, Hosni, 591
Mullen, Harryette, 432
Muller, Eddie, 160, 161, 397
Munro, Alice, 58, 391
Murphy, Eddie, 340
Murphy, George, 471
Musial, Stan, 143
Mussolini, Benito, 260, 540
Myers, Carmel, 635
Myles, Eileen, 42, 272, 313, 314

Nabokov, Vladimir, 320, 351, 370
Nash, Ogden, 240
Nazimova, Alla, 261, 354
Neal, Patricia, 52
Neame, Ronald, 413
Necker, Jacques, 373
Neeson, Liam, 47, 556
Nelson, Cary, 63
Nelson, Maggie, 215
Neutra, Richard, 552
Newcombe, Anton, 50, 51
Newman, Paul, 566
Newton, Thandie, 490
Nicholas, John, 552
Nicholls Jr., George, 608

Patti, Adelina, 486
Pattinson, Robert, 456
Paulik, Johan, 133
Pavan, Marisa, 115, 116
Pavarotti, Luciano, 193
Payard, François, 585–587
Payne, Ethel, 611–613
Payton, Barbara, 537
Pearce, Guy, 528
Pearl, Minnie, 374
Pears, Peter, 660
Peck, Dale, 458
Peck, Gregory, 52, 75, 76, 409
Peet, Amanda, 489
Penn, Arthur, 86, 161, 492
Penn, Sean, 460
Perec, Georges, 619, 620
Perkins, Anthony, 161
Perrin, Jacques, 268
Persky, Lester, 41
Persky, Stan, 487, 488
Peters, Bernadette, 296
Petit, Catherine, 359
Petit, Roland, 492
Pfeiffer, Michelle, 300, 301
Philipe, Gérard, 261
Philips, Lee, 61
Phillippe, Ryan, 261
Phillips, Ian, 77
Phillips, John, 524
Phillips, Lisa, 37
Phillips, Michelle Gilliam, 524
Picano, Felice, 361, 362
Picasso, Pablo, 66, 100, 202, 275, 397, 551, 639
Pickett, Bobby, 176
Pickford, Mary, 356
Pidgeon, Walter, 537
Pierre et Gilles, 582
Pinter, Harold, 476
Plante, David, 427
Plath, Sylvia, 30, 31, 69, 505, 602
Plato, 102, 139, 167, 478
Plummer, Christopher, 336, 368
Pocahontas, 368
Podhoretz, Norman, 442
Poitier, Sidney, 86, 104, 160, 269, 375
Polanski, Roman, 341
Pollock, Jackson, 265
Polo, Theresa Elizabeth, 193

Pomus, Doc, 205
Ponti, Carlo, 328
Pontius, Chris, 330
Poole, Wakefield, 295
Porges, Maria, 657
Porter, Bern, 432
Porter, Cole, 81, 90, 107
Porter, Darwin, 307
Porter, Katherine Anne, 118, 119, 365
Portman, Natalie, 522, 523
Postlethwaite, Pete, 312
Potrero, Sidney, 269
Potter, Beatrix, 172
Pound, Ezra, 25, 63, 630
Powell Jr., Adam Clayton, 612
Powell, Doug, 606
Powell, Eleanor, 531
Powell, Michael, 122, 123
Powell, William, 125
Power, Tyrone, 104
Powers, John Robert, 246
Powers, Stefanie, 404, 437
Powley, Bel, 623, 624
Preminger, Erik Lee, 375
Preminger, Otto, 82, 83, 223, 374–376, 392, 393, 439
Prendergast, Maurice, 219
Presle, Micheline, 268
Presley, Elvis, 211, 429, 477, 543, 544, 610, 624
Presley, Priscilla, 446
Pressburger, Emeric, 122, 123
Preston, John, 168, 523, 524
Prevallet, Kristin, 451–453
Previn, André, 181
Price, Leontyne, 72, 73, 441
Price, Vincent, 209
Prince, 90, 433, 617
Prince, Richard, 273
Prinz, LeRoy, 471
Prinze, Freddie, 414
Proust, Marcel, 221, 238, 594, 628
Prouty, Olive Higgins, 68, 69
Pryor, Richard, 271
Pullman, Bill, 265
Purcell, Henry, 660
Purdy, James, 362
Pynchon, Thomas, 166, 285, 292

Quaid, Randy, 167

ABOUT THE AUTHORS

Kevin Killian (1952–2019) was a San Francisco–based poet, playwright, novelist, biographer, editor, critic, and artist. Highly prolific and radically queer, he published several volumes of poetry and short stories, as well as four novels. Killian's trio of memoirs, *Fascination*, was published by Semiotext(e) in 2018. He also wrote and produced fifty plays, and was a preeminent scholar on the poet Jack Spicer. Killian was a core participant in San Francisco's New Narrative writing circle, and with his wife, Dodie Bellamy, he coedited *Writers Who Love Too Much: New Narrative 1977–1997*. In addition to reviewing for Amazon, Killian published criticism in *Art in America, Artforum, Artweek*, the *Brooklyn Rail, BOMB, Framework*, and elsewhere.

Dodie Bellamy was married to Kevin Killian for 33 years. She has published three books with Semiotext(e)—*Bee Reaved*, an essay/memoir collection circling around grief, loss and mortality; a new edition of her 1998 PoMo vampire novel *The Letters of Mina Harker*; and another essay collection, *When the Sick Rule the World*. With Kevin Killian, she co-edited *Writers Who Love Too Much: New Narrative 1977–1997*. In 2018–19 she was the subject of *On Our Mind*, a yearlong series of public events, commissioned essays and reading-group meetings organized by the CCA Wattis Institute. She received a 2023 Guggenheim fellowship for non-fiction writing.

Wayne Koestenbaum—poet, critic, fiction-writer, artist, filmmaker—has published over twenty books, including *Stubble Archipelago*, Ultramarine, *The Cheerful Scapegoat, Figure It Out, Camp Marmalade, My 1980s & Other Essays, Humiliation, Hotel Theory, Circus, Andy Warhol, Jackie Under My Skin*, and *The Queen's Throat* (nominated for a National Book Critics Circle Award). Recipient of a Guggenheim Fellowship in Poetry, an American Academy of Arts and Letters Award in Literature, and a Whiting Award, he is a Distinguished Professor of English, French, and Comparative Literature at the CUNY Graduate Center.